SERVICES MARKETING

Valarie A. Zeithaml

Partners for Service Excellence

Mary Jo Bitner

Arizona State University

THE McGRAW-HILL COMPANIES, INC.

New York St. Louis San Francisco Auckland Bogotá Caracas Lisbon
London Madrid Mexico City Milan Montreal New Delhi
San Juan Singapore Sydney Tokyo Toronto

McGraw-Hill

A Division of The McGraw·Hill Companies

SERVICES MARKETING
International Editions 1996

Exclusive rights by McGraw-Hill Book Co.–Singapore for manufacture and export. This book cannot be re-exported from the country to which it is consigned by McGraw-Hill.

1 2 3 4 5 6 7 8 9 0 KKP PMP 9 8 7 6

This book was set in Times Roman by Ruttle, Shaw & Wetherill, Inc.
The editors were Karen Westover, Caroline Iannuzzo, and Sheila H. Gillams;
the production supervisor was Denise L. Puryear.
The cover was designed by Joseph A. Piliero.
The photo editor was Anne Manning.

Library of Congress Cataloging-in-Publication Data

Zeithaml, Valarie A.
    Services marketing / Valarie A. Zeithaml. – 1st ed.
      p.   cm.
    Includes bibliographical references and index.
    ISBN 0-07-078250-4
    1. Service industries–Marketing.   2. Customer services.
  3. Marketing.   I. Bitner, Mary Jo.   II. Title.
HD9980.5.Z45   1996
658.8–dc20   95-44395

When ordering this title, use ISBN 0-07-114881-7

Printed in Singapore

ABOUT THE AUTHORS

VALARIE A. ZEITHAML (*seated*) is principal of Partners for Service Excellence, a consulting firm specializing in strategy, measurement, and implementation of services marketing and management. She obtained a Master's of Business Administration and a doctorate from the University of Maryland and spent twelve years as a business school professor, most recently on the faculty of the Fuqua School of Business, Duke University. She is the author of more than fifty articles, ten monographs, and three books, including the best-selling business book entitled *Delivering Quality Service: Balancing Customer Perceptions and Expectations.* Dr. Zeithaml has consulted with IBM, John Hancock Financial Services, AT&T, General Electric, U.S. West, BellSouth, Aetna, Ameritech, Sears, Marriott, and GTE.

MARY JO BITNER, Ph.D., is an Associate Professor of Marketing and Research Director at the First Interstate Center for Services Marketing at Arizona State University. She has taught services marketing for over ten years and is a frequent presenter on executive education programs in services marketing and management. She is the author of numerous articles on services topics appearing in the *Journal of Marketing, Journal of Retailing, Journal of Business Research, Journal of the Academy of Marketing Science,* and others. She obtained her Ph.D. from the University of Washington, Seattle.

To my husband, Jim Palmer, with love and gratitude.
And to "Aunt," who gave me the foundation I needed.
—V.A.Z.

To my wonderful family—
husband Rich and daughters Andrea and Christa.
—M.J.B.

We dedicate this textbook to the pioneering services marketing researchers
who developed the field through their passion, persistence, and creativity.
Without their vision and tenacity, neither this textbook nor the field would exist.

CONTENTS

CASES

PREFACE

This is a textbook for students and business people who recognize the vital role that services play in the economy and its future. The economies of the world are now dominated by services: the percent of GDP and the labor force in the United States, France, the United Kingdom, Canada and Japan are 72.3, 64.3, 62.9, 62, and 56.8, respectively. In 1995, for the first time, the Fortune 500 included service firms, recognizing the important and dominant role these companies play in the U.S. economy. Of the top ten companies on the list, four were services and over half of the entire list were service companies. Furthermore, manufacturing companies recognize the potential of service as one of the few sustainable competitive advantages they can develop.

We wrote this book in recognition of the ever-growing importance of services and the unique challenges faced by managers of services.

Why a Services Marketing Textbook?

Since the beginning of our academic careers in marketing, we have devoted our research and teaching efforts to the topic of services marketing. We strongly believe that services marketing is different from goods marketing in several significant ways, and that it requires different strategies and tactics that traditional marketing textbooks do not fully reflect. This textbook is unique in both content and structure, and we hope that you will learn from it as we have in writing it.

New Content   The foundation of the text is the recognition that services present special challenges that must be identified and addressed. Problems commonly encountered in service businesses not faced by goods businesses—the inability to inventory, difficulty in synchronizing demand and supply, and challenges in controlling the performance quality of human interactions—need to be articulated and tackled by managers. Many of the strategies required include information that is new to marketing. We wrote the text to help students and managers understand and address these special problems of services marketing.

For the most part, we do not repeat material from marketing principles or marketing strategy textbooks. Instead, we adjust, when necessary, standard content on distribution, pricing, and promotion to account for service differences of tangibility, heterogeneity, and perishability.

In addition to standard marketing topics (e.g., the marketing mix), this textbook introduces students to entirely new topics that include management and measurement of service quality, the linking of customer measurement to performance measurement, and cross-functional treatment of issues through integration of marketing with disciplines such as operations and human resources. Each of these topics represents pivotal content for tomorrow's corporations as they structure around process rather than task, flatten the corporate hierarchy, use teams to manage tasks, and develop customer intimacy.

Distinguishing Content Features   The distinguishing features of our textbook include:

1 Greater emphasis on the topic of service quality than existing marketing and service marketing textbooks

2 Increased focus on customer expectations and perceptions and what they imply for marketers, a perspective consistent with the prevailing philosophy of market-driven and customer-driven quality

3 Description of the measurement of service quality and its relationship to performance measures, Malcolm Baldrige criteria, and operations measures, including a partial chapter on market-driven performance measurement systems

4 A chapter on customer-defined service standards

5 Cross-functional treatment of issues through integration of marketing with other disciplines such as operations and human resources

6 Consumer-based pricing and value pricing strategies

7 Description of a set of tools that must be added to basic marketing techniques when dealing with services rather than goods

8 A chapter on marketing services internationally

9 Introduction of three service Ps to the traditional marketing mix and increased focus on customer relationships and relationship marketing strategies

10 An entire chapter that recognizes human resource challenges and human resource strategies for delivering customer-focused services

11 A detailed and complete introduction to service blueprinting—a tool for describing, designing, and positioning services

12 Coverage of the customer's role in service delivery and strategies for making customers productive partners in service creation

13 A chapter on the role of physical evidence, particularly the physical environment or "servicescapes"

Conceptual and Research Foundations   We synthesized research and conceptual material from many talented academics and practitioners to create this book. We relied on pioneering work of researchers and business people from diverse disciplines such as marketing, human resources, operations, and management. Because the field of services marketing is international in its roots, we also drew from work originating around the globe. The framework of the book is managerially focused, with every chapter presenting company examples and strategies for addressing issues in the chapter.

Conceptual Frameworks in Chapters   We developed integrating frameworks in most chapters. For example, we created new frameworks for understanding service pricing, managing expectations, customer relationships, customer roles, and internal marketing.

Unique Structure   The text features a structure completely different from the standard 4P (marketing mix) structure of introductory marketing texts. Beginning with Chapter 3, it is organized around the gaps model of service quality, and begins with the customer. Chapters 3, 4, and 5 each focus on a specific topic about the customer: customer expectations, perceptions, and consumer behavior. The managerial content in the rest of the chapters is framed by the gaps model.

Fully Integrated Text   In the 1980s, the field of services marketing was so new that insufficient material had been written on the topic to create a traditional textbook. For that reason, the books used as texts contained cases and readings that had to be interpreted by educators for their students. These 1980s service marketing books were therefore different from standard textbooks—where the major function is to synthesize and conceptualize the material—and placed a burden on the professor to blend the components. We wanted to create a textbook that contained integrated text materials, thereby removing from professors and students the tremendous burden of synthesis and compilation.

What Courses and Students Can Use the Text?

In our years of experience teaching services marketing, we have found that a broad cross-section of students are drawn to learning about services marketing. Students with career interests in services industries as well as goods industries with high service components (e.g., industrial productions, high tech products, durable products) want and need to understand these topics. Students who wish to become consultants and entrepreneurs want to learn the strategic view of marketing, which includes not just physical goods but also the myriad of services that envelop them. Virtually all students—even those who will work for packaged goods firms—will face employers needing to understand the basics of services marketing.

While services marketing courses are usually designated as marketing electives, a large number of enrollees in our classes have been finance students seeking to broaden their knowledge and career opportunities in financial services. Business students with human resource, accounting, and operations majors also enroll as do non-business students from such diverse disciplines as health administration, recreation and parks, public and nonprofit administration, law, and library sciences.

Students need only a basic marketing course as a prerequisite for a services marketing course and this textbook. The primary target audience for the textbook is services marketing classes at the undergraduate (junior or senior elective courses), graduate (both master's and doctoral courses), and executive student levels. Secondary target audiences are (1) service *management* classes at both the undergraduate and graduate levels and (2) marketing management classes at the graduate level where a professor wishes to provide more comprehensive teaching of services than is possible with a standard marketing management textbook. A subset of chapters will provide a more concise text for use in a quarter-length or mini-semester course. A further-reduced set of chapters may be used to supplement undergraduate and graduate basic marketing courses to enhance the treatment of services.

What Can We Provide Educators to Teach Services Marketing?

As a team, we have accumulated nearly twenty years of experience teaching the subject of services marketing. We set out to create a textbook that represents the approaches we have found most effective. We incorporated all that we have learned in our many years of teaching services marketing—teaching materials, student exercises, case analyses, and overhead masters.

How Many Sections and Chapters Are Included and What Do They Cover?

The textual material includes eighteen chapters divided into six parts. Part One introduces the topic. Part Two discusses the customer. Part Three describes ways that services marketing firms can and do listen to their customers. Part Four describes ways that companies align strategy, service design, and service standards with customer expectations. Part Five contains information dealing with service delivery, and Part Six describes managing service promises.

The Supplementary Materials

Cases   We include carefully selected cases to illustrate services marketing principles and strategy. Almost all have been written since 1990, and have not been included in other services marketing textbooks. A majority of the cases are international, focusing on companies doing business outside the United States. The cases illustrate business-to-business marketing challenges as well as consumer marketing issues.

Instructor's Manual   We have provided teaching notes for the cases included in the textbook that specifically relate to the teaching of services principles. We include notes, overheads, and follow-up conceptual material where relevant and questions for each case that allow students to focus on aspects of the case that are most important.

The instructor's manual uses the "active learning" educational paradigm that involves students in constructing their own learning experiences and exposes them to the collegial patterns present in work situations. Active learning offers an educational underpinning for the pivotal work force skills required in business, among them oral and written communication skills, listening skills, and critical thinking and problem solving.

ACKNOWLEDGMENTS

We owe a great deal to the pioneering service researchers and scholars who developed the field of services marketing. They include John Bateson, Leonard Berry, Bernard

Booms, Dave Bowen, Steve Brown, Larry Crosby, John Czepiel, Ray Fisk, William George, Christian Gronroos, Steve Grove, Evert Gummesson, Chuck Lamb, Christopher Lovelock, Ben Schneider, Parsu Parasuraman, Lynn Shostack, and Carol Surprenant.

We are particularly indebted to Parsu Parasuraman and Len Berry, who have been research partners of Dr. Zeithaml's since 1982. The gaps model, around which this textbook was organized, was developed in collaboration with them, as was the model of customer expectations used in Chapter 4. Much of the research and measurement content in this textbook has been shaped by what our team found in a fifteen-year program of research on service quality.

Dr. Bitner expresses special thanks to Steve Brown, Michael Mokwa, the First Interstate Center for Services Marketing and Department of Marketing at Arizona State University. Without their support and encouragement this book would not be a reality. She also thanks Bernard Booms, Mike Hutt, Bruce Walker and Larry Crosby for their valued advice and mentorship throughout the process.

We wish to express our gratitude to our friends and fellow researchers John Graham and Mary Gilly for researching and writing the chapter on international marketing. We sought—and fortunately were able to involve—international service experts who could provide the experience and insight to present an integrated and up-to-the-minute discussion of this part of the services discipline that is growing the fastest and yet remains the most difficult to understand.

Bonnie Binkert, the former McGraw-Hill editor who started this project, deserves credit for so many things: her skill and experience, her ability to motivate and encourage, and her support. Michael Houston, consulting editor for McGraw-Hill, provided insights throughout the project. We also thank Karen Westover, Caroline Iannuzzo, and Sheila Gillams of the McGraw-Hill staff for their talents in seeing the project through to completion.

Chuck Lamb and Bernie Booms, our friends and colleagues, were generous enough with their case teaching talents to serve as advisors on the cases selected for the text. With Bernie's persistence and investigative talents, we have been able to draw together a body of cases that best illustrates the service marketing concepts and practices we discuss. Lauren Wright was our partner in developing an instructor's manual that incorporated active learning approaches to enliven the teaching and learning of services marketing. Michael Guiry created the test bank.

Dr. Zeithaml acknowledges the clients that she worked with during the writing of this book who provided real-world anchoring for the conceptual and research material. Thanks to Dick Jones, Jane Hemphill, and Bob Signorello of IBM for their enthusiasm and missionary zeal for service during the period when IBM was transitioning to services in the early 1990s. She also wishes to thank Les Hemmings of John Hancock Financial Services, Stefanie Shelley, Karen Amico, and Karen Horn of GE Capital, Jim Gadd and Pat Eidson of BellSouth, Nancy Clifford of Aetna, and John Kinney of GE Aircraft Engines, all of whom taught her a great deal in these past three years.

Dr. Bitner is grateful to the charter member companies of the First Interstate Center for Service Marketing, and particularly thanks its Board of Advisors, who have shared their time and valued ideas over the years. Their insights provided the grounding for many strategies and examples included in the book. The charter member companies include AT&T, Baxter Healthcare Corporation, Blue Cross and Blue Shield, Co-operators Financial Services, Cummins Engine Company, Dial Corporation, Elrick and Lavidge, Federal Express Corporation, First Interstate Bank, Ford Motor Company, Harley-Davidson, IBM Canada and US, Johnson and Higgins, Johnson & Johnson Health Care Systems, Marriott Corporation, MicroAge, The Promus Corporation, Samaritan Health System, Walker Group, Xerox Corporation, and Yellow Freight Systems, Inc.

Finally, we want to acknowledge the suggestions and improvements made by James G. Barnes, Memorial University of Newfoundland; Ruth N. Bolton, University of Maryland; Barbara Coe, University of North Texas; Catherine Cole, University of Iowa; Peter B. Everett, Pennsylvania State University; Raymond P. Fisk, University of Central Florida; Mary C. Gilly, University of California, Irvine; Cathy Goodwin, University of Manitoba; Dennis Guseman, California State University, Bakersfield; John M. Gwin, University of Virginia; Mike Houston, University of Minnesota; John Lindgren, University of Virginia; Jagdip Singh, Case Western Reserve University; Michael Soloman, Rutgers University, New Brunswick; and Lauren K. Wright, California State University, Chico.

Valarie A. Zeithaml
Mary Jo Bitner

INTRODUCTION

1

INTRODUCTION
TO SERVICES

*Imagine that you are Julia Brennan, a recent Master of Business Administration gradu-
ate, who has been offered the job of marketing director of Johnson, MacMillan, & Allen
(JM&A), a regional chemical and environmental consulting firm. Julia will be the first
marketing director.*

*Julia has a combined undergraduate degree in chemical engineering and business.
She worked for three years in sales for an industrial products manufacturer before returning to study for her MBA. During her MBA program she worked on a marketing plan
for a local parts manufacturer. The plan focused on demand projections, competitive
analysis, and promotion and pricing strategies for the product.*

*JM&A provides advice and training to companies in the areas of air pollution and in-
dustrial hygiene. The industrial hygiene group assists clients in meeting federal industrial environment regulations including safety compliance inspections, employee monitoring, process ventilation efficiency studies, employee training, and indoor air quality
investigation. The firm's air pollution group offers services including air pollution sampling, consultation, and regulatory agency enforcement for industrial plants. The partners and staff at JM&A have degrees in chemical engineering, industrial engineering,
and industrial hygiene. Their clients represent a broad range of industries from mining
to chemical and aerospace industries, hospitals, state and federal government, and
power utilities.*

*Despite her technical background and knowledge of basic marketing, Julia realizes
that she is in for a challenge in marketing chemical and environmental consulting services. None of the seven partners or 22 associates has a marketing background, but
many of them have done some reading about the importance of customer orientation and
total quality management. They are confident that in hiring Julia they will be able to
grow and win more jobs in their ever more competitive marketplace.*

3

While the firm grew steadily in its first six years of operation, increasing competition and a changing economic climate have resulted in declining sales in the past six months. The partners do not know exactly why sales have declined nor do they have a clear picture of their current or potential customers. They realize that they have lost clients from time to time, and that they don't always win when they submit a bid for a job, but they don't know why. Technically, the firm's personnel are highly competent. The partners have asked Julia to develop, in her first six months, a marketing plan for the organization.

If you were Julia, where would you start? What does Julia need to know about the service economy and service businesses to prepare her for the job? What are the differences between marketing services like JM&A's and marketing goods like those of the parts manufacturer in her MBA project, or selling a manufactured product like Julia did in her previous job? Simply defining the product being offered by JM&A may not be easy. What are the components of the product? What is the bundle of benefits from the customer's point of view? How can she describe to customers what the engineering service is? How does JM&A's product differ from the products of their major competitors? Do the partners and associates understand what marketing is, and what their individual marketing roles are? Certainly the actions and attitudes of the employees of the firm have tremendous marketing impact on customers. Who are the current customers, anyway? How do they feel about the firm? What is the demand pattern for the type of services offered by the firm? What happens when there isn't enough business? What happens when there is too much business?

As the opening vignette illustrates, and as Julia quickly discovered, services are different from goods, and managing a service business is different from managing in the manufacturing sector—not unique, but different. This chapter will set the stage for the rest of the text in illuminating these key differences and challenges and in giving you a foundation for understanding the management of services. Many of the ideas and strategies you have learned and will learn in other business courses certainly apply (either totally, or to some extent) to service businesses and to the management of services within manufacturing. What we will focus on in this book, therefore, are those aspects that are different, and the special tools and strategies you will need to be an effective manager and marketer of services.

The objectives of the first chapter are to:

1 Explain what services are and clarify certain myths about services such as "the service economy produces services at the expense of other sectors."

2 Explain the need for special services marketing concepts and practices and why the need has developed and accelerated over the last two decades.

3 Outline the basic differences between goods and services (intangibility, heterogeneity, simultaneous production and consumption, perishability), and the resulting challenges for service businesses.

4 Introduce the services marketing triangle and the expanded marketing mix for services as powerful concepts that can aid in addressing the challenges of service businesses.

WHAT ARE SERVICES?

Put in the most simple terms, *services are deeds, processes, and performances.* Our opening vignette illustrates what is meant by this definition. The services offered by Johnson, MacMillan, & Allen are not tangible things that can be touched, seen, and felt, but rather are intangible deeds and performances. To be concrete, JM&A offers industrial hygiene compliance services that can include everything from compliance inspections to employee monitoring, process ventilation efficiency studies, and employee training. Each of these services may include a final, tangible report or, in the case of employee training, tangible instructional materials. Otherwise, the entire service is represented to the client through problem analysis activities, meetings with the client, follow-up calls, and reporting—a series of deeds, processes, and performances. Similarly, the core offerings of hospitals, hotels, banks, and utilities comprise primarily deeds and actions performed for customers.

Relying on the simple, broad definition of *services*, it quickly becomes apparent that services are produced not only by service businesses such as those just described but are a¹so integral to the offerings of many manufactured-goods producers. For example, car manufacturers offer warranties and repair services for their cars; computer manufacturers offer warranties, maintenance contracts, and training; industrial equipment producers offer delivery, inventory management, and maintenance services. All of these services are examples of deeds, processes, and performances.

While we will rely on the simple, broad definition of services, you should be aware that over time services and the service sector of the economy have been defined in subtly different ways. The variety of definitions can often explain the confusion or disagreements people have when discussing services and when describing industries that comprise the service sector of the economy. Compatible with our simple, broad definition is one that defines services to "include all economic activities whose output is not a physical product or construction, is generally consumed at the time it is produced, and provides added value in forms (such as convenience, amusement, timeliness, comfort or health) that are essentially intangible concerns of its first purchaser."[1] This definition has been used also to delineate the service sector of the economy, as illustrated in Table 1-1. When we refer to the service sector, we will be assuming this broad range of industries.

More limited definitions of services may exclude the retail sector or government services or some other group of services. For example, *Business Week,* in its special issue on industry projections, does *not* include financial services (banking, insurance, securities, real estate), telecommunications, or government under its "Services" section.[2] When statistics regarding the growth and contribution of services to the economy are cited, discrepancies often occur if these more limited definitions of the service sector are used and people are thus comparing apples and oranges.

Tangibility Spectrum

The broad definition of services implies that intangibility is a key determinant of whether an offering is or is not a service. While this is true, it is also true that very few products are purely intangible or totally tangible. Instead, services tend to be *more in-*

TABLE 1-1 INDUSTRIES CLASSIFIED WITHIN THE SERVICE SECTOR*

Transportation and public utilities
  Transportation
    Railroad transportation
    Local and interurban passenger transit
    Trucking and warehousing
    Water transportation
    Air transportation
    Pipelines, except natural gas
    Transportation services
  Communication
    Telephone and telegraph
    Radio and television broadcasting
  Electric, gas, and sanitary services
Wholesale trade
Retail trade
Finance, insurance, and real estate
  Banking
  Credit agencies other than banks
  Security and commodity brokers, and services
  Real estate
  Holding and other investment companies

Other services
  Hotels and other lodging places
  Personal services
  Business services
  Auto repair, services, and garages
  Miscellaneous repair services
  Motion pictures
  Amusement and recreation services
  Health services
  Legal services
  Educational services
  Social services and membership
    organizations
  Miscellaneous professional services
  Private household services
Federal government
  Civilian
  Military
Government enterprises
State and local government
  Education
  Other services

*Using the broad definition of service industries, this list was compiled from *Survey of Current Business,* 1988.

tangible than manufactured products, and manufactured products tend to be *more tangible* than services. For example, the fast-food industry, while classified as a service, also has many tangible components such as the food, the packaging, and so on. Automobiles, while classified within the manufacturing sector, also supply many intangibles, for example, transportation. The tangibility spectrum shown in Figure 1-1 captures this idea. Throughout this text, when we refer to services we will be assuming the broad definition of services and acknowledging that there are very few "pure services" or "pure goods." The issues and approaches we discuss are directed toward those offerings that lie on the right side, the intangible side, of the spectrum shown in Figure 1-1.

As suggested earlier, intangibles are *not* produced only in the service sector of the economy. Manufacturers such as Boeing Airplane Company and Ford Motor Company also produce products on the right end of the spectrum, both for sale to external consumers and to support internal production processes. For example, Boeing has provided consulting services and demand forecasting services for its airline customers. And within the Boeing Airplane Company there are large departments (such as data processing, legal services) that provide internal services to the organization.

Trends in the Service Sector

While we often hear and read that many modern-day economies are dominated by services, the United States and other countries did not become service economies

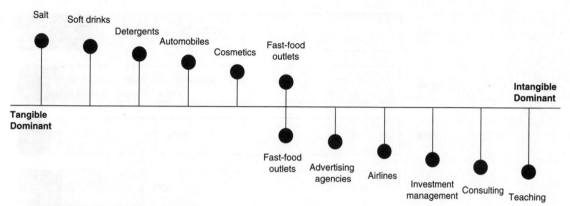

FIGURE 1-1   Tangibility spectrum.

Source: G. Lynn Shostack, "Breaking Free from Product Marketing," *Journal of Marketing,* 41 (April 1977): 73–80. Reprinted with permission of the American Marketing Association.

overnight. As early as 1929, 55 percent of the working population was employed in the service sector in the United States, and approximately 54 percent of the gross national product was generated by services in 1948. The data in Figures 1-2 and 1-3 show that the trend toward services has continued, until in the early 1990s services represent 73 percent of the gross domestic product and 78 percent of employment. Note also that these data do not include internal services provided within a manufacturing company (such as Xerox or Boeing) or services that these manufacturers sell externally. The number of employees and value of the services they produce would be classified as manufacturing sector data.

While the growth in services is remarkable, not *all* service industries have grown at the same rate. A disproportionate amount of the growth in employment has come from "producer services" (e.g., accounting, legal, banking, architecture, engineering) and government services. In some service industries, such as retail, the percentage of total employment they represent has remained relatively flat, whereas in others, such as wholesale or distribution services, it has actually fallen.

WHY SERVICES MARKETING?

Why is it important to learn about services marketing, service quality, and service management? What are the differences in services versus manufactured-goods marketing that have led to the demand for books and courses on services? Many forces have led to the growth of services marketing, and many industries, companies, and individuals have defined the scope of the concepts, frameworks, and strategies that define the field.

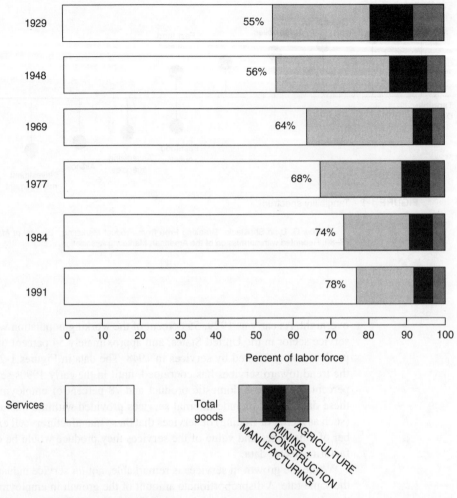

FIGURE 1-2 Percent of U.S. labor force by industry.

Source: Survey of Current Business; July 1988, Table 6.6B, and July 1992, Table 6.4C; Eli Ginzberg and George J. Vojta, "The Service Sector of the U.S. Economy," Scientific American 244, 3 (1981): 31–39.

A Service-Based Economy

First, services marketing concepts and strategies have developed in response to the tremendous growth of service industries resulting in their increased importance to the U.S. and world economies. As was noted, in 1991 the service sector represented 78 percent of total employment and at least 73 percent of the gross domestic product of the United States. Almost all of the absolute growth in numbers of jobs and the fastest growth rates in job information are in service industries. One study reported the "25 hottest careers" for 1993 as being in one of the five major segments of information tech-

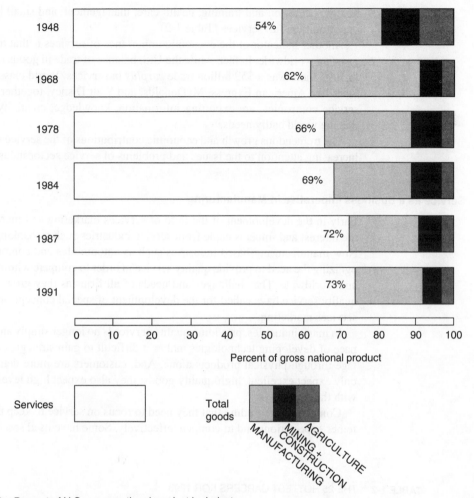

FIGURE 1-3 Percent of U.S. gross national product by industry.

The data for 1984, 1987, and 1991 are based on industry percentages of gross domestic product (GDP) rather than gross national product (GNP), because the *Survey of Current Business* now reports GDP as the primary measure of U.S. production. For the United States, the dollar levels of GDP and GNP differ very little. Thus the earlier data and the data from 1984 forward are comparable.

Source: Survey of Current Business, July 1988, Table 6.1, and May 1993, Table 2; Eli Ginzberg and George J. Vojta, "The Service Sector of the U.S. Economy," *Scientific American,* 244, 3 (1981): 31–39.

nology, education and training, health care, management, and small [service] business opportunities—all services (Table 1-2).

Another indicator of the economic importance of services is that trade in services is growing worldwide. In fact, while the U.S. balance of trade in goods remains in the red, in 1992 there was a $59 billion trade *surplus* in services. World class providers of services like American Express, McDonalds, and Walt Disney, together with many small service companies, are exporting information, knowledge, creativity, and technology that the world badly needs.[3]

The tremendous growth and economic contributions of the service sector have drawn increasing attention to the issues and problems of service sector industries.

Service as a Business Imperative in Manufacturing

Early in the development of the field of services marketing and management, most of the interest and impetus came from service industries such as banking and health care. Now manufacturing-based industries such as automobiles and computers are also recognizing the need to provide quality service in order to compete within the United States and worldwide. The challenges and needs of all firms as they grow toward delivering quality service have called for the development of special concepts and approaches for services marketing.

In many industries, providing quality service is no longer simply an option. The quick pace of developing technologies makes it difficult to gain strategic competitive advantage through physical products alone. And, customers are more demanding. They not only expect excellent, high-quality goods; they also expect high levels of service along with them.

Companies are finding that they need to focus on service to keep up with rising customer expectations and to compete effectively. Some have used service extremely well

TABLE 1-2   THE 25 HOTTEST CAREERS FOR 1993

Information technology	Managed-care manager
Computer programmer	Nurse practitioner
Database manager	Physical therapist
LAN (Local Area Network)	Management
Systems analyst	Diversity manager
Telecommunications manager	Environmental manager
Education, training	Human resources manager
Cross-cultural trainer	Ombudsman
Employee trainer	Product manager
Environmental consultant	Small-business opportunities
50-Plus marketer	Employee leasing
School administration	Financial planning
Health care	Private investigation
Family physician	Professional-practice management
Home health-care nurse	Professional-temp management

Source: Working Woman, July 1993, pp. 41–51.

for competitive advantage. For example, in the word-processing software industry, WordPerfect Corporation has clearly distinguished itself by providing easy access and consistent service to its users. The company has differentiated itself through four flexible customer service programs: Classic Service, Priority Service, Premium Services, and Electronic Services.[4] The Classic Service is a toll-free hotline service available to all WordPerfect customers for a limited period after purchase. The other services are designed for specific market segments, to meet all customers' varying needs. WordPerfect emphasizes its services through its advertising and public relations and, because of their effective delivery, it is able to compete very successfully, serving as a service benchmark for many companies both within and outside the software industry.

Deregulated Industries and Professional Service Needs

Specific demand for services marketing concepts has come from the deregulated industries and professional services as both of these groups have gone through rapid changes in the ways they do business. In the past two decades, many very large service industries including airlines, banking, telecommunications, and trucking have been deregulated by the U.S. government. Similar deregulatory moves have taken place in many other countries as well. As a result, marketing decisions that used to be tightly controlled by the government are now partially, and in some cases totally, within the control of individual firms. For example, until 1978 all airline fares, routes, and commissions paid to travel agents were determined and monitored by the government. Now individual airlines are free to set their own pricing structures and determine which routes they will fly. Needless to say, deregulation created turmoil in the airline industry, accelerating the need for more sophisticated, customer-based, and competition-sensitive marketing. The same is true in all deregulated industries.

Providers of professional services (such as dentists, lawyers, accountants, engineers, and architects) have also demanded new concepts and approaches for their businesses as these industries have become increasingly competitive and as professional standards have been modified to allow at least limited advertising. The challenges faced by Julia Brennan in our opening vignette are common across the professions. While traditionally the professions avoided even using the word *marketing,* they are now seeking better ways to understand and segment their customers, to ensure the delivery of quality services, and to strengthen their positions amidst a growing number of competitors.

Many service industries, such as health care, traditionally dominated by an operations perspective have also sensed the need to be more customer focused and are implementing new approaches for understanding their customers' needs. For example, Hospital Corporation of America is equipping its 96 hospitals with a portable computer system that can collect on-site customer reactions to the hospital experience.[5] As these traditionally operations-focused industries listened to their customers, they recognized their needs for new tools and approaches for delivering quality service.

New Technologies Spawn Need for Service Concepts

Because of the advances in information-based technologies, a multitude of new service concepts have exploded into the marketplace. Facsimile (FAX) machines, voice messaging, and cellular phones are examples of technology-based service concepts that have substituted for traditional ways of delivering similar services. FAX machines have substituted for mail and phone calls, voice messaging can substitute for secretarial services, and cellular phones have made phone communication accessible from any location. In each of these cases marketing has played a role in educating customers about the service concept and teaching them how to use it.

Sometimes, as in the case of Caller ID services (see the following Technology Spotlight), people need considerable education before they are willing to try new services. A prime example of initial consumer resistance to a new service concept is the case of the automated teller machine (ATM). When ATMs were first introduced, a tremendous marketing effort was needed to communicate the benefits of the new service and to educate people in its use. People were skeptical of the computer technology itself (many bank customers had no experience at all with computers), and some feared that the machine would make an error, forget to record a deposit, or steal their bank card. People simply had to learn that what they had always viewed as a personal service delivered by a human bank teller *could* be delivered reliably through technology and that they, the consumers, were capable of learning to use the technology. Ongoing marketing research identified problems in the early machines and has led to technical enhancements and ease-of-use improvements over time.

Educating customers on how to use the new technologies and communicating the benefits they can derive from them are continuing challenges for service marketers. The roles of technology both in improving the efficiency of service delivery and in the development of radically new service concepts are themes that are explored throughout this text.

Services Marketing Is Different

As the forces described above coincided, those involved soon realized that there was something different about marketing services and managing services. There were issues and problems they hadn't faced in manufacturing and packaged-goods companies. For example, when a firm's core offering is a deed performed by an employee (such as engineering consulting), how can the firm ensure consistent product quality to the marketplace? As service businesses began to turn to marketing and decided to hire marketing people, they naturally recruited from the best marketers in the world—Procter and Gamble, General Foods, Kodak. People who moved from marketing in packaged-goods industries to marketing in health care, banking, and other service industries found their skills and experiences were not directly transferable. They faced issues and dilemmas in marketing services that their experiences in packaged goods and manufacturing had not prepared them for. These people realized the need for new concepts and approaches for marketing and managing service businesses.

Service marketers responded to these forces and began to work across disciplines and with academics and business practitioners from around the world to develop and document marketing practices for service industries. As the field evolved, it expanded to address the concerns and needs of *any* business where service is an integral part of the offering.[6] Frameworks, concepts, and strategies developed to address the fact that "services marketing is different."

TECHNOLOGY SPOTLIGHT

NEW TECHNOLOGY-BASED SERVICES REQUIRE CUSTOMER EDUCATION: THE CASE OF CALLER IDENTIFICATION

"If only the phone would stop ringing." "I'm just a slave to the telephone." "Sometimes I just unplug the telephone so I can get something done." Perhaps even you or someone you know has said this. These are some of the frustrations people voice against the telephone, which, needless to say, is a service very few people choose to live without. The real frustration underlying these quotes is a sense of loss of control over time and an anger at strangers and other unwanted callers who seem to have the right to invade one's privacy whenever they choose.

Enter Caller ID, a service of US WEST Communications, and similar services offered by other telecommunication companies. Caller ID is made possible through advances in information technology that allow identification of the person calling before the telephone is answered. By attaching a special display unit to the telephone, subscribers to US WEST's service can view the name and phone number of the person making an incoming call and decide whether to answer the phone. Thus, if there are people a subscriber really wants to talk to no matter when they call, the call won't be missed by having the phone unplugged or using an answering machine. And subscribers can choose to completely avoid unwanted calls. The display unit also stores the names and numbers of those who called so that calls can be returned when it's more convenient.

Despite the many benefits of this service (and others like it) and the fact that it and related services satisfy real needs of modern-day consumers, US WEST and other companies have faced considerable challenges when introducing the service. First, the privacy issue needs explaining. Whose privacy is being protected by Caller ID? What about the persons calling? What if for some reason they don't *want* their name and number to be displayed (e.g., people calling into hotlines, people calling from battered person shelters)? Blocking options are available that allow callers to stop their name and number from being displayed. But what if innocent people aren't aware of this service or don't know how to use it?

Another marketing challenge relates to educating customers on how the technology works. Considerable information is required so that consumers understand what equipment they might need and how the technology would work in their home or business. Using caller identification services in conjunction with complementary blocking, tracing, and other services also have to be explained. For example, a service of US WEST called Priority Call allows subscribers to program their telephones to use a unique ring when certain people call; the service Call Rejection features the ability to have a recorded message for particular numbers indicating that the subscriber is not accepting calls from those numbers.

While very successful in the communities where it has been introduced, Caller ID is an example of a new technology-based service that has required considerable consumer education and public relations efforts to gain acceptance.

MYTHS ABOUT SERVICES

While the growth and dominance of services is apparent in most advanced economies, until very recently little attention was paid to the businesses and organizations that make up the service sector. Why? Explanation for the inattention to the service sector can be found in several myths surrounding services since the mid-1800s. A myth is a popular belief, usually oversimplified, that tends to explain only *part* of the phenomena. The following are commonly held myths about services.[7] While there is *some* truth in each of the myths, the ideas are generally overly simplistic and logically flawed.

Myth 1: A Service Economy Produces Services at the Expense of Other Sectors

There are those who fear that because services continue to grow at an accelerated pace, eventually advanced economies will produce *only* services, and there will be no manufactured goods output at all. A related belief is that because service production is growing, other sectors cannot grow simultaneously. These fears are largely unfounded. First, in an absolute sense, both manufacturing and services have grown. There are more workers in the manufacturing sector now than there were twenty years ago, and total industrial production has grown as well. Second, much of the employment in the service sector is linked directly to manufacturing; there has been an increasing need for services in support of manufactured products. The tendency of businesses to outsource service support functions (that is, to hire someone outside the firm to provide services that used to be provided by company employees) will result in continued growth of services in support of manufacturing, but *not at the expense of manufacturing.*

A subtle corollary to the misconception that services are produced at the expense of other sectors is that services have no value, or at least that they have less value than manufactured goods. This corollary has its roots in early economic theories. Both Karl Marx and Adam Smith believed that services were less important and less valuable than manufactured goods, and therefore investments in service should be avoided.

However, the value and need for services can be easily seen from the point of view of consumers, manufacturers themselves, other businesses, and the economy as a whole. Modern-day consumers who spend a large proportion of their personal budgets on services place a higher priority on maintaining their spending for services than for manufactured goods. Just think of your own weekly or monthly expenditures. How much do you spend on services? Or try explaining to a consumer that child care, health care, air transportation, entertainment, education, and household services have "no value." Similarly, manufacturers and other businesses value highly the services of design engineers, transportation specialists, inventory systems engineers, and those in other particular high-value-added fields. Such services can improve productivity and enhance the ultimate value of the goods produced. Finally, data suggest that traditionally the service sector has served as a stabilizing force for the economy across business cycles. A 1987 study revealed that employment in services is more stable than employment in the manufacturing sector during recessionary periods,[8] because spending for services and employment in the service sector holds more steady. Although this buffering effect may be diminishing somewhat as more services become tied directly to manufacturing cycles through outsourcing, the traditional macroeconomic value of services should not be overlooked.

Myth 2: Service Jobs Are Low Paying and Menial

Intuitively, many people believe that service employees are primarily small retailers, fast-food employees, hairdressers, store clerks, and low-skilled workers. There is some truth to this perception in that *many* small businesses are services *and* when people are laid off in low-skilled manufacturing jobs they typically see their employment alternatives as limited to low-paying, low-skilled service jobs. However, easily half of all service workers in the United States are in highly skilled, white-collar occupations such as law, accounting, education, banking, and medicine. And much of the growth in service jobs has come in the more highly skilled sectors. People in these professional service jobs are not at the low-pay end of the wage scale.

Related to the low-skilled, low-paid misconception is the idea that the firms who employ service workers are primarily "mom and pop" operations, or businesses operating at a very small scale. What this suggests is that, while the service sector may employ large numbers and dominate the gross domestic product (GDP), the businesses that make up the sector are small, numerous, and individually not very powerful. However, both Profit Impact of Market Strategy (PIMS) and *Fortune* 500 data suggest that concentration and scale among larger service industries are comparable to those of larger manufacturing industries. Examples are easy to cite. Think of the airline, banking, telecommunication, and credit industries, for example, which are all relatively concentrated. And think of specific companies such as AT&T, American Express, Federal Express, Marriott Hotel Corporation—not exactly "mom and pop" operations.

Myth 3: Service Production Is Labor Intensive and Low in Productivity

Common images of the service economy suggest businesses where investments in labor far outweigh capital investments and where productivity is sluggish, creating a drag on the entire economy. Such images are certainly not very positive. While *some* service industries are labor intensive (e.g., many personal services, restaurants, professional services), as many or more are high in capital intensity. For example, one study revealed that of 145 industries studied, nearly half of the 30 most capital intensive were services, and few service industries were classified in the lowest capital-intensity categories.[9] In the late 1980s, aggregate investment in plant and equipment by the service sector surpassed that of manufacturing.[10] One simply has to think of examples of highly capital-intensive service industries—airlines, telecommunications, utilities—to know that the labor intensity myth is not generally true.

With regard to productivity, for a long time people have stated as unquestioned fact that service sector productivity is low and that rates of improvement are almost nonexistent.[11] The low-productivity issue is complex and is complicated by difficulties in measuring service productivity and in accounting for trade-offs between quantity and quality as determinants of productivity.[12] With traditional measures, gains in productivity generally show up as either lower costs (for the same value/quality) or higher value/quality to the customer (for the same costs). The problem for many services is in determining how to measure value or quality. For example, day-care centers now handle more children per worker, which on the surface would appear to be a productivity gain on the basis of lower costs for the same "output." But many would say the likely decline in quality of care offsets the lower cost productivity gain.[13] Such issues have caused the Bureau of Labor Statistics simply to not attempt to measure productivity in many service industries, including health care, real estate, and insurance.

A number of studies using measurement approaches adapted for services show mounting evidence that service sector productivity is gaining and in many cases may actually surpass gains in manufacturing productivity. Among the new evidence is a study by McKinsey & Co. that concluded that five major U.S. service industries (airlines, telecommunications, retail banks, retailing, and restaurants) outperformed their European and Japanese counterparts in productivity gains, most by a wide margin.[14] Recent Bureau of Labor Statistics data support the McKinsey findings, as does research by Stephen Roach of Morgan Stanley, suggesting that for the service sector "the productivity gains are real."[15] Further evidence is the tremendous success of U.S. service exports, which has resulted in a rising trade surplus in services.

Myth 4: The Growth of Government Is the Reason We Are a Service Economy

This is an easy one to counter. While it is true that employment in the public sector has grown tremendously in the United States over the last fifty years, the U.S. economy would still be a service-based one without government. In fact, over half of the U.S. labor force is employed in private sector services.[16]

Myth 5: Service Is a Necessary Evil for Manufacturing Firms

Historically, many manufacturers viewed service (defined as after-sale support) as something they *had* to provide, essentially a cost of doing business and not in any way profitable. This historic view typically equated service with repair, maintenance, and complaint handling. More recently, the view of service has broadened and includes anything intangible added to the product that will increase its utility or value to the customer. Many manufacturers now view services as profit centers and as vehicles to differentiate their products from those of the competition. IBM is an example of a company in which service is coming to be viewed in this way (see introductory paragraphs in chapter 2 for more details on IBM's approach). Similarly, Xerox Corporation reoriented itself in the early 1980s to emphasize the service components of its offerings. Figure 1-4 shows a Xerox copier advertisement that clearly establishes the importance of service to Xerox's core product offering. Many have suggested that the competitive battleground in manufacturing has shifted to service as a logical next step in the competitive chain that starts with product technology, then moves to cost-based competition, then to quality, and then to service.[17]

Myth 6: Managing Services Is Just Like Managing Manufacturing Businesses

This is the myth that really drives the need for this book and the development of courses on services marketing and management. If this myth were true, there would be no need for special tools and approaches for service businesses.

In the late 1970s and early 1980s, the debate over "is the marketing of services different?" raged among marketing scholars. Many took the position that the differences between products and services were more of emphasis than of nature or kind. Regardless of the position taken, such differences were thought to lead to significant variations in the strategies necessary for service organizations to market their products successfully. In 1979, Gary Knisely, a management consultant, decided to take this question to actual service marketers. Conclusions from his interviews are captured in Box 1-1; they give a historical sense of the challenges faced by early services marketers.[18] Although scholars debated whether marketing management was different for goods than for services, for top managers with experience in both areas the differences were pronounced

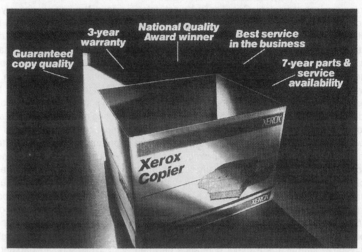

Some of the best features of our copiers don't come in the box.

When you buy a copier, don't forget you're also buying a company.

And when the name on the box is Xerox, you get a lot more than a copier. You get a company dedicated to your complete satisfaction.

For example, only Xerox offers a three-year warranty on all desktop copiers that it makes—that's 12 times longer than any other manufacturer.

Xerox also guarantees copy quality. So you can be sure your 20,000th copy will be just as good as your first.

Equally unique is our guarantee to provide parts and service for all our copiers for up to seven years.

Add to that the fact that every Xerox copier is backed by the best supplies and the best service organization in the business.

And that—when it comes to documents —no company has more experience than Xerox.

All of which are just a few of the reasons that Xerox was recently honored with the Malcolm Baldrige National Quality Award.

So make your next copier a Xerox. And get the best features in a copier— plus the best features in a company.

For information about any Xerox copier, call 1-800 TEAM-XRX. Ext. 250A.

Xerox

© 1990 XEROX Corporation. XEROX® is a trademark of XEROX CORPORATION

FIGURE 1-4

Source: Reprinted with permission, courtesy of Worldwide Strategic Advertising, Xerox Corporation.

BOX 1-1

**IS THE MARKETING OF SERVICES DIFFERENT?
A HISTORICAL PERSPECTIVE**

In 1979, Gary Knisely, a principal of the consulting firm Johnson Smith & Knisely, asked the above question to practicing services marketers. Specifically, Knisely interviewed several high-ranking marketing executives who had all gone to work in the consumer service industry after extensive experience in the consumer package goods industry (known for its marketing prowess).

These executives found differences, all right. Their discoveries came from attempts to apply (with mixed success, it turned out) consumer-goods marketing practices directly to services. James L. Schorr of Holiday Inns Inc., formerly with Procter & Gamble, found that he could not overlay a consumer-goods firm's marketing system onto a service firm. He, and the other executives interviewed, expressed certain recurring themes. First, more variables exist in the marketing mix for services than for consumer goods. Schorr claimed that in a service business, marketing and operations are more closely linked than in a manufacturing business. Thus the service production process is part of the marketing process. Second, customer interface is a major difference between goods marketing and services marketing. Executives from package goods companies never had to think in terms of a direct dialogue with their customers. For Schorr, the marketing of hotel rooms boiled down to a "people-on-people" sale. Robert L. Catlin, in relating his experience in the airline industry, stated that "Your people are as much of your product in the consumer's mind as any other attribute of the service." People buy products because they believe they work. But with services, people deal with people they like and they tend to buy services because they believe they will like them. This makes the customer/employee interface a critical component of marketing.

The executives also commented on how the marketing mix variables common to both goods and services have vastly different implications for marketing strategy in the two industries. In the distribution and selling of services, the firm cannot rely on well-stocked shelves past which the consumer can push a cart and make selections. Consumers' exposure to the full range of need-fulfilling service products may be limited by the salesperson's "mental inventory" of services and how he or she prioritizes them. We can say that the service product manager is competing for the "mental shelf space" of the firm's sales personnel. For Rodney Woods, group marketing officer at United States Trust Co., pricing was the most critical factor in the marketing of services versus products. For Woods, determining the costs associated with service production and delivery proved very difficult, much more of a challenge than he had faced in his earlier career working with such large package goods companies as Pillsbury, Procter & Gamble, and Bristol-Myers. Also, the benefits of using price as a promotional weapon were not as apparent. Promotional price cuts tended to erode hard fought positioning and image.

While scholars debated early on the issue of whether marketing management differs for goods versus services, for top managers with experience in both areas the differences were pronounced in 1979. They still are today. The differences these early service marketers noted were the impetus for many of the ideas, concepts, and strategies practiced today.

Source: This discussion is based on interviews conducted by Gary Knisely that appeared in *Advertising Age* on January 15, 1979, February 19, 1979, March 19, 1979, and May 14, 1979.

in 1979 and still are today. The differences these early services marketers noted are categorized and discussed in the next section.

DIFFERENCES IN GOODS VERSUS SERVICES MARKETING

There is general agreement that inherent differences between goods and services exist and that they result in unique, or at least different, management challenges for service businesses and for manufacturers that offer services as a core offering.[19] These differences and associated marketing implications are shown in Table 1-3.

TABLE 1-3 SERVICES ARE DIFFERENT

Goods	Services	Resulting implications
Tangible	Intangible	Services cannot be inventoried. Services cannot be patented. Services cannot be readily displayed or communicated. Pricing is difficult.
Standardized	Heterogeneous	Service delivery and customer satisfaction depend on employee actions. Service quality depends on many uncontrollable factors. There is no sure knowledge that the service delivered matches what was planned and promoted.
Production separate from consumption	Simultaneous production and consumption	Customers participate in and affect the transaction. Customers affect each other. Employees affect the service outcome. Decentralization may be essential. Mass production is difficult.
Nonperishable	Perishable	It is difficult to synchronize supply and demand with services. Services cannot be returned or resold.

Source: Adapted from Valarie A. Zeithaml, A. Parasuraman, and Leonard L. Berry, "Problems and Strategies in Services Marketing," *Journal of Marketing* 49 (Spring 1985): 33–46.

Intangibility

The most basic, and universally cited, difference between goods and services is intangibility. Because services are performances or actions rather than objects, they cannot be seen, felt, tasted, or touched in the same manner that we can sense tangible goods. For example, health-care services are actions (e.g., surgery, diagnosis, examination, treatment) performed by providers and directed toward patients and their families. These services cannot actually be seen or touched by the patient, although the patient may be able to see and touch certain tangible components of the service (e.g., equipment, hospital room). In fact, many services such as health care are difficult for the consumer to grasp even mentally. Even after a diagnosis or surgery has been completed the patient may not fully comprehend the service performed.

Resulting Marketing Implications Intangibility presents several marketing challenges: Services cannot be inventoried, and therefore fluctuations in demand are often difficult to manage. For example, there is tremendous demand for resort accommodations in Phoenix in February, but little demand in July. Yet resort owners have the same number of rooms to sell year-round. Services cannot be patented legally, and new service concepts can therefore easily be copied by competitors. Services cannot be readily displayed or easily communicated to customers, so quality may be difficult for consumers to assess. Decisions about what to include in advertising and other promotional materials are challenging, as is pricing. The actual costs of a "unit of service" are hard to determine and the price/quality relationship is complex.

Heterogeneity

Because services are performances, frequently produced by humans, no two services will be precisely alike. The employees delivering the service frequently *are* the service in the customer's eyes, and people may differ in their performance from day to day or even hour to hour. Heterogeneity also results because no two customers are precisely alike; each will have unique demands or experience the service in a unique way. Thus, the heterogeneity connected with services is largely the result of human interaction (between and among employees and customers) and all of the vagaries that accompany it. For example, a tax accountant may provide a different service experience to two different customers on the same day depending on their individual needs and personalities and on whether the accountant is interviewing them when he or she is fresh in the morning or tired at the end of a long day of meetings.

Resulting Marketing Implications   Because services are heterogeneous across time, organizations, and people, ensuring consistent service quality is challenging. Quality actually depends on many factors that cannot be fully controlled by the service supplier, such as the ability of the consumer to articulate his or her needs, the ability and willingness of personnel to satisfy those needs, the presence (or absence) of other customers, and the level of demand for the service. Because of these complicating factors, the service manager cannot always know for sure that the service is being delivered in a manner consistent with what was originally planned and promoted.

Simultaneous Production and Consumption

Whereas most goods are produced first, then sold and consumed, most services are sold first and then produced and consumed simultaneously. For example, an automobile can be manufactured in Detroit, shipped to San Francisco, sold two months later, and consumed over a period of years. But restaurant services cannot be provided until they have been sold, and the dining experience is essentially produced and consumed at the same time. Frequently this also means that the customer is present while the service is being produced and thus views and may even take part in the production process. This also means that frequently customers will interact with each other during the service production process and thus may affect each others' experiences. For example, strangers seated next to each other in an airplane may well affect the nature of the service experience for each other. That passengers understand this fact is clearly apparent in the way business travelers will often go to great lengths to be sure they are not seated next to families with small children. Another outcome of simultaneous production and consumption is that service producers find themselves playing a role as part of the product itself and as an essential ingredient in the service experience for the consumer.

Resulting Marketing Implications   Because services often are produced and consumed at the same time, mass production is difficult if not impossible. The quality of service and customer satisfaction will be highly dependent on what happens in "real time," including actions of employees and the interactions between employees and customers. Similarly, it is not usually possible to gain significant economies of scale through centralization. Usually operations need to be relatively decentralized so that the service can be delivered directly to the consumer in convenient locations. Also because of simultaneous production and consumption, the customer is involved in and observes the production process and thus may affect (positively or negatively) the outcome of the service transaction. In a related vein, "problem customers" (those who disrupt the service process) can cause problems for themselves or others in the service setting, resulting in lowered customer satisfaction. For example, in a restaurant setting, an over-demanding and intoxicated patron will command extra attention from the service provider and negatively impact the experiences of other customers.

Perishability

Perishability refers to the fact that services cannot be saved, stored, resold, or returned. A seat on an airplane or in a restaurant, an hour of a lawyer's time, or telephone line capacity not used cannot be reclaimed and used or resold at a later time. This is in contrast to goods that can be stored in inventory or resold another day, or even returned if the consumer is unhappy. Wouldn't it be nice if a bad haircut could be returned or resold to another consumer? Perishability makes this an unlikely possibility for most services.

Resulting Marketing Implications   A primary issue that marketers face in relation to service perishability is the inability to inventory. Demand forecasting and creative planning for capacity utilization are therefore important and challenging decision areas. The fact that services cannot typically be returned or resold also implies a need for strong recovery strategies when things do go wrong. For example, while a bad haircut cannot be returned, the hairdresser can and should have strategies for recovering the customer's good will if and when such a problem occurs.

Challenges and Questions for Service Marketers

Because of these basic differences between goods and services, marketers of services face some very real and distinctive challenges. The challenges revolve around understanding customer needs and expectations for service, tangibilizing the service offering, dealing with a myriad of people and delivery issues, and keeping promises made to customers. Answers to questions such as the ones listed here still elude managers of services.

How can service quality be defined and improved when the product is intangible and nonstandardized?

How can new services be designed and tested effectively when the service is essentially an intangible process?

How can the firm be certain it is communicating a consistent and relevant image when so many elements of the marketing mix communicate to customers, and some of these elements are the service providers themselves?

How does the firm accommodate fluctuating demand when capacity is fixed and the service itself is perishable?

How can the firm best motivate and select service employees who, because the service is delivered in real-time, become a critical part of the product itself?

How should prices be set when it is difficult to determine actual costs of production and price may be inextricably intertwined with perceptions of quality?

How should the firm be organized so that good strategic and tactical decisions are made when a decision in any of the functional areas of marketing, operations, and human resources may have significant impact on the other two areas?

How can the balance between standardization and personalization be determined to maximize both the efficiency of the organization and the satisfaction of its customers?

How can the organization protect new service concepts from competitors when service processes cannot be legally patented?

How does the firm communicate quality and value to consumers when the offering is intangible and cannot be readily tried or displayed?

How can the organization ensure the delivery of consistent quality service when both the organization's employees and the customers themselves can affect the service outcome?

THE SERVICES MARKETING TRIANGLE

The preceding questions are some of the many raised by managers and marketers in service businesses that we will address throughout this text. A useful way to conceptualize the questions and decisions that need to be made is presented in the services marketing triangle shown in Figure 1-5. The triangle suggests that there are three types of marketing that must be successfully carried out for a service organization to succeed, and that all of them revolve around making and keeping promises to customers.

On the right side of the triangle are the external marketing efforts that the firm engages in to set up its customers' expectations and make promises to customers regarding what is to be delivered. *Anything* that communicates to the customer before service delivery can be viewed as part of this external marketing function. In service firms there are many factors that communicate to customers beyond the traditional elements of advertising, special promotions, sales, and public relations, for example, the firm's personnel and the physical facilities themselves.

On the bottom of the triangle is what has been termed *interactive marketing,* or what some refer to as *real-time marketing.* Here the actual service delivery takes place—the firm's employees interact directly with customers. It is at this point that the promise is delivered (or not delivered). Having a positive link between what is promised through external marketing and what is delivered through interactive marketing is critical. All the external marketing in the world is useless if promises cannot be kept.

The left side of the triangle suggests the critical role played by internal marketing, which enables employees to keep the promises that have been made to customers. In-

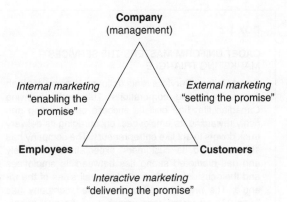

FIGURE 1-5   The services marketing triangle.

Source: Adapted by permission of Prentice-Hall, Englewood Cliffs, N.J., based on Philip Kotler, *Marketing Management: Analysis, Planning, Implementation, and Control,* 8th ed., (1994), p. 470.

ternal marketing (discussed extensively in a later chapter) refers to the activities the firm must carry out to train, motivate, and reward its employees. Unless service employees are able and willing to deliver on the promises made, the firm will not be successful in keeping its promises and the services marketing triangle will collapse. Internal marketing hinges on the assumption that employee satisfaction and customer satisfaction are inextricably linked.

What the triangle implies is that all three sides are critical to successful services marketing and management, that without one of the sides in place the triangle, or the total marketing effort, cannot be supported. Each side represents significant challenges for most service businesses, and as we proceed through the text we will find approaches and strategies for dealing with all three. Cadet Uniform Services, a successful Canadian company, has captured the essence of the triangle in its marketing efforts, as illustrated in Box 1-2.

THE SERVICES MARKETING MIX

Another way to begin addressing the challenges of services marketing is to think creatively about the marketing mix—through an expanded marketing mix for services.

Traditional Marketing Mix

One of the most basic concepts in marketing is the *marketing mix,* defined as the elements an organization controls that can be used to satisfy or communicate with customers. The traditional marketing mix is composed of the four p's: product, price, place (distribution), and promotion.[20] These elements appear as core decision variables in any marketing text or marketing plan. The notion of a mix implies that all of the variables are interrelated and depend on each other to some extent. Further, the marketing mix philosophy implies that there is an optimal mix of the four factors for a given market segment at a given point in time.

Key strategy decision areas for each of the four p's are captured in the first four columns in Table 1-4. Careful management of *product, place, promotion,* and *price* will

BOX 1-2

CADET UNIFORM MASTERS THE SERVICES MARKETING TRIANGLE

Cadet Uniform Services rents uniforms to some of North America's leading corporations. This small, growing Canadian firm has built its success on recruiting and richly rewarding its employees, encouraging its delivery truck drivers to act like entrepreneurs. The company has also managed its customers' expectations effectively and has promoted strong ties between its employees and their customers, thus mastering all sides of the triangle. The reward for this determined company has been 22 percent average growth over the past twenty years and double-digit gross profit margins that exceed the industry norms. In 1993 the company was a certificate-of-merit winner in the Awards for Business Excellence, the Canadian equivalent of the Baldrige award. Turnover rate among Cadet's employees is very low, at about 7 percent, and customers don't leave either. The company loses only 1 percent of its customers annually due to factors within the company's control. Cadet offers a clear illustration of a company that has excelled in the three types of marketing in the services triangle.

External marketing: "setting the promise"

By staying in close touch with its customers Cadet understands their needs and is able to design its services around customer expectations. Because drivers are assigned to accounts and stay with those same accounts over long periods of time, the drivers are able to build relationships and understand customers' changing needs over time. Everything that Cadet communicates to its customers says "quality service," from the people it hires, to the way employees dress, to employees' personalities, to the trucks they drive and the quality of the uniforms they supply.

Interactive marketing: "delivering the promise"

Promises of quality service are delivered to Cadet's cus-

tomers through its drivers. Delivery drivers—called customer service representatives (CSRs)—are assigned an account, and that account then belongs to the driver for the life of the account. Customers thus interact regularly with the same person and get to know their driver. If a customer leaves the company for what are determined to be "controllable" causes, the driver loses income. Drivers spend most of their nine-hour days delivering and collecting uniforms, interacting with customers, and building new business. In the afternoon drivers are on the phone handling requests and complaints from their own clients. Says one driver, "What I like about this job is the rapport you get to build with customers. You become their focal point." Some 50 to 60 percent of a driver's pay is based on customer satisfaction and retention.

Internal marketing: "enabling the promise"

To ensure that its drivers are able to interact effectively with customers and retain their business, Cadet is very careful about who it recruits for those jobs, and then it trains its employees to be successful at customer retention. Seven interviews are the norm for Cadet's CSRs. The company looks for employees who are obsessively neat, proud of their work, physically fit, and exceptionally friendly. Says one of the company recruiters, "I'm looking for someone with a positive attitude, someone who wants to work, who's ready to work." Once they are hired, Cadet employees go through three months of training to learn the whole scope of the business before setting foot in a delivery truck. After that they ride with experienced CSRs for nine months to watch how they interact with customers. Only then are they eligible for their own routes. Cadet also pays its CSRs well—about $40,000, nearly twice the industry average.

Sources: The following two articles featured information about Cadet Uniform Services: "How to Keep Customers for Life: Some Clues for Putting Theory Into Practice," *The Service Edge* 5, 9 (September 1992): 1–3; Ronald Henkoff, "Finding, Training and Keeping the Best Service Workers," *Fortune,* October 3, 1994, pp. 110–122.

clearly also be essential to the successful marketing of services. However, the strategies for the four p's require some modifications when applied to services. For example, traditionally promotion is thought of as involving decisions related to sales, advertising, sales promotions, and publicity. In services, these factors are also important, but because services are produced and consumed simultaneously, service delivery people (such as clerks, ticket-takers, nurses, phone personnel) are involved in "real time" promotion of the service even if their jobs are typically defined in terms of the operational

TABLE 1-4 EXPANDED MARKETING MIX FOR SERVICES

Product	Place	Promotion	Price	People	Physical evidence	Process
Physical good features	Channel type	Promotion blend	Flexibility	Employees	Facility design	Flow of activities
Quality level	Exposure	Salespeople	Price level	Recruiting	Aesthetics	Standardized
Accessories	Intermediaries	Number	Terms	Training	Functionality	Customized
Packaging	Outlet locations	Selection	Differentiation	Motivation	Ambient conditions	Number of steps
Warranties	Transportation	Training	Discounts	Rewards	Equipment	Simple
Product lines	Storage	Incentives	Allowances	Teamwork	Signage	Complex
Branding	Managing channels	Advertising		Customers	Employee dress	Level of customer involvement
		Targets		Education	Other tangibles	
		Media types		Training	Reports	
		Types of ads		Communicating culture and values	Business cards	
		Copy thrust		Employee research	Statements	
		Sales promotion			Guarantees	
		Publicity				

function they perform. Pricing also becomes very complex in services where "unit costs" needed to calculate prices may be difficult to determine, and where the customer frequently uses price as a cue to quality.

Expanded Mix for Services

Because services are usually produced and consumed simultaneously, customers are often present in the firm's factory, interact directly with the firm's personnel, and are actually part of the service production process. Also, because services are intangible customers will often be looking for any tangible cue to help them understand the nature of the service experience. These facts have led services marketers to conclude that they can use additional variables to communicate with and satisfy their customers. For example, in the hotel industry the design and decor of the hotel as well as the appearance and attitudes of its employees will influence customer perceptions and experiences.

Acknowledgment of the importance of these additional communication variables has led services marketers to adopt the concept of an expanded marketing mix for services shown in the three remaining columns in Table 1-4.[21] In addition to the traditional four p's, the services marketing mix includes *people, physical evidence,* and *process.*

People   All human actors who play a part in service delivery and thus influence the buyer's perceptions; namely, the firm's personnel, the customer, and other customers in the service environment.

All of the human actors participating in the delivery of a service provide cues to the customer regarding the nature of the service itself. How these people are dressed, their personal appearance, and their attitudes and behaviors all influence the customer's perceptions of the service. The service provider or contact person can be very important. In fact, for some services, such as consulting, counseling, teaching, and other professional relationship-based services, the provider *is* the service. In other cases the contact person .may play what appears to be a relatively small part in service delivery, for instance, a telephone installer, an airline baggage handler, or an equipment delivery dispatcher. Yet research suggests that even these providers may be the focal point of service encounters that can prove critical for the organization.

Physical Evidence   The environment in which the service is delivered and where the firm and customer interact, and any tangible components that facilitate performance or communication of the service.

The physical evidence of service includes all of the tangible representations of the service such as brochures, letterhead, business cards, report formats, signage, and equipment. In some cases it includes the physical facility where the service is offered, for example, the retail bank branch facility. In other cases, such as telecommunication services, the physical facility may be irrelevant. In this case other tangibles such as billing statements and appearance of the repair truck may be important indicators of quality. Especially when consumers have little on which to judge the actual quality of service they will rely on these cues, just as they rely on the cues provided by the people and the service process. Physical evidence cues provide excellent opportunities for the firm to send consistent and strong messages regarding the organization's purpose, the intended market segments, and the nature of the service.

Process   The actual procedures, mechanisms, and flow of activities by which the service is delivered—the service delivery and operating systems.

The actual delivery steps the customer experiences, or the operational flow of the service, will also provide customers with evidence on which to judge the service. Some services are very complex, requiring the customer to follow a complicated and extensive series of actions to complete the process. Highly bureaucratized services frequently follow this pattern, and the logic of the steps involved often escapes the customer. Another distinguishing characteristic of the process that can provide evidence to the customer is whether the service follows a production-line/standardized approach or whether the process is an empowered/customized one. None of these characteristics of the service is inherently better or worse than another. Rather, the point is that these process characteristics are another form of evidence used by the consumer to judge service. For example, two successful airline companies, Southwest in the United States and Singapore Airlines, follow extremely different process models. Southwest is a no-frills (no food, no assigned seats), no exceptions, low-priced airline that offers frequent, relatively short-length domestic flights. All of the evidence it provides is consistent with its vision and market position. Singapore Airlines, on the other hand, focuses on the business traveler and is concerned with meeting individual traveler needs. Thus, its process is highly customized to the individual, and employees are empowered to provide nonstandard service when needed. Both airlines have been very successful.

The three new marketing-mix elements (people, physical evidence, and process) are included in the marketing mix as separate elements because they are within the control of the firm and any or all of them may influence the customer's initial decision to purchase a service, as well as the customer's level of satisfaction and repurchase decisions. The traditional elements as well as the new marketing-mix elements will be explored in depth in future chapters.

SUMMARY

This chapter has set the stage for further learning about services marketing by presenting information about changes in the world economy and business practice that have driven the focus on service: the fact that services dominate the modern economies of the world; the focus on service as a competitive business imperative; specific needs of the deregulated and professional service industries; the role of new service concepts growing from technological advances; and the realization that services marketing is different. A broad definition of services as deeds, processes, and performances was presented, and several myths about services were dispelled.

Building on this fundamental understanding of the service economy, the chapter went on to present the key differences between goods and services that underlie the need for distinct strategies and concepts for managing service businesses. These basic differences are that services are intangible, heterogeneous, produced and consumed simultaneously, and perishable. Because of these basic differences, service managers face a number of challenges in marketing, including the complex problem of how to deliver quality services consistently.

Two powerful concepts—the services marketing triangle and the services marketing mix—were introduced as conceptual frameworks for beginning to address the unique challenges of services marketing. The remainder of the text will focus on exploring the unique challenges further and on developing solutions for dealing with these challenges that will help you to become an effective service manager.

DISCUSSION QUESTIONS

1 The U.S. GDP and the GDP of most developed economies are dominated by services. In your opinion is this good, bad, or irrelevant?

2 In your other business courses, how much attention is paid to the distinct issues facing service businesses? Why have services received relatively little attention in business schools and management strategies compared with package and other manufactured goods?

3 What are the basic differences in marketing goods versus services? What are the implications of these differences for Johnson, MacMillan, & Allen, the engineering consulting firm described in the chapter's opening vignette?

4 One of the underlying frameworks for the text is the services marketing mix. Discuss why each of the three new mix elements (process, people, and physical evidence) is included. How might each of these communicate with or help to satisfy an organization's customers?

5 Think of a service job you have had or currently have. How effective, in your opinion, was or is the organization in managing the elements of the services marketing mix?

6 Again, think of a service job you have had or currently have. How did or does the organization handle relevant problems listed in Table 1-3?

7 How can quality service be used in a manufacturing context for competitive advantage? Think of your answer to this question in the context of automobiles or computers or some other manufactured product you have actually purchased.

8 Choose an organizational context you are familiar with. Discuss each of the three sides of the services marketing triangle in the context of that organization.

EXERCISES

1 Roughly calculate your budget for an average month. What percentage of your budget goes for services versus goods? Do the services you purchase have value? In what sense? If you had to cut back on your expenses what would you cut out?

2 Visit two local retail service providers that you believe are positioned very differently (e.g., K-Mart and Macy's, or Burger King and a fine-dining restaurant). From your own observations, compare their strategies on the elements of the services marketing mix.

3 What are the implications of the services marketing triangle for the organization you work for, the business school, your project company, or another relevant unit/department? Who occupies each of the three points on the triangle? How can each of the types of marketing (external, interactive, and internal) be carried out more effectively? Are there specific challenges or barriers to effective marketing in any of the three areas?

NOTES

1   James Brian Quinn, Jordan J. Baruch, and Penny Cushman Paquette, "Technology in Services," *Scientific American* 257, 6 (December 1987): 50–58.

2   *Business Week,* "1993 Industry Outlook," January 11, 1993.

3   Ralph T. King, Jr., "U.S. Service Exports Are Growing Rapidly, but Almost Unnoticed," *Wall Street Journal,* April 21, 1993, p. 1.

4   "Setting a Quality Standard: WordPerfect Support," from *WordPerfect Report,* Summer/Fall 1994.

5   "Portable Computer Allows Hospitals to Measure Service 'Anytime, Anyplace,' " *The Service Edge* 6, 6 (June 1993): 7.

6   The evolution of the services marketing field and literature is documented in two companion articles in the Spring 1993 issue of *Journal of Retailing*: "Building a New Academic Field—The Case of Services Marketing," by Leonard L. Berry and A. Parasuraman, pp. 13–60, and "Tracking the Evolution of the Services Marketing Literature," by Raymond P. Fisk, Stephen W. Brown, and Mary Jo Bitner, pp. 61–103.

7   Many of the points in this section were raised by James Brian Quinn, *Intelligent Enterprise* (New York: Free Press, 1992), chap. 1, and Ronald K. Shelp, "The Service Economy Gets No Respect," *Across the Board,* February 1984 (New York: The Conference Board).

8   G. Moore, "The Services Industries and the Business Cycle," *Business Economics,* April 1987.

9   R. Kutscher and J. Mark, "The Service Sector: Some Common Perceptions Reviewed," *Monthly Labor Review,* April 1983.

10 "Services Are Supplying the Steam for Business Investment," *Fortune,* June 5, 1989.

11 Stephen S. Roach, "Services under Siege—The Restructuring Imperative," *Harvard Business Review,* September–October 1991, pp. 82–91.

12 "Productivity Statistics for the Service Sector May Understate Gains," *Wall Street Journal,* August 12, 1992, p. 1.

13 Ibid.

14 This study and others were cited in Myron Magnet, "Good News for the Service Economy," *Fortune,* May 3, 1993, pp. 47–52.

15 Ibid.

16 Shelp, "The Service Economy Gets No Respect."

17 William H. Davidow, "The Coming Service Crisis," *Field Service Manager,* October 1986.

18 This discussion is based on interviews conducted by Gary Knisely that appeared in *Advertising Age* on January 15, 1979; February 19, 1979; March 19, 1979; and May 14, 1979.

19 Discussion of these issues is found in many services marketing publications. The discussion here is based on Valarie A. Zeithaml, A. Parasuraman, and Leonard L. Berry, "Problems and Strategies in Services Marketing," *Journal of Marketing* 49 (Spring 1985): 33–46; and Stephen W. Brown and Mary Jo Bitner, "Services Marketing," *AMA Management Handbook,* 3d Edition (New York: AMACOM Books, 1994), pp. 15-5 to 15-15.

20 E. Jerome McCarthy and William D. Perreault, Jr., *Basic Marketing, A Global Managerial Approach* (Boston: Richard D. Irwin, 1993).

21 Bernard H. Booms and Mary Jo Bitner, "Marketing Strategies and Organizational Structures for Service Firms," in *Marketing of Services*, eds. J. H. Donnelly and W. R. George (Chicago: American Marketing Association, 1981) pp. 47–51.

2

KEY COMPETITIVE TRENDS
AND CONCEPTUAL
FRAMEWORK
OF THE BOOK

Time: *January 1993*
Location: *Boardrooms across the United States*
Situation: *Frustrated and dissatisfied board members of the corporate pillars of American business history—General Motors, American Express, Sears, Westinghouse, and IBM—are trying to decide how to rescue their troubled companies from ruin. Never has a period in business history seen so many ousted CEOs (including GM's Roger Stempl, IBM's John Akers, American Express's James Robinson), so much retrenching and restructuring, so little growth, and so much fear for the future. No business prognosticator in the high-growth 1980s could have forecast the slow-moving 1990s that brought about a virtual revolution in competition. What happened to these model corporations of the past? Where did they falter? What are they not doing that other giants (like AT&T and GE) are doing to succeed? Can they regain viability? What strategies are needed?*

    At least one of these companies, IBM, has recognized that the revenue decline, sluggish growth, and diminishing profits in manufacturing require a new corporate focus: services. Rather than emphasizing high-end systems such as mainframes, which are being replaced by smaller machines, or personal computers, plagued by devastating price wars, the company is now transitioning itself to a services firm, developing three major categories of services: professional and systems integration services, functional consulting, and management consulting.

Few would argue that the competitive environment in the United States and the world is changing rapidly in the 1990s. Intense rivalry within and between industries downsizing of companies, internationalization and commoditization of markets—all of these forces present challenges to today's companies that arguably exceed those at any time in the past. To adjust to this metamorphosis, the shape, configuration, and behavior of companies are being scrutinized. Many powerful market leaders of the past were too slow in recognizing change and remained tethered to tradition for too long. Market domination by size and scale, the credo of many of these giants, no longer seems to lead to revenues or profits.

Competitive changes are critical to all companies that engage in services marketing. Most experts agree that change for these companies is no longer optional or incremental but instead is inevitable and revolutionary. The new ways to win seem counter to tradition: act small, like an entrepreneur. Even if you are as large as GE, AT&T, or Johnson and Johnson, mimic or become many small companies. Drop out of markets you can't serve well. Stay nimble. Be intimate with the customer. Focus on strengthening relationships with your best customers and walk away from others. Openly share information.

Managers of service companies must understand the environmental and competitive changes and assess their impact on designing and delivering services. For this reason we will incorporate information about them in this chapter and throughout the text.

The objectives of this chapter are to:

1 Introduce seven of the most powerful competitive trends currently shaping marketing and business strategy:

* Customer satisfaction and customer focus
* Value
* Total quality management (TQM) and service quality
* Emphasis on service as a key differentiator in manufacturing firms
* New measurement systems that link customer satisfaction with financial goals and operational measurements
* Emerging technology
* Internationalization of service

2 Present a conceptual framework for delivering service that will serve as the structure for this textbook.

COMPETITIVE TRENDS FOR THE 1990S AND BEYOND

Customer Satisfaction and Customer Focus

Many of the historic sources of company superiority—technology, innovation, economies of scale—allowed companies to focus their efforts internally and prosper. Today, internal focus in many companies is shifting to an external focus on the customer. Companies are acknowledging that unless customer needs are taken into account in designing and delivering both services and goods, all the technical superiority in the world will not bring success.

While the requirement for customer focus may seem obvious to a marketing student or practitioner, the reality is that many organizations—private, public, and even nonprofit—have historically viewed the customer as a distant and sometimes even bothersome necessity. To these companies, external focus on the customer brings with it a major culture change. High-tech companies driven by research and development (R&D) and invention, in fact, sometimes see an inherent conflict in focusing on the customer, believing that the creativity and autonomy of the company will be stifled. Yet the reality is that customers today will not buy overly complicated services or overengineered products, not just because they are too expensive but also because the extras and complications actually detract from the worth of the offering.

Customer focus is also anathema to many professional services organizations in medicine, law, accounting, even higher education. To these and other professions, there seems to be a conflict between technical excellence and customer-perceived excellence. Lawyers, for example, sometime see customer focus as a paradox: customers, they believe, are not knowledgeable enough to know what they need. What legal clients want, they contend, is to receive the least costly, least constraining advice—the opposite in many cases of what the experts know they need. Physicians and dentists sometimes offer a credible argument about the difficulty of simultaneously providing high technical quality and customer satisfaction: courses of treatment needed to eliminate disease are often painful and uncomfortable. Professors and other educators, too, may fear that customer focus means they must compromise their ethics and standards by focusing on what they believe students want: no homework, easy A's, and twenty-four-hour access to professors.

When customers become scarce in an industry and competition heats up, however, the customer gains power. In the early 1990s, when competition for master of business administration students intensified and *Business Week* conducted "customer surveys" of students to rank the best business schools in the United States, the business school "customer" assumed a more central position in these organizations. What students wanted in courses and experiences began to drive curricula, content, and peripherals associated with business degrees. Business schools overhauled their MBA programs to make them more relevant to the students and the business environment. Many B-schools revamped the course content of their programs, recognized their key constituents (students, faculty, administrators, alumni, and corporate recruiters), and acknowledged that they needed research to understand their customers' expectations.

In the 1990s, few organizations can ignore the centrality of the customer in remaining financially viable. Few organizations can develop winning services and products without understanding customers' wants and needs and using them as foundation for development and delivery.

Value

Another key competitive factor defining the way services are bought and sold is value. In the words of one business observer, the marketing of value has "gone from a groundswell to a tidal wave."[1] Value reflects the growing customer concern of getting more for money, time, and effort invested. Experts can point to many reasons why value is critical to today's consumers: economic problems, loss of jobs due to company restructuring, and a return to the real and practical. While the 1980s could easily have been termed the decade of extravagance, the customer priority of the 1990s is turning out to be value. To thrive, companies must understand the demographic and psychographic changes that reflect this new perspective.

Companies that did not recognize and adapt to the customer's criterion of value early enough have suffered. Witness American Express, the service titan of the 1980s, that failed to foresee that its positioning as provider of the luxury card was not as viable in the 1990s as it was in the 1980s. While no competitors had been able to best American Express in its own positioning, rival cards created new positioning for the value decade, most by offering more for less: GM offered a rebate on dollars spent; Citibank created a card that offered frequent flier miles from American Airlines for every dollar spent, and others dropped their rates.[2] Compared with these value offerings, American Express's prestige positioning was outdated. American Express finally responded to customer demand for value with its own airline mileage bonuses, but not until its market share had been seriously eroded by competing cards and its chairman and 1980s' hero, James Robinson, had been forced out.

Other companies that have maintained closer touch with their customers are adjusting their offerings to feature value, sometimes in combination with quality. Federal Express developed an offering different from its traditional high-quality, high-price positioning to correspond with the value desired by a large segment of its customers. The company added afternoon delivery at a cheaper price than the regular 10:30 a.m. morning delivery. In fact, the company widened the options available to include several "value" offerings—afternoon, two-day, government overnight, overnight freight, and two-day freight.

Many companies are confused in attempting to deliver customer value, largely because value is an amorphous concept that means different things to different customers. The first steps in creating value involve understanding what value means from the customer's point of view, how value perceptions are formed, how they can be influenced, and how consumers relate quality, price, and value in their deliberations about products and services. In this textbook we describe how customers perceive value and discuss how value relates to price and perceived quality. We also detail both the strategies service companies are developing to deliver value offerings and the ways that manufacturing firms use service as a key value-add accompanying their goods.

Total Quality Management and Service Quality

Many experts considered the 1980s the decade of manufacturing quality because efforts to improve quality—to make products that conformed to requirements—were initiated in some form in many companies during that time. *Total quality management* (TQM) is the term widely used to capture the movement, although this concept is used in a myriad of ways. In a general sense, TQM has most often been defined as a management philosophy or way of doing business based on continuous quality improvement. TQM has subsumed a diverse group of quality techniques and strategies, among them statistical process control, process management, employee participation, management commitment and leadership, empowerment, and team building. Unfortunately, there is not a universally accepted definition of TQM, nor a set of guidelines concerning the strategies and tactics that fall within it. Companies using any combination of these techniques, indeed any particular quality technique, tend to refer to them or it as TQM.

TQM approaches were embraced by manufacturing firms far earlier than by service firms, but some or all of the techniques listed here are rapidly penetrating a widening group of service organizations. The movement has spread to colleges and universities, city and state governments, and even the U.S. government. When these institutions faced strict budgets, diminishing markets, and reduced resources, they began to compete the way for-profit companies do. Organizations from the Internal Revenue Service to the legal departments of major American corporations are implementing TQM and attempting to provide superior customer service.

In an effort to be somewhat more precise about terminology, this textbook will use the term *service quality* to mean the delivery of excellent or superior service. Rather than use the vague *TQM* term, we will discuss the specific quality techniques and strategies as they relate to services and discuss ways that companies have implemented service quality programs. In fact, the framework of the textbook, described later in this chapter, is based on service quality.

Emphasis on Service as a Key Differentiator in Manufacturing Firms

As noted in chapter 1, service companies are not the only firms stressing service as a competitive weapon. Financial officers of 50 of America's largest companies, most of them in manufacturing, ranked customer service as more critical to viability in the 1990s than all other strategies, including innovation and cost reduction.[3] These and other companies that manufacture tangible products contend that customer service is critical to prospering, even surviving, in today's markets. One reason for this focus is that competitive parity has been reached in many manufactured goods (such as personal computers, video cassette recorders, and other electronic products, to name just a few) meaning that product quality alone no longer differentiates one producer from another. Low price as a differentiating strategy is also disappearing, especially as companies face the reality that they and their competitors accomplish little more in price wars than to eliminate their own margins. One of the few remaining strategies that can set one goods company apart from others is customer service, broadly defined as developing strong relationships with customers. Goods firms in industries such as automobiles, computers, and most industrial firms are heavily focusing on service. Some of them, like IBM as discussed at the beginning of this chapter, are even transforming themselves into services companies. Because virtually all companies have some service component of their offerings, and because many are increasing this emphasis, we include many goods company examples in this textbook.

New Measurement Systems That Link Customer Satisfaction with Financial Goals and Operational Measurements

As companies pursue service quality and customer satisfaction strategies to differentiate themselves in their marketplaces, their measurement systems are changing to reflect these priorities. The Malcolm Baldrige Quality Award, the prestigious national quality award spearheaded by the U.S. Commerce Department, specifies that company measurement must focus on the customer:

> . . . indicators should be selected to best represent the attributes that link to customer requirements, customer satisfaction, and competitive performance as well as to operational effectiveness and efficiency. A system of indicators thus represents a clear and objective basis for aligning all activities of the company toward well-defined goals and for tracking progress toward the goals.

Before the early 1990s, few companies had measurement systems that viewed the customer as a focus. While most companies were drowning in measurement, emphasis was typically on short-term financial performance, productivity, and efficiency—not on long-term customer satisfaction and value. Xerox pioneered the centrality of customer satisfaction measures in the late 1980s when David Kearns, its top executive, made the decision that customer satisfaction was to be the ultimate goal of the corporation. Kearns believed that if customers were satisfied, profits and revenues would follow. Focusing on customers' priorities led the company to many changes, one of the most important being a companywide measurement effort emphasizing customer satisfaction.

To anticipate corporate performance in intensely competitive marketplaces where the customer is pivotal, other measures are being added to corporate report cards. These new report cards also allow executives to link financial, operational, and customer measures so that they can identify whether customer satisfaction and service quality positively impact performance and the bottom line. When committing resources to improve service quality, company executives want to be sure that these investments will pay off. To document the payoff, many organizations have put in place measures that capture both the costs and gains of service quality. We will devote part of a chapter to describing these new types of measurement systems.

Emerging Technology

The services sector currently owns more than 85 percent of America's installed base of technology.[4] Technology is used in services businesses to lower costs, increase productivity, improve the way service is delivered, put more information in the hands of service representatives, personalize the service, collect data on customer needs, add value for the customer, differentiate the service, and build relationships with customers.

Technological advances such as relational data bases, expert systems, image processing, and local area networks are but a few of the technologies that offer service opportunities. Interactive, on-line services, such as Prodigy, CompuServe, and AmericaOnline, allow consumers to make their own airline reservations, choose restaurants in cities far from their home computer, talk to other users through electronic billboards, and check the weather in all parts of the world. Other electronic services offer the customer access to extensive library services and on-demand cable programming and movies.

Technology also revolutionizes the types of new services created by companies. Perhaps the most exciting emerging technology is *virtual reality,* the use of simulated environments (see the Technology Spotlight). This technology uses multiple sensory information and data to render, recreate, and simulate a "world" that is described in data.[5]

TECHNOLOGY SPOTLIGHT

VIRTUAL REALITY

Virtual reality is a type of information technology that uses multiple sensory information and data to render, recreate, and simulate a "world" that is described in data. According to *Business Week,* in virtual reality the mind can see "previously hidden relationships in complex sets of data and . . . absorb, manipulate, and interpret information more quickly and completely." Consider this example:

> You sit in a wood-paneled room as Colonel Jack Thorpe, special assistant for simulation at the Pentagon's Defense Advanced Research Projects Agency, douses the lights, flips on a computer—and sends three 5-foot screens in front of you thundering into ac-

tion. Instantly you're transported inside a tank rolling across the Iraqi desert. You are performing the same maneuvers as a unit of the 2nd Armored Cavalry during "73 Easting," an actual battle in the Persian Gulf War. The graphics on the screens are only video-game quality. Yet the illusion works: You duck as shells scream toward you and explode in ear-splitting fury.[6]

This computer-simulated fight is so realistic that soldiers participating in it improve their scores for battlefield acumen dramatically, one reason the military is spending more than $500 million on simulations of this type. Virtual reality has many potential applications to service provision, among them boosting of productivity and provision of more cost-effective training. In a later chapter we will describe some of the applications.

Technology also offers efficiencies in the ways in which other services are performed. The United States Automobile Association, a San Antonio insurance company that specializes in military officers and their families, joined with IBM to create a computer imaging system that completely eliminated file cabinets, paperwork, and the clerks that used to be needed to run the files around. Employees scan an average of 14 million pieces of incoming mail (except checks) a year.[7] Because of this, all telephone contact personnel can almost immediately call up a customer's account information, allowing the company to give highly customized and personalized service at a greatly reduced price. USAA has also used the system to process claims; claim dossiers that fill a filing cabinet can then be compressed on an optical disk and multimedia can recreate the accident reports, show color videos of the damage—all by conference call.[8]

Technology, particularly information technology, is so important in the service sector that we will feature a technology spotlight (like the one you have just read) in each chapter of the textbook. The most innovative and promising developments in technology that affect services marketing, services design, and service provision will be featured.

Internationalization of Services

At one time—and indeed, not so long ago—the potential for services to be provided on a global basis was limited by the belief that services cannot be transported. That time is now past, for the internationalization of services has become a reality. U.S. companies now transport everything from the McDonald's eating experience to worldwide consulting services, and the services of other countries are rapidly competing with those in the United States. An important impact of the internationalization of services is that many markets are becoming global. Probably the most dramatic examples of global service markets are in the airline and financial services industries.

In a sense, international services marketing can be viewed as a form of customization. While most standardized services marketing strategies must be customized somewhat when implemented in different localities, the customization associated with international services often must be radical. Cultures are different. Language changes. The meanings of words, symbols, brand names, slogans, service environments, and experiences are likely to vary and these must be adapted. Even McDonalds, as global as any service business operating today, must adjust some aspects of its services marketing in other countries. Transporting and marketing services to new cultures, new countries, and new geographic regions requires additional attention to ensure success.

All of these competitive trends affect the way goods and services businesses will operate in the 1990s and beyond. Unless managers of companies providing services understand these changes and adjust for their impact when designing, marketing, and delivering services, they are unlikely to prosper. We will describe the way successful service organizations are adapting to the changes throughout this textbook, which is organized around the framework discussed in the next section.

THE GAPS MODEL OF SERVICE QUALITY

This textbook is structured around a conceptual model that positions the key concepts, strategies, and decisions in services marketing. We will develop the model called the gaps model of service quality in this chapter.[9]

The Customer Gap: The Difference between Customer Perceptions and Expectations

Customer perceptions are subjective assessments of actual service experiences. Figure 2-1 shows a pair of boxes that correspond to two concepts—*customer expectations* and *customer perceptions*—that play a major role in services marketing. Customer expectations are the standards of or reference points for performance against which service experiences are compared, and are often formulated in terms of what a customer believes should or will happen. For example, when you visit a fast-food restaurant you expect a

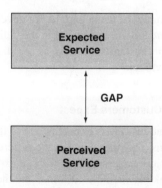

FIGURE 2-1   The customer GAP.

certain level of service, one that is considerably different from the level you would expect in an expensive restaurant.

The sources of customer expectations consist of marketer-controlled factors (such as pricing, advertising, sales promises) as well as factors that the marketer has limited ability to affect (innate personal needs, word-of-mouth communications, competitive offerings). In a perfect world, expectations and perceptions would be identical: customers would perceive that they receive what they thought they would and should. In practice these concepts are often, even usually, separated by some distance. Broadly, it is the goal of services marketing to bridge this distance, and we will devote virtually the entire textbook to describing strategies and practices designed to close this customer gap.

Considerable evidence exists that consumer evaluation processes differ for goods and services and that these differences affect the way service providers market their organizations. Unfortunately, much of what is known and written about consumer evaluation processes pertains specifically to goods. The assumption appears to be that services, if not identical to goods, are at least similar enough in the consumer's mind that they are chosen and evaluated in the same manner. We want to show that services' unique characteristics—intangibility, heterogeneity, inseparability of production and consumption, and perishability—necessitate different consumer evaluation processes from those used when assessing goods.

Because customer satisfaction and customer focus are so critical to competitiveness of firms in the 1990s, any company interested in delivering quality service must begin with a clear understanding of its customers. For this reason we will devote the first section of the textbook to describing the relevant customer concepts so that the focus of everything can relate back to them. We will detail what is known about customer expectations and perceptions of service as well as what is known about customer behavior in services. Knowing what customers want and how they assess what they receive is the best way to design effective services in the competitive 1990s.

In a broad sense, the process of closing the customer gap shown in Figure 2-1 can be subdivided into four "company gaps," discrepancies within the organization that inhibit delivery of quality service. These are:

Provider gap 1: Not knowing what customers expect
Provider gap 2: Not selecting the right service designs and standards
Provider gap 3: Not delivering to service standards
Provider gap 4: Not matching performance to promises

We will build a model of these gaps as we develop this chapter. Because customer expectations and perceptions are central in the delivery of excellent service, we will keep the customer gap constantly in view as we discuss the four provider gaps here and throughout the textbook.

Provider Gap 1: Not Knowing What Customers Expect

Not knowing what customers expect is one of the root causes of not delivering to customer expectations. Provider gap 1 is the difference between customer expectations of service and company understanding of those expectations. Notice that in Figure 2-2 we have created a link between the customer and the company, showing customer expecta-

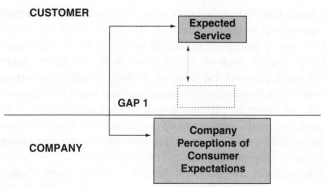

FIGURE 2-2   Provider GAP 1.

tions above the line that dissects the model and provider perceptions of those expectations below the line. When we use the term *company* in this gap, we refer to anyone in the organization who has the responsibility and authority to create or change service policies, procedures, and standards. This could include top executives, middle managers, supervisors, and—in many of the more innovative companies today—empowered teams. In earlier versions of the gaps model, the term *manager* was used rather than company because in the past most changes in service policies and procedures were established and approved by management.

Why does this first provider gap occur? Many reasons exist: no direct interaction with customers, unwillingness to ask about expectations, and/or unpreparedness in addressing them. When people with the authority and responsibility for setting priorities do not fully understand customers' service expectations, they may trigger a chain of bad decisions and suboptimal resource allocations that result in perceptions of poor service quality. One example of misplaced priorities stemming from an inaccurate understanding of customers' expectations is spending far too much money on buildings and the appearance of a company's physical facilities when customers may be much more concerned with how convenient, comfortable, and functional the facilities are. Another example is illustrated by the management of Sears in the early 1990s, when the company failed to understand that customers had changed their desires and modes of shopping. The company kept its traditional catalogue store long after customers had decided to take their business elsewhere. In the mid-1990s, Sears management rediscovered its customers, now defined primarily as women, and began once again to be profitable and satisfying to customers.

In this textbook we have broadened the responsibility for the first provider gap from managers alone to any employee in the organization with the authority to change or influence service policies and procedures. In today's changing organizations, the authority to make adjustments in service delivery is delegated to empowered teams and frontline people. For example, when AT&T asked its long-distance operators to improve quality service to customers, the team identified key customer segments and conducted its own customer research to determine expectations. Provider gap 1 was closed without involving management as it is traditionally defined.

An inaccurate understanding of what customers expect and what really matters to them leads to service performance that falls short of customer expectations. The necessary first step in improving quality of service is for management or empowered employees to acquire accurate information about customers' expectations (i.e., close provider gap 1). Formal and informal methods to capture information about customer expectations can be developed through market research. Techniques involving a variety of traditional research approaches must be used to stay close to the customer, among them customer visits, survey research, complaint systems, and customer panels. More innovative techniques, such as quality function deployment, structured brainstorming, and service quality gap analysis, are often needed.

Market segmentation is the grouping of customers sharing similar requirements, expectations, and demographic or psychographic profiles. While segmentation has been used by marketers for decades, it may be more critical today than at any other time. Customers are no longer satisfied by homogeneous products and services for the mass market; now, more than ever before, they are seeking and buying services that fit their unique configuration of needs. Many marketers are achieving success with *niche marketing*—targeting segments of customers and developing services and strategies that fit their needs better than other companies' offerings. Other marketers are embracing the concept of *mass customization*—creating services for a large group of customers that can be customized or appear to be customized through technological innovations. Finally, service companies must manage the customer mix, an issue more critical in services marketing, where customers often interact with each other while receiving service, than in goods marketing. Managing the customer mix, in a broad sense, means determining and choosing a mix of customers to target who are compatible or at least separated from each other if incompatible.

Another trend related to provider gap 1 involves current company strategies to retain customers and strengthen relationships with them. The term *relationship marketing* is used to describe this approach, which emphasizes strengthening the bonds with existing customers. When organizations have strong relationships with their customers, gap 1 is less likely to occur. One of the major marketing factors that is leveraged in relationship marketing, particularly in manufacturing companies, is service. Technology affords companies the ability to acquire and integrate vast quantities of data on customers that can be used to build relationships. Frequent flyer travel programs conducted by airlines, car rental companies, and hotels are among the most familiar programs of this type. Frequent buyer programs used by bookstores such as Waldenbooks and B. Dalton Bookseller also encourage loyalty and frequent purchase among customers. Relationship marketing is distinct from *transactional marketing,* the term used to describe the more conventional emphasis on acquiring new customers rather than on retaining them. When companies focus too much on attracting new customers, they may fail to understand the changing needs and expectations of their current customers.

Provider Gap 2: Not Selecting the Right Service Designs Standards

Accurate perceptions of customers' expectations are necessary, but not sufficient, for delivering superior quality service. Another prerequisite is the presence of service designs and performance standards that reflect those accurate perceptions. A recurring theme in service companies is the difficulty executives, managers, and other policy-setters experience in translating their understanding of customers' expectations into service quality specifications.

Provider gap 2 is the difference between company understanding of customer expectations and development of *customer-driven service designs and standards* (Figure 2-3). Customer-driven standards are different from the conventional performance standards that most services companies establish (this other type of standard we will call *company-driven standards*) in that they are based on pivotal customer requirements that are visible to and measured by customers. They are operations standards set to correspond to customer expectations and priorities rather than to company concerns such as productivity or efficiency.

Provider gap 2 exists in service organizations for a variety of reasons. Those responsible for setting standards, typically management, sometimes believe that customer expectations are unreasonable or unrealistic. They may also believe that the degree of variability inherent in service defies standardization and therefore that setting standards will not achieve the desired goal. Further, they may contend that the demand for service is too hard to predict or that the way the company and its personnel operate cannot be changed. Although some of these assumptions are valid in some situations, they are often only rationalizations for management's reluctance to tackle head-on the difficult challenge of setting service standards to deliver excellent service.

Perhaps a more fundamental reason for the potential gap between awareness of customers' expectations and the translation of that awareness into appropriate service designs and standards is the absence of wholehearted management or company commitment to service quality. In the face of short-term financial deadlines, many service companies are reluctant to pursue or continue customer satisfaction or quality efforts. It

FIGURE 2-3   Provider GAP 2.

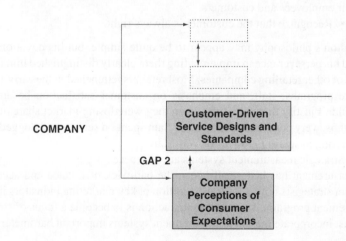

takes perseverance, as Bob Allen, chief executive officer of AT&T, stated in an address to many of his employees when the company won two Malcolm Baldrige Quality awards in 1992: "We need the patience to stay with it [quality and customer satisfaction efforts] when short-term revenues and profits are in the spotlight."[10]

The quality of service delivered by customer-contact personnel is critically influenced by the standards against which they are evaluated and compensated. Standards signal to contact personnel what management priorities are and which types of performance really count. When service standards are absent or when the standards in place do not reflect customers' expectations, quality of service as perceived by customers is likely to suffer. In contrast, when standards do reflect what customers expect, the quality of service they receive is likely to be enhanced. Therefore, closing provider gap 2—by demonstrating strong leadership commitment and by setting customer-defined performance standards—has a powerful positive impact on closing the customer gap.

Leadership plays a pivotal role in providing service excellence. In particular, management must perceive that customer expectations can and should be met and must be visibly committed to delivering high service quality. Leaders such as the late Sam Walton of Wal-Mart, Michael Eisner of Disney, and Robert Crandall of American Airlines are role models for service companies in that they clearly indicate that customers and service are among the top priorities in their companies. Their management philosophies, usually very basic yet powerful, reveal their strong commitment to service. Sam Walton, a quintessential service leader, used the following philosophy to spur his people and his company to preeminence in retailing:

- Realize that customer service is key.
- Design for comfort and convenience.
- Provide one-stop shopping.
- Customize.
- Invert the organizational chart so that the customer is on top and company management is on the bottom.
- Empower the sales staff.
- Provide servant leadership—Wal-Mart's managers are servants to the needs of their employees and customers.
- Recognize that the customer is always right.

Walton's philosophy may appear to be quite simple, but his devotion to the principles and his perseverance in implementing them clearly distinguished him from service leaders of other retailing companies. Most retailers retrenched in the early 1990s, cutting service programs, staff, and emphasis on customer satisfaction because they felt they couldn't justify them at a time when they were losing market share and customers. Yet in those very competitive few years, Sam spent on service and doggedly led the charge, resulting in soaring growth for Wal-Mart.

Strategic measurement systems are also necessary to close this gap. While company measurement has historically been the bailiwick of finance and accounting, management strategists now call for the addition of key marketing indicators in the overall measurement program. If customer satisfaction is to become a focus of strategy, companies must incorporate into their measurement systems important barometers of customer satisfaction and perceived service quality. To achieve competitive superiority in an era when satisfying customers is a priority, companies need measurement systems that incorporate and align measures of customer perceptions and satisfaction with pivotal operational and performance indicators.

Provider Gap 3: Not Delivering to Service Standards

Provider gap 3 is the discrepancy between development of customer-driven service standards and actual service performance by company employees (Figure 2-4). Even when guidelines exist for performing services well and treating customers correctly, high-quality service performance is not a certainty. Standards must be backed by appropriate resources (people, systems, technology) and also must be supported to be effective—that is, employees must be measured and compensated on the basis of performance along those standards. Thus, even when standards accurately reflect customers' expectations, if the company fails to provide support for them—if it does not facilitate, encourage, and require their achievement—standards do no good. When the level of service delivery performance falls short of the standards (provider gap 3), it falls short of what customers expect as well. Narrowing gap 3, by ensuring that all the resources needed to achieve the standards are in place, reduces the gap.

Research and company experience have identified many of the critical inhibitors to closing gap 3. These include employees who do not clearly understand the role they are to play in the company, employes who feel in conflict between customers and company management, the wrong employees, inadequate technology, inappropriate compensation and recognition, and lack of empowerment and teamwork. These factors all relate to the company's human resource function, involving internal practices such as recruit-

FIGURE 2-4   Provider GAP 3.

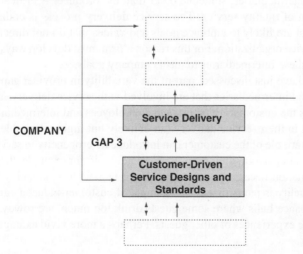

ment, training, feedback, job design, motivation, and organizational structure. To close provider gap 3, the issues must be addressed across functions (e.g., with both marketing and human resources) if they are to be effective.

Most companies have, in addition to external customers, a variety of *internal customers,* employees or departments that directly interact with customers and sell, advise, maintain, or troubleshoot for other departments or functions in the company. For example, company salespeople who interact directly with the external customer can be considered internal customers of many other departments and functions in the company (such as the market research function, the administrative staff, and the product development department). Salespeople depend on these other functions to perform effectively for them, the internal customer, so that they in turn can perform for the external customer. Unless the company acknowledges the importance of internal customers, these internal intermediaries may have different goals, incentives, and motives than the department developing the service.

One of the difficulties associated with gap 3 involves the challenge in delivering service through such intermediaries as retailers, franchisees, agents, and brokers. Because quality in service occurs in the human interaction between customers and service providers, control over the service encounter by the company is crucial, yet it rarely is fully possible. Most service (and many manufacturing) companies face an even more formidable task: attaining service excellence and consistency in the presence of intermediaries who represent them, interact with their customers, and yet are not under their direct control. Among the intermediaries that play a central role in service delivery are retailers, franchisees, and dealers.

Franchisers of services depend on their franchisees to execute service delivery as they have specified it. And it is in the execution by the franchisee that the customer evaluates the service quality of the company. When a McDonald's franchisee cooks the Mc-Nuggets too short a time, the customer's perception of the company—and of other Mc-Donald's franchisees—is tarnished. When one Holiday Inn franchise has unsanitary conditions, it reflects on all others and on the company itself. With franchises and other types of intermediaries, someone other than the producer is critically important to the fulfillment of quality service. The service delivery process is complicated by outside parties that are likely to embrace goals and values that do not directly align with those of the service organization. For this reason a firm must develop ways to either control or motivate these intermediaries to meet company goals.

As we have just discussed, part of the variability in provider gap 3 comes from employees and intermediaries that are involved with service delivery. The other important variable is the customer. Even if contact employees and intermediaries are 100 percent consistent in their service delivery (an unlikely but highly desirable state!), the uncontrollable variable of the customer can introduce heterogeneity in service delivery. If customers do not perform their roles appropriately—if, for example, they fail to provide all the information necessary to the provider or neglect to read and follow instructions—service quality is jeopardized. An example of customer-induced variability is in nightclubs or dance halls where some guests drink too much, are rowdy, and interfere with the service experiences of other guests. Perhaps a more vivid example is the behavior of airline passengers when a flight cancellation is announced. Both business and leisure customers, all intending to get to their destination at a promised time and frustrated with their inability to do so, become "customers from hell," demanding and even abusive. Their behavior affects the performance of service providers and also may incite other passengers or, at a minimum, create uncomfortable confrontations and competition for seats on the next available plane.

Effective service organizations acknowledge the role of customer variability and develop strategies to teach customers to perform their roles appropriately. Airlines, for example, have contingency plans for canceled flights, corralling employees from other parts of the business to assist in dealing with the crisis. Other companies develop customer education or communication programs to teach customers to be good customers. Service companies can and do use strategies to improve their own productivity and effectiveness by enlisting the customer's cooperation.

Another issue in gap 3 is the need in service firms to synchronize demand and capacity. Because services are perishable and cannot be inventoried, service companies frequently face situations of overdemand or underdemand. Lacking inventories to handle overdemand, companies lose sales when capacity is inadequate to handle customer needs. On the other hand, capacity is frequently underutilized in slow periods. Most companies rely on operations strategies such as cross training or varying the size of the employee pool to synchronize supply and demand. The use of marketing strategies in many companies is limited. Marketing strategies for managing demand, such as price changes, advertising, promotion, and alternative service offerings, can supplement approaches for managing supply.

Provider Gap 4: Not Matching Performance to Promises

The fourth provider gap, shown in Figure 2-5, illustrates the difference between service delivery and the service provider's external communications. Promises made by a service company through its media advertising, sales force, and other communications may potentially raise customer expectations that serve as the standard against which customers assess service quality. The discrepancy between actual and promised service therefore broadens the customer gap. Broken promises can occur for many reasons: overpromising in advertising or personal selling, inadequate coordination between operations and marketing, and differences in policies and procedures across service outlets. For instance, when a bank participating in a study conducted by one of the authors introduced a new student loan program, the marketing arm of the bank sold too many of the loans too fast without verifying in advance whether the operations group was geared up to mail out the loan checks as promised. As you may imagine, broken promises and irate customers were the result. During the month following the introduction of the loan service the bank received over 500 complaint letters from frustrated customers asking, "Where's my check?"

In addition to unduly elevating expectations through exaggerated claims, there are other, less obvious ways in which external communications influence customers' service quality assessments. Customers are not always aware of everything done behind the

CUSTOMER

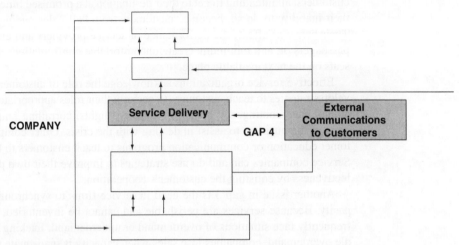

COMPANY

FIGURE 2-5   Provider GAP 4.

scenes to serve them well. One bank executive indicated that customers were unaware of the bank's behind-the-counter, on-line teller terminals, which would translate into visible effects on customer service. By neglecting to inform customers of such behind-the-scenes efforts, the bank was foregoing an opportunity to favorably influence service perceptions.

For instance, a securities brokerage company that participated in a study done by one of the authors had a "forty-eight-hour rule" prohibiting its account executives from buying or selling securities for their personal accounts for the first forty-eight hours after information about the securities was supplied by the company. The brokers could advise clients and buy or sell on their behalf right away, but they themselves had to wait forty-eight hours before buying or selling for their own accounts. The company did not communicate this information to its customers, perhaps contributing to a perception that "all the good deals are probably made by the brokers for themselves" (a perception that surfaced in the securities brokerage focus groups). Customers who are aware that a company is taking concrete steps to serve their best interests are likely to perceive a delivered service in a more favorable way.

Customers' service perceptions may also be enhanced if the company educates them to be better users of the service. Service companies frequently fail to capitalize on opportunities to improve customers' perceptions. As one bank executive observed, "We don't teach our customers how to use us well and why we do the things we do."

External communications can affect not only customers' expectations but also customers' perceptions of the delivered service. Discrepancies between service delivery and external communications about it (provider gap 4) adversely affect customers' assessments of service quality. Gap 4 reflects a breakdown in coordination between employees responsible for delivering the service and employees in charge of describing and/or promoting the service to customers. When employees who promote the service do not fully understand the reality of service delivery, they are likely to make exaggerated promises or fail to communicate to customers aspects of the service intended to serve them well. The result is poor service quality perceptions. Effectively coordinating actual service delivery with external communications, therefore, narrows provider gap 4 and favorably affects the customer gap as well.

In service companies, a fit between communications about service and actual service delivery is necessary. Accurate and appropriate communications—advertising, personal selling, and publicity—that do not overpromise or misrepresent are essential to delivering services that customers perceive as high in quality. One of the major difficulties associated with these types of communications is that they involve issues that cross disciplinary boundaries. Because service advertising promises what *people* do, and because what people do cannot be controlled in the way that machines that produce physical goods can be controlled, this type of communication involves functions other than the marketing department. Successful company communications are the responsibility of both marketing and operations: marketing must accurately but beguilingly reflect what happens in actual service encounters, and operations must deliver what is promised in advertising. If communications set up unrealistic expectations for customers, the actual encounter will disappoint the customer. Another function that must be involved in communication is human resources. For employees to deliver excellent customer service, firms must serve the employees through training, motivation, compensation, and recognition to have a powerful impact on the quality of service the employees deliver.

Another issue related to gap 4 is associated with the pricing of services. In packaged goods (and even in durable goods), many customers possess enough price knowledge before purchase to be able to judge whether a price is fair or in line with competition. With services, customers often have no internal reference point for prices before purchase and consumption. Pricing strategies such as discounting, "everyday prices," and couponing obviously need to be different with services in cases where the customer has no sense of the price to start with! Techniques for developing prices for services are more complicated than those for pricing of tangible goods.

Because services are largely intangible, customers look to the physical or tangible representations of them for information about the service. Tangible factors such as buildings, offices, service personnel, invoices, credit cards, and interior design all play a strong role in service provision.

In summary, external communications—whether from advertising, pricing, or the tangibles associated with the service—can create a larger customer gap by raising expectations about service delivery. In addition to improving service delivery, companies must also manage all communications to customers so that inflated promises do not lead to higher expectations.

PUTTING IT ALL TOGETHER: CLOSING THE GAPS

The full conceptual model shown in Figure 2-6 conveys a clear message to managers wishing to improve the quality of their company's service: The key to closing the cus-

CUSTOMER

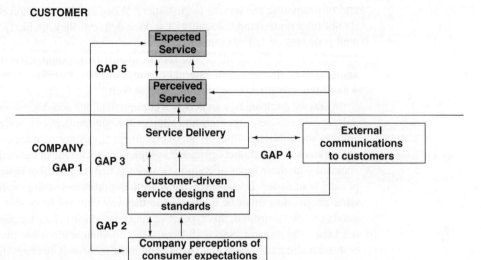

FIGURE 2-6 GAPs model of service quality.

tomer gap is to close gaps 1 through 4 and keep them closed. To the extent that one or more of gaps 1 through 4 exist, customers perceive service quality shortfalls. The model, called the gaps model, serves as a framework for service organizations attempting to improve quality service and services marketing.

The model also serves as the overall framework of this textbook. The textbook begins where the process of improving service quality begins: gaining an understanding of the nature and extent of the customer gap. Given the strong focus on the customer and the need to use knowledge about the customer to drive business strategy, we believe this foundation of emphasis is warranted.

Following the section on the customer gap, other sections will deal with the provider gaps. Our ordering of the gaps for the textbook matches the optimal ordering of the gaps for improving services marketing or quality service in organizations: Start by understanding customer expectations (provider gap 1), establish customer-driven standards to address key priorities (provider gap 2), and then align service performance with customer-driven standards (provider gap 3). Provider gap 4, which involves matching promises with service performance, follows.

One way companies use the gaps model is to search for evidence of gaps 1 through 4 in a service organization, taking corrective action wherever necessary. In the sections and chapters covering the provider gaps, we show you the potential causes underlying each of the gaps (summarized in Exhibit 2-1) as well as corrective actions available to eliminate those factors. We also show you the marketing and marketing research tools available to identify, quantify, and monitor customer perceptions and expectations so that the effectiveness of these actions can be monitored.

EXHIBIT 2-1   KEY FACTORS LEADING TO THE PROVIDER GAPS

Gap 1

Inadequate marketing research orientation

Insufficient marketing research
Research not focused on service quality
Inadequate use of market research

Lack of upward communication

Lack of interaction between management and customers
Insufficient communication between contact employees and managers
Too many layers between contact personnel and top management

Insufficient relationship focus

Lack of market segmentation
Focus on transactions rather than relationships
Focus on new customers rather than relationship customers

Gap 2

Absence of customer-driven standards

Lack of customer-driven service standards
Absence of process management to focus on customer requirements
Absence of formal process for setting service quality goals

Inadequate service leadership

Perception of infeasibility
Inadequate management commitment

Poor service design

Unsystematic new service development process
Vague, undefined service designs
Failure to connect service design to service positioning

Gap 3

Deficiencies in human resource policies

Ineffective recruitment
Role ambiguity and role conflict
Poor employee–technology job fit
Inappropriate evaluation and compensation systems
Lack of empowerment, perceived control, and teamwork

Failure to match supply and demand

Failure to smooth peaks and valleys of demand
Inappropriate customer mix
Overreliance on price to smooth demand

Customers not fulfilling roles

Customers lacking knowledge of their roles and responsibilities
Customers negatively impacting each other

Gap 4

Ineffective management of customer expectations

Failure to manage customer expectations through all forms of communication
Failure to educate customers adequately

Overpromising

Overpromising in advertising
Overpromising in personal selling
Overpromising through physical evidence cues

Inadequate horizontal communications

Insufficient communication between sales and operations
Insufficient communication between advertising and operations
Differences in policies and procedures across branches or units

SUMMARY AND CONCLUSION

This chapter described seven of the most powerful competitive trends currently shaping marketing and business strategy: (1) customer satisfaction and customer focus, (2) value, (3) total quality management and service quality, (4) use of customer service as a key differentiator in manufacturing firms, (5) new measurement systems that link customer satisfaction with financial goals, (6) emerging technology, (7) internationalization of service. Each of these competitive trends influences the effectiveness of services marketing and will therefore serve as a key theme throughout the textbook.

The chapter also presented the gaps model of service quality (shown in Figure 2-6), a framework for understanding and improving service delivery. The textbook is organized around the gaps model, which focuses on five pivotal gaps in delivering and marketing services:

- Customer gap: Difference between expectations and perceptions
- Provider gap 1: Not knowing what customers expect
- Provider gap 2: Not selecting the right service designs and standards
- Provider gap 3: Not delivering to service standards
- Provider gap 4: Not matching performance to promises

DISCUSSION QUESTIONS

1 How have the companies described in the beginning of this chapter (IBM, GM, American Express, Sears) fared since 1993? For the companies that have turned around their fate, what strategies did they pursue to do so? For the companies that have continued to decline, what have they done wrong?

2 Name three of the most successful services companies you can think of. Have any of these companies achieved success without focus on the customer? If so, what were the keys to their success?

3 Define the term *value* from the customer's point of view.

4 How are customer expectations different from customer perceptions?

5 Which of the four service provider gaps do you believe is the most difficult to close? Why?

6 Which of the four service provider gaps can be closed in the marketing function alone?

7 What specific examples can you give for the key factors responsible for gap 1?

8 What specific examples can you give for the key factors responsible for gap 2?

9 What specific examples can you give for the key factors responsible for gap 3?

10 What specific examples can you give for the key factors responsible for gap 4?

EXERCISES

1 Select a service organization and interview an employee of that firm. Ask how the seven competitive trends discussed in this chapter influence the way the company does business.

2 Assume that we measured overall service quality (gap 5) of an airline company's service and found that customers' perceptions of the service quality were very low compared with perceptions of the competition. On the basis of the gaps model, why might this low

quality perception occur and how might each of the other four gaps contribute? Be as detailed and specific as you can, and use concrete airline examples.

NOTES

1 Gary Strauss, "Marketers' Plea: Let's Make a Deal," *USA Today*, September 29, 1992, p. B1-2.

2 Christopher Power et al., "Value Marketing," *Business Week,* November 11, 1991.

3 Howard Schlossberg, "U.S. Firms: Quality Is the Way to Satisfy," *Marketing News,* February 4, 1991, p. 1.

4 Stephen S. Roach, "Services under Siege—the Restructuring Imperative," *Harvard Business Review,* September–October, 1991, p. 83.

5 Joan O'C. Hamilton, Emily Smith, Gary McWilliams, Evan Schwartz, and John Carey, "Virtual Reality: How a Computer-generated World Could Change the Real World," *Business Week,* October 5, 1992, p. 97.

6 Ibid.

7 Thomas Teal, "Service Comes First: An Interview with USAA's Robert McDermott," *Harvard Business Review,* September–October, 1991.

8 Myron Magnet, "Who's Winning the Information Revolution," *Fortune,* November 30, 1992, pp. 110–117.

9 Valarie A. Zeithaml, A. Parasuraman, and Leonard L. Berry, *Delivering Quality Service: Balancing Customer Perceptions and Expectations* (New York: Free Press, 1990).

10 Speech given by Robert Allen at AT&T Quality Conference, October 22, 1992.

FOCUS ON THE CUSTOMER

3

CONSUMER BEHAVIOR IN SERVICES

Consumer problem: Time deficiency
The solution: Services

> *Today's dual-career couple, single parent, and two-job families are realizing a burning consumer need: more time. Individuals in these and other nontraditional family configurations are overstressed with their work and home obligations and find dealing with many of life's everyday tasks overwhelming. In a recent study, 50 percent of dual-income primary shoppers with children and 35 percent of their single-income counterparts contend that shopping and service tasks contribute to life's stresses. For many customers all types of shopping have become "drudgery or worse."[1]*
>
> *The antidote to time deficiency? New services and service features of retailers that recover time for consumers. Innovative new services—pet sitting, plant watering, mail packaging, wedding advising, baby-proofing, executive organizing, personal shopping, even health form preparing—are emerging to deal with tasks that used to be performed by the household but now can be purchased by the time-buying consumer.[2] Conventional services such as retailing and banking are also adding peripheral services to make shopping easier, increasing their hours to suit customer schedules, reducing transaction time, accessing sales and service personnel more easily, improving delivery, and providing merchandise or services at home or work.[3]*
>
> *And there is an increasingly popular parallel phenomenon in business today called* outsourcing, *which means purchasing whole service functions (such as billing, secretarial services, maintenance, inventory, computer operations, and marketing) from other firms rather than executing them in-house. The motivation in corporations, however, is not so much time saving as it is dollar saving. Companies that are becoming leaner through corporate restructuring have discovered that in many cases purchasing*

services outright from another company can be far more economical than the payroll and capital costs of performing them inside.

The primary objective of service producers and marketers is identical to that of all marketers: to develop and provide offerings that satisfy consumer needs and expectations, thereby ensuring their own economic survival. In other words, service marketers need to be able to close the customer gap between expectations and perceptions described in chapter 2 and shown in Figure 3-1. To achieve this objective, service providers need to understand how consumers choose and evaluate their service offerings. Unfortunately, most of what is known about consumer evaluation processes pertains specifically to goods. The assumption appears to be that services, if not identical to goods, are at least similar enough in the consumer's mind that they are chosen and evaluated in the same manner.

This chapter challenges that assumption and shows that services' unique characteristics necessitate different consumer evaluation processes from those used in assessing goods. Recognizing these differences and thoroughly understanding consumer evaluation processes are critical for the customer focus on which effective services marketing is based. Because the premise of this textbook is that the customer is the heart of effective services marketing, we will begin with the customer and maintain this focus throughout the textbook.

Consumers have a more difficult time evaluating and choosing services than goods, partly because services are intangible and nonstandardized and partly because consumption is so closely intertwined with production. These characteristics lead to differences in consumer evaluation processes for goods and services in all stages of the buying process. The chapter is organized into four categories of customer behavior that correspond roughly to stages in the buying process: (1) information search, (2) evaluation of alternatives, (3) purchase and consumption, and (4) postpurchase evaluation. As shown in Figure 3-2, lack of understanding of the way customers assess and choose services in these four fundamental stages leads to a customer gap that must be closed by service marketers.

The objectives of this chapter are to:

1 Overview the generic differences in consumer behavior between services and goods.

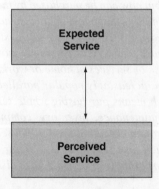

FIGURE 3-1   The customer GAP.

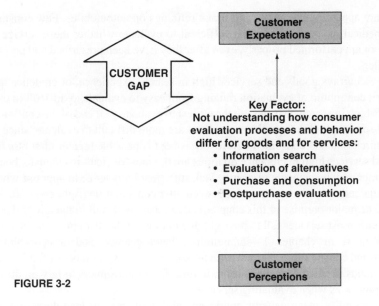

FIGURE 3-2

2 Introduce the aspects of consumer behavior that a marketer must understand in four categories of consumer behavior:

- Information search
- Evaluation of service alternatives
- Service purchase and consumption
- Postpurchase evaluation

3 Provide a set of propositions that will serve as a foundation for customer focus in the services marketing topics and strategies presented in the remainder of the textbook.

SERVICES: SEARCH VERSUS EXPERIENCE VERSUS CREDENCE PROPERTIES?

One framework for isolating differences in evaluation processes between goods and services is a classification of properties of offerings proposed by economists.[4] Economists first distinguished between two categories of properties of consumer products: *search qualities,* attributes that a consumer can determine before purchasing a product; and *experience qualities,* attributes that can only be discerned after purchase or during consumption. Search qualities include color, style, price, fit, feel, hardness, and smell; experience qualities include taste and wearability. Goods such as automobiles, clothing, furniture, and jewelry are high in search qualities, for their attributes can be almost completely determined and evaluated before purchase. Goods and services such as vacations and restaurant meals are high in experience qualities, for their attributes cannot be known or assessed until they have been purchased and are being consumed. A third category, *credence qualities,* are characteristics that the consumer may find impossible to evaluate even after purchase and consumption.[5] Examples of offerings high in credence qualities are appendix operations and brake relinings on automobiles. Few consumers possess medical or mechanical skills sufficient to evaluate whether these services are necessary or are performed properly, even after they have been prescribed and produced by the seller.

Figure 3-3 arrays goods and services high in search, experience, or credence qualities along a continuum of evaluation ranging from easy to evaluate to difficult to evaluate. Goods high in search qualities are the easiest to evaluate (left end of the continuum). Good and services high in experience qualities are more difficult to evaluate, since they must be purchased and consumed before assessment is possible (center of continuum). Goods and services high in credence qualities are the most difficult to evaluate, because the consumer may be unaware of or may lack sufficient knowledge to appraise whether the offerings satisfy given wants or needs even after consumption (right end of the continuum). The major premise of this chapter is that most goods fall to the left of the continuum, while most services fall to the right due to three of the distinguishing characteristics described in chapter 1—intangibility, heterogeneity, and inseparability of production and consumption. These characteristics make services more difficult to evaluate than goods. Difficulty in evaluation, in turn, forces consumers to rely on different cues and processes when evaluating services.

The intangibility, heterogeneity, and inseparability of services lead them to possess few search qualities and many experience qualities. Intangibility means services cannot be displayed, physically demonstrated, or illustrated; heterogeneity means that consumers cannot be certain about performance on any given day, even if they use the same service provider on a regular basis; and inseparability of production and consumption means the buyer usually participates in producing the service, thereby affecting the performance and quality of the service. A doctor's accurate diagnosis, the desired haircut from a salon, effective stain removal from a dry cleaner—all these depend on the consumer's specification, communication, and participation in the production of the service.

FIGURE 3-3 Continuum of evaluation for different types of products.

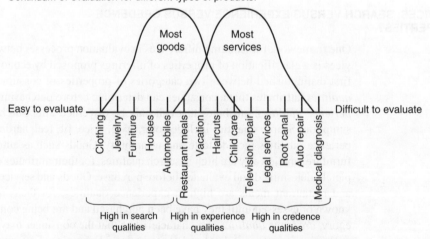

Credence qualities also dominate many services, especially those provided by professionals and specialists. Consumers may find it impossible to judge services performed by professionals and specialists with extensive training or experience in a specialized skill.

Because experience and credence qualities dominate in services, consumers employ different evaluation processes than those they use with goods, where search qualities dominate. They are also likely to experience the steps in the decision-making process in different orders and at different times from the steps in the classic goods-driven decision-making process (see Exhibit 3-1). Specific areas where characteristics of services may lead to divergent evaluation processes and altered consumer behavior are information search, evaluative criteria, size and composition of the evoked set of alternatives, perceived risk, adoption of innovations, brand loyalty, assessment of value, and attribution of dissatisfaction. Specific topics that need to be understood for services that are not issues in physical goods include services as drama, emotions and mood, role playing, and customer compatibility. Each of these areas will be described and discussed in this chapter.

EXHIBIT 3-1   REVIEW OF SELECTED BASIC MARKETING PRINCIPLES: CONSUMER BEHAVIOR

If you took a basic marketing course before the services marketing course you are currently taking, you learned certain core material about consumer behavior. In writing this textbook, we set out to extend the basic marketing information you currently possess and convey to you: (1) completely new material not contained in basic marketing courses, and (2) ways to adjust familiar marketing principles to make them effective in services marketing.

In many of the chapters that are not completely new material (such as this chapter), we will offer you an "Exhibit" like this one that provides a concise overview of marketing basics you should already possess to fully understand the chapter. For most of you, this overview will jog your memory and position the chapter material in the context of what you already know. For others, this overview may alert you to information you missed in your basic course or that is wholly new because you have not taken a previous marketing course. For those in the latter category, we provide references in the exhibits that can be examined to bring you to the same level as those who have taken a marketing course previously.

Now, to get back to marketing basics about consumer behavior. Among these basics are the following:

Marketing Basic 3-1   Consumers go through a decision-making process that can include up to five steps. We will use an adapted version of these steps to organize the information in this chapter:[6]

1 *Need recognition*
The customer has a need to fulfill or a problem to solve

2 *Information search*
The customer seeks out information to help satisfy the need

3 *Evaluation of alternatives*
The customer selects a subset of the alternatives and evaluates them

4 *Purchase*
The customer chooses a particular brand and then buys it

5 *Purchase outcome*
The customer evaluates the choice made and decides whether it lives up to expectations

For More Information   "Consumer Buying Behavior," chapter 6 in *Marketing,* Courtland L. Bovee, Michael J. Houston, and John V. Thill (New York, McGraw-Hill, 1995).

SERVICES: CATEGORIES IN THE DECISION-MAKING PROCESS AND FRAMEWORK OF THE CHAPTER

Using an adaptation of the basic consumer decision-making process shown in the Exhibit 3-1, we have organized this chapter into four main categories: (1) information search, (2) evaluation of alternatives, (3) purchase and consumption, and (4) postpurchase evaluation (Figure 3-4). In purchase of services, these categories do not occur in a linear sequence the way they most often do in the purchase of goods. As you will see in this chapter, one of the major differences between goods and services is that a greater portion of the evaluation of services succeeds purchase and consumption than is the case with goods. Therefore, while our categorization here follows the sequence consumers use with goods, we will show how these stages in services depart from evaluation of goods.

Information Search

Use of Personal Sources   Consumers obtain information about products and services from personal sources (e.g., friends or experts) and from nonpersonal sources (e.g., mass or selective media). When purchasing goods, consumers make generous use of both personal and nonpersonal sources because both effectively convey information about search qualities.

When purchasing services, on the other hand, consumers seek and rely to a greater extent on personal sources, for several reasons. First, mass and selective media can convey information about search qualities but can communicate little about experience

FIGURE 3-4   Categories in consumer decision-making and evaluation of services.

Information Search
- Use of personal sources
- Perceived risk

Evaluation of Alternatives
- Evoked set
- Emotion and mood

Purchase and Consumption
- Service provision as drama
- Service roles and scripts
- Compatibility of customers

Postpurchase Evaluation
- Attribution of dissatisfaction
- Innovation diffusion
- Brand loyalty

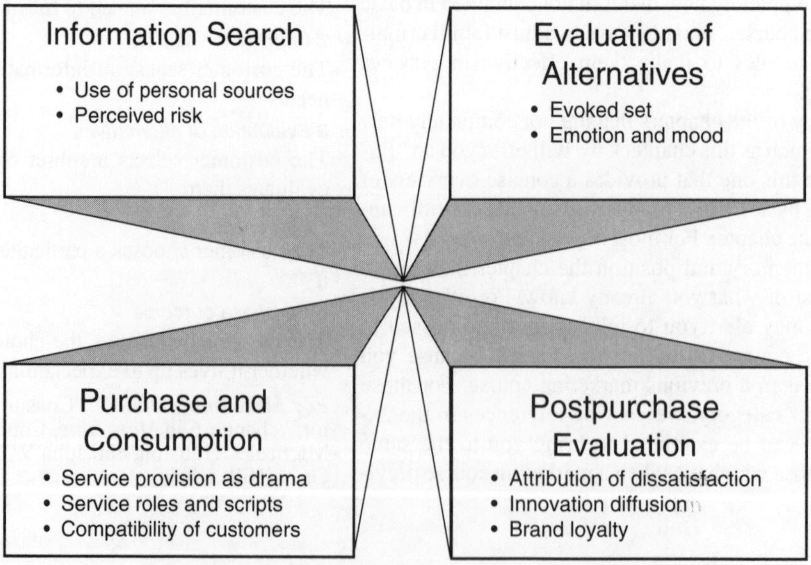

qualities. By asking friends or experts about services, however, the consumer can obtain information vicariously about experience qualities. Second, nonpersonal sources of information may not be available because (1) many service providers are local, independent merchants with neither the experience nor the funds for advertising; (2) "cooperative" advertising, or advertising funded jointly by the retailer and the manufacturer, is used infrequently with services because most local providers are both producer and retailer of the service; and (3) professional associations banned advertising for so many years that both professionals and consumers tend to resist its use even though it is now permitted. Third, since consumers can discover few attributes before purchase of a service, they may feel greater risk in selecting a little-known alternative.

Personal influence becomes pivotal as product complexity increases and when objective standards by which to evaluate a product decrease (i.e., when experience qualities are high).[7] Most managers in service industries recognize the influence of word of mouth in services, which leads us to our first proposition (see Exhibit 3-2):

Proposition 1:

Consumers seek and rely more on information from personal sources than from nonpersonal sources when evaluating services before purchase.

EXHIBIT 3-2   PROPOSITIONS: WHAT ARE THEY AND WHY ARE WE USING THEM IN THIS CHAPTER?

In this chapter on consumer behavior we use *propositions* to present the material, a different approach from that in any of the other chapters. Propositions are statements set forth as explanations for behavior or phenomena. We assert them here as conjectures to guide your thinking about consumer behavior in services.

As you read through the chapter, think of yourself as the consumer and keep in mind the services that you purchase. Consider whether each of these propositions holds true for your own purchasing and consuming behavior in services. Or, you may want to decide under which conditions (for example, types of services or times of purchase or consumption) they hold true. Or, you may want to think about how you and a friend differ in consuming services; this will help you recognize that not all consumers behave the same way and will prepare you for chapter 6 in which we discuss market segmentation.

Another way you can use the propositions in this chapter is in thinking about a particular service company's consumers. (At the end of the chapter we suggest a similar exercise as a class project.) Consider each

proposition as an assertion about these customers and evaluate (either on your own, or better yet, by talking with customers directly) whether it holds true. If it does, the proposition should form the basis for any services marketing strategy designed for that company. Obviously, a services strategy that acknowledges and incorporates consumer behavior and evaluation processes will hit the mark far more frequently than one that makes assumptions about—or worse yet, completely ignores—these concerns.

A final way these propositions can be useful is in preparing you to understand the customers of any current or future services that you design or market. In preparing a marketing plan or strategy, the first step should be to carefully consider customers and the contexts in which they purchase and consume services. We believe that the list of propositions we offer in this chapter will lead you to contemplate the most critical aspects of consumer behavior.

While propositions might be useful in other chapters in the textbook, we reserve them for this one to give you a means to carry the customer with you throughout the rest of this textbook.

Next, consumers may find postpurchase evaluation more essential with services than with goods because services possess experience qualities that cannot be adequately assessed before purchase. One model of audience response to communication[8] describes the situation that occurs frequently when consumers select services: (1) The consumer selects from among virtually indistinguishable alternatives. (2) Through experience the consumer develops an attitude toward the service. (3) After the development of an attitude, the consumer learns more about the service by paying attention to messages supporting his or her choice. In contrast to the conventional view of audience response to communication, where consumers seek information and evaluate products before purchase, with services most evaluation follows purchase.

Proposition 2:

Consumers engage in greater postpurchase evaluation and information-seeking with services than with goods.

Proposition 3:

Consumers engage in more postpurchase evaluation than prepurchase evaluation when selecting and consuming services.

Perceived Risk   While some degree of perceived risk probably accompanies all purchase transactions, more risk would appear to be involved in the purchase of services than in the purchase of goods because services are intangible, nonstandardized, and usually sold without guarantees or warranties.

First, the intangible nature of services and their high level of experience qualities imply that services generally must be selected on the basis of less prepurchase information than is the case for products. Second, because services are nonstandardized, there will always be uncertainty about the outcome and consequences each time a service is purchased.

Third, service purchases may involve more perceived risk than product purchases because, with few exceptions, services are not accompanied by warranties or guarantees. The dissatisfied service purchaser can rarely "return" a service, since he has already consumed it by the time he realizes his dissatisfaction.

Finally, many services (e.g., medical diagnosis, pest control) are so technical or specialized that consumers possess neither the knowledge nor the experience to evaluate whether they are satisfied, even after they have consumed the service. This line of reasoning leads to our fourth proposition.

Proposition 4:

Consumers perceive greater risks when buying services than when buying goods.

The hypothesized increase in perceived risk involved in purchasing services suggests the use of strategies to reduce risk. Where appropriate, guarantees of satisfaction may be offered. To the extent possible, service providers should emphasize employee training and other procedures to standardize their offerings, so that consumers learn to expect a given level of quality and satisfaction.

TECHNOLOGY SPOTLIGHT

CONSUMER RESISTANCE TO CHANGING TECHNOLOGY: VOICE MAIL

Among the changes technology has served up to consumers is voice mail electronic phone-answering systems. These systems have both supporters and detractors. Supporters tout the benefits in terms of efficiency and productivity for the company, but also the consumer benefits of the systems: no more busy signals or endlessly ringing telephones, time spent waiting allows quicker access to a knowledgeable person, and callers can leave detailed messages that do not require actual conversations to relay. Detractors, on the other hand, claim that voice mail is often confusing, frustrating (callers cannot always be sure that messages are received), and impersonal, sending a message that the company doesn't have time to interact with the customer. Because of these dissatisfiers, many companies, including Delta Airlines and First Union Bank in Charlotte, North Carolina, discontinued them.

One service area in which voice mail is being tested is in hotels. More than 1,000 hotel properties in the United States (among them ITT Sheraton and Westin Hotels and Resorts) now have ordered the service for their guests. When guests are out of their rooms, callers can leave messages on the system rather than directly with an operator. When guests return (or access messages from a remote location by pushing a code), they pick up their messages from the system rather than from the hotel operator. Perhaps surprisingly, many hotels have found that callers leave guests more messages on voice mail than with operators, particularly foreign or multilingual guests who find it easier to communicate through the systems than through operators.[9]

It is well documented that consumers tend to resist new and changing technology, even when it results in improvements in services. In the early 1980s, when automatic teller machines were introduced by the banking industry, customers balked. They didn't like the idea of putting their bank cards or deposits into a strange machine. During that time, banks exerted great effort to make the machines more friendly. One bank purchased an ATM system that allowed customers to insert their bank cards half way and hold on to the other half while transactions were occurring, a strategy that made them more willing to make the transition to automation. Another bank created an advertising campaign called "Harvey Wallbanker," endowing their machines with a sociable and friendly personality complete with a big party where the bank took photographs of city businessmen with Harvey Wallbangers (a popular drink of the time) and using the machines. Still another installed mirrors at eye level in the ATMs to allow customers to view a personal and (very) familiar face while banking the new way.

Among the criteria for customer acceptance of new technology are (1) that the technology have a clear customer benefit; (2) that the technology be simple to use, particularly in its introduction stage; and (3) that the technology be implemented correctly. In voice mail, that means allowing callers an easy escape to a human being, indicating to callers how quickly they can expect a call back, not using the systems as screening devices, and testing systems with external customers to make sure the messages and systems meet their needs.[10]

So will customers embrace voice mail? If ATMs are any indication, absolutely!

Evaluation of Service Alternatives

Evoked Set   The evoked set of alternatives—that group of products a consumer considers acceptable options in a given product category—is likely to be smaller with services than with goods. One reason involves differences in retailing between goods and services. To purchase goods, consumers generally shop in retail stores that display competing products in close proximity, clearly demonstrating the possible alternatives. To purchase services, on the other hand, the consumer visits an establishment (e.g., a bank, a dry cleaner, or a hair salon) that almost always offers only a single "brand" for sale. A second reason for the smaller evoked set is that consumers are unlikely to find more than one or two businesses providing the same services in a given geographic area, whereas they may find numerous retail stores carrying the identical manufacturer's product. A third reason for a smaller evoked set is the difficulty of obtaining adequate prepurchase information about services.

Faced with the task of collecting and evaluating experience qualities, consumers may simply select the first acceptable alternative.

Proposition 5:

The consumer's evoked set of alternatives is smaller with services than with goods.

For nonprofessional services, consumers' decisions often entail the choice between performing the services for themselves or hiring someone to perform them. Working wives may choose between cleaning their own homes or hiring housekeepers, between altering their families' clothes or taking them to a tailor, even between staying home to take care of their children or engaging a day-care center to provide child care. Consumers may consider themselves as sources of supply for many services, including lawn care, tax preparation, and preparing meals.

Proposition 6:

For many nonprofessional services, the consumer's evoked set frequently includes self-provision of the service.

Nonprofessional service providers must recognize that they often replace or compete with the consumer, which may imply more exacting standards from the consumer and may require more individualized, personal attention from the service provider. Consumers know what they expect from providers of housecleaning or lawn care or day care because they know what they are accustomed to providing for themselves. The alert service marketer will be certain to research consumers' expectations and demands in such situations.

Emotion and Mood   Emotion and mood are feeling states that influence people's (and therefore customers') perceptions and evaluations of their experiences. Moods are distinguished from emotions in that moods refer to transient feeling states that occur at specific times and in specific situations, whereas emotions are more intense, stable, and pervasive.[11]

Because services are experiences, moods and emotions are critical factors that shape the perceived effectiveness of service encounters. If a service customer is in a "bad mood" when he enters a service establishment, service provision will likely be interpreted more negatively than if he were in a buoyant, positive mood. Similarly, if a service provider is irritable or sullen, her interaction with customers will likely be colored by that mood. Furthermore, when another customer in a service establishment is cranky or frustrated, whether from problems with the service or from existing emotions unrelated to the service, his or her mood affects the provision of service for all customers who sense the negative mood. In sum, any service characterized by human interaction is strongly dependent on the moods and emotions of the service provider, the service customer, and other customers receiving the service at the same time.

In what specific ways can mood affect the behavior of service customers? First, positive moods can make customers more obliging and willing to participate in behaviors that help service encounters succeed.[12] A customer in a good emotional state is probably more willing to follow an exercise regimen prescribed by a physical therapist, bus his own dishes at a fast-food restaurant, and overlook delays in service. A customer in a negative mood may be less likely to engage in behaviors essential to the effectiveness of the service but that seem difficult or overwhelming: abstaining from chocolates when on a diet program with Weight Watchers, taking frequent aerobic classes from a health club, or completing homework assigned in a class.

Proposition 7:

Positive (negative) moods and emotions enhance (decrease) the likelihood of performance of behaviors with positive expected outcomes.[13]

A second way that moods and emotions influence service customers is to bias the way they judge service encounters and providers. Mood and emotions enhance and amplify experiences, making them either more positive or more negative than they might seem in the absence of the moods and emotions.[14] After losing a big account, a saleswoman catching an airline flight will be more incensed with delays and crowding than she might be on a day when business went well. Conversely, the positive mood of a services customer at a dance or restaurant will heighten the experience, leading to positive evaluations of the service establishment. The direction of the bias in evaluation is consistent with the polarity (that is, positive or negative) of the mood or emotion.

Proposition 8:

Mood and emotion bias the customer's evaluation of service encounters in "mood-congruent" directions.[15]

Finally, moods and emotions affect the way information about service is absorbed and retrieved. As memories about a service are encoded by a consumer, the feelings associated with the encounter become an inseparable part of the memory. If travelers fall in love during a vacation in the Bahamas, they may hold favorable assessments of the destination due more to their emotional state than to the destination itself. Conversely, if a customer first realizes his level of fitness is poor when on a guest pass in a health club, the negative feelings may be encoded and retrieved every time he thinks of the health club or, for that matter, any health club.

Proposition 9:

The mood of the customer influences the way impressions of a service are encoded, retained, and retrieved by the customer.[16]

The last three propositions suggest that service marketers need to be aware of the moods and emotions of customers and of service employees and should attempt to influence those moods and emotions in positive ways. They need to cultivate positive moods and emotions such as joy, delight, and contentment and discourage negative emotions such as distress, frustration, anger, and disgust. Many service factors can be used to influence moods: the ambiance and design of the physical setting, the processes associated with service delivery, exertion of control over unruly customers (such as specifying a limit to the number of alcoholic drinks a customer can buy on an airplane or after the seventh inning of a baseball game), limiting of waiting time in lines, scheduling of customers, and training and motivation of service personnel. The characteristics of service employees who interact with customers (rather than the service facility itself) have a stronger impact on customer satisfaction with services, which leads us to the next proposition:

Proposition 10:

The greater the human interaction in the service encounter, the more likely the consumer's evaluation of the service will be influenced by moods and emotion.[17]

Service Purchase and Consumption

Service Provision as Drama   Researchers and managers of service businesses have compared service provision with drama, observing that both aim to create and maintain a desirable impression before an audience, and both recognize that the way to accomplish this is by carefully managing the actors and the physical setting of their behavior.[18] In fact, the service marketer must play many drama-related roles (including director, choreographer, and writer) to be sure the performances of the actors are pleasing to the audience. The Walt Disney Company explicitly considers its service provision a "performance," even using show-business terms like "cast member," "onstage," and "show" to describe the operations at Disneyland and Walt Disney World.[19]

The skill of the service "actors" in performing their routines, the way they appear, and their commitment to the "show" are all pivotal to service delivery. While service actors are present in most service performances, their importance increases when the degree of direct personal contact increases (such as in a hospital, resort, or restaurant), when the services involve repeat contact, and when the contact personnel as actors have discretion in determining the nature of the service and how it is delivered (as in education, medical services, and legal services).[20]

The physical setting of the service can be likened to the staging of a theatrical production including scenery, props, and other physical cues to create desired impressions. Among a setting's features that may influence that character of a service are the colors or brightness of the service's surroundings; the volume and pitch of sounds in the setting; the smells, movement, freshness, and temperature of the air; the use of space; the style and comfort of the furnishings; and the setting's design and cleanliness.[21] The setting increases in importance when the nature of a service is distinguished by its environment, as is the case with Steak and Ale and Ponderosa Steakhouses or a "downtown" law firm.[22]

Proposition 11:

The delivery of service can be conceived as drama where: service personnel are the "actors," service customers are the "audience," physical evidence of the service is the "setting," and the process of service assembly is the "performance."[23]

The drama metaphor offers a useful way to conceive of service performances. Among the aspects of a service that can be considered in this way are selection of personnel (auditioning the actors), training of personnel (rehearsing), clearly defining the role (scripting the performance), creation of the service environment (setting the stage), and deciding which aspects of the service should be performed in the presence of the customer (onstage) and which should be performed in the back room (backstage).[24]

Service Roles and Scripts   If we think of services performances as drama, we can view each player as having a role to perform. Roles have been defined as combinations of social cues that guide and direct behavior in a given setting.[25] The success of any service performance depends in part on how well the "role set" or players—both service employees and customers—act out their roles.[26] Service employees need to perform their roles according to expectations of the customer; if they do not, the customer may be frustrated and disappointed. As we discussed earlier in this chapter, the customer's role must also be performed well. If customers are informed and educated about the expectations and requirements of the service (i.e., if the customer plays the proper role), and if the customer cooperates with the service provider to deliver the best possible service (i.e., if he or she is reading from the same script), the service performance is likely to be successful.

Proposition 12:

Service encounters can be viewed as role performances.[27]

One of the factors that most influences the effectiveness of role performance is a script—a "coherent sequence of events expected by the individual, involving her either as a participant or as an observer."[28] Service scripts consist of a set of ordered actions, actors, and objects that, through repeated involvement, define what the customer expects.[29] Conformance to scripts is satisfying to the customer, while deviations from the script lead to confusion and dissatisfaction.

Consider the script that you hold for the first day of class in a college course. Among the actions you expect are the following: (1) enter the classroom; (2) see other students in the room who are taking the class; (3) see the professor in the front of the room; (4) listen to the professor describe the course; (5) get a syllabus of the class; and (6) leave class early and start the actual education on the second class day. If a professor performs in accordance with the script you hold, you feel comfortable, familiar, and satisfied with the service encounter. Experiencing a script that is incongruent with this expected pattern leads to confusion and dissatisfaction. What if you showed up and there were no other students in the class with you the first day? What if the professor sent a graduate student instead of coming herself? Suppose the professor told you he hadn't had time to write a syllabus? In these and other situations,

Proposition 13:

Negative departures from the customer's expected script will detract from service performance.

Positive discrepancies from the script are not as easy to specify—they may also detract or could "surprise" and add to the service encounter. Suppose the college class we just discussed was filled to capacity on the first day. Would you interpret that as positive—a sure sign that the class was popular—or negative—a signal that personal attention from the professor may be reduced? What if the professor was unusually friendly and so engaged students that they stayed to the end of the period? While some students might be delighted because the friendliness of the professor exceeded expectations, others might be disgruntled, having counted on more free time between classes. Still others may be suspicious, not trusting the friendliness because it doesn't follow the expected pattern. More personalization or attention is not always better.[30]

Proposition 14:

Departures from the customer's expected script, including provision of more of an attribute than expected, may detract from or add to the service experience.

Related to the ideas of scripts and roles is the concept of *mutual understanding* between service customers and employees. Mutual understanding results when service customers and employees are similar cognitively and they can accurately sense what the role of the other person is.[31] When employees can sense and understand the customer's perspective and be empathetic, and when service customers can appreciate the role and constraints of the service employee, customer satisfaction with the service encounter intensifies.

The Compatibility of Service Customers   We have just discussed the roles of employees and customers receiving service. We now want to focus on the role of *other* customers receiving service at the same time. Consider how central the mere *presence* of other customers is in churches, restaurants, dances, bars, lounges, and spectator sports: If no one else shows up, customers will not get to socialize with others, one of the primary expectations in these types of services. However, if the number of customers becomes so dense that crowding occurs, customers may also be dissatisfied.[32] The way other customers behave with many services such as airlines, education, clubs, and social organizations also exerts a major influence on a customer's experience.[33] In general, the presence, behavior, and similarity of other customers receiving services has a strong impact on the satisfaction and dissatisfaction of any given customer.[34]

Customer compatibility[35] has been identified as important in services experiences, especially in situations where:

Customers are in close physical proximity to each other, such as in crowded airlines,

Verbal interaction among customers is likely, such as in full-service restaurants, night clubs, and bars,

Customers are engaged in numerous and varied activities, such as in a library or swimming pool,

The service environment attracts a heterogeneous customer mix, such as public parks or bowling alleys,

The core service is compatibility, such as Big Brothers, Big Sisters, or escort or dating services,

Customers must occasionally wait for the service, such as in physicians' offices or waiting for a table in a restaurant,

Customers are expected to share time, space, or service utensils with one another the way patrons in health clubs share shower facilities, golfers share fairways and greens, and residents of a retirement community share laundry facilities.[36]

Customers can be incompatible for many reasons—differences in beliefs, values, experiences, abilities to pay, appearance, age, and health, to name just a few. The service marketer must anticipate, acknowledge, and deal with heterogeneous consumers who have the potential to be incompatible. The service marketer can also bring homogeneous customers together and solidify relationships between them, which increases the cost to the customer of switching service providers.[37]

Proposition 15:

Customer compatibility is a factor that influences customer satisfaction, particularly in high contact services.

Post-Purchase Evaluation

Attribution of Dissatisfaction   When consumers are disappointed with purchases—because the products did not fulfill the intended needs, did not perform satisfactorily, or were not worth their price—they may attribute their dissatisfaction to a number of different sources, among them the producers, the retailers, or themselves. Because consumers participate to a greater extent in the definition and production of services, they may feel more responsible for their dissatisfaction when they purchase services than when they purchase goods. As an example, consider a female consumer purchasing a haircut; receiving the cut she desires depends in part upon her clear specifications of her needs to the stylist. If disappointed, she may blame either the stylist (for lack of skill) or herself (for choosing the wrong stylist or for not communicating her own needs clearly).

The quality of many services depends on the information the customer brings to the service encounter: A doctor's accurate diagnosis requires a conscientious case history and a clear articulation of symptoms; a dry cleaner's success in removing a spot depends on the consumer's knowledge of its cause; and a tax preparer's satisfactory performance relies on the receipts saved by the consumer. Failure to obtain satisfaction with any of these services may not be blamed completely on the retailer or producer, since the consumer must adequately perform his or her part in the production process also.

With products, on the other hand, a consumer's main form of participation is the act of purchase. The consumer may attribute failure to receive satisfaction to her own decision-making error, but she holds the producer responsible for product performance. Goods usually carry warranties or guarantees with purchase, emphasizing that the producer believes that if something goes wrong, it is not the fault of the consumer.

Proposition 16:

Consumers attribute some of their dissatisfaction with services to their own inability to specify or perform their part of the service.

Proposition 17:

Consumers may complain less frequently about services than about goods due to their belief that they themselves are partly responsible for their dissatisfaction.

Innovation Diffusion   The rate of diffusion of an innovation depends on consumers' perceptions of the innovation with regard to five characteristics: relative advantage, compatibility, communicability, divisibility, and complexity.[38] An offering that has a relative advantage over existing or competing products; that is compatible with existing norms, values, and behaviors; that is communicable; and that is divisible (i.e., that can be tried or tested on a limited basis) diffuses more quickly than others. An offering that is complex, that is, difficult to understand or use, diffuses more slowly than others.

Considered as a group, services are less communicable, less divisible, more complex, and probably less compatible than goods. They are less communicable because they are intangible (e.g., their features cannot be displayed, illustrated, or compared) and because they are often unique to each buyer (as in a medical diagnosis or dental care). Services are less divisible because they are usually impossible to sample or test on a limited basis (e.g., how does one "sample" a medical diagnosis? a lawyer's services in settling a divorce? even a haircut?). Services are frequently more complex than goods because they are composed of a bundle of different attributes, not all of which will be offered to every buyer on each purchase.

Finally, services may be incompatible with existing values and behaviors, especially if consumers are accustomed to providing the service for themselves. As an illustration, consider a novel day-care center that cooks breakfast for children so that parents can arrive at work early. Mothers accustomed to performing this service for their children may resist adopting the innovation because it requires a change in habit, in behavior, even in values.

Proposition 18:

Consumers adopt innovations in services more slowly than they adopt innovations in goods.

Marketers may need to concentrate on incentives to trial when introducing new services. The awareness-interest-evaluation stages of the adoption process may best be bypassed because of the difficulty and inefficiency of communicating information about intangibles. Offering free visits, dollars-off coupons, and samples may be appropriate strategies to speed diffusion of innovations in services.

Brand Loyalty   The degree to which consumers are committed to particular brands of goods or services depends on a number of factors: the cost of changing brands (switching cost), the availability of substitutes, the perceived risk associated with the purchase, and the degree to which they have obtained satisfaction in the past. Because it may be more costly to change brands of services, because they may have more difficulty being aware of the availability of substitutes, and because higher risks may accompany services, consumers are more likely to remain customers of particular companies with services than with goods.

Greater search costs and monetary costs may be involved in changing brands of services than in changing brands of goods. Because of the difficulty of obtaining information about services, consumers may be unaware of alternatives or substitutes for their brands, or may be uncertain about the ability of alternatives to increase satisfaction over present brands. Monetary fees may accompany brand switching in many services: Physicians often require complete physicals on the initial visit; dentists sometimes demand new X-rays; and health clubs frequently charge "membership fees" at the outset to obtain long-term commitments from customers.

If consumers perceive greater risks with services, as is hypothesized here, they probably depend on brand loyalty to a greater extent than when they purchase products. Brand loyalty, described as a "means of economizing decision effort by substituting habit for repeated, deliberate decision," functions as a device for reducing the risks of consumer decisions.

A final reason consumers may be more brand loyal with services is the recognition of the need for repeated patronage in order to obtain optimum satisfaction from the seller. Becoming a "regular customer" allows the seller to gain knowledge of the customer's tastes and preferences, ensures better treatment, and encourages more interest in the consumer's satisfaction. Thus, a consumer may exhibit brand loyalty to cultivate a satisfying relationship with the seller.

Proposition 19:

Brand switching is less frequent with services than with products.

Brand loyalty has two sides. The fact that a service provider's own customers are brand loyal is not a problem. The fact that the customers of the provider's competition are difficult to capture, however, creates special challenges. The marketer may need to direct communications and strategy to the customers of competitors, emphasizing attributes and strengths that he or she possesses and the competitor lacks. Marketers can also facilitate switching from competitors' services by reducing switching costs. AT&T promised MCI customers that it would handle the transfer from MCI to AT&T, and also guaranteed it would pay to allow the customer to switch back if necessary, making it virtually costless for customers to switch long-distance carriers.

SUMMARY AND CONCLUSION

Intangibility, heterogeneity, and inseparability of production/consumption lead services to possess high levels of experience and credence properties, which in turn make them more difficult to evaluate than tangible goods. We isolated and discussed four categories of consumer behavior that reflect the differences between goods and services: (1) information search, (2) evaluation of service alternatives, (3) service purchase and consumption, (4) postpurchase evaluation. Nineteen specific hypotheses about consumer behavior in services were offered, accompanied by strategic implications for marketers. To be effective, service providers may need to alter their marketing mixes to recognize different consumer behaviors and evaluation processes.

DISCUSSION QUESTIONS

1 This chapter focused on aspects of consumer behavior that are different depending on whether goods or services are being purchased. What aspects of consumer behavior in the purchase of goods and services are similar?

2 Where does a college education fit on the continuum of evaluation for different types of products? Where does computer software fit? Consulting? Retailing? Fast food?

3 What are examples (other than those given in the chapter) of services that are high in credence properties?

4 For what types of services might consumers depend on mass communication (nonpersonal sources of information) in the purchase decision?

5 Which of the propositions in the chapter describe your behavior when it comes to purchasing services?

6 For what types of services would consumers tend to engage in the most postpurchase evaluation? The least?

7 Name three high-technology services (other than ATMs) that consumers resisted in the early stages of introduction but then accepted and used.

8 What is the impact of a service guarantee on the perceived risk customers experience in purchasing services?

9 List five services for which customer compatibility is essential.

10 What are examples of services where brand switching is difficult for consumers?

EXERCISES

1 Choose a particular end-consumer services industry and one type of service provided in that industry (such as the financial services industry for mortgage loans or the legal services industry for wills). Talk to five customers who have purchased that service and determine to what extent the propositions in this chapter described their behavior in information search, evaluating alternatives, purchase and consumption, and postpurchase and consumption for that service.

2 Choose a particular business-to-business service industry and one type of service provided in that industry (such as the information services industry for computer maintenance services or the consulting industry for management consulting). Talk to five customers in that industry and determine to what extent the propositions in this chapter described their behavior in information search, evaluation of alternatives, purchase and consumption, and postpurchase evaluation for that service.

NOTES

1 Eugene H. Fram, "Stressed-out Consumers Need Timesaving Innovations," *Marketing News,* March 2, 1992, p. 10.

2 Leonard L. Berry, "The Time-Buying Customer," *Journal of Retailing,* Vol. 55, No. 4, Winter 1979, 58–69.

3 Fram, "Stressed-out Consumers."

4 Phillip Nelson, "Information and Consumer Behavior," *Journal of Political Economy* 78, 20 (1970): 311–329.

5 M. R. Darby and E. Karni, "Free Competition and the Optimal Amount of Fraud," *Journal of Law and Economics* 16 (April 1973): 67–86.

6 Courtland L. Bovee and John V. Thill, *Marketing* (New York: McGraw-Hill, 1992).

7 T. S. Robertson, *Innovative Behavior and Communication* (New York: Holt, Rinehart & Winston, 1971).

8 N. L. Ray, "Marketing Communication and the Hierarchy of Effects," unpublished research paper 180, Stanford University, Stanford, Calif., August 1973.

9 "While Some Sing the Praises of Voice Mail, Other Exasperated Companies Pull the Plug," *The Service Edge,* Vol. 5, April 1992.

10 "Voice Processing: A Fine Line between Customer-Friendly and Customer-Deadly," *The Service Edge,* March 1992, p. 7.

11 Meryl Paula Gardner, "Mood States and Consumer Behavior: A Critical Review," *Journal of Consumer Research* 12 (December 1985): 281–300.

12 Ibid., p. 288.

13 Ibid.

14 Silvan S. Tomkins, "Affect as Amplification: "Some Modifications in Theory," in *Emotion: Theory, Research, and Experience,* ed. R. Plutchik and H. Kellerman (New York: Academic Press, 1980), pp. 141–164.

15 Gardner, "Mood States and Consumer Behavior," p. 288.

16 Ibid. Also see Martin L. Hoffman, "Affect, Cognition, and Motivation," in *Handbook of Motivation and Cognition: Foundations of Social Behavior,* ed. R. M. Sorrentino and E. T. Higgins (New York: Guilford Press, 1986), pp. 244–280.

17 Madeline Johnson and George M. Zinkhan, "Emotional Responses to a Professional Service Encounter," *Journal of Services Marketing,* Vol. 5, No. 2, Spring 1991, pp. 5–16.

18 Steven J. Grove, Raymond P. Fisk, and Mary Jo Bitner, "Dramatizing the Service Experience: A Managerial Approach," in *Advances in Services Marketing and Management,* ed. Theresa A. Swartz, David E. Bowen, and Steven W. Brown (Greenwich, CT: JAI Press) Vol. 1 (1992), pp. 91–121.

19 Leonard L. Berry, "The Employee as Customer," *Journal of Retail Banking,* 3 (March, 1981): 33–40.

20 Grove, Fisk, and Bitner, "Dramatizing the Service Experience."

21 Ibid.

22 Ibid., pp. 104–105.

23 Ibid.

24 Ibid.

25 Michael R. Solomon, Carol Surprenant, John A. Czepiel, and Evelyn G. Gutman, "A Role Theory Perspective on Dyadic Interactions: The Service Encounter," *Journal of Marketing* 49 (Winter, 1985), 99–111.

26 Ibid.

27 Ibid., p. 108.

28 Robert F. Abelson, "Script Processing in Attitude Formation and Decision Making," in *Cognition and Social Behavior,* ed. John S. Carroll and John S. Payne (Hillsdale, N.J.: Erlbaum, 1976).

29 Ruth A. Smith and Michael J. Houston, "Script-based Evaluations of Satisfaction with Services," in *Emerging Perspectives on Services Marketing,* ed. L. Berry, G. Lynn Shostack, and G. Upah (Chicago: American Marketing Association, 1982), pp. 59–62.

30 Solomon, Surprenant, Czepiel, and Gutman, "Dyadic Interactions."

31 Lois A. Mohr and Mary Jo Bitner, "Mutual Understanding between Customers and Employees in Service Encounters," *Advances in Consumer Research* 18 (1991): 611–617.

32 John E. G. Bateson and Michael K. M. Hui, "Crowding in the Service Environment," in *Creativity in Services Marketing: What's New, What Works, What's Developing,* ed. M. Venkatesan, Diane M. Schmalensee, and Claudia Marshall (Chicago: American Marketing Association, 1986), pp. 85–88.

33 Julie Baker, "The Role of the Environment in Marketing Services: The Consumer Perspective," in *The Services Challenge: Integrating for Competitive Advantage,* ed. John A. Czepiel, Carole A. Congram, and James Shanahan (Chicago: American Marketing Association, 1987), pp. 79–84.

34 Charles L. Martin and Charles A. Pranter, "Compatibility Management: Customer-to-Customer Relationships in Service Environments," *Journal of Services Marketing* 3 (Summer 1989).

35 Ibid.

36 Ibid., pp. 10–11.

37 Ibid.

38 E. M. Rogers, *Diffusion of Innovations* (New York: Free Press, 1962).

4

CUSTOMER EXPECTATIONS OF SERVICE

Problem: Rapid escalation of customer expectations
Root cause: Fierce competition

Managers of service companies bemoan what they perceive as an unprecedented escalation of customer expectations in many service industries. In services from airlines to education, customers are being offered new features, fresh perks, and lower prices than ever to choose and use companies' services. Each competitive advance raises customer expectations, as has been dramatically demonstrated in the airline industry in the 1990s. Airlines have granted so many bonus miles, free trips, and first-class upgrades—and discounted those that customers pay for—that business travelers' expectation levels are higher than they have ever been at a time when few major airlines can manage to make a profit.

But the credit-card industry is perhaps the best example of elevated customer expectations driven by competitive warfare. Competition for customer dollars has been unusually brutal in the 1990s, increasing the expectations customers hold for credit-card services. In the 1980s, credit-card companies competed on brand image and coverage. With a premium image, American Express did not have to match the reduced annual fees or interest rates competitors charged customers, nor the service fees billed merchants. Its principal competitors, MasterCard and VISA, battled for position as cards that were accepted everywhere the customer wanted to go. Industry status quo for nearly two decades was followed by a revolution in a short six months in 1993.

An entirely new set of competitors entered the industry, spurred by regulations allowing companies outside the financial services industry the right to issue credit cards. Companies in retailing, automobile manufacturing, and other industries immediately recognized the opportunity for profits at a time when their own industries were stable or *declining. Armed with the knowledge that customers could be swayed by value and that they had to offer something different to play in the game, these companies made a major impact at the end of 1992, forever altering the expectations customers had of credit cards. Instead of image and coverage, the new weapons were lower interest rates, longer grace periods before payment was due, frequent flyer miles, no annual fees, rebates, discounts, prizes, and merchandise. Here is a sample of the competitive offerings that intensified customer expectations at that time:*

The *AT&T Universal Card* dropped annual fees for life for charter members, reduced interest rates, and offered a 10 percent discount on AT&T calling-card long-distance calls.

The *Citibank AAdvantage Card* offered frequent flyer miles on American Airlines for every dollar spent.

The *GM Card* wiped out annual fees, dropped its interest rates, and added altogether different bells and whistles, including: (1) a 5 percent rebate on all purchases and transferred balances to be used to buy or lease GM cars and trucks, and (2) an extra 5 percent rebate bonus on purchases from GM card corporate partners including Avis, MCI, and Marriott.

The *GE Rewards MasterCard* charged no annual fee the first year (with $1,500 cash balance transfers) and granted $10 Reward Savings Certificates every three months plus $10 GE Rewards Checks for every $500 in purchases to be redeemed at 25 GE partners merchants and service companies ranging from Cinemax to Toys R Us.

Given these offerings, what happened to the expectations of credit-card customers? They escalated at a rapid pace. The new entrants established an enhanced meaning of value to card holders and forced experienced players such as American Express to match their offerings. For the first time in its history, Amex bowed to the pressure by cutting the fees it charged merchants and offering Membership Miles, a program for free frequent flyer miles on a list of airlines.

Customer expectations are beliefs about service delivery that function as standards or reference points against which performance is judged. Because customers compare their perceptions of performance with these reference points when evaluating service quality, thorough knowledge about customer expectations is critical to services marketers. Knowing what the customer expects is the first and possibly most critical step in delivering quality service. Being wrong about what customers want can mean losing a customer's business when another company hits the target exactly. Being wrong can also mean expending money, time, and other resources on things that don't count to the customer. Being wrong can even mean not surviving in a fiercely competitive market such as the credit card industry we just described.

Among the aspects of expectations that need to be explored and understood for successful services marketing are the following: What types of expectation standards do customers hold about services? What factors most influence the formation of these expectations? What role do these factors play in changing expectations? How can a service company meet or exceed customer expectations?

Figure 4-1 highlights the expectations portion of the Gaps Model that is the focus of this chapter. We will examine the highlighted portion of the model in detail in an effort to fully understand the concept of customer expectations.

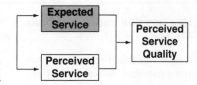

FIGURE 4-1   The role of expectations in service.

The objectives of this chapter are to:

1 Recognize that customers hold different types of expectations for service performance.

2 Discuss the sources of customer expectations of service including those that are controllable and uncontrollable by marketers.

3 Distinguish between customers' global expectations of their relationships with service providers and their expectations of the service encounter.

4 Acknowledge that the types and sources of expectations are similar for end consumers and business customers, for pure service and product-related service, for experienced customers and inexperienced customers.

5 Delineate the most important current issues surrounding customer expectations.

In this chapter we provide a framework for thinking about customer expectations. The chapter is divided into four main sections: (1) the meaning and types of expected service, (2) factors that influence customer expectations of service, (3) a model of service expectations, and (4) current issues involving customer service expectations.[1]

MEANING AND TYPES OF SERVICE EXPECTATIONS

While most everyone has an intuitive sense of what expectations are, service marketers need a far more thorough and clear definition of expectations in order to comprehend, measure, and manage them. To address this need, research has been conducted recently (see Exhibit 4-1). We will use many of the observations developed in that research to give you a framework for thinking about customer expectations. We will also use quotes from customers in that research to illustrate the concepts and sources of expectations.

Expected Service: Two Levels of Expectations

One of the findings of this study is that customers hold several different types of expectations about service. The first can be termed *desired service* and defined as the level of service the customer hopes to receive—the "wished for" level of performance. Desired service is a blend of what the customer believes "can be" and "should be."[2] For example, consumers who sign up for a computer dating service expect to find compatible, attractive, interesting people to date, and perhaps even someone to marry. The expectation reflects the hopes and wishes of these consumers—without these hopes and wishes and the belief that they may be fulfilled, they would probably not purchase the dating service. In a similar way, you will engage the services of your college's placement office

---

EXHIBIT 4-1   METHODOLOGY FOR UNDERSTANDING CUSTOMER EXPECTATIONS

The model used in this chapter was based on consistent patterns of responses in an exploratory research study designed specifically to determine the nature and sources of customer expectations.[3] In chapter 6 we will describe the techniques used in exploratory research as well as other ways to conduct market research related to services marketing. For now, a brief explanation of the way this study was conducted will give you the background for the concepts and quotes in this chapter.

Sixteen focus group interviews were held in six different service sectors: commercial property and casualty insurance, automobile insurance, business equipment repair, automobile repair, hotels, and truck and tractor rental/leasing.

These sectors were chosen to represent both pure service and product-related service, both end customers and business customers, and both experienced customers and inexperienced customers.

Common themes emerging from the focus group interviews and insights from previous research led to the development of the conceptual model of customer service expectations. Although differences were anticipated across the different comparison pairs, the nature and sources of expectations appeared to be similar across the groups. Expectations of end- and business-customer groups, of experienced and inexperienced customers, and of customers of pure and of product-related services had fundamentally the same nature and antecedents.

---

when you are ready to graduate. What are your expectations of the service? In all likelihood, you want the office to find you a job—the right job in the right geography for the right salary—because that is what you hope and wish for.

However, you probably also see that the economy may constrain the availability of ideal job openings in companies. In this situation and in general, customers hope to achieve their service desires but recognize that this is not always possible. For this reason they hold another, lower level expectation for the threshold of acceptable service.[4] This lower expectation has been termed *adequate service*—the level of service the customer will accept. Many college graduates in the early 1990s, trained for high-level, highly skilled jobs, accepted entry-level positions at fast-food restaurants and mail-order retailers or internships for no pay. Their hopes and desires (that is, their desired service expectations) were still high but they recognized that they could not attain those desires in the market that existed at the time. Their standard of adequate service was much lower than that of their desired service: Some graduates accepted any job for which they could earn a salary, and others agreed to nonpaying, short-term positions as interns to gain experience. Adequate service represents the "minimum tolerable expectation,"[5] the bottom level of performance acceptable to the customer, and reflects the level of service customers believe they will get on the basis of their experience with services.

Figure 4-2 shows these two expectation standards as the upper and lower boundaries for the expectation "box" in Figure 3-1. This figure portrays the idea that customers assess service performance on the basis of two standards: what they desire and what they deem acceptable.

Among the intriguing questions about service expectations is whether customers hold the same or different expectation levels for service firms in the same industry. For example, are desired service expectations the same for all restaurants? Or just for all fast-food restaurants? Do the levels of adequate service expectations vary across restaurants? Consider the following quote:

FIGURE 4-2   Dual customer expectation levels.

Levels of expectation are why two organizations in the same business can offer far different levels of service and still keep customers happy. It is why McDonald's can extend excellent industrialized service with few employees per customer and why an expensive restaurant with many tuxedoed waiters may be unable to do as well from the customer's point of view.[6]

This quote illustrates that customers hold similar desired expectations across categories of service but that these categories are not as broad as whole industries. Among subcategories of restaurants are the following: expensive restaurants, fast-food restaurants, airport restaurants. A customer's desired service expectation for fast-food restaurants is quick, convenient, tasty food in a clean setting. The desired service expectation for an expensive restaurant, on the other hand, is elegant surroundings, gracious employees, candlelight, and fine food. In essence, desired service expectations seem to be the same for service providers within a subcategory that is defined by the customer.

The adequate service expectation level, however, is likely to vary for different firms within a category. Within fast-food restaurants, a customer may hold a higher expectation for McDonald's than for Burger King, having experienced consistent service at McDonald's over time and somewhat inconsistent service at Burger King. It is possible, therefore, that a customer can be more disappointed with service from McDonald's than from Burger King even though the level of service at McDonald's is higher than the level at Burger King.

The Zone of Tolerance

As we discussed in earlier chapters of this textbook, services are heterogeneous in that performance may vary across providers, across employees from the same provider, and even within the same service employee. The extent to which customers recognize and are willing to accept this variation is called the *zone of tolerance* and is shown in Figure 4-3. If service drops below adequate service—the minimum level considered acceptable—customers will be frustrated and their satisfaction with the company undermined. If service performance is outside the zone of tolerance at the top end—where performance exceeds desired service—customers will be very pleased and probably quite surprised as well. You might consider the zone of tolerance as the range or window in which customers do not particularly notice service performance. When it falls outside the range (either very low or very high), the service gets the customer's attention in either a positive or negative way. As an example, consider the service an airline passenger receives

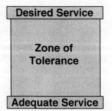

FIGURE 4-3   The zone of tolerance.

from the ticket counter when checking luggage. Most customers hold a range of acceptable times for this service encounter—probably somewhere between five and ten minutes. If service consumes that period of time, customers probably do not pay much attention to the wait. If a customer enters the line and finds sufficient airline personnel at their stations to serve her in the first two or three minutes, she may notice the service and judge it as excellent. On the other hand, if a customer has to wait in line for fifteen minutes, he (and most likely all the other passengers in the line) begins to grumble, looks at his watch, and glares at the personnel behind the stations marked "position not open" who are not waiting on customers. The longer the wait is outside the zone of tolerance, the more frustrated he becomes.

Customers' service expectations are characterized by a range of levels, bounded by desired and adequate service, rather than a single level. This tolerance zone, representing the difference between desired service and the level of service considered adequate, can expand and contract within a customer. An airline customer's zone of tolerance will narrow when he is running late and is concerned about making his plane. A minute seems much longer and his adequate service level increases. On the other hand, a customer who arrives at the airport early may have an expanding tolerance zone, making the wait in line far less noticeable than when he or she is pressed for time. This example shows that the marketer must understand not just the size and boundary levels for the zone of tolerance but also when and how the tolerance zone fluctuates within a given customer.

Another aspect of variability in the range of reasonable services is that different customers possess different tolerance zones. Some customers have narrow zones of tolerance, requiring a tighter range of service from providers, while other customers allow a greater range of service. For example, very busy customers would likely always be pressed for time and therefore desire short wait times in general and also hold a constrained range for the length of acceptable wait times. When it comes to meeting plumbers or repair personnel at their homes for appliance problems, customers who work outside the home have a more restricted window of acceptable time duration for that appointment than would customers who work in their homes or do not work at all.

An individual customer's zone of tolerance increases or decreases depending on a number of factors, including company-controlled factors such as price. A business insurance customer commented, "Price increases don't really drive up expectations. But my tolerance level will become more stringent/less flexible with an increase." A business equipment repair customer claimed, "My expectations are higher when I've paid for a maintenance agreement, because I've paid money up front."[7] Later in this chapter we will describe many different factors, some company controlled and others customer controlled, that lead to the narrowing or widening of the tolerance zone.

Customers' tolerance zones also vary for different service attributes or dimensions. The more important the factor, the narrower the zone of tolerance is likely to be. In general, customers are likely to be less tolerant about unreliable service (broken promises, service errors) than other service deficiencies, which means that they have higher expectations for this factor. In addition to higher expectations for the most important service dimensions and attributes, customers are likely to be less willing to relax these expectations than those for less important factors, making the zone of tolerance for the most important service dimension smaller and the desired and adequate service levels higher.[8] Figure 4-4 portrays the likely difference in tolerance zones for the most important and the least important factors.[9]

Figure 4-5 shows the difference in zones of tolerance for first-time service and for recovery service. While customers' expectations are higher for both the result of the service (the service outcome) and the way the service is delivered (the process) during recovery service, the opportunity for recovery is greater with the process dimensions because of lower expectations and a larger zone of tolerance. It is also possible that for service attributes that customers assess in categorical terms (i.e., either the service provider possesses the attribute or does not) the zone of tolerance could be zero (i.e., adequate and desired service will be at the same level).[10]

The fluctuation in the individual customer's zone of tolerance is more a function of changes in the adequate service level, which moves readily up and down due to situational circumstances, than in the desired service level, which tends to move upward incrementally due to accumulated experiences. Desired service is relatively idiosyncratic and stable compared with adequate service, which moves up and down and in response to competition and other factors. Fluctuation in the zone of tolerance can be likened to

FIGURE 4-4   Zones of tolerance for different service dimensions.

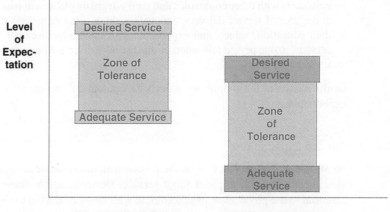

Source: Berry, Parasuraman, and Zeithaml (1993).

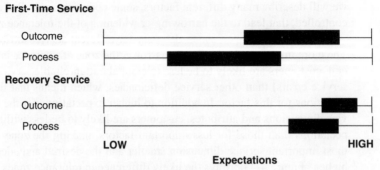

FIGURE 4-5   Zones of tolerance for first-time and recovery service.

Source: Parasuraman, Berry, and Zeithaml (1991).

an accordion's movement, but with most of the gyration coming from one side (the adequate service level) rather than the other (the desired service level).

In summary, customers have two different levels of expectations: desired service and adequate service. The desired service level is less subject to change than the adequate service level. A zone of tolerance separates these two levels. This zone of tolerance varies across customers and expands or contracts within the same customer.

FACTORS THAT INFLUENCE CUSTOMER EXPECTATIONS OF SERVICE

Because expectations play such a critical role in customer evaluation of services, marketers need and want to understand the factors that shape them. Marketers would also like to have control over these factors as well, but many of the forces that influence customer expectations are uncontrollable:

> [Service] expectations are formed by many uncontrollable factors, from the experience of customers with other companies and their advertising to a customer's psychological state at the time of service delivery. Strictly speaking, what customers expect is as diverse as their education, values, and experience. The same advertisement that shouts "personal service" to one person tells another that the advertiser has promised more than it can possibly deliver.[11]

In this section of the chapter we will try to separate out the many influences on customer expectations.

Sources of Desired Service Expectations

As shown in Figure 4-6, two of the largest influences on desired service level are personal needs and philosophies about service. *Personal needs,* those states or conditions essential to the physical or psychological well being of the customer, are pivotal factors that shape the level of desired service. Personal needs can fall into many categories, including physical, social, psychological, and functional. A fan who regularly goes to

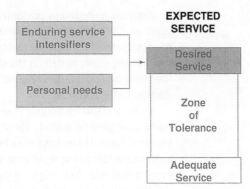

FIGURE 4-6   Factors that influence desired service.

baseball games right from work, and is therefore thirsty and hungry, hopes and desires that the food and drink vendors will pass by his section frequently, whereas a fan who regularly has dinner elsewhere has a low or zero level of desired service from the vendors. A customer with high social and dependency needs may have relatively high expectations for a hotel's ancillary services, hoping, for example, that the hotel has a bar with live music and dancing. The impact of personal needs on desired service is illustrated by the different expectations held by two business insurance customers:

> Most of my expectations pertain to brokers. I expect the broker to do a great deal of my work because I don't have the staff. . . . I expect the broker to know a great deal about my business and communicate that knowledge to the underwriter.

> My expectations are different . . . I do have a staff to do our certificates, etc., and use the broker minimally.[12]

Some customers are more demanding than others, having greater sensitivity to, and higher expectations of, service. *Enduring service intensifiers* are individual, stable factors that lead the customer to a heightened sensitivity to service. One of the most important of these factors can be called *derived service expectations,* which occur when customer expectations are driven by another person or group of people. A niece from a big family who is planning a ninetieth birthday party for a favorite aunt is representing the entire family in selecting a restaurant for a successful celebration. Her needs are driven in part by the derived expectations from the other family members. A parent choosing a vacation for the family, a spouse selecting a home-cleaning service, an employee choosing a rental office for the firm—all these customers' individual expectations are intensified because they experience derived expectations from other parties who will receive the service. In the context of business-to-business service, customer expectations are driven by the expectations of their own customers. The head of an information services department in an insurance company, who is the business customer of a large computer vendor, has expectations based on those of the insurance customers he serves: when the computer equipment is down, his customers complain. His need to keep the system up and running is not just his own expectation but is derived from the pressure of his customers.

Business-to-business customers may also derive their expectation from their managers and supervisors. Employees of a marketing research department may speed up project cycles (i.e., increase their expectations for speed of delivery) when pressured by their management to deliver the study results. Purchasing agents may increase demands for faster delivery at lower costs when company management is emphasizing cost reduction in the company.

Another enduring service intensifier is *personal service philosophy*—the customer's underlying generic attitude about the meaning of service and the proper conduct of service providers. If you have ever been a waitress or a waiter in a restaurant, you are likely to have standards for restaurant service that were shaped by your training and experience in that role. You might, for example, believe that waitresses should not keep customers waiting longer than fifteen minutes to take their orders. Knowing the way a kitchen operates, you may be less tolerant of lukewarm food or errors in the order than others who have not held the role of waitperson. In general, customers who are themselves in service businesses or have worked for them in the past seem to have especially strong service philosophies. The focus group interviews discussed earlier in the chapter yielded two comments that illustrate personal service philosophies:

An automobile insurance customer: You expect to be treated the way you treat other people.

A business insurance customer: Your own basic philosophies and attitudes about how to do business carry over into what you expect from insurance companies.[13]

To the extent that customers have personal philosophies about service provision, their expectations of service providers will be intensified. Personal service philosophies and derived service expectations elevate the level of desired service.

Sources of Adequate Service Expectations

A different set of determinants affect adequate service, the level of service the customer finds acceptable. In general, these influences are short term in nature and tend to fluctuate more than the somewhat stable factors that influence desired service. In this section we explain the five factors shown in Figure 4-7 that lead to adequate service: (1) transitory service intensifiers, (2) perceived service alternatives, (3) customer self-perceived service role, (4) situational factors, and (5) predicted service.

The first set of elements, *transitory service intensifiers,* are temporary, usually short term, individual factors that make a customer more aware of the need for service. Personal emergency situations in which service is urgently needed (such as an accident and the need for automobile insurance, or a breakdown in office equipment during a busy period) raise the level of adequate service expectation, particularly the level of responsiveness required and considered acceptable. A mail-order company that depends on 800-number phone lines for receiving all customer orders will tend to be more demanding of the telephone service during peak periods of the week, month, and year. Any system breakdown or lack of clarity on the lines will be tolerated less during these intense periods than at other times. The impact of transitory service intensifiers is evident in

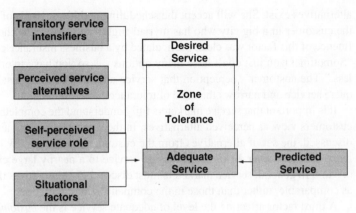

FIGURE 4-7   Factors that influence adequate service.

these two comments by two focus group participants in the study described earlier in the chapter.

> An automobile insurance customer: The nature of my problem influences my expectations, for example, a broken window versus a DWI accident requiring brain surgery.

> A business equipment repair customer: I had calibration problems with the X-ray equipment. They should have come out and fixed it in a matter of hours because of the urgency.[14]

Problems with the initial service can also lead to heightened expectations. Performing a service right the first time is very important, because customers value service reliability above all other dimensions. If the service fails in the recovery phase, fixing it right the second time (that is, being reliable in service recovery) is even more critical than it was the first time. Automobile repair service provides a case in point. If a problem with your automobile's brakes sends you to a car repair provider, you expect the company to fix the brakes. If you experience further problems with the brakes after the repair (a situation that is not all that uncommon with car repair), your adequate service level will increase. In general, service recovery expectations are higher than initial service expectations, as shown earlier in Figure 4-5. As one auto repair customer put it: "I am willing to be understanding the first time but would expect much more and be more impatient the second time around." In these and other situations where transitory service intensifiers are present, the level of adequate service will increase and the zone of tolerance will narrow.

Perceived service alternatives are other providers from whom the customer can obtain service. If customers have multiple service providers to choose from, or if they can provide the service for themselves (such as lawn care or personal grooming), their levels of adequate service are higher than those of customers who believe it is not possible to get better service elsewhere. An airline customer who lives in a very small town with a tiny airport, for example, has a reduced set of options in airline travel. This customer will be more tolerant of the service performance of the carriers in the town because few alternatives exist. She will accept the scheduling and lower levels of service more than the customer in a big city who has myriad flights and airlines to choose from. The influence of this factor was clearly articulated by a business insurance customer who said: "Sometimes you just don't have many options . . . so you have to effectively settle for less." The customer's perception that service alternatives exist raises the level of adequate service and narrows the zone of tolerance.

It is important that service marketers fully understand the complete set of options that customers view as perceived alternatives. In the small town–small airport example just discussed, the set of alternatives from the customer's point of view is likely to include more than just other airlines—limousine service to a nearby large city, rail service, or driving. In general, service marketers must discover the alternatives the customer views as comparable, rather than those in the company's competitive set.

A third factor affecting the level of adequate service is the *customer's self-perceived service role.* We define this as customer perceptions of the degree to which customers exert an influence on the level of service they receive. In other words, customers' expectations are partly shaped by how well they believe they are performing their own roles in service delivery.[15] One role of the customer is specifying the level of service expected. A customer who is very explicit with a waiter about how rare he wants his steak cooked in a restaurant will probably be more dissatisfied if the meat comes to the table overcooked than a customer who does not articulate the degree of doneness expected. The customer's active participation in the service also affects this factor. A customer who doesn't show up for many of her allergy shots will probably be more lenient on the allergist when she experiences symptoms than one who conscientiously shows up for every shot.

A final way the customer defines his or her role is in assuming the responsibility for complaining when service is poor. A dissatisfied customer who complains will be less tolerant than one who does not voice his or her concerns. An automobile insurance customer acknowledged his responsibility in service provision this way: "You can't blame it all on the insurance agent. You need to be responsible too and let the agent know what exactly you want." A truck-leasing customer recognized her role by stating: "There are a lot of variables that can influence how you get treated, including how you deal with them."[16]

Customers' zones of tolerance seem to expand when they sense they are not fulfilling their roles. When, on the other hand, customers believe they are doing their part in delivery, their expectations of adequate service are heightened. The comment of an automobile repair customer illustrates: "Service writers are not competent. I prepare my own itemized list of problems, take it to the service writer, and tell him or her: 'Fix these.' "

Levels of adequate service are also influenced by *situational factors,* defined as service performance conditions that customers view as beyond the control of the service provider. For example, where personal emergencies such as serious automobile accidents would likely intensify customer service expectations of insurance companies (because they are transitory service intensifiers), catastrophes that affect a large number of people at one time (tornadoes or earthquakes) may lower service expectations because customers recognize that insurers are inundated with demands for their services. Cus-

---

TECHNOLOGY SPOTLIGHT

INFORMATION TECHNOLOGY AND REENGINEERING COMBINE TO CHANGE CUSTOMER EXPECTATIONS OF SERVICE

The union of two major trends—information technology and reengineering of work processes—are resulting in customer service breakthroughs that significantly alter customer expectations. Reengineering, which involves changing the processes and assumptions by which work gets accomplished, is facilitated by technology that includes electronic mail, video conferencing, laptop computers, car faxes, cellular phones, personal computer networks, and handheld wireless terminals. These information technologies increase the speed of processes such as billing, solving of customer problems, handling of customer complaints, product delivery, and handling of applications. Here are just two of the customer service improvements that have resulted:

1 Billing and invoicing changes. DuPont processes bills electronically with many of its vendors instead of using invoices. With about 4 percent of its suppliers the company doesn't bother with purchase orders. Instead, outside vendors are linked electronically with DuPont's internal inventory system. When the suppliers see that DuPont is running short on an item, they automatically deliver replacement goods.

2 Sales process changes. Phoenix Designs, Inc., a Herman Miller subsidiary, revamped its traditional way of selling office furniture. The old way: a salesperson goes to the customer's office, gathers ideas to take to a designer, returns to the office for the designer to work up a draft, goes back and forth between the office and the customer for six weeks, and—finally—delivers a proposal to the customer. The arrangement was frustrating to buyers and not profitable to Phoenix. The new way: Using PCs and a custom software program called "Z-Axis," salespeople are their own designers and can generate proposals in four or five days. The effectiveness of the system is stunning. One dealer made a sale each of the 70 times it first used the system. Small dealers reported an average increase in sales of 1,000 percent. Now underway is a portable system that will allow sales reps to work on designs right in the customer's office.

Source: Business Week Special Report: The Technology Payoff, June 14, 1993, pp. 46–68.

---

tomers who recognize that these contingencies are not the fault of the service company may accept lower levels of adequate service given the context. In general, situational factors temporarily lower the level of adequate service, widening the zone of tolerance.

The final factor that influences adequate service is *predicted service* (Figure 4-8), the level of service customers believe they are likely to get. This type of service expectation can be viewed as predictions made by customers about what is likely to happen during an impending transaction or exchange. Predicted service performance implies some objective calculation of the probability of performance or estimate of anticipated service performance level. If customers predict good service, their levels of adequate service are likely to be higher than if they predict poor service. For example, full-time residents in a college town usually predict faster restaurant service during the summer months when students are not on campus. This will probably lead them to have higher standards for adequate service in restaurants during the summer than during school months. On the other hand, customers of telephone companies and utilities know that installation service from these firms will be difficult to obtain during the first few weeks of school when a myriad of students are setting up their apartments for the year. In this case, levels of adequate service decrease and zones of tolerance widen.

Predicted service is typically an estimate or calculation of the service a customer will receive in an individual transaction rather than in the overall relationship with a service provider. Where desired and adequate service expectations are global assessments com-

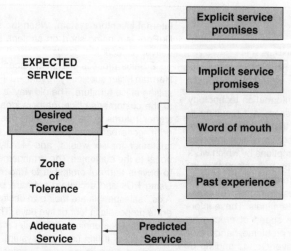

FIGURE 4-8 Factors that influence desired and predicted service.

prising many individual service transactions, predicted service is almost always an estimate of what will happen in the next service encounter or transaction that the customer experiences. This is one of the reasons why predicted service is viewed in this model as an influencer of adequate service.

Because predictions are about individual service encounters, they are likely to be more concrete and specific than the types of expectation levels customers hold for adequate service or desired service. For example, your predicted service expectations about the length of time you will spend in the waiting room the next time you visit your doctor will likely be expressed in terms of the number of minutes or hours you have sat in the waiting room this time.

Service Encounter Expectations versus Overall Service Expectations

In chapter 5 we will discuss the difference between overall service quality and service encounter quality, viewing the service encounter as a discrete event occurring over a definable period of time (such as a particular hotel stay or a particular check-in experience at the hotel). Customers hold expectations of the quality of each service encounter, just as they hold expectations about the overall service quality of a firm. When the expectations are about individual service encounters, they are likely to be more specific and concrete (for example, the number of minutes one must wait for a front desk clerk) than the expectations about overall service quality (for example, speedy service).

Sources of Both Desired and Predicted Service Expectations

When consumers are interested in purchasing services, they are likely to seek or take in information from several different sources. For example, they may call a store, ask a friend, or deliberately track newspaper advertisements to find the needed service at the lowest price. They may also receive service information by watching television or hearing an unsolicited comment from a colleague about a service that was performed well. In addition to these active and passive types of external search for information, consumers may conduct an internal search by reviewing the information held in memory about the service. This section discusses one internal and three external factors that influence both desired service and predicted service expectations: (1) explicit service promises, (2) implicit service promises, (3) word-of-mouth communications, and (4) past experience.

Explicit service promises are personal and nonpersonal statements about the service made by the organization to customers. The statements are personal when they are communicated by salespeople or service or repair personnel; they are nonpersonal when they come from advertising, brochures, and other written publications. Explicit service promises are one of the few influences on expectations that are completely in the control of the service provider.

Promising exactly what will ultimately be delivered would seem a logical and appropriate way to manage customer expectations and ensure that reality fits the promises. However, companies and the personnel who represent them often deliberately overpromise to obtain business or inadvertently overpromise by stating their best estimates about delivery of a service in the future. An auto insurance customer in the focus groups described in Exhibit 4-1 commented: "They say in their advertising that they are the 'good driver' company, and yet my premiums kept going up even though I had no accidents. When I inquired they said it was because of the average number of accidents in my group." In addition to overpromising, company representatives simply do not always know the appropriate promises to make because services are often customized and therefore not easily defined and repeated; the representative may not know how long or in what final form the service will be delivered.

All types of explicit service promises have a direct impact on desired service expectation. If the sales visit portrays a banking service that is available twenty-four hours a day, the customer's desires for that service (as well as the service of competitors) will be shaped by this promise. A hotel customer describes the impact of explicit promises on expectations: "They get you real pumped up with the beautiful ad. When you go in you expect the bells and whistles to go off. Usually they don't." A business equipment repair customer states: "When you buy a piece of equipment you expect to get a competitive advantage from it. Service is promised with the sale of the equipment."

Explicit service promises influence both the levels of desired service and predicted service: They shape what customers desire in general as well as what they predict will happen in the next service encounter from a particular service provider or in a certain service encounter.

Implicit service promises are service-related cues other than explicit promises that lead to inferences about what the service should and will be like. These quality cues are dominated by price and the tangibles associated with the service. In general, the higher the price and the more impressive the tangibles, the more a customer will expect from the service. Consider a customer who shops for insurance, finding two firms charging radically different prices. She may make the inference that the firm with the higher price should and will provide higher quality service and better coverage. Similarly, a customer who stays at a posh hotel is likely to desire and predict a higher standard of service than from a hotel with less impressive facilities.

The importance of *word-of-mouth communication* in shaping expectations of service is well documented.[17] These personal and sometimes nonpersonal statements made by parties other than the organization convey to customers what the service will be like and influence both predicted and desired service. As we discussed in Chapter 3, word-of-mouth communication carries particular weight as an information source because it is perceived as unbiased. Word of mouth tends to be very important in services that are difficult to evaluate before purchase and direct experience of them. Experts (including *Consumer Reports,* friends, and family) are also word-of-mouth sources that can affect the levels of desired and predicted service. In the words of one focus group participant: "What I hear from others about higher service levels in their companies can influence my expectation levels. . . . I will check around to see why my company isn't providing the same level of service."

Past experience, the customer's previous exposure to service that is relevant to the focal service, is another force in shaping predictions and desires. The service relevant for prediction can be previous exposure to the focal firm's service. For example, you probably compare each stay in a particular hotel with all previous stays in that hotel. But past experience with the focal hotel is likely to be a very limited view of your past experience. You may also compare each stay with your experiences in other hotels and hotel chains. Customers also compare across industries: hospital patients, for example, compare hospital stays against the standard of hotel visits. Cable service customers tend to compare cable service with the standards set by telephone service, one reason why cable service is often judged to be poor. In a general sense, past experience may incorporate previous experience with the focal brand, typical performance of a favorite brand, experience with the brand last purchased or the top-selling brand, as well as the average performance a customer believes represents a group of similar brands.[18] Sample quotes from the focus groups described in Exhibit 4-1:

> My expectations are definitely influenced by my past experience . . . my expectations are more realistic because of the knowledge I've gained.

> The more years you spend in this business the more you expect because the more you learn and know.

A MODEL OF CUSTOMER SERVICE EXPECTATIONS

The full model of customer expectations and the forces that influence them is shown in Figure 4-9. At the center of the model is the detailed view of expectations showing the two levels, desired and adequate, and the zone of tolerance that separates them. The sources or antecedents of each type of expectation are shown along the sides of the model.

How might a manager of a service organization use this model to create, improve, or market services? First, managers need to know the pertinent expectation sources and their relative importance for a customer population, a customer segment, and perhaps even a particular customer. They need to know, for instance, the relative weight of word of mouth, explicit service promises, and implicit service promises in shaping desired

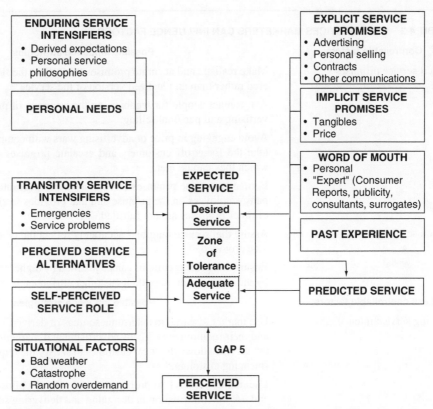

FIGURE 4-9 Nature and determinants of customer expectations of service.

Source: Zeithaml, Berry, and Parasuraman (1993).

service and predicted service. Some of these sources are more stable and permanent in their influence (e.g., enduring service intensifiers and personal needs) than the others, which fluctuate considerably over time (e.g., perceived service alternatives and situational factors).

The different sources vary in terms of their credibility as well as their potential to be influenced by the marketer. Exhibit 4-2 shows the breakdown of typically controllable and uncontrollable factors and offers suggestions about the ways services marketers can influence the factors. Chapter 16 of this textbook will detail these and other strategies that services marketers can use to match delivery to promises and thereby manage expectations.

The Customer Gap Revised: Service Superiority versus Service Adequacy

The gap between customer expectations and perceptions shown at the beginning of this chapter can now be revised to reflect the two comparison standards for customer expec-

EXHIBIT 4-2 WAYS SERVICES MARKETERS CAN INFLUENCE FACTORS

Controllable factors	Possible influence strategies
Explicit service promises	Make realistic and accurate promises that reflect the service actually delivered rather than an idealized version of the service.
	Ask contact people for feedback on the accuracy of promises made in advertising and personal selling.
	Avoid engaging in price or advertising wars with competitors because they take the focus off customers and escalate promises beyond the level at which they can be met.
	Formalize service promises through a service guarantee that focuses company employees on the promise and that provides feedback on the number of times promises are not fulfilled.
Implicit service promises	Assure that service tangibles accurately reflect the type and level of service provided.
	Ensure that price premiums can be justified by higher levels of performance by the company on important customer attributes.

Less controllable factors	Possible influence strategies
Enduring service intensifiers	Use market research to determine sources of derived service expectations and their requirements. Focus advertising and marketing strategy on ways the service allows the focal customer to satisfy the requirements of the influencing customer.
	Use market research to profile personal service philosophies of customers and use this information in designing and delivering services.
Personal needs	Educate customers on ways the service addresses their needs.
Transitory service intensifiers	Increase service delivery during peak periods or in emergencies.
Perceived service alternatives	Be fully aware of competitive offerings and, where possible and appropriate, match them.
Self-perceived service role	Educate customers to understand their roles and perform them better.
Word-of-mouth communications	Simulate word-of-mouth in advertising by using testimonials and opinion leaders.
	Identify influencers and opinion leaders for the service and concentrate marketing efforts on them.
	Use incentives with existing customers to encourage them to say positive things about the service.
Past experience	Use marketing research to profile customers' previous experience with similar services.
Situational factors	Use service guarantees to assure customers about service recovery regardless of the situational factors that occur.
Predicted service	Tell customers when service provision is higher than what can normally be expected so that predictions of future service encounters will not be inflated.

tations: desired and adequate service. The comparison between desired service and perceived service is the *perceived service superiority gap.* The smaller the gap between desired service and perceived service, the higher the perceived service superiority of the firm. The measure of the difference between these two concepts can be termed the *measure of service superiority (MSS),* and is equivalent to the difference between the two concepts, or perceived service minus desired service (Figure 4-10).

The comparison between adequate service and perceived service is the *perceived service adequacy gap.* The smaller the gap between adequate service and perceived service, the higher the perceived service adequacy of the firm. The difference between the two can be called the *measure of service adequacy (MSA)* and is equivalent to the difference between the two concepts, or perceived service minus adequate service.

These two service quality assessments (of perceived service superiority and perceived service adequacy) therefore replace the single customer gap in the gaps model. In essence, this states that two types of service quality assessments are made by consumers: perceived service superiority, which results from a comparison between desired service and perceived service; and perceived service adequacy, which results from a comparison between adequate service and perceived service.

CURRENT ISSUES INVOLVING CUSTOMER SERVICE EXPECTATIONS

The following issues represent current topics of particular interest to service marketers regarding customer expectations. In this section we will discuss four of the most frequently asked questions about customer expectations:

1 What does a service marketer do if customer expectations are "unrealistic"?
2 How does a company exceed customer service expectations?
3 Do customer service expectations continually escalate?

FIGURE 4-10   The customer GAP revisited.

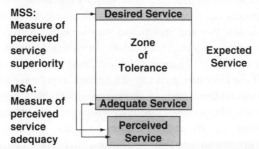

Measure of service superiority (MSS) = perceived service minus desired service
Measure of service adequacy (MSA) = perceived service minus adequate service

Source: Zeithaml, Berry, and Parasuraman (1993).

4 How does a service company stay ahead of competition in meeting customer expectations?

What Does a Services Marketer Do if Customer Expectations Are "Unrealistic"?

One of the inhibitors to learning about customer expectations is management's and employee's fear of asking. This apprehension often stems from the belief that customer expectations will be extravagant and unrealistic, and that by asking about them a company will set itself up for even loftier expectation levels (i.e., "unrealistic" levels). Compelling evidence, shown in Exhibit 4-3, suggests that customers' main expectations of service are quite simple and basic: "simply put, customers expect service companies to do what they are supposed to do. They expect fundamentals, not fanciness; performance, not empty promises."[19] Customers want service to be delivered as promised. Unfortunately, many service customers are disappointed and let down by companies' inability to provide this basic service expectation.

Asking customers about their expectations does not so much raise the levels of the expectations themselves but rather heightens the belief that the company will do something with the information that surfaces. Arguably the worst thing a company can do is show a strong interest in understanding what customers expect and then never act on the information. At a minimum, a company should acknowledge to customers that it has received and heard their input and that it will expend effort trying to address their issues. The company may not be able to—and indeed does not always have to—deliver to expressed expectations. An alternative and appropriate response would be to let customers know the reasons desired service is not being provided at the present time, and describe the efforts planned to address them. Another approach could be a campaign to educate customers about ways to use and improve the service they currently receive. Giving customers progress updates as service is improved to address their needs and desires is sensible because it allows the company to get credit for iterative efforts in service delivery.

Some observers recommend deliberately underpromising the service to increase the likelihood of meeting or exceeding customer expectations.[20] While underpromising makes service expectations more realistic, thereby narrowing the gap between expectations and perceptions, it also may reduce the competitive appeal of the offer. Also, some research has indicated that underpromising may have the inadvertent effect of lowering customer *perceptions* of service, particularly in situations where customers have little experience with a service.[21] In these situations, customer expectations may be self-fulfilling; that is, if the customer goes into the service experience expecting good service, he or she will focus on the aspects of service provision that are positive, and vice versa. Thus, a salesperson who pitches a customer with a realistic promise may lose the sale to another who inflates the offering. In chapter 16 of this textbook we will describe various techniques for controlling a firm's promises, but for now consider two options. First, if the salesperson knows that no competitor can meet an inflated sales promise in an industry, he or she could point that fact out to the customer, thereby refuting the promise made by competitive salespeople

The second option is for the provider to follow a sale with a "reality check" about ser-

EXHIBIT 4-3   SERVICE CUSTOMERS WANT THE BASICS

Type of service	Type of customer	Principal expectations
Automobile repair	Consumers	*Be competent* ("Fix it right the first time"). *Explain things* ("Explain why I need the suggested repairs—provide an itemized list"). *Be respectful* ("Don't treat me like a dumb female").
Automobile insurance	Consumers	*Keep me informed* ("I shouldn't have to learn about insurance law changes from the newspaper"). *Be on my side* ("I don't want them to treat me like I am a criminal just because I have a claim"). *Play fair* ("Don't drop me when something goes wrong"). *Protect me from catastrophe* ("Make sure my estate is covered in the event of a major accident"). *Provide prompt service* ("I want fast settlement of claims").
Hotel	Consumers	*Provide a clean room* ("Don't have a deep-pile carpet that can't be completely cleaned . . . you can literally see germs down there"). *Provide a secure room* ("Good bolts and peephole on door"). *Treat me like a guest* ("It is almost like they're looking you over to decide whether they're going to let you have a room"). *Keep your promise* ("They said the room would be ready, but it wasn't at the promised time").
Property and casualty insurance	Business customers	*Fulfill obligations* ("Pay up"). *Learn my business and work with me* ("I expect them to know me and my company"). *Protect me from catastrophe* ("They should cover your risk exposure so there is no single big loss"). *Provide prompt service* ("Fast claim service").
Equipment repair	Business customers	*Share my sense of urgency* ("Speed of response. One time I had to buy a second piece of equipment because of the huge down time with the first piece"). *Be competent* ("Sometimes you are quoting stuff from their instruction manuals to their own people and they don't even know what it means"). *Be prepared* ("Have all the parts ready").
Truck and tractor rental/leasing	Business customers	*Keep the equipment running* ("Need to have equipment working all of the time—that is the key"). *Be flexible* ("The leasing company should have the flexibility to rent us equipment when we need it"). *Provide full service* ("Get rid of all the paperwork and headaches").

Source: Parasuraman, Berry, and Zeithaml (1991).

vice delivery. One of the authors of this textbook bought a new house from a builder. Typical sales promises were made about the quality of the home, some less than accurate, in order to make the sale. Before closing on the house, the buyer and builder conducted a final check on the house. At the front door, the builder turned to the buyer and pointed out that each new home has between 3,000 and 5,000 individual elements and that in his experience the typical new home had 100 to 150 defects. Armed with this "reality check," the buyer thought the 32 defects found in the house seemed minor. Consider the buyer's response in the absence of that reality check.

How Does a Company Exceed Customer Service Expectations?

Many companies today talk about exceeding customer expectations—delighting and surprising them by giving more than they expect. AT&T's Universal Card Service, a winner of the 1992 Malcolm Baldrige Quality Award, uses "delighting the customer" as a key service theme. This philosophy raises the question: Should a service provider try simply to meet customer expectations or to exceed them?

First, it is essential to recognize that exceeding customer expectations of the basics is virtually impossible. Honoring promises—having the reserved room available, meeting deadlines, showing up for meetings, delivering the core service—is what the company is *supposed* to do. Companies are supposed to be accurate and dependable and provide the service they promised to provide.[22] As you examine the examples of basic expectations of customers in Exhibit 4-3, ask yourself if a provider doing any of these things would delight you. The conclusion you should reach is that it is very difficult to surprise or delight customers consistently by delivering reliable service.

How, then, does a company delight its customers and exceed their expectations? In virtually any service, developing a customer relationship is one approach for exceeding service expectations. The United States Automobile Association (USAA), a provider of insurance to military personnel and their dependents, illustrates how a large company that never interacts personally with its customers can surprise and delight them with its personalization of service and knowledge of the customer. Using a state-of-the-art imaging system, all USAA employees can access any customer's entire information file in seconds, giving them full knowledge of the customer's history and requirements and the status of the customer's recent interactions with the company. Expecting a lower level of personalization from an insurance company and from most any service interaction on the telephone, USAA's customers are surprised and impressed with the care and concern employees demonstrate.

Using a similar type of information technology, Ritz-Carlton Hotels, another winner of the 1992 Malcolm Baldrige Quality Award, provides highly personalized attention to its customers. The company trains each of its employees to note guest likes and dislikes and to record these into a computerized guest history profile. The company now has information on the preferences of more than 240,000 repeat Ritz-Carlton guests, resulting in more personalized service. The aim is not simply to meet expectations of guests but to provide them with a "memorable visit." The company uses the guest history information to exceed customers' expectations of the way they will be treated. When a repeat customer calls the hotel's central reservations number to book accommodations, the reservation agent can call up the individual's preference information. He or she then sends this information electronically to the particular hotel at which the reservation is made. The hotel outputs the data in a daily guest recognition and preference report that is circulated to employees. Employees then greet the repeat guest personally at check-in and ensure that the guest's needs/preferences are anticipated and met.[23]

How well does this approach work? According to surveys conducted for Ritz-Carlton by an independent research firm, 92 to 97 percent of the company's guests leave satisfied.[24] A survey by Gallup Surveys found the Ritz-Carlton Hotel Company to be the first choice of its customers for the last two years, a 95 percent satisfaction rating, compared with a 57 percent satisfaction rating for the nearest competitor. And the Ritz-Carlton maintains a 10 percent performance gap over the next best competitor out of those hotels rated four or five stars by the *Mobil Travel Guide*.[25]

Do Customer Service Expectations Continually Escalate?

As we illustrated in the beginning of this chapter, customer service expectations are dynamic. In the credit-card industry, as in many competitive service industries, battling companies seek to best each other and thereby raise the level of service above that of competing companies. Service expectations—in this case adequate service expectations—rise as quickly as service delivery or promises rise. In a highly competitive and rapidly changing industry, expectations can thus rise quickly. For this reason companies need to monitor adequate service expectations continually—the more turbulent the industry, the more frequent the monitoring needed.

Desired service expectations, on the other hand, are far more stable. Because they are driven by more enduring factors, such as personal needs and enduring service intensifiers, they tend to be high to begin with and remain high.

How Does a Service Company Stay Ahead of Competition in Meeting Customer Expectations?

All else being equal, a company's goal is to meet customer expectations better than its competitors. Given the fact that adequate service expectations change rapidly in a turbulent environment, how can a company ensure that it stays ahead of competition? Figure 4-11, which depicts a company's competitive position from a service quality standpoint, gives a framework for answering this question. A company's measure of service adequacy and measure of service superiority scores, discussed earlier in this chapter, will determine how well it is positioned. Depending on the relative levels of customer perceptions and expectations, a company can operate at a competitive disadvantage, a competitive advantage, or at the customer franchise (loyal customer) service level.[26]

The adequate service level reflects the minimum performance level expected by customers after they consider a variety of personal and external factors (Figure 4-7) including the availability of service options from other providers. Companies whose service performance falls short of this level are clearly at a competitive disadvantage, with

Customer perception and expectation levels	Measure of service adequacy and superiority	Competitive status
Perceived service ——————▶ Desired service ——————▶	MSA = positive MSS = negative	Customer franchise
Perceived service ——————▶ Adequate service ——————▶	MSA = positive MSS = negative	Competitive advantage
Perceived service ——————▶	MSA = negative MSS = negative	Competitive disadvantage

FIGURE 4-11   Relative competitive status defined by measures of service adequacy (MSA) and superiority (MSS).

Source: Parasuraman, Berry, and Zeithaml (1991).

the disadvantage escalating as the gap widens. These companies' customers may well be "reluctant" customers, ready to take their business elsewhere the moment they perceive an alternative.

If they are to use service quality for competitive advantage, companies must perform above the adequate service level. A favorable MSA score, however, may signal only a temporary advantage. Customers' adequate service levels, which are less stable than desired service levels, will rise rapidly when competitors promise and deliver a higher level of service. If a company's MSA score is barely positive to begin with, a competitor can quickly erode that advantage and change the MSA score from positive to negative into the area of competitive disadvantage. Companies currently performing in the region of competitive advantage must stay alert to the need for service increases to meet or beat competition.

To develop a true customer franchise—immutable customer loyalty—companies must consistently exceed not only the adequate service level but also the desired service level. Exceptional service can intensify customers' loyalty to a point where they are impervious to competitive options. ChemLawn, a Columbus, Ohio, commercial lawn maintenance company since the 1970s, illustrates the development of a customer franchise.

In the late 1980s, competition from smaller lawn maintenance companies such as Orkin and Barefoot eroded ChemLawn's domination of the market, leading ChemLawn to recognize that its former strategy of simply selling to customers had to be replaced by listening and responding to customers.[27] At an all-day meeting of its largest commercial customers, ChemLawn discovered that it was perceived as a lawn maintenance company, rather than as a total lawn-care provider. Recognizing the strategic benefit in meeting the need for total lawn care, ChemLawn changed its approach to view its services as a business asset: "We started telling these companies, 'We can give you more than green grass and a weed-free lawn We can improve your bottom line by making your appearance a marketing tool.' "[28]

The company then set out to create a customer franchise and far exceed the expectations of lawn-care customers. Most of ChemLawn's corporate customers were banks, restaurants, and hotels—all businesses that needed to pay special attention to their landscaping because it contributed to the overall image of the business. Sales reps were taught to approach customers in a very customized and personal way. They began by photographing the ground of potential customers and then, with picture in hand, demonstrated the improvements possible with proper landscaping. They also refocused their sales and service efforts on marketing vice presidents of the company, rather than maintenance personnel. These were the people who cared about issues such as occupancy rates and customer traffic patterns, and who needed to be convinced that ChemLawn's services could make a difference to the bottom line. They got their message across: commercial sales have been growing over 20 percent a year.[29]

SUMMARY

Using a conceptual model of the nature and determinants of customer expectations of service, we showed in this chapter that customers hold different types of service expectations: (1) *desired service,* which reflects what customers want; (2) *adequate service,* what customers are willing to accept; and (3) *predicted service,* what customers believe they are likely to get. Customers have global expectations of their relationships with service providers and also expectations of individual service encounters.

Customer expectations are influenced by a variety of factors, some controllable and others uncontrollable by service marketers. The types and sources of expectations are the same for end consumers and business customers, for pure service and product-related service, and for experienced customers and inexperienced customers.

DISCUSSION QUESTIONS

1 What is the difference between desired service and adequate service? Why would a services marketer need to understand both types of service expectations?

2 Consider a recent service purchase that you have made. Which of the factors influencing expectations (shown in Figure 4-11) were the most important in your decision? Why?

3 Why are desired service expectations more stable than adequate service expectations?

4 How do the technology changes discussed in the Technology Spotlight in this chapter influence customer expectations?

5 Describe several instances where a service company's explicit service promises were inflated and led you to be disappointed with the service outcome.

6 Consider a small business preparing to buy a computer system. Which of the influences on customer expectations (shown in Figure 4-11) do you believe will be pivotal? Which factors will have the most influence? Which factors will have the least importance in this decision?

7 Which of the revised service gaps—measure of service adequacy (MSA) or measure of service superiority (MSS)—is most important? Why?

8 What strategies can you add to Exhibit 4-2 for influencing the factors?

9 Do you believe any of your service expectations are unrealistic? Which ones? Should a service marketer try to address unrealistic customer expectations?

10 In your opinion, what service companies have effectively built customer franchises (immutable customer loyalty)?

EXERCISES

1 What factors do you think influenced your professor to adopt this textbook? In the case of textbook adoption, what do you think are the most important factors? After you have formulated your ideas, ask your professor in class to talk about the sources of his or her expectations.

2 Keep a service journal for a day and document your use of services. Ask yourself before each service encounter to indicate your predicted service of that encounter. After the encounter, note whether your expectations were met or exceeded. How does the answer to this question relate to your desire to do business with that service firm again?

3 List five incidences when a service company has exceeded your expectations. How did you react to the service? Did these incidences change the way you viewed subsequent interactions with the companies? In what way?

4 Intuitively, it would seem that managers would want their customers to have wide tolerance zones for service. But if customers do have these wide zones of tolerance for service, is it more difficult for firms with superior service to earn customer loyalty? Would superior service firms be better off to attempt to narrow customers' tolerance zones to reduce the competitive appeal of mediocre providers?

NOTES

1 The model on which this chapter is based is taken from Valarie A. Zeithaml, Leonard L. Berry, and A. Parasuraman, "The Nature and Determinants of Customer Expectations of Service," *Journal of the Academy of Marketing Science* 21, 1 (1993): 1–12.

2 See sources such as Christian Gronroos, *Strategic Management and Marketing in the Service Sector* (Helsingfors: Swedish School of Economics and Business Administration, 1982); Uolevi and Jarman R. Lehtinen, "Service Quality: A Study of Quality Dimensions," unpublished working paper, Helsinki, Finland OY, Service Management Institute, 1982); and Stephen W. Brown and Teresa A. Swartz, "A Dyadic Evaluation of the Professional Services Encounter," *Journal of Marketing* 53 (April 1989): 92–98.

3 See note 2.

4 Robert B. Woodruff, Ernest R. Cadotte, and Roger L. Jenkins, "Expectations and Norms in Models of Consumer Satisfaction," *Journal of Marketing Research* 24 (August 1987): 305–314.

5 John A. Miller, "Studying Satisfaction, Modifying Models, Eliciting Expectations, Posing Problems, and Making Meaningful Measurements," in *Conceptualization and Measurement of Consumer Satisfaction and Dissatisfaction,* ed. H. Keith Hunt, (Bloomington: Indiana University School of Business, 1977), pp. 72–91.

6 W. H. Davidow and B. Uttal, "Service Companies: Focus or Falter," *Harvard Business Review,* July–August 1989, pp. 77–85.

7 Zeithaml, Berry, and Parasuraman, "Customer Expectations of Service," p. 6.
8 A. Parasuraman, Leonard L. Berry, and Valarie A. Zeithaml, "Understanding Customer Expectations of Service," *Sloan Management Review,* 32, 3 (Spring 1991): 42.
9 Leonard L. Berry, A. Parasuraman, and Valarie A. Zeithaml, "Ten Lessons for Improving Service Quality," *Marketing Science Institute,* Report No. 93-104, May 1993.
10 Zeithaml, Berry, and Parasuraman, "Customer Expectations of Service."
11 Davidow and Uttal, "Service Companies," p. 85.
12 Zeithaml, Berry, and Parasuraman, "Customer Expectations of Service," p. 7.
13 Ibid.
14 Ibid., p. 8.
15 David Bowen, "Leadership Aspects and Reward Systems of Customer Satisfaction," speech given at CTM Customer Satisfaction Conference, Los Angeles, March 17, 1989.
16 Zeithaml, Berry, and Parasuraman, "Customer Expectations of Service," p. 8.
17 Duane L. Davis, Joseph G. Guiltinan, and Wesley H. Jones, "Service Characteristics, Consumer Research and the Classification of Retail Services," *Journal of Retailing* 55 (Fall 1979): 3–21; William R. George and Leonard L. Berry, "Guidelines for the Advertising of Services," *Business Horizons* 24 (May–June 1981): 52–56.
18 Ernest R. Cadotte, Robert B. Woodruff, and Roger L. Jenkins, "Expectations and Norms in Models of Consumer Satisfaction," *Journal of Marketing Research* 14 (August 1987): 353–364.
19 Parasuraman, Berry, and Zeithaml, "Understanding Customer Expectations," p. 40.
20 Davidow and Uttal, "Service Companies."
21 William Boulding, Ajay Kalra, Richard Staelin, and Valarie A. Zeithaml, "A Dynamic Process Model of Service Quality: From Expectations to Behavioral Intentions," *Journal of Marketing Research,* 30 (February 1993): 7–27.
22 Parasuraman, Berry, and Zeithaml, "Understanding Customer Expectations," p. 41.
23 "How the Ritz-Carlton Hotel Company Delivers 'Memorable' Service to Customers," *Executive Report on Customer Satisfaction* 6, 5 (March 15, 1993): 1–4.
24 Ibid.
25 Ibid.
26 Parasuraman, Berry, and Zeithaml, "Understanding Customer Expectations."
27 Susan Caminiti, "Finding New Ways to Sell More," *Fortune,* July 27, 1992, pp. 100–103.
28 Ibid., p. 102.
29 Ibid.

5

CUSTOMER PERCEPTIONS OF SERVICE

A poll of 1,507 consumers done by the Wall Street Journal and NBC found that consumers give U.S. businesses only a so-so rating on service.[1] Another study mentioned in the article found that two of five customers who stop doing business with a company do so over service-related issues.[2] These customers clearly are unhappy and value high-quality service enough to search for it elsewhere. The Wall Street Journal/NBC poll suggested that many consumers are even willing to pay more for good service if and when they find it.

As for specific industries, consumers in the WSJ/NBC poll felt that the services offered by some industries are actually improving (e.g., supermarkets and restaurants), while the services in many industries (e.g., airlines, gas stations, and insurance companies) are getting worse (Figure 5-1). On what criteria are these customers judging quality? What makes consumers feel positive about service quality in one industry, or for one firm, and negative in other instances?

And what about cultural differences? Do customers perceive quality service the same in different countries? A recent study by the American Quality Foundation suggests that the answer to this question is no. The authors found that in Germany quality is associated with meeting "standards," while in Japan it means "perfection," in France "luxury," and in the United States "that it works."[3] In Russia, perceptions of quality and quality criteria are rapidly changing.[4] Whereas in the past customers may have had to bribe waiters to get a table in a restaurant and then be faced with dirty glasses, forks, and knives, now many restaurants and hotels have begun retraining employees to smile, greet customers, and anticipate their needs.

What about you? Take a minute to reflect on your experiences as a consumer of services. How do you judge quality of service when you go to the bank or the library, when

"How would you rate the overall level of service these industries provide customers?"

	GETTING BETTER	GETTING WORSE	STAYING ABOUT THE SAME	NOT SURE
Supermarkets	31%	18%	50%	1%
Automobiles	24	37	31	8
Restaurants	22	19	56	3
Department stores	20	29	48	3
Hotels	20	16	45	19
Banks	17	29	50	4
Airlines	11	36	40	13
Insurance	10	49	34	7
Gas stations	6	59	32	3

FIGURE 5-1   Customer ratings of service industries.

you eat a restaurant meal, or when you take a trip on an airplane? Think about a service firm that recently disappointed you in terms of its quality. Why were you disappointed? Think about a service firm you have a long relationship with. Why do you stay with the firm? How do you judge its quality?

How customers perceive services and how they assess whether they have experienced quality service, whether they are satisfied, and whether they have received good value are the subjects of this chapter. Our purpose is to understand the criteria customers use to evaluate service. We will be focusing on the "perceived service" box in Figure 5-2. As we go through this chapter, keep in mind that perceptions are always considered relative to expectations. Thus, because expectations are dynamic, evaluations may also shift—over time, from person to person, and from culture to culture, as implied in the opening paragraphs. Ten years from now Russian consumers may well use very different criteria to judge the quality of a restaurant meal than they are using currently.

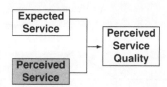

FIGURE 5-2   The role of perceptions in service.

The objectives of this chapter are to:

1 Present the four primary factors that influence customer perceptions of service: service encounters ("moments of truth"), the evidence of service, image, and price.

2 Show how these perceptions are organized to form impressions of service quality, customer satisfaction, and value.

3 Highlight strategies whereby organizations can influence and manage customer perceptions of service.

FACTORS THAT INFLUENCE CUSTOMER PERCEPTIONS OF SERVICE

Figure 5-3 illustrates the primary factors influencing customer perceptions of service. Each of the four factors shown in the boxes in the figure will be discussed and illustrated in this section. Two of the factors—service encounters and evidence of service—will be covered in greater depth than the others since they are unique and clearly distinguish perceptions of service from perceptions of manufactured products. Later in the chapter we will see how these factors work together to form overall customer perceptions of quality, satisfaction, and value, as shown in the circle in Figure 5-3.

When we refer to customer perceptions we assume that the dimensions of service and the ways in which customers evaluate encounters are similar whether the customer is internal or external to the organization.[5] By *external customers* we mean *those individuals and businesspeople who buy goods and services from the organization,* the people we usually think of when we use the word "customer." To illustrate, in a telecommunications setting external customers include residential telephone users, business customers, and government at all levels. In this same setting, *internal customers* are *em-*

FIGURE 5-3   Factors influencing customer perceptions of service.

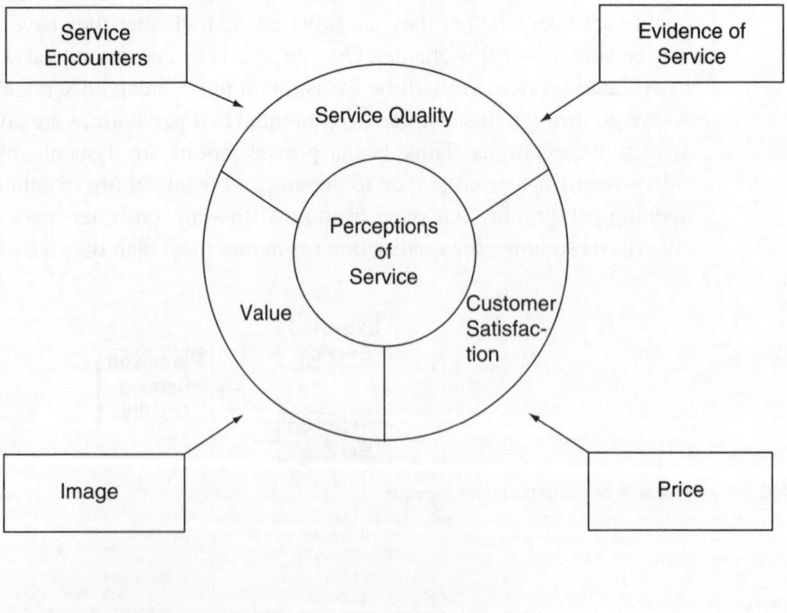

ployees within the firm who in their jobs depend on others in the organization for internally provided goods and services. For example, a telephone repair person depends on services provided by dispatchers and vehicle maintenance crews to do her job effectively. For the dispatchers and the vehicle maintenance crew, the repair person is their internal customer. If they fail to provide quality service to the repair person, it is more difficult for the repair person to do the same for external customers. When we refer to customer perceptions and how customers evaluate services, you can assume that we include both internal and external customers.

Service Encounters, or "Moments of Truth"

From the customer's point of view, the most vivid impression of service occurs in the service encounter, or the "moment of truth," when the customer interacts with the service firm. For example, among the service encounters a hotel customer experiences are checking in to the hotel, being taken to a room by a bellperson, eating a restaurant meal, requesting a wake-up call, and checking out. Among the service encounters that a business-to-business customer experiences in purchase and use of a piece of equipment are sales contact, delivery, installation, billing, and servicing. You could think of the linking of these moments of truth as a service encounter cascade (see Figures 5-4 and 5-5). It is in these encounters that customers receive a snapshot of the organization's service quality, and each encounter contributes to the customer's overall satisfaction and willingness to do business with the organization again. From the organization's point of view, each encounter thus presents an opportunity to prove its potential as a quality service provider and to increase customer loyalty.

Some services have few service encounters, and others have many. The Disney Corporation estimates that each of its amusement park customers experiences about 74 service encounters, and that a negative experience in any one of them can lead to a negative overall evaluation. Mistakes or problems that occur in the early levels of the service cascade are particularly critical, because a failure at one point results in greater risk for dissatisfaction at each ensuing level. Marriott Hotels learned this through their extensive

FIGURE 5-4 A service encounter cascade for a hotel visit.

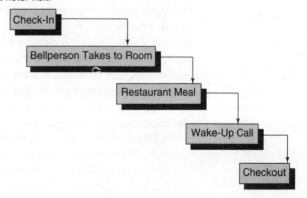

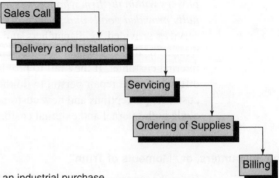

FIGURE 5-5 A service encounter cascade for an industrial purchase.

customer research to determine what service elements contribute most to customer loyalty. They found that four of the top five factors came into play in the first ten minutes of the guest's stay.[6]

The Importance of Encounters   While early events in the encounter cascade are likely to be especially important, *any* encounter can potentially be critical in determining customer satisfaction and loyalty. If a customer is interacting with a firm for the first time, that initial encounter will create a first impression of the organization. In these first encounter situations, the customer frequently has no other basis for judging the organization, and the initial phone contact or face-to-face experience with a representative of the firm can take on excessive importance in the customer's perceptions of quality. A customer calling for repair service on a household appliance may well hang up and call a different company if he is treated rudely by a customer service representative, put on hold for a lengthy period, or told that two weeks is the soonest someone can be sent out to make the repair. Even if the technical quality of the firm's repair service is superior, the firm may not get the chance to demonstrate it if the initial telephone encounter drives the customer away.

Even when the customer has had multiple interactions with a firm, each individual encounter is important in creating a composite image of the firm in the customer's memory. Many positive experiences add up to a composite image of high quality, while many negative interactions will have the opposite effect. On the other hand, a combination of positive and negative interactions will leave the customer feeling unsure of the firm's quality, doubtful of its consistency in service delivery, and vulnerable to the appeals of competitors. For example, a customer of a health maintenance organization (HMO) could have a poor encounter with the appointment-scheduling phone person, a very positive encounter with a nurse practitioner, an OK encounter with a lab technician, and an OK encounter with a physician. This mixture of experiences will leave the customer wondering about the quality of the organization and unsure of what to expect on the next visit. Each encounter adds to or detracts from the potential for a continuing relationship.

Logic suggests that not all encounters are equally important in building relationships. For every organization, certain encounters are probably key to customer satisfaction.

For Marriott Hotels, as noted, it is the early encounters that are most important. In a hospital context, a study of patients revealed that encounters with nursing staff were more important in predicting satisfaction than were encounters with meal service or patient discharge personnel.[7] And research at GTE Laboratories documents that small business customers' relationships with GTE depend on specific installation, repair, and sales encounters.[8]

Aside from common key encounters, there are some momentous encounters that, like the proverbial "one bad apple," simply ruin the rest and drive the customer away no matter how many or what type of encounters have occurred in the past. These can occur in connection with very important events (such as the failure to deliver an essential piece of equipment before a critical deadline) or they may seem inconsequential, as in the story of the bank customer described in Exhibit 5-1. Similarly, momentous positive encounters can sometimes bind a customer to an organization for life.

Types of Service Encounters   A service encounter occurs every time a customer interacts with the service organization. There are three general types of service encounters: *remote encounters, phone encounters,* and *face-to-face encounters.*[9] A customer may experience any of these types of encounters or a combination of all three, in his or her relations with a service firm.

First, encounters can occur without any direct human contact (*remote encounters*), such as when a customer interacts with a bank through the ATM system, or with Ticketron through an automated ticketing machine, or with a mail-order service through automated dial-in ordering. Remote encounters also occur when the firm sends its billing statements or communicates other types of information to customers by mail. Although there is no direct human contact in these remote encounters, each represents an opportunity for the firm to reinforce or establish quality perceptions in the customer. In remote encounters the tangible evidence of the service and the quality of the technical processes and systems become the primary bases for judging quality.

EXHIBIT 5-1   ONE CRITICAL ENCOUNTER DESTROYS THIRTY-YEAR RELATIONSHIP

"If you have $1 in a bank or $1 million, I think they owe you the courtesy of stamping your parking ticket," said John Barrier. One day in 1989 Mr. Barrier paid a visit to his bank in Spokane, Washington. He was wearing his usual shabby clothes and pulled up in his pickup truck, parking in the lot next to the bank. After cashing a check, he went outside to drive away and was stopped by a parking attendant who told him there was a 60-cent fee, but that he could get his parking slip validated in the bank and park for free. No problem, Barrier thought, and he went back into the bank (where, by the way he had been banking for thirty years). The teller looked him up and down and refused to stamp his slip, telling him that the bank validated parking only for people who have transactions with the bank, and that cashing a check wasn't a transaction. Mr. Barrier then asked to see the bank manager, who also looked him up and down, stood back, and "gave me one of those kinds of looks," also refusing to validate the parking bill. Mr. Barrier then said, "Fine. You don't need me, and I don't need you." He withdrew all his money and took it down the street to a competing bank, where the first check he deposited was for $1,000,000.

Source: "Shabby Millionaire Closes Account, Gives Bank Lesson about Snobbery," United Press International, in *The Arizona Republic,* Feb. 21, 1989, p. A3.

In many organizations (for example insurance companies, utilities, telecommunications), the most frequent type of encounter between an end customer and the firm occurs over the telephone (*phone encounter*). Almost all firms (whether goods manufacturers or service businesses) rely on phone encounters in the form of customer-service, general inquiry, or order-taking functions. The judgment of quality in phone encounters is more complex than that in remote encounters because there is greater potential variability in the interaction.[10] Tone of voice, employee knowledge, and effectiveness/efficiency in handling customer issues become important criteria for judging in these encounters.

For example, to ensure quality in telephone encounters at AT&T's Universal Card, employees have direct access to computerized data on all customers. Thus when a customer calls, the employee can immediately pull up that customer's information and respond to any inquiries with specific, factual information. If it is necessary to transfer the customer to another point of contact within the company, the first employee will introduce the customer by name to the next employee who can handle the inquiry, as follows: "Ms. Johnson, I'll be transferring you to Beth who will put a hold on charges on your missing card." The next thing Ms. Johnson hears is, "Hello, Ms. Johnson, this is Beth. I understand your new card has not yet arrived in the mail."

A third type of encounter is the one that occurs between an employee and a customer in direct contact (*face-to-face encounters*). At Disney theme parks, face-to-face encounters occur between customers and ticket-takers, maintenance personnel, actors in Disney character costumes, ride personnel, food and beverage servers, and others. For a company like Xerox, in a business-to-business setting direct encounters occur between the business customer and salespeople, delivery personnel, and repair and maintenance representatives. Determining and understanding service quality issues in face-to-face contexts is the most complex of all. Verbal and nonverbal behaviors are both important determinants of quality, as are tangible cues such as employee dress and other symbols of service (e.g., equipment, informational brochures, physical setting). In face-to-face encounters the customer also plays a role in creating quality service for herself through her own behavior during the interaction.

Sources of Pleasure and Displeasure in Service Encounters Because of the importance of service encounters in building quality perceptions and ultimately influencing customer satisfaction with the organization, researchers have extensively analyzed service encounters in many contexts to determine the sources of customers' favorable and unfavorable perceptions. The research uses the Critical Incident Technique to get customers and employees to provide verbatim stories about satisfying and dissatisfying service encounters they have experienced.[11] With this technique, customers (either internal or external) are asked the following questions:

> Think of a time when, as a customer, you had a particularly *satisfying (or dissatisfying)* interaction with _____.
> When did the incident happen?
> What specific circumstances led up to this situation?
> Exactly what did the employee (or firm) say or do?
> What resulted that made you feel the interaction was *satisfying (or dissatisfying)?*
> What could or should have been done differently?

Sometimes contact employees are asked to put themselves in the shoes of a customer and answer the same questions: "Put yourself in the shoes of *customers* of your firm. In other words, try to see your firm through your customers' eyes. Now think of a recent time when a customer of your firm had a particularly *satisfying/unsatisfying* interaction with you or a fellow employee." The stories are then analyzed to determine common themes of satisfaction/dissatisfaction underlying the events. On the basis of thousands of service encounter stories, four common themes—recovery (after failure), adaptability, spontaneity, and coping—have been identified as the sources of customer satisfaction/dissatisfaction in memorable service encounters.[12] Each of the themes is discussed here, and sample stories of both satisfying and dissatisfying incidents are given in Exhibits 5-2 through 5-5. The themes encompass service behaviors in encounters spanning a wide variety of industries.

Recovery—Employee Response to Service Delivery System Failures   The first theme includes all incidents in which there has been a failure of the service delivery system and an employee is required to respond in some way to consumer complaints and disappointments. The failure may be, for example, a hotel room that isn't available, an airplane flight that is delayed six hours, an incorrect item sent from a mail-order company, a critical error on an internal document. The content or form of the employee's response is what causes the customer to remember the event either favorably or unfavorably. Examples of recovery incidents, both good and bad, are given in Exhibit 5-2. The source of the story is also identified, either an external customer, an internal customer, or an employee who has been asked to assume the point of view of the customer.

Adaptability—Employee Response to Customer Needs and Requests   A second theme underlying satisfaction/dissatisfaction in service encounters is how adaptable the service delivery system is when the customer has special needs or requests that place demands on the process. In these cases, customers judge service encounter quality in terms of the flexibility of the employees and the system. Incidents categorized within this theme all contain an implicit or explicit request for customization of the service to meet a need. Much of what customers see as special needs or requests may actually be rather routine from the employee's point of view; what is important is that the customer perceives that something special is being done for her based on her own individual needs. External customers and internal customers alike are pleased when the service provider puts forth the effort to accommodate and adjust the system to meet their requirements. On the flip side, they are angered and frustrated by an unwillingness to try to accommodate and by promises that are never followed through. Contact employees also see their abilities to adapt the system as being a prominent source of customer satisfaction, and often they are equally frustrated by constraints that keep them from being flexible. Examples of adaptability incidents, both good and bad, are given in Exhibit 5-3.

Spontaneity—Unprompted and Unsolicited Employee Actions   Even when there is no system failure and no special request or need, customers can still remember service encounters as being very satisfying or very dissatisfying. Employee spontaneity in delivering memorably good or poor service is the third theme. Satisfying incidents in this group represent very pleasant surprises for the customer (special attention, being treated like royalty, receiving something nice but not requested), whereas dissatisfying incidents in this group represent negative and unacceptable employee behaviors (rudeness,

EXHIBIT 5-2   SERVICE ENCOUNTER THEME 1: RECOVERY

EMPLOYEE RESPONSE TO SERVICE DELIVERY SYSTEM FAILURES

Satisfactory

They lost my room reservation but the manager gave me the V.P. suite for the same price. (external customer)

Even though I didn't make any complaint about the hour and a half wait, the waitress kept apologizing and said the bill was on the house. (external customer)

My shrimp cocktail was half frozen. The waitress apologized, and didn't charge me for any of my dinner. (external customer)

I contacted the department that was responsible for correcting a problem in a monthly report that is prepared for a regulatory agency. The employee I was referred to dropped everything and worked to get a new report finished. I was favorably impressed because this employee cared, even though it [the report] was not her direct responsibility. (internal customer)

A gentleman left his shoes outside his room door to be shined. When he went to retrieve them, they were gone, and could not be found. The hotel staff took responsibility and within an hour a representative of Nordstrom had arrived with six pairs of shoes for the gentleman to choose from. (employee)

Dissatisfactory

We had made advance reservations at the hotel. When we arrived we found we had no room— no explanation, no apologies, and no assistance in finding another hotel. (external customer)

For weeks I had been waiting for my medical identification card and it had not arrived . . . so I went to the clinic. They told me to wait while they checked. After ten minutes they gave me the excuse "It's in the mail." The reason I felt so dissatisfied was that nobody knew anything. They kept giving me the run around. . . . (external customer)

One of my suitcases was all dented up and looked like it had been dropped from 30,000 feet. When I tried to make a claim for my damaged luggage, the employee insinuated that I was lying and trying to rip them off. (external customer)

A loan officer's signature was missing on the application of a new VISA account. I contacted the loan officer who sent the paperwork. She stated that the paperwork had never been required and refused to fill it out. She had a very snippy attitude and refused to assist me. (internal customer)

Passengers had been on the plane on the ground for about an hour, delayed due to weather. One flight attendant, after repeated inquiries from customers, became short with his answers to them. He used an unpleasant tone of voice and exhibited an annoyed behavior. The employee fueled the passengers' frustrations by acting annoyed. (employee)

---

stealing, discrimination, ignoring the customer). Examples of spontaneity incidents are shown in Exhibit 5-4.

Coping—Employee Response to Problem Customers   The incidents categorized in this group came to light when *employees* were asked to describe service encounter incidents in which customers were either very satisfied or dissatisfied. In addition to describing incidents of the types outlined under the first three themes, employees described many incidents in which customers were the cause of their own dissatisfaction. Such customers were basically uncooperative, that is, unwilling to cooperate with the service provider, other customers, industry regulations, and/or laws. In these cases nothing the employee could do would result in the customer feeling pleased about the en-

---

EXHIBIT 5-3   SERVICE ENCOUNTER THEME 2: ADAPTABILITY

EMPLOYEE RESPONSE TO CUSTOMER NEEDS, PREFERENCES, AND REQUESTS

Satisfactory	Dissatisfactory
The flight attendant helped me calm and care for my airsick child. (external customer)	*The waitress refused to move me from a window table on a hot day because there was nothing left in her section. (external customer)*
I didn't have an appointment to see a doctor, however, my allergy nurse spoke to a practitioner's assistant and worked me in to the schedule. I received treatment after a ten-minute wait. I was very satisfied with the special treatment I received, the short wait, and the quality of the service. (external customer)	*My young son, flying alone, was to be assisted by the stewardess from start to finish. At the Albany airport she left him alone in the airport with no one to escort him to his connecting flight. (external customer)*
It was snowing outside—my car broke down. I checked 10 hotels and there were no rooms. Finally, one understood my situation and offered to rent me a bed and set it up in one of their small banquet rooms. (external customer)	*Despite our repeated requests, the hotel staff wouldn't deal with the noisy people partying in the hall at 3 a.m. (external customer)*
Although it was not our regular order time, I needed some supplies that we did not have in stock. I called the supply office and the gentleman on the phone said, "no problem. I will send that to you through interbranch mail today." I received the supplies the next day. His word was as good as gold. (internal customer)	*I called a branch to get the specifics on a customer's NSF notice. It turned out that a deposit slip was encoded improperly—our mistake—but the fee for the NSF was taken out at another branch. The employee said, "oh, you made the mistake and we have to pay for it." Even though the mistake was made at our branch, I am still an employee of the same bank and should be treated with respect. I was made to feel real bad. (internal customer)*
The weather was very cold and I got off work at 7 a.m. as night auditor. Three groups of hotel guests were having trouble starting their cars in the cold. I told them that if they would like to sit in the lobby and have some coffee, I would jump start their cars. I assured them that this was a common problem in the cold and told them I shouldn't have any problem getting them started. (employee)	*A guest explained to the bellman that he had to get to the airport in ten minutes. This was very short notice. The employee contacted the hotel van driver, Chuck. Chuck says "no way!" Chuck gets mad at both the bellman and the guest. The bellman ends up having to call a cab for the guest. (employee)*

---

counter. We use the term "coping" to describe these incidents because this is the behavior generally required of employees to handle problem customer encounters. As is apparent in the examples of these given in Exhibit 5-5, rarely are such encounters satisfying from the customers' point of view.[13] Also of interest is that customers themselves didn't relate any "problem customer" incidents. That is, customers either do not see, or choose not to remember or retell, stories of the times when they themselves were unreasonable to the point of causing their own dissatisfactory service encounter.

General Service Behaviors   Table 5-1 summarizes the specific behaviors that cause satisfaction and dissatisfaction in service encounters according to the four themes

EXHIBIT 5-4 SERVICE ENCOUNTER THEME 3: SPONTANEITY

UNPROMPTED AND UNSOLICITED EMPLOYEE ACTIONS

Satisfactory	Dissatisfactory
The waiter treated me like royalty. He really showed he cared about me. (external customer)	The lady at the front desk acted as if we were bothering her. She was watching TV and paying more attention to the TV than to the hotel guests. (external customer)
We always travel with our teddy bears. When we got back to our room at the hotel we saw that the maid had arranged our bears very comfortably in a chair. The bears were holding hands. (external customer)	I needed a few more minutes to decide on a dinner. The waitress said, "If you would read the menu and not the road map, you would know what you want to order." (external customer)
The anesthesiologist took extra time to come and explain exactly what I would be aware of and promised to take special care in making sure I did not wake up. It impressed me that the anesthesiologist came to settle my nerves and explain to me the difference in the medicine I was getting because of my cold. It was a nice bit of extra attention that he did not have to give. (external customer)	Victoria never seemed to hear what I said. She asked me to repeat everything. After the first few times, I grew annoyed. Very calmly, I asked once again if she could tell me whether I'd keep the same number. "It all depends" was her stock answer. She offered me a service package (call waiting/forwarding) which I declined. She offered again, saying she couldn't understand why anyone wouldn't want call waiting. Now I was angry. (external customer)
I was preparing a presentation and needed input from another department. An employee from the department provided the needed input and agreed to review the presentation. I was favorably impressed because of (1) the employee's enthusiasm in providing input, and (2) the subsequent constructive criticism the employee made on improving the presentation. (internal customer)	I returned a call to an employee at one of our branches and a different employee answered the phone. I did not identify myself as an employee, but just asked for the person I wanted to talk to. The employee said, "Okay, What are you doing?" I hesitated because I didn't know if she was speaking to me, so she repeated, "What are you doing? Are you chewing gum?" I answered that I was not. The employee's tone of voice was rude, as was her question. (internal customer)
A manager from the mall called in an order to go over the phone. She said she'd be over to pick it up as soon as she could, but it might be a while because she was so busy. When her food was ready, I had a waitress cover my tables and I took her food to her personally. (employee)	There was a woman who came into the restaurant every morning. The one waitress on the floor didn't like this woman and gave her minimal service. The woman asked for a refill and marmalade, but the waitress wouldn't go back to the table. I brought her what she wanted, the waitress came back to the table and began to verbally abuse the customer. (employee)

just presented. The left side of the table suggests what employees do that results in positive encounters, while the right side summarizes negative behaviors within each theme.

This section of the chapter has examined in some depth the service encounter, or the "moment of truth," as the building block of consumer perceptions of service. Individual encounters are the most fundamental, concrete, and vivid events through which consumers can begin building their overall impressions of an organization. Because of the

EXHIBIT 5-5   SERVICE ENCOUNTER THEME 4: COPING

EMPLOYEE RESPONSE TO PROBLEM CUSTOMERS

No problem customer incidents were reported by either external or internal customers. Only three percent of the incidents in this group were satisfactory.

Satisfactory

A person who became intoxicated on a flight started speaking loudly, annoying the other passengers. The flight attendant asked the passenger if he would be driving when the plane landed and offered him coffee. He accepted the coffee and became quieter and friendlier. (employee)

Dissatisfactory

An intoxicated man began pinching the female flight attendants. One attendant told him to stop, but he continued and then hit another passenger. The co-pilot was called and asked the man to sit down and leave the others alone, but the passenger refused. The co-pilot then "decked" the man, knocking him into his seat. (employee)

While a family of three were waiting to order dinner, the father began hitting his child. Another customer complained about this to the manager who then, in a friendly and sympathetic way, asked the family to leave. The father knocked all of the plates and glasses off the table before leaving. (employee)

Five guests were in a hotel room two hours past check out time. Because they would not answer the phone calls or let the staff into the room, hotel security staff finally broke in. They found the guests using drugs and called the police. (employee)

When a man was shown to his table in the nonview dining area of the restaurant, he became extremely angry and demanded a window table. The restaurant was very busy, but the hostess told him he could get a window seat in a half hour. He refused to wait and took his previously reserved table, but he complained all the way through the dinner and left without tipping. (employee)

potential importance of these immediate events, many organizations have found it useful to capture customer impressions of service encounters on the spot before the memory of the event has faded. Our Technology Spotlight features examples of how this "real-time" research can be done.

The Evidence of Service

Another major set of factors influencing customer perceptions of service is referred to as the "evidence of service."[14] Because services are intangible, customers are searching for evidence of service in every interaction they have with an organization. Figure 5-6 depicts the three major categories of evidence as experienced by the customer: people, process, and physical evidence. These categories together represent the service and provide the evidence that tangibilizes the offering. Note the parallels between the elements comprising evidence of service and the new marketing-mix elements presented in chapter 1. The new mix elements essentially *are* the evidence of service.

All of these evidence elements, or a subset of them, are present in every service encounter a customer has with a service firm, and are critically important in managing service encounter quality and creating customer satisfaction. For example, when an HMO patient has an appointment with a doctor in a health clinic, the first encounter of the visit is frequently with a receptionist in a clinic waiting area. The quality of that encounter

TABLE 5-1 GENERAL SERVICE BEHAVIORS—DO'S AND DON'TS

Theme	Do	Don't
Recovery	Acknowledge problem	Ignore customer
	Explain causes	Blame customer
	Apologize	Leave customer to "fend for him/herself"
	Compensate/upgrade	Downgrade
	Lay out options	Act as if nothing is wrong
	Take responsibility	"Pass the buck"
Adaptability	Recognize the seriousness of the need	Ignore
	Acknowledge	Promise, but fail to follow through
	Anticipate	Show unwillingness to try
	Attempt to accommodate	Embarrass the customer
	Adjust the system	Laugh at the customer
	Explain rules/policies	Avoid responsibility
	Take responsibility	"Pass the buck"
Spontaneity	Take time	Exhibit impatience
	Be attentive	Ignore
	Anticipate needs	Yell/laugh/swear
	Listen	Steal from customers
	Provide information	Discriminate
	Show empathy	
Coping	Listen	Take customer's dissatisfaction personally
	Try to accommodate	Let customer's dissatisfaction affect others
	Explain	
	Let go of the customer	

will be judged by how the appointment registration *process* works (is there a line? how long is the wait? is the registration system computerized and accurate?), the actions and attitude of the *people* (is the receptionist courteous, helpful, knowledgeable? does he treat the patient as an individual? does he handle inquiries fairly and efficiently?), and the *physical evidence* of the service (is the waiting area clean and comfortable? is the signage clear?). The three types of evidence may be differentially important depending on the type of service encounter (remote, phone, face-to-face). All three types will operate in face-to-face service encounters as in the one just described.

Image

Beyond impressions from the immediate service encounter and evaluations of service evidence, customer perceptions can be influenced by the image or reputation of the organization. Here we define *organizational image* as *perceptions of an organization reflected in the associations held in consumer memory*.[15] These associations can be very concrete, such as hours of operation, number of flights per day, length of time in busi-

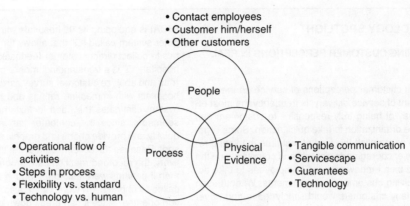

- Contact employees
- Customer him/herself
- Other customers

People

Process

Physical
Evidence

- Operational flow of
  activities
- Steps in process
- Flexibility vs. standard
- Technology vs. human

- Tangible communication
- Servicescape
- Guarantees
- Technology

FIGURE 5-6 The evidence of service (from the customer's point of view).

ness, ease of access. Or they can be less concrete and even emotional, such as excitement, trustworthiness, tradition, ingenuity, fun, reliability. The associations can relate to the service experience itself, the company, or the user of the service. Thus McDonald's could be linked in consumers' memories to the character Ronald McDonald, a specific consumer segment such as kids, a feeling such as "fun," a service characteristic such as consistent or fast, a symbol such as the golden arches, or a life-style such as harried.[16] This image is built up in the customer's mind through communication (e.g., advertising, public relations, physical images, word of mouth) combined with actual experiences at McDonalds.

Organizational image can exist on several levels. A large service organization with multiple outlets or branches has a corporate image. But it also has a local image that is closely associated with a specific location. Continuing the preceding example, McDonalds has: an international corporate image, an image in the United States, an image in Japan, and an image in many other countries. But it also has a local image linked directly to the specific outlet that a customer visits in his or her community. A favorable and well-known image—corporate and/or local—is an asset for any organization because image can impact perceptions of quality, value, and satisfaction.[17]

Organizational image serves as a filter that influences customer perceptions of the service organization's operations. A very positive image will serve as a buffer against incidents of poor service. In other words, if a customer has an overall very positive image of the organization, one bad experience will likely not be fatal. However, further bad experiences will erode the positive image, removing its protection. This filtering function of organizational image can work in the opposite way as well. When consumers have an unfavorable image of an organization they are likely to be very angry and dissatisfied when things go wrong. And it will likely take multiple good experiences to begin changing the overall poor image.

TECHNOLOGY SPOTLIGHT

CAPTURING CUSTOMER PERCEPTIONS IN REAL TIME

Capturing customer perceptions of service on the spot, at the point of service delivery, is frequently the most effective way of being truly responsive to customers and allows the organization to take quick action. Some organizations accomplish this kind of real-time marketing research by encouraging comments and complaints on the spot, and then empowering their employees to take action in solving customer disappointments. Without such action, many customers would simply leave and never come back. At its Heathrow Airport gates, British Airways tried another approach to getting immediate customer feedback. It installed video cameras in booths where disgruntled passengers could record their feelings and complaints verbally and on camera right after disembarking the plane. The video booths were able to capture the immediate reactions and feelings of customers, and the tapes provided vivid examples of customer perceptions that managers were required to view.

To collect this sort of firsthand, anytime, customer-perceptions data the Hospital Corporation of America (HCA) is equipping its 96 hospitals with a portable computer system called "Q" that allows the individual hospitals to collect direct customer feedback anywhere in the hospital. "Q" is a freestanding, mobile computer that can read and analyze customer survey cards and provide the hospitals with immediate ratings and reports. The new system eliminates the need for external, third-party researchers, since the computer can analyze the data quickly and provide charts and graphic summaries on the spot. Because "Q" collects data at the time of service delivery, the recorded reactions are probably more reliable than if patients were asked to send in a survey or were called by phone a few weeks later. Also, the system is action oriented, since it can break down customer perceptions very specifically, allowing for more focused strategies. For example, a broad issue like "care and concern of nurses for patients" can be broken down to actionable information like day received, time of day, shift, floor, or gender of respondent.

Source: How to Handle Customers' Gripes," by Patricia Sellers, *Fortune,* Oct. 24, 1988, p. 87–100; "Portable Computer Allows Hospitals to Measure Service 'Anytime, Anyplace,' *The Service Edge* 6, 6, (June 1993): p. 7.

Price

The price of the service can also greatly influence perceptions of quality, satisfaction, and value. Because services are intangible and often difficult to judge before purchase, price is frequently relied on as a surrogate indicator that will influence quality expectations and perceptions. If the price is very high, customers are likely to expect high quality, and their actual perceptions will be influenced by this expectation. If the price is too high, the organization may be sending a message of unconcern for customers, or "rip-off." On the other hand, if the price is too low, customers may doubt the organization's ability to deliver quality. The price charged will also figure greatly into customers' perceptions of value, particularly following consumption of the service when customers assess whether the benefits they received were worth the cost of the service. Because price is such an important variable in determining customer expectations and perceptions of service, we devote an entire chapter later in the book to the dynamics of pricing and pricing strategies for services. For now, it is enough to state that price can have a strong impact on customer perceptions of service.

HOW ARE CUSTOMER PERCEPTIONS ORGANIZED?

Customers perceive services in terms of the quality of the service, how satisfied they are with the service, and the overall value of the service (Figure 5-3). These customer-oriented terms—quality, satisfaction, and value—have been the focus of attention for executives and researchers alike over the last ten years. In fact, we identified all three of these concepts in chapter 2 as key competitive trends for the 1990s and beyond. Companies today recognize that they can compete more effectively by distinguishing themselves with respect to service quality, improved customer satisfaction, and value. In this part of the chapter we focus on these three encompassing constructs to show how customer perceptions of service are organized. We will spend disproportionate space on service quality, since it is the primary focus of the book. Customer perceptions of value will be briefly discussed here and covered in much greater depth later in the book in the pricing chapter.

Service Quality

Earlier we defined *service quality* as *the delivery of excellent or superior service relative to customer expectations.* How customers judge service quality is the focus of this section. First we discuss the distinctions between process and technical outcome quality; then we examine the five dimensions of service quality.

Process vs. Technical Outcome Quality

Ultimately, consumers judge the quality of services on their perceptions of the technical outcome provided and on how that outcome was delivered. For example, a legal services client will judge the quality of the outcome, or how the court case was resolved, and also the quality of the process. Process quality would include such things as the lawyer's timeliness, his responsiveness in returning phone calls, his empathy for the client, his courtesy and listening skills. Similarly, a restaurant customer will judge the service on her perceptions of the meal (technical outcome quality) and on how the meal was served and how the employees interacted with her (process quality).

If the service has a specific outcome, as in the winning or losing of a lawsuit, the customer can judge the effectiveness of the service on the basis of that outcome. However, many services offered by lawyers, doctors, engineers, college professors, accountants, and architects, among others—as well as many routine services such as termite inspection and automobile repair—are highly complex and a clear outcome is not always evident. In these situations, the technical quality of the service—the actual competence of the provider or effectiveness of the outcome—is not easy for the customer to judge. The customer may never know for sure whether the service was performed correctly or even if it was needed in the first place. This explains why a major automobile repair retailer was able to so oversell and overcharge for car-repair services that it was accused of fraud; customers were not knowledgeable enough about the increasingly sophisticated service of car repair to recognize that recommended repairs were unnecessary.

The existence of both process and outcome quality can also explain why an architect with superb technical skills and certifications can fail to compete effectively with architects who can deliver superior interpersonal quality as well. In this example, if customers cannot judge the technical quality of the outcome effectively (or even if they can, but they believe other equally competent architects are available), they will base their quality judgments on process dimensions such as the architect's ability to solve problems, her ability to empathize, whether she meets deadlines, and her courtesy.

When customers cannot accurately evaluate the technical quality of a service, they form impressions of the service including its technical quality from whatever sources exist, using their own "shorthand" or cues that may not be apparent to the provider. Consider the services that college professors provide to their students. Most students are in school to learn what they do not know. However, not knowing the subjects they are studying does not prevent them from making judgments about their professors. Cues such as the tangibles that accompany the service (overheads and other presentation materials) the professor's appearance of nervousness, the degree of confidence communicated, or even whether the professor starts and ends class on time, are used to infer competence. Understanding the cues used to signal the presence or absence of technical quality allows professors and other marketers some control over their customers' impressions.

In a study investigating the cues influential in assessing legal services, researchers found that courtesy was an extremely powerful signal: the level of the lawyer's courtesy accounted for at least 60 percent of the variation in how happy or angry a respondent was with the attorney.[18] In another study, researchers found that courtesy was the only evaluative criterion common to all four of the services under review.[19] Thus, courtesy of the provider was used as a signal of quality for a service whose technical quality could not be accurately evaluated. In the first study referenced, less than 15 percent of the variation in how happy or angry the respondent was with the lawyer could be attributed to the outcome itself, the rest being attributed to interpersonal characteristics of the lawyers.[20]

Service Quality Dimensions   Research suggests that customers do not perceive quality as a unidimensional concept—that is, customers' assessments of quality include perceptions of multiple factors.[21] For example, it has been suggested that the following eight dimensions of quality are applied to all goods and services: performance, features, reliability, conformance, durability, serviceability, aesthetics, and perceived quality (roughly equivalent to prestige).[22] Others have argued that dimensions of quality are meaningful when applied to *categories of products* (for example durable goods, packaged goods, services). To illustrate, research on perceptions of quality in automobiles has shown that quality is assessed on six dimensions: reliability, serviceability, prestige, durability, functionality, and ease of use.[23] Research on food products suggests that rich/full flavor, natural taste, fresh taste, good aroma, and appetizing looks determined perceptions of quality in 33 food categories.[24]

Other researchers have found that consumers consider five dimensions in their assessments of service quality, as shown in Figure 5-7 and defined here[25]:

- **Reliability:** Ability to perform the promised service dependably and accurately
- **Responsiveness:** Willingness to help customers and provide prompt service
- **Assurance:** Employees' knowledge and courtesy and their ability to inspire trust and confidence
- **Empathy:** Caring, individualized attention given to customers
- **Tangibles:** Appearance of physical facilities, equipment, personnel, and written materials

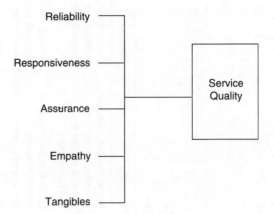

FIGURE 5-7   Dimensions of service quality.

These dimensions represent how consumers organize information about service quality in their minds. On the basis of exploratory and quantitative research, these five dimensions were found relevant for banking, insurance, appliance repair and maintenance, securities brokerage, long-distance telephone service, automobile repair service, and others. The dimensions are also applicable to retail and business services, and logic suggests they would be relevant for internal services as well. Sometimes customers will use all of the dimensions to determine service quality perceptions, at other times not. For example, in a remote encounter such as an encounter with an ATM, empathy is not likely to be a relevant dimension. And in a phone encounter such as scheduling a repair call, tangibles will not be relevant.

We will expand on each of the five dimensions of service quality and provide illustrations of how customers judge each dimension. Table 5-2 gives examples of each for consumer services (car repair, airline, medical care), business-to-business service (architecture), and internal service (information processing within a company).

Reliability: Delivering on promises   Of the five dimensions, reliability has been consistently shown to be the most important determinant of perceptions of service quality among U.S. customers.[26] Reliability is defined as the ability to perform the promised service dependably and accurately. In its broadest sense, reliability means that the company delivers on its promises—promises about delivery, service provision, problem resolution, and pricing. Customers want to do business with companies that keep their promises, particularly their promises about the core service attributes. We saw this in the earlier section on service encounters: A major group of incidents that customers remember are those related to failure of the core service delivery system and the subsequent efforts (if any) to recover.

One company that effectively communicates and delivers on the reliability dimension is Federal Express. The reliability message of Federal Express—when it "absolutely, positively has to get there"—reflects the company's service positioning. In a later chapter we will discuss specifically how Federal Express has managed to ensure that it keeps this promise. But even when firms don't choose to position themselves explicitly on reliability as Federal Express has, this dimension is extremely important to

TABLE 5-2 EXAMPLES OF HOW CUSTOMERS JUDGE THE FIVE DIMENSIONS OF SERVICE QUALITY

	Reliability	Responsiveness	Assurance	Empathy	Tangibles
Car repair (consumer)	Problem fixed the first time and ready when promised	Accessible; no waiting; responds to requests	Knowledgeable mechanics	Acknowledges customer by name; remembers previous problems and preferences	Repair facility; waiting area; uniforms; equipment
Airline (consumer)	Flights to promised destinations depart and arrive on schedule	Prompt and speedy system for ticketing, in-flight, baggage handling	Trusted name; good safety record; competent employees	Understanding of special individual needs; anticipates customer needs	Aircraft; ticketing counters; baggage area; uniforms
Medical care (consumer)	Appointments are kept on schedule; diagnoses prove to be accurate	Accessible; no waiting; willingness to listen	Knowledge, skills, credentials, reputation	Acknowledges patient as a person; remembers previous problems; good listening; patience	Waiting room; exam room; equipment; written materials
Architecture (business)	Delivers plans when promised and within budget	Returns phone calls; adapts to changes	Credentials; reputation; name in the community; knowledge and skills	Understands client's industry; acknowledges and adapts to specific client needs; gets to know the client	Office area; reports; plans themselves; billing statements; dress of employees
Information processing (internal)	Provides needed information when requested	Prompt response to requests; not "bureaucratic"; deals with problems promptly	Knowledgeable staff; well-trained; credentials	Knows internal customers as individuals; understands individual and departmental needs	Internal reports; office area; dress of employees

consumers. Think of the service companies you are most loyal to. Unless you have no choice about whom you do business with, we would surmise that those service companies you are most loyal to are reliable in delivering the core service.

All firms need to be aware of customer expectations of reliability. Firms that do not provide the core service that customers think they are buying fail their customers in the most direct way. The importance of reliability is further dramatized by the finding that customers' expectations for service are likely to go up when the service is not performed as promised. When service failures occur, customers' tolerance zones are likely to shrink and their adequate and desired service levels are likely to rise.[27]

Responsiveness: Being Willing to Help   Responsiveness is the willingness to help customers and to provide prompt service. This dimension emphasizes attentiveness and promptness in dealing with customer requests, questions, complaints, and problems. Again, recall the research on service encounters and note the parallels between responsiveness and the large group of incidents that were listed under "adaptability" . . . There are strong similarities between the employee behaviors noted in those critical service encounters and the responsiveness dimension of service quality. Responsiveness is communicated to customers by the length of time they have to wait for assistance, answers to questions, or attention to problems. Responsiveness also captures the notion of flexibility and ability to customize the service to customer needs.

To excel on the dimension of responsiveness, a company must be certain to view the process of service delivery and the handling of requests from the customer's point of view rather than from the company's point of view. Standards for speed and promptness that reflect the company's view of internal process requirements may be very different from the customer's requirements for speed and promptness.

Catalog retailers such as L.L. Bean and Talbot's focus on responsiveness in achieving their reputations for service excellence. To truly distinguish themselves on responsiveness, companies need well-staffed customer-service departments as well as responsive front-line people in all contact positions. Responsiveness perceptions diminish when customers wait to get through to a company by telephone, are put on hold, or are put through to a phone mail system. Structure and training are the keys. L.L. Bean has three separate groups of customer-service people (one to receive telephone orders, another to handle telephone inquiries, and still another for mail order) because it finds that asking contact representatives to do all three creates confusion and role stress.

Assurance: Inspiring Trust and Confidence   Assurance is defined as employees' knowledge and courtesy and the ability of the firm and its employees to inspire trust and confidence. This dimension is likely to be particularly important for services that the customer perceives as involving high risk and/or about which they feel uncertain about their ability to evaluate outcomes, for example, banking, insurance, brokerage, medical, and legal service.

Trust and confidence may be embodied in the person who links the customer to the company, for example securities brokers, insurance agents, lawyers, counselors. In such service contexts the company seeks to build trust and loyalty between key contact people and individual customers. The "personal banker" concept captures this idea—customers are assigned to a banker who will get to know them individually and who will coordinate all of their banking services. (An inherent risk for the company when these types of personal relationships are built up is that the customer will follow the service provider if and when the provider leaves the company.)

In other situations, trust and confidence are embodied in the organization itself. Insurance companies such as Allstate ("You're in good hands with Allstate") and Prudential ("Own a piece of the rock") illustrate efforts to create trusting relationships between customers and the company as a whole.

In the early stages of a relationship, the customer may use tangible evidence to assess the assurance dimension. Visible evidence of degrees, honors, and awards and special certifications may give a new customer confidence in a professional service provider. In its mammography screening program, Lutheran Health Services informs all new patients that the hospital's screening center is certified by the American College of Radiologists and explains the extensive criteria that must be met to receive the certification. In addition, an official sticker notifying patients of the certification is glued to the X-ray machine at eye level where patients will see it. Such evidence is meant to engender trust in the process and outcome.

Empathy: Treating Customers as Individuals Empathy is defined as the caring, individualized attention the firm provides its customers. The essence of empathy is conveying, through personalized or customized service, that customers are unique and special. Customers want to feel understood by and important to firms that provide service to them. Personnel at small service firms often know customers by name and build relationships that reflect their personal knowledge of customer requirements and preferences. When such a small firm competes with larger firms, the ability to be empathetic may give the small firm a clear advantage.

In business-to-business services, customers want supplier firms to understand their industries and issues. Many small computer consulting firms successfully compete with large vendors by positioning themselves as specialists in particular industries. Even though larger firms have superior resources, the small firms are perceived as more knowledgeable about customer's issues and needs and able to offer more customized services.

Tangibles: Representing the Service Physically Tangibles are defined as the appearance of physical facilities, equipment, personnel, and communication materials. All of these provide physical representations or images of the service that customers, particularly new customers, will use to evaluate quality. Service industries that emphasize tangibles in their strategies include hospitality services where the customer visits the establishment to receive the service, such as restaurants and hotels, retail stores, and entertainment companies.

While tangibles are often used by service companies to enhance their image, provide continuity, and signal quality to customers, most companies combine tangibles with another dimension to create a service quality strategy for the firm (e.g., Jiffy Lube emphasizes both responsiveness and tangibles—providing fast, efficient service and a comfortable, clean waiting area). In contrast, firms that don't pay attention to the tangibles dimension of the service strategy can confuse and even destroy an otherwise good strategy.

Customer Satisfaction

Practitioners and writers in the popular press tend to use the terms "satisfaction" and "quality" interchangeably, but researchers have attempted to be more precise about the meanings and measurement of the two concepts. Early in the debate over the differences in meaning, some researchers considered satisfaction an evaluation made only at the level of the individual transaction (such as eating a particular meal at McDonald's) instead of a global assessment (the accumulation of an individual's experiences with the fast-food chain). While the debate is not yet resolved, current thinking suggests that both service quality and customer satisfaction can be viewed at the individual service encounter (transaction) level or at a more global level.[28] Thus, rather than distinguishing quality and satisfaction in terms of level of analysis, consensus is growing that the two concepts are fundamentally different in their underlying causes and outcomes.[29] While they have certain things in common, satisfaction is generally viewed as a broader concept than service quality assessment, which focuses specifically on dimensions of service. With this view, perceived service quality is a component of customer satisfaction.

Figure 5-8 graphically illustrates growing agreement on the distinctions between the two constructs. As shown, service quality is a focused evaluation that reflects the customer's perception of the five specific dimensions of service. Satisfaction, on the other

FIGURE 5-8   Customer perceptions of quality and customer satisfaction.

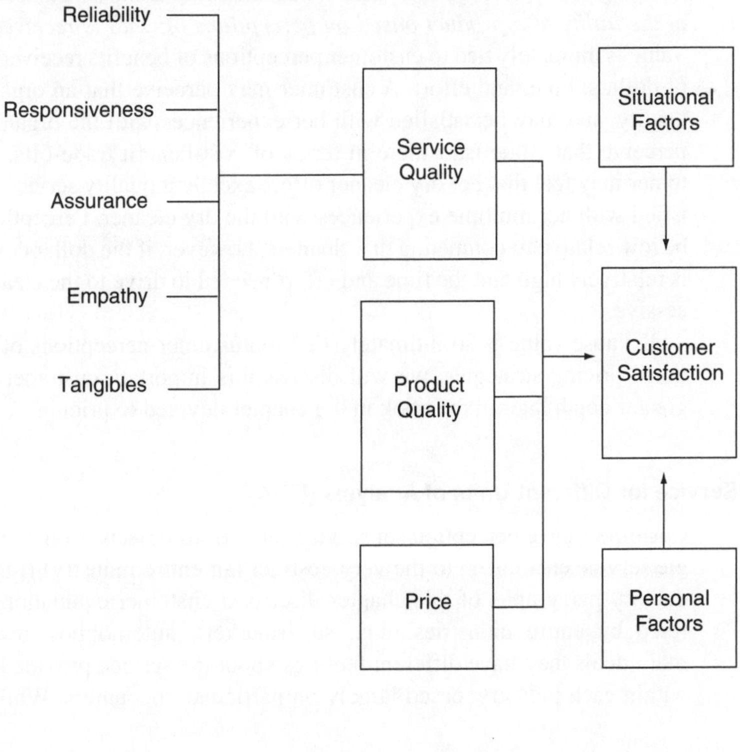

hand, is more inclusive: It is influenced by perceptions of service quality, product quality, and price as well as situational factors and personal factors. For example, service quality of a health club is judged on attributes such as whether equipment is available and in working order when needed (reliability), how responsive staff members are to customer needs (responsiveness/empathy), how skilled the trainers are (assurance), and whether the facility is well maintained (tangibles). Customer satisfaction with the health club is a broader concept that will certainly be influenced by perceptions of service quality but will also include perceptions of product quality (e.g., quality of products sold in the pro shop), the price of membership,[30] personal factors such as the consumer's emotional state, and even uncontrollable situational factors such as weather conditions and experiences driving to and from the health club.[31]

Another distinction generally drawn between quality and satisfaction is that quality perceptions can occur in the absence of actual experience with an organization ("I know that the Four Seasons Hotel offers a high level of service quality, even though I've never stayed there"), whereas customer satisfaction can only be assessed following an actual experience with an organization ("I cannot tell you how satisfied I am with the Four Seasons until I've actually stayed there").

Perceived Value

In addition to judging products and services on the basis of quality and satisfaction, customers also evaluate them according to their perceived value. While value has different meanings to different people, here we define *value* as *the consumer's overall assessment of the utility of a product based on perceptions of what is received and what is given.* Value is intimately tied to customer perceptions of benefits received versus cost in terms of dollars, time, and effort. A customer may perceive that an organization offers good quality, and may be satisfied with her experiences with the organization, but she may perceive that value isn't there in terms of cost-benefit trade-offs. For example, a customer may feel that her dry cleaner offers excellent quality service, and she may be satisfied with her multiple experiences with the dry cleaner. Perceptions of value can still be low relative to competing dry cleaners, however, if the dollar cost of the dry cleaning is relatively high and the time and effort needed to drive to the cleaning location are excessive.

Because value is so intimately tied to customer perceptions of price and organizations' pricing strategies, we will discuss this important customer perception in much greater depth later in the book in the chapter devoted to pricing.

Perceptions of Service for Different Units of Analysis (UOA)

Customers have perceptions of service for various objects, from the most specific (a single service encounter) to the very abstract (an entire industry) (Figure 5-9). The introductory paragraphs of this chapter discussed customer evaluations of the services offered by entire industries (e.g., supermarkets, automobiles, restaurants). However, individuals may have different feelings about the service provided by a particular firm within each industry, based largely on particular encounters. While a person's evalua-

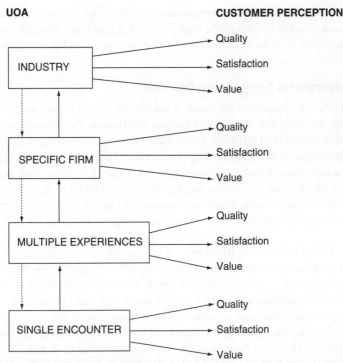

FIGURE 5-9 Customer perceptions of service for different units of analysis (UOA).

tions of individual service encounters will likely affect higher level evaluations, the correlation between the two is not necessarily perfect. For example, you may have a favorite restaurant (specific firm UOA) where you go all the time. One evening you have a terrible meal there (single encounter UOA). Given your many past excellent experiences (multiple experiences UOA), however, your perceptions of the firm's quality (specific firm UOA) would remain high. On a similar note, it is often said that people distrust and dislike the legal profession (industry UOA), but they are very satisfied with *their* lawyer (specific firm UOA).

Figure 5-9 illustrates the various UOAs and the associated customer perceptions. The arrows between types of units indicate that we expect the more specific evaluations to affect evaluations at higher levels. However, in some cases a person's perceptions of an industry or a specific firm may influence that person's evaluation of a specific encounter.

STRATEGIES FOR INFLUENCING CUSTOMER PERCEPTIONS

The primary purpose of this chapter is to orient you to the factors that influence customer perceptions of service and to show how these are organized around broader perceptions of quality, satisfaction, and value. Next we will describe management strategies used to influence perceptions of service directly. We cover these strategies only briefly here since much of the rest of the book is aimed at providing in-depth understanding of such strategies to influence effectively both expectations and perceptions of service.

Aim for Customer Satisfaction in Every Service Encounter

Because every service encounter is potentially critical to customer retention, many firms aim for "zero defects," or 100-percent satisfaction. To achieve this requires, first, clear documentation of all of the points of contact between the organization and its customers. Development of understanding of customer expectations for each of these encounters is the next step, so that strategies can be built around meeting those expectations. Each of the four themes underlying satisfaction/dissatisfaction in service encounters presented earlier in the chapter—recovery, adaptability, spontaneity, and coping—suggests specific types of actions that would aid an organization aiming for zero defects.

Plan for Effective Recovery   The examples presented in Exhibit 5-2 illustrate that service failures and subsequent recovery efforts create strong memories for customers and for employees who empathize with their customers. When service customers have been disappointed on the first try, "doing it very right the second time" is essential to maintaining customer loyalty.[32] This implies a need for service process and system analysis to determine the root causes of failure so that a redesign can ensure higher reliability.[33] However, because of the inherent variability of services, failures are inevitable even for the best of firms. Thus, organizations need recovery systems that allow employees to turn the failure around and leave the customer satisfied.[34] Recovery strategies are discussed more in Chapter 7.

Facilitate Adaptability and Flexibility   As shown in Exhibit 5-3, customer perceptions of organizational adaptability and flexibility also create feelings of satisfaction or dissatisfaction in service encounters. The existence of this encounter theme suggests a need to know when and how the system can be flexed, and when and how to explain to customers why a particular request cannot be granted. Knowledge of the service concept, the service delivery system and its operation, and the system standards enables employees to inform customers about what happened, what can be done, and why their needs or requests can or cannot be accommodated. Such knowledge and willingness to explain can leave a lasting positive impression on customers even when their specific request cannot be met.

Encourage Spontaneity   Memorable encounters occur for customers even when there is no system failure and no special request, as shown in Exhibit 5-4. While employee behaviors within this third theme would appear to be somewhat random and relatively uncontrollable, there are things that organizations can do to encourage positive spontaneous behaviors and discourage negative behaviors. Recruitment and selection procedures can be used to hire employees with strong service orientation, whose natural tendency is to be service-minded.[35] A strong service culture, employee empowerment, effective supervision and monitoring, and quick feedback to employees also will control to some extent the seeming randomness of these behaviors. Because of their extreme importance for service quality, we will discuss these human resource issues in depth in chapter 11.

Help Employees Cope with Problem Customers   The service encounters classified within the coping theme (Exhibit 5-5) represent times when customers were the cause of their own dissatisfaction. Several management strategies are suggested by this last theme. First, managers and customers need to acknowledge that the customer isn't always right, nor will she always behave in acceptable ways. Contact employees who have been on the job any length of time know this, but frequently they are told that the "customer is king" and are not given the appropriate training and tools to deal with problem customers. Employees need appropriate coping and problem-solving skills to handle difficult customers as well as their own feelings in such situations. Another implication is the need for "training customers" so that they will know what to expect and know the appropriate behaviors in given situations. Issues relevant to this theme will be explored further in chapters 11 and 13.

Manage the Dimensions of Quality at the Encounter Level   While the five dimensions of service quality—reliability, responsiveness, assurance, empathy, and tangibles—are generally applied to the overall quality of the firm, it is certainly possible to relate them to each individual encounter. If we think of each encounter in terms of these five themes, we can formulate strategies for ensuring satisfaction in the "moment of truth" that will add to the broad strategies around the four themes just discussed. Many of the strategies related to the four encounter themes will reinforce the quality dimensions directly. For example, strategies aimed at improving adaptability of service employees should enhance customer perceptions of responsiveness and empathy.

Manage the Evidence of Service to Reinforce Perceptions

The evidence of service—people, process, physical evidence—shown in Figure 5-6 provides a framework for planning marketing strategies that address the expanded marketing-mix elements for services. These new elements, or a subset of them, essentially tangibilize the service for the customer and thus represent important means for creating positive perceptions. Because of their importance, the new elements need to be treated as strategic marketing variables, as are product, price, place, and promotion, the traditional mix elements. Entire chapters of this book are devoted to strategies relevant to people (chapters 11, 13), process (chapter 10), and physical evidence (chapter 18).

Communicate Realistically and Use Customer Experiences to Reinforce Images

Because an organization's image can have a strong impact on customer perceptions, many organizations with poor images are quick to jump to the conclusion that "we need to change our image." Often, the first thing they do is develop a new advertisement or brochure, remodel the service facility, or change the corporate slogan to suggest "customer satisfaction is our number one priority." However, experts have noted that "image is reality—therefore, image development and improvement programs have to be based on reality."[36] Strategies to build positive images should be based on what can be delivered, or they will backfire when customers experience the service and realize that nothing has changed, or that the communication efforts of the organization are setting up false promises.

This is what happened to a large retailing chain in Europe that suffered from an image of being less service oriented than its competitors. It invested in a corporate image-building campaign to communicate good service, customer-conscious employees, a nice store atmosphere, and other aspects of good service. Unfortunately, this was basically all that was done. While sales increased in the short term, in the long term sales returned to where they were before and the chain's image was even worse. This example illustrates the lesson that if market communication does not fit reality, reality normally wins.[37] Chapters 16 through 18 of this book cover a wide range of strategies that can be used to manage service images in positive ways through communication efforts, pricing, and management of physical evidence.

An organization's image is reinforced (or confused) by actual service experiences, so in the long term it is critical to manage all customer experiences to solidify the desired image. Companies like Federal Express, Southwest Airlines, and McDonalds, which have very strong and positive images in their customers' minds, have built those images on excellent communication combined with consistent delivery that matches the communication.

Use Price to Enhance Customer Perceptions of Quality and Value

Service prices are powerful cues that aid customers in forming expectations of service levels and later help them to evaluate actual quality and value received. Pricing strategies therefore need to be developed in conjunction with service positioning and communication strategies; they cannot be based on cost considerations alone. Because pricing is so important and such a powerful influence on customers' expectations and perceptions, a full chapter (chapter 17) is devoted to pricing issues and strategies.

SUMMARY

This chapter described the primary factors influencing customer perceptions of service. We began with an in-depth discussion of service encounters, the building blocks of customer perceptions. The importance of encounters, types of encounters, and sources of customer satisfaction and dissatisfaction in such encounters were presented as a foundation for understanding of perceptions. From customers' points of view, the service encounter is the most vivid impression they have of the organization's quality.

The "evidence of service," or the three new marketing-mix elements for services, were also presented as a set of factors that are critical in forming customer perceptions. Management of these three new elements—people, process, and physical evidence—is as critical for service success as management of the other strategic marketing-mix variables. The roles of organizational image and price were also discussed in relation to forming customer perceptions of service.

The second half of the chapter examined broader, more abstract perceptions, namely customer impressions of service quality, satisfaction, and value. The difference between process and outcome quality in services was discussed. Service quality and its five dimensions—reliability, responsiveness, assurance, empathy, tangibles—were examined in detail. We noted that service quality and satisfaction are similar ideas and that current thinking suggests satisfaction is a broader concept, influenced by quality. Value was defined, but a thorough discussion of value concepts is left for a later chapter. The chapter ended with a brief look at strategies relevant to the four factors influencing customer perceptions.

Chapters 3, 4, and 5 have provided you with a grounding in customer issues relevant to services. The three chapters together are intended to give you a solid understanding of customer behavior issues and of service expectations and perceptions. We will proceed through the rest of the book to illustrate ways to close this most important gap, the Customer GAP, through closing the four Provider GAPs.

DISCUSSION QUESTIONS

1 Is your opinion of the service offered by the industries in the *Wall Street Journal*/NBC poll (Figure 5-1) different from the survey results or do you agree with what they found? Why do you agree or disagree?

2 What are the four general sets of factors that influence customer perceptions of service (Figure 5-3)? Describe a service you have experienced and how (or whether) each of the factors influenced your personal perceptions.

3 Describe a remote encounter, a phone encounter, and a face-to-face encounter that you have had recently. How did you evaluate the encounter, and what were the most important factors determining your satisfaction/dissatisfaction in each case?

4 What is the difference between an external and an internal customer? Use the university as an example, and list as many different types of both external and internal customers as you can think of.

5 Describe an "encounter cascade" for an airplane flight. In your opinion, what are the most important encounters in this cascade for determining your overall impression of the quality of the airline?

6 List and define the five dimensions of service quality. Describe the services provided by a firm you do business with (your bank, your doctor, your favorite restaurant) on each of the dimensions. In your mind, has this organization distinguished itself from its competitors on any particular service quality dimension?

7 Why did the gentleman described in Exhibit 5-1 leave his bank after thirty years? What were the underlying causes of his dissatisfaction in that instance, and why do you think that would cause him to leave the bank?

8 Discuss the differences between perceptions of service quality and customer satisfaction.

9 Think of a specific service provider you frequently do business with. Using Figure 5-9 as a guide, assess quality for the different units of analysis (UOA) starting with your most recent encounter with that service provider. In other words, what is your opinion of the quality of that one encounter? What is your opinion of the quality of all the en-

counters you've had personally with that provider? What is your opinion of the quality of that company/organization? What is your opinion of quality in the industry that company/organization is part of? Are your perceptions of quality the same for each UOA?

EXERCISES

1 Keep a journal of your service encounters with different organizations (at least five) during the week. For each journal entry ask yourself the following questions: What circumstances lead up this encounter? What did the employee say or do? How did you evaluate this encounter? What exactly made you evaluate the encounter that way? What should they have done differently (if anything)? Categorize your encounters according to the four themes of service encounter satisfaction/dissatisfaction (recovery, adaptability, spontaneity, coping) identified in the text.

2 Write a letter of complaint (or make an in-person complaint) to an organization you believe has failed to meet your expectations. What was the firm's response? Analyze the adequacy of the response (or recovery) from your perspective as a customer.

3 Interview someone with a non-U.S. cultural background. Ask the person about service quality, whether the five dimensions of quality are relevant, and which are most important in determining quality of banking services (or some other type of service) in the person's country.

4 Think of an important service experience you have had in the last several weeks. Analyze the encounter according to the "evidence of service" provided (see Figure 5-6). Which of the three evidence components was (or were) most important for you in evaluating the experience, and why?

5 Interview an employee of a local service business. Ask the person to discuss each of the five dimensions of quality with you as it relates to the person's company. Which dimensions are most important? Are any dimensions **not** relevant in this context? Which dimensions does the company do best? Why? Which dimensions could benefit from improvement? Why?

NOTES

1 "Many Consumers Expect Better Service and Say They Are Willing to Pay for It," *Wall Street Journal,* November 12, 1990, p. B1.

2 Ibid., study done by Forum Corporation.

3 "The Stuff Americans Are Made Of," American Quality Foundation, New York, 1993.

4 Jack Kelley, "Service without a Smile, Russians Find a Friendly Face Works Better," *USA Today,* January 21, 1991.

5 Dwayne Gremler, Mary Jo Bitner, and Kenneth R. Evans, "The Internal Service Encounter," *International Journal of Service Industry Management* 5, 2 (1994): 34–56.

6 "How Marriott Makes a Great First Impression," *The Service Edge* 6, 5 (May 1993): 5.

7 Arch G. Woodside, Lisa L. Frey, and Robert Timothy Daly, "Linking Service Quality, Customer Satisfaction, and Behavioral Intention," *Journal of Health Care Marketing* 9, 4 (December 1989): 5–17.

8 Ruth N. Bolton and James H. Drew, "Mitigating the Effect of Service Encounters," *Marketing Letters* 3, 1 (1992): 57–70.

9 G. Lynn Shostack, "Planning the Service Encounter," in *The Service Encounter,* ed. John A. Czepiel, Michael R. Solomon, and Carol F. Surprenant, Lexington, Mass.: Lexington Books, 1985, pp. 243–254.

10 Ibid.

11 For detailed discussions of the Critical Incident Technique see: John C. Flanagan, "The Critical Incident Technique," *Psychological Bulletin* 51 (July 1954): 327–358; Mary Jo Bitner, Jody D. Nyquist, and Bernard H. Booms, "The Critical Incident as a Technique for Analyzing the Service Encounter," in *Services Marketing in a Changing Environment* ed. T. M. Bloch, G. D. Upah, and V. A. Zeithaml, (Chicago: American Marketing Association, 1985), pp. 48–51; Sandra Wilson-Pessano, "Defining Professional Competence: The Critical Incident Technique 40 Years Later," presentation to the Annual Meeting of the American Educational Research Association, New Orleans, 1988.

12 For a complete discussion of the research on which this section is based see: Mary Jo Bitner, Bernard H. Booms, and Mary Stanfield Tetreault, "The Service Encounter: Diagnosing Favorable and Unfavorable Incidents," *Journal of Marketing* 54 (January 1990): 71–84; Mary Jo Bitner, Bernard H. Booms, and Lois A. Mohr, "Critical Service Encounters: The Employee's View," *Journal of Marketing* 58, 4 (1994): 95–106; Dwayne Gremler and Mary Jo Bitner, "Classifying Service Encounter Satisfaction across Industries," in *Marketing Theory and Applications,* ed. Chris T. Allen et al. (Chicago: American Marketing Association, 1992), pp. 111–118; Dwayne Gremler, Mary Jo Bitner, and Kenneth R. Evans, "The Internal Service Encounter," *International Journal of Service Industry Management* 5, 2 (1994): 34–56.

13 Bitner, Booms, and Mohr, op cit.

14 Mary Jo Bitner, "Managing the Evidence of Service," in *The Service Quality Handbook,* ed. Eberhard Scheuing and William Christopher, (New York: AMACOM Press, 1993), pp. 358–370.

15 Kevin Lane Keller, "Conceptualizing, Measuring, and Managing Customer-Based Brand Equity," *Journal of Marketing,* January 1993, pp. 1–22.

16 David A. Aaker, *Managing Brand Equity* (New York: Free Press, 1991), chap. 5.

17 This section on the role of image in services is based on material presented in chapter 7, "Managing Total Market Communication and Image," of Christian Gronroos, *Service Management and Marketing* (Lexington, Mass: Lexington Books, 1990).

18 Madeline Johnson and George M. Zinkhan, "Emotional Responses to a Professional Service Encounter," *The Journal of Services Marketing* 5 (Spring 1991): 5–15.

19 F. G. Crane and T. K. Clarke, "The Identification of Evaluative Criteria and Cues Used in Selecting Services," *Journal of Services Marketing* 2 (Spring 1989): 53–59.

20 Johnson and Zinkhan, op cit, p. 12.

21 Much of this section draws on material presented in Valarie A. Zeithaml, A. Parasuraman, and Leonard L. Berry, "Strategic Positioning on the Dimensions of Service Quality," in *Advances in Services Marketing and Management,* Vol. 2, ed. Teresa A. Swartz, David E. Bowen, and Stephen W. Brown (Greenwich, Conn.: JAI Press, 1993), pp. 207–228.

22 David Garvin, "Competing on the Eight Dimensions of Quality," *Harvard Business Review,* November–December 1987, pp. 101–109.

23 Merrie Brucks and Valarie A. Zeithaml, "Price as an Indicator of Quality Dimensions," Marketing Science Institute Working Paper, Cambridge, Mass., 1991.

24 P. Bonner and R. Nelson, "Product Attributes and Perceived Quality: Foods," in *Perceived Quality,* ed. J. Jacoby and J. Olson (Lexington, Mass.: Lexington Books, 1985), pp. 64–79.

25 A. Parasuraman, Valarie A. Zeithaml, and Leonard L. Berry, "SERVQUAL: A Multiple-Item Scale for Measuring Consumer Perceptions of Service Quality," *Journal of Retailing* 64 (Spring 1988): 12–40.

26 Ibid.

27 A. Parasuraman, Valarie A. Zeithaml, and Leonard L. Berry, "Understanding Customer Expectations of Service," *Sloan Management Review* 32 (Spring 1991): 39–48.

28 For more discussion of the debate on the distinctions between quality and satisfaction see: A. Parasuraman, Valarie A. Zeithaml, and Leonard L. Berry, "Reassessment of Expectations as a Comparison Standard in Measuring Service Quality: Implications for Future Research," *Journal of Marketing* 58, 1 (January 1994): 111–124; Richard L. Oliver, "A Conceptual Model of Service Quality and Service Satisfaction: Compatible Goals, Different Concepts," in *Advances in Services Marketing and Management,* Vol. 2, ed. Swartz, Bowen, and Brown, op. cit., pp. 65–85; Mary Jo Bitner and Amy R. Hubbert, "Encounter Satisfaction vs. Overall Satisfaction vs. Quality: The Customer's Voice," in *Service Quality: New Directions in Theory and Practice,* ed. Roland T. Rust and Richard L. Oliver (Newbury Park, Calif.: Sage, 1993), pp. 71–93; Dawn Iaccabucci, et al., "The Calculus of Service Quality and Customer Satisfaction: Theory and Empirical Differentiation and Integration," in *Advances in Services Marketing and Management,* Vol. 3, ed. Teresa A. Swartz, David E. Bowen, and Stephen W. Brown (Greenwich, Conn.: JAI Press, 1994), pp. 1–67.

29 See in particular Parasuraman, Zeithaml, and Berry (1994), op cit, and Oliver, op cit.

30 Parasuraman, Zeithaml, and Berry (1994), op cit.

31 Oliver, op cit.

32 Leonard L. Berry and A. Parasuraman, *Marketing Services* (New York: Free Press, 1991), chap. 3.

33 G. Lynn Shostack, "Designing Services that Deliver," *Harvard Business Review,* January–February 1984, pp. 133–139; G. Lynn Shostack, "Service Positioning through Structural Change," *Journal of Marketing* 51 (1987): 34–43.

34 For good coverage of recovery strategies see Berry and Parasuraman, op cit, and Christopher W. L. Hart, James L. Heskett, and W. Earl Sasser, Jr., "The Profitable Art of Service Recovery," *Harvard Business Review,* July–August 1990, pp. 148–156. Recovery strategies will also be discussed further in chapter 7 of this book.

35 Benjamin Schneider and Daniel Schechter, "Development of a Personnel System for Service Jobs," in *Service Quality: Multi-disciplinary and Multi-national Perspectives,* ed. Stephen W. Brown, Evert Gummesson, and Bo Edvardsson (Lexington, Mass.: Lexington Books, 1991), pp. 217–236.

36 Gronroos, op cit, p. 171.

37 Ibid.

LISTENING TO CUSTOMER REQUIREMENTS

PART

THREE

LISTENING TO CUSTOMER
REQUIREMENTS

6

UNDERSTANDING
CUSTOMER EXPECTATIONS
THROUGH
MARKETING RESEARCH

The contest: Best graduate business schools
The judges: Graduates of business schools
Corporate recruiters
The approach: Marketing research

Until 1988, students contemplating a graduate business school education could find only limited information about the various schools, particularly about the experience and evaluations of students who had matriculated at the schools. Published ratings of schools rested on test scores of entering students and starting salaries of graduates. The only available school rankings used deans of business schools as judges, rather than the students attending the schools. Finding out student perceptions of schools required informal word-of-mouth communication and networking, activities that were time consuming and whose results were difficult to compare across schools.

But in 1988, Business Week *revolutionized business school choice by providing potential students with the information they wanted: opinions and attitudes of students themselves. In a pioneering marketing research study, the magazine began its now-annual rankings of business schools by their primary "customers"— recent graduates and corporate recruiters. The study ranks the institutions on the basis of customer satisfaction: how the schools determine and satisfy the needs of both graduates and the corporations who hire them.[1]*

In the 1994 version of the study, Business Week *mailed 6,353 surveys to recent master's of business administration graduates and 354 to corporate recruiters. A full 73 percent of the graduates and 72 percent of the corporate recruiters responded to the survey—a very high rate of return by research standards.[2]*

Here's how the student survey worked. Questionnaires were mailed to a random sam-

ple of MBA candidates from 44 business schools. The recipients answered 86 questions about the school's performance which were subsequently weighted to reflect how closely they related to overall satisfaction. A composite index was created from the results of the 1994 surveys (weighted 50%), the 1992 surveys (weighted 25%), and the 1990 surveys (weighted 25%). Graduates judged only their own schools on teaching quality, program content, and career placement.

The survey of recruiters polled companies that hired MBAs and asked them to rate the top 10 schools on the basis of the rate of of success of a school's graduates in their companies. The 1994 rankings were:

1 Pennsylvania's Wharton
2 Northwestern's Kellogg School
3 Chicago
4 Stanford
5 Harvard
6 Michigan
7 Indiana
8 Columbia
9 UCLA
10 Massachusetts Institute of Technology[3]

The Business Week *research-derived rankings have led to many changes in schools, including revamped curricula, refocusing of efforts to topics such as teamwork and global concerns, and greater emphasis on the satisfaction of students and corporations.*

One reaction to the survey and its findings is a response that occurs frequently in market research: When managers do not like the findings, they question a study's accuracy and claim the results are biased. Other schools heard that first-year MBA students at one of the schools organized a letter-writing campaign in which 85 students sent personal letters to the magazine raving about the program at their school. Bias did not result, however, because graduated students rather than current ones were surveyed.

Despite a genuine interest in meeting customer expectations, many companies miss the mark by thinking inside out—they believe they know what customers *should* want and deliver that, rather than finding out what they *do* want (Figure 6-1). When this happens, companies provide services that do not match customer expectations: important features are left out, and the levels of performance on features that are provided are inadequate. Because services have few clearly defined and tangible cues, this difficulty may be considerably larger than it is in manufacturing firms. A far better approach involves thinking outside in—determining customer expectations and then delivering to them. Thinking outside in involves using marketing research to understand customers and their requirements fully. Marketing research, the subject of this chapter, involves far more than conventional surveys. It consists of a portfolio of listening strategies that allow the company to deliver to expectations.

Figure 6-2 shows the main factors that lead to a gap between customer expectations and company perceptions of customer expectations. These factors include insufficient marketing research, inadequate use of marketing research, lack of interaction between

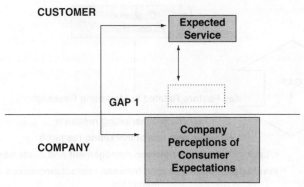

FIGURE 6-1   Provider GAP 1.

customers and company management, and lack of interaction between contact personnel and management. This chapter discusses each of these factors and then focuses on ways services companies can address these factors to close Provider GAP 1.

The objectives of this chapter are to:

1 Present the types of and guidelines for marketing research in services.

2 Show the ways that marketing research information can and should be used for services.

3 Describe the strategies by which companies can facilitate interaction and communication between management and customers.

4 Present ways that companies can and do facilitate interaction between contact people and management.

USING MARKETING RESEARCH TO UNDERSTAND CUSTOMER EXPECTATIONS

Finding out what customers expect is essential to providing service quality, and marketing research is a key vehicle for understanding customer expectations and perceptions of services. In services, as with any offering, a firm that does no marketing research at all is unlikely to understand its customers. A firm that does marketing research, but not on the topic of customer expectations, may also fail to know what is needed to stay in tune with changing customer requirements. Marketing research must focus on service issues such as what features are most important to customers, what levels of these features customers expect, and what customers think the company can and should do when problems occur in service delivery. Even when a service firm is small and has limited resources to conduct research, avenues are open to explore what the customer expects.

Exhibit 6-1 reviews the basics of marketing research that you are likely to remember from a marketing principles course. In this section we discuss the elements of services marketing research programs that help companies to identify customer expectations and perceptions.

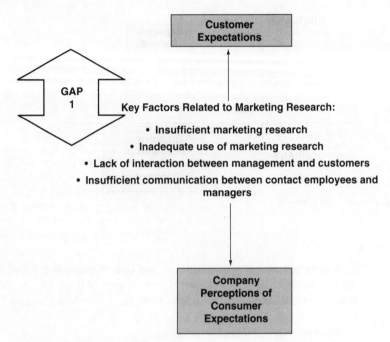

FIGURE 6-2 Key factors leading to provider GAP 1.

Figure 6-3 shows the stages in the marketing research process for services. As you can see, these stages and the general process for marketing research shown in Exhibit 6-1 are conceptually equivalent except for one major difference. In the figure we added a stage following the definition of the research problem and objectives that focuses on developing a services measurement strategy. This stage views research and measurement in a strategic, rather than tactical, way. Inclusion of this stage allows managers to invest research dollars wisely and to grasp the overall need for service and research. Far too many service companies are rushing to conduct research (i.e., jumping to stage 3) in a piecemeal fashion without considering the overall strategic purpose of the research.

In the following sections we will discuss the research process in each stage using examples in services and focusing on the ways the tactics of general marketing research may need to be adjusted to maximize their effectiveness in services.

Stage 1: Define the Problem and Research Objectives

The first stage of the services marketing research process is without doubt the most critical: defining the problem and research objectives. This is the stage in which the services marketer poses the questions to be answered or problems to be solved with the research. Does the company want to know how customers view the service provided by the company, what customer requirements are, how customers will respond to a new service introduction, or what customers will want from the company five years from now? Each

EXHIBIT 6-1   REVIEW OF BASIC MARKETING PRINCIPLES: MARKETING RESEARCH

Stages in the Marketing Research Process
1 Defining the problem and research objectives
2 Developing the research plan
3 Collecting the information
4 Analyzing the information
5 Presenting the findings

Kinds of Data
Primary Data: Original information gathered for the specific purpose at hand
Secondary Data: Data that already exist and were collected for purposes other than to answer the specific research questions now being studied

Types of Marketing Research
Exploratory research: The gathering of preliminary data to shed light on the real nature of the problem and suggest some hypotheses or new ideas
Observational research: The gathering of primary data by observing relevant people, actions, and situations
Survey research: Collection of descriptive information about people's knowledge, attitudes, preferences, or buying behavior by direct questions
Causal research: Collection of information to test cause and effect relationships

Characteristics of Good Marketing Research
Use of scientific method
Research creativity
Use of multiple methods
Balances the value and cost of research information

Commonly Used Types of Statistical Analysis
Regression analysis: Shows the impact of many factors (such as age, income, marital status) on a variable of interest (such as sales). The researcher's intent is to predict the variable of interest using the factors.
Correlation analysis: Provides statistical evidence of the relationships of variables to each other.
Factor analysis: A technique used for data reduction and interpretation that is based on correlation analysis.
Discriminant analysis: Involves the investigation of group differences. Two or more groups (such as purchasers or nonpurchasers of a service) are compared on a set of variables to identify and understand the differences.
Cluster analysis: A technique for identifying interdependence among variables that shows how they group together.
Conjoint analysis: Often called trade-off analysis, measures the customer's preference for attributes considered jointly. Customers typically provide their preference ordering for various combinations of attributes.

Source: Philip Kotler, "Marketing Information Systems and Marketing Research," *Marketing Management,* 7th ed. (New York: Prentice Hall, 1991), pp. 94–117

---

of these research questions requires a different research strategy. Thus it is essential to devote time and resources to define the problem thoroughly and accurately. In spite of the importance of this first stage, many marketing research studies are initiated without adequate attention to objectives, as evidenced in this thirty-year-old observation that remains accurate today:

> Despite a popular misconception to the contrary, objectives are seldom given to the researcher: The decision-maker seldom formulates his objectives accurately. He is likely to state his objectives in the form of platitudes which have no operational significance. Consequently, objectives usually have to be extracted by the researcher. In so doing, the researcher may well be performing his most useful service to the decision-maker.[4]

Research objectives translate into action questions like those just listed. While many different questions and objectives are likely to be part of a marketing research program, the following are the most common in services:

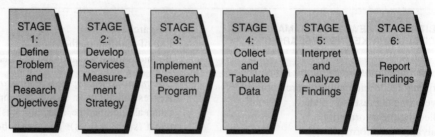

FIGURE 6-3   Stages in the marketing research process for services.

- To identify dissatisfied customers, so that service recovery can be attempted
- To discover customer requirements or expectations for service
- To monitor and track service performance
- To assess overall company performance compared with that of competition
- To assess gaps between customer expectations and perceptions
- To gauge effectiveness of changes in service delivery
- To appraise the service performance of individuals and teams for evaluation, recognition, and rewards
- To determine customer expectations for a new service
- To monitor changing customer expectations in an industry
- To forecast future expectations of customers

These research objectives are similar in many ways to the research conducted for physical products: both aim to assess customer requirements, dissatisfaction, and demand. Services research, however, incorporates additional elements that require specific attention.

First, services research must continually monitor and track service performance because performance is subject to human variability and heterogeneity. Conducting performance research at a single point in time, as might be done for a physical product such as an automobile, would be insufficient in services. A major focus of services research involves capturing human performance—at the level of the individual employee, the team, the branch, the organization as a whole, and the competition. Another focus of services research is documenting the process by which service is performed. Even when service employees are performing well, a service provider must continue to track performance because the potential for variation in service delivery is always present.

A second distinction in services research is the need to consider and monitor the gap between expectations and perceptions. This gap is dynamic because both perceptions and expectations can fluctuate. Does the gap exist because performance is declining, because performance varies with demand and supply level, or because expectations are escalating?

Table 6-1 lists a number of services research objectives. Once objectives such as these have been identified, they will point the way to decisions about the most appropriate type of research, methods of data collection, and ways to use the information. We will describe the additional columns in this table in the following sections of this chap-

TABLE 6-1 ELEMENTS IN AN EFFECTIVE MARKETING RESEARCH PROGRAM FOR SERVICES

Type of research	Primary research objectives	Qual./Quan.	Costs of information		Frequency	Expectation/ Perception	Statistically valid?	Shows priorities?
			Monetary	Time				
Complaint solicitation	To identify/attend to dissatisfied customers To identify common service failure points	Qual.	Low	Low	Continuous	P	No	No
Critical incident studies	To identify "best practices" at transaction level To identify customer requirements as input for quantitative service To identify common service failure points To identify systemic strengths and weaknesses in customer-contact services	Qual.	Low	Moderate	Periodic	P	No	No
Reqm'nts research	To identify customer requirements as input for quantitative research	Qual.	Moderate	Moderate	Periodic	E	No	No
Relationship surveys	To monitor and track service performance To assess overall company performance compared with that of competition To determine links between satisfaction and behavioral intentions	Quan.	Moderate	Moderate	Annual	P	Yes	Yes
	SERVQUAL Surveys: To assess gaps between customer expectations and perceptions	Quan.	Moderate	Moderate	Annual	E, P	Yes	Yes
Trailer calls	To obtain immediate feedback on performance of service transactions To measure effectiveness of changes in delivery To assess service performance of individuals and teams To use as input for process improvements To identify common service failure points	Quan.	Moderate	Moderate	Continuous	P	Yes	Yes
Key client studies	To create dialogue with important customers To close the loop with important customers To identify common service failure points	Qual./Quan.	Moderate	Moderate	Annual	E, P	No	Yes
"Mystery" shopping	To measure individual employee performance for evaluation, recognition, and rewards To identify systemic strengths and weaknesses in customer-contact services	Quan.	Low	Low	Quarterly	P	Yes	No
Customer panels	To monitor changing customer expectations To provide a forum for customers to suggest and evaluate new service ideas	Qual.	Moderate	Moderate	Continuous		No	No
Lost customer research	To identify reasons for customer defections	Qual.	Low	Low	Continuous		No	No
Future expectations research	To forecast future expectations of customers To develop and test new service ideas	Qual./Quan.	High	High	Periodic	E	No/Yes	No/Yes

ter. But first, let's look at a service organization that established a services research program by building on a clearly defined set of objectives.

IBM's education and training business (called Skill Dynamics in the early 1990s), one of the world's largest professional and technical education companies, faced major challenges in 1992. Temporarily separated from its parent company, Skill Dynamics faced declining revenues from internal IBM customers and the need to grow market share by pursuing new customers. The company's vision was to be a world-class provider of education, training, and related offerings both inside and outside IBM. To meet this goal, the company embarked on a research program designed to determine and improve customer satisfaction, service quality, and value.

While the underlying goals were to improve service delivery to customers and to attain financial success, the company needed to translate these very general goals into specific research objectives. The company began its service research program with the following objectives:

- To identify the most important customer requirements for its services and offerings
- To monitor and track service performance
- To determine the relationship between service quality and positive consequences of satisfaction such as willingness to recommend the company to others and intent to continue doing business with the company
- To identify dissatisfied customers and attempt service recovery

Stage 2: Develop a Services Measurement Strategy

The second research stage requires that the company match its research objectives with a *measurement strategy,* the strategic view of the measures that will constitute the outcomes of the program and will guide the organization in improving service delivery. The measurement strategy for Skill Dynamics was developed by outlining the information the company would need at the end of the project. The strategy is represented in Table 6-2. The aspects of service that were identified as critical to be measured were: (1) key *predictors of satisfaction,* those aspects of service that had the largest impact on satisfaction; (2) *overall satisfaction,* measures; and (3) *consequences of satisfaction,* positive or negative expected outcomes of satisfaction.

In the planning stage of the measurement strategy, the company did not know what aspects of its services best predicted customer satisfaction because no comprehensive research had been conducted to identify them. The six categories of predictors listed in the table (education planning/course selection, enrollment/logistics, course content, instructor effectiveness, and postclass use) represent the categories of requirements customers have when interacting with the firm. Students first select courses, then register, attend class, and finally use the information in their jobs. The company wanted to identify the most important service requirements in each of these categories and to determine their relative importance in predicting satisfaction with the encounters and with the company as a whole. Next, the company knew that it needed overall satisfaction measures at various company levels (individual course, business unit, and overall company) to track performance and to use in decisions involving compensation, recognition, and re-

TABLE 6-2   "FAMILY OF MEASURES": MEASUREMENT STRATEGY FOR SKILL DYNAMICS

	Customer segment		
What will be measured	Executive	Student Manager	Student
Key predictors of satisfaction			
Education planning/course selection	X	X	X
Enrollment logistics		X	X
Course content			X
Instructor effectiveness			X
Postclass	X	X	X
Overall satisfaction measures			
Class/program	X	X	X
Business unit	X	X	X
Relationship with Skill Dynamics	X	X	
Consequences of satisfaction			
Value	X	X	X
Loyalty	X	X	X
Repurchase intentions	X	X	X
Intent to recommend	X	X	X

wards. Finally, the company wanted to relate the impact of satisfaction to company performance; therefore the measurement strategy incorporated the positive consequences of satisfaction such as value, loyalty, repurchase intentions, and intent to recommend.

The company targeted three customer segments: executives, student managers, and students. The X's in the table indicate the positions where company executives decided that measures were needed. As you can see, the measurement strategy is an overall blueprint that allows the company to view the types of measures required.

While development of a measurement strategy is a very important step, many service companies do not approach measurement this way; instead, they conduct projects on an ad hoc basis, usually because they have an immediate need or want the answers for program or tactics. Incorporating the measurement strategy step before the research program step can save the company considerable time and effort, ensure that research dollars are well spent, and guarantee that measurement supports the strategic goals of the company.

Stage 3: Implement the Research Program

This stage involves both developing and implementing a plan to collect all the primary data needed to fulfill the measurement strategy. It involves many different decisions. What type of research approach should we use? How will we collect the information? When will we collect the information? How do we make sure that the information is accurate? How much will the research cost?

Criteria for an Effective Services Research Program   The services *research program* can be defined as the composite of separate research studies and types needed to address research objectives and execute the measurement strategy. A myriad of types of research could be considered in a research program. Before we discuss the major types, we offer criteria for an effective services research program. Understanding these criteria will help a company evaluate different types of research and choose the ones most appropriate for its research objectives.

Includes Qualitative and Quantitative Research[5]   Marketing research is not limited to surveys and statistics. Some forms of research are exploratory and preliminary, called *qualitative research,* and are conducted to clarify problem definition and prepare for more formal empirical research.[6] *Quantitative research* in marketing, on the other hand, is designed to describe the nature, attitudes, or behaviors of customers empirically and to test specific hypotheses that a services marketer wants to examine. Both types of research are important and need to be included in services marketing research programs. Insights gained through qualitative methods such as customer focus groups, informal conversations with individual customers, critical incidents research (described in chapter 5), and direct observation of service transactions show the marketer the right questions to ask of consumers and make the numbers in computer printouts meaningful. Qualitative research also gives managers the perspective and sensitivity that are critical in interpreting the data and initiating improvement efforts.[7]

Because the results of qualitative research play a major role in designing quantitative research, it often is the first type of research conducted. The Skill Dynamics company talked informally with many different customers in preparation for designing a survey for the company. In responding to open-ended questions about their likes and dislikes about the company, customers told Skill Dynamics the attributes that most needed to be contained in its questionnaires. Difficulties associated with class enrollment and instruction emerged as dominant themes in the initial interviews, so the company incorporated questions about these aspects of its service on its structured surveys.

Quantitative research clearly is important in assessing and improving service delivery and design. Quantitative research gives managers data from which they can make broad inferences about customer groups. These studies are essential for quantifying customer satisfaction, the importance of service attributes, the extent of service quality gaps, and perceptions of value. They also provide managers with yardsticks to evaluate and track the firm's service performance and show how the firm compares with competitors.

Results from empirical studies often trigger the need to conduct further qualitative research. Empirical data can highlight specific service deficiencies for deeper qualitative probing. For instance, Skill Dynamics found that perceived performance of instructors was a critical dimension on which student satisfaction depended. In the company's early surveys, only one question pertained to instruction. Postsurvey focus groups asked respondents to share specific aspects of instruction to illustrate the low performance they had experienced. The company found that three different aspects of instructor knowledge (subject matter expertise, practical experience, and class management skills) were critical. The company then added questions to its quantitative survey to capture these aspects, providing far better diagnostics than the original single questionnaire item. Such focus group discussions can be very productive for understanding the basis of the quantitative findings and in generating ideas for improvement.[8]

Includes both Perceptions and Expectations of Customers   As we discussed in chapter 4, expectations serve as standards or reference points for customers. In evaluating service quality, customers compare what they perceive they get in a service encounter with their expectations of that encounter. For this reason, a measurement program that captures only perceptions of service is missing a critical part of the service quality equation. Companies need also to incorporate measures of customer expectations.

Measurement of expectations can be included in a research program in multiple ways. First, basic research that relates to customers' requirements—that identifies the service features or attributes that matter to customers—can be considered expectation research. In this form, the *content* of customer expectations is captured, initially in some form of qualitative research such as focus group interviews. Research on the *levels* of customer expectations also is needed. This type of research quantitatively assesses the levels of customer expectations and compares these with perception levels, usually by calculating the gap between expectations and perceptions.

Balances the Cost of the Research and the Value of the Information   One of the major criteria for deciding the types of research to include in a services marketing research program is an assessment of the cost of the research compared with its benefits or value for the company. One type of cost is the monetary outlay in terms of direct costs to marketing research companies, payments to respondents, and internal company costs incurred by employees collecting the information (as in complaint solicitations). Time costs are also a factor, including the length of time between the start of a research study and the time the data are available for use by employees, as well as the time commitment needed internally by employees to administer the research. These and other costs must be traded off against the value of the information to the company in terms of better decision-making, retained customers, and successful new service launches. As in many other marketing decisions, the costs are easier to estimate and track than the value of the information. For this reason, we include only costs in the columns of Table 6-1. In chapter 9 we describe approaches to estimating the value of customers to a company, approaches that are useful as input to the trade-off analysis needed to address this criterion.

Includes Statistical Validity When Necessary   We have already shown that research has multiple and diverse objectives. These objectives determine the appropriate type of research and methodology. To illustrate, some research is used within companies not so much to measure as to build relationships with customers—to allow company contact people to learn what customers desire, to diagnose the strengths and weaknesses of their and the firm's efforts to address the desires, to prepare a plan to meet requirements, and to confirm after a period of time (usually one year) that the company has executed the plan. The underlying objective is to allow contact people to identify specific action items that will gain the maximum return in customer satisfaction for individual customers. This type of research does not need sophisticated quantitative analysis, anonymity of customers, careful control of sampling, or strong statistical validity.

On the other hand, research used to track overall service quality that will be used for bonuses and salary increases of salespeople must be carefully controlled for sampling bias and statistical validity. One of us (VZ) has worked with a company that paid salespeople on the basis of customers' satisfaction scores while allowing the salespeople to control the customers sampled. Obviously, the salespeople quickly learned that they could have surveys sent only to satisfied customers, artificially inflating the scores and—of course—undermining the confidence in the measurement system. Not all forms of research have statistical validity, and not all forms need it. Most forms of qualitative research, for example, do not possess statistical validity.

Measures Priorities or Importance   Customers have many service requirements, but not all are equally important. One of the most common mistakes managers make in trying to improve service is spending resources on the wrong initiatives, only to become discouraged because the firm's service does not improve! Measuring the relative importance of service dimensions and attributes helps managers to channel resources effectively; therefore, research must document the priorities of the customer. Prioritization can be accomplished in multiple ways. First, *direct importance measures* ask customers to prioritize items or dimensions of service. Several alternatives are available for measuring importance directly, among them asking respondents to rank-order service dimensions or attributes, or to rate them on a scale from "not at all important" to "extremely important." One effective approach involves asking respondents to allocate a total of 100 points across the various service dimensions. Still another form of direct importance measures involves the use of anchored rating scales that ask the respondent to choose the most important item on the list, assign it a score of 10, then rate the other items relative to this most important item. *Indirect importance measures* are estimated using the statistical procedures of correlation and regression analysis, which show the relative contribution of questionnaire items or requirements to overall service quality. Both indirect and direct importance measures provide evidence of customer priorities, and the technique that is chosen depends on the nature of the study and the number of dimensions or attributes that are being evaluated.

Occurs with Appropriate Frequency   Because customer expectations and perceptions are dynamic, companies need to institute a service quality research process, not just do isolated studies. A single study of service provides only a "snapshot" view of one moment in time. For full understanding of the marketplace's acceptance of a company's service, marketing research must be ongoing. Without a pattern of studies repeated with appropriate frequency, managers cannot tell whether the firm is moving forward or falling back, and which of their service-improvement initiatives are working and which are not. Just what does "ongoing research" mean in terms of frequency? The answer is specific to the type of service and to the purpose and method of each type of service research a company might do.[9] As we discuss the different types in the following section, you will see in Table 6-1 the frequency with which each type of research could be conducted.

Includes Measures of Loyalty or Behavioral Intentions   An important trend in services research involves measuring the positive and negative consequences of service quality along with overall satisfaction or service quality scores. Among the most important generic behavioral intentions are willingness to recommend the service to others and repurchase intent. These behavioral intentions can be viewed as positive and negative consequences of service quality. Positive behavioral intentions include saying positive things about the company, recommending the company to others, remaining loyal, spending more with the company, and paying a price premium. Negative behavioral intentions include saying negative things to others, doing less business with the company, switching to another company, and complaining to outside organizations such as the Better Business Bureau. Other more specific behavioral intentions differ by service; for example, behavioral intentions related to medical care include following instructions from the doctor, taking medications, and returning for follow-up. Tracking these areas can help a company estimate the relative value of service improvements to the company and can also identify customers who are in danger of defecting.

Summary   Most of the research criteria are incorporated in the columns of Table 6-1. As we discuss the elements in an effective services marketing research program, we will indicate how these approaches satisfy the criteria. In addition to the types and techniques of research shown in the table, the Technology Spotlight in this chapter shows the way that electronic and other technology adds to the information managers can collect.

Elements in an Effective Services Marketing Research Program   A good services marketing research program includes multiple types of research studies. The composite of studies and types of research will differ by company because the range of uses for service quality research—from employee performance assessment to advertising campaign development to strategic planning—requires a rich, multifaceted flow of information. The particular portfolio for any company will match company resources and address the key areas needed to understand the customers of the business. If a company were to engage in virtually all types of service research, the portfolio would look like Table 6-1. So that it will be easier for you to identify the appropriate type of research for different research objectives, we list the objectives in column 2 of the table. In the following sections we describe each major type of research and show the way each type addresses the criteria just delineated.

Complaint Solicitation   In this form of research, the firm collects and documents complaints of customers, then uses that information to identify dissatisfied customers, correct individual problems where possible, and identify common service failure points. While this research is used both for goods and services, it has a critical real-time purpose in services—to improve failure points and improve or correct the performance of contact personnel. Research on complaints is one of the easiest types of research for firms to conduct; many companies depend solely on customer complaints to stay in touch with customers. Unfortunately, research conducted by TARP, a research organization in Washington, has provided convincing evidence that customer complaints alone are a woefully inadequate source of information: only 4 percent of customers with problems actually complain to the company. The other 96 percent will stay dissatisfied, telling an average of 9 to 10 other people about their dissatisfaction.[10]

To be effective, the technique requires rigorous recording of numbers and types of complaints through many channels, and then working to eliminate the most frequent ones. Companies must both solve individual customer problems and seek overall patterns to eliminate failure points. More sophisticated forms of complaint resolution define "complaint" broadly to include all comments—both negative and positive—as well as questions from customers. The firm must build a depository for this information and report results frequently, perhaps weekly or monthly.

TECHNOLOGY SPOTLIGHT

HOW TECHNOLOGY IMPROVES THE PRACTICE OF MARKETING
RESEARCH

Technological changes in the way market research is
conducted, analyzed, and used are making the job of the
marketing research department far easier than it used to
be. Here are just a few of the innovations that technology
has brought to market research.

• *Compute This!* Computers are becoming an invaluable resource for analyzing data and facilitating the collection of marketing research information. "We talk to
50,000 to 70,000 of our customers every year, and since
we got computers, we save a pot full of money, as well as
a few forests," according to Steven Underwood, senior
research analyst at Mervyn's Department Stores.[11] Researchers have traded in their clipboards and lengthy
forms for pen-based computers that allow them simultaneously to take down data, analyze it, and reconfigure
follow-on questions. According to John Fiedler, president
of the marketing research company Populus, Inc.: "It's as
close to artificial intelligence as anything in market research."[12] With statistical programs loaded into the computers, researchers can do their own analysis and adjust
to responses immediately by changing media placement, advertising copy, or even plans for new services.
When outside firms handled the data, changes might
take six weeks to implement. Another, perhaps surprising, benefit of using computers as interviewers is that
consumers tend to be more honest and willing to divulge
private information than they would with a human researcher. "Face to face, if you ask their income, they'll
say 'none of your business.' On the computer, it's an
anonymous transaction."[13] Finally, when surveys come
on computer diskettes rather than paper, response rates
in some hard-to-reach populations (such as doctors and
business executives) are sometimes higher.

• *"James Bond Hits the Supermarket."*[14] Electronic
and infrared surveillance equipment now provides retailers with improved data about shopper's traffic patterns
and buying habits while in stores. One Chicago company
used infrared sensors in store ceilings to track shopping
carts and thereby reveal insights about shoppers that
weren't possible without the technology. The data were
useful in pinpointing sections that were not visited and in
revealing merchandising missteps. One Southern grocery chain, for example, noticed that foot traffic in the important and profitable produce area began falling off in
one of its stores but not another, even though the stores
had identical layouts. A research study revealed that a
manager in the problem store had installed a salad bar
near the produce section that was diverting people from
the produce. Another finding was that a larger-than-ex-
pected percentage of shoppers were "dippers" who
parked their carts at the ends of aisles and then walked
down the aisles, filling their arms with items from the
shelves as they went. The company documented that
such shoppers buy less because they are limited by what
they can carry. The real payback in this technologically
sophisticated market research is the improved ability to
document the effects of altering display space or moving
products from aisle to aisle. By pinpointing peak or ideal
spots, retailers could raise margins and profits by such
strategies as highlighting their own store brand products.
The techniques could go so far as to assign values to
particular sections and aisles and charge manufacturers
more money for shelf space in peak locations.[15]

• *Stroll through My Virtual Aisle.* Visionary Shopper,
a PC-based marketing research system, allows customers to stroll through store aisles on a computer
screen, examining merchandise (in a simulated grocery
store or department store) and responding to the shopping environment. The software allows shoppers to
zoom in on shelves and place merchandise in their grocery carts for purchase. Shelf configurations and service
atmospheres can be varied and compared in terms of respondent preferences. Because the marketing research
interaction is unique, it often feels like fun for respondents who then will spend more time with the research
than in conventional store surveys.[16]

Critical Incidents Studies   In chapter 5 we discussed the Critical Incident Technique, whereby customers provide verbatim stories about satisfying and dissatisfying
service encounters they have experienced. Studies using critical incidents are appropriate to address many different research objectives. They are effective alternatives to complaint solicitation because they too identify dissatisfied customers and common service
failure points. Critical incidents are powerful and vivid in eliciting customer requirements, particularly when the research is focused on behavioral dimensions of employee

performance at the transaction level. The critical incident technique is also an ideal way to have customers describe "best practices" at the transaction level.

Requirements Research   Requirements research involves identifying the benefits and attributes that customers expect in a service. This type of research is very basic and essential for it determines the type of questions that will be asked on surveys and ultimately the improvements that will be attempted by the firm. Because these studies are so basic, qualitative techniques are appropriate to begin them. Quantitative techniques may follow, usually during a pretest stage of survey development. Unfortunately, many companies do not do an adequate job in requirements research, often developing surveys on the basis of intuition or company direction rather than thorough customer probing.

An example of requirements research is *structured brainstorming,* a technique developed by researchers in IBM's Advanced Business Systems unit.[17] In this technique a sample of customers and potential customers is assembled. A facilitator leads the group through a series of exercises on creativity and then has the customers describe the ideal provider of the service—what they would want if they could have their ideal service. The facilitator asks "what" customers want (to elicit fundamental requirements), "why" they want it (to elicit the underlying need or benefit sought), and "how" they will know when they receive it (to elicit specific service features).

Another approach to requirements research that has been effective in services industries is to examine existing research about customer requirements in similar service industries. The five dimensions of quality service are generalizable across industries, and sometimes the way these dimensions are manifest is also remarkably similar. Hospital patients and customers of hotels, for example, expect many of the same features when using these two services. Besides expert medical care, patients in hospitals expect comfortable rooms, courteous staff, and food that tastes good—the same features that are salient to hotel customers. In these and other industries that share common customer expectations, managers may find it helpful to seek knowledge from existing research in the related service industry. Because hotels have used marketing and marketing research longer than hospitals have, insights about hotel guests' expectations can inform about patients' expectations. Hospital administrators at Albert Einstein Medical Center in Philadelphia, for example, asked a group of nine local hotel executives for advice in understanding and handling patients. Many improvements resulted, including better food, easier-to-read name tags, more prominent information desks, and radios in many rooms.[18]

"Relationship" Surveys   One category of surveys could appropriately be named *relationship surveys,* for they pose questions about all elements in the customer's relationship with the service (including service, product, and price). This comprehensive approach can help a company make a useful diagnosis of strengths and weaknesses. These surveys are also used to monitor and track service performance, usually being conducted annually with the initial survey providing a baseline for service performance. When used for this purpose, respondents must be chosen randomly to ensure that the surveys are statistically valid. Relationship surveys are also used to compare company performance with that of competitors, often using the best competitor's performance as a benchmark. When used for this purpose, the sponsor of the survey is often not identified and questions are asked about both the focal company and one or more competitors.

One type of relationship survey that is used to evaluate service is the *SERVQUAL Survey.* As we have emphasized throughout this text, customers evaluate a firm's service quality by comparing perceptions of service with their expectations of service. SERVQUAL, a multidimensional scale for measuring customer perceptions and evaluations, was created in the mid-1980s to capture customer assessments of service quality. The scale reflects the five dimensions of service quality, each dimension containing multiple items that capture the fundamental attributes of service. Exhibit 6-2 shows the items on the basic SERVQUAL scale, as well as the phrasing of the expectations and perceptions portions of the scale.

Trailer Calls or Posttransaction Surveys While the purpose of relationship surveys is to gauge the overall relationship with the customer, the purpose of transaction surveys is to capture information about one or all of the key service encounters with the customer. In this method, customers are asked a short list of questions immediately after a particular transaction (hence the name *trailer calls*) about their satisfaction with the transaction and contact personnel with whom they interacted. Because the surveys are administered continuously to a broad spectrum of customers, they are more effective than complaint solicitation (where the information comes only from dissatisfied customers).

At checkout, immediately after staying at Fairfield Inns, customers are asked to use a computer terminal to answer four or five questions about their stay in the hotel. This novel approach has obvious benefits over the ubiquitous comment cards left in rooms—the response rate is far higher because it engages customers and takes only a few minutes. Frequently these surveys are administered by telephone several days after a transaction such as installation of durable goods or claims adjustment in insurance. Because they are timed to occur close to service transactions, these surveys are useful in identifying sources of dissatisfaction and satisfaction. A strong benefit of this type of research is that it often appears to customers that the call is following up to assure that they are satisfied; consequently the call does double duty as a market research tool and as a customer service. This type of research is simple and fresh and provides management with continuous information about interactions with customers. Further, the research allows management to associate service quality performance with individual contact personnel so that high performance can be rewarded and low performance corrected. It also serves as an incentive for employees to provide better service because they understand how and when they are being evaluated. A comprehensive research approach using transaction-based surveys will be described in chapter 8.

Key Client Studies When the firm sells to businesses or to intermediate customers rather than to end-consumers, some clients are large and important enough to be studied individually and in depth. To General Electric Company's aerospace group, for example, key clients included the Army, Navy, Air Force, and several airframe and electronics companies. To fully understand these clients' needs, as well as the strengths and weaknesses of the aerospace group vis-á-vis competitors, the GE group interviewed 600 customers at all management levels of these key clients.[19] These in-depth research studies can also be appropriate for end-customers when key clients, who are larger or more important than others, can be identified. Law firms, for example, might focus on clients involved in major cases, banks might study their top depositors or borrowers, and airlines might research key corporate clients.

"Mystery" Shopping   In this form of research,[20] companies hire outside research organizations to send people into service establishments and experience the service as if they were customers. These "mystery" shoppers are trained in the criteria important to customers of the establishment and deliver objective assessments of the performance of service personnel. This type of research has benefits in that service personnel know they might be evaluated at any time and are therefore on their best service behavior. However, the research can be viewed as punitive and stressful, and a company needs to handle this potential drawback in its communication about the research.

Customer Panels   Customer panels are ongoing groups of customers assembled to provide attitudes and perceptions about a service over time. They offer a company regular and timely customer information, virtually a pulse on the market. Firms can use customer panels to represent large segments of end-customers. USAir, for example, instituted business-traveler panels that meet several times a year. Panelists are frequent travelers of both USAir and other airlines and provide insights and suggestions about airline service and facilities.

Lost Customer Research   This type of research involves deliberately seeking customers who have dropped the company's service to inquire about their reasons for leaving. Some lost customer research is similar to "exit interviews" with employees, in that it asks open-ended, in-depth questions to expose the reasons for defection and the particular events that led to dissatisfaction. It is also possible to use more standard surveys on lost customers. For example, a midwestern manufacturer used a mail survey to ask former customers about its performance during different stages of the customer–vendor relationship. The survey also sought specific reasons for customers' defections and asked customers to describe problems that triggered their decreases in purchases.[21]

One benefit of this type of research is that it identifies failure points and common problems in the service and can help establish an early-warning system for future defectors. Another benefit is that the research can be used to calculate the cost of lost customers, something that will be discussed more fully in chapter 9.

Future Expectations Research   Customer expectations are dynamic and can change very rapidly in markets that are highly competitive and volatile. As competition increases, as tastes change, and as consumers become more knowledgeable, companies must continue to update their information and strategies. One such "industry" is interactive video, representing the merger of computer, telecommunications, and cable television. The technologies available in this industry are revolutionary. In situations like these, companies want to understand not just current customer expectations but also future expectations—the service features desired in the future. This type of research is the newest and includes different types. First, *features research* involves environmental scanning and querying of customers about desirable features of possible services. *Lead user research* brings in customers who are opinion leaders/innovators and asks them what requirements are not currently being met by existing products or services. Another form of this research is the *synectics approach,* which defines lead users more broadly than in standard lead user research. For example, when Polaroid conducted a study on electronic imaging, it asked questions of art museum directors, designers, people from the medical field, and others who might potentially be interested in the technology and services possible with the technology. In these and other approaches, customers talk not about technology but about their own needs. The Delphi approach, a group consensus

EXHIBIT 6-2   SERVQUAL: A MULTIDIMENSIONAL SCALE TO CAPTURE CUSTOMER PERCEPTIONS AND EXPECTATIONS OF SERVICE QUALITY[22]

The SERVQUAL scale was first published in 1988[23] and has undergone numerous improvements and revisions since then. The scale currently contains 21 perception items that are distributed throughout the five service quality dimensions. The scale also contains expectation items. While many different formats of the SERVQUAL scale are now in use, we show here the basic 21 perception items, as well as a sampling of ways the expectation items have been posed. Depictions of the data from the SERVQUAL scale are shown later in this chapter in Figures 6-4 and 6-5.

PERCEPTIONS

Perceptions Statements in the Reliability Dimension

	Strongly Disagree						Strongly Agree
1. When XYZ Company promises to do something by a certain time, it does so.	1	2	3	4	5	6	7
2. When you have a problem, XYZ Company shows a sincere interest in solving it.	1	2	3	4	5	6	7
3. XYZ Company performs the service right the first time.	1	2	3	4	5	6	7
4. XYZ Company provides its services at the time it promises to do so.	1	2	3	4	5	6	7
5. XYZ Company keeps customers informed about when services will be performed.	1	2	3	4	5	6	7

Statements in the Responsiveness Dimension

1. Employees in XYZ Company give you prompt service.	1	2	3	4	5	6	7
2. Employees in XYZ Company are always willing to help you.	1	2	3	4	5	6	7
3. Employees in XYZ Company are never too busy to respond to your request.	1	2	3	4	5	6	7

Statements in the Assurance Dimension

1. The behavior of employees in XYZ Company instills confidence in you.	1	2	3	4	5	6	7

	Strongly Disagree						Strongly Agree
2. You feel safe in your transactions with XYZ Company.	1	2	3	4	5	6	7
3. Employees in XYZ Company are consistently courteous with you.	1	2	3	4	5	6	7
4. Employees in XYZ Company have the knowledge to answer your questions.	1	2	3	4	5	6	7

Statements in the Empathy Dimension

1. XYZ Company gives you individual attention.	1	2	3	4	5	6	7
2. XYZ Company has employees who give you individual attention.	1	2	3	4	5	6	7
3. XYZ Company has your best interests at heart.	1	2	3	4	5	6	7
4. Employees of XYZ Company understand your specific needs.	1	2	3	4	5	6	7

Statements in the Tangibles Dimension

1. XYZ Company has modern-looking equipment.	1	2	3	4	5	6	7
2. XYZ Company's physical facilities are visually appealing.	1	2	3	4	5	6	7
3. XYZ Company's employees appear neat.	1	2	3	4	5	6	7
4. Materials associated with the service (such as pamphlets or statements) are visually appealing at XYZ Company.	1	2	3	4	5	6	7
5. XYZ Company has convenient business hours.	1	2	3	4	5	6	7

EXPECTATIONS: Several Formats for Measuring Customer Expectations Using Versions of SERVQUAL

Matching Expectations Statements (paired with the previous perception statements)

	Strongly Disagree						Strongly Agree
When customers have a problem, excellent firms will show a sincere interest in solving it.	1	2	3	4	5	6	7

EXHIBIT 6-2 (CONTINUED)

Referent Expectations Formats

1. Considering a "world class" company to be a "7," how would you rate XYZ Company's performance on the following service features?

	Low						High
Sincere, interested employees	1	2	3	4	5	6	7
Service delivered right first time	1	2	3	4	5	6	7

2. Compared with the level of service you expect from an excellent company, how would you rate XYZ Company's performance on the following?

	Low						High
Sincere, interested employees	1	2	3	4	5	6	7
Service delivered right first time	1	2	3	4	5	6	7

Combined Expectations/Perceptions Statements

For each of the following statements, circle the number that indicates how XYZ Company's service compares with the level you expect:

	Lower than my desired service level			The same as my desired service level			Higher than my desired service level	
1. Prompt service	1	2	3	4	5	6	7	8	9
2. Courteous employees	1	2	3	4	5	6	7	8	9

Expectations Distinguishing between Desired Service and Adequate Service

For each of the following statements, circle the number that indicates how XYZ Company's performance compares with your *minimum service level* and with your *desired service level*.

	Compared with My *Minimum* Service Level XYZ's Service Performance Is:									Compared with My *Desired* Service Level XYZ's Service Performance Is:								
When it comes to . . .	Lower				Same				Higher	Lower				Same				Higher
1. Prompt service	1	2	3	4	5	6	7	8	9	1	2	3	4	5	6	7	8	9
2. Employees who are consistently courteous	1	2	3	4	5	6	7	8	9	1	2	3	4	5	6	7	8	9

technique, can be used to narrow down the choices and identify services that hold out the most promise to customers.

Summary and Example of a Multifaceted Service Research Program Federal Express, the first major service company to win the Malcolm Baldrige National Quality Award, has a strong and comprehensive program of marketing and customer satisfaction research.[24] Its program includes:

1 *Customer requirements and expectations,* gleaned from multiple qualitative and quantitative research studies, feedback from sales professionals, and feedback from customer service professionals.

2 *800 numbers for complaints,* which are systematically captured and dispatched to responsible parties. Trends are also tracked and analyzed.

3 *Customer satisfaction study,* with objectives of assessing satisfaction, identifying reasons for dissatisfaction, and monitoring satisfaction over time. This involves 2,400 telephone interviews per quarter measuring 17 domestic service attributes, 22 export service attributes, 8 drop-box attributes, and 8 service center attributes.

4 *Ten targeted satisfaction studies,* on specialized business functions. These are direct mail, self-administered surveys.

5 *Satisfaction monitoring,* at every point of interaction with the customer, some through transaction-based studies and others using operational measures driven by customer requirements.

6 *Comment card program,* monitoring satisfaction with counter service.

7 *Customer satisfaction studies in world markets,* focusing on understanding how service delivery must be adapted to global markets.

Stage 4: Collect and Tabulate the Data

We have described the types of research that are useful in an effective marketing research program for services. Most research studies yield information that can be assessed and analyzed in many different ways with the use of many different techniques. Therefore, the objectives of the research guide the type of analysis conducted as well as the specific choice of research method and questions asked.

The types of analysis used in qualitative research are different from those used in quantitative research. Qualitative research involves information that needs to be combined and organized in a meaningful manner. Rigor can and must be present in qualitative analysis, just as it is in quantitative research.

Many different types of quantitative analysis can be conducted for services research, some very basic and others highly sophisticated. Among the most basic calculations are means (averages) and standard deviations (which indicate variability) of expectation and perception scores, importance means and standard deviations, and cross tabulations that reveal statistically significant differences across categories of customers. More technical yet widely used forms of analysis are discussed in depth in marketing research textbooks.

The purpose of analysis is to put research findings in the appropriate format for answering research questions. In many cases this involves developing a *marketing information system* to store, analyze, and regularly report results of the data collected. Skill Dynamics, for example, measures student satisfaction at the end of each of the classes its instructors teach. The data from student satisfaction surveys go immediately to a central location where they are analyzed by computer and sent to instructors and class managers. Averages and standard deviations are calculated.

Stage 5: Analyze and Interpret the Findings

One of the biggest challenges facing a marketing researcher is converting a complex set of data to a form that can be read and understood quickly by executives, managers, and other employees who will make decisions from the research. Many of the people who use marketing research findings have not been trained in statistics and have neither the time nor the expertise to analyze computer printouts and other technical research information. The goal in this stage of the marketing research process is to communicate information clearly to the right people in a timely fashion. Among considerations are the following: Who gets this information? Why do they need it? How will they use it? When users feel confident that they understand the data, they are far more likely to apply it appropriately. When managers do not understand how to interpret the data, or when they lack confidence in the research, the investment of time, skill, and effort will be lost.

Exhibit 6-3 shows a sample management summary sent to each business unit in Skill Dynamics to report monthly levels of satisfaction and behavioral intentions of students. This management summary communicated information quickly and simply about the business unit's classes, and could be used by the organization for multiple purposes including compensation.

Figure 6-4 shows how a graphic can be useful in communicating information about service performance. In this figure, average SERVQUAL scores for the five service quality dimensions are illustrated. Remember that SERVQUAL scores are expressed as the difference between expectations and perceptions (P–E) and are most often negative numbers because customer perceptions typically fall short of customer expectations. For example, the only dimension in Figure 6-4 where customer perceptions exceeded expectations (as shown by a positive SERVQUAL score) is tangibles. The others are all negative, demonstrating the company's service shortfalls, particularly in the dimensions of reliability and responsiveness.

Reporting of research findings must be timely, and the timeliness is determined by the research objective. For example, feedback about individual courses taught at Skill Dynamics is most helpful when it occurs as quickly after the class as possible so that adjustments can be made before the course is taught again. On the other hand, new services research has a longer lead time and does not need to be collected and reported immediately, for these decisions are more deliberate.

Stage 6: Report the Findings

Presenting the research findings is the sixth stage in the marketing research process. In most cases, depicting the findings graphically is a powerful way to communicate re-

---

EXHIBIT 6-3   MONTHLY RESULTS REPORTED TO BUSINESS UNITS OF SKILL DYNAMICS*

Questions	Satisfaction			Questions	Satisfaction		
Overall Satisfaction	% Sat.	% Neutral	% Dissat.	Likely to	% High	% Neutral	% Low
How satisfied w/				Apply skills taught? 90		8	2
class?	87	10	3	Use class materials? 83		13	4
How satisfied w/				Recommend this	86	10	4
instructor?	94	5	1	class?			
Time well spent?	86	10	4	Take another class	91	8	1
				w/ us?			
				Consider us your	79	17	4
				first choice?			

*Actual percentages have been disguised in this example.

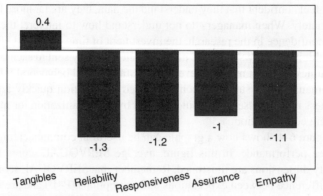

FIGURE 6-4   Mean SERVQUAL scores by service dimension.

search information. Here are a sample of graphic representations of the types of marketing research data we have discussed throughout this chapter.

Tracking of Performance, Gap Scores, and Competition[25]   A simple way of tracking performance is shown in Figure 6-5. Both expectations and perceptions are plotted and the gap between them shows the service quality shortfall. Competitor service performance is another frequently tracked service quality measurement. It allows managers to have a better grasp of service improvement priorities for their firm by comparing the firm's service strengths and weaknesses against those of key competitors.

Salience of Dimensions and Attributes   Figure 6-6 shows a way to present findings about the salience of service quality dimensions. The summary findings shown come from a research study conducted in four service industries[26] and are consistent with general findings of many different service quality studies: customers consider reliability the most important service dimension overall. The relative importance of the other service quality dimensions varies across industries, although tangibles typically is evaluated as less important overall than the other dimensions.

Zones of Tolerance Charts[27]   When companies collect data on the dual expectation levels described in chapter 4—desired service and adequate service—along with performance data, they can convey the information concisely on zones of tolerance charts. Figure 6-7 plots customer service quality perceptions relative to customers' zones of tolerance. Perceptions of company performance are indicated by the circles, and the zones of tolerance boxes are bounded on the top by the desired service score and on the bottom by the adequate service score. When the perception scores are within the boxes, as in Figure 6-7, the company is delivering service that is above customers' minimum level of expectations. When the perception scores are below the boxes, the company's service performance is lower than the minimum level, and customers are indeed dissatisfied with the company's service.

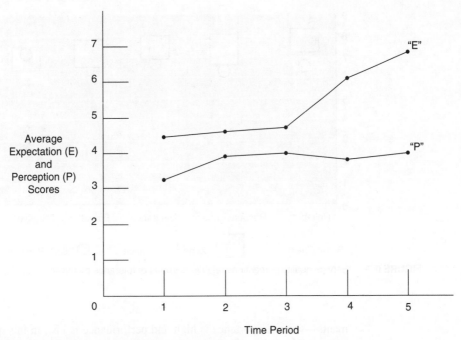

FIGURE 6-5   Tracking of customer expectations and perceptions.

Importance/Performance Matrices   One of the most useful forms of analysis in marketing research is the importance/performance matrix. This chart combines information about customer perceptions and importance ratings. An example is shown in Figure 6-8. Importance is represented on the vertical axis from high (top) to low (bottom). Performance is shown on the horizontal axis from low (left) to high (right). There are many variations of these matrices: some companies define the horizontal axis as the gap between expectations and perceptions, or as performance relative to competition. The shading on the chart indicates the area of highest leverage for service quality improve-

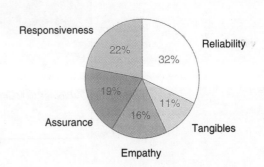

FIGURE 6-6   Relative importance of service dimensions when respondents allocate 100 points.

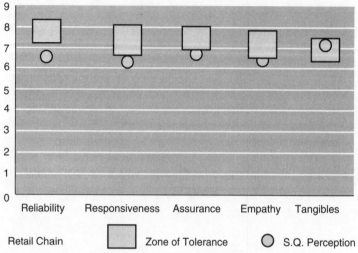

FIGURE 6-7   Service quality perceptions relative to zones of tolerance by dimensions.

ments—where importance is high and performance is low. In this quadrant are the attributes that most need to be improved. In the adjacent upper quadrant are attributes to be maintained, ones that a company performs well and that are very important to customers. The lower two quadrants contain attributes that are less important, some of which are performed well and others poorly. Neither of these quadrants merit as much attention in terms of service improvements as the upper quadrants because customers are not as concerned about the attributes that are plotted in them as they are the attributes in the upper quadrants.

FIGURE 6-8   Importance/performance matrix.

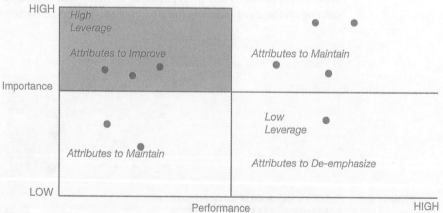

Customer Satisfaction Indices   A customer satisfaction index is a composite of the perceptual satisfaction or service quality measures collected in an organization. This type of presentation summarizes large amounts of company data and is useful in tracking service performance over time. A well-known and widely-used customer satisfaction index was developed by J. D. Power and Associates, a full-service marketing research company recognized for its customer satisfaction studies of cars and trucks. Among the service measurements tracked are (1) "after delivery quality," including such things as number of times serviced, number of times returned due to unsatisfactory service, delays at dealership; (2) service advisor promptness, understanding of the problem and overall importance; and (3) the overall experience, including fairness of fees, ease of obtaining an appointment, cleanliness of facility, explanation of charge, and loaner car availability.

With all of this different marketing research data collected, J. D. Power needed an efficient and simple way to communicate the findings to its customers, the automotive companies and their customers. It developed the CSI index, which provides an overall ranking as well as rankings within each of two key factors: technical factor and people factor, the two important components in overall satisfaction and ownership experience. J. D. Power summarizes the results of the data so that management can grasp the bottom line quickly. It offers an overall (CSI) index, a people factor index, and a technical factor index. Each index reflects the weighted average of the scores making up the variables within each factor. The overall average for all manufacturers is converted into an index score of 100. Scores over 100 show better-than-average performance, and those under 100 are below average. The indexing methods allow manufacturers to see where they stand relative to competition and where to concentrate their efforts to best stay ahead of competition.[28]

USE OF MARKETING RESEARCH INFORMATION

Conducting research about customer expectations is only the first part of understanding the customer, even if the research is appropriately designed and executed. A service firm must also use the research findings in a meaningful way—to drive change or improvement in the way service is delivered. The misuse—or worse yet, nonuse—of research data can lead to a large gap in understanding of customer expectations. When managers do not read research reports because they are too busy dealing with the day-to-day challenges of the business, companies fail to use the resources available to them. And when customers participate in marketing research studies but never see changes in the way the company does business, they feel frustrated and annoyed with the company. Understanding how to make the best use of research—to apply what has been learned to the business—is a key way to close the gap between customer expectations and management perceptions of customer expectations.

Managers must learn to turn research information and insights into action, to recognize that the purpose of research is to drive improvement and customer satisfaction. As one executive of a marketing research firm commented,

Rather than simply capturing data and measuring trends, companies need to get immediate, actionable feedback that they can use to change behaviors that are causing dissatisfaction and thus keep more customers in the long run. It isn't satisfying customers that makes the profit wheel spin. Bottom line, what makes a company's profit wheel spin is getting customers to buy from you again.[29]

The research plan should specify the mechanism by which customer data will be used. The research should be actionable: timely, specific, and credible. It can also have a mechanism that allows a company to respond to dissatisfied customers immediately. Consider the following examples of firms that have developed truly actionable research programs:

• Sky Alland, a customer satisfaction management firm from Laurel, Maryland, interviews customers of one of its clients, an automobile manufacturer, after they have experienced dealer service. If a dissatisfied customer is identified by the interviewer, a "Customer Alert" is faxed within two hours to the dealer contact to allow the dealer to respond immediately by calling the customer and responding to the complaint. Because the auto manufacturer has found that not all dealers follow up on the complaints, the research firm itself calls customers back to verify that action has been taken. If it hasn't, a "Critical Alert" is faxed immediately to the dealer principal and to the manufacturer. If a sufficient number of these are issued, the manufacturer will coach or counsel the dealer.[30]

• At First National Bank of Chicago, customer satisfaction telephone surveys are conducted every six weeks by employees from different parts of the bank (Cash Management, Systems Operations, Human Relations, Financial Administrations, Sales, Marketing). A decision to use internal interviewers, rather than a third-party research firm, was made because it allowed a true dialogue between the company and the customer. Customers believed that if they talked with bank personnel themselves, rather than market researchers, they might have a chance to get their issues resolved. Bank personnel were trained in conducting surveys: "This kind of training is to get [interviewers] focused on the future and the transformation of the system or how things are delivered rather than harping on the data." After the interview is over, the interviewer completes a follow-up activator whereby required action is taken, including solving the problem or calling the customer back.[31]

• At many hospitals, patients are asked to evaluate quality of food, cleanliness, and staff courtesy. But at St. Barnabas Medical Center in New Jersey, patient feedback is used for a very important purpose: evaluating and paying vendors. The hospital's contracts with vendors specify a certain level of patient satisfaction; if the services do not receive sufficiently high patient scores, payment to the vendor is limited. Vendors earn as much as 150 percent of a base amount (covering overhead and a pretax profit) or as little as 60 percent of base, depending on quarterly survey scores.[32]

• Goodyear Tire & Rubber Company conducts enough customer telephone interviews each week to obtain reliable information on their satisfaction with each of its 1,200 retail stores. When dissatisfied customers are identified, they are asked if they would like to be contacted by the store or district manager to address unresolved complaints or problems. The company also follows some buyers up to two years to track their experiences, attitudes, and satisfaction. These results are compiled and regularly reported back to managers in marketing, production, and product development.[33]

- Complaints can provide important information about failures or breakdowns in the service system if compiled, analyzed, and fed back to employees who can correct the problem. L. L. Bean, for example, tracks complaints by product, tallying and summarizing them daily, and places them in a problem file accessible to all employees. The approach allows top management to overview the key areas of customer dissatisfaction on a regular basis, and to make changes swiftly to meet customer expectations. Customer service representatives are also able to act knowledgeably and helpfully when providing service to customers.[34]

- U.S. Healthcare, a major health maintenance organization, surveys its members to see how they like their doctors and then ties physicians' incentive pay to the scores on the survey. Among the patient issues that affect the level of incentive pay are the following: ease of making appointments, waiting time in the office; personal concern shown to patients; and ease of obtaining follow-up test results.[35]

UPWARD COMMUNICATION

In some service firms, especially small and localized firms, owners or managers may be in constant contact with customers, thereby gaining firsthand knowledge of customer expectations and perceptions. But in large service organizations, managers do not always get the opportunity to experience firsthand what their customers want. This problem is illustrated in a comment from a bank's customer service representative:

> We have three floors. Our manager, when he first got here, sat on the second floor. Now he is on the third floor in his enclosed office. He told us he doesn't want to be with the public. He needs time for himself. What are his priorities? He doesn't know what's going on on the first floor. I've had lots of customers ask for the manager. I say, "I'm sorry, he's on a month's vacation."[36]

The larger a company is, the more difficult it will be for managers to interact directly with the customer and the least firsthand information they will have about customer expectations. Even when they read and digest research reports, managers can lose the reality of the customer if they never get the opportunity to experience the actual service. A theoretical view of how things are supposed to work cannot provide the richness of the service encounter. To truly understand customer needs, management benefits from hands-on knowledge of what really happens in stores, on customer service telephone lines, in service queues, and in face-to-face service encounters. If GAP 1 is to be closed, managers in large firms need some form of customer contact. Robert Crandall, CEO of American Airlines, illustrates the value in experiencing the service firsthand.

> ... commitment and dedication on the part of your people only happens when there's that same commitment and dedication on the part of the boss. Top management must confront the realities of the marketplace daily. I don't sit on some mountaintop, telling the American Airlines passenger service department how to deal with problems. I get out there and watch them work. I take regular trips on American—not because I have to go somewhere, but because I want to see for myself how we're doing.[37]

Objectives for Upward Communication

Table 6-3 shows the major research objectives for improving upward communication in an organization. They include gaining firsthand knowledge about customers, improving internal service quality, gaining firsthand knowledge of employees, and obtaining ideas for service improvement. These objectives can be met by two types of interactive activities in the organization, one designed to improve the type and effectiveness of communications from customers to management, and the other designed to improve communications between employees and management.

Research for Upward Communication

Executive Visits to Customers This approach is frequently used in business-to-business services marketing. In some visits, executives of the company make sales or service calls with customer contact personnel (e.g., salespeople). In other situations, executives of the selling company arrange meetings with executives at a similar level in client companies. When Lou Gerstner became CEO of IBM, one of his first actions was to arrange a meeting with 175 of the company's biggest customers for a discussion of how IBM can better meet their needs. The meeting was viewed as a signal that the new IBM would be more responsive and focused on the customer than it had become in the late 1980s and early 1990s.

Executive or Management Listening Approaches (Customers) The marketing director at Milliken called his experience working the swing shift "naive listening," and he described its benefits as follows:

TABLE 6-3 ELEMENTS IN AN EFFECTIVE PROGRAM OF UPWARD COMMUNICATION

Type of interaction or research	Research objective	Qual./Quan.	Cost of information		
			Money	Time	Frequency
Executive visits to customers	To gain firsthand knowledge about customers	Qual.	Moderate	Moderate	Continuous
Executive listenings	To gain firsthand knowledge about customers	Qual.	Low	Low	Continuous
Research on intermediate customers	To gain in-depth information on end-customers	Quan.	Moderate	Moderate	Annual
Employee internal satisfaction surveys	To improve internal service quality	Quan.	Moderate	Moderate	Annual
Employee visits or listenings	To gain firsthand knowledge about employees	Qual.	Moderate	Moderate	Continuous
Employee suggestions	To obtain ideas for service improvements	Qual.	Low	Low	Continuous

Getting close to the customer is a winner! . . . I worked the second shift (3:00 p.m. to midnight) and actually cleaned carpeting as well as hard-surface floors. I operated all the machinery they used daily, plus handled the same housekeeping problems. . . . Now I can put together my trade advertising as well as my entire merchandising program based directly upon the needs of my customers as I observed them. . . . I'm learning—from new-product introduction to maintenance of existing products—exactly what our health care customers require.[38]

As this example illustrates, direct interaction with customers adds clarity and depth to the manager's understanding of customer expectations and needs.

Managers can also spend time on the line, interacting with customers and experiencing service delivery. A formal program for encouraging informal interaction is often the best way to ensure that the contact takes place. First National Bank of Chicago's survey process involves having senior managers, among them the senior vice president and his department heads, trained and certified to conduct survey interviews. Benefits of the program in terms of opening management's eyes about customers are clear:

Because senior management's contact with customers tends to be at the highest level, they may assume that those customers are completely satisfied . . . until they make a survey call to the receivables manager or clerk and find out that it's a different story. The shock and reality of it gets [senior managers] to realize, "Maybe I'm not as connected with the customer as I thought I was."[39]

Another example of a formal program of executive listening is the "Listen to Customers" program at Universal Card. A wide range of managers in the company, from accounting to legal, visit customers twice a year. And 95 percent of the senior management team conducts service observations during which they monitor customer service calls for a minimum of two hours a month.[40]

Research on Intermediate Customers   Intermediate customers (such as contact employees, dealers, distributors, agents, brokers) are people the company serves who serve the end-customer. Researching the needs and expectations of these customers *in serving the end-customer* can be a useful and efficient way both to improve service to and obtain information about end-users. The interaction with intermediate customers provides opportunities for understanding the end-customer's expectations and problems. It can also help the company learn about and satisfy the service expectations of intermediate customers, a process critical in their providing quality service to end-customers.

Research on Internal Customers   Employees who perform services are themselves customers of internal services on which they depend heavily to do their jobs well. There is a strong and direct link between the quality of internal service that employees receive and the quality of service they provide to their own customers. For this reason it is important to conduct employee research that focuses on the service internal customers give and receive. In many companies this requires adapting existing employee opinion research to focus on service satisfaction. Employee research complements customer research when service quality is the issue being investigated. Customer research provides insight into what is occurring, whereas employee research provides insight into why. The two types of research play unique and equally important roles in improving service quality. Companies that focus service quality research exclusively on external customers are missing out on a rich and vital source of information.[41]

Metropolitan Life Insurance Company, New York, markets personal insurance to policyholders, group health and life coverage to corporations, and pension plans to both groups. The company developed a comprehensive program of measuring expectations of all its customers, including internal (employee) customers. According to the company, the importance of measuring service quality "applies equally across the board, not excluding internal customers. Maybe only 25 percent of our people are servicing an outside customer."[42] Using a customized version of SERVQUAL, Met Life regularly monitors expectations and perceptions of all their customers.

Executive or Management Listening Approaches (Employees)   Employees who actually perform the service have the best possible vantage point for observing the service and identifying impediments to its quality. Customer-contact personnel are in regular contact with customers and thereby come to understand a great deal about customer expectations and perceptions.[43] If the information they know can be passed on to top management, top managers' understanding of the customer may improve. In fact, it could be said that in many companies, top management's understanding of the customer depends largely on the extent and types of communication received from customer-contact personnel and from noncompany contact personnel (e.g., independent insurance agents, retailers) who represent the company and its services. When these channels of communication are closed, management may not get feedback about problems encountered in service delivery and about how customer expectations are changing.

Sam Walton, the late founder of Wal-Mart, the highly successful discount retailer, once remarked, "Our best ideas come from delivery and stock boys."[44] To stay in touch with the source of new ideas, he spent endless hours in stores working the floor, helping clerks, or approving personal checks, even showing up at the loading dock with a bag of doughnuts for a surprised crew of workers.[45] He was well known for having his plane drop him next to a wheat field where he would meet a Wal-Mart truck driver. Giving his pilot instructions to meet him at another landing strip 200 miles down the road, he would make the trip with the Wal-Mart driver, listening to what he had to say about the company.

Upward communication of this sort provides information to upper-level managers about activities and performances throughout the organization. Specific types of communication that may be relevant are formal (e.g., reports of problems and exceptions in service delivery) and informal (e.g., discussions between contact personnel and upper-level managers). Managers who stay close to their contact people benefit not only by keeping their employees happy but also by learning more about their customers.[46] These companies encourage, appreciate, and reward upward communication from contact people. Through this important channel, management learns about customer expectations from those employees in regular contact with customers and can thereby reduce the size of GAP 1.

Employee Suggestions Most companies have some form of employee suggestion program whereby contact personnel can communicate to management their ideas of improving work. Suggestion systems have come a long way from the traditional suggestion box. Effective suggestion systems are ones in which employees are empowered to see their suggestions through, where supervisors can implement proposals immediately, where employees participate for continuous improvement in their jobs, where supervisors respond quickly to ideas, and where coaching is provided in ways to handle suggestions. The National Association of Suggestion Systems (NASS) reports that U.S. companies receive fewer suggestions than their counterparts in Japan, and that the typical financial return for an idea is much higher than the return in Japan.[47] In today's companies, suggestions from employees are facilitated by self-directed work teams that encourage employees to identify problems and then work to develop solutions to those problems. At GE Mobile Communications, Inc., 16,000 ideas and solutions were submitted by company employees in a four-year period, resulting in $33 million of direct savings to the company.[48]

SUMMARY

This chapter identified several of the key problems that result in Provider GAP 1, the discrepancy between what customers expect and what management perceives that they expect. These problems include insufficient marketing research, inadequate use of marketing research findings, insufficient communication between management and customers, and insufficient upward communication from contact employees to managers. The chapter discussed strategies to address each of these problems in order to close the gap.

DISCUSSION QUESTIONS

1 Give five reasons research objectives must be established before marketing research is conducted.
2 Using the "Review of Basic Marketing Principles" shown in Exhibit 6-1, see whether you can recall the points made here from previous courses. If you do not, find a copy of a basic marketing textbook and review the material. Do you believe that the basic principles are appropriate for services marketing?
3 Why are both qualitative and quantitative research methods needed in a services marketing research program?
4 Why does the frequency of research differ across the research methods shown in Table 6-1?
5 Compare and contrast the types of research that help a company identify common failure points (see column 2 in Table 6-1). Which of the types do you think produces better information? Why?
6 In what situations does a service company need requirements research?
7 What reasons can you give for companies' lack of use of research information? How might you motivate managers to use the information to a greater extent? How might you motivate front-line workers to use the information?
8 Given a specific marketing research budget, what would be your recommendations for

the percentage to be spent on customer research versus upward communication (Exhibit 6-3)? Why?

9   What kinds of information could be gleaned from research on intermediate customers? What would intermediate customers know that service providers might not?

EXERCISES

1   Choose a local services organization to interview about marketing research. Find out what the firm's objectives are and the types of marketing research it currently uses. Using the information in this chapter, think about the effectiveness of its marketing research. What are the strengths? Weaknesses?

2   Choose one of the services you consume. If you were in charge of creating a survey for that service, what questions would you ask on the survey? Give several examples. What type of survey (relationship versus transaction based) would be most appropriate for the service? What recommendations would you give to management of the company about making such a survey actionable?

3   If you were the marketing director of your college or university, what types of research (see Table 6-1) would be essential for understanding of both external and internal customers? If you could choose only three types of research, which ones would you select? Why?

NOTES

1   "The Best B Schools," *Business Week,* October 24, 1994, pp. 62–67.
2   Ibid., p. 70.
3   Ibid.
4   Russell L. Ackoff, *Scientific Method,* (New York: Wiley, 1961), p. 71.
5   A. Parasuraman, Leonard L. Berry, and Valarie A. Zeithaml, "Guidelines for Conducting Service Quality Research," *Marketing Research: A Magazine of Management and Applications,* December 1990, pp. 34–44.
6   Courtland Bovée and John Thill, *Marketing* (New York: McGraw-Hill, 1992), p. 122.
7   Parasuraman, Berry, and Zeithaml, *"Guidelines."*
8   Ibid.
9   Leonard L. Berry, A. Parasuraman, and Valarie A. Zeithaml, "Ten Lessons for Improving Service Quality," *Marketing Science Institute* Report No. 93-104, May 1993.
10   Karl Albrecht and Ron Zemke, *Service America! Doing Business in the New Economy* (Homewood, Ill.: Dow Jones-Irwin, 1985).
11   "More Market Researchers Swear by PCs," *Wall Street Journal,* March 15, 1993.
12   Ibid.
13   Ibid.
14   "James Bond Hits the Supermarket: Stores Snoop on Shoppers' Habits to Boost Sales," *Wall Street Journal,* August 25, 1993, p. B1.
15   Ibid.
16   "Shoppers Virtually Stroll through Store Aisles to Examine Packages," *Marketing News,* June 7, 1993, p. 2.
17   Edith E. Lueke and Thomas W. Suther, III, "Market-Driven Quality: A Market Research and Product Requirements Methodology," *IBM Technical Report,* June 1991.

18 J. Carey, J. Buckley, and J. Smith, "Hospital Hospitality," *Newsweek,* February 11, 1985, p. 78.

19 As discussed in "Customer Perceptions of GE Aerospace," *Customer Focus.* General Electric Company publication, December 1986.

20 For examples, see Stephen J. Grove and Raymond P. Fiske, "Observational Data Collection Methods for Services Marketing: An Overview," *Journal of the Academy of Marketing Science* 20 (Summer, 1992): 117–214.

21 "Knowing What It Takes to Keep (or Lose) Your Best Customers," *Executive Report on Customer Satisfaction* 5 (October 30, 1992).

22 A. Parasuraman, Valarie A. Zeithaml, and Leonard L. Berry, "SERVQUAL: A Multiple-Item Scale for Measuring Consumer Perceptions of Service Quality," *Journal of Retailing* 64, 1 (Spring 1988).

23 Ibid.

24 "Multiple Measures Give FedEx Its 'Good' Data," *The Service Edge,* June 1991, p. 6.

25 Parasuraman, Berry, and Zeithaml, *Guidelines.*

26 Valarie A. Zeithaml, A. Parasuraman, and Leonard L. Berry, *Delivering Quality Service: Balancing Customer Perceptions and Expectations,* (New York: Free Press, 1990), p. 28.

27 A. Parasuraman, Valarie A. Zeithaml, and Leonard L. Berry, "Moving Forward in Service Quality Research," *Marketing Science Institute* Report No. 94-114, September 1994.

28 "Toyota Is Standout Once Again on J. D. Power's Quality Survey," *Wall Street Journal,* May 28, 1993, p. B1.

29 "Are You a Gatherer of Data—or a Driver of Improvement?" *Executive Report on Customer Satisfaction* 6, 14 (July 30, 1993): 2.

30 Ibid.

31 "First Chicago Continuously Monitors Satisfaction," *Executive Report on Customer Satisfaction* 6, 12 (June 30, 1993): 1–3.

32 "Pleasing Hospital Patients Can Pay Off," *Wall Street Journal,* May 13, 1993, p. B1.

33 Don Lee Bohl, ed., *"Close to the Customer," An American Management Association Research Report on Consumer Affairs* (New York: American Management Association, 1987).

34 Thomas J. Peters and Nancy Austin, *A Passion for Excellence* (New York: Random House, 1985).

35 "More Managed Health-Care Systems Use Incentive Pay to Reward 'Best' Doctors," *Wall Street Journal,* January 25, 1993, p. B1.

36 Leonard L. Berry, A. Parasuraman, and Valarie A. Zeithaml, "The Service-Quality Puzzle," *Business Horizons,* September–October 1988, pp. 35–43.

37 As quoted in speech by Richard C. Whiteley, "Creating Customer Focus," The Forum Corporation, Philadelphia, Pa.

38 Peters and Austin, *A Passion for Excellence,* p. 16.

39 "First Chicago Continuously Monitors Satisfaction," p. 3.

40 "Baldrige Winner Co-Convenes Quality Summit," *Executive Report on Customer Satisfaction,* October 30, 1992.

41 Parasuraman, Berry, and Zeithaml, *Guidelines.*

42 Kate Bertrand, "In Service, Perception Counts," *Business Marketing,* April 1989, p. 46.

43 Mary Jo Bitner, Bernard Booms, and Lois Mohr, "Critical Service Encounters: The Employee's Viewpoint," *Journal of Marketing,* October 1994, 58, 4, 95–106.

44 Stephen Koepp, "Make that Sale, Mr. Sam," *Time,* May 18, 1987.

45 Ibid.

46 Zeithaml, Parasuraman, and Berry, *Delivering Quality Service,* p. 64.

47 "Empowerment Is the Strength of Effective Suggestion Systems," *Total Quality Newsletter,* August 1991.

48 "Who Really Knows Best When It Comes to Improving Quality?," *Total Quality Newsletter,* August 1991.

7

BUILDING CUSTOMER RELATIONSHIPS THROUGH SEGMENTATION AND RETENTION STRATEGIES

The Issue: Customer churn

Rapid customer turnover and the effects of discontinued customer relationships are critical issues for many businesses today. The effects of growing competition, coupled with industry maturity and recessionary pressures, mean that organizations can't totally depend on new customers to take the place of lost customers.

Customer turnover, sometimes referred to as "customer churn," was the issue facing Browning-Ferris Industries, Inc., the number two trash hauler in the United States.[1] Although 86 percent of Browning-Ferris's customers remained loyal, 70,000 old customers were lost each year. What the loss of customers effectively meant was that the company had to bring in more than 70,000 new customers (103,000 in 1992) to continue its growth. As in many industries, this turnover was viewed as unavoidable for a long time. Now, however, stiffer competition means that growth can no longer be ensured through attraction of new customers alone—customer retention has become a priority for Browning-Ferris.

To begin addressing the rate of turnover, Browning-Ferris is using some of the research tools presented in chapter 6 to understand and build better relationships with its current customers. First, the company surveyed 30,000 current customers to design a satisfaction index that rates the performance of each of the company's two-hundred hauling districts. In addition, it has begun asking thousands of current customers to respond each month to questions about service. Through these efforts the company can begin to identify why some customers are dissatisfied and transfer their business to another garbage hauler.

Whereas customers frequently mention price issues when they switch service providers, usually there's something more to it. Asking them to describe their service experiences in detail helps to expose these underlying issues. By talking to its current customers and learning what can be done to improve service, Browning-Ferris is showing a commitment to customer retention and long-term relationship building. Instead of relying solely on new customers, their strategy now focuses on retention of customers as a cornerstone for future growth.

Sometimes companies fail to understand customers accurately because they fail to focus on customer relationships. They tend to fixate on acquiring new customers rather than viewing customers as assets that they need to retain. By concentrating on new customers, firms can easily fall into the traps of short-term promotions, price discounts, or catchy ads that bring customers in but are not enough to keep customers coming back. By adopting a relationship philosophy, on the other hand, companies begin to understand customers over time and in greater depth, and are better able to meet their changing needs and expectations.

Marketing strategies aimed at closing GAP 1 (Figure 7-1) by understanding market segments and building long-term relationships with customers are the subjects of this chapter. Unless markets are carefully segmented, customer expectations, needs, and requirements may be defined too broadly, satisfying no one. And when an organization focuses too much on new customer needs and requirements, it may lose current customers whose needs aren't being met.

Figure 7-2 shows the factors contributing to GAP 1 that will be discussed in this chapter. The figure suggests that there may be a gap between customer expectations and company perceptions of expectations when the organization focuses solely on transactions rather than relationships, when it is preoccupied with new customers rather than current customers, and when there is a lack of effective market segmentation.

The objectives of the chapter are to:

1 Explain relationship marketing and the foundations of a retention marketing strategy

FIGURE 7-1   Provider GAP 1.

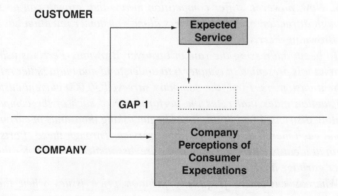

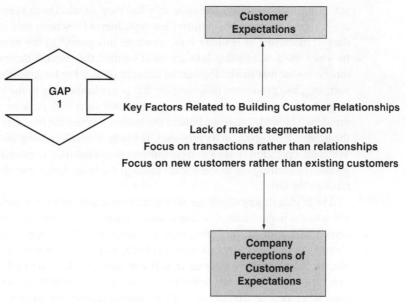

FIGURE 7-2   Key factors leading to provider GAP 1.

2 Show the benefits of customer retention to both the consumer and the organization

3 Discuss how to segment and why market segmentation must be the foundation for effective relationship strategies

4 Present retention strategies used by organizations to build relationships with their customers

RELATIONSHIP MARKETING

> There has been a shift from a transactions to a relationship focus [in marketing]. Customers become partners and the firm must make long-term commitments to maintaining those relationships with quality, service and innovation.[2]

Relationship marketing (or relationship management) is a philosophy of doing business, a strategic orientation, that focuses on *keeping and improving* current customers, rather than on acquiring new customers. This philosophy assumes that consumers prefer to have an ongoing relationship with one organization than to switch continually among providers in their search for value. Building on this assumption and the fact that it is usually much cheaper to keep a current customer than to attract a new one, successful marketers are working on effective strategies for retaining customers. Our opening example showed how a successful service company in the garbage collection industry was shifting its focus from one of relying on *new* customers for growth to one of relying on customer retention.

It has been suggested that firms frequently focus on attracting customers (the "first act"), but then pay little attention to what they should do to keep them (the "second act").[3] Ideas expressed in an interview with James L. Schorr, then executive vice president of marketing at Holiday Inns, illustrate this point.[4] In the interview he stated that he was famous at Holiday Inns for what's called the "bucket theory of marketing." By this he meant that marketing can be thought of as a big bucket: it's what the sales, advertising, and promotion programs do that pours business in to the top of the bucket. As long as these programs are effective, the bucket stays full. However, "There's only one problem," he said, "there's a hole in the bucket." When the business is running well and the hotel is delivering on its promises, the hole is small and few customers are leaving. When the operation is weak and customers are not satisfied with what they get, however, people start falling out of the bucket through the holes faster than they can be poured in through the top.

The bucket theory illustrates why a relationship strategy that focuses on plugging the holes in the bucket makes so much sense. Historically, marketers have been more concerned with acquisition of customers, so a shift to a relationship strategy often represents changes in mind set, organizational culture, and employee reward systems. For example, the sales incentive systems in many organizations are set up to reward bringing in new customers. There are fewer (or no) rewards for retaining current accounts. Thus, even when people see the logic of customer retention, the existing organizational systems may not support its implementation.

Goals of Relationship Marketing

The primary goal of relationship marketing is to *build and maintain a base of committed customers who are profitable for the organization.* To achieve this goal, the firm will focus on the *attraction, retention, and enhancement of customer relationships.*[5] First, the firm will seek to attract customers who are likely to become long-term relationship customers. Through market segmentation (discussed in detail later in the chapter), the company can come to understand the best target markets for building lasting customer relationships. As the number of these relationships grows, the loyal customers themselves will frequently help to attract (through word of mouth) new customers with similar relationship potential.

Once they are attracted to begin a relationship with the company, customers will be more likely to stay in the relationship when they are consistently provided with quality products and services and good value over time. They are less likely to be pulled away by competitors if they feel the company understands their changing needs and seems willing to invest in the relationship by constantly improving and evolving its product and service mix. The United States Automobile Association (USAA), one of the most profitable insurance companies in the United States, has this kind of relationship with its members.[6] USAA's business is focused on a very targeted segment—U.S. military officers and their families. It supplies them with insurance and financial services to meet their lifelong needs. According to their former president and CEO, Robert F. McDermott, the goal of the company with respect to its customers is to "think about the events in the life of a career officer and then work out ways of helping him get through them."[7] As an example of how focused the company is on adjusting its services to fit the life event needs of its customers, during the Gulf War the company encouraged members sent to the Gulf to *downgrade* their automobile insurance to save themselves money. For instance, if their cars were just going to sit in garages while they were gone, they wouldn't need liability coverage. And when two-car families had one spouse in the Gulf, USAA gave them the rates for a single person with two cars. Actions such as these clearly indicate USAA's commitment to its current members.

Finally, the goal of customer enhancement suggests that loyal customers can be even better customers if they buy more products and services from the company over time. Loyal customers not only provide a solid *base* for the organization, they may represent growth potential. This is certainly true for USAA, whose officer members' needs for insurance increase over their lifetimes as well as the lifetimes of their children. Other examples abound. A bank checking account customer becomes a better customer when she sets up a savings account, takes out a loan, and/or uses the financial advising services of the bank. And a corporate account becomes a better customer when it chooses to do 75 percent of its business with a particular supplier rather than splitting the business equally among three suppliers. In recent years, in fact, many companies have aspired to be the "exclusive supplier" of a particular product or service for their customers. Over time these enhanced relationships can increase market share and profits for the organization.

Benefits of Customer Retention

Both parties in the customer/firm relationship can benefit from customer retention. That is, it is not only in the best interest of the *organization* to build and maintain a loyal customer base, but *customers* themselves also benefit from long-term associations.

Benefits for Customers   Assuming they have a choice, customers will remain loyal to a firm when they receive greater *value* relative to what they expect from competing firms. Remember that perceived value is the consumer's overall assessment of the utility of a product based on perceptions of what is received and what is given. Value represents a trade-off for the consumer between the "give" and the "get" components. Consumers are more likely to stay in a relationship when the gets (quality, satisfaction, specific benefits) exceed the gives (monetary and nonmonetary costs). When firms can consistently deliver value from the customer's point of view, clearly the customer benefits and has an incentive to stay in the relationship.

In addition to the specific inherent benefits of receiving service value, customers also benefit from long-term relationships because such associations contribute to a sense of well-being and quality of life. Building a long-term relationship with a service provider can reduce consumer stress as initial problems, if any, are solved; special needs are accommodated; and the consumer learns what to expect. This is particularly true for complex services (e.g., legal, medical, education), for services where there is high ego involvement (e.g., hair styling, health club, weight-loss program), and for services that require large dollar investments (e.g., corporate banking, insurance, architecture). After a time the consumer begins to trust the provider and to count on a consistent level of quality service.

Human nature is such that most of us would prefer not to change service providers, particularly when we have a considerable investment in the relationship. If the service provider knows us, knows our preferences, and has tailored services to suit our needs over time, then changing providers would mean educating a new provider on all of these factors. The costs of switching are frequently high in terms of both dollar costs of transferring business and the psychological and time-related costs. In fact, one of the stressful and unsettling aspects of relocating to a new geographic area is the need to establish new relationships with service providers such as banks, schools, retailers, doctors, and hairdressers.

Most consumers (whether individuals or businesses) have many competing demands for their time and money and are continually searching for ways to balance and simplify decision-making to improve the quality of their lives. When they can maintain a relationship with a service provider, they free up time for other concerns and priorities. An excellent example is the case of dual-career families, for whom the decision about who should care for their children during the workday is one of the most important decisions they make. Once they have identified and established a satisfying relationship with a good caregiver (whether it be an individual, a day-care center, or a preschool) family stress is reduced and the quality of family life is improved. Should something happen that requires a change in caregivers, or should the relationship quality deteriorate for any reason, family stress levels immediately increase. Thus, a stable relationship with a good child-care provider is directly reflected in quality of life. Frequently families are willing to pay premium prices to maintain stable, predictable, high-quality care for their children.

In some long-term customer/firm relationships a service provider may actually become part of the consumer's social support system.[8] For example, hairdressers often serve as personal confidantes. Less common examples include proprietors of local retail stores who become central figures in neighborhood networks; the health club or restaurant manager who knows her customers personally; the private school principal who knows an entire family and its special needs; or the river guide who befriends patrons on a long rafting trip.[9] These types of personal relationships can develop for business-to-business customers as well as for end-consumers of services. The social support benefits resulting from these relationships are important to the consumer's quality of life (personal and/or work life) above and beyond the technical benefits of the service provided.

Benefits for the Organizations   The benefits to an organization of maintaining and developing a loyal customer base are numerous. They can be linked directly to the firm's bottom line.

Increasing Purchases   Results of studies reported by Frederick Reichheld and W. Earl Sasser show that across industries customers tend to spend more each year with a particular relationship partner than they did in the preceding period.[10] Figure 7-3 graphically illustrates this trend for a variety of businesses. As consumers get to know a firm and are satisfied with the quality of its services relative to that of its competitors, they will tend to give more of their business to the firm. And as customers mature (in terms of age, life cycle, growth of business), they frequently require more of a particular service.

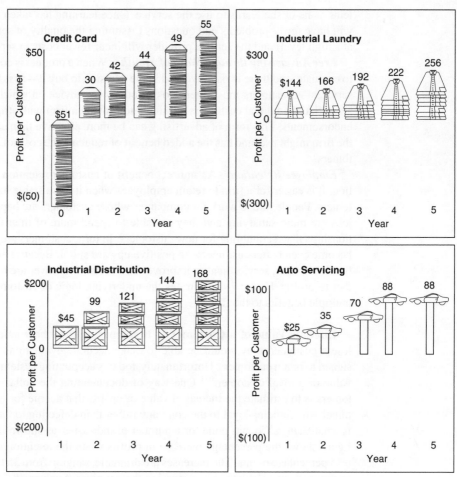

FIGURE 7-3   Profit generated by a customer over time.

Source: Reprinted by permission of *Harvard Business Review.* An exhibit from "Zero Defection: Quality Comes to Services," by Frederick F. Reichheld and W. Earl Sasser, Jr., September–October 1990. Copyright © by the President and Fellows of Harvard College; all rights reserved.

Lower Costs   There are many start-up costs associated with attracting new customers. They include advertising and other pron otion costs, operating costs of setting up accounts and systems, and time costs of getting to know the customer. Sometimes these initial costs can outweigh the revenue expected from the new customer in the short term. A prime example occurs in the insurance industry. Typically the insurer doesn't recover its up-front selling costs until the third of fourth year of the relationship. Thus, from a profit point of view there would seem to be great incentive to keep new customers once the initial investment has been made.

Even ongoing relationship maintenance costs are likely to drop over time. For example, early in a relationship a customer is likely to have questions and to encounter problems as he or she learns to use the service. Once learning has taken place the customer will have fewer problems and questions (assuming the quality of service is maintained at a high level) and the service provider will incur fewer costs in serving the customer.

Free Advertising through Word of Mouth   When a product is complex and difficult to evaluate, and there is risk involved in the decision to buy it—as is the case with many services—consumers most often look to others for advice on which providers to consider. Satisfied, loyal customers are likely to provide a firm with strong word-of-mouth endorsements. This form of advertising can be more effective than any paid advertising the firm might use, and has the added benefit of reducing the costs of attracting new customers.

Employee Retention   An indirect benefit of customer retention is employee retention. It is easier for a firm to retain employees when it has a stable base of satisfied customers. People like to work for companies whose customers are happy and loyal. Their jobs are more satisfying and they are able to spend more of their time fostering relationships than scrambling for new customers. In turn, customers are more satisfied and become even better customers—a positive upward spiral. Because employees stay with the firm longer, service quality improves and costs of turnover are reduced, adding further to profits. Figure 7-4 illustrates the underlying logic of customer retention and its multiple benefits to the firm.

Lifetime Value of a Customer   "If companies knew how much it really costs to lose a customer, they would be able to make accurate evaluations of investments designed to retain customers. Unfortunately, today's accounting systems do not capture the value of a loyal customer."[11] One way of documenting the dollar value of loyal customers is to estimate the increased value or profits that accrue for each additional customer who remains loyal to the company rather than defecting to the competition. This is what Bain & Co. has done for a number of industries, as shown in Figure 7-5.[12] The figure shows the percentage increase in profits when the retention or loyalty rate rises by 5 percentage points. The increases are dramatic, ranging from 35 to 95 percent. These increases were calculated by comparing the net present values of the profit streams for the average customer life at current retention rates with the net present values of the profit streams for the average customer life at 5-percent higher retention rates.

A somewhat less complex yet equally convincing approach to understanding the life-

FIGURE 7-4   Underlying logic of customer retention benefits to the organization.

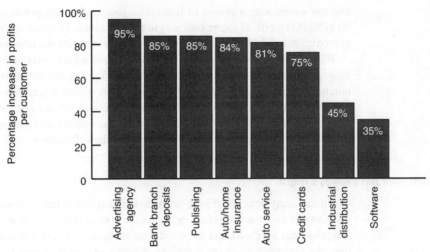

FIGURE 7-5   Profit impact of 5% increase in retention rate.

> *Source:* Reprinted with permission of the American Marketing Association. From Frederick E. Reich-held, "Loyalty and the Renaissance of Marketing," *Marketing Management* (1994):15.

time value of a customer is simply to multiply out the customer's average dollar purchases over the average lifetime of the customer in a particular industry. The numbers can soon become very large. Tom Peters used this approach to calculate the lifetime value of his small firm as a customer of Federal Express,[13] as follows:

Tom Peters estimated that his 20-person office had approximately $1500 per month in business with Federal Express. Assuming a 10-year average lifetime for a customer in the express mail industry, the value of his firm to Federal Express becomes:

$$\$1500/\text{month} \times 12 \text{ months/year} \times 10 \text{ years} = \$180,000$$

Going even further, he estimated that in this industry a happy customer will create *at least* one new customer via word of mouth:

$$\$180,000 \times 2 \text{ new customers} = \$360,000$$

Thus the value of his company's business for Federal Express was about $360,000.

Peters also estimated that the average Federal Express delivery person stops at 40 businesses the size of his each day:

$$\$360,000/\text{company} \times 40 \text{ companies} = \$14,000,000$$

Thus the average employee at Federal Express is managing a $14,000,000 portfolio of lifetime business for the company.

Similarly, Stew Leonard, the very successful Connecticut grocer, has calculated the lifetime value of one of his store patrons at $50,000.[14] He arrived at this figure by multiplying an average $100 per week grocery bill by 50 weeks per year times an estimated 10-year life of a loyal customer. These relatively simple calculations can be used to assess at least preliminarily the lifetime value of customers in a variety of industries.[15] The average waiter with a station of five tables in a moderately priced restaurant is waiting on $750,000 worth of future business in a given night. The average nurse is dealing with approximately $2,000,000 worth of lifetime business for the hospital.

With more sophisticated systems to document actual costs and profit streams over time, a firm can be more scientific about documenting the dollar value and costs of retaining customers. A more complex calculation would attempt to estimate the dollar value of *all* the benefits associated with a loyal customer, not just the long-term revenue stream. The value of word-of-mouth advertising, employee retention, and declining account maintenance costs would also enter into the calculation.

The Customer Isn't Always Right

Given the many benefits of long-term customer relationships, it would seem that a company would not want to refuse or terminate a relationship with any customer. The assumption that all customers are good customers is also very compatible with the belief that "the customer is always right," an almost sacrosanct tenet of business in the 1990s. Yet any service worker can tell you that this statement isn't *always* true, and in some cases it may be preferable for the firm and the customer to not continue their relationship. This section presents a view of customer relationships that suggests all relationships may not be beneficial, and that every customer is not right all of the time.

The Wrong Segment   A company cannot target its services to all customers; some segments will be more appropriate than others. It would not be beneficial to either the company or the customer for a company to establish a relationship with a customer whose needs the company cannot meet. For example, a school offering a lock-step, daytime MBA program would not encourage full-time working people to apply for its program, nor would a law firm specializing in government issues establish a relationship with individuals seeking advice on trusts and estates. These examples seem obvious. Yet firms frequently do give in to the temptation to make a sale by agreeing to serve a customer who would be better served by someone else.

Similarly, it would not be wise to forge relationships simultaneously with incompatible market segments. In many service businesses (e.g., restaurants, hotels, tour package operators, entertainment, education), customers experience the service together and can influence each other's perceptions about value received. Thus, to maximize service to core segments an organization may choose to turn away marginally profitable segments that would be incompatible. For example, a conference hotel may find that mixing executives in town for a serious educational program with students in town for a regional track meet may not be wise. If the executive group is a key long-term customer, the hotel may choose to pass up the sports group in the interest of retaining the executives. The importance of compatible segments is discussed further in the next major section of this chapter.

Not Profitable in the Long Term   In the absence of ethical or legal mandates, organizations will prefer *not* to have long-term relationships with unprofitable customers. Some segments of customers will not be profitable for the company even if their needs *can* be met by the services offered. This may be the case when there are not enough customers in the segment to make it profitable to develop a marketing approach, when the segment cannot afford to pay the cost of the service, or when the projected revenue flows from the segment would not cover the costs incurred to originate and maintain the business. For example, a small rural community in Illinois may desire airline service to Chicago, but the fixed costs of providing the service would not be covered by the limited number of travelers desiring the service. If the airline were to charge enough to cover the costs, people could not afford the air fare. To illustrate further, in the banking industry it has been estimated that 40 to 70 percent of customers served in a typical bank are not profitable in the sense that the costs of serving these customers exceed the revenues generated.[16]

At the individual customer level, it may not be profitable for a firm to engage in a relationship with a particular customer who has bad credit or who is a poor risk for some other reason. Retailers, banks, mortgage companies, and credit-card companies routinely refuse to do business with individuals whose credit histories are unreliable. While the short-term sale may be beneficial, the long-term risk of nonpayment makes the relationship unwise from the company's point of view. Similarly, some car rental companies have begun to check into the driving records of customers and are rejecting bad-risk drivers.[17] This practice, while controversial, is logical from the car rental companies' point of view since they can cut back on insurance costs and accident claims (thus reducing rental costs for *good* drivers) by not doing business with accident-prone drivers. Consumer activists, however, cite privacy issues and inconvenience to unsuspecting travelers as arguments against the practice.

Beyond the monetary costs associated with serving the wrong customers, there can be substantial time investments in some customers that, if actually computed, would make them unprofitable for the organization. Everyone has had the experience of waiting in a bank, a retail store, or even in an education setting while a particularly demanding customer seems to use more than his share of the service provider's time. The dollar value of the time spent with a specific customer is typically not computed or calculated into the price of the service.

In a business-to-business relationship, the variability in time commitment to customers is even more apparent. Some customers may use considerable resources of the supplier organization through inordinate numbers of phone calls, excessive requests for information, and other time-consuming activities. In the legal profession, clients are billed for every hour of the firm's time that they use in this way, since time is essentially the only resource the firm has. Yet in other service businesses all clients essentially pay the same regardless of the time demands they place on the organization. For example, meetings and conventions are very big business for hotels. Yet hotel convention staff know that some companies are wonderful to work with—they are efficient and place reasonable demands on the organization. Others are not organized and constantly change their plans and requirements. Both types of organizations may bring in the same revenue to the hotel, but the costs are clearly unequal.

It should be noted that the best customers are not just the ones that generate the most profit. Especially in business-to-business settings, those customers that inspire the best ideas and innovations are also good relationship customers even if they don't necessarily generate the highest profits.[18] Customers who are willing to be involved in new service development or who are on the cutting edges of their own industries can help the organization develop and maintain quality services for the entire marketplace. These customers benefit the organization beyond the profits they generate.

Difficult Customers   Managers have repeated the phrase "the customer is always right" so often that it should be accepted by every employee in every service organization. Why isn't it? Perhaps because it simply isn't true. The customer isn't always right. No matter how frequently it is said, it doesn't become reality, and service employees know it.[19]

Employees recognize that beyond the monetary and time loss that can be traced to some customers, there are customers who are simply difficult to work with for a variety of reasons. Because of the stress they place on the organization and its employees, some organizations may choose to avoid relationships with these customers.

As discussed in chapter 5 of this book, when employees of hotels, restaurants, and airlines were interviewed about critical service encounters that had caused customers to leave their firms dissatisfied, they reported a whole category of incidents that resulted from the customer's *own* behavior.[20] Customer behaviors such as verbal/physical abuse of employees, refusal to follow policies or laws, drunkenness, and "pigheadedness" were found to result in dissatisfaction for the customer. In other words, from the employees' perspectives, "problem customers" frequently cause their own dissatisfaction.

Although often these difficult customers will be accommodated and employees can be trained to recognize and deal with them appropriately, at times the best choice may be to not maintain the relationship at all—especially at the business-to-business level where long-term costs to the firm can be substantial. Take for example the view of some of Madison Avenue's major ad agencies. "Some ad agencies say some accounts are so difficult to work with that they simply cannot—or will not—service them."[21] Difficult clients paralyze the ad agency for a variety of reasons. Some ask that a particular ad campaign work for all of their diverse constituencies at the same time, which in some cases may be next to impossible. Others require so much up-front work and ad testing before selecting the agency that the work is essentially done, and for free by those agencies not selected. Other clients are stingy, require *dozens* of storyboards before settling on a concept, or require a lot of direct, frequently disruptive, involvement in the production process. As a result agencies have become more wary of chasing every client that comes along. "As in a marriage, all agencies and all clients don't work well together."[22]

Thus, while in general firms will seek to maintain strong relationships with customers because of the benefits discussed, companies will want to acknowledge that *all* customer segments and all individual customers are not necessarily good long-term relationship customers. Knowing who the best relationship customers are requires careful market segmentation.

THE FOUNDATION FOR RELATIONSHIPS: MARKET SEGMENTATION

The foundation of an effective customer relationship strategy is market segmentation—learning and defining *who* the organization wants to have relationships with. In earlier chapters we discussed consumers of services and described their behavior, expectations, and perceptions. If we were to aggregate all the behavior, expectation, and perception information for all the customers in a particular market, we would probably be overwhelmed with the variations across customers. At one extreme, service firms—historically those with a relatively small number of customers, each of whom is vitally important—treat customers as individuals and develop individual marketing plans for each customer. For example, a law firm, an advertising agency, or even a large manufacturer like the Boeing Airplane Company will develop service offerings customized specifically and individually for their large corporate clients.

At the other extreme, some service firms offer one service to all potential customers as if their expectations, needs, and preferences were homogeneous. Providers of gas or electricity, for example, often view the needs of customers as varying only in terms of quantity purchased; for this reason their marketing approach is standardized. Between these two extremes are options that most service marketers choose—offering different services to different *groups* of customers. To do this effectively, companies need market segmentation and targeting.

Market segmentation is the process of aggregating customers with similar wants, needs, preferences, or buying behavior. *Market targeting* involves evaluating the attractiveness of the segments and selecting ones the firm will serve. In other words, segmentation is the analysis conducted about customers and targeting is the managerial decision about whom to serve. Both of these are required for effective *market positioning,* which involves establishing the competitive position for the service in the mind of the customer and creating or adapting the service mix to fit the position.

Process for Market Segmentation and Targeting in Services

Many aspects of segmentation and targeting for services are the same as those for manufactured goods. For that reason we include Exhibit 7-1 as a review of basic marketing principles for segmentation and targeting.[23] There are differences, however. The most powerful difference involves the need for compatibility in market segments. Because other customers are typically present when a service is delivered, service providers must recognize the need to choose compatible segments or to ensure that incompatible segments are not receiving service at the same time. A second difference between goods and services is that service providers have a far greater ability to customize service offerings than manufacturing firms have. Consequently a services marketer can choose a broader set of segments or subsegments to serve than can many manufacturing firms, particularly if they can keep these segments separate from or compatible with each other. We describe these differences and other aspects of market segmentation and targeting for services in the following sections. Figure 7-6 illustrates the steps involved in segmenting and targeting services.

Step 1: Identify Bases for Segmenting the Market Market segments are formed by grouping customers who share common characteristics that are in some way meaningful to the design, delivery, promotion, or pricing of the service. Common segmentation bases for consumer markets are shown in Exhibit 7-1, including demographic seg-

EXHIBIT 7-1   REVIEW OF BASIC MARKETING PRINCIPLES: MARKET SEGMENTATION AND MARKET TARGETING

Bases for Market Segmentation

Demographic Segmentation: dividing the market to form groups based on variables such as age, sex, family size, income, occupation, or religion

Geographic Segmentation: dividing the market to form different geographic units such as nations, counties, or states

Psychographic Segmentation: dividing buyers to form groups based on social class, life style, or personality characteristics

Behavioral Segmentation: dividing buyers to form groups based on knowledge, attitude, uses, or responses to a service

Requirements for Effective Segmentation

Measurability: The degree to which the size and purchasing power of the segments can be measured

Accessibility: The degree to which the segments can be reached and served

Substantiality: The degree to which the segments are large or profitable enough

Actionability: The degree to which effective programs can be designed for attracting and servicing of the segments

Criteria for Evaluating Market Segments for Market Targeting

Segment Size and Growth: includes information on current dollar sales, projected growth rates, and expected profit margins

Segment Structural Attractiveness: includes current and potential competitors, substitute products and services, relative power of buyers, and relative power of suppliers

Company Objectives and Resources: involves whether the segment fits the company's objectives

---

mentation, geographic segmentation, psychographic segmentation, and behavioral segmentation. Segments may be identified on the basis of *one* of these characteristics or a combination. For instance, an urban YMCA may provide services for demographic segments determined by age: preschool and gymnastics for those under 6; basketball for boys and girls ages 5 to 16; and weight training and fitness classes for adults. Within these demographic segments there may be more finely defined services based on lifestyle or usage, for example, fitness classes offered at 5 a.m. and 5:30 p.m. for adults who work from 8 a.m. to 5 p.m. Two general patterns have characterized the selection of segmentation bases: *a priori segmentation,* where the marketing manager decides on the appropriate basis for segmentation in advance of doing any research on a market, and *post hoc segmentation,* where individuals are grouped into segments on the basis of research findings.[24]

Demographic Segmentation   Often, demographic variables (age, gender, income, ethnicity, occupation, religion) are the easiest to identify, and thus they form the underlying basis of the segmentation strategy. For example, because of the tremendous population growth among Hispanics in the United States, many services are focused on this demographic segment of the population. Since 1990 the number of Hispanic radio stations in the United States has grown 21 percent, and the number of newspapers targeted at Hispanics is expanding rapidly as well.[25] In this case a service concept has been developed to appeal to a segment based on ethnicity. School-based health insurance for kids who have no insurance through their parents' health plans or Medicaid is another service targeted toward a demographic segment, on the basis of age characteristics and income as well.[26]

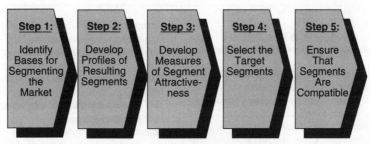

FIGURE 7-6   Steps in market segmentation and targeting for services.

In business-to-business markets, characteristics of the firm itself (such as size, industry, or financial situation) are used to segment markets. An architectural firm, for example, may specialize in new design and construction for the restaurant industry. The firm may further segment the restaurant market by customer size, developing a specific marketing strategy for large restaurant chains and another strategy for small, independent restaurants.

Geographic Segmentation   In other cases, geographic variables (nations, counties, states, regions) form the base for dividing the marketplace or identifying potential unmet needs. For instance, faced with mounting competitive and cost-cutting pressures in the United States, the need for health care services in Mexico, and the potential of the Mexican economy, many U.S. hospitals are expanding their services to Mexico[27] (see Box 7-1). Here the fundamental segmentation basis is a nation—Mexico.

Psychographic Segmentation   Many times it is not a particular demographic or geographic variable that defines the market segment, but rather a shared sense of values, a common life-style, or common personality characteristic among consumers in the segment. A service based on psychographic segmentation will focus on such factors in the design and delivery of the service. For example, the big three weight-loss programs in the United States (Weight Watchers, Nutri/System, Jenny Craig) are positioning themselves to attract market segments concerned not only with weight loss but also with staying healthy—in other words, the focus is on weight *management* rather than solely on weight *loss.* Staying healthy and being concerned about weight management are common values shared by customers in this example.

Behavioral Segmentation   At other times a segmentation strategy may be formed around behavioral characteristics of consumers such as their knowledge, attitudes, or usage patterns. Marriott International has segmented the market for hotel services primarily on usage. The corporation has four lodging segments and products: Marriott Hotels, Resorts and Suites; Courtyard by Marriott; Residence Inn; and Fairfield Inn. Each type of hotel is designed to fit a different usage segment, from full-service convention centers in the Marriott Hotels, Resorts and Suites group to the short-stay, economy segment at the Fairfield Inn. The Residence Inn properties are designed to serve those who need an extended-stay hotel (e.g., a week to 10 days or more) (see Box 7-2).

In business-to-business marketing, the applications situations of the organization form the basis for segmentation. Such applications situations as technology needs, product usage, or service requirements are examples. To illustrate, an institutional food ser-

---

BOX 7-1
REACHING OUT: Services Being Offered by U.S. Hospitals and Medical Groups to Attract Mexican Business

- **Scripps Memorial Hospitals, San Diego** Consulting on development of 80-bed hospital in Aguascalientes state. Training Mexican nurses and medical technicians. Seminars for Mexican physicians.
- **University Medical Center, Tucson** Continuing education for Mexican physicians in both countries. Toll-free telephone consultation line into Mexico. Air transport service.
- **Samaritan Health System, Phoenix** Seminars for visiting Mexican physicians. Air transport service into Mexico. Spanish-language brochures. Marketing to Arizona employers with Mexican plants.

- **Carondelet Holy Cross Hospital, Nogales, Ariz.** Continuing education classes for Mexican physicians. Translation services. Laboratory services for Mexican hospitals. Yellow Pages advertising.
- **Dallas Medical Resource, Dallas** Observational fellowships for Mexican doctors. Travel services. Toll-free consultation line. Building computer link with Monterrey medical group.
- **Texas Medical Center, Houston** Continuing education for Mexican physicians. Physician exchanges. Travel and translation services. Foreign newspapers for patients.

Source: Tomsho, 1993. Reprinted by permission of *Wall Street Journal* © 1993, Dow Jones & Company, Inc. All rights reserved worldwide.

---

vice provider may have different service configurations for the large manufacturer segment that requires full-service executive dining facilities and large-volume cafeterias than it would have for the hospital market segment that uses a centralized kitchen facility to disperse a wide variety of dietary configurations. Still another service package would be required for the large university market segment that requires a variety of dining options including an array of vending machines.

Another critical aspect of commercial or industrial market segmentation is that the consumer is usually a group of people rather than an individual; the decision-making unit for commercial services is rarely just the user of the service but instead includes influencers, decision-makers, and purchasers—all of whom might be different people and departments.

Step 2: Develop Profiles of Resulting Segments Once the segments have been identified it is critical to develop profiles of them. In consumer markets these profiles usually involve demographic characterizations of psychographic or usage segments. Of most importance in this stage is clearly understanding how and whether the segments differ from each other in terms of their profiles. If they are not different from each other, the benefits to be derived from segmentation, that is, from more precisely identifying sets of customers, will not be realized.

Table 7-1 is an illustration of profiles developed for customers of a business-to-business equipment service supplier. The market was first segmented on the basis of the type of environment in which the equipment was found: office, manufacturing, distribution, and special markets. Situational and usage profiles of these four equipment environments were then developed to help gain understanding of their needs, so that marketing approaches and service configurations could be developed for the segment. As can be seen in the table, the segments clearly differ in major environmental characteristics, required response time for repair, technological complexity of the equipment used, type of equipment, existence of hardware and software issues, and other factors. If the four segments had been found to have identical profiles on these situational and usage characteristics, there would have been no need to segment the market.

BOX 7-2

**MARRIOTT CORPORATION TARGETS
EXTENDED-STAY GUESTS WITH RESIDENCE INNS**

Marriott's Residence Inn is positioned as a home-away-from-home for travelers who need a place to stay for a week to 10 days, or even for a month. At the Residence Inn the services provided to the guest support a warm, homelike feeling and cover a gamut of needs from free grocery shopping to same-day laundry and even self-service guest laundry facilities. Suites include kitchen facilities, a living room, and bedroom(s), and even a fireplace in many. To encourage socializing among guests there is a free continental breakfast buffet in the mornings and complimentary beverages and snacks in the hospitality area in the evenings. On arrival, guests are welcomed with a personal letter from the manager welcoming them "home."

Source: Reprinted courtesy of Marriott Residence Inn.

Grocery List

Brand/Amount

- ☐ Milk _____
- ☐ Eggs _____
- ☐ Bread _____
- ☐ Cereal _____
- ☐ Juice _____
- ☐ Soda _____
- ☐ Produce _____

- ☐ Meat _____
  _____

- ☐ Coffee _____
- ☐ Ice Cream _____
- ☐ Other _____
  _____
  _____
  _____

Signature _____ Suite _____

Please leave this list at the Front Desk by 9:00
a.m. to assure same day delivery. There is no
charge for this service, and grocery costs will be
billed directly to your suite.

**SORRY, WE ARE UNABLE TO PURCHASE
ANY BEER, WINE OR LIQUOUR.**

Welcome Home!

I am very pleased you chose to stay at Residence Inn Annapolis. Our service culture, "Residence Inn . . . where caring people make you feel at home", is our daily goal! With that in mind, I would like to acquaint you with some of our features.

Chances are you didn't have an opportunity to do any shopping before you arrived. On the breakfast bar is a first nighter basket. Enjoy the popcorn this evening and of course, the coffee tomorrow morning. If you need any type of grocery item, we will be more than happy to do the shopping for you. Feel free to check with our professional front desk staff on how this works.

The cleaning of your suite will be scheduled Monday-Friday between 8:30 a.m.-5:00 p.m., Saturday between 9:00 a.m.-5:30 p.m., and Sunday between 9:30 a.m.-6:00 p.m. Sheets are changed every other day. If there are any specific service requests, please contact our front desk. Our housekeeping staff is always prepared to exceed the expectations of our guests.

We hope you enjoy the complimentary continental breakfast served each morning in our gatehouse. On Monday-Thursday evenings from 5:30 p.m. to 7:00 p.m., enjoy our social hour activities.

Our team's passion is the love of serving people. Exceeding your expectations and fulfilling your needs is the standard for our success. Enjoy your stay with us!

Respectfully,

*Roger L. Kruse
General Manager*

Step 3: Develop Measures of Segment Attractiveness The fact that segments of customers exist does not justify a firm's choice of them as targets. Segments must be evaluated in terms of their attractiveness, some aspects of which are shown in Exhibit 7-1.[28] The size and purchasing power of the segments must be measurable so that the company can determine if the segments are worth the investment in marketing and relationship costs associated with the group. Recall from our earlier discussion that not all customers or customer segments are good potential relationship customers. They must be profitable in the long term in terms of revenues generated, and they also should not place a disproportionate drain on the firm's time and/or human energy. These costs are not always easy to determine in advance.

The chosen segments also must be accessible, meaning that advertising or marketing vehicles must exist to allow the company to reach the customers in the segments. The legal profession views direct contact or solicitation of clients from another attorney or

TABLE 7-1 PROFILES OF EQUIPMENT SERVICE CUSTOMER SEGMENTS

Market segment	Major features	Service factors				
		Response and repair time	Technological complexity of products	Type of equipment	Hardware/ software issues	Other
Office environment	Unsophisticated users "White-collar" environment Growing complexity & mix of products supported Low-density installed base at each site	8–24 hours	Medium	Electromechanical (e.g., word processing & photocopying equipment)	Generally no	Many service groups present
Manufacturing environment	Sophisticated users High-technology orientation High-density installed base at each site	1–4 hours	Very high	Electronic (e.g., CAD/CAM equipment)	Generally yes	Generally single vendor service
Distribution environment	Sophisticated users "Blue-collar" environment High-density installed base at each site	2–8 hours	High	Electronic, electromechanical & network related (e.g., order processing, inventory control systems)	Generally yes	Service becoming increasingly important due to technology and regulation changes
Special markets	Unsophisticated users Requires special knowledge of customer Medium-density installed base at each site	8–24 hours	Low to medium	Electromechanical (e.g., systems designed for hospitals & hotel/motels)	Yes—very specialized	Typically, specifically oriented suppliers & system integrated

Source: Donald F. Blumberg, "Developing Service as a Line of Business," *Management Review,* February 1987, pp. 58–62. Reprinted, by permission of the publisher, from *Management Review,* February, 1987. © 1987. American Management Association, New York. All rights reserved.

law firm as unethical. Therefore, even when a firm can identify specific potential clients in a segment, it may not be able to access these clients except through impersonal mailings. Service firms must also seek actionable segments, ones for which services and marketing mixes for the services can be designed to attract and serve them.[29]

Step 4: Select the Target Segments Based in part on the evaluation criteria in step 3, the services marketer will select the target segment or segments for the service. The service firm must decide if the segment is large enough and trending toward growth. Market size will be estimated and demand forecasts completed to determine whether the segment provides strong potential. Competitive analysis, including an evaluation of current and potential competitors, substitute products and services, and relative power of buyers and relative power of suppliers, will also help in the final selection of target segments. Finally, the firm must decide whether serving the segment is consistent with company objectives and resources.[30]

Step 5: Ensure That the Target Segments Are Compatible   This step, of all the steps in segmentation strategy, is arguably more critical for service companies than for goods companies. Because services are often performed in the presence of the customer, the services marketer must be certain that the customers are compatible with each other. If during the nonpeak season a hotel chooses to serve two segments that are incompatible with each other—for example, families who are attracted by the discounted prices and college students on their spring break—it may find that the two groups do not merge well. It may be possible to manage the segments in this example so that they do not directly interact with each other, but if not, they may negatively influence each others' experiences, hurting the hotel's future business. In identifying segments it is thus important to think through how they will use the service and whether segments will be compatible. Later in the book (in chapters 13 and 14) we will examine specific strategies for balancing demand for service while serving the right segments and strategies for managing the customer mix.

Individualized Service: Segments of One

The preceding section discussed the basics of segmentation and the importance of identifying relevant segments of relationship customers. When carried to their logical conclusions, both segmentation and customization lead to "segments of one" or "mass customization"—products and services designed to fit each individual's needs. The inherent characteristics of services lend themselves to customization and support the possibility of segmenting to the individual level. That is, because services are delivered to people by people, they are difficult to standardize and their outcomes and processes may be inconsistent from provider to provider, from customer to customer, and even from one time period to the next. This inherent heterogeneity is at once a curse and a blessing. On the one hand it means that service delivery is difficult to control and predict, and the resulting inconsistencies may cause customers to question a firm's reliability. On the other hand it presents opportunities to customize and tailor the service in ways typically not possible for manufacturers of goods. Because the service itself is frequently delivered in "real time" by "real people" there is an opportunity for one-to-one customization of the offering. Heterogeneity pursued in a purposeful manner can be turned into an effective customization strategy.

While segments of one may be practically unrealistic in some cases, the underlying idea of crafting a customized service to fit each individual's needs fits very well with today's consumers, who demand to be treated as individuals and who want their own particular needs satisfied. (Remember from chapter 5 that customer perceptions of service are clearly linked to adaptability, flexibility, and responsiveness of the service.)

For service providers who have a limited number of large customers, the segment of one marketing strategy may be obvious. For example, a food management company that provides cafeteria and other types of food service for large manufacturing facilities will customize its services for each large account on the basis of the specific needs of the organization. Or an advertising agency that specializes in providing communication services for Fortune 500 companies will develop individualized plans for each client. In such situations, a relationship manager or an account manager will likely be assigned to a particular customer or client to develop a marketing plan tailored to that client's needs.

But even in consumer markets where a company may have hundreds, thousands, or even millions of moments of truth per day, technology combined with employee empowerment is leading the way to mass customization. Our technology spotlight features two very different companies that are successfully using information technologies to customize their offerings: Fingerhut, a mail-order company targeting low-income consumers, and the Ritz-Carlton, a high-end luxury hotel.

In his book, *Mass Customization,* Joe Pine describes a number of different approaches for working toward a mass customization goal.[31] Some of these approaches include:

Customizing the service around a standardized core. A standard core service such as airline transportation or hotel accommodations can be customized through addition of

---

TECHNOLOGY SPOTLIGHT

CUSTOMER INFORMATION SYSTEMS ALLOW MASS CUSTOMIZATION OF SERVICES

The potential of today's customer information systems far exceeds any traditional marketing information system that has gone before. These new systems differ from the old in their scale (thousands of bits of information on tens of millions of customers), the depth of information that can be captured on each individual or household, and the ways in which the information can be used. In many cases, access to this type of information about individual customers allows the organization to customize to the individual level what previously would have been undifferentiated services.

For example, the Ritz-Carlton Hotel Company, winner of the 1992 Malcolm Baldrige National Quality Award, targets its services to industry executives, meeting and corporate travel planners, and affluent travelers. While there are many dimensions to their success, one of the keys is the quality of their customer data base. By training each employee to note the likes and dislikes of regular guests and to enter this information immediately into the customer's file, employees at any Ritz-Carlton Hotel are able to personalize services to the Ritz-Carlton's 240,000 repeat customers. They can know in advance the guest's preferences and be prepared to provide individualized service even before the guest's arrival. For example, if a guest prefers a feather pillow, wants extra brown sugar with her oatmeal, or always orders a glass of sherry before retiring, this information can be entered

into the data base and these needs anticipated—often much to the guest's surprise.

In a very different realm, Fingerhut, the fourth largest U.S. mail-order company, has used an advanced customer information system to customize communication strategies for individual customers. Fingerhut's primary market segment is households with less than $25,000 in annual income, a segment that would typically be viewed as poor credit risks. The company is successful in serving this segment because of its sophisticated use of customer information. Its data base captures as many as 1,400 pieces of information on an individual household and then uses this information to determine who within the segment are the best customers to pursue long-term relationships with. The data base is then used to determine an individualized communication strategy for high-potential relationship customers. Customers are segmented into different groups on the basis of their purchasing histories and are then targeted for particular promotions or catalogs. The catalogs themselves may be further customized to the individual level by including personalized promotional offers and messages. For example, a personal message included in her catalog might thank Mrs. Smith for her recent purchase of a VCR and then go on to congratulate her on her fourteenth anniversary as a Fingerhut customer.

Sources: Jim Bessen, "Riding the Marketing Information Wave," *Harvard Business Review,* September–October 1993, pp. 150–160; and "1992 Award Winner," publication of the Ritz-Carlton Hotel Company.

features or through creative delivery options. Hotels, for example, offer in-room variations (e.g., smoking/nonsmoking, size and number of beds) as well as add-ons such as office services for business travelers and exercise facilities.

Creating customizable services. Here the firm offers the same service to everyone, using a design that can be customized by the consumer. Interactive computer services (Prodigy, Compuserve), ATM's, and automated ticketing systems are examples of this type of service customization. Other examples are self-service salad bars, or entertainment environments such as Disney World.

Offering point-of-delivery customization. Using this option the provider allows customers to communicate what they need/want at the point of service delivery. The service is customized in real time by the employee to fit those needs. Classic examples include professional services, health care, counseling, and personal care services.

Offering standard modules that can be combined in unique ways. This is the approach used by tour companies that offer the traveler different vacation components (hotels, airlines, destinations, lengths of stay) that they can combine to design their own unique trip. University degree programs operate in this way as well. For example, in an MBA program a student who is interested in service industry management might take all of the MBA core courses and then design a concentration that includes a course on services marketing, one on quality, one on service operations, and one on human resources. In this way the MBA product is customized to the individual student's career needs.

It should be noted that not all industries or individual companies offer appropriate settings for the implementation of mass customization.[32] For example, it may be very difficult to customize commodity services such as electricity or gas, and in other cases government regulation may prohibit customization. Some companies may be too hierarchical and bureaucratic in their structure to facilitate a mass customization strategy. And there may be cases when consumers simply do not value customization or when they would be too confused by all the possible options. Any company that is considering a shift to mass customization of its services will therefore want to analyze carefully the need for as well as the feasibility of such a change.

RETENTION STRATEGIES

To this point in the chapter we have focused on the rationale for relationship marketing, the benefits of customer retention, and the importance of identifying the right market segment(s) for relationship building. In this section we will look at some of the specific strategies and tactics used by firms to build relationships and tie customers closer to the firm. That is, once a firm has carefully identified its market segments, what are some of the specific tactics it can use to accomplish the goal of retaining the customer?

Monitor Relationships

A basic strategy for customer retention is to implement a thorough means of monitoring and evaluating relationship quality over time. Basic market research in the form of (at a minimum) annual customer relationship surveys can be the foundation for such a monitoring strategy. Current customers should be surveyed to determine their perceptions of value received, quality, satisfaction with services, and satisfaction with the provider relative to competitors. The organization will also regularly communicate with its *best* customers in person or over the telephone. In a competitive market it is difficult to retain customers unless they are receiving a base level of quality and value.

A well-designed customer data base is also a foundation for customer retention strategies. Knowing who the organization's current customers are (names, addresses, phone numbers, etc.), what their buying behavior is, the revenue they generate, the related costs to serve them, their preferences, and relevant segmentation information (e.g., demographics, life-style, usage patterns) forms the foundation of a customer data base. In cases of customers leaving the organization, information on termination would also exist in the data base. By having such a detailed data base on its customers, American Express is able to tailor its corporate card member newsletter on the basis of card holders' spending patterns and preferences. The result of this tailoring is 1,349 versions of the newsletter, targeted at specific customer needs and interests.[33]

These two basics (relationship survey and customer data base) are combined with a variety of other types of marketing research as described in chapter 6, for example, trailer calls, complaint monitoring, lost-customer surveys, and customer visits, to develop a profile of the organization's customer relationships. With a foundation of customer knowledge combined with quality offerings and value, a firm can engage in retention strategies to hold on to its customers.

Three Levels of Retention Strategies

Leonard Berry and A. Parasuraman have developed a framework for understanding types of retention strategies, as shown in Table 7-2.[34] The framework suggests that retention marketing can occur at three different levels and that each successive level of strategy results in ties that bind the customer a little closer to the firm. At each successive level, the potential for sustained competitive advantage is also increased. Also note that each level brings with it increasingly greater customization, or individualized service.

Level 1   At level 1, the customer is tied to the firm primarily through financial incentives—lower prices for greater volume purchases or lower prices for customers who have been with the firm a long time. Examples of level 1 relationship marketing are not hard to find. Think about the airline industry and related travel service industries like hotels and car rental companies. "Frequent flyer" programs provide financial incentives and rewards for travelers who bring more of their business to a particular airline. Hotels and car rental companies do the same. Long-distance telephone companies in the United States are engaged in a similar battle, trying to provide volume discounts and other price incentives to retain market share and build a loyal customer base. One reason these financial incentive programs proliferate is that they are not difficult to initiate and frequently result in at least short-term profit gains. Unfortunately, financial incentives do not generally provide long-term advantages to a firm since, unless combined with another relationship strategy, they don't serve to differentiate the firm from its competitors in the long run. Many travelers belong to several frequent flyer programs and don't hesitate to trade off among them. And there is considerable customer switching every month among the major telecommunication suppliers. While price and other financial incen-

TABLE 7-2   THREE LEVELS OF RETENTION STRATEGIES

Level	Type of bond(s)	Marketing orientation	Degree of service customization	Primary marketing mix element	Potential for sustained competitive differentiation
1	Financial	Customer	Low	Price	Low
2	Financial and social	Client	Medium	Personal communications	Medium
3	Financial, social, and structural	Client	Medium to high	Service delivery	High

Source: Reprinted with the permission of The Free Press, an imprint of Simon & Schuster. From Berry and Parasuraman, 1991. Copyright © 1991.

tives are important to customers, they are generally not difficult for competitors to imitate, since the only customized element of the marketing mix is price.

Level 2   Level 2 strategies bind customers to the firm through more than pricing incentives. While price is still assumed to be important, level 2 retention marketers build long-term relationships through social as well as financial bonds. Customers are viewed as "clients," not nameless faces, and become individuals whose needs and wants the firm seeks to understand. Services are customized to fit individual needs, and marketers find ways of staying in touch with their customers, thereby developing social bonds with them. For example, in a study of customer-firm relationships in the insurance industry, it was found that behaviors such as staying in touch with clients to assess their changing needs, providing personal touches like cards and gifts, and sharing personal information with clients all served to increase the likelihood that the client would stay with the firm.[35]

Social bonds are common among professional service providers (e.g., lawyers, accountants, teachers) and their clients as well as among personal care providers (hairdressers, counselors, health care providers) and their clients. A dentist who takes a few minutes to review her patient's file before coming in to the exam room is able to jog her memory on personal facts about the patient (occupation, family details, interests, dental health history). By bringing these personal details into the conversation, the dentist reveals her genuine interest in the patient as an individual and builds social bonds.

Technology can help to create social bonds with the organization even in mass markets where consumers don't necessarily interact with the same employee every time. Ritz-Carlton's personalized consumer information system, discussed in the technology spotlight, fits here. The hotel keeps personal information on all of its 240,000 repeat guests so that it can anticipate guest needs and be prepared to customize elements of the stay even before the guest arrives. The computerized information is updated whenever something new is learned about a particular guest, and the information is available to all hotels in the chain. The guest then feels special and valued as an individual, and a social bond with the *hotel chain* is created.

Sometimes relationships are formed with the organization due to the social bonds that develop *among customers* rather than between customers and the provider of the service. This is frequently the case in health clubs, country clubs, educational settings, and other service environments where customers interact with each other. Over time the social relationships they have with other customers are important factors that keep them from switching to another organization. Women who exercise together regularly at a health club may develop social ties and friendships that bind them to each other and to the particular fitness center where they work out. People who vacation at the same place during the same weeks every year build bonds with others who vacation there at the same time. Loyalty to the vacation spot is partially a function of loyalty to a group of friends they have made over the years. Organizations that encourage bonding among customers are also engaging in level 2 retention strategies.

While social bonds alone may not tie the customer permanently to the firm, they are much more difficult for competitors to imitate than are price incentives. In the absence of strong reasons to shift to another provider, social bonds can encourage customers to stay in a relationship. In combination with price incentives, social bonding strategies may be very effective.

Level 3   Level 3 strategies are the most difficult to imitate and involve structural as well as financial and social bonds between the customer and the firm. Structural bonds are created by providing services to the client that are highly customized and frequently designed right into the service delivery system for that client. Structural bonds often are created by providing customized services to the client that are technology based and serve to make the customer more productive. Some concrete examples will help to demonstrate the effectiveness of structural bonds in building relationships.

By working closely with its hospital customers, Baxter Healthcare has developed ways to improve hospital supply ordering, delivery, and billing that have greatly enhanced their value as a supplier. For example, they developed "hospital-specific pallet architecture" that meant all items arriving at a particular hospital were shrink-wrapped with labels visible for easy identification. Separate pallets were assembled to reflect the individual hospital's storage system, so that instead of miscellaneous supplies arriving in boxes (sorted at the convenience of Baxter's internal needs), they arrived on "client-friendly" pallets designed to suit the distribution needs of the particular hospital. By linking the hospital into a data-based ordering system of this nature and providing enhanced value in the actual delivery, Baxter has structurally tied itself to the hospital, making it less likely that the hospital will seek other suppliers.

An exclusive conference center assured itself of significant continued business from one of the Big Six accounting firms when it partnered with the accounting firm in an investment to build a training facility. The training facility was built on the grounds of the conference center and was custom designed for the needs of the accounting firm. To recapture its investment, the accounting firm committed itself to holding all of its midmanagement training at the facility. The investment was a wise one for both organizations, resulting in a structural tie between them that assured the conference center of continued business.

Another example of level 3 strategy can be seen in the competitive battle between UPS and Federal Express.[36] Both firms are attempting to tie their clients closer to them by providing them with free computers—Federal Express's PowerShips and UPS's MaxiShips—that store addresses and shipping data, print mailing labels, and help track packages. By tieing into one of the systems a company can save time overall and keep better track of daily shipping records. But there is also a potential downside to this arrangement from the customer's perspective: Customers may fear that tieing themselves too closely to one provider may not allow them to take advantage of potential price savings from other providers in the future.

Recovery—Retaining Customers When Things Go Wrong

As we have seen, reliability and "doing it right the first time" are extremely important factors in customers' judgments of service quality. Yet for even the best of firms, service failures and mistakes are inevitable. And because service is often performed in the presence of the customer, errors and failures are difficult to hide or disguise. It is usually not possible to "start over" as it might be with a manufactured product. When things go wrong, the consumer is presented with a good reason to switch providers and to tell others to not use the service. Effective recovery is thus essential to save and even build the relationship. If the organization fails in recovery, it has failed the customer twice—a double deviation from customer expectations.

Studies in different industries have shown that *dissatisfied* complaining consumers will tell between 9 and 16 people about their poor experience, whereas *satisfied* complainants will tell only 4 or 5 people about their positive experience.[37] Studies by the Technical Assistance Research Programs (TARP) Institute reveal that the impact of complaints on repeat purchase intentions is dramatic.[38] Only 19 percent of people whose complaints about products and services over $100 in value are *not* satisfactorily resolved intend to repurchase from the same provider. The percentage is higher, 46.5 percent, for complaints about products and services from $1 to $5 in value. When a complaint *is* satisfactorily resolved, the intent to repurchase goes up to 54.3 percent (over $100) and 70 percent ($1–$5). Interestingly, those dissatisfied consumers who don't complain at all have the lowest intent to repurchase.

Given the potential impact of service failures on repurchase and negative word of mouth, effective recovery strategies are essential to a comprehensive customer retention approach. Recall from chapter 5 the consumer research that showed the importance of effective recovery in distinguishing satisfying from dissatisfying service encounters. In the absence of effective recovery, the organization may lose a customer as well as potential customers who hear about the failure secondhand. So what is an effective service recovery strategy? The following paragraphs outline some of the essential ingredients.[39]

Track and Anticipate Recovery Opportunities   "The customer who complains is your friend." Customers who don't complain are likely not to come back, and further they may influence other customers to not try the service. Building on this notion, organizations need systems to track and identify failures, viewing them as opportunities to save and retain customer relationships.

An effective service recovery strategy requires identification of failure points in the system through listening to customers. This means not only monitoring complaints, but really listening and being active in searching out potential failure points. A variety of types of market research can be used to unearth recovery opportunities (e.g., collecting critical incidents, monitoring complaints, soliciting feedback through trailer calls, and offering an 800 number). Effective service guarantees and suggestion boxes for both contact employees and customers can bring to light problem areas within the service system.

Take Care of Customer Problems on the Front Lines   From the customer's point of view, the most effective recovery is accomplished when a front-line worker can take the initiative to solve the problem on the spot. Acknowledgement of the problem, an apology, an explanation when appropriate, and a solution to the problem are often all the customer wants. Sometimes the solution may be a refund: retailers with liberal return policies build customer loyalty through refunding or trading in defective merchandise, no questions asked. Or the solution may be an upgrade, as when an airline or hotel provides a customer with a better seat or a better room at the same price when the original reservation is not available. Sometimes the solution may be more customized and even appear "heroic," as in the story of a service hero described in Box 7-3. Whatever the recovery solution, customers want it right away—not after a number of phone calls, red tape, or being passed from one person to another.

Solve Problems Quickly   Once the failure points are identified, employees must act quickly to solve problems as they occur. A problem not solved can quickly escalate. Sometimes employees can even anticipate problems before they arise and surprise customers with a solution. For example, flight attendants on a flight severely delayed due to weather anticipated everyone's hunger, particularly the young children's. Once in flight they announced to the harried travelers: "Thank you for your extreme patience in waiting with us. Now that we're on our way, we'd like to offer you complementary beverages and dinner. Because we have a number of very hungry children on board, we'd like to serve them first, if that's OK with all of you." The passengers nodded and applauded their efforts, knowing that hungry, crying children could make the situation even worse. The flight attendants had anticipated a problem and solved it before it escalated.

Empower the Front Line to Solve Problems   For service employees there is a specific and real need for recovery training. Because customers demand that service recovery take place on the spot and quickly, front-line employees need the skills, authority, and incentives to engage in effective recovery. Effective recovery skills include hearing the customer's problems, identifying solutions, improvising, and perhaps bending the rules from time to time. Recovery skills are invoked when exceptions to the normal routine occur. Thus, to be effective at recovery front-line service employees have to be versatile, since they must typically follow rules, stick to a routine, and treat all customers alike.

They must also be empowered to employ their skills; they must have the authority, usually within certain defined limits, to solve the customer's immediate problem. Fur-

---

BOX 7-3

STORY OF A SERVICE HERO

"A good recovery can turn angry, frustrated customers into loyal ones. It can, in fact, create more goodwill than if things had gone smoothly in the first place. Consider how Club Med-Cancun, part of the Paris-based Club Mediterranée, recovered from a service nightmare and won the loyalty of one group of vacationers.

The vacationers had nothing but trouble getting from New York to their Mexican destination. The flight took off six hours late, made two unexpected stops, and circled thirty minutes before it could land. Because of all the delays and mishaps, the plane was en route for ten hours more than planned and ran out of food and drinks. It finally arrived at two o'clock in the morning, with a landing so rough that oxygen masks and luggage dropped from overhead. By the time the plane pulled up to the gate, the soured passengers were faint with hunger and convinced that their vacation was ruined before it had even started. One lawyer on board was already collecting names and addresses for a class-action lawsuit.

Silvio de Bortoli, the general manager of the Cancun resort and a legend throughout the organization for his ability to satisfy customers, got word of the horrendous flight and immediately created an antidote. He took half the staff to the airport, where they laid out a table of snacks and drinks and set up a stereo system to play lively music. As the guests filed through the gate, they received personal greetings, help with their bags, a sympathetic ear, and a chauffeured ride to the resort. Waiting for them at Club Med was a lavish banquet, complete with mariachi band and champagne. Moreover, the staff had rallied other guests to wake up and greet the newcomers, and the partying continued until sunrise. Many guests said it was the most fun they'd had since college.

In the end, the vacationers had a better experience than if their flight from New York had gone like clockwork. Although the company probably couldn't measure it, Club Mediterranée won market share that night. After all, the battle for market share is won not by analyzing demographic trends, ratings points, and other global measures, but rather by pleasing customers one at a time."

---

ther, they should not be punished for taking action. In fact, incentives should exist that encourage employees to exercise their recovery authority.

Learn from Recovery Experiences   "Problem-resolution situations are more than just opportunities to fix flawed services and strengthen ties with customers. They are also a valuable—but frequently ignored or underutilized—source of diagnostic, prescriptive information for improving customer service."[40] By tracking service recovery efforts and solutions, managers can often learn about systematic problems in the delivery system that need fixing. By conducting root-cause analysis, they can identify the sources of the problems and can modify processes, sometimes eliminating almost completely the *need* for recovery.

Customer Appreciation

One obvious, but often neglected, way to retain customers is to show appreciation for their business.[41] By first providing the services as promised, and then thanking the customer for the business, firms can go a long way toward retaining individual customers. Especially in business-to-business situations, customers would like their suppliers to extend appreciation either in person or over the phone, and not just take their business for granted. Letters addressed to "Dear Valued Customer" are not really the answer, especially for the organization's best customers. Such an impersonal approach may well communicate exactly the opposite of what was intended. Instead, a personal letter (addressed to the right person with correct spelling and current title), or a personal phone call will have greater impact.

SUMMARY

In this chapter we have focused on the rationale for, benefits of, and strategies for developing long-term relationships with customers. It should be obvious by now that organizations that focus only on getting new customers may well fail to understand their current customers and thus may be bringing customers through the front door while equal or greater numbers are exiting through the back door. The particular strategy an organization uses to retain its current customers can and should be customized to fit the industry, the culture, and the customer needs of the organization. However, the basics of a good relationship strategy require (1) effective market segmentation to identify *who* the organization wants to have relationships with, (2) continuous development of services that evolve to suit the needs of these relationship customers, and (3) monitoring of current customer relationships through relationship surveys and an up-to-date customer data base. By working with current customers in these ways, the organization has a good chance of accurately understanding current customer expectations and of narrowing service quality GAP 1.

DISCUSSION QUESTIONS

1 Discuss how relationship marketing or retention marketing is different from the traditional emphasis in marketing.
2 Think about a service organization that retains you as a loyal customer. Why are you loyal to this provider? What are the benefits to you of staying loyal and not switching to another provider? What would it take for you to switch?
3 With regard to the same service organization, what are the benefits to the organization of keeping you as a customer? Calculate your "lifetime value" to the organization.
4 Have you ever worked as a front-line service employee? Can you remember having to deal with difficult or "problem" customers? Discuss how you handled such situations. As a manager of front-line employees, how would you help your employees deal with difficult customers?
5 What are the basic steps in market segmentation? What specific challenges exist for service organizations when it comes to segmentation?
6 Explain the logic behind the "segments of one" idea. Why are services particularly amenable to this form of segmentation?
7 Describe the three levels of retention strategies, and give examples of each type. Again, think of a service organization to which you are loyal. Can you describe the reason(s) you are loyal in terms of the three different levels? In other words, what ties you to the organization?
8 Why is it important for a service firm to have a strong recovery strategy? Think of a time when you received less-than-desirable service from a particular service organization. Was any effort made to recover? What should/could have been done differently? Do you still buy services from the organization? Why or why not? Did you tell others about your experience?

EXERCISES

1 Interview the manager of a local service organization. Discuss with the manager who the target market(s) is for the service. Estimate the lifetime value of a customer in one or more of the target segments. To do this you will need to get as much information from the manager as you can. If the manager cannot answer your questions, make some assumptions.

2 In small groups in class debate the question, "Is the customer always right?" In other words, are there times when the customer may be the wrong customer for the organization?

3 Write a letter of complaint to a service organization (or voice your complaint in person) where you have experienced less-than-desirable service. What do you expect the organization to do to recover? (Later, report to the class the results of your complaint, whether you were satisfied with the recovery, what could/should have been done differently, and whether you will continue using the service.)

4 Design a "customer appreciation" program for the organization you currently work for. Why would you have such a program, and whom would it be directed toward?

5 Choose a specific company context (e.g., your class project company, the company you work for, or a company in an industry you are familiar with). Calculate the lifetime value of a customer for this company. You will need to make assumptions to do this, so make your assumptions clear. Using ideas and concepts from this chapter, describe a relationship marketing strategy to increase the number of lifetime customers for this firm.

NOTES

1 Jeff Bailey, "Why Customers Trash the Garbage Man," *Wall Street Journal,* March 17, 1993, p. B1.

2 Frederick E. Webster, Jr., "The Changing Role of Marketing in the Corporation," *Journal of Marketing,* October 1992, pp. 1–17.

3 Leonard L. Berry and A. Parasuraman, *Marketing Services* (New York: Free Press, 1991), chap. 8.

4 Gary Knisely, "Comparing Marketing Management in Package Goods and Service Organizations," a series of interviews appearing in *Advertising Age,* January 15, February 19, March 19, and May 14, 1979.

5 Leonard L. Berry, "Relationship Marketing," in *Emerging Perspectives on Services Marketing,* eds. Leonard L. Berry, G. Lynn Shostack, and Gregory D. Upah (Chicago: American Marketing Association, 1983), pp. 25–28.

6 See Thomas Teal, "Service Comes First: An Interview with USAA's Robert F. McDermott," *Harvard Business Review,* September—October 1991, pp. 117—127; and Robert F. McDermott, "USAA: Employee Satisfaction Equals Customer Satisfaction," in *Managing Quality in America's Most Admired Companies,* ed. Jay W. Spechler (San Francisco: Berrett-Koehler Publishers, 1993), pp. 279–288.

7 Teal, "Service Comes First," p. 124.

8 See Mara B. Adelman, Aaron Ahuvia, and Cathy Goodwin, "Beyond Smiling: Social Support and Service Quality," in *Service Quality, New Directions in Theory and Practice,* eds. Roland T. Rust and Richard L. Oliver (Thousand Oaks, Calif.: Sage Publications, 1994), pp. 139–172; Cathy Goodwin, "Private Roles in Public Encounters: Communal Relationships in Service Exchanges," unpublished manuscript, University of Manitoba, 1993.

9 Eric J. Arnould and Linda L. Price, "River Magic: Extraordinary Experience and the Extended Service Encounter," *Journal of Consumer Research* 20, 1 (1993): 24–45.

10 Frederick F. Reichheld and W. Earl Sasser, Jr., "Zero Defections: Quality Comes to Services," *Harvard Business Review,* September–October 1990, pp. 105–111.

11 Ibid., p. 106.

12 Ibid., p. 110.

13 Thomas J. Peters, *Thriving on Chaos: Handbook for a Management Revolution,* New York: HarperCollins Publishers, 1987.

14 "The Stew Leonard's Story," video produced by Stew Leonard's Dairy, Norwalk, Connecticut.

15 Peters, op. cit.

16 Peter Carroll and Sanford Rose, "Revisiting Customer Retention," *Journal of Retail Banking* 15, 1 (1993): 5–13.

17 Jonathan Dahl, "Rental Counters Reject Drivers without Good Records," *Wall Street Journal,* October 23, 1992, p. B1.

18 Michael Schrage, "Fire Your Customers," *Wall Street Journal,* March 16, 1992, p. A8.

19 Kathleen D. Sanford, "The Customer Isn't Always Right," *Supervisory Management,* October 1989, pp. 29–33.

20 Mary Jo Bitner, Bernard H. Booms, and Lois Mohr, "Critical Service Encounters: The Employee's Viewpoint," *Journal of Marketing* 58 (October 1994): 95–106.

21 Laura Bird, "The Clients That Exasperate Madison Avenue," *Wall Street Journal,* November 2, 1993, p. B1.

22 Ibid.

23 See Philip Kotler and Gary Armstrong, "Marketing Segmentation, Targeting and Positioning," *Principles of Marketing,* 5th ed. (Prentice Hall: Englewood Cliffs, NJ, 1991), pp. 216–249.

24 Yoram Wind, "Issues and Advances in Segmentation Research," *Journal of Marketing Research,* August 1978, pp. 317–37.

25 See Andrea Gerlin, "Radio Stations Gain by Going after Hispanics," *Wall Street Journal,* July 14, 1993, p. B1; and "Publications in Spanish on the Rise," cover story, *USA Today,* August 31, 1993.

26 Sarah Lubman, "School-based Health Insurance for Kids Catches On as Way to Cover Uninsured," *Wall Street Journal,* August 31, 1993, p. B1.

27 Robert Tomsho, "U.S. Hospitals See Opportunity in Mexico," *Wall Street Journal,* August 13, 1993, p. B1.

28 Kotler and Armstrong, "Marketing Segmentation," pp. 216–249.

29 Ibid.

30 Ibid.

31 B. Joseph Pine II. *Mass Customization* (Boston: Harvard Business School Press, 1993).

32 B. Joseph Pine II, Bart Victor, and Andrew C. Boynton, "Making Mass Customization Work," *Harvard Business Review,* September–October 1993, pp. 108–119.

33 Wendy Marx, "The New Segment of One," *Direct Magazine,* September 1994, pp. 45–48.

34 Berry and Parasuraman, *Marketing Services,* pp. 136–142.

35 Lawrence A. Crosby, Kenneth R. Evans, and Deborah Cowles, "Relationship Quality in Services Selling: An Interpersonal Influence Perspective," *Journal of Marketing,* July 1990, pp. 68–81.

36 Laurie M. Grossman, "Federal Express, UPS Face Off on Computers," *Wall Street Journal,* September 17, 1993, p. B1.

37 "Consumer Complaint Handling in America: An Update Study, Part II," Technical Assistance Research Programs (TARP) Institute, a study performed at the request of the U.S. Office of Consumer Affairs, 1986.

38 Ibid.

39 Sources of service recovery strategy ideas: Christopher W. L. Hart, James L. Heskett, and W. Earl Sasser, Jr., "The Profitable Art of Service Recovery," *Harvard Business Review,* July–August 1990, pp. 148–156; Rom Zemke, "The Art of Service Recovery: Fixing Broken Customers—and Keeping Them on Your Side," in *The Service Quality Handbook,* eds. Eberhard E. Scheuing and William F. Christopher (New York: AMACOM, 1993), pp. 463–476; Berry and Parasuraman, *Marketing Services,* chap. 3.

40 Berry and Parasuraman, *Marketing Services,* p. 52.

41 Richard R. Shapiro, "Retaining Profitable Customers: A Target Approach," presented at QUIS 3, University of Karlstad, Karlstad, Sweden, June 1992.

PART FOUR

ALIGNING STRATEGY, SERVICE DESIGN, AND STANDARDS

CUSTOMER-DEFINED SERVICE STANDARDS

Marketing research data aren't the only numbers Federal Express tracks to run its business. The company drives its operations with the aid of the most comprehensive, customer-defined index of service standards and measures in the world. FedEx's service quality indicator (SQI) was designed as "unforgiving internal performance measurement" to ensure that the company delivered to its goal of "100 percent customer satisfaction after every interaction and transaction and 100 percent service performance on every package handled."[1] The development and implementation of SQI led to a Malcolm Baldrige National Quality Award.

What makes this service index different from those of other companies is its foundation in customer feedback. Since the 1980s, FedEx has documented customer complaints and used the information to improve internal processes. Its composite listing of the eight most common customer complaints, called the "Hierarchy of Horrors," included: wrong day delivery, right day late delivery, pickup not made, lost package, customer misinformed by Federal Express, billing and paperwork mistakes, employee performance failures, and damaged package. Although this list was useful, it fell short of giving management the ability to anticipate and eliminate customer complaints before they occurred.

In 1988 the company developed the 12-item statistical SQI to be a more "comprehensive, pro-active, customer-oriented measure of customer satisfaction and service quality."[2] The SQI consists of the following components and weighting (based on relative importance of each component to customers):

Indicator	Weight
Right Day Late Deliveries	1
Wrong Day Late Deliveries	5
Traces Not Answered	1
Complaints Reopened	5
Missing Proofs of Delivery	1
Invoice Adjustments	1
Missed Pickups	10
Damaged Packages	10
Lost Packages	10
Aircraft Delay Minutes	5
Overgoods	5
Abandoned Calls	1
International	1

Another distinguishing feature of the SQI is its reporting in terms of numbers *of errors rather than* percentages. *Management of the company strongly believed that percentages distanced the company from the consumer: to report 1 percent of packages late diminished the reality of 15,000 unhappy customers (1% of the approximately 1.5 million packages shipped a day). The service quality indicator report is disseminated weekly to everyone in the company. On receipt of the report, root causes of service failures are investigated. With a senior officer assigned to each component, and with bonuses for everyone in the company tied to performance on the SQI, the company drives continuously closer to its goal of 100 percent satisfaction with every transaction.*[3]

As we saw in chapters 6 and 7, understanding customer expectations is the first step in delivering high service quality. Once managers of service businesses accurately understand what customers expect, they face a second critical challenge: using this knowledge to set service quality standards and goals for the organization. Service companies often experience difficulty in setting standards to match or exceed customer expectations partly because doing so requires that the marketing and operations departments within a company work together. In most service companies, integrating the work of the marketing function and the operations function (appropriately called functional integration) is not a typical approach; more frequently these two functions operate separately—setting and achieving their own internal goals—rather than pursuing a joint goal of developing the operations standards that best meet customer expectations.

Creating service standards that address customer expectations is not a common practice in U.S. firms. Doing so often requires altering the very process by which work is accomplished, which is ingrained in tradition in most companies. Often, change requires new equipment or technology. Change also necessitates aligning executives from different parts of the firm to understand collectively the comprehensive view of service quality from the customer's perspective. And almost always, change requires a willingness to be open to different ways of structuring, calibrating, and monitoring the way service is provided.

Figure 8-1 highlights Provider GAP 2, which reflects the discrepancy between customer expectations and the service standards set to correspond to those expectations. In

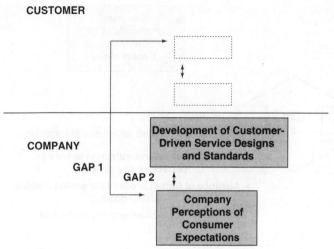

CUSTOMER

COMPANY

GAP 1

GAP 2

Development of Customer-Driven Service Designs and Standards

Company Perceptions of Consumer Expectations

FIGURE 8-1   Provider GAP 2.

this chapter we will take the highlighted portion of the model and examine it in detail to understand fully the concept of customer-defined service standards. Figure 8-2 shows the main factors that lead to GAP 2 that will be addressed in this chapter. These factors include inadequate standardization for service behaviors and actions, absence of a formal process for setting service quality goals, and lack of customer-defined standards. This chapter discusses each of these factors and then focuses on ways service companies can address them to close Provider GAP 2.

The objectives of this chapter are to:

1 Differentiate between company-defined and customer-defined service standards.

2 Distinguish among one-time service fixes, and "hard" and "soft" customer-defined standards.

3 Explain the critical role of the service encounter sequence (discussed in chapter 5) in developing customer-defined standards.

4 Illustrate how to translate customer expectations into behaviors and actions that are definable, repeatable, and actionable.

5 Explain the process of developing customer-defined service standards.

6 Emphasize the importance of service performance indices in implementing strategy for service delivery.

MAIN FACTORS LEADING TO PROVIDER GAP 2

Inadequate Standardization of Service Behaviors and Actions

The translation of customer expectations into specific service quality standards depends on the degree to which tasks and behaviors to be performed can be standardized or routinized. Some executives and managers believe that services cannot be standardized—

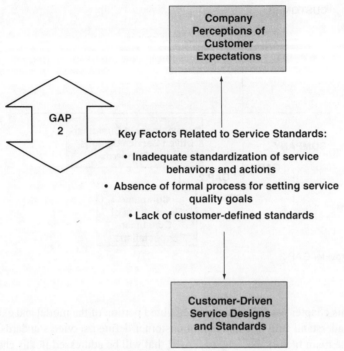

FIGURE 8-2   Key factors leading to provider GAP 2.

that customization is essential for providing high-quality service. In certain "expert" services such as accounting, consulting, engineering, and dentistry, for example, professionals provide customized and individualized services; standardizing of the tasks is perceived as being impersonal, inadequate, and not in the customer's best interests. Managers also may feel that standardizing tasks is inconsistent with employee empowerment—that employees will feel controlled by the company if tasks are standardized. Further, they feel that services are too intangible to be measured. This view leads to vague and loose standard setting with little or no measurement or feedback.

In reality, many service tasks are routine (such as those needed for opening checking accounts or spraying lawns for pests), and for these, specific rules and standards can be fairly easily established and effectively executed. Employees may welcome knowing how to perform actions most efficiently, for it frees them to use their ingenuity in the more personal and individual aspects of their jobs. If services are customized for individual customers (e.g., investment portfolio management or estate planning), specific standards (such as those relating to time spent with the customer) may not be appropriate. Even in highly customized services, however, many aspects of service provision can be routinized. Physicians and dentists, for example, can and do standardize recurring and nontechnical aspects of the service such as checking patients in, weighing patients, billing patients, collecting payment, and taking routine measurements. In delegating these routine tasks to assistants, physicians and dentists can spend more of their time on the more expert services of diagnosis or patient care.

According to one long-term observer of service industries, standardization of service can take three forms: (1) substitution of technology for personal contact and human effort, (2) improvement in work methods, and (3) combinations of these two methods.[4] Examples of technology substitution include automatic teller machines, automatic car washes, and airport X-ray machines. Improvements in work methods are illustrated by restaurant salad bars and routinized tax and accounting services developed by firms such as H&R Block and Comprehensive Accounting Corporation.

Technology and work improvement methods facilitate the standardization of service necessary to provide consistent delivery to customers. By breaking tasks down and providing them efficiently, technology also allows the firm to calibrate service standards such as the length of time a transaction takes, the accuracy with which operations are performed, and the number of problems that occur. In developing work improvements, the firm comes to understand completely the process by which the service is delivered. With this understanding, the firm more easily establishes appropriate service standards.

How does a company change the way work is done to make the process of delivering service match what customers expect? The concept of *reengineering* of company processes plays a major role. Reengineering involves rethinking the way the company is organized to perform its work. Often it involves creating completely new processes and approaches and ignoring the way work has been accomplished in the past. We will discuss reengineering and process management in other chapters, but these go hand in hand with the standards material we describe in this chapter.

Standardization, whether accomplished by technology or by improvements in work processes, reduces GAP 2. Both technology and improved work processes structure important elements of service provision and also facilitate goal setting. It is important to recognize that standardization does not mean that service is performed in a rigid, mechanical way. Customer-defined standardization ensures that the most critical elements of a service are performed as expected by customers, not that every action in a service is executed in a uniform manner. Using customer-defined standardization can, in fact, allow for and be compatible with employee empowerment. One example of this compatibility involves the time limits many companies establish for customer service calls. If their customers' highest priorities involve feeling good about the call or resolving problems, then setting a limit for calls would be decidedly company defined and not in customers' best interests. In other words, this would be standardization that both constrains employees and works against customer priorities. Companies like American Express and L. L. Bean, in using customer priorities rather than company priorities, have no set standard for the amount of time an employee spends on the telephone with a customer. Instead, they have standards that focus on making the customer satisfied and comfortable, allowing telephone representatives to use their own judgment about the time limits.

Absence of Formal Goal Setting

Companies that have been successful in delivering consistently high service quality are noted for establishing formal standards to guide employees in providing service. These companies have an accurate sense of how well they are performing service that is critical to their customers—how long it takes to conduct transactions, how frequently service fails, how quickly they settle customer complaints—and strive to improve by defining goals that lead them to meet or exceed customer expectations.

Several types of formal goal setting are relevant in service businesses. First, a target for an individual behavior or action needs to be established. As an example, consider the behavior "calls the customer back quickly," an action that signals responsiveness in contact employees. If the service goal for employee behavior is stated in such a general term as "call the customer back quickly," the standard provides little direction for service employees. Different employees will interpret this vague objective in their own ways, leading to inconsistent service: some may call the customer back in ten minutes whereas others may wait two to four days. And the firm itself will not be able to determine when or if individual employees meet the goal because its expression is not measurable—one could justify virtually any amount of time as "quickly." On the other hand, if the individual employee's service goal is to call each customer back within four hours, employees have a specific and unambiguous guideline about how quickly they should execute the action (four hours). Whether the goal is met is also unequivocal: if it occurs within four hours it meets the goal, otherwise it does not.

Another type of formal goal setting involves the overall department or company target, most frequently expressed as a percentage, across all executions of the behavior or action. For example, a department might set as its overall goal "to call the customer back within four hours 97 percent of the time" and collect data over a month's or year's time to evaluate the extent to which it meets the target.

Service firms that produce consistently excellent service—firms like Walt Disney, Federal Express, and Merrill Lynch—have very specific, quantified, measurable service goals. Walt Disney calibrates employee performance on myriad behaviors and actions that contribute to guest perceptions of high service quality. Whether they are set and monitored using audits (such as timed actions) or customer perceptions (such as opinions about courtesy), service standards provide a means for formal goal setting.

Lack of Customer-defined Standards

Virtually all companies possess service standards and measures that are *company defined*—they are established to reach internal company goals for productivity, efficiency, cost, or technical quality. To close GAP 2, standards set by companies must be based on customer requirements and expectations rather than just on internal company goals. In this chapter we make the case that company-defined standards are not typically successful in driving behaviors that close Provider GAP 2. Instead, a company must set *customer-defined standards:* operational standards based on pivotal customer requirements that are visible to and measured by customers. These standards are deliberately chosen to match customer expectations and to be calibrated the way the customer views and expresses them. Because these are the goals that are essential to the provision of excellent service, the rest of this chapter will focus on customer-defined standards.

Knowing customer requirements, priorities, and expectation levels can be both effective and efficient. Anchoring service standards on customers can save money by identifying what the customer values, thus eliminating activities and features that the customer either does not notice or will not pay for. Through precise measurement of expectations, the company often discovers that it has been overdelivering to many customer needs:

> . . . a bank might add several extra tellers and reduce the average peak waiting time in line from 7 minutes to 5 minutes. If customers expect, however, to wait up to 8 minutes during peak time, the investment in extra tellers may not be effective. An opportunity thus exists to capture the value of this information through reduced teller costs and higher profits.[5]

While customer-defined standards need not conflict with productivity and efficiency, they do not originate with these company concerns. Rather they are anchored in and steered by customer perceptual measures of service quality or satisfaction. The service standards that evolve from a customer perspective are likely to be different from company-defined service standards.

Virtually all organizations have lists of things they measure regularly, most of which fall into the category of company-defined standards. Often these standards deal with activities or actions that reflect the history of the business rather than the reality of today's competitive marketplace or the needs of current customers.

CUSTOMER-DEFINED SERVICE STANDARDS

The type of standards that close Provider GAP 2 are *customer-defined standards,* operational goals and measures based on pivotal customer requirements that are visible to and measured by customers. They are operations standards set to correspond to customer expectations and priorities rather than to company concerns such as productivity or efficiency. They are the translation of customer requirements into goals and guidelines for employee performance. Two major types of customer-defined service standards can be distinguished.

"Hard" Customer-defined Standards

All of the Federal Express standards that comprise the SQI fall into the category of "hard" standards and measures: things that can be counted, timed, or observed through audits. Many of Federal Express's standards relate to on-time delivery and not making mistakes, and for good reason. As we stressed earlier in this textbook, customer expectations of reliability—fulfillment of service promises—are high. A series of 35 studies across numerous industries from the Arthur D. Little management consulting firm found that the most frequently cited customer complaint was late product and service delivery (44 %), followed by product and service quality mistakes (31%).[6]

To address the need for reliability, companies can institute a "do it right the first time" and an "honor your promises" value system by establishing reliability standards. An example of a generic reliability standard that would be relevant to virtually any service company is "right first time," which means that the service performed is done correctly the first time according to the customer's assessment. If the service involves delivery of products, "right first time" to the customer might mean that the shipment is accurate—that it contains all that the customer ordered and nothing that the customer did not order.

If the service involves installation of equipment, "right first time" would likely mean that the equipment was installed correctly and was able to be used immediately by the customer. Another example of a reliability standard is "right on time," which means that the service is performed at the scheduled time. The company representative arrives when promised or the delivery is made at the time the customer expects it. In more complex services, such as disaster recovery or systems integration in computer service, "right on time" would likely mean that the service was completed by the promised date.

When it comes to providing service across cultures and continents, service providers need to recognize that customer-defined service standards often need to be adapted. In the United States we expect waiters to bring the check promptly. In fact, if we do not receive it shortly after the last course, and without our asking for it, we evaluate the service as slow and nonresponsive. In Spain, however, customers consider it rude for the waiter to bring the check to the table without being asked to do so. They feel rushed, a state they dislike during meals. While bringing the check to the table (whether sooner or later, requested or not) is an activity that restaurants need to incorporate as a customer-defined service standard, the parameters of the standard must be adapted to the culture.

Hard service standards for responsiveness are set to ensure the speed or promptness with which companies deliver products (within two working days), handle complaints (by sundown each day), answer questions (within two hours), and arrive for repair calls (within thirty minutes of estimated time). In addition to standard setting that specifies levels of response, companies must have well-staffed customer service departments. Responsiveness perceptions diminish when customers wait to get through to the company by telephone, are put on hold, or are dumped into a phone mail system. A well-structured and well-trained body of employees is also essential. L. L. Bean has three separate groups of customer service people (one to receive orders, another to handle telephone inquiries, and still another for mail order) because it finds that asking contact representatives to do all three creates confusion and role stress. New contact employees are trained in specific responsiveness interpersonal skills including opening, tone, problem solving, summarizing actions/outcome, and closing/offering future assistance. The company also has three specialized support groups to facilitate and assist contact personnel: research teams (who deal with complex service issues and correspondence), merchandise information teams (for sporting goods, soft goods, and parts), special services teams (for international orders, special orders, and repairs), and outbound services teams (who focus on missing information and problems with orders).

Table 8-1 shows a sampling of the hard standards that have been established by service companies. This list is a small subset of all of these standards because we include only those that are customer defined—based on customers' requirements and perspectives. Because Federal Express has a relatively simple and standard set of services, it can translate most of its customers' requirements into hard standards and measures. Not all standards, however, are as easily quantifiable as those at Federal Express.

"Soft" Customer-defined Standards

All customer priorities cannot be counted, timed, or observed through audits. As Albert Einstein once said, "Not everything that counts can be counted, and not everything that

TABLE 8-1   EXAMPLES OF HARD CUSTOMER-DEFINED STANDARDS

Company	Customer priorities	Customer-defined standard
Honeywell (Home and Building Division	Fast response; on-time delivery; order accuracy	Orders entered same day received; orders delivered when promised; order correct
Southern Pacific	19 Key attributes	Operational measures to correspond with the 19 key attributes
Federal Express	On-time delivery	# of Packages right day late; # of packages wrong day late; # of missed pickups
Dun and Bradstreet Information Services	Fast turnaround on company investigations	36-Hour response time (previous standard: 7 days)
University Microfilms	Fast processing of theses	Theses processed in 60 days (previous average, 150 days)
Great Plains Software	Rapid response to technical problems	Response time guaranteed at 1 or 3 hours (or get $25 coupon)
Canadian Imperial Bank of Commerce	Accessibility	5-Minute early opening and late closing
Land's End	Personal attention	No standard or measurement for length of telephone call
U.S. Healthcare	Fast response; regular contact with customers	20-Second average call answering; 95% same-day problem resolution; 2-hour response time for requests; proactive service calls 3X per year
Granite Rock	Getting the concrete when the crew is ready	On-time delivery (now at 93.5% ± 15 min.) (was at 70% ± 30 min.)
Lenscrafters (optical retailer)	Quick turnaround on glasses	Glasses in 1 hour (now at 95%)
Texas Instruments (Defense Systems Electronics Group)	Compliance with commitments; more personal contact	On-time delivery; product compliance to requirements; customer visits
Florida Power & Light	Short wait time	Wait time (segmented by type of call)

can be counted, counts." For example, "understanding and knowing the customer" is not a customer priority for which a standard that counts, times, or observes employees can adequately capture. In contrast to hard measures, which are operational, soft measures are those that must be documented using perceptual measures. We call the second category of customer-defined standards *soft standards and measures* because they are opinion-based measures that cannot be observed and must be collected by talking to customers, employees, or others. Soft standards provide direction, guidance, and feedback to employees in ways to achieve customer satisfaction and can be quantified by measuring customer perceptions and beliefs. These are especially important for person-to-person interactions such as the selling process and the delivery process for professional services. Table 8-2 shows examples of soft customer-defined standards.

TABLE 8-2   EXAMPLES OF SOFT CUSTOMER-DEFINED STANDARDS

Company	Customer priorities	Customer-defined standards
General Electric	*Interpersonal skills of operators:* *Tone of voice* *Problem solving* *Summarizing actions* *Closing*	Taking ownership of the call; following through with promises made; being courteous and knowledgeable; understanding the customer's question or request

Ritz-Carlton	*Treat me with respect*	"Gold Standards"
		    Uniforms are to be immaculate
		    Wear proper and safe footware
		    Wear name tag
		    Adhere to grooming standards
		    Notify supervisor immediately of hazards
		    Use proper telephone etiquette
		    Ask the caller, "May I place you on hold?"
		    Do not screen calls
		    Eliminate call transfers where possible

Nationwide Insurance	*Responsiveness*	Human voice on the line when customers report problems
L. L. Bean	*Calming human voice; minimize customer anxiety*	Tone of voice; other tasks not done (arranging gift boxes) while on the telephone with customers
Florida Power & Light	*Telephone responsiveness*	Customers not put on hold or transferred; ability to answer questions; courteous and professional; caring and concern
American Express	*Resolution of problems*	Resolve problem at first contact (no transfers, other calls, or multiple contacts); communicate and give adequate instructions; Take all the time necessary
	Treatment	Listen; do everything possible to help; be appropriately reassuring (open and honest)
	Courtesy of representative	Put card member at ease; be patient in explaining billing process; display sincere interest in helping card member; listen attentively; address card member by name; thank card member at end of call

At GE's industrial answer center, soft standards and measures have been incorporated to ensure that customer requirements are met. A percentage of all callers to the 800 number is surveyed to determine if the customer service agents exhibited the behaviors customers think are most important:

Taking ownership of the call
Following through with promises made
Being courteous and knowledgeable
Understanding the customer's question or request.

Results are reported and discussed weekly and are used as the basis for identifying problems and developing approaches to correct them and thereby satisfy customers.

Mini Maid Services, a firm that franchises home and office janitorial services, successfully built a business by developing a repertoire of 22 customer-defined soft standards for daily cleaning chores. The company sends out crews of four who perform these 22 tasks in an average time of fifty-five minutes for a fee of $39.50 to $49.50. Follow-up trailer calls survey customer perceptions of the effectiveness of these soft standards.

The Ritz-Carlton, winner of the 1992 Malcolm Baldrige Award, uses a set of "Gold Standards" to drive the service performance it wants. Among the soft standards established are the following:

> Uniforms are to be immaculate. Wear proper and safe footwear (clean and polished), and your correct name tag. Take pride and care in your personal appearance (adhering to all grooming standards).
>
> Notify your supervisor immediately of hazards, injuries, equipment or assistance that you need.
>
> Use proper telephone etiquette. Answer within three rings and with a "smile." When necessary, ask the caller, "May I place you on hold?" Do not screen calls. Eliminate call transfers where possible.[7]

One-Time Fixes

When customer research is undertaken to find out what aspects of service need to be changed, requirements can sometimes be met using *one-time fixes*. One-time fixes are technology, policy, or procedure changes that, when instituted, address customer requirements. Performance standards do not typically need to be developed for these dissatisfiers because the one-time change in technology, policy, or procedures accomplishes the desired change.

To illustrate policy and procedure changes in an international context, consider London's Central Middlesex Hospital. At one time almost everything about Central Middlesex, from the architectural design of the buildings to staff processes and activities, centered on the in-patient aspects of the business, despite the fact that 90 percent of the hospital's patients were out-patients. When the hospital became a self-governing trust under the British government's National Health Service reforms, plans were announced to convert it to a patient-focused hospital. The most important one-time fix was to reverse the emphasis from in-patients to out-patients. With the recognition for this change, the hospital was reorganized around 14 ambulatory centers such as rehabilitation services and a family care center that combines obstetrics, pediatrics, and gynecology.

Examples of successful one-time fixes include Marriott Hotel's express checkout and check-in, GM Saturn's one-price policy for automobiles, and Granite Rock's twenty-four-hour express service. In each of these examples, customers had expressed a desire to be served in ways different from the past. Marriott's customers had clearly indicated their frustration at waiting in long checkout lines. Saturn customers disliked haggling over car prices in dealer showrooms. And Granite Rock, a 1992 Malcolm Baldrige National Quality Award winner with a "commodity" product, had customers who desired twenty-four-hour availability of ground rock from its quarry.

Where most companies in their industries decided for various reasons not to address these customer requirements, Marriott, Saturn, and Granite Rock each responded with one-time fixes that virtually revolutionized the service quality delivered by their companies. Marriott used technology to create Express Checkout, a one-time fix that also resulted in productivity improvements and cost reductions. The company recently announced a similar one-time fix for hotel Express Check-In, again in response to customers' expressed desires. Saturn countered industry tradition and offered customers a one-price policy that eliminated the haggling characteristics of automobile dealerships. And Granite Rock created an ATM-like system for twenty-four-hour customer access to rock ground to the 14 most popular consistencies. The company created its own Granite Xpress Card that allowed customers to enter, select, and receive their supplies at any time of the day or night.

One-time fixes are often accomplished by hard technology. Hard technology can simplify and improve customer service, particularly when it frees company personnel by handling routine, repetitive tasks and transactions. Customer service employees can then spend more time on the personal and possibly more essential portions of the job. American Airlines, whose standardized and automated baggage handling process is legendary, learned long ago that the standardization of its baggage system with hard technology could free the company to provide highly personalized service in cases where baggage was lost:

> A phone call to the lost-baggage number from any location at any hour is answered by a live sales rep at a center manned around the clock. The live voice didn't know any more than the tape message did but the reality was the sympathetic response the living person provided—a degree of comfort no tape machine could match.[8]

Some hard technology, in particular computer data bases that contain information on individual needs and interests of customers, allows the company to standardize the essential elements of service delivery. Basic delivery standards can then be established and measured. Some types of hard technology useful in standard setting include information data bases, automated transactions, and scheduling and delivery systems. Effective use of information data bases is illustrated in the following examples:

> Campbell Soup receives regular requests for information about product ingredients, nutritional value, and flavors. Because many of these requests are repetitive, the company created a large computer data base to respond. The data base allows Campbell to define service protocols, standard ways to respond quickly to customer requests, that appear to give individualized attention and provide answers to all questions. The data base frees up employees, because the only questions they must handle personally are those not within the categories covered by the data base.[9]

> Marshall Field's eliminated "task-interfering duties" for salespeople. The retail store automated check approval, implemented in-store telephone directories to allow employees to contact other departments and other stores quickly, reorganized wrapping stations, and simplified order forms, all of which resulted in faster checkout and more attention to the customer. Each of these tasks had previously required varying amounts of time and blocked employees from responding quickly to customer requests.

Pizza Hut centralized and computerized its home delivery operations. Rather than having the separate tasks of order taking, baking, and delivery all in the same location, the company developed a system that works more effectively for both the company and the customer. Operators in a customer service center (not a bakery) take requests for pizza. Working from a data base that shows past orders, trained operators take an average of seventeen seconds to verify directions to a caller's home and enter his or her request. Operators then route the orders to the closest bake shops, which are strategically located throughout cities to ensure fast deliveries. Cooks in the satellite bake shops prepare pizzas on instructions sent to bake shop printers from ordertakers' computers. Drivers aim to complete their deliveries within a half hour of a customer's call, and usually succeed.

One-time fixes also deal with the aspects of service that are affected by things other than human performance: rules and policies, operating hours, product quality, and price. An example of a one-time fix involving a policy change is that of allowing front-line employees to refund money to dissatisfied customers. An example of operating hour changes is one allowing retail establishments to be open on Sundays.

Building Blocks: The Service Encounter Sequence

Customer-defined standards are established to define processes or human performance operationally to meet the expectations of customers. Performance requirements are rarely the same across all parts of a company; instead, they are associated with particular service processes and encounters. Consider Figure 8-3, a representation of AT&T General Business Systems's customer contact processes, which decomposes the relationship between the customer and AT&T across the entire business.[10] Except for the top branch, labeled "Product" (which reflects the tangible equipment the company sells), each of the business process branches represents a company process during which customers and the firm interact. The first customer-firm interaction point is sales, followed by installation, repair, and billing. AT&T recognized that its customers' requirements and priorities differed across these processes. Because of these differences, internal measurements chosen to drive behavior differ across the processes and correspond to customers' priorities in each individual encounter.

A customer's overall service quality evaluation is the accumulation of evaluations of multiple service experiences. Service encounters, therefore, are the building blocks for service quality and the component pieces needed to establish service standards in a company. In establishing standards we are concerned with service encounter quality, for we want to understand for each service encounter the specific requirements and priorities of the customer. When we know these priorities we can focus on them as the aspects of service encounters for which standards should be established. Therefore, one of the first steps in establishing customer-defined standards is to delineate the service encounter sequence. The top half of Figure 8-4 shows such a sequence defined by a computer manufacturer.

Defining service encounter sequences has other advantages for the company. The service encounter view provides information that allows service companies to better diag-

Business Process	Customer Need		Internal Metric
30% Product	Reliability	(40%)	% Repair Call
	Easy to Use	(20%)	% Calls for Help
	Features / Functions	(40%)	Functional Performance Test
30% Sales	Knowledge	(30%)	Supervisor Observations
	Responsive	(25%)	% Proposal Made on Time
	Follow-up	(10%)	% Follow Up Made
10% Installation	Delivery Interval Meets Needs	(30%)	Average Order Interval
	Does Not Break	(25%)	% Repair Reports
	Installed When Promised	(10%)	% Installed on Due Date
15% Repair	No Repeat Trouble	(30%)	% Repeat Reports
	Fixed Fast	(25%)	Average Speed of Repair
	Kept Informed	(10%)	% Customers Informed
15% Billing	Accuracy, No Surprise	(45%)	% Billing Inquiries
	Resolve on First Call	(35%)	% Resolved First Call
	Easy to Understand	(10%)	% Billing Inquiries

(Total Quality brackets Product and Sales)

FIGURE 8-3   AT&T's process map for measurements.

Source: AT&T General Business Systems

nose their strengths and weaknesses, translating requirements into specific behaviors customers are expecting. Understanding behaviors at the level of a service encounter facilitates behavior change in employees by clearly describing what customers expect. It is also easier to identify the appropriate customers to survey and satisfy at the service encounter level than at the overall relationship level. For example, in the "sales contact before sale" interaction, it would be desirable to survey and satisfy the decision-maker, whereas in "hardware service," the appropriate person would be the user. Furthermore, employees can easily identify which service encounters they are responsible for. Next, research by service encounter can be readily incorporated when companies redesign service processes because it is specific and detailed. Finally, measurement by interaction can occur continuously rather than periodically, offering an opportunity to constantly monitor customer feedback and the impact of changes in marketing and selling.

In developing customer-defined standards, companies frequently find that their own views of the service encounter sequence may not mesh with the customer's view. In establishing standards for the company depicted in Figure 8-4, researchers found that customers explicitly stated that they did not always want to interact with the company in the manner the company had established. Companies often distinguish service interactions by the role of the company personnel involved (such as salesperson, technical person, manager), rather than by the customer's purpose.

The bottom half of Figure 8-4 shows the customer version of the service encounter sequence. The steps are much more specific than the company-defined steps. For example, the customer wanted the "contact before the sale" interaction to be more than just a selling interaction. In fact, customers could distinguish between two separate interac-

Defined by a Computer Manufacturer

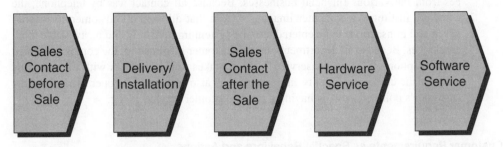

Defined by a Computer Manufacturer's Customer

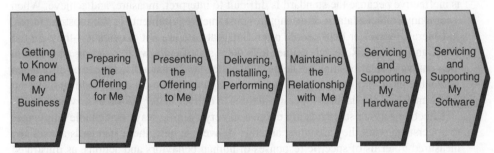

FIGURE 8-4   Service encounter sequences.

tions: (1) getting to know me and (2) selling to me. Customers felt that careful listening and understanding of their needs were central to virtually all other issues. Specifying a separate presale interaction for getting to know customers and determining their requirements was the way the company addressed the customer's desire to be known and understood.

The differences between the company's and the customer's views in Figure 8-4 are not extreme, they simply represent recasting of the interactions. For many service companies, however, the difference between the company's view of the interactions and customers' desired ways to interact with the company are radically different. Consider, for example, most insurance companies and financial services firms, which are organized internally by "product"—the type of insurance or financial product offered. Each product part of the business deals individually with customers, even though customers overlap across products. Residential insurance customers, for example, buy property, casualty, and automobile insurance. But because the companies view the external world from their internal perspectives, there is no organization or integration by customer. Instead, a customer wanting to change an address record within the company is forced to make multiple calls to locate the right parts of the company.

Some insurance and financial service organizations have made this change. USAA, United Service Automobile Association, believes strongly in its "one company" image. The company discovered that customers wanted contact personnel to be familiar with them and their needs across the business, rather than having to talk to different employees from the various financial businesses. Because all contact was by telephone, the company instituted a computer imaging system that allowed all customer correspondence and transactions to be entered into the system immediately and be available to all employees. Because all departments shared customer information, the company created the perception of "seamless service," which makes doing business with the company easy for the customer. Fidelity Investments has also integrated its operations from the customer's point of view by having a single customer service center.

Expressing Customer Requirements as Specific Behaviors and Actions

Setting a standard in broad conceptual terms, such as "improve skills in the company," is ineffective because the standard is difficult to interpret, measure, and achieve. When a company collects data, it often captures customer requirements in very abstract terms. In general, contact or field people often find that data are not diagnostic—they are too broad and general. Research neither tells them specifically what is wrong and right in their customer relationships nor helps them understand what activities can be eliminated so that the most important actions can be accomplished. In most cases, field people need help translating the data into specific actions to deliver better customer service.

Effective service standards are defined in very specific ways that enable employees to understand what they are being asked to deliver. At best, these standards are set and measured in terms of specific responses of human behaviors and actions, as illustrated by the following quote from an American Airlines executive:

> We have standards for almost every area of the operation, and we check them on a regular basis. We are constantly measuring how long it takes us to answer a reservations call, or process a customer in a ticket line, or get a plane-load of passengers on board the aircraft, or open the door of the airplane once it reaches its destination, or get food on, or get trash off.[11]

While all of the examples in this quote are hard standards, soft standards can also be described and measured using perceptions data. The measures of these activities form the baseline for performance at American Airlines and the standard against which all ensuing transactions are measured.

Figure 8-5 shows different levels of abstraction/concreteness for a service firm arrayed from top (most abstract) to bottom (most concrete and specific). At the very abstract level are customer requirements that are too general to be useful to employees: customers want satisfaction, value, and relationships. One level under these very general requirements are abstract dimensions of service quality already discussed in this book: reliability, responsiveness, empathy, assurance, and tangibles. One level further are attributes more specific in describing requirements. If we dig still deeper beneath the attribute level, we get to specific behaviors and actions that are at the right level of specificity for setting standards. Exhibit 8-1 defines and describes the concepts related to these levels of abstraction and customer-defined standards.

A real-world example of the difference in requirements across these levels will illustrate the practical significance of these levels. In Skill Dynamics's traditional measure-

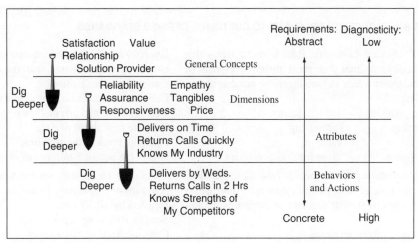

FIGURE 8-5   What customers expect: getting to actionable steps.

ment system, only one aspect of the instructor was included in its class evaluation: ability of instructor. During qualitative research relating to the attributes that satisfy students of Skill Dynamics, three somewhat more specific requirements were elicited: (1) instructor's style, (2) instructor's expertise, and (3) instructor's management of class. While the articulation of the three attributes was more helpful to instructors than the broad "ability of instructor," management found that the attributes were still too broad to be helpful to instructors wanting to improve their course delivery. When the company invested in a customer-defined standards project in 1993, the resulting measurement system was far more useful in diagnosing student requirements because the research focused on *specific behaviors and actions* of instructors that met student requirements. Instead of a single broad requirement or three general attributes, the requirements of students are articulated in 14 specific behaviors and actions that relate to the instructor and 11 specific behaviors and actions that relate to the course content. These behaviors and actions are clearly more diagnostic for communicating what was good and bad in the courses. An additional benefit of this approach is that feedback on behaviors and actions is less personal than feedback on traits or personal characteristics. It is also easier for employees of a company to make changes that relate to behaviors rather than to personality traits.

In summary, the level of customer requirements appropriate for customer-defined standards is concrete behaviors and actions. These are equivalent to features and functions in products, whereas the most abstract level is equivalent to product benefits. It is relatively easy to distinguish between a product feature (the color is red and the instrument panel has 25 buttons) and a benefit (the car has prestige or high performance). But distinguishing between behaviors and actions and attributes or dimensions of service is more complicated, and requires a researcher's experience and familiarity with services. The difficulty in distinguishing among these levels is one of the main reasons quality approaches used in manufacturing (for example, "voice of the customer" and a widely used

---

EXHIBIT 8-1   CONCEPTS RELEVANT TO CUSTOMER-DEFINED STANDARDS

General, Abstract Concepts: Broad, vague terms that could incorporate many or most different aspects of what a customer wants and are therefore not diagnostic. Examples:

Solution provider	Service quality
Relationship	Partnership
Quality	Value
Total solution	Value for the investment

Service Dimensions: More specific (and therefore more diagnostic) than general abstract concepts, *dimensions* are subgroups of similar features or attributes. Examples:

Reliability	Responsiveness
Empathy	Tangibles
Courtesy	Competence
Assurance	Understanding the customer

Attributes: Specific features or characteristics that describe aspects of service. Because attributes are more specific than the terms above, they are more diagnostic. Examples:

Answers calls quickly	Respects my point of view
Meets deadlines	Acknowledges problems
Delivers on time	Shares knowledge with me
Asks me what I want	Keeps me informed
Adjusts the system	Apologizes
Listens	Provides information

Behaviors and Actions: Concrete and tangible representations of requirements that fully define the performance expected. Examples:

Delivers or installs on promised date
Gets price we had originally agreed upon
Tells me cost ahead of time
Fixes the product the first time
Greets me within 5 minutes of entering store

Standards: Guidelines set for behaviors, actions, and activities of employees. Examples:

Delivers by 10:30 a.m.
Sends a follow-up letter
Calls me back within 4 hours
Resolves every complaint by end of day
Opens airplane door within 16 seconds
Proposals have fewer than 10 pages

Measures: Metrics that allow tracking of conformance to standards. Examples:

Number of times packages are delivered late
Percentage of total packages delivered late
Number of complaints resolved by end of day
Percentage of complaints resolved by end of day
Percentage of proposals with correct number of pages

---

method of quality analysis called "quality function deployment") have been more difficult to apply in service companies than in product companies.

Measurements of Behaviors and Actions

Hard Measurements   Hard measurements consist of counts or audits or timed actions that provide feedback about the operational performance of a service standard. What distinguishes these data from soft measurements is that they can be captured continuously without asking the customer's opinion about them. To demonstrate, here are some of the actual hard measurements for components of the Federal Express SQI:

Missing Proofs of Delivery. The number of invoices that do not include proof-of-delivery paperwork

Overgoods. Lost and found packages that lack, or have lost, identifying labels for the sender and the addressee and are sent to the Overgoods Department

Wrong Day Late Deliveries. Packages delivered after the commitment date

Traces. The number of "proof of performance" requests from customers that cannot be answered through data contained in the computer system.[12]

In these and other hard measurements, the actual gauge involves a count of the number and type of actions or behaviors that are correct or incorrect. Somewhere in the operation system these actions and behaviors are tabulated, frequently through information technology (see the technology spotlight). Other gauges of hard measures include service guarantee lapses (the number of times a service guarantee is invoked because the service did not meet the promise), amounts of time (as in the number of hours or days to respond to a question or complaint, or minutes waited in line), and frequencies associated with relevant standards (such as the number of visits made to customers).

TECHNOLOGY SPOTLIGHT

THE ROLE OF INFORMATION TECHNOLOGY IN CUSTOMER-DEFINED STANDARDS

Performance measurement has been facilitated, in fact made possible, in large part through dramatic improvements in information technology, particularly in computer hardware and software. Information technology allows companies to generate, analyze, store, and disseminate large data bases of information.

Federal Express's state of the art information tracking system, called COSMOS IIB, is able to track and process real-time data in a very short period of time:

Beginning when a courier picks up a package, and repeated each time that a package changes hands within the delivery process, a Federal Express employee uses a hand-held SuperTracker computer to scan an identifying bar code preprinted on the package's airbill. The SuperTracker automatically records the time and date of each scan and downloads the information to COSMOS IIB. When the package is delivered, the delivery courier performs a proof-of-delivery scan of the bar code, while entering the first initial and last name of the person who signed for the package. Thus, when a customer calls to inquire, "Where is my package?" "Who signed for it?" "What time did it arrive?," a customer service agent can access COSMOS IIB to describe the package's complete history. Even if the package was delivered just minutes before, the customer service agent will be able to confirm where and at what time the package arrived, and who received it.[13]

Among the information technology innovations that are leading the way to better service:

• *Computerized performance monitoring and control systems.* CPMCSs have been developed to gather and track employee service performance data. Performance measures such as length of service calls, speed of answering, and number of abandoned calls can be documented automatically by these systems. Some employee confusion and resistance may accompany the use of these systems, which have historically triggered opposition from trade unions. The impact of the systems depends on the way they are designed and used within companies. Creating a balance among the design factors—behavioral aspects measured, frequency of measurement, recipients of data, and tasks monitored by the system—can improve employee receptivity. If employees are well trained and knowledgeable about the system and if the computer data are managed in a positive manner for continuous improvement, they should be able to be successfully integrated.[14]

• *PowerShips and MaxiShips.* Federal Express Corporation and United Parcel Service are competing head to head on innovative technology. Both systems store addresses and shipping data, print mailing labels, and tack the whereabouts of packages. PowerShips are kits that FedEx has given to more than 26,500 of its best customers. UPS has given out about 15,000 MaxiShips to its customers. Both systems allow the shipping companies essentially to bring their customers into their operations. By using these technologies the companies gain loyalty of customers and reduce comparison shopping. FedEx offers "FedExtras," tracking software and prizes such as photocopiers and cellular phones, to companies that boost their usage with FedEx.[15]

In the 1980s, American Express Company's Travel-Related Services division found customer expectations about credit-card services increased tremendously as competition in the industry intensified. Rather than accept performance that departed more and more from expectations as the competitive pressure built, the company decided that computer improvements were the answer to meeting customer expectations. Through the computer improvements they developed, many important customer requests were met. The division reduced personal card processing from an average of thirty-five days to fifteen days, replaced cards in an average of two days rather than fifteen days, dropped response time to card holder inquiries from sixteen to ten days, answered merchant inquiries in four days rather than fourteen, and reduced emergency service for card replacement to within twenty-four hours worldwide.[16]

Computer information systems are often the basis for setting standards to improve customer service. L. L. Bean, the direct marketer, earned its reputation for outstanding customer service using a computer data base that supplies moment-to-moment information about models, colors, and sizes of products in stock. With this system the company can set and achieve high standards of customer service. The data base enables them to fill an incredible 99.8 percent of orders accurately.[17]

The appropriate hard measure to deliver to customer requirements is not always intuitive or obvious, and the potential for counting or tracking an irrelevant aspect of operations is high. For this reason it is desirable to link the measure of operational performance with soft measures (surveys or trailer calls) to be sure that they are strongly correlated.

Soft Measurements   Two types of perceptual measurement that were described in chapter 6 can document customers' opinions about whether performance met the standards established: trailer calls and relationship surveys. Relationship surveys cover all aspects of the customer's relationship with the company, are typically expressed in attributes, and are usually completed once per year. Trailer calls are associated with specific service encounters, are short (approximately six or seven questions), and are administered as close in time to a specific service encounter as possible. An example of a trailer questionnaire for a complaint-handling service encounter is shown in Exhibit 8-2. Trailer calls can be administered in various ways: company-initiated telephone calls following the interactions, postcards to be mailed, letters requesting feedback, customer-initiated calls to an 800 number, or on-line electronic surveys. For requirements that are longer term and at a higher level of abstraction (e.g., at the attribute level), annual relationship surveys can document customer perceptions on a periodic basis. Trailer calls are administered continuously, whenever a customer experiences a service encounter of the type being considered, and they provide data on a continuous basis. The company must decide on a survey strategy combining relationship surveys and trailer calls to provide soft measurement feedback.

PROCESS FOR DEVELOPING CUSTOMER-DEFINED STANDARDS

Figure 8-6 shows the general process for setting customer-defined service standards.

EXHIBIT 8-2   TRAILER QUESTIONNAIRE FOR COMPLAINT HANDLING SERVICE ENCOUNTER

1. How satisfied were you with the way we handled your recent comment or complaint to the company? *Completely* 1 2 3 4 5 *Not at all*	c. Listen to /understand your complaint Yes No d. Ask what solution you prefer Yes No e. Follow through on promises Yes No
2. When you contacted us, did we:	3. If you answered "No" above, please explain._____
a. Respond quickly Yes No	_____
b. Respond courteously	_____

Step 1: Identify Existing or Desired Service Encounter Sequence

The first step involves delineating the service encounter sequence. Some companies will view this sequence as AT&T General Business Systems did in Figure 8-3. Ideally, the company would be open to discovering customers' desired service encounter sequences, exploring the ways customers want to do business with the firm.

Step 2: Translate Customer Expectations into Behaviors and Actions for Each Service Encounter

The input to step 2 is existing research on customer expectations. In this step, abstract customer requirements and expectations must be translated into concrete, specific behaviors and actions associated with each encounter in the service encounter sequence. Abstract requirements (e.g., reliability) can call for a different behavior or action in each service encounter, and these differences must be probed. Eliciting these behaviors and actions is likely to require additional qualitative research because most service company's marketing information has not been collected for this purpose.

Information on behaviors and actions must be gathered and interpreted by an objective source such as a research firm or an inside department with no stake in the ultimate decisions. If the information is filtered through company managers or front-line people with an internal bias, the outcome would be company-defined rather than customer-defined standards.

Research techniques discussed in chapter 6 that are relevant for eliciting behaviors and actions include in-depth interviewing of customers, focus group interviews, and other forms of research such as partnering.

Focus groups or in-depth interviews can use funnel techniques (funneling thinking about the general service or transaction down to the specific behaviors that interviewees associate with good or poor performance) or critical incident techniques to identify behaviors and actions that signaled that the service was performed especially well or poorly. Customer panels—groups of customers that meet regularly—are also effective. IBM U.S., in developing its AS/400 computer (admittedly a product rather than a service, but some elements of the offering involved services), used the partnering approach in attaining the Baldrige Award. Before developing the computer, company designers and marketers assembled 250 customers to determine their needs and priorities. In a

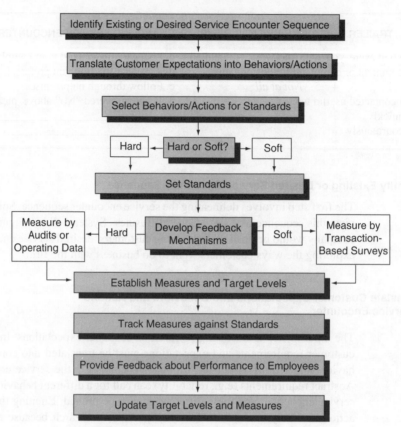

FIGURE 8-6 Process for setting customer-defined standards.

series of meetings and discussions, the company asked for customer needs and reactions to what was developed. In a sense, partnering results in customer-defined standards through negotiation with customer about their needs and the company's ability to fulfill those needs.

When customers are small in number or large in importance to companies, partnering is a useful approach. Partnering is the process by which a company and its customers (or suppliers or distributors) engage in a dialogue in which they agree to trust and share formerly proprietary information to improve products and services as well as customer satisfaction.

Step 3: Select Behaviors and Actions for Standards

This stage involves prioritizing the behaviors and actions, of which there will be many, into those for which customer-defined standards will be established. The following are the most important criteria for creation of the standards.

1 The standards are based on behaviors and actions that are very important to customers. Customers have many requirements for the products and services that companies provide. Customer-defined standards need to focus on what is *very important* to customers. Unless very important behaviors/actions are chosen, a company could show improvement in delivering to standards with no impact on overall customer satisfaction or business goals.

2 The standards cover performance that needs to be improved or maintained. Customer-defined standards should be established for behavior that needs to be improved or maintained. The company gets the highest leverage or biggest impact from focusing on behaviors and actions that need to be improved. Figure 8-7 shows a commonly used tool in marketing research called an importance/performance matrix for a computer manufacturer. It combines the importance and performance criteria and indicates by shading in the cell in the matrix where behaviors and actions should be selected to meet those criteria.

3 The standards cover behaviors and actions employees can improve. Employees perform according to standards consistently only if they understand, accept, and have control over the behaviors and actions specified in the standards. Holding contact people to standards that they cannot control (such as product quality or time lag in introduction of new products) does not result in improvement. For this reason, service standards should cover controllable aspects of employees' jobs.

FIGURE 8-7   Importance/performance matrix: delivering, installing, performing.

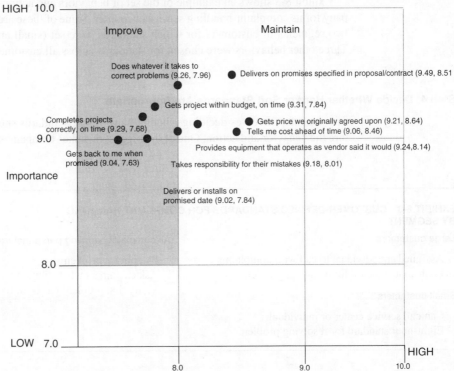

4 The standards are accepted by employees. Employees will perform to standards consistently only if they understand and accept the standards. Imposing standards on unwilling employees often leads to resistance, resentment, absenteeism, even turnover. Many companies establish standards for the amount of time it should take (rather than for the time it does take) for each service job and gradually cut back on the time to reduce labor costs. This practice inevitably leads to increasing tensions among employees. In these situations, managers, financial personnel, and union employees can work together to determine new standards for the tasks. Through this participation, commitment of the line organization can be obtained and standards will be accepted and more accurate.

5 The standards are predictive rather than reactive. Customer-defined standards should not be established on the basis of complaints or other forms of reactive feedback. Reactive feedback deals with past concerns of customers, rather than with current and future customer expectations. Rather than waiting for dissatisfied customers to complain, the company should actively seek both positive and negative perceptions of customers in advance of complaints. Research information that covers the full scope of customer requirements is the best foundation for customer-defined standards.

6 The standards are challenging but realistic. A large number of studies on goal setting show that highest performance levels are obtained when standards are challenging but realistic. If standards are not challenging, employees get little reinforcement for mastering them. On the other hand, unrealistically high standards leave an employee feeling dissatisfied with performance and frustrated by not being able to attain the goal.

Exhibit 8-3 shows an example of the set of behaviors and actions selected by a company for its complaint-handling service encounter. Some of these are different across the two segments of customers for which standards were set (small and large customers). Three other behaviors were chosen for standards across all customers.

Step 4: Decide Whether Hard or Soft Standards Are Appropriate

The next step involves deciding whether hard or soft standards should be used to capture the behavior and action. One of the biggest mistakes companies make in this step is

---

EXHIBIT 8-3 CUSTOMER-DEFINED STANDARDS FOR COMPLAINT HANDLING BY SEGMENT

Large customers

Assigned an individual to call with complaints
Four-hour standard for resolving problems

Small customers

Can call service center or individual
Eight-hour standard for resolving problems

All complaint handling personnel trained to:

Paraphrase problems
Ask customers what solution they prefer
Verify that problem has been fixed

---

to choose a hard standard hastily. Companies are accustomed to operational measures and have a bias toward them. However, unless the hard standard adequately captures the expected behavior and action, it is not customer defined. The best way to decide whether a hard standard is appropriate is to first establish a soft standard by means of trailer calls and then determine over time which operational aspect most correlates to this soft measure. Figure 8-8 shows the linkage between speed of complaint handling (a hard measure) and satisfaction (a soft measure); the figure illustrates that satisfaction strongly depends on the number of hours it takes to resolve a complaint.

Hard standards can be developed for each of the five service quality dimensions. First, reliability standards usually relate to service behaviors and actions that are performed right the first time. Therefore, establishing a standard for "right first time" may be appropriate. If the service involves delivery of products, "right first time" to the customer might mean that the shipment is accurate—that it contains all that the customer ordered and nothing that the customer did not order. If the service involves installation of equipment, "right first time" may mean equipment installed correctly so that it is immediately usable by the customer.

Another customer-defined reliability indicator is "right on time," which means that the service is performed at the scheduled time. The company representative arrives when promised or the delivery is made at the time the customer expects it. In more complex services, such as disaster recovery or systems integration, "right on time" would likely mean that the service was completed by the promised date.

Responsiveness can be translated into the amount of time the customer expects to wait between calling the company and receiving a call back with an answer or a solution. Responsiveness standards are usually stated in terms of time or speed.

FIGURE 8-8   Linkage between soft measures and hard measures for speed of complaint handling.

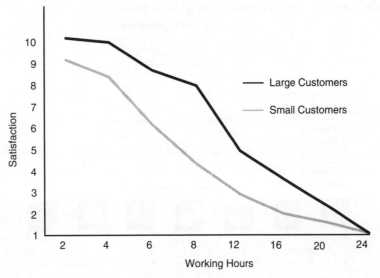

Standards for empathy and assurance are more difficult to translate into hard standards and may more appropriately be captured in soft standards and measures.

Step 5: Develop Feedback Mechanisms for Measurement to Standards

To be effective, standards must be measured and reviewed regularly. Without measurement and feedback, corrections to quality problems will probably not occur. American Airlines's service goal approach illustrates the effective use of measurement and feedback:

> Reservation phones must be answered within 20 seconds, 85% of flights must take off within five minutes of departure time and land within 15 minutes of arrival time. Cabins must have their proper supply of magazines. Performance summaries drawn up every month tell management how the airline is doing and where the problems lie. The late arrivals may have been caused by disgruntled air controllers which can't be helped. But an outbreak of dirty ashtrays may be traced to a particular clean-up crew. The manager responsible for the crew will hear about it. His pay and promotion depend on meeting standards.[18]

One critical aspect of developing feedback mechanisms is ensuring that they capture the process from the customer's view rather than the company's view. This is a difficult step for most companies. Figure 8-9 demonstrates the subtle but critical difference between viewing the process from the customer's perspective and viewing it from the company's perspective. Through research, a large credit-card company found that a pivotal customer expectation is replacement of a lost card. From the customer's point of view, quick replacement means forty-eight hours between the time the customer calls the company and the customer receives a new credit card (top part of Figure 8-9).

FIGURE 8-9   Aligning company processes with customer expectations.

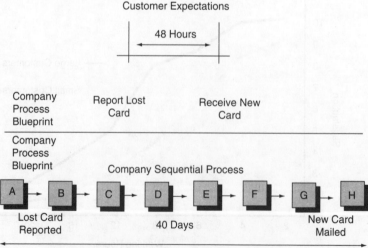

The lower half of the figure displays the company's view of the card replacement process. Replacing a card requires activities in eight departments. Each department has its own company-defined standard about the length of time needed to complete its portion of the transaction. From the company's internal perspective and time frame, card replacement consumes forty days. And while the starting point for the company is the same as the customer's, the end points are different. The end point in the company's process is mailing out the new card, whereas in the customer's it is receiving the new card. This difference could easily consume another forty-eight hours—the equivalent of the entire process according to the customer's requirement.

This example illustrates the difference between a customer-defined process standard and a company-defined process standard. A company cannot deliver market-defined service if its process for standard setting does not correspond to the customer's process.

An additional step involves creating an internal process to monitor and track, for example, the amount of time between the customer's call about a lost card and the customer's receipt of a new card. The measure must reflect the way the customer views the process and the exact way the customer measures this process.

Large companies need to set up complete systems of transaction-based surveys (also called event-triggered surveys) to capture their performance on customer-defined standards. American Express measures 13 different card member transactions and 10 service establishment transactions to track company performance on important service encounters. The individual standards for several of these service encounters are listed in Table 8-2.

Figure 8-10 shows the links among the various feedback vehicles we have described in this chapter. The M's in the figure indicate either hard or soft measurements. In each

FIGURE 8-10   Links among customer feedback vehicles.

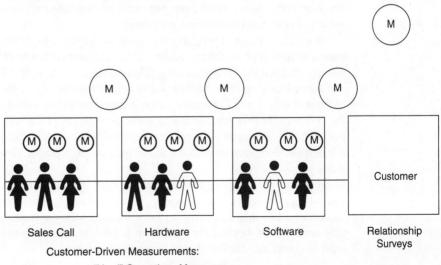

Sales Call   Hardware   Software   Relationship Surveys

Customer-Driven Measurements:

"Hard" Operations Measures
Transaction-Based "Soft" Measures

service encounter either hard, operational measurements or trailer calls are established. There is also an annual measure in the form of relationship surveys. In chapter 9 we will discuss the desirability of linking all these measurements together in a company data base. Doing so could provide invaluable information about the impact of different aspects of service delivery on overall satisfaction.

Step 6: Establish Measures and Target Levels

The next step requires that companies establish target levels for the standards. Without this step the company lacks a way to quantify whether the standards have been met. Figure 8-9 shows the approach used to set standards for timeliness in a service company. Each time a complaint was made to the company, and each time one was resolved, employees logged in the times. They also asked each customer his or her satisfaction with the performance in resolving the complaint. The company was then able to plot the information from each complaint on the chart, to determine how well the company was performing as well as where the company wished to be in the future. The vertical axis in the figure shows the satisfaction levels of customers, and the horizontal axis shows the number of hours it took the company to resolve customer problems. This technique is but one of several for determining the target level.

Simple Perception–Action Correlation Studies When the service consists of repetitive processes, companies can simply relate levels of customer satisfaction with actual performance of a behavior or task. This type of approach is called a correlation study and can be the basis for setting the optimal level for the standard. Consider, for example, a simple study to determine the standard for customers' wait time in line. The information needed includes customer perceptions of their wait in line (soft perceptual measure) and the amount of time they actually stand in line (hard operations measure). The joint collection of these data over many transactions provides evidence of the sensitivity of customers to different wait times.

An airline conducted precisely this study by having a flight attendant intercept customers as they approached the ticket counter. As each customer entered the line, the attendant stamped the entry time on a ticket (using a machine like those in parking lots) and handed the customer the stamped ticket. As the customer exited the line at the end of the transaction, the flight attendant restamped the ticket with the exit time and asked the customer three or four questions about perceptions of the wait in line and satisfaction with the transaction. Aggregating the individual customer data provided a graph that allowed the company to evaluate the impact on perceptions of various levels of line waits.

Of course, the company can also include both short-term and long-term costs in this evaluation to understand the trade-offs in cost and satisfaction. Decisions made only on short-term costs may be counter to those for long-term satisfaction. Therefore, companies need to look beyond the short term in settling customer-defined standards; long-term customer satisfaction should be the driving force.

Hypothetical Satisfaction–Performance Surveys In situations where perception–action correlation studies cannot be conducted, a similar result can be achieved using what are called hypothetical satisfaction–performance surveys. In these short (usually twenty-minute) quantitative surveys, customers are asked how satisfied they would be (from completely to not at all) if the company provided certain levels of service. For example, asking how satisfied customers would be with waiting for marketing reps to arrive for appointments for 1, 3, 5, 7, 10, . . . 120 minutes or waiting for call backs for 1/4, 1/2, 1, 1 1/2, . . . 8 hours will produce results similar to the perception–action correlation analysis and allow the company to use the same logic to select standards.

Some transactions or services fall into a gray area between hard and soft and are best handled with survey questions that examine what actions customers desire or expect. For example, assume the initial satisfaction research showed customers found the salespeople were unresponsive to requests for information. The best means for determining which information is desired and not forthcoming is a simple survey where customers rate the desirability of the information types and indicate whether the company now provides it when asked.

Competitive Benchmarking   David Kearns, former chief executive officer of Xerox Corporation, defined benchmarking as the "continuous process of measuring products, services, and practices against the toughest competitors or those companies recognized as industry leaders."[19] Rooted in the Japanese concept of *dantotsu,* meaning the best of the best, benchmarking is based on seeking the best practices (and measures of those practices) to attain superiority. One of the most important aspects of benchmarking is in setting operations standards:

> [Benchmarking] is a new way to establish operating targets—not how they have been established in the past, but established based on the best of the best practices, constantly reviewed and updated to ensure the best and most structured way to obtain long-term superiority.[20]

The use of benchmarking, however, does not always lead to customer-defined standards. Four types of benchmarking exist: *internal* (against the best internal operations), *competitive* (against external direct product competitors), *functional* (against external functional best operations or industry leaders), and *generic* (against generic functions or processes regardless of industries).[21] Both internal and competitive benchmarking run the risk of being defined internally by the company, either by looking only within the organization for best practices and measures or by defining the competitive set for the business. In both of these types of benchmarking, company-defined rather than customer-defined standards could be generated.

The company's decision about the benchmarking company may be limited to the product class, whereas the customer's view of the set of competitors may include many different companies from multiple industries. In the rapidly changing computer industry, for example, choosing companies to benchmark solely from the set of hardware vendors would be shortsighted. Most customers do not limit their scope of the information services industry to only mainframes and hardware. The best approximation to customer-defined standards would involve benchmarking the best of breed in each subset of the information services industry: hardware, software, consulting, systems integration, education, personal computers, laptops, networking, and so on. Because competition is intense in the information services industry, customer expectations are shaped by many different companies.

Step 7: Track Measures against Standards

Roger Milliken, head of Milliken Industries, is reported to have said: "In God we trust, all others bring data." Successful service businesses, such as Federal Express and Walt Disney, have careful and comprehensive fact-based systems about their operations. One company that lives and thrives through management by fact is Granite Rock in Watsonville, California. The ninety-year-old, family-run business (concrete, asphalt, and crushed stone) that won the 1992 Baldrige Award in the small-business category has been described as a "huge mechanism for gathering, analyzing, and acting on information."[22] Statistical process control and other types of charts are everywhere tracking characteristics of its concrete and crushed stone and processes such as the time it takes customers to fill their trucks. Customer complaints are also tracked through what the company calls "product-service discrepancy reports" and root-cause analysis (a Total Quality Management approach to analysis that is designed to identify the source of a problem as a first step in eliminating the problem) and updates are distributed to all 14 plants. The reports show how long it takes to resolve complaints and provide detailed quarterly analyses of trends. Plants can track their trends for four years running. As a result, the company has reduced its product liability costs to one-tenth the industry average. When it comes to product quality and customer service, Granite Rock leaves nothing to chance. According to Dave Franceschi, manager of quality support,

> We simply have to know how we're doing. And as soon as we see a dip in the numbers, we need to do some root-cause analysis. If something goes wrong, we have to figure out what happened and prevent it from happening again, so we can get back on that upward climb.[23]

Step 8: Provide Feedback about Performance to Employees

Federal Express communicates the performance on its service quality indicator daily so that everyone in the company knows how it is performing. When problems occur, they can be identified and corrected. The SQI measurement gives everyone in the company immediate feedback on activity that is strongly related to customer perceptions. In a general sense, data and facts need to be analyzed and distributed to support evaluation and decision-making at multiple levels within the company. The data also must be deployed quickly enough that the people who need it to make decisions about service or processes can do so. Responsibility for meeting service requirements must also be communicated throughout the organization. All parts of the organization must be measuring their service to internal customers, and ultimately measuring how that performance relates to external customer requirements.[24]

Step 9: Periodically Update Target Levels and Measures

The final step involves revising the target levels, measures, and even customer requirements on a regular enough basis to keep up with customer expectations.

SERVICE PERFORMANCE INDICES

One outcome from following the process just described is a service performance index. Service performance indices are comprehensive composites of the most critical performance standards. Development of an index begins by identifying the set of customer-defined standards that the company will use to drive behavior. Next, the standards and measures strategy is translated into data that are reported using a structure such as the one shown in Figure 8-11. Not all service performance indices contain customer-defined standards, but the best ones, like FedEx's SQI, are based on them. Most companies build these indices by (1) understanding the most important requirements of the customer, (2) linking these requirements to tangible and measurable aspects of service provision, and (3) using the feedback from these indices to identify and improve service problems. The most progressive companies also use the feedback for reward and recognition systems within the company. Here are a few examples of the service performance indices of U.S. companies.

Farm Credit Business' Service Quality Index In this bank's farm credit business, the organization sorted its product and service factors into two categories: *intrinsic factors,* which included components of quality that were inherent in the product or service itself, and *extrinsic factors,* which included behaviors of contact people and the prestige of the institution. Qualitative and quantitative research was then conducted and the following steps used to create the index:

1 Identify the key customer concerns that determine new purchases and retention of repeat customers.
2 Assess the relative importance to customers of intrinsic versus extrinsic concerns.
3 Assign to each concern a percentage weight to reflect its relative importance to the customer when choosing among service providers.

FIGURE 8-11 Structure for a customer service performance index.

Customer Satisfaction	Service Performance Index				
Service Encounters	Reliability	Responsiveness	Assurance	Empathy	Tangibles
Overall Satisfaction					

4 Obtain ratings of the bank and its three largest competitors from the customer's point of view.

5 Convert the bank's customer ratings into an index of quality, as follows. If the bank beats the competition by more than 1 point on a given factor, that factor's percentage of customer concern is considered "superior". If the bank is within 1 point of the competitive average, then the percentage for that factor is considered equivalent. Or, if the bank is more than 1 point below the competition, the customer concern percentage is considered inferior. The total SQI is equal to the total of the superior percentages minus the inferior percentages. If the score is positive, the company has a service quality advantage over competition.[25]

American Express's "Service Tracking Report"   This report systematically measures both customer satisfaction and employee performance worldwide. Compiled on a monthly basis, the document uses statistics to measure the performance of business units throughout the world against more than 100 service quality factors related to customers' three major service dimensions: responsiveness, timeliness, and accuracy. In the first three years of the tracking study's use, American Express improved service delivery by 78 percent and reduced each transaction's average cost by 21 percent.[26]

Southern Pacific   At one time Southern Pacific was rated lowest in its industry on customer satisfaction. Since then it has passed the competition in many areas because of a revised customer satisfaction measurement program and service performance index. It began by redesigning its survey around 19 key attributes that drove customer satisfaction. After gaining management commitment to these priorities, it linked these attributes to real operational measures and also to financial performance. It eliminated any operational measures that could not be directly linked to the 19 customer requirements. It now compares itself to best of breed in the railroad and trucking industries.

First National Bank of Chicago   This bank's tracking system won an award for excellence in 1988 from the International Customer Service Association. First Chicago tracks 650 service quality measures relating to timely, accurate, and responsive service. Measures include speed of telephone answering, number of abandoned calls, accuracy of check encoding, turnaround time on inquiries, and the speed at which the bank transfers securities. One department's clerical errors decreased from 1 per 4,000 in 1982 to 1 per 10,000 in 1989. The system saves First Chicago $7 to $10 million per year.[27]

USAA's Family of Measures (FOM)   The United Services Automobile Association tracks the quality of individual and unit performance to ensure that persons or groups are showing improvement in service delivery. The company focuses on continuous improvement—that people want an ongoing picture of how they're doing, that they want to be measured in accordance with standards they themselves have helped to set, and that they value the opportunity to improve performance without direct reference to compensation—and therefore it focuses on improvement over time, rather than on giving grades. Every month FOM tracks five areas: quality, quantity of work completed, service timeliness, resource utilization, and customer satisfaction. The FOM is a flexible evaluation process that is developed by a representative group of employees from a work unit. To develop their index, each group asks itself four questions: (1) Is the activity under our control? (2) Is it significant? (3) Does it involve some form of data that we can collect? (4) Can we easily analyze the results? They decide which measures to include and on the relative weight of each measure in the system. Two measures—quality and quantity—are weighted for each unit.[28]

Airline Performance Index   This index (developed by the National Institute for Aviation Research, Wichita State University) identifies a comprehensive set of factors that influence airline service perceptions and rates all U.S. airlines annually on the index. These factors include:

1 On-time flights
2 Number of accidents
3 Flight problems
4 Pilot errors
5 Overbookings
6 Mishandled baggage
7 Fare complaints
8 Frequent-flier awards
9 Other complaints
10 Refund complaints
11 Service complaints
12 Ticket complaints[29]

Among the issues companies must tackle when developing service performance indices are: (1) the number of components to be contained, (2) what overall or summary measures will be included, (3) whether the index should be weighted or unweighted (to put greater emphasis on the performance of the attributes considered most important to customers), and (4) whether all parts of the business (departments, sectors, or business units) will be held to the same performance measures. One of the most important goals of an index is to simply and clearly communicate business performance in operational and perceptual terms. Companies must develop the rigor in these measurement areas that they have in financial performance.

SUMMARY

This chapter discussed Provider GAP 2, the discrepancy between company perceptions of customer expectations and the standards they set to deliver to these expectations. Among the major causes for Provider GAP 2 are inadequate standardization of service behaviors and actions, absence of formal process for setting service quality goals, and lack of customer-defined standards. These problems were discussed and detailed, along with strategies to close the gap.

Customer-defined standards are at the heart of delivery of service that customers expect: they are the link between customer's expressed expectations and company actions to deliver to those expectations. Creating these service standards is not a common practice in U.S. firms. Doing so requires that companies' marketing and operations departments work together by using the marketing research as input for operations. Unless the operations standards are defined by customer priorities, they are not likely to have an impact on customer perceptions of service.

DISCUSSION QUESTIONS

1 How does the service measurement that we describe in this chapter differ from the service measurement in chapter 6? Which of the two types do you think is most important? Why?

2 In what types of service industries are standards most difficult to develop? Why? Recommend three standards that might be developed in one of the firms from the industries you specify. How would employees react to these standards? How could you gain buy-in for them?

3 Given the need for customer-defined service standards, do firms need company-defined standards at all? Could all standards in a company be customer defined? Why or why not? What functional departments in a firm would object to having all standards customer defined?

4 What is the difference between hard and soft standards? Which do you think would be more readily accepted by employees? By management? Why?

5 Consider the university or school you currently attend. What are examples of hard standards, soft standards, and one-time fixes that would address student requirements? Does the school currently use these standards for delivery of service to students? Why or why not? Do you think your reasons would apply to private-sector companies as well? To public or nonprofit companies?

6 Think about a service that you currently use, then map out the service encounter sequence for that service. What is your most important requirement in each interaction? Document these requirements, and make certain that they are expressed at the concrete level of behaviors and actions.

7 Which of the service performance indices described at the end of this chapter is the most effective? Why? What distinguishes the one you selected from the others? How would you improve each of the others?

8 Get a copy of your school's student questionnaire and compare it with the Skill Dynamics examples shown in Exhibit 8-3. Which of the two shown in the exhibit most resembles the one from your school? How would you improve on the existing survey?

EXERCISES

1 Select a local service firm. Visit the firm and ascertain the service measurements the company tracks. What hard measures do they monitor? Soft measures? On the basis of what you find, complete the customer service performance index shown in Figure 8-11.

2 Choose one of the peripheral services (such as computer, library, placement) provided by your school. What hard standards would be useful to track to meet student expectations? What soft standards? What one-time fixes would improve service?

3 Think about a service company you have worked for or know about. Using Figure 8-6, write in customer requirements at each of the levels. How far down in the chart can you describe requirements? Is that far enough?

NOTES

1 "Taking the Measure of Quality," *Service Savvy,* March 1992, p. 3.
2 Ibid.
3 Speech by Federal Express Manager in Baltimore, Md., June 1993.
4 Ted Levitt, "Industrialization of Service," *Harvard Business Review,* September–October 1976, pp. 63–74.
5 Brian S. Lunde and Sheree L. Marr, "Customer Satisfaction Measurement: Does It Pay Off?" (Indianapolis: Walker Customer Satisfaction Measurements, 1990).
6 "Fast, Reliable Delivery Processes Are Cheered by Time-Sensitive Customers," *The Service Edge* 4, 3 (1993): 1.
7 "The Ritz-Carlton Basics," flyer distributed by the Ritz-Carlton to all employees.
8 W. E. Crosby, "American Airlines—A Commitment to Excellence," in *Services Marketing in a Changing Environment* (Chicago: American Marketing Association, 1985).
9 Don Lee Bohl, ed., "Close to the Customer," An American Management Association Research Report on Consumer Affairs (New York: American Management Association, 1987).
10 Raymond E. Kordupleski, Roland T. Rust, and Anthony J. Zaharik, "Why Improving Quality Doesn't Improve Quality (or Whatever Happened to Marketing?)," *California Management Review* 35, 3 (Spring 1993): 89.
11 Crosby, "American Airlines," pp. 11–12.
12 "Taking the Measure of Quality," p. 3.
13 AMA Management Briefing, "Blueprints for Service Quality—the Federal Express Approach" (New York: AMA Membership Publishing Division, 1991), pp. 55–56.
14 Rebecca Grant and Christopher Higgins, "Monitoring Service Workers via Computer: The Effect on Employees, Productivity, and Service," *National Productivity Review,* Spring 1989, pp. 101–104.
15 Laurie M. Grossman, "Federal Express, UPS Face Off on Computers," *Wall Street Journal,* September 17, 1993, p. B1.
16 "Boosting Productivity at American Express," *Business Week,* October 5, 1981, pp. 62, 66.
17 George Russell, "Where the Customer Is Still King," *Time,* February 2, 1987.
18 Jeremy Main, "Toward Service without a Snarl," *Fortune,* March 23, 1981, p. 61.
19 Robert Camp, *Benchmarking: The Search for Industry Best Practices that Lead to Superior Performance* (Milwaukee: American Society for Quality Control, 1989).
20 Ibid.
21 Ibid.
22 "Managing by Fact: It's Exhaustive, Expensive, and Essential," *The Service Edge* 6, 5 (May 1993).
23 Ibid., p. 2.
24 Ibid., p. 3.
25 Thomas Thamara, "Quality Converts Customers into Long-Term Partners," *The Bankers Magazine,* September–October 1990, pp. 54–57.
26 Kate Bertrand, "In Service, Perception Counts," *Business Marketing,* April 1989, pp. 48–50.
27 Ibid.
28 Tom Ehrenfeld, "Merit Evaluation and the Family of Measures," *Harvard Business Review,* September–October 1991, p. 122.
29 Doug Carroll, "Expert: Being on Time Isn't Everything for Airlines," *USA Today,* March 5, 1992, page 6B.

9

LEADERSHIP AND MEASUREMENT SYSTEMS FOR MARKET-DRIVEN SERVICE PERFORMANCE

"He's wild, he's crazy, he's in a tough business—and he has built the most successful airline in the U.S."[1]

When Fortune *magazine chose Herb Kelleher of Southwest Airlines as its 1994 "CEO of the Year," it summed up the essence of service leadership. Herb Kelleher created and now runs the airline that the U.S. Department of Transportation calls the "principal driving force for changes occurring in the airline industry." Southwest scores higher than any other airline on the DOT's three pivotal measures of airline performance: on-time flights, accurate baggage handling, and customer satisfaction. And Southwest performs well financially too: it is the only U.S. airline that has been consistently profitable over the past five years.*

Why is Herb Kelleher a model service leader? Some of the reasons—which parallel the general factors signaling service leadership that will be discussed more fully in this chapter—include:

1 Service Vision. *Kelleher has uniquely positioned his airline as a low-cost, short-haul carrier with its own brand of service. The average Southwest flight is 375 miles and costs only $58. Among the reasons Kelleher can deliver good service at this low price are his decision to eliminate the frills of flying and his unwillingness to pay the $30 million annual fee to link up with computer reservation systems used by travel agents. Customers must buy Southwest tickets directly from the airline, carry their own bags, and bring their own snacks on board. Customers in his target segment don't seem to mind at all, for the advantages more than compensate for the inconveniences.*

2 Role Model. *Kelleher is an "in-the-field" service leader.[2] With respect to service to customers, he is the kind of leader "who will stay out with a mechanic in some bar* *until four o'clock in the morning to find out what is going on. And then he will fix whatever is wrong." With respect to employees,* Fortune *described his behavior this way:*

> *Kelleher reigns over his band of 12,000 loyalists like some sort of manic father figure. He is often at the center of the festivities that break out frequently on the headquarters party deck overlooking the flat Texas countryside. Whatever the occasion—a holiday, someone's retirement, Friday—Kelleher can be found in the middle of a worshipful crowd.*

3 Selection and Training of Service Personnel. *Kelleher works hard to choose employees that match his vision of service. He explains:*

> *What we are looking for, first and foremost, is a sense of humor . . . then we are looking for people who have to excel to satisfy themselves and who work well in a collegial environment. We don't care that much about education and expertise, because we can train people to do whatever they have to do. We hire attitudes.*

4 Motivation of Employees. *Kelleher instills in his people what he calls "an insouciance, an effervescence," something others call a "hoo-hah brio." Southwest workers are known to go to great lengths to "amuse, surprise, or somehow entertain passengers." During delays at the gate, for example, ticket agents give prizes to passengers with the largest holes in their socks. To add a bit of pleasant surprise while passengers board, flight attendants sometimes hide in the overhead luggage bins and then pop out when passengers start filing in.*

5 Team-building. *When Southwest acquired Morris Air in 1993, Southwest demonstrated its willingness to have the merged airlines' employees as part of its team. Spurred by Kelleher, "hundreds of Southwest employees spontaneously began sending cards, candy, and company T-shirts to Morris employees as a way of welcoming them into the fold."*

Does Kelleher himself make the difference in the success of Southwest Airlines? Only time—and his eventual successor—will determine the answer to this question. But Fortune *concluded, in naming Kelleher America's best CEO in 1994:*

> *Nobody inside the company, or outside for that matter, could likely fill the many roles he plays for his employees—inspirational leader, kindly uncle, cheerleader, clown. It may cost his company someday, but in the dictionary beneath the words, "one of a kind," there should be a picture of Herb Kelleher, grinning.*

For a company to deliver quality service requires leadership and commitment from top management. Without this commitment—and top management's willingness to accept temporarily the difficulties involved in change—quality service performance simply will not happen. Contact employes and middle management will not and cannot improve service quality without strong leadership from top management. Strong leadership in service almost always focuses on the customer, as illustrated by the message on a poster prominently displayed at L. L. Bean, the successful direct-mail marketer.

> What is a Customer? A Customer is the most important person ever in this office . . . in person or by mail. A Customer is not dependent on us . . . we are dependent on him. A Customer is not an interruption of our work . . .. he is the purpose of it. We are not doing a

favor by serving him . . . he is doing us a favor by giving us the opportunity to do so. A Customer is not someone to argue or match wits with. Nobody ever won an argument with a Customer. A Customer is a person who brings us his wants. It is our job to handle them profitably to him and to ourselves.[3]

Among companies that sell to other businesses, rather than to the end-customer, are those whose customer-oriented philosophies lead them to be the best in their fields. DuPont, the top-rated firm among chemical companies, captures the reason for its success simply: "Our marketing effort starts with the customer."[4]

Management may not be willing (or able) to put the systems in place that can match or exceed customer expectations. A variety of factors involving leadership, including management indifference, short-term profit orientation, market conditions, and resource constraints, may account for Provider GAP 2, the discrepancy between managers' perceptions of customer expectations and the standards and designs they implement for service delivery (Figure 9-1). Factors discussed in this chapter include (1) inadequate service leadership, (2) lack of recognition that service quality is a profit strategy, and (3) imbalanced performance scoreboard (Figure 9-2).

The objectives of this chapter are to:

1 Discuss the role that leadership plays in meeting or exceeding customer expectations.

2 Profile successful service leaders and describe what they do within their organizations to deliver quality service.

3 Provide a framework to examine the impact of service quality on profits.

4 Discuss the need for market-driven measurement systems that integrate perceptual, operational, and financial measurements.

KEY REASONS FOR GAP 2

Inadequate Service Leadership

The absence of service leadership virtually guarantees a wide GAP 2. Service leadership does not mean meeting a company's self-defined productivity or efficiency standards, many of which the customers does not notice or desire. Service leadership means driving for service that the customer wants and is willing to pay for. When managers are not committed to service quality from the customer's point of view, they fail to view the customer as the focus of organizational efforts. They fail to establish necessary service quality initiatives, and they do not see that attempts to improve service quality lead to better company performance.

Not Recognizing that Quality Service Is a Profit Strategy

In the 1980s, executives of leading service companies were willing to trust their intuitive sense that better service would lead to improved financial success, and thus they committed resources to improving service before they had any documentation of the financial payoff. Some of these companies, such as Federal Express and Xerox, have been richly rewarded for their leap of faith that service quality would lead to financial gain.

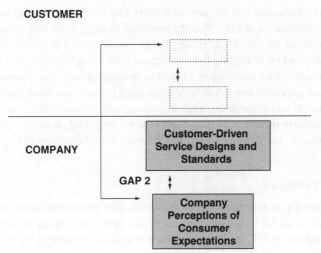

FIGURE 9-1   Provider GAP 2.

Executives in other companies have withheld judgment on (and sometimes support for) service quality, waiting for solid evidence for its financial soundness. In the current era of downsizing and streamlining, virtually all companies hunger for tools to ascertain and monitor the payoff and payback of new investments in service quality.

FIGURE 9-2   Key factors leading to provider GAP 2.

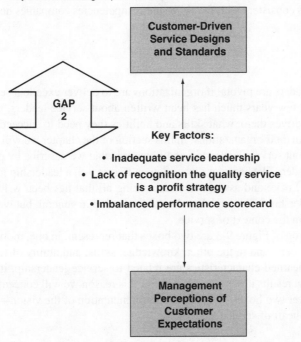

Many managers still see service quality as a cost rather than as a contributor to profits, partly because of the difficulty involved in tracing the link between service quality and financial returns. Determining the financial impact of service quality parallels the age-old problem of finding the connection between advertising and sales. Service quality's results—like advertising's results—are cumulative, and therefore evidence of the link may not come immediately or even quickly. And, like advertising, service quality is only one of many variables, such as pricing, advertising, efficiency, and image, that simultaneously influence profits. Furthermore, spending on service per se does not guarantee results, for strategy and execution must both be considered.

Imbalanced Performance Scorecard

Traditionally, organizations have measured their performance almost completely on the basis of financial indicators such as profit, sales, and return on investment. This "imbalanced scorecard" leads companies to emphasize financials to the exclusion of other performance indicators. Today's corporate strategists recognize the limitations of evaluating corporate performance on financials alone, contending that

. . . income-based financial figures are better at measuring the consequences of yesterday's decisions than they are at indicating tomorrow's performance . . . many executives saw their companies' strong financial records deteriorate because of unnoticed declines in quality or customer satisfaction or because global competitors ate into their market share.[5]

A "balanced performance scorecard"—one that captures other areas of performance, such as customer perceptions and operational indicators, along with financial performance—is consistent with the skills and competencies companies need today to survive and prosper.

SERVICE LEADERSHIP

Service leaders are pivotal if organizations are to deliver excellent service to customers. In the last few years much has been written about service leaders, including who they are, what drives them, what skills and abilities they need to succeed, and how they behave within their organizations. In this section of the chapter we will summarize what is known about service leadership and illustrate what we describe by profiling successful service leaders. We base our discussion on Figure 9-3, a leadership model developed by Edwin E. Locke and associates summarizing all that has been written and researched about leadership.[6] The model applies to leadership in general, but we will focus on how it applies in the context of service.

At the top of Figure 9-3 are two boxes that represent, in one, motives and traits common to leaders, and in the other, knowledge, skills, and ability of leaders. While these innate or learned characteristics are related to service leadership, it is the *behavior* of leaders that results in service success. For this reason we will concentrate our discussion on the lower two boxes—vision, and implementation of the vision—because these represent the heart of service leadership.

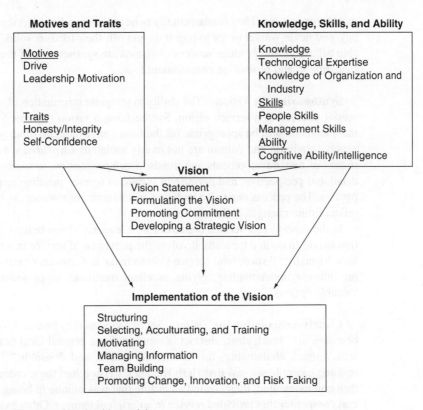

Motives and Traits	**Knowledge, Skills, and Ability**
Motives Drive Leadership Motivation Traits Honesty/Integrity Self-Confidence	Knowledge Technological Expertise Knowledge of Organization and Industry Skills People Skills Management Skills Ability Cognitive Ability/Intelligence

Vision

Vision Statement
Formulating the Vision
Promoting Commitment
Developing a Strategic Vision

Implementation of the Vision

Structuring
Selecting, Acculturating, and Training
Motivating
Managing Information
Team Building
Promoting Change, Innovation, and Risk Taking

FIGURE 9-3   Essence of leadership model.

Source: Locke et al., 1991.

A Leader Creates a Service Vision

An organizational vision is "an ideal and unique image of the future."[7] Experts express leadership vision as follows:

> . . . a leader must first have developed a mental image of a possible and desirable future state of the organization. This image, which we call vision, may be as vague as a dream or as precise as a goal or a mission statement. The critical point is that a vision articulates a view of a realistic, credible, attractive future for the organization, a condition that is better in some important ways than what now exists. A vision is a target that beckons.[8]

Most observers and writers in management assert that vision is a prerequisite for service excellence; Ron Zemke offers documentation that service visions are effective: "Organizations with concise, understandable, and actionable service strategies are four times as likely to receive superior service ratings from the customers as those without them."[9]

Excellent service to the customer is virtually always a central component of service visions that succeed. "True service leaders see the power of superior service as fundamental for success. They fundamentally believe that excellent service is a winning strategy, and never waiver or try to turn it on and off; their focus is solid."[10] Service leadership behaviors that produce successful visions are synthesizing of the vision, clearly articulating it, and promoting commitment to it.

Synthesizing the Vision   The ability to integrate information of various types is essential in creating a service vision. Synthesizing a vision requires *foresight,* to ensure that the vision will be appropriate for the future environment; *hindsight,* so that organizational tradition and culture are not overly violated; a *worldview,* to capitalize on the impact of new developments and trends; *depth perception,* to see the whole picture in detail and perspective; and *peripheral vision,* to foresee possible responses from competitors. The process must also include a mechanism for revision, so that the vision will reflect future changes in the environment.[11]

In the context of a service organization, a leader's vision defines what the organization strives to do and typically involves the provision of service in a unique or different way. Virtually all successful service visions make the customer central, either by showing intimate understanding, giving excellent treatment, or providing more and more valuable options.

Clearly Articulating the Vision   Service visions may be simple or complex, but the best ones are "brief, clear, abstract in representing a general ideal rather than a specific achievement, challenging, future-oriented, stable, and desirable."[12] In this chapter's opening example we saw that Herb Kelleher's vision met these criteria; he envisioned, then communicated, then created an airline that was unique in being a short-haul, low-cost competitor that provided service in an original manner. Other examples of successful service visions that meet these criteria include:

For P. T. Barnum: "The greatest show on earth."
For AT&T: "Anytime, anywhere communications."
For Manor Care: To become the "best nursing care system in the world."[13]
For the florist Podesta Baldocci: "Selling beauty, not just flowers."[14]
For USAA Insurance: "The mission . . . in one word, service. As a company objective, service comes ahead of either profits or growth."[15]

Promoting Commitment to the Service Vision   Service leaders constantly and visibly express their commitment to the troops of service employees on which they depend for execution of the vision. Bill Marriott, Jr., continues his father's legendary commitment to customers by traveling the country to oversee operations personally. Each year he "visits 80 percent of the company's hotels, inspects a third of the flight kitchens and eats at company restaurants as often as five times a week."[16] He claims: "It's a commitment. I'm the first in and the last out. If you are a leader, you better lead—and you lead by example. You have to motivate people, let them know you want to see what they can do."[17]

Many successful service leaders practice this kind of "in the field" leadership.[18] David Glass, CEO of Wal-Mart since the death of Sam Walton, the company's founder, spends two or three days a week in Wal-Mart stores, claiming, "Not much constructive ever gets done in Bentonville," the company's headquarters.[19] A typical day in the stores:

A day of touring stores in upstate New York begins with a 6:15 a.m. breakfast with the buyers from Bentonville and local associates . . . At the stores, Glass's style consists largely of breezing along the aisles, notebook in hand, and asking about a million questions, not counting, "How y'all doing? . . . What's the competition doing? How is apparel selling? Who's the biggest competitor in men's wear? Department 19 isn't doing well; got any ideas? Should we be doing something different? Where did you work before you came to Wal-Mart? Are you challenged enough by the work?" He is absolutely at ease on the sales floor, bantering with associates and customers, and injecting wry comments. One department head complains that the store doesn't have ecologically correct trash bags: "No? Well, the buyer's up here today. Just go and hang him."[20]

A Leader Implements the Service Vision

Promoting commitment to the service vision is critical if leaders are to translate service vision into specific actions. According to the model shown in Figure 9-3, the leader must also engage in other actions and activities to implement the vision, including structuring the organization; selecting, acculturating, and training employees; motivating; managing information; building teams; and promoting change, innovation, and risk taking. Figure 9-4 shows model service leaders from companies that have excelled at these activities. In the following sections we will discuss each of the activities and the reasons our model leader exemplifies effectiveness.

Structuring the Organization for Service Excellence   A service organization must be configured in a way that accomplishes the leader's vision. Among the structural

FIGURE 9-4   Model service leaders at implementing the vision.

Key Leadership Activities	Model Service Leaders
Structuring the Organization	Robert Allen, AT&T
Selecting, Acculturating, and Training	Bernard Marcus, Home Depot Eugene Johnson III, Fidelity Investments
Motivating	Mary Kay Ash, Mary Kay Jan Carlzon, SAS
Managing Information	Sam Walton, Wal-Mart Bill Marriot, Jr., Marriott Hotels
Team Building	Robert Allen, AT&T
Promoting Change, Innovation, Risk Taking	Robert Allen, AT&T Roger McDermott, USAA

elements that inhibit service excellence are bureaucracy, rigid hierarchy, strict definition of functional boundaries, centralization, myriad layers of management, and command-and-control approaches. With these elements a company is a "typical vertical organization, a company in which staffers look up to bosses instead of out to customers."[21] Prominent in correcting these structural problems is a reorganization called the "horizontal corporation." Horizontal organizations organize work flow around processes that ultimately link to customer needs, instead of around functions, departments, or tasks.[22] The seven key elements of the horizontal corporation include:

1 Organize around process, not task. Build three to five "core processes," with specific performance goals. Assign an "owner" to each process.

2 Flatten the hierarchy by eliminating work that fails to add value.

3 Use teams to manage everything, giving teams a common purpose and limiting supervision.

4 Let customers drive performance, making customer satisfaction (rather than profits or stock appreciation) the measure of performance.

5 Reward team performance rather than just individual performance.

6 Maximize supplier and customer contact.

7 Inform and train all employees and entrust employees with data.[23]

In its purest state, the horizontal corporation centers around a company's core processes—its flow of activity, information, decision, and materials—that deliver what customers expect. Redesigning processes appropriately can improve performance and allow employees to interact more directly with customers, and to respond more quickly to customer needs.

Robert Allen's Restructuring of AT&T   AT&T's service leader, Robert Allen, had the foresight to recognize that aspects of the company's size and structure needed to be changed dramatically. He subsequently built a new organization based on the precepts of the horizontal corporation. In an interview with *Fortune* magazine, Allen commented, "We're trying to create an atmosphere of turning the organization chart upside down, putting the customers on top. The people close to the customer should be doing the key decision-making."[24] This approach was developed when a 1991 survey revealed that fewer than one of five employees thought top management's statements were credible. As a result, Allen implemented an upward feedback approach by which he and all other executives were rated by their subordinates. "He supports his managers, who support the employees. His customers, he says, are all those who work for him."[25]

AT&T is currently organized into four major business groups—the telephone network itself, equipment for telecommunications networks, end-user products like telephones and answering machines, and computers. The corporate structure encourages cooperation and communication among otherwise independent businesses, including cross-unit teams that seek new opportunities. Allen does not carry the title of president and has no chief operating officer. Instead, the four executives responsible for the groups and the company CEO comprise a five-man presidency known as the Operations Committee. It meets for several days a month and is responsible for the day-to-day affairs of the company.

The structure Allen uses at the top has been implemented in other areas of the company, such as the Network Services Division. From a beginning number of 130 processes, the Division culled 13 core processes. Each core process has an owner, who focuses on day-to-day operations of the process, and a champion, who ensures that the process remains linked with overall business strategies and goals. The Network Services Division also sets budgets by process and awards bonuses to employees on the basis of customer evaluations.

Selecting, Acculturating, and Training Service Personnel   As we will see in chapter 11, a major part of implementing service excellence involves hiring and training the right people. Selecting, acculturating, and training are three related and critical leadership activities. Selecting involves choosing the right service worker for each job. Acculturating involves instilling the organization's culture and vision in those selected. Training helps employees understand and perform their responsibilities and duties. The best service leaders, like Herb Kelleher in this chapter's opener, are actively involved in these activities.

Training by Bernard Marcus of Home Depot   Home Depot, the do-it-yourself retailing chain founded in 1979, has demonstrated outstanding growth even during recession years. Customer service is one of the cornerstones of the firm's success, and training of personnel is the bedrock of its customer service. Service people are trained rigorously, sometimes by Marcus himself, in such interpersonal skills as helping customers choose the right tools and in such technical skills as tile laying and electrical installation. Marcus spends much of his time in the stores furthering the skills of his salespeople.

Training through Delegation by Fidelity's Eugene Johnson III   Eugene Johnson III of Fidelity Investments has a unique way of delegating.

Johnson divides power in the company among small divisions with aggressive, entrepreneurial leadership. "When we do something new, we put one person in charge and let him go," says Johnson.[26]

Fidelity Investments began with one manager and a secretary. Today it's the nation's second largest brokerage house. That combination of individualism and cooperation extends to the managers of Fidelity's 112 funds. "We have no investment committees, no one comes down from the mountain with orders on how to invest."[27]

Motivating Subordinates   Motivating subordinates involves generating "enthusiasm for the work, commitment to task objectives, and compliance with orders and requests."[28] The means by which leaders motivate subordinates include (1) use of formal authority, (2) role modeling, (3) building self-confidence, (4) delegating, (5) creating challenge through goal setting, and (6) rewarding and punishing.[29] While all of these approaches can be effective, we will illustrate only three of them, along with a service leader who is particularly effective at motivating service personnel.

Mary Kay's Motivational Approach: Recognition and Confidence Building   Mary Kay Ash, whose makeup company grew from $198,000 in sales in 1963 to over $613 million today, personifies effective motivational leadership. Through her stewardship of the 300,000-person Mary Kay sales force, women "who have never led anything more demanding than the family dog for a walk have been transformed into sales managers leading up to 20,000 people each."[30] Other women who have had careers as certified public accountants, lawyers, and corporate managers find that they are more successful and satisfied working for her than they were in their previous jobs.

Mary Kay motivates her salespeople the way she wanted to be motivated as an employee: She wanted to be treated well, to be recognized for her accomplishments, and to be given the chance to achieve her potential. Legend holds that after eleven years as head of sales training for another company, she returned from a business trip one day to discover that her male assistant, whom she had just spent nine months training, had been made her boss—at twice her salary. When she appealed the discrimination and was ignored, she determined to convert her experience into a business plan for a company that would treat women right, "not ruin their self-esteem" or limit how much money they could make.

Motivation by recognition and confidence building are the approaches currently used in the company. At the company's annual convention, called Seminar, saleswomen assemble to reward and recognize each other with Cadillacs, five-star vacations, diamonds, and furs. Symbols abound: the color of the women's suits, the diamond bracelets they wear, the Cadillacs all signify how successful they have been as Mary Kay salespeople. The culmination of the annual event involves Mary Kay personally crowning four Queens of Seminar—women who have excelled at sales or recruiting. "That feting is the key to the company's success. Emotional compensating matters almost as much as the cash," observers report.

> . . . Mary Kay calls you her daughter and looks you dead in the eye. She makes you feel you can do anything. She's sincerely concerned about your welfare. By these soft touches, every "daughter" in the company learns a lesson: When somebody takes an interest in you, it feels good. The 300,000 sales consultants try to treat customers the same way, remembering their birthdays, sending them little notes, showing they're interested. That's what sells the makeup.[31]

Jan Carlzon's Motivating through the "Art of Loving"   Jan Carlzon became the leader of Scandinavian Airline Systems (SAS) at a time when the airline market was stagnant, the airline was losing $20 million a year, employee morale was low due to layoffs, and customer service was worsening. Rather than support the direction of decline, Carlzon created and implemented a service vision of being "the best airline in the world for the frequent business traveler."

Carlzon motivated employees in a dramatic and positive way, a way that differed from techniques used by other managers in his culture. He believed in turning the organizational chart upside down: Anyone serving the customer was at the top, and everyone else, including middle management, served and supported them. Carlzon's style was described as outgoing and bold and he gained attention using flair and fun to communicate his customer-focused ideas. When he launched SAS's makeover of airplanes and uniforms, he invited frequent flyers to tour the new planes, then led a company chorus line to a disco version of "Love Is in the Air."

Carlzon possessed a sensitivity both to customers and employees. He created the "moments of truth" concept and believed strongly that the company needed to be successful in the 50,000 moments of truth with customers every day. Employees praised his ability to listen and his openness, and his top managers were motivated personally:

> He has great charisma and he's a preacher . . . he's very eager to spread his ideas. He's been talking and talking and I think that was necessary to make the shift in the organization to marketing/service orientation from technical/production orientation.[32]

Part of Carlzon's strength as a leader came from his philosophy about motivating employees, expressed in the following statement he made during an interview:

> In my experience, there are two great motivators in life. One is fear. The other is love. You can manage an organization by fear, but if you do you will ensure that people don't perform up to their real capabilities. A person who is afraid doesn't dare perform to the limits of his or her capabilities. People are not willing to take risks when they feel afraid or threatened.[33]

Carlzon's approach worked. SAS returned to profitability the year after he took over, won multiple service awards, and remains today one of the strongest airline competitors.

Managing Information   Effective leaders are information gatherers who listen to their subordinates and to sources outside the organization, especially customers: "They are around and available, not remote and unapproachable. They read. They develop wide information networks. They share and disseminate information appropriately within the organization."[34] Service leaders, in particular, are typically "deeply and personally involved in the customer service function of their business. They personally read complaint logs and letters, took phone calls, and were highly visible and available to the rank and file."[35] They are unwilling to delegate this most important function to others in the firm, but want to be involved and knowledgeable themselves.

Leaders who keep their ears tuned to employees are using upward communication to understand the activities and performance in the company. Specific types of communication that may be relevant are formal (e.g., reports of problems and exceptions in service delivery) and informal (e.g., discussions between contact people and upper-level managers). Leaders who stay close to their contact people benefit not only by keeping their employees happy but also by learning more about the customer. Consider the following examples of leaders managing information effectively.

Sam Walton, the Information Gatherer   Sam Walton, the late founder of Wal-Mart, the highly successful discount retailer, once remarked, "Our best ideas come from delivery and stock boys."[36] To be sure he stayed in touch with the source of new ideas, he spent most of his time in his stores, working the floor, helping clerks or approving personal checks, even showing up at the loading dock with a bag of doughnuts for a surprised crew of workers. "He would have the plane drop him next to a wheat field where he would meet a Wal-Mart truck driver. Giving his pilot instructions to meet him at another landing strip 200 miles down the road, he could make the trip with the Wal-Mart driver, listening to what he has to say about the company."[37]

Bill Marriott, Jr., the Listener   Each year, Bill Marriott, Jr., visits most of the company's hotels to listen to customers and employees, and he eats at company restaurants as often as five times a week.[38] He is known for walking around his hotels at all hours, surveying breakfast preparations at 6:15 a.m., or looking over rooms for the slightest imperfection. Staying close to the customer is part of the Marriott tradition. William Marriott, Bill's father and Marriott founder, is said to have read almost all of the customer comment cards for the entire fifty-six years of his leadership.[39]

Building Teams   Service leaders need to build cooperation among their followers, to teach subordinates to work effectively together to achieve goals. Among the strategies used to ensure that employees work together are creating cooperative goals that can only be reached together, using project teams and task forces, and implementing group-based reward systems.[40] Building an effective top-management team—to demonstrate to all in the organization that teamwork is essential—is symbolic as well as practical.

Robert Allen's Top-Management Teamwork   David Nadler of New York's Delta Consulting Group calls AT&T's Operations Committee, which serves as a five-man presidency, "a team that's unique at this level in corporate America."[41] All members must thoroughly understand what the others are doing, which results in "synergy and carefully considered tradeoffs among groups when conflicts arise."[42] Allen supports the team leadership approach by basing members' bonuses on the performance of their group and of AT&T as a whole.

The Operations Committee is supported by other high-level teams, particularly teams built on six high-potential areas of opportunity: video, wireless, data transmission, voice recognition and processing, messaging, and computing. Each team is represented by members from the four major business groups, a team leader, and an Operations Committee member who services as the team's champion. "The intent is to mix it up, get people talking, and figure out the businesses and structures that AT&T as a company will need next."[43]

Promoting Change, Innovation, and Risk Taking   Leaders of unsuccessful service organizations often demonstrate short-term, narrow thinking—an unwillingness to think creatively and optimistically about customer needs, and an excuse for maintaining the status quo. Successful service leaders tend to be open to innovation and receptive to different and possibly better ways of doing business. These leaders operate with the philosophy that almost anything the customer wants could be considered and evaluated. They are willing to transform the way they do business as well as to invest money, time, and effort to fully satisfy their customers.

Robert McDermott's Vision of Technology for USAA   Robert F. McDermott, former CEO of USAA, the fifth largest U.S. insurer of homes and cars, claims that willingness to make large investments in new technology was one of the most important elements in the success of his service company.

USAA has used technology not only to increase productivity but also to improve the quality of service. For example, USAA's state-of-the-art electronic imaging system means that each day some 30,000 pieces of mail never leave the mailroom. Instead, an exact image of the correspondence is placed electronically in the customer's policy service file and, simultaneously, in a sort of electronic in-basket where it will be handled by the first available service representative anywhere in the building.[44]

Sam Walton's Retailing Risks   Sam Walton, former chairman and founder of Wal-Mart, revolutionized retailing. Some of the risks he took include (1) setting up a distribution center with 18 regional distribution centers and a fleet of trucks when he couldn't convince existing distributors to deliver to his rural markets; (2) locating in rural markets that were underserved by other retailers; and (3) fully computerizing inventory and sales information.

Robert Allen's "Anytime, Anywhere Communications"   The cover of a *Business Week* article made the following comment on Allen's risk taking: "1-800-GUTS."[45] Allen's futuristic vision includes creating a "high-tech communications system that will actually track people down and deliver a phone call or a fax, whether they're in the office, on a ski lift, or sitting in an airplane." In implementing his vision, the company plans to take many risks, among them "voice, electronic mail, and even video, all zapped across AT&T's digital-information superhighway and delivered to conventional phones, computers, TVs, cellular handsets, and soon, to a new generation of wireless devices."[46] Allen is "betting billions that his view of the communications world is the right one, to build a global network and pump it full of every kind of traffic: voice, data, video, entertainment—you name it."[47]

Fidelity Investments and its leader, chairman and CEO Edward C. Johnson, also typify the innovation that characterizes service leaders:

> Fidelity was the first to let customers move money between funds with a toll-free telephone call. It was the first to let customers write checks on money-market mutual-fund accounts. Today, Fidelity lets customers switch money among funds by telephone—without talking with a service representative—or via personal computer.[48]

The Challenge of Middle Management

Thus far in this chapter we have talked about the role of service leaders in implementing service excellence in their companies. We have also focused on front-line employees and their roles in service implementation throughout this book. What remains to be discussed is the role of middle management in implementing the service vision. Middle management is the link from leadership to the troops—it must pass along the service leader's commitment to quality by setting and communicating service standards for employees' work units and by reinforcing the standards with motivation and support.

Middle management has been in turmoil in the 1990s; during reengineering and restructuring, middle managers are often the first group targeted to leave. The American Management Association reported that even though middle managers account for only 5 percent of the work force, they constitute 22 percent of the layoffs.[49] One reason they seem expendable is that companies are moving to self-managed work teams that assume the two primary roles of middle managers—supervision of employees and gathering and processing of data. Many existing middle managers are redefining their jobs from supervising to coaching, sponsoring, and empowering their subordinates.

> Middle managers who master skills such as team building . . . and who acquire broad functional expertise will likely be in the best position to get tomorrow's top corporate jobs. That's because the role of the top executive is becoming more like that of a team player and broker of others' efforts, not that of an autocrat.[50]

The new middle manager has been described as one who:

Thinks of self as a sponsor, team leader, or internal consultant.
Deals with anyone necessary to get the job done.
Changes organizational structures in response to market change.
Invites others to join in decision making.
Shares information.
Tries to master a broad array of managerial disciplines.
Demands results.[51]

In other words, the middle manager must become an integral part of the team of service workers who interact with the customer. Financial incentives linked to behavior that fosters high service quality in addition to more typical performance goals (such as sales) help to communicate to these managers that service is a priority. One large service organization instituted a 60/40 bonus plan to support the company's quest for service excellence: instead of managerial bonuses based 100 percent on sales, the company rewarded managers on both sales (60 percent) and service quality (40 percent).

SERVICE QUALITY AS A PROFIT STRATEGY

Service leadership is the first essential ingredient necessary to close GAP 2. The second ingredient also involves leadership: leaders must recognize that quality service is a profitable strategy for their companies. They need to believe and validate that investments in quality service will pay off for the company financially. As executives have sought to understand the relationship between service quality and profits, they are finding evidence to support the relationship but are also realizing that the link between service quality and profits is neither straightforward nor simple.

Service quality affects many economic factors in a company, some of them leading to profits through variables not traditionally in the domain of marketing. For example, the traditional total quality management (TQM) approach expresses the financial impact of service quality in lowered costs or increased productivity. These relationships involve operational issues that concern marketing only in the sense that marketing research is used to identify service improvements that customers notice and value.

In addressing questions about the impact of service quality on profits, scholars distinguish between *offensive effects* (i.e., market capture and market share) and *defensive effects* (retaining customers, lowering marketing and promotional costs).[52] The model shown in Figure 9-5 summarizes the linkages between service quality and profits that involve both effects. Improved service will attract new customers to the business (the offensive effect) and it will enable the business to retain its current customers (the defensive effect).[53]

The Role of Service Quality in Offensive Marketing: Attracting More and Better Customers

Service quality can help companies attract more and better customers to the business. When service is good, a company gains a positive reputation and through that reputation

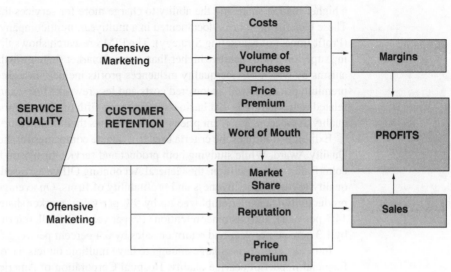

FIGURE 9-5   Service quality spells profits.

EXHIBIT 9-1   THE MALCOLM BALDRIGE NATIONAL QUALITY AWARD

One of the most pervasive frameworks for incorporating quality and the customer into the management process of U.S. organizations is the Malcolm Baldrige National Quality Award criteria. The Baldrige Quality Award is given annually to U.S. companies that excel in quality management and quality achievement.

Created as a joint venture between the U.S. Department of Commerce and private industry, the Award was designed to promote (1) awareness of the importance of quality to competitiveness, (2) understanding of the requirements for excellence in quality, and (3) sharing of information on successful quality strategies.

Companies compete in one of three categories: manufacturing, service, and small business. Companies first submit application packages that describe their company's quality activities. On the basis of the information submitted, members of the Board of Examiners evaluate the applications, conduct site visits to companies that score well, and choose winners from finalists.

Winners are chosen on the basis of a set of core values and concepts that include customer-driven quality, leadership, continuous improvement, employee participation and development, fast response, design quality and prevention, long-range outlook, management by fact, partnership development, and corporate responsibility and citizenship. These core values are embodied in the Award criteria on which companies are judged:

1.0 Leadership
2.0 Information and Analysis
3.0 Strategic Quality Planning
4.0 Human Resource Development and Management
5.0 Management of Process Quality
6.0 Quality and Operational Results
7.0 Customer Focus and Satisfaction

These criteria are nonprescriptive (i.e., they allow wide latitude in how requirements are met), comprehensive, and interrelated. They emphasize quality system alignment and are part of a diagnostic or assessment system. Companies that enter the competition but do not win are provided feedback on ways to make improvements. Among the winners in the service category are Federal Express, Ritz-Carlton Hotels, AT&T Universal Card, and AT&T Network Systems.

Source: Malcolm Baldrige National Quality Award 1994 Criteria, U.S. Department of Commerce Technology Administration, Gaithersburg, Md., 1994.

a higher market share and the ability to charge more for services than the competition. These benefits have been documented in a multiyear, multicompany study called PIMS (Profit Impact of Marketing Strategy). The PIMS research shows that companies offering superior service achieve higher-than-normal market share growth and that the mechanisms by which service quality influences profits include increased market share and premium prices as well as lowered costs and less rework.[54] An example of one finding related to marketing is that businesses in the top fifth of competitors on relative service quality average an 8 percent price premium versus their competitors.[55]

Exhibit 9-1 outlines the criteria used to evaluate companies for the Malcolm Baldrige Quality Award. While studying both product and service firm semi finalists in the Malcolm Baldrige competition, the General Accounting Office assessed the contribution of quality to the competitiveness and profitability of firms. On average, quality increased productivity (sales per employee up by 9% per year), market share (up an average of 14% per year), and customer retention (1% per year). Overall, return on assets improved by 1.3 percent per year and return on sales by 0.4 percent per year.[56]

Individual companies large enough to have multiple outlets have also confirmed the financial impact of service quality. Hospital Corporation of America, for example, reported a strong link between patient perceptions of high-quality care and a hospital's profitability across its many hospitals.[57] And U.S. automotive companies have demonstrated that dealers with high service quality scores have higher-than-normal profit, return on investment, and profit per new vehicle sold, among other favorable financial indicators.

The Role of Service Quality in Defensive Marketing: Retaining Customers

In chapter 10 we will explain that customer defection (or "customer churn") is widespread in service businesses. Lost customers must be replaced by new customers, and replacement comes at a high cost, because it involves advertising, promotion, and sales costs as well as start-up operating expenses. New customers are often unprofitable for a time after acquisition: In the insurance industry, for example, the insurer typically doesn't recover selling costs until the third or fourth year of the relationship. Capturing customers from other companies is also an expensive proposition: A greater degree of service improvement is necessary to make a customer switch from a competitor than to retain a current customer.[58] In general, the longer a customer remains with the company, the more profitable the relationship is for the organization:

> Served correctly, customers generate increasingly more profits each year they stay with a company. Across a wide range of businesses, the pattern is the same: the longer a company keeps a customer, the more money it stands to make.[59]

The money a company makes from retention comes from four sources (shown in Figure 9-5): costs, volume of purchases, price premium, and word-of-mouth communication.

Lower Costs   Lowering customer defection rates saves money. It has been found that attracting a new customer is five times as costly as retaining an existing one.[60] Consultants who have focused on these relationships assert that customer defections have a stronger impact on a company's profits than market share, scale, unit costs, and many other factors usually associated with competitive advantage.[61] They also claim that, depending on the industry, companies can increase profits from 25 to 85 percent by retaining just 5 percent more of their customers. The General Accounting Office study of semifinalists in the Malcolm Baldrige competition found that quality reduced costs: order processing time decreased on average by 12 percent per year, errors and defects fell by 10 percent per year, inventory shrank by 7.2 percent, and cost of quality declined by 9 percent per year.

Consider the following facts about the role of service quality in lowering costs:

• The annual cost of dissatisfaction with hospital services for a hospital with 5,000 annual discharges has been estimated at more than $750,000.[62]

• "Our highest quality day was our lowest cost of operations day" (Fred Smith, Federal Express).

• "Our costs of not doing things right the first time were from 25 to 30 percent of our revenue" (David F. Colicchio, Regional Quality Manager, Hewlett-Packard Company).

• Profit on services purchased by a ten-year customer is on average three times greater than for a five-year customer.[63]

• Bain & Company, a consulting organization specializing in retention research, estimates that in the life insurance business, a 5-percent annual increase in customer retention lowers a company's costs per policy by 18 percent.

Volume of Purchases   Customers who are satisfied with a company's services are likely to increase the amount of money they spend with that company or the types of services purchased. A customer satisfied with a broker's services, for example, will likely invest more money when it becomes available. Similarly, a customer satisfied with a bank's checking services is likely to open a savings account with the same bank, and to use the bank's loan services as well.

Price Premium   Evidence suggests that a customer who notices and values the services provided by a company will pay a price premium for those services. Granite Rock, a 1992 winner of the Baldrige Award, has been able to command prices up to 30 percent higher than competitors for its rock (a product that many would claim is a commodity!) because it offers off-hour delivery and twenty-four-hour self-service.

Word of Mouth   In chapter 3 of this book we described the valuable role of word-of-mouth communications in purchasing service. Because word-of-mouth communication is considered more credible than other sources of information, the best type of promotion for a service may well come from other customers who advocate the services provided by the company. Word of mouth brings new customers to the firm, and the financial value of this form of advocacy can be calibrated by the company in terms of the promotional costs it saves as well as the streams of revenues from new customers.

THE BALANCED PERFORMANCE SCORECARD

The final leadership factor concerns senior executives' views of performance. Some executives view, measure, and evaluate performance only in financial terms. Others recognize that financial return is limited:

> Financial measures emphasize profitability of inert assets over any other mission of the company. They do not recognize the emerging leverage of the soft stuff—skilled people and employment of information—as the new keys to high performance and near-perfect customer satisfaction .... If the only mission a measurement system conveys is financial discipline, an organization is directionless.[64]

Other measures of performance must be captured and quantified to predict future financial performance and to drive the performance of companies. One leading expert on corporate performance claims that "... within the next five years, every company will have to redesign how it measures its business performance in order to remain competitive."[65] This view, gaining in popularity, maintains that company measurement systems must go beyond traditional financial measures to include the full range of critical gauges of performance. They recommend that companies create a "balanced scorecard," described as follows:

> ... a set of measures that gives top managers a fast but comprehensive view of the business ... (that) complements the financial measures with operational measures of customer satisfaction, internal processes, and the organization's innovation and improvement activities—operational measures that are the drivers of future financial performance.[66]

As shown in Figure 9-6, the balanced performance scorecard captures three perspectives in addition to the financial perspective: customer, operational, and learning.

FIGURE 9-6   The balanced scorecard.

Source: Kaplan and Norton, 1992.

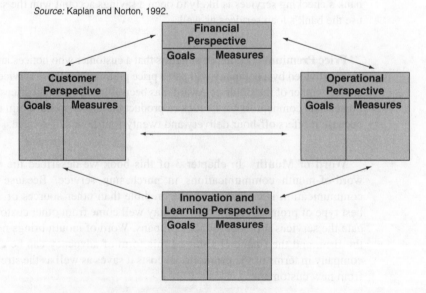

TECHNOLOGY SPOTLIGHT

IMPLEMENTING A BALANCED SCORECARD IN HEALTH CARE

"We are building health policy on the notion that the health-care system can be held accountable for its performance."

So said president Sheila Leatherman of United HealthCare's Center for Health Care Policy and Evaluation in Minneapolis, acknowledging that there were insufficient data in her firm's industry to monitor performance. Her company was one of the first to develop and collect health-care measures because standard methods did not exist for comparing plans on their quality and value of care. An industry effort involving the National Committee for Quality Assurance and more than 30 HMOs and insurers is trying to remedy this lack of data by developing a common set of quality indicators and standards.

As we described in this chapter, more and more companies believe that developing objective measures of quality and efficiency—and compiling them in a balanced report card that goes beyond financial measures—provides strategic information for the company and valuable data for customers.

United HealthCare Corporation was one of the first HMOs to disclose its results across different aspects of quality (shown in the accompanying table) and efficiency.

Technical quality, which tracks objective medical data, is represented in measures such as rates of childhood immunizations at age 2 to 6 months, eye exams for diabetics, and caesarean section births. Customer-perceived quality is captured in measures such as patient satisfaction with quality of doctors and overall patient satisfaction. Administrative efficiency is gauged by administrative costs per member per month.

The measurement plan was developed in part for customers, who face increased complexity and difficulty in choosing medical care and insurance. It was also created to help firms bring health-care costs under control as they try to expand their networks and develop ways to care for uninsured Americans.

Issues that surround the development of the measurement plan in the health-care industry parallel those in other industries that have attempted to develop them. Companies who score low invariably claim that their patients were worse off to start with. The tone of punishment implicit in the system is considered by some to be detrimental to overall quality because risky patients needing help may not be able to get it. Further, standard data are hard to agree on because technical quality can be measured in different ways.

Source: Ron Winslow, "Report Card on Quality and Efficiency of HMOs May Provide a Model for Others," *Wall Street Journal,* March 9, 1993, p. B1.

The balanced scorecard brings together, in a single management report, many of the seemingly disparate elements of a company's competitive agenda. Second, the scorecard guards against sub-optimization by forcing senior managers to consider all the important operational measures together.[67]

Methods for measuring financial performance are the most developed and established in corporations, having been created more than four hundred years ago. In contrast, efforts to measure market share, quality, innovation, human resources, and customer satisfaction have only recently been created. The Technology Spotlight shows how one company went about measuring. Service leaders can close GAP 2 by developing a discipline of performance measurement in all four categories.

Financial Measurement

One way service leaders are changing financial measurement involves calibrating the defensive impact of retaining and losing customers. The monetary value of retaining customers can be estimated from projecting average revenues over the lifetimes of customers. The number of customer defections can then be translated into lost revenue to the firm and become a critical company performance standard:

> Ultimately, defections should be a key performance measure for senior management and a fundamental component of incentive systems. Managers should know the company's defection rate, what happens to profits when the rate moves up or down, and why defections occur.[68]

Companies can also measure actual increases or decreases in revenue from retention or defection of customers by capturing the value of a loyal customer, including expected cash flows over a customer's lifetime.[69] Other possible financial measures (as shown in Figure 9-7) include (1) value of price premiums, (2) volume increases, (3) value of customer referrals, (4) value of cross sales, and (5) long-term value of customers.

Customer Perception Measurement

These measures reflect customer beliefs and feelings about the company and its products and services and can be considered predictors of how the customer will behave in the future. Aggregate forms of the measurements we discussed in chapter 6 regarding marketing research could be captured in this category. Among the measures that would be valuable to track (shown in Figure 9-7) are overall service perceptions and expectations, perceptual measures of value, and behavioral intention measures such as loyalty and intent to switch.

Operational Measurement

These measures involve the translation of customer perceptual measures into the standards or actions that must be set internally to meet customers' expectations. While virtually all companies count or calculate operational measures in some form, the balanced scorecard requires that these measures stem from the business processes that have the greatest impact on customer satisfaction. In other words, these measures are not independent of customer perceptual measures but instead are intricately linked with them. In chapter 8 we called these customer-linked operational measures *customer-defined standards,* operational standards determined through customer expectations and calibrated the way the customer views and expresses them.

Innovation and Learning Measurement

This final area of measurement involves a company's ability to innovate, improve, and learn—by launching new products, creating more value for customers, and improving operating efficiencies. This is the measurement area that is most difficult to capture quantitatively but can be accomplished using performance-to-goal percentages.

The balanced performance scorecard gives managers and their companies four different strategic perspectives from which to choose measures. It goes beyond traditional financial indicators by also calibrating customer perceptions and expectations, operational processes, and innovation and improvement activities. By reducing the measures

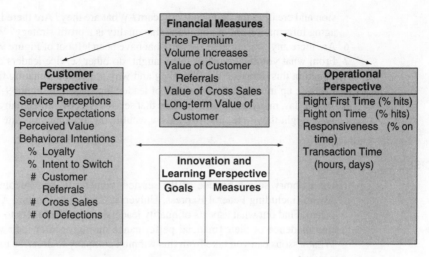

FIGURE 9-7   Sample measurements for the balanced scorecard.

to those that are essential in each of the perspectives, the scorecard becomes an extension of the company's strategic vision. Companies can customize their scorecards to fit their mission, strategy, technology, and culture.

SUMMARY

To lead a service organization effectively, managers must create the service vision and then implement it through structuring the organization; selecting, acculturating, training, and motivating employees; managing information; building teams; and promoting change and risk taking. These activities were described in this chapter, along with model service leaders who practice the activities effectively. The chapter also discussed the need for viewing service quality as a profit strategy and for creating a balanced performance scorecard.

DISCUSSION QUESTIONS

1 Is it possible for a service company to be successful without the support of top management? Why or why not?

2 Review the list of ways that management implements the service vision. Which of these ways do you believe are the most difficult for a leader to do? The easiest? If you were a service leader, in what order would you engage in these activities?

3 List successful service visions that you are aware of (over and above the ones we mentioned in this chapter). Why are they successful?

4 Is motivating subordinates a more difficult task in service businesses than in goods businesses? Why or why not? Is it also more important? Why or why not?

5 Are there links between "managing information" as part of implementing the service vi-

sion and creating the balanced scorecard? What are they? Are there links between managing information and recognizing that quality is a profit strategy? What are they?

6 Are there any aspects of leadership that have been left out of Figure 9-3? What are they?

7 From what you have read or been taught, do other service leaders deserve to be mentioned in this chapter? Who are they and why are you nominating them? How do they measure up in terms of the essence of leadership shown in Figure 9-3?

8 To this day, many companies believe that service is a cost rather than a revenue producer. Why might they hold this view? How would you argue the opposite view?

EXERCISES

1 Do a library search on one of the service winners of the Malcolm Baldrige Quality Award (including Federal Express, Universal Card, Ritz Carlton, AT&T Network Services). Find out what aspects of quality leadership qualified them to win. See if you can find evidence of their financial performance during or after their winning the award. What lessons can you take from this winning company to describe to other service businesses?

2 Select a service industry (such as fast food) or company (such as McDonald's) you are familiar with, either as a customer or an employee, and create a balanced scorecard. Use the table in the Technology Spotlight and Figure 9-6 as models, then describe the operational, customer, financial, and learning measures that could be used to capture performance.

NOTES

1 Kenneth Labich, "Is Herb Kelleher America's Best CEO?," *Fortune,* May 2, 1994. Unless otherwise indicated, all quotations in the chapter opener are from this article.

2 Leonard Berry, "Quality Leadership Requires Clear Demonstration of the 'Vision,' " *Total Quality,* August 1991, p. 7.

3 Thomas J. Peters and Nancy Austin, *A Passion for Excellence* (New York: Random House, 1985), p. 95.

4 "At DuPont, Everybody Sells," *Sales and Marketing Management,* December 3, 1984, p. 33.

5 Robert S. Kaplan and David P. Norton, "The Balanced Scorecard—Measures that Drive Performance," *Harvard Business Review,* January–February 1992.

6 Edwin A. Locke et al., *The Essence of Leadership: The Four Keys to Leading Successfully* (New York: Lexington Books, 1991).

7 J. M. Kouzes and B. Z. Posner, *The Leadership Challenge: How to Get Extraordinary Things Done in Organizations* (San Francisco, Calif.: Jossey-Bass, 1987).

8 W. G. Bennis and B. Nanus, *Leaders: The Strategies for Taking Charge* (New York: Harper and Row, 1985), p. 89.

9 Ron Zemke, "Making the Case for Service 'Visions,' " *The Service Edge,* March 1991, p. 8.

10 Berry, "Quality Leadership Requires Clear Demonstration of the 'Vision,' " p. 7.

11 Bennis and Nanus, *Leaders,* pp. 102–3.

12 Locke et al., *The Essence of Leadership.*

13 R. Ackoff, *The Art of Problem Solving* (New York: Wiley, 1978).

14 Kouzes and Posner, *The Leadership Challenge.*

15 Thomas Teal, "Service Comes First: An Interview with USAA's Robert F. McDermott," *Harvard Business Review,* September–October 1991.

16 Mike Sheridan, "J. W. Marriott, Jr., Chairman and President, Marriott Corporation," *Sky,* March 1987, p. 48.

17 Ibid.

18 Berry, "Quality Leadership Requires Clear Demonstration of the 'Vision,' " p. 7.

19 Bill Saporito, "David Glass Won't Crack under Fire," *Fortune,* February 8, 1993, p. 78.

20 Ibid., p. 80.

21 John Byrne, "The Horizontal Corporation," *Business Week,* December 20, 1993, p. 76.

22 Ibid.

23 Ibid.

24 David Kirkpatrick, "Could AT&T Rule the World?", *Fortune,* May 17, 1993, p. 57.

25 Ibid., pp. 65–66.

26 John Waggoner, "Johnson Embraces 'Kaisan,'" *USA Today,* June 9, 1993.

27 Ibid.

28 Gary Yukl, *Leadership in Organizations,* 2d ed. (Englewood Cliffs, N.J.: Prentice Hall).

29 Locke et al., *The Essence of Leadership.*

*0 Alan Farnham, "Mary Kay's Lessons in Leadership," *Fortune,* September 20, 1993.

31 Ibid.

32 John Kao, "Scandinavian Airlines System," case published by Harvard Business School, 1987, p. 5.

33 "The Art of Loving," interview with Jan Carlzon, president and CEO of SAS, *Inc. Magazine,* Fall 1989.

34 Locke et al., *The Essence of Leadership.*

35 W. H. Davidow and B. Uttal, *Total Customer Service* (New York: Harper & Row, 1989), p. 98.

36 Stephen Koepp, "Make that Sale, Mr. Sam." *Time,* May 18, 1987, pp. 54–55.

37 Ibid.

38 Sheridan, "J. W. Marriott, Jr.," p. 48.

39 Ibid.

40 Kouzes and Posner, *The Leadership Challenge.*

41 Kirkpatrick, "Could AT&T Rule the World?," p. 62.

42 Ibid.

43 Ibid.

44 Teal, "Service Comes First."

45 Bart Ziegler, "AT&T's Bold Bet," *Business Week,* August 30, 1993, p. 26.

46 Ibid.

47 Ibid., p. 32.

48 Waggoner, p. B1.

49 Brian Dumaine, "The New Non-Manager Managers," *Fortune,* February 22, 1993.

50 Ibid., p. 81.

51 Ibid.

52 Claus Fornell and Birger Wernerfelt, "Defensive Marketing Strategy by Customer Complaint Management: A Theoretical Analysis," *Journal of Marketing Research,* November 1987, pp. 337–46.

53 Anthony Zahorik and Roland Rust, "Modeling the Impact of Service Quality on Profitability—A Review," in *Advances in Service Marketing and Management,* Vol. 1, ed. Teresa Schwartz, Greenwich, CT: JAI Press, 247–76.

54 L. W. Phillips, D. R. Chang, and R. D. Buzzell, "Product Quality, Cost Position and

Business Performance: A Test of Some Key Hypotheses," *Journal of Marketing,* 2, Spring 1993, pp. 26–43.

55 Bradley Gale, "Monitoring Customer Satisfaction and Market-Perceived Quality," *American Marketing Association Worth Repeating Series,* number 922CS01, Chicago, 1992.

56 "Proof that Quality Pays Off," presentation by Alan Mendelowitz, General Accounting Office, at the Customer Satisfaction and Quality Measurement Conference, San Francisco, March 8–10, 1992, sponsored by the American Marketing Association and the American Society for Quality Control.

57 Mary T. Koska, "High Quality Care and Hospital Profits: Is There a Link?" *Hospitals,* March 5, 1990, pp. 62–63.

58 Eugene W. Anderson and May W. Sullivan, "Customer Satisfaction and Retention across Firms," presentation at the TIMS College of Marketing Special Interest Conference on Services Marketing, Nashville, Tenn., September 1990.

59 Frederick Reichheld and Earl Sasser, "Zero Defections: Quality Comes to Services," *Harvard Business Review,* September–October 1990, p. 106.

60 Peters and Austin, *A Passion for Excellence.*

61 Reichheld and Sasser, "Zero Defections," p. 105.

62 Steven R. Steiber and William J. Krowinski, *Measuring and Monitoring Patient Satisfaction* (Chicago American Hospital Publishing Inc., 1990), p. 4.

63 S. Rose, "The Coming Revolution in Credit Cards," *Journal of Retail Banking,* Summer 1990, pp. 17–19.

64 Dave Zielinski, "A Sole Focus on Finances Can Trouble the Heart of Business," *Total Quality Newsletter,* July 1994, p. 3.

65 Robert G. Eccles, "The Performance Measurement Manifesto," *Harvard Business Review,* January–February 1991, pp. 131–37.

66 Robert S. Kaplan and David P. Norton, "The Balanced Scorecard—Measures that Drive Performance," *Harvard Business Review,* January–February 1992.

67 Ibid.

68 Reichheld and Sasser, "Zero Defections," p. 111.

69 Ibid.

10

SERVICE DESIGN AND POSITIONING

Have you ever considered starting your own service business? What type of service would it be? What would you do first? Assuming you understood your market and had a good feel for potential customers' needs and expectations, how would you go about designing the service to meet those needs? If you were starting a business to manufacture a new product, you would most likely begin by designing and building a prototype of your new product. But how could you do this for a service?

These were some of the questions US West had to answer when it started a new service for the home-based office customer segment. More and more people are operating home offices, whether as a second office for work done away from the primary employer or as the primary business location. US West knows that a home office needs a smooth and efficient system for placing and receiving calls, sending and receiving faxes, and accepting messages when out of the office. The company thus introduced a Home Office Consulting Center to assist home office workers in setting up the needed systems, including automated voice mail and FAX mail.[1] While the technology exists, customers often don't know how to use it to their advantage. US West's consultants can educate them and help them design an appropriate communication system for their needs. The Center eventually will serve a region with an estimated 2.6 million work-at-home customers.

The home office consulting service represents a new concept for US West, targeted at a new and growing customer segment. To introduce the idea the company had to clearly define it and figure out how to communicate it to customers. Even more important, the company had to figure out how to communicate the concept to employees who would implement it and develop the internal processes and systems to facilitate delivery. Such design challenges are no easy task when a service is new to the market, is highly intangible, and is highly dependent on employees for delivery.

263

Did US West succeed with its home office consulting service? As of this writing, the answer is yes. What causes new products and services to succeed or fail? If you decide to start your own business, what can you do to protect yourself as much as possible from failure?

A recent study of 11,000 new products launched by 77 manufacturing, service, and consumer products companies found that only 56 percent of new offerings are still on the market five years later.[2] Failures can be traced to a number of causes: no unique benefits offered; insufficient demand; unrealistic goals for the new product/service; poor fit between the new service and others within the organization's portfolio; poor location; insufficient financial backing; failure to take the necessary time to develop and introduce the product.[3] Frequently a good service idea fails due to design and specification flaws, as emphasized in this chapter.

As we have already seen, understanding customer expectations is but the first essential step in the delivery of quality service. Given accurate understanding of expectations, service standards and designs must then match customer expectations and allow employees and systems to deliver quality services, as suggested by GAP 2 of the service quality model (Figure 10-1).

Chapter 8 focused on customer-defined standards as a way of closing GAP 2, while chapter 9 focused on leadership issues. In this chapter we will concentrate on service design and positioning approaches that further contribute to closing GAP 2 (Figure 10-2).

The objectives of the chapter are to:

1 Describe the challenges inherent in service design and positioning.
2 Present helpful steps in the new service development process.
3 Show the value of service blueprinting in new service design, service improvement, and positioning strategies.

FIGURE 10-1   Provider GAP 2.

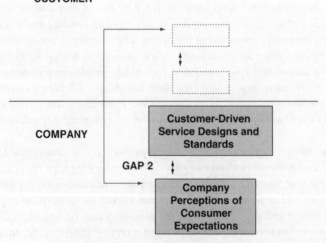

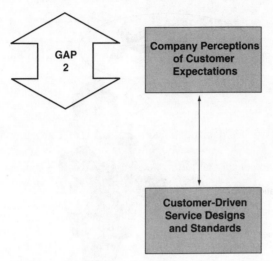

FIGURE 10-2   Key factors leading to provider GAP 2.

4 Demonstrate how to build a service blueprint.

5 Explain service positioning and the role of the service quality dimensions, service evidence, and blueprinting in positioning strategies.

CHALLENGES OF SERVICE DESIGN AND POSITIONING

Because services are intangible, for example, a hospital stay, a golf lesson, an NBA basketball game, they are difficult to describe and communicate. When services are delivered over a long period—a week's resort vacation, ten weeks on a Weight Watchers program—their complexity increases and they become even more difficult to define and describe. Further, because services are delivered by employees to customers, they are heterogeneous: rarely are two services alike, or experienced in the same way. These characteristics of services, which we explored in the first chapter of this book, are the heart of the challenge involved in designing and positioning services.

Because services cannot be photographed, touched, examined, and tried out, people frequently resort to words in their efforts to describe them. Lynn Shostack, a pioneer in developing design concepts for services, has pointed out four risks of attempting to describe services in words alone, as illustrated in Figure 10-3.[4] The first risk is *oversimplification*. Shostack points out that "to say that 'portfolio management' means 'buying and selling stocks' is like describing the space shuttle as 'something that flies.' Some people will picture a bird, some a helicopter and some an angel" (p. 76). Words are simply inadequate to describe a whole complex service system.

The second risk is *incompleteness*. In describing services, people (employees, managers, customers) tend to omit details or elements of the service with which they are not

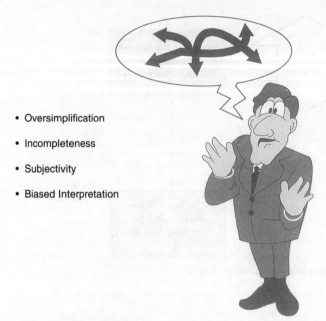

- Oversimplification

- Incompleteness

- Subjectivity

- Biased Interpretation

FIGURE 10-3   Risks of relying on words alone to describe services.

familiar. A person might do a fairly credible job of describing how a discount stock brokerage service takes orders from customers. But would that person be able to describe
fully how the monthly statements are created, how the interactive computer system
works, and how these two elements of the service are integrated into the order-taking
process?

The third risk is *subjectivity.* Any one person describing a service in words will be biased by personal experiences and degree of exposure to the service. There is a natural
(and mistaken) tendency to assume that because all people have gone to a fast-food
restaurant, they all understand what that service is. Persons working in different functional areas of the same service organization (e.g., a marketing person, an operations
person, a finance person) are likely to describe the service very differently as well, biased by their own functional blinders.

A final risk of describing services using words alone is *biased interpretation.* No two
people will define "responsive," "quick," "flexible," in exactly the same way. For example, a supervisor or manager may suggest to a front-line service employee that the
employee should try to be more flexible or responsive in providing service to the customer. Unless flexibility is further defined, the employee is likely to interpret the word
differently from the manager.

All of these risks become very apparent in the new service development process,
when organizations may be attempting to design services never before experienced by
customers. It is critical that all involved (managers, front-line employees, and behind-

the-scenes support staff) be working with the same concepts of the new service, based on customer needs and expectations. For a service that already exists, any attempt to improve it will also suffer unless everyone has the same vision of the service and associated issues. The risks of using words alone are also apparent in service positioning where the organization is attempting through all of the service quality and marketing-mix elements to establish or retain a particular market position in the customer's mind. Again, unless everyone in the organization has a clear and shared picture of the service, its position may not be portrayed consistently to the customer.

In the following sections of this chapter we will present approaches for new service development, design, and positioning that attempt to address these unique challenges.

NEW SERVICE DEVELOPMENT

Research suggests that products that are designed and introduced by following the steps in a structured planning framework have a greater likelihood of ultimate success than those not developed within a framework.[5] The fact that services are intangible makes it even more imperative for a new service development system to have four basic characteristics: (1) It must be objective, not subjective. (2) It must be precise, not vague. (3) It must be fact driven, not opinion driven. (4) It must be methodological, not philosophical.[6]

Often, new services are introduced on the basis of managers' and employees' subjective opinions about what the services should be and whether they will succeed, rather than on objective designs incorporating data about customer perceptions, market needs, and feasibility. A new service design process may be imprecise in defining the nature of the service concept because the people involved believe either that intangible processes *cannot* be defined precisely or that "everyone knows what we mean." Neither of these explanations or defenses for imprecision is justifiable, as we will illustrate in the model for new service development described in this chapter.

Because services are produced and consumed simultaneously and often involve interaction between employees and customers, it is also critical that the new service development process involve *both* employees and customers. Employees frequently *are* the service, or at least they *perform* or *deliver* the service, and thus their involvement in choosing which new services to develop and how these services should be designed and implemented can be very beneficial. Contact employees are psychologically and physically close to customers and can be very helpful in identifying customer needs for which new services can be offered. Involving employees in the design and development process also increases the likelihood of new service success because employees can identify the organizational issues that need to be addressed to support the delivery of the service to customers.[7] For example, at Metropolitan Life Insurance Co., cross-functional teams comprising representatives from administration, claims, marketing, and information systems are included to ensure that all aspects of the service and delivery process are considered before full-scale development of a new insurance service concept begins.

Because customers are often active participators in service delivery, they too should be involved in the new service development process. Beyond just providing input on their own needs, customers can help design the service concept and the delivery process, particularly in cases where the customer personally carries out part of the service process. Marriott Corporation is well known for involving its guests in the design of its hotel rooms, to ensure that the features and placement of furnishings in the rooms will work for the guests and not just for the staff or the architects who design the rooms.

Types of New Services

As we build the new service development process, remember that not all new services are "new" to the same degree. Box 10-1 covering travel industry innovations shows how airlines, hotels, and airplane manufacturers are adding new service options for business travelers in an attempt to revitalize demand and compete in this market segment. While some are contemplating adding new services (e.g., FAX machines, desks, computers), others are planning improvements in the core service (e.g., adding more first-class seating for frequent-flier upgrades).[8] The types of new service options can run the gamut from major innovations to minor style changes, as described in the following.[9]

Major innovations are new services for markets as yet undefined. Past examples include the first broadcast television services and Federal Express's introduction of nationwide, overnight small-package delivery service. Many innovations now and in the future will evolve from information and computer-based technologies. Examples are highlighted in this chapter's technology spotlight.

Start-up businesses consist of new services for a market that is already served by existing products that meet the same *generic* needs. Service examples include: the creation of health maintenance organizations to provide an alternative form of health care delivery, ATMs for bank transactions, door-to-door airport shuttle services that compete with traditional taxi and limousine services.

New services for the currently served market represent attempts to offer existing customers of the organization a service not previously available from the company (although it may be available from other companies). Examples include Barnes and Noble (a very successful retail bookstore) offering coffee service, a health club offering nutrition classes, and airlines offering FAX and phone service during flights.

Service line extensions represent augmentations of the existing service line, such as a restaurant adding new menu items, an airline offering new routes, a law firm offering additional legal services, a university adding new courses or degrees.

Service improvements represent perhaps the most common type of service innovation. Changes in features of services that are already offered might involve faster execution of an existing service process, extended hours of service, or augmentations such as added amenities in a hotel room.

Style changes represent the most modest service innovations, although they are often highly visible and can have significant impact on customer perceptions, emotions, and attitudes. Changing the color scheme of a restaurant, revising the logo for an organization, or painting aircraft a different color all represent style changes. These do not fundamentally change the service, only its appearance, similar to how packaging changes are used for consumer products.

BOX 10-1

NEW SERVICES FOR BUSINESS TRAVELERS

Airline companies and hotels are stepping up their efforts to regain and build relationships with their most prized customers: business travelers. Because they frequently travel on short notice, business travelers take less advantage of discounted rates than do leisure customers, and are therefore more profitable customers. To attract and retain this market segment, firms are developing a variety of new services. In the hotel industry, the focus has been on the hotel room itself. Hookups for laptop computers, phones with multiple lines, FAX machines, and voice mail are some of the features being added to make the room more functional for business travelers. Radisson Hotels International Inc. tested "business class" accommodations that included in-room coffee, breakfast, computer hookups, in-room movies, newspapers, and quick FAX delivery. Hyatt Hotels is addressing the need for business services through special floors with rooms including free FAXes, office supplies, and other business amenities. At the upscale Four Seasons Hotels rooms can have everything from sophisticated telephone-messaging systems to in-room FAXes and twenty-four-hour concierge service.

In the airline industry, companies are focusing on the business traveler both on the ground and in the air. British Airways opened an arrival lounge at London's Heathrow Airport that offers private rooms with showers, clothes-pressing service, and a breakfast room for its top-fare passengers. Other airlines are targeting the in-flight experience for improvements. American Airlines offers premium service on its flights between New York and Los Angeles in which business-class passengers get first-class-type cuisine as well as individual head and leg

rests. Taking another tack, USAir Group Inc. provides abundant first-class seating for frequent-flyer upgrades.

Looking further into the future, McDonnell Douglas Corp. is designing various aircraft configurations that include in-flight office setups. In one design there is a stand-up booth for single-aisle planes that includes a fold-down table where passengers could send a FAX, make a call, and use the computer before returning to their seat. An even longer-term strategy is to develop an "office in the sky," where passengers could buckle up and stay right at a work station through the entire flight.

Hotels, airlines, and car rental companies as well have been working on speedier check-in and checkout services to retain their business travelers. The check-in counter for all of these services is a common source of customer complaints. Counter-bypass programs using computerized check-in and checkout are one way to expedite the process. Hilton Hotels Corp. and Marriott Hotel Corp. have both introduced variations of free express check-in in the context of their larger-scale efforts to make the front-desk experience more efficient. Express check-in guests are usually served in a separate line and are handed an envelope that includes their contract and key in exchange for their credit-card number. UAL Corp.'s United Airlines now permits full-fare travelers flying between Chicago and five other airports to pick up their reserved tickets at the gate instead of the ticket counter.

Sources: James S. Hirsch, "Travel Industry Speeds Up Check-Ins and Check-Outs," *Wall Street Journal,* September 20, 1993, p. B1; Pauline Yoshihashi, "Hotels Turn Guest Rooms into Well-stocked Offices," *Wall Street Journal,* September 20, 1993, p. B1; Michael J. McCarthy, "Airlines Retool Services to Attract More Full-Fare Fliers," *Wall Street Journal,* October 27, 1993, p. B1.

Stages in New Services Development

Here we will focus on the actual steps to be followed in new service development. The steps can be applied to any of the types of new services just described. Much of what is presented in this section has direct parallels in the new product development process for manufactured goods.[10] Due to inherent characteristics of services, however, the development process for new services requires unique and complex adaptations. Figure 10-4 shows the basic principles and steps in new service development. While these may be similar to those for manufactured goods, their implementation is significantly different.[11] In addition, for many service industries (e.g., telecommunication, transportation, utilities, banking), government agencies that regulate the industries greatly influence the nature and speed of new service development.

TECHNOLOGY SPOTLIGHT

TECHNOLOGY REVOLUTIONIZES SERVICE OFFERINGS

Information technologies have dramatically revolutionized the service offerings and delivery processes in many service industries. Not long ago architectural services—the actual drawings, that is—were rendered totally by hand. Now computer-assisted design (CAD) systems are commonplace in that industry, freeing the architect to design and make modifications to his or her drawings on a computer screen. Another technological advancement in the architecture industry allows the designer to create what appears to be a photograph of a building, interior, or landscape by combining pieces of unrelated photographs stored in the computer into one design. By doing this the designer can try out different colors, different layouts, and different furnishings and present realistic photos to the client before the client makes a final decision. In a similar way, a landscape architect can show a client how the exterior of a proposed home or building will look with various types and combinations of plantings.

Law is another industry that has changed the way its services are provided through use of technology. Legal research that in the past was conducted by staff attorneys and paralegals working in libraries can now be done on-line using systems such as Lexis/Nexis. Lexis is the leading full-text computer-assisted legal research service that includes case law, statutes, and specialized

law libraries. A legal researcher can call up a particular document, read it, and locate related references quickly on the computer screen without ever leaving the law office. Nexis, the other half of the service, is a computer-assisted electronic service that offers full-text articles from leading news and business sources. Both services can be accessed from a personal computer. These vast information data bases, and others, have revolutionized the way legal research is done. The process is now more efficient, far ranging, and more immediately responsive to client needs.

Technology is also reshaping education—at home and at school. Students from preschool to university level can have information at their fingertips that would once have required a long and arduous search through the library shelves. And more than information is available via computer. Educational software in the form of reading ("Reader Rabbit"), math ("Math Blaster"), and geography ("Where in the World is Carmen Sandiego?") is making learning more fun and often more effective for youngsters. Through vivid pictures, imaginative sound accompaniment, and rules and outcomes, kids can learn a variety of basic skills. More advanced learners find that the computer can assist them with writing, locating specific information, and learning about more advanced subjects. With a product called "The Body Illustrated," teenagers can learn about human anatomy and can even watch a heart beat on the screen.

In all of the cases just described, technology has changed the nature of the offerings, resulting in new services that provide greater value to consumers.

An underlying assumption of new product development process models is that new product ideas can be dropped at any stage of the process if they do not satisfy the criteria for success at that particular stage.[12] Figure 10-4 shows the checkpoints that precede critical stages of the development process. The checkpoints specify requirements that a new service must meet before it can proceed to the next stage of development. (Some organizations are finding that, to speed up the process of new service development, some steps can be worked on simultaneously, and in some instances a step may even be skipped. In all cases, however, the critical tests that allow the service to pass through each checkpoint must be passed.)

Business Strategy Development   It is usually assumed that an organization will have an overall strategic vision and mission. Clearly a first step in new service development is to review that vision and mission. If these are not clear, the overall strategic direction of the organization must be determined and agreed on. The new services strategy and specific new service ideas must fit within the larger strategic picture of the organization.

Business Strategy Development or Review

New Service Strategy Development

Idea Generation

| Screen ideas against new service strategy |

Concept Development and Evaluation

| Test concept with customers and employees |

Business Analysis

| Test for profitability and feasibility |

Service Development and Testing

| Conduct service prototype test |

Market Testing

| Test service and other marketing-mix elements |

Commercialization

Postintroduction Evaluation | _____ | = checkpoint

FIGURE 10-4   New service development process.

Source: Booz-Allen & Hamilton, 1982; Bowers, 1985; Cooper, 1993.

New Service Strategy Development   The types of new services that will be appropriate will depend on the organization's goals, vision, capabilities, and growth plans. By defining a new service strategy (possibly in terms of markets, types of services, time horizon for development, profit criteria, or other relevant factors), the organization will be in a better position to begin generating specific ideas. For example, the organization may choose to focus its growth on new services at a particular level of the described continuum from major innovations to style changes. Or the organization may define its new services strategy even more specifically in terms of particular markets or market segments, or in terms of specific profit generation goals.

One way to begin formulating a new services strategy is to use the framework shown in Figure 10-5 for identifying growth opportunities.[13] The framework allows an organization to identify possible directions for growth and can be helpful as a catalyst for creative ideas. The framework may also later serve as an initial idea screen if, for example, the organization chooses to focus its growth efforts on one or two of the four cells in the matrix. The matrix suggests that companies can develop a growth strategy around current customers or for new customers, and can focus on current offerings or new service offerings.

Idea Generation   The next step in the process is the formal solicitation of new ideas. The ideas generated at this phase can be passed through the new service strategy screen described in the preceding step. Many methods and avenues are available for

Offerings	Markets	
	Current Customers	New Customers
Existing Services	SHARE BUILDING	MARKET DEVELOPMENT
New Services	SERVICE DEVELOPMENT	DIVERSIFICATION

FIGURE 10-5   New service strategy matrix for identifying growth opportunities.

searching out new service ideas. Formal brainstorming, solicitation of ideas from employees and customers, and learning about competitors' offerings are some of the most common approaches.

To illustrate how the matrix shown in Figure 10-5 might function as a catalyst for idea generation, consider growth strategies pursued by Taco Bell, one of the world's fastest growing and most successful fast-food chains.

Share-building (current customers, existing services). This strategy is pursued by Taco Bell in the rapid expansion of Taco Bell outlets throughout the United States in recent years.

Market Development (new customers, existing services). Taco Bell has expanded by offering its services in nontraditional locations, using creative formats to reach new customers. For example, Taco Bells can now be found in airports, universities, and schools. Often the outlets in these locations are scaled-back "express" versions of the service with a limited menu and small space requirement. Another form of market development is expansion into international markets.

Service Development (current customers, new services). Taco Bell has new menu items, improved service delivery, and lowered prices to better serve its current customers.

Diversification (new customers, new services). This growth option, involving new services for consumers not currently served, is frequently the most challenging, since it takes the organization into unfamiliar territories on both the product and market dimensions. Taco Bell has pursued this type of growth by selling its branded products in grocery stores and by buying significant interests in other restaurant chains such as Chevy's (Mexican restaurants) and California Pizza Kitchen.

In service businesses, contact personnel, who actually deliver the services and interact directly with consumers, can be particularly good sources of ideas for complementary services to those already in the marketplace and how to improve current offerings.

Whether the source of a new idea is inside or outside the organization, there should exist some *formal* mechanism for ensuring an ongoing stream of new service possibilities. This mechanism might include: a formal new service development department or function with responsibility for generating new ideas; suggestion boxes for employees and customers; new service development teams that meet regularly; surveys and focus groups with customers and employees; or formal competitive analysis to identify new services. While new service ideas *may* arise outside the formal mechanism, total dependence on luck is not advisable.

Service Concept Development and Evaluation   Once an idea surfaces that is regarded as a good fit with both the basic business and the new service strategies, it is ready for initial development. In the case of a tangible product, this would mean formulating the basic product definition and then presenting consumers with descriptions and drawings to get their reactions.

The inherent characteristics of services, particularly intangibility and simultaneous production and consumption, place complex demands on this phase of the process. Drawing pictures and describing an intangible service in concrete terms are difficult. It is therefore important that agreement be reached at this stage on exactly what the concept is. By involving multiple parties in sharpening the concept definition, it often becomes apparent that individual views of the concept are not the same. For example, in describing the design and development of a new discount brokerage service, Lynn Shostack relates that initially the bank described the concept as a way "to buy and sell stocks for customers at low prices."[14] Through the initial concept development phase it became clear that not everyone in the organization had the same idea about how this description would translate into an actual service, and that there were a variety of ways the concept could be developed. Only through multiple iterations of the service—and the raising of hundreds of issues, large and small—was an agreement finally reached on the discount brokerage concept.

After clear definition of the concept, it is important to produce a description of the service that represents its specific features and characteristics and then to determine initial customer and employee responses to the concept. The service design document would describe the problem addressed by the service, discuss the reasons for offering the new service, itemize the service process and its benefits, and provide a rationale for purchasing the service.[15] The roles of customers and employees in the delivery process would also be described. The new service concept would then be evaluated by asking employees and customers whether they understand the idea of the proposed service, whether they are favorable to the concept, and whether they feel it satisfies an unmet need.

Business Analysis   Assuming the service concept is favorably evaluated by customers and employees at the concept development stage, the next step is to determine its feasibility and potential profit implications. Demand analysis, revenue projections, cost analyses, and operational feasibility are assessed at this stage. Because the development of service concepts is so closely tied to the operational system of the organization, this stage will involve preliminary assumptions about the costs of hiring and training personnel, delivery system enhancements, facility changes, and any other projected operations costs.

The organization will pass the results of the business analysis through its profitability and feasibility screen to determine whether the new service idea meets the minimum requirements.

Service Development and Testing In the development of new tangible products, this stage involves construction of product prototypes and testing for consumer acceptance. Again, because services are intangible and largely produced and consumed simultaneously, this step is difficult. To address the challenge, this stage of service development should involve all who have a stake in the new service: customers and contact employees as well as functional representatives from marketing, operations, and human resources. During this phase, the concept is refined to the point where a detailed service blueprint representing the implementation plan for the service can be produced. The blueprint is likely to evolve over a series of iterations on the basis of input from all of the parties listed. For example, when a large state hospital was planning a new computer-based information service for doctors throughout its state, it involved many groups in the service development and evaluation stage, including medical researchers, computer programmers and operators, librarians, telecommunications experts, and record clerks as well as the physician customers.[16]

A final step is for each area involved in rendering the service to translate the final blueprint into specific implementation plans for its part of the service delivery process. Because service development, design, and delivery are so intricately intertwined, all parties involved in any aspect of the new service must work together at this stage to delineate the details of the new service. If not, seemingly minor operational details can cause an otherwise good new service idea to fail. For example, often services are promoted without the backup needed to take calls and answer customer questions. When one telecommunication company promoted a new service to its heavy-user customer segment and then didn't have enough customer service representatives to take the volume of inquiries that came in, the company aggravated its best customer segment and at the same time lost potential sales of the new service. The tourism office in one of the western states had the same problem when it promoted the state through a beautiful *Sunset* magazine advertisement offering information and brochures about the state, but then failed to adequately staff the 800 number given in the ad.

Market Testing It is at this stage of the development process that a tangible product might be test marketed in a limited number of trading areas to determine marketplace acceptance of the product as well as other marketing-mix variables such as promotion, pricing, and distribution vehicles. Again, the standard approach for a new manufactured product is typically not possible for a new service due to its inherent characteristics. Because new service offerings are often intertwined with the delivery system for existing services, it is difficult to test new services in isolation. And in some cases, for example a one-site hospital, it may not be possible to introduce the service to an isolated market area since the organization has only one point of delivery. There are alternative ways of testing the response to marketing-mix variables, however. The new service might be offered to employees of the organization and their families for a time to assess their responses to variations in the marketing mix. Or the organization might decide to test variations in pricing and promotion in less realistic contexts by presenting customers with hypothetical mixes and getting their responses in terms of intentions to try the service under varying circumstances. While this approach certainly has limitations compared with an actual market test, it is better than not assessing market response at all.

It is also extremely important at this stage in the development process to pilot run the service to be sure that the operational details are functioning smoothly. Frequently this purpose is overlooked and the actual market introduction may be the first test of whether the service system functions as planned. By this point, mistakes in design are harder to correct. As one noted service expert says, "There is simply no substitute for a proper rehearsal" when introducing a new service.[17] In the case of the discount brokerage service described earlier, a pilot test was run by offering employees a special price for one month. The offer was marketed internally, and allowed the bank to observe the service process in action before it was actually introduced to the external market.

Commercialization   At this stage in the process, the service goes live and is introduced to the marketplace. This stage has two primary objectives. The first is to build and maintain acceptance of the new service among large numbers of service delivery personnel who will be responsible day to day for service quality. This task is made easier if acceptance has been built in by involving key groups in the design and development process all along. However, it will still be a challenge to maintain enthusiasm and communicate the new service throughout the system; excellent internal marketing (discussed in chapter 11) will help.

The second objective is to carry out monitoring of all aspects of the service during introduction and through the complete service cycle. If the customer needs six months to experience the entire service, then careful monitoring must be maintained through at least six months. Every detail of the service should be assessed—phone calls, face-to-face transactions, billing, complaints, and delivery problems. Operating efficiency and costs should also be tracked.

Postintroduction Evaluation   At this point, the information gathered during commercialization of the service can be reviewed and changes made to the delivery process, staffing, or marketing-mix variables on the basis of actual market response to the offering. No service will ever stay the same. Whether deliberate or unplanned, changes will always occur. Therefore, formalizing the review process to make those changes that enhance service quality from the customer's point of view is critical. The service blueprint serves a valuable purpose in providing a focal point for discussing and planning changes in the offering.

Use of a Formal New Service Development Model by Service Firms

The model we have presented shows what service firms *should* do and what many *strive* to do in developing new services. This ideal model may not always be followed, for a variety of reasons. Some reasons are logical, for example when a very minor service modification is being introduced. In this case a full-scale new service development process would not be necessary, although some level of assessment of consumer desire for the modification and monitoring of the effectiveness of the modification would still be important. At other times a promising and well-developed new service idea may surface from outside the formal new service development process. Ways to integrate such ideas into the system must be found.

Sometimes the model is not followed because it is viewed as too difficult, or because those in control of the new idea (managers, employees) become anxious and excited to introduce the service before the operational details have been worked out. Professor Michael Bowers collected information about new services from 253 companies in three different service industries (insurance, banks, and hospitals). He found that many of the steps in the new service development process were not likely to be followed in these companies (see Table 10-1).[18] For each of the stages of new service development, the companies indicated on a scale from 1 to 5 whether they engaged in that step all of the time (5) or never (1). The table shows that the steps most unlikely to be followed are idea generation, product development and testing, and market testing. Product development (average score 2.48) and market testing (average score 2.33) appear to be most difficult or unlikely. The steps most likely to be completed were the development of a business strategy (average score 3.79) and business analysis (average score 3.88) of the feasibility and profitability of the new service. In the research, Bowers asked new product managers in the organizations surveyed what the greatest problems in new service development were. Their responses are shown in Table 10-2.

While it can't be assumed that all service firms or industries follow the same patterns as the banks, insurance companies, and hospitals in this study, similar lack of a formal new service development process has been noted by others.[19] This is particularly disturbing given that research suggests companies that *do* follow a systematic new service development process generally achieve a higher level of performance with their new introductions. This positive relationship (between following a systematic process and ultimate success) has been noted in Bowers's study as well as in a series of studies by Robert G. Cooper on new tangible products.[20]

TABLE 10-1   EXTENT TO WHICH BANKS, INSURANCE COMPANIES, AND HOSPITALS EMPLOY A SYSTEMATIC PROCESS OF NEW SERVICE DEVELOPMENT (PERCENT RESPONDING IN EACH CATEGORY)

	Never	Seldom	Occasionally	Often	All the time	Average score[a]
Business strategy development	4	11	19	34	32	3.79
New product strategy development	9	17	26	31	16	3.29
Idea generation	12	26	31	24	8	2.92
Concept development and evaluation	6	18	27	38	12	3.33
Business analysis	2	6	23	38	30	3.88
Product development and testing	27	30	20	13	10	2.48
Market testing	24	39	20	11	5	2.33
Commercialization	6	10	25	35	24	3.61

[a]The average score is the mean across all of the companies' responses, with 1 = never and 5 = all the time.
Source: Reprinted with permission from Bowers, 1985.

TABLE 10-2 SOURCE OF PROBLEMS IN DEVELOPING NEW SERVICES

Problem	Percent reporting[a]
Lack of commitment (money, time, personnel, senior management, support)	48
Lack of knowledge about the environment (consumers, competition, economy)	44
Poor management (lack of strategic planning, problems with coordination, no assigned responsibility, cost)	34
Inexperience in new service development	11
Lack of motivation	4
Miscellaneous	10

[a]Respondents were allowed to provide more than one response. Therefore, the percentage figures should be read as "48% of the respondents cited lack of commitment to new service development as one of the biggest problems."
Source: Bowers, 1985.

SERVICE BLUEPRINTING

A major stumbling block in developing new services (and in improving existing services) is seeming inability to describe and depict the service at the concept development, product development, and market test stages. As pointed out in the opening pages of this chapter, one of the keys to closing GAP 2 (matching service specifications to customer expectations) is the ability to describe key service process characteristics objectively and to depict them so that employees, customers, and managers alike know what the service is, can see their role in its delivery, and understand all of the steps and flows involved in the service process. In this section of the chapter we will look in depth at service blueprinting, a technique that addresses the challenges of designing and specifying intangible service processes.[21]

What Is a Service Blueprint?

The manufacturing and construction industries have a long tradition of engineering and design. Can you imagine a house being built without detailed specifications? Can you imagine a car, a computer, or even a simple product like a child's toy or a shampoo, being produced without concrete and detailed plans, written specifications, and engineering drawings? Yet services commonly lack concrete specifications. A service, even a complex one, might be introduced without any formal, objective depiction of the process.

A service blueprint is a picture or map that accurately portrays the service system so that the different people involved in providing it can understand and deal with it objectively regardless of their roles or their individual points of view. Blueprints are particularly useful at the design and redesign stages of service development. A service blueprint visually displays the service by simultaneously depicting the process of service delivery, the roles of customers and employees, and the visible elements of the service. It provides a way to break a service down into its logical components and to depict the steps or tasks in the process, the means by which the tasks are executed, and the evidence of service as the customer experiences it.

Origins of Blueprinting.   Blueprinting has its origins in a variety of fields and techniques, including logistics, industrial engineering, decision theory, and computer systems analysis—all of which deal with the definition and explanation of *processes*.[22] Logistics typically involves diagramming, measuring, and designing work flows and human tasks. Industrial engineering, a related discipline, offers a well-developed diagramming vocabulary and an orientation toward time as the critical "raw material" of any process. Logistics and industrial engineering contribute useful ideas for using time efficiently and productively to accomplish given tasks, without wasted motion or activity. Like logistics and industrial engineering, decision theory provides helpful input for blueprinting through its analytical approach to describing processes and a well-developed symbolic vocabulary. But decision theory is oriented toward choices, probabilities, and outcomes rather than tasks. Thus decision theory is most useful for describing service processes that require judgment and choices such as those found in the professions or in highly personalized and customized services. The final discipline, computer systems analysis, also offers unique concepts for service system design and analysis. Systems analysis deals largely with relationships, sequences, and dependencies. For a computer to produce a given result, the analyst must chart out where the computer must go to find all the pieces of data it needs; what intermediate sorts, calculations, or combinations must be done to those data; the order in which these steps must be done; and whether the execution of the steps will interfere with or unintentionally alter any other task the computer is trying to do.

These concepts are extremely relevant to services where the entire system must operate and be understood as an integrated whole if it is to achieve its intended objective. None of these disciplines is adequate by itself for fully understanding and designing service systems. Elements of each are useful for conceptualizing services, however, as well as for quantifying and measuring various parts of the service system. The two pioneers in applying and adapting these concepts to service design and marketing are Lynn Shostack and Jane Kingman-Brundage.

Blueprint Components   The key components of service blueprints are shown in Figure 10-6.[23] They are customer actions, "onstage" contact employee actions, "backstage" contact employee actions, and support processes. The conventions for drawing service blueprints are not rigidly defined, and thus the particular symbols used, the number of horizontal lines in the blueprint, and the particular labels for each part of the blueprint may vary somewhat depending on what one reads and the complexity of the blueprint being described. This is not a problem, as long as one keeps in mind the purpose of the blueprint and views it from the point of view of its usefulness as a tool, rather than as a set of cast-in-stone rules for designing services.

The *customer actions* area encompasses the steps, choices, activities, and interactions that the customer performs in the process of purchasing, consuming, and evaluating the service. In a legal services example, the customer actions might include a decision to contact an attorney, a phone call to the attorney, a face-to-face meeting(s), additional phone calls, receipt of documents, and receipt of a bill.

Paralleling the customer actions are two areas of contact employee actions. The steps

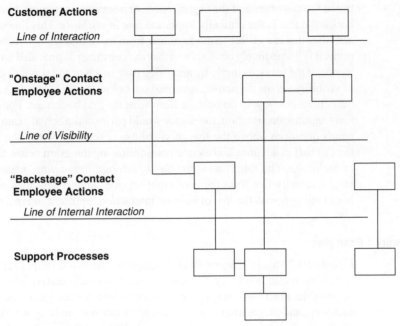

Customer Actions

Line of Interaction

"Onstage" Contact Employee Actions

Line of Visibility

"Backstage" Contact Employee Actions

Line of Internal Interaction

Support Processes

FIGURE 10-6   Service blueprint components.

and activities that the contact employee performs that are visible to the customer are the *"onstage" employee actions*. In the legal services setting, the actions of the attorney (the contact employee) that are visible to the client are, for example, the initial interview, intermediate meetings, and final delivery of legal documents.

Those contact employee actions that occur behind the scenes to support the onstage activities are the *"backstage" contact employee actions*. In the example, anything the attorney does behind the scenes to prepare for the meetings or to prepare the final documents will appear in this section of the blueprint, together with phone call contacts the customer has with the attorney or other front-line staff in the firm.

The *support processes* section of the blueprint covers the internal services, steps, and interactions that take place to support the contact employees in delivering the service. Again in the legal example, any service support activities such as legal research by staff, preparation of documents, and secretarial support to set up meetings will be shown in the support processes area of the blueprint.

One of the most significant differences in service blueprints compared with other types of process flow diagrams is the inclusion of customers and their view of the service process. In fact, in designing effective service blueprints it is recommended that the diagramming start with the customer's view of the process and work backward into the delivery system. The boxes shown within each action area depict steps performed or experienced by the actors at that level.

The four key action areas are separated by three horizontal lines. First is the *line of interaction,* representing direct interactions between the customer and the organization. Anytime a vertical line crosses the horizontal line of interaction, a direct contact between the customer and the organization, or a service encounter, has occurred. The next horizontal line is the critically important *line of visibility*. This line separates all service activities that are visible to the customer from those that are not visible. In reading blueprints it is immediately obvious whether the consumer is provided with much visible evidence of the service simply by analyzing how much of the service occurs above the line of visibility versus the activities carried out below the line. This line also separates what the contact employees do onstage from what they do backstage. For example, in a medical examination situation, the doctor would perform the actual exam and answer the patient's questions above the line of visibility, or onstage, while she might read the patient's chart in advance and dictate notes following the exam below the line of visibility, or backstage. The third line is the *line of internal interaction,* which separates contact employee activities from those of other service support activities and people. Vertical lines cutting across the line of internal interaction represent internal service encounters.

Service Blueprint Examples

Figures 10-7 and 10-8 show service blueprints for two different services: express mail and an overnight hotel stay.[24] These blueprints are deliberately kept very simple, showing only the most basic steps in the services. Complex diagrams could be developed for each step, and the internal processes could be much more fully developed. In addition to the four action areas separated by the three horizontal lines, these blueprints also show the physical evidence of the service from the customer's point of view at each step of the process.

In examining the express mail blueprint in Figure 10-7, it is clear that from the customer's point of view there are only three steps in the service process: the phone call, the package pickup, and the package delivery. The process is relatively standardized, the people that perform the service are the phone order-taker and the delivery person, and the physical evidence is the document package, the transmittal forms, the truck, and the hand-held computer. The complex process that occurs behind the line of visibility is of little interest or concern to the customer. However, for the three visible-to-the-customer steps to proceed effectively, invisible internal services are needed. What these steps are and the fact that they support the delivery of the service to the external customer are apparent from the blueprint.

Any of the steps in the blueprint could be exploded into a detailed blueprint if needed for a particular purpose. For example, if it were learned that the "unload and sort" step was taking too long and causing unacceptable delays in delivery, that step could be blueprinted in much greater detail to isolate the problems.

In the case of the overnight hotel stay depicted in Figure 10-8, the customer obviously is more actively involved in the service than he or she is in the express mail service just described. The guest first checks in, then goes to the hotel room where a variety of steps take place (receiving bags, sleeping, showering, eating breakfast, etc.), and finally checks out. Imagine how much more complex this process could be and how many more interactions might occur if the service map depicted a week-long vacation at the hotel, or even a three-day business conference. From the service map it is also clear (by reading across the line of interaction) with whom the guest interacts and thus who the peo-

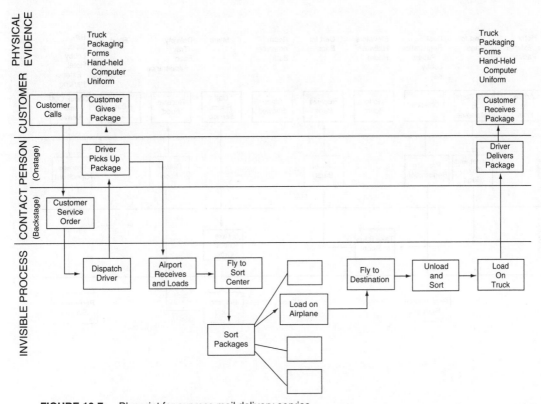

FIGURE 10-7   Blueprint for express mail delivery service.

Source: Reprinted with permission of the publisher from Bitner, 1993. All rights reserved.

ple are who provide evidence of the service to the customer. Several interactions occur with a variety of hotel employees including the bellperson, the front desk clerk, the food service order-taker, and the food delivery person. Each of the steps in the customer action area is also associated with various forms of physical evidence, from the hotel parking area and hotel exterior and interior, to the forms used at guest registration, the lobby, the room, and the food. The hotel facility itself is critical in communicating the image of the hotel company, in providing satisfaction for the guest through the manner in which the hotel room is designed and maintained, and in facilitating the actions and interactions of both the guest and the employees of the hotel. In the hotel case, the process is relatively complex (although again somewhat standardized), the people providing the service are a variety of front-line employees, and the physical evidence includes everything from the guest registration form to the design of the lobby and room to the uniforms worn by front-line employees.

A final example of a more complex blueprint is shown in Figure 10-9. This blueprint was developed in support of the discount brokerage service referred to several times in the new service development section of this chapter.[25] While all of the horizontal lines

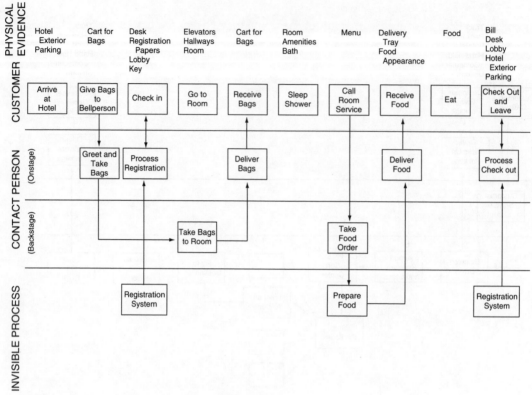

FIGURE 10-8   Blueprint for overnight hotel stay service.

Source: Reprinted with permission of the publisher from Bitner, 1993. All rights reserved.

are not depicted in this blueprint, it is clear that the internal, nonvisible aspects of the service are very complex, whereas from the customer's point of view the service is relatively simple. This blueprint shows why the service development process for this new service involved so many iterations.

Reading and Using Service Blueprints

A service blueprint can be read in a variety of ways, depending on one's purpose. If the purpose is to understand the customer's view of the process, the blueprint can be read from left to right, tracking the events in the customer action area. Questions that might be asked are: How is the service initiated by the customer? What choices does the customer make? Is the customer highly involved in creating the service, or are there few actions required of the customer? What is the physical evidence of the service from the customer's point of view? Is the evidence consistent with the organization's strategy and positioning?

If the purpose is to understand the contact employees' roles, the blueprint can also be

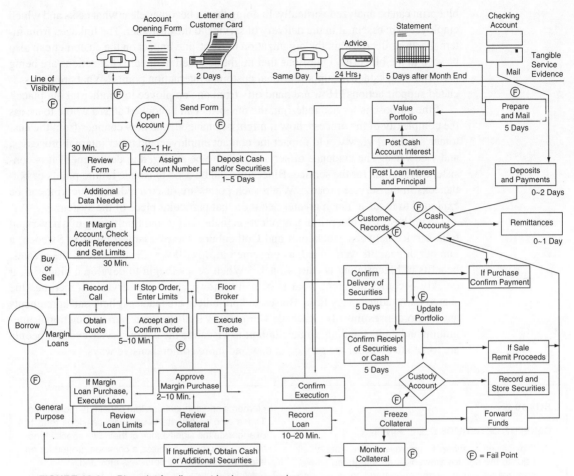

FIGURE 10-9   Blueprint for discount brokerage service.

Source: Reprinted with permission of the American Marketing Association, from Shostack, 1984, p. 43.

read horizontally but this time focusing on the activities directly above and below the line of visibility. Questions that might be asked are: How rational, efficient, and effective is the process? Who interacts with our customers, when, and how often? Is one person responsible for the customer, or is the customer passed off from one contact employee to another? Recognition that the patient was passed from one employee to another with little or no individual attention resulted in a hospital in Florida reorganizing itself so that each patient was assigned to a "care pair" (usually a nurse and an assistant) that serves the patient's needs from check-in to discharge. The result was a reduction in operating costs in pilot units of greater than 9 percent, and higher patient satisfaction.[26]

If the purpose is to understand the integration of the various elements of the service process, or to identify for particular employees where they fit into the bigger picture, the blueprint can be analyzed vertically. In doing this, it becomes clear what tasks and which employees are essential in the delivery of service to the customer. The linkages from internal actions deep within the organization to front-line impact on the customer can also be seen in the blueprint. Questions that might be asked include: What actions are being performed backstage to support critical customer interaction points? What are the associated support actions? How are hand offs from one employee to another taking place?

If the purpose is service redesign, the blueprint can be looked at as a whole to assess the complexity of the process, how it might be changed, and how changes from the customer's point of view would impact the contact employee and other internal processes, and vice versa. The evidence of service can also be analyzed to determine if it is consistent with goals for the service. Blueprints can be used to isolate failure points or bottlenecks in the service process. When such points are discovered, the blueprint can be exploded to focus in much greater detail on that particular piece of the system.

On the basis of a blueprinting application in the design and fine-tuning of a new rapid train service between Stockholm and Gothenburg, the two largest cities in Sweden, a number of benefits were noted, as presented in Box 10-2.[27] Clearly, one of the greatest benefits of blueprinting is educational.[28] When people begin to develop a blueprint, it quickly becomes apparent what is actually known about the service. Sometimes the shared knowledge is very little. Biases and prejudices are made explicit, and agreements and compromises must be reached. The process itself promotes cross-functional integration and understanding. In the attempt to visualize the entire service system, people are forced to consider the service in new and more comprehensive ways.

BOX 10-2

BENEFITS OF SERVICE BLUEPRINTING

1 Provides an overview so employees can relate "what I do" to the service viewed as an integrated whole, thus reinforcing a customer-oriented focus among employees.
2 Identifies fail points, that is, weak links of the chain of service activities, which points can be the target of continuous quality improvement.
3 Line of interaction between external customers and employees illuminates the customer's role and demonstrates where the customer experiences quality, thus contributing to informed service design.
4 Line of visibility promotes a conscious decision on what customers should see and which employees will be in contact with customers, thus facilitating rational service design.
5 Line of internal interaction clarifies interfaces across departmental lines, with their inherent interdependencies, thus strengthening continuous quality improvement.
6 Stimulates strategic discussions by illuminating the elements and connections that constitute the service. Those who participate in strategic sessions tend to exaggerate the significance of their own special function and perspective unless a common ground for an integrated view of the service is provided.
7 Provides a basis for identifying and assessing cost, revenue, and capital invested in each element of the service.
8 Constitutes a rational basis for both external and internal marketing. For example, the service map makes it easier for an advertising agency or an in-house promotion team to overview a service and select essential messages for communication.
9 Facilitates top-down, bottom-up approach to quality improvement. It enables managers to identify, channel, and support quality improvement efforts of grassroots employees working on both front-line and support teams. Employee work teams can create service maps and thus more clearly apply and communicate their experience and suggestions for improvements.

Source: Reprinted with permission, from Gummesson and Kingman-Brundage, 1991.

Building a Blueprint

Recall that many of the benefits and purposes of building blueprints evolve from the process of doing it. Thus the final product is not necessarily the only goal. Through the process of developing the blueprint, many intermediate goals can be achieved: clarification of the concept, development of a shared service vision, recognition of complexities and intricacies of the service that are not initially apparent, and delineation of roles and responsibilities, to name a few. The development of the blueprint needs to involve a variety of functional representatives as well as information from customers. Drawing or building a blueprint is not a task that can be assigned to one person or one functional area. Box 10-3 identifies the basic steps in building a blueprint.

Step 1: Identify the Service Process to Be Blueprinted   Blueprints can be developed at a variety of levels, and there needs to be agreement on the starting point. For example, the express mail blueprint shown earlier is at the basic service concept level. Little detail is shown, and variations based on market segment or specific services are not shown. Specific blueprints could be developed for overnight express mail, two-day express mail, large accounts, and/or store-front drop-off centers. Each of these blueprints would share some features with the concept blueprint, but would also include unique features. Or, if the "sort packages" and "loading" elements of the process were found to be problem areas or bottlenecks that were slowing service to customers, a detailed blueprint of the subprocesses at work at those two steps could be developed. Identifying the process to be mapped will be determined by the underlying purpose for building the blueprint in the first place.

Step 2: Map the Service Process from the Customer's Point of View   This step involves charting the choices and actions that the customer performs or experiences in purchasing, consuming, and evaluating the service. If the process being mapped is an internal service, then the customer will be an employee who is the recipient of the service. Identifying the service from the customer's point of view first will help to avoid focusing on processes and steps that have no customer impact. This step forces agreement on who the customer is (sometimes no small task) and may involve considerable research to determine exactly how the customer experiences the service. If market segments ex-

---

BOX 10-3

BUILDING A SERVICE BLUEPRINT

1 Identify the process to be blueprinted.
   Basic business concept
   A service (within a family of services)
   A specific service component
2 Map the process from the customer's point of view.
3 Draw the line of interaction.

4 Draw the line of visibility.
5 Map the process from the customer contact person's point of view, distinguishing on-stage from backstage actions.
6 Draw the line of internal interaction.
7 Link customer and contact person activities to needed support functions.
8 Add evidence of service at each customer action step.

perience the service in different ways, then separate blueprints will be done for each significant segment.

Sometimes the beginning and ending of the service from the customer's point of view may not be obvious. For example, research in a hair-cutting context revealed that customers viewed the process as beginning with the phone call to the salon and setting of the appointment, while the hair stylists did not typically view the making of appointments as part of the service process.[29] Similarly, in a mammography screening service, patients viewed driving to the clinic, parking, and locating the screening office as part of the service experience. If the blueprint is being developed for an existing service, it may be helpful at this point in the process to videotape or photograph the service process from the customer's point of view. Often managers and others who are not on the front lines do not actually know what the customers are experiencing and what it all looks like from their point of view.

Steps 3–5: Map Contact Employee Actions, Both Onstage and Backstage   First the lines of interaction and visibility are drawn, and then the process from the customer contact person's point of view is mapped, distinguishing visible or onstage activities from invisible backstage activities. For existing services this will involve questioning front-line operations employees to learn what they do and which activities are performed in full view of the customer versus those activities that are carried out behind the scenes.

Steps 6–7: Map Internal Support Activities   The line of internal interaction can then be drawn and linkages from contact person activities to internal support functions can be identified. It is in this process that the direct and indirect impact of internal actions on customers becomes apparent. Internal service processes take on added importance when viewed in connection with their link to the customer. Alternatively, certain steps in the process may be viewed as unnecessary if there is no clear link to the customer's experience or to an essential internal support service.

Step 8: Add Evidence of Service at Each Customer Action Step   Finally, the evidence of service can be added to the blueprint to illustrate what it is that the customer sees and receives as tangible evidence of the service at each step in the customer experience. The photographic blueprint including photos, slides, or video of the process can be very useful at this stage as well to aid in analyzing the impact of tangible evidence and its consistency with the overall strategy and service positioning.

SERVICE POSITIONING

How the service is designed (its process blueprint and associated evidence) will impact the image of the service in the customer's mind. Likewise, the image, or position, that the organization chooses will dictate to some extent the essential features and design of the service process. Service design, specifications, and positioning are thus inextricably intertwined. We turn now to a discussion of positioning and its relationship to service design elements.

A service offering's *position* is the way it is perceived by consumers, particularly in relation to competing offerings. The service position is what is in the customer's mind, whether or not it is the image planned or desired by the organization. An organization or a particular offering of an organization is successfully positioned if it has established and maintains a distinctive and desirable place for itself in the consumer's mind relative to competing organizations or offerings. If a service is successfully positioned, the mention of the service will conjure up in the customer's mind an image that is distinct from images of similar service offerings. Service positioning is useful in establishing a new service image, as well as for maintaining and repositioning existing services.

First, positioning is critical in establishing a *new service image.* When the first ten-minute lube and oil change service was introduced in the 1970s, no one was familiar with the concept nor had anyone experienced it. (With the proliferation of such services today it is difficult to imagine a time, such a short while ago, when they did not exist.) The idea was to distinguish this new service from the corner gas station where, until then, people had their cars attended to almost exclusively. The first such company communicated its desired position as a fast, efficient, affordable, no-appointment-necessary service through a variety of vehicles including its name (Speedi-Lube), its colors (blue and white), the design of its facilities (clean, uncluttered, functional), its signage (clear, unambiguous instructions to the customer), its employees (professional, clean uniforms), and the simplicity of its process.

There is a tendency to assume that market positions are established primarily through advertising. This may be true for consumer package goods, but for services and other more complex products all elements of the services marketing mix can and should reinforce the chosen position. Through the consistency of communication using all of the mix factors, Speedi-Lube quickly established an image for itself. (See the opening paragraphs of chapter 18 for more details on this example.)

Positioning is also important for existing services in *maintaining and reinforcing an established image* in customers' minds. For example, Marriott's Residence Inn (described in chapter 7) is a hotel positioned for extended-stay guests needing a "home-away-from-home." Marriott has effectively established this position in the minds of its consumers using all elements of the services marketing mix. The name of the hotel itself communicates the nature of the target market, and the words "home" and "neighborhood" are used frequently in the hotel's communications. The physical facility also communicates a residential or homelike feel with rooms that include kitchens, separate living room areas, and often fireplaces. Services provided go beyond the typical hotel and extend into support services that people need over extended periods such as laundry, dish washing, grocery shopping, and planned social activities.

Sometimes service *repositioning* is used to change the image of the service in the minds of consumers. This was the case for Charles Schwab & Co., a large U.S. discount brokerage company founded in 1975 at the time commission rates were deregulated. During the first twelve years of its existence the company gradually evolved its position from one of focusing on discount financial services for independent investors based almost entirely on price as the differentiator to one focusing more on value plus price. The value component was added to the service position by rapid automation and a proliferation of branches. Through these changes, customers came to see Charles Schwab & Co. as a broker with: good value for the commission; few transaction errors; trade anytime, anywhere; quick buy and sell confirmation; and easy to understand commission struc-ture.[30] Through consistent communication strategies and the addition of automated systems and extensive branching, the company was able to move customers along as the company's position evolved. After 1987, Charles Schwab again sought out a new position, this time attempting to expand the value theme through serving a wider range of investor segments. Recently, the company has further enhanced its position as a highly customized convenient self-serve broker by adding Saturday and evening hours and providing "Windows"-based investment software for customers under the advertising tag "Helping Investors Help Themselves."

Positioning Dimensions

Services can be positioned on a variety of dimensions: according to the needs they satisfy, the benefits they deliver, specific service features, when and how they are used, or who uses them. What is essential is to position the service on something that is important to consumers, something that can serve to distinguish the service from its competitors, and something that can be delivered consistently. The following sections will develop various means of positioning services on the basis of important differentiating factors. We begin first with positioning on the dimensions of service quality identified in chapter 5. Clearly, if service quality is important to consumers, then it should be possible to develop successful positioning on important dimensions of quality. We will also examine the practice of positioning service on the evidence of service.

Positioning on the Five Dimensions of Service Quality

Organizations may choose to focus on one or more of the five dimensions of service quality in developing an effective position, namely, reliability, responsiveness, assurance, empathy, and tangibles.

Reliability   Federal Express is probably the most well-known example of a company that has focused on reliability. Its message is, "When it absolutely, positively, has to get there." Another company that has successfully positioned itself on reliability is Florida Power & Light Company. Serving a part of the country that annually averages eighty days of thunderstorms with associated lightning-caused service interruptions, company engineers teamed with suppliers to develop advanced surge protectors that insulate transformers from lightning damage. They also developed a sophisticated, computer-based lightning tracking system to anticipate where weather-related problems might occur, and then strategically position crews at these locations to quicken recovery response time. The company reduced service unavailability (customer minutes-interrupted divided by customers served) from 70 minutes at year-end 1987 to 48.37 minutes at year-end 1988.[31] The company's reputation for reliability was severely tested in 1989, however, when a strong and unexpected cold front caused massive power outages in Florida, proving that companies whose reputations are built on reliability still need contingency plans for those occasions when even these plans will fail.

For Federal Express and Florida Power & Light the strategy will work well as long as reliability can be maintained as a distinguishing characteristic among their set of competitors. In many cases, however, reliability is not a good distinguishing characteristic even though it is a critically important quality dimension. Think about the banking industry, telecommunications, or the airline industry. In these industries, reliability of the core service is assumed, it is a basic requirement that they must meet just to play the game. Thus reliability is not likely to be a successful differentiating factor for positioning in those industries.

Responsiveness   Some organizations choose to focus on *responsiveness* in their positioning. They are responding to customers' desire for prompt, "willing to help" service. The Four Seasons Hotels reflect this type of positioning. Its ads communicate the Four Seasons' willingness to respond quickly to just about any idiosyncratic demand a customer might have. A woman in one of its ads needs a "couple of raincoats cleaned overnight" and the small print in the ad suggests that the staff can accomplish just about anything, even at 11 p.m.:

> There's nothing like a challenge at 11 p.m. to test our staff's dogged determination. Say the word, and our valets will clean and deliver your clothing by morning. If it's wrinkled, they'll press it with equal dispatch. We will polish your shoes with a virtuoso's touch, and if need be, even provide new laces—all with our compliments . . . .

Another organization that has always focused on responsiveness is American Express. This company has set responsiveness standards for nearly all of its processes. Among these are the number of hours to replace a lost card, the number of days to process a card application, and the number of hours for a retailer to receive an answer to a billing question. The standards are based on customer requirements for responsiveness and customer perceptions of speed and promptness, rather than on company definitions.

Assurance   The third quality dimension, *assurance,* is used effectively for positioning in industries where trust and confidence in the service provider are particularly critical. Insurance companies frequently use assurance-based advertising tag lines to build customer confidence: "You're in good hands with Allstate," "The Quiet Company" (Northwestern Mutual Life), and "Own a Piece of the Rock" (Prudential). As with reliability in banking, however, assurance may be assumed in the insurance industry, so that having established a secure position with regard to assurance an insurance company would have to distinguish itself on other quality dimensions or service features.

Assurance is also critically important in health care, and the Mayo Clinic has effectively used an assurance-based advertising message ("Trust Your Health to the Name You Know") to reinforce its strong, long-standing image of quality and confidence. With the turmoil in the U.S. health care industry, the Mayo Clinic's clearly differentiated position in the marketplace is a strong competitive advantage for them.

Empathy   Firms can also position themselves on *empathy,* which builds on the customer's desire for caring, individualized attention. Lufthansa, a German airline company, has established its position as a carrier that understands individual needs of customers from a variety of cultures, as shown in the ad insert: ". . . over the years, every

experience with every traveler from every corner of the world has helped us to understand you. We've grown accustomed to differences in custom." It captures this idea in
its advertising tag line as well ("The difference between worldwide and worldwise")
(Figure 10-10) and by showing a very touching, intimate interaction between a pilot and
a small child.

When companies pursue a course directed at "mass customization" or "segments of
one" as presented in chapter 7, they are by definition positioning themselves at least partially on the empathy dimension. Travel agents that develop personal travel preference
profiles on frequent travelers, recording such information as preferred form of payment,
secretary's name, and seating preferences in a computerized client file, are focusing their
strategy on the empathy dimension. The advertising of the Principal Financial Group

FIGURE 10-10   Lufthansa emphasizes empathy and individual service.
Source: Reprinted courtesy of Lufthansa.

suggests positioning on empathy. Their ad shows one egg in a single-compartment egg carton and the copy reads:

> Processing customers by the dozen. That's how most companies today provide financial services. But Financial Strategies from the Principal Financial Group takes a fresh approach. Because no two customers, like no two eggs, are exactly alike, Financial Strategies lets our representatives focus on each person's unique financial needs . . . .

Tangibles   The final quality dimension, *tangibles,* may also be the focus of a positioning strategy. For a long time Alaska Airlines has positioned itself as a quality airline by emphasizing the extra leg and seat room it provides passengers. This focus on tangibles is consistent with its pricing (infrequent discounts) and customer service (better-than-average quality food; attentive in-flight servers) strategies as well. Tangibles are also a common positioning element for resorts, hotels, restaurants, and retailers. In positioning its highly successful bookstore chain, Barnes and Noble has supported its position as an "entertaining, social environment" through providing plenty of welcoming public space, sophisticated and stylish displays, cafes where people can drink coffee and read, and restrooms so people can stay a long time if they wish.

Because tangibles, particularly the physical environment, associated with a service organization are so highly visible to customers, it is important that they be designed in ways consistent with the positioning strategy, whatever it is. This is true even when tangibles are not the focus of the positioning strategy. For example, a high-volume law firm that focuses on providing reasonably priced, uncomplicated services to the public from a mall location would want to design its tangibles to be consistent with that position rather than design a facility that looked like a downtown, high-rise law firm.

Positioning on Service Evidence

Services can also be positioned by focusing on the evidence of service from the customers' point of view. Recall from chapter 5 that the evidence of service falls into three broad categories: people, physical evidence, and process. Because services are largely intangible, these tangible manifestations take on added importance in establishing and reinforcing the service position. If the evidence matches a desired position, it can serve to reinforce and solidify the strategy; if the evidence doesn't match the positioning strategy, confusion will result, and in the worst case the strategy may fail. Any one or all three of the evidence elements can be effectively used either in support of a positioning strategy based on the quality dimensions or as the primary focus of the strategy.

People: Service Contact Employees and Other Customers   Here we are referring to the contact employees (or any visible employee) and customers who may be in the service facility. How these people look, how they act, and who they are will influence the service position in the customer's mind. Imagine yourself arriving in a city for the first time, seeking a place to have dinner. As you wander down a street with a number of different restaurants, you glance through the windows, noticing the service personnel (what are they wearing? is there a host/hostess?) and the other customers (are they dressed in business attire, or casual? are they young or middle-aged? are there families?). Your impressions help to position each restaurant in your mind relative to the other restaurants.

The Disney Corporation works hard to hire and train contact employees so that they all convey a consistent image and reinforce the position of the Disney theme parks as places that guarantee you a fun experience. All employees, from the street cleaners to the ticket-takers to the entertainers, are trained to be helpful and knowledgeable, and to exhibit an "onstage" persona anytime they are within view of customers.

Employee uniforms and dress codes can also serve to reinforce or convey a particular service position. One service expert has suggested that uniforms "package the service provider" like plastics and boxes package tangible products.[32] The uniform (or whatever clothing is specified by the dress code) provides a physical representation of the service that customers will incorporate into their image and mental positioning of the service. Southwest Airlines has effectively used employee uniforms to reinforce its image as a fun-loving, casual airline by allowing both flight and ground crews to wear shorts and tennis shoes. For other services a uniform may reinforce the provider's credibility (e.g., a physician's white coat) or suggest consistency of service by reinforcing a message of standardization and unchanging quality. The communicative power of the uniform is perhaps most apparent when it works at cross purposes to the desired service position. For example, a lawyer wearing a loud suit or a hotel concierge wearing blue jeans would project an image inconsistent with the desired image of the firm. Similarly, a standardized uniform may work at cross purposes if the desired image is one of flexibility and personalized service.

Because the customers who use the service will influence a service organization's position, some organizations "train" their customers to act in ways consistent with their position. The "Q," a large U.S. health club chain, has a dress and behavior code for members that is consistent with its targeted position. Because the organization's strategy is to appeal to middle-aged adults, who may be overweight and self-conscious, the dress code does not allow trendy, tight-fitting exercise clothing but rather requires that members wear loose-fitting clothing and shirts of a certain length.

Physical Evidence: Tangible Communication, Price, Physical Environment, Guarantees Physical evidence is similar to the tangibles element described previously. While tangibles may not be rated high by consumers in terms of their influence on quality, tangibles/physical evidence are critical for positioning and solidifying an image. All forms of tangible communication (brochures, advertising, business cards, billing statements), the price, the physical environment where the service is delivered, and any guarantees should be consistent to ensure that the position is well established in the customer's mind. For example, an executive education program that conveys an image of high quality through its brochure (excellent graphics, attractive paper stock and colors), program content (well-known presenters, comprehensive and current content), and pricing strategy (several hundred dollars per day) will attract a mid- to high-level executive. The promised position must then be solidified by actual quality program delivery, excellent materials, prime accommodations, responsive service, and excellent food quality. The tangible evidence used to position this type of high-end executive education experience would be different from the evidence used to position a day-long seminar aimed at mass audiences and priced at less than one hundred dollars.

Process: Flow of Activities, Steps in the Process, Flexibility of Process   The basis of any service positioning strategy is the service itself, but we have little knowledge of how to craft service processes for positioning purposes.[33] The work on service blue-printing has forged a connection between service processes as structural elements that can be engineered for strategic service positioning purposes.

Service process can be defined in terms of two variables: complexity and divergence.[34] *Complexity* reflects the number of steps involved in delivering the service, and *divergence* reflects the executional latitude, or variability of those steps. Whether a service is high or low in complexity and in divergence can be readily determined by looking at its blueprint. Service positions, and possibilities for repositioning, can then be defined in terms of these variables. For example, a physician's service is high in both complexity and divergence. Hotel services are high in complexity (lots of steps in the service delivery process) but low in divergence (they have standardized their service processes for every sequence from room cleaning to checkout). Other services are low in complexity but high in divergence; for example a singer simply "sings," a painter simply "paints," and a minister "preaches," but every time they perform the service is different. Services that are low in both complexity and divergence include movie theaters, car washes, and vending machines. In these cases there are few steps in the service process, and the steps are all quite standardized.

Figure 10-11 shows how within the health-care industry alone, variations in structural

FIGURE 10-11   Relative positions of health care services based on process dimensions of complexity and divergence.

Source: Reprinted with permission of the American Marketing Association, from Shostack, 1987.

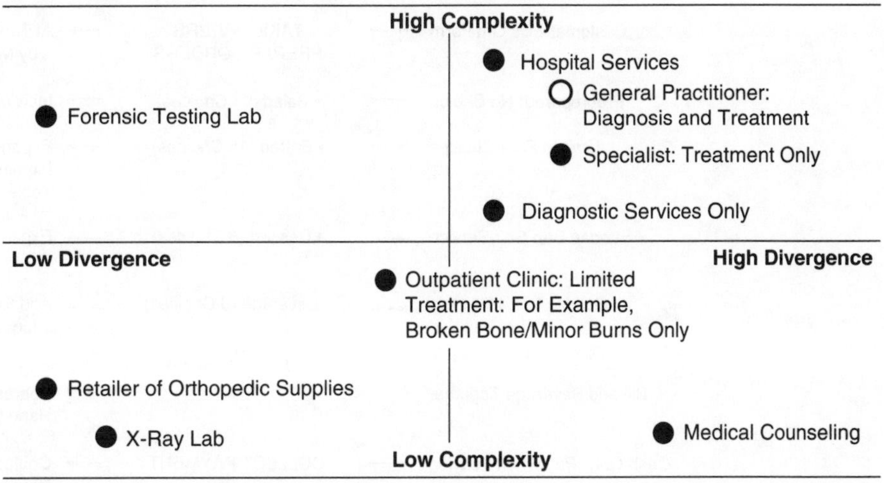

forms divide services among the four cells defined by complexity and divergence. While an X-ray lab would be viewed as low in both complexity and divergence, a general practitioner's services would be relatively high in both dimensions.

By defining the organization's current position in structural terms, the opportunities for repositioning around structural dimensions are more apparent. For example, Figure 10-12 shows in simplified terms some changes in process that a mid-priced family restaurant might consider to reposition itself in terms of divergence or complexity. The restaurant's current process characteristics are described in the middle column of the figure. To move toward a higher complexity/higher divergence position, the restaurant might consider the changes suggested in the right column, while to reposition itself as a low complexity/low divergence restaurant, it would look at the changes suggested in the left column. Sometimes the types of changes suggested by Figure 10-12 are made for reasons other than positioning, for example, to gain operating efficiencies, or for financial reasons, without attention being paid to the impact such structural changes may have on the organization's position.

FIGURE 10-12   Repositioning alternatives for a mid-priced restaurant based on process dimensions of complexity and divergence.

Source: Reprinted with permission of the American Marketing Association, from Shostack, 1987.

LOWER COMPLEXITY/DIVERGENCE	CURRENT PROCESS	HIGHER COMPLEXITY/DIVERGENCE
No Reservations ←	TAKE RESERVATION →	Specific Table Selection
Self-Seating. Menu on Blackboard ←	SEAT GUESTS, GIVE MENUS →	Recite Menu: Describe Entrees & Specials
Eliminate ←	SERVE WATER, AND BREAD →	Assortment of Hot Breads and Hors d'Oeuvres
Customer Fills Out Form ←	TAKE ORDERS PREPARE ORDERS	→ At Table. Taken Personally by Maitre d'
Preprepared: No Choice ←	• Salads (4 Choices)	→ Individually Prepared at Table
Limit to Four Choices ←	• Entree (15 Choices)	→ Expand to 20 Choices: Add Flaming Dishes; Bone Fish at Table; Prepare Sauces at Table
Sundae Bar: Self-Service ←	• Dessert (6 Choices)	→ Expand to 12 Choices
Coffee, Tea, Milk Only ←	• Beverage (6 Choices)	→ Add Exotic Coffees; Wine List; Liqueurs
Serve Salad & Entree Together: Bill and Beverage Together ←	SERVE ORDERS	→ Separate Course Service: Sherbert Between Courses; Hand Grind Pepper
Cash Only: Pay when Leaving ←	COLLECT PAYMENT	→ Choice of Payment, Including House Accounts; Serve Mints.

SUMMARY

To close GAP 2, service providers must effectively match customer expectations to actual service process designs and positioning strategies. However, because of the very nature of services—their intangibility and heterogeneity specifically—the design, development, and positioning of service offerings are complex and challenging. Many services are only vaguely defined before their introduction to the marketplace. This chapter has outlined some of the challenges involved in designing and positioning services, and some strategies for effectively overcoming the challenges.

Through adaptations of the new product development process that is commonplace in goods production and manufacturing companies, service providers can begin to make their offerings more explicit and avoid failures. The new service development process presented in the chapter includes nine stages, beginning with the development of a business and new service strategy and ending with postintroduction evaluation of the new service. Between these initial and ending stages are a number of careful steps and checkpoints designed to maximize the likelihood of new service success. Carrying out the stages requires the inclusion of customers, contact employees, and anyone else who will affect or be affected by the new service. Because successful new service introduction is often highly dependent on service employees (often they *are* the service), integration of employees at each stage is critical.

Service blueprinting is a particularly useful technique in the new service development process. A blueprint can make a complex and intangible service concrete through its visual depiction of all of the steps, actors, processes, and physical evidence of the service. The key feature of service blueprints is their focus on the customer—the customer's experience is documented first and is kept fully in view as the other features of the blueprint are developed. This chapter has provided the basic tools needed to build, use, and evaluate service blueprints.

The final sections of the chapter have illustrated the linkages between service design and positioning. Because of the nature of services, their positions are affected by much more than advertising and promotion. All dimensions of service quality, as well as the people, process, and physical evidence of the service, can be used to reinforce the positioning strategy.

DISCUSSION QUESTIONS

1 Why is it challenging to design and develop services?
2 What are the risks of attempting to describe services in words alone?
3 According to the research reported in the chapter and shown in Table 10-1, which steps in the new service development process are least likely to be carried out? Which are most likely? Discuss these findings. Discuss their implications for new services success.
4 Compare and contrast the three blueprints included in the chapter in Figures 10-7, 10-8, and 10-9.
5 How might a service blueprint be used for marketing, human resource, and operations decisions? Focus on one of the blueprint examples shown in the text to give yourself a context for your answer.
6 Assume that you are a multiproduct service company that wants to grow through adding new services. Describe a logical process you might use to introduce a new service to the

marketplace. What steps in the process might be most difficult and why? How might you incorporate service blueprinting into the process?

7 What is service positioning? Discuss how the dimensions of service quality can be used for positioning strategies. Describe an example of a service you believe is clearly positioned on one or more of the service quality dimensions.

8 Discuss how the service evidence elements can be used in positioning strategies. Describe an example of a service you believe is clearly positioned on one or more of the service evidence elements.

9 How can service blueprints be used to improve service positioning strategies?

EXERCISES

1 Think of a new service you would like to develop if you were an entrepreneur. How would you go about it? Describe what you would do and where you would get your information.

2 Find a new and interesting service in your local area, or a service offered on your campus. Document the service process via a service blueprint. To do this you will probably need to interview one of the service employees. After you have documented the existing service, use blueprinting concepts to redesign the service or change it in some way.

3 Choose a service you are familiar with and document the customer action steps through a photographic blueprint. What is the "evidence of service" from your point of view as a customer?

4 Blueprint your experiences as a customer of two firms with very different positions within the same industry (e.g., Southwest Airlines vs. Delta; a fast-food restaurant vs. a sit-down restaurant; an HMO vs. a private physician). How does the process contribute to (or detract from or confuse) the intended service position in each case?

NOTES

1 Guy Webster, "Home-based Firms Get Help," *Arizona Republic,* March 3, 1994, p. D1.

2 "Flops, Too Many New Products Fail. Here's Why—and How to Do Better," cover story, *Business Week,* August 16, 1993, pp. 76–82.

3 Ibid.; and Robert G. Cooper, *Winning at New Products,* 2d ed., (Reading, Mass.: Addison-Wesley, 1993).

4 G. Lynn Shostack, "Understanding Services through Blueprinting," in *Advances in Services Marketing and Management,* Vol. 1, eds. Teresa A. Swartz, David E. Bowen, and Stephen W. Brown (Greenwich, Conn.: JAI Press, 1992), pp. 75–90.

5 Cooper, *Winning at New Products.*

6 G. Lynn Shostack, "Service Design in the Operating Environment," in *Developing New Services,* eds. William R. George and Claudia Marshall (Chicago: American Marketing Association, 1984), pp. 27–43.

7 Benjamin Schneider and David E. Bowen, "New Services Design, Development and Implementation and the Employee," in *Developing New Services,* ed. George and Marshall, pp. 82–101.

8 Michael J. McCarthy, "Airlines Retool Services to Attract More Full-Fare Fliers," *Wall Street Journal,* October 27, 1993, p. B1.

9 Adapted from Donald F. Heany, "Degrees of Product Innovation," *Journal of Business Strategy,* Spring 1983, pp. 3–14, appearing in Christopher H. Lovelock, "Developing

and Implementing New Services," in *Developing New Services,* eds. George and Marshall, pp. 44–64.

10 Cooper, *Winning New Products.*

11 The steps shown in Figure 10-4 and discussed in the text are based primarily on the model developed by Michael J. Bowers, "An Exploration into New Service Development: Organization, Process and Structure," doctoral dissertation, Texas A & M University, 1985. Bowers' model is adapted from Booz-Allen & Hamilton, *New Product Management for the 1980's* (New York: Booz-Allen & Hamilton, 1982).

12 Robert G. Cooper, "Stage Gate Systems for New Product Success," *Marketing Management* 1, 4 (1992): 20–29.

13 While the basic framework shown in Figure 10-5 has been developed and adapted by many researchers and authors over the last thirty years, its original form can be found in H. Igor Ansoff, *Corporate Strategy* (New York: McGraw-Hill, 1965).

14 Shostack, "Service Design."

15 Eberhard E. Scheuing and Eugene M. Johnson, "A Proposed Model for New Service Development," *Journal of Services Marketing* 3, 2 (1989): 25–34.

16 Michael R. Bowers, "Developing New Services for Hospitals: A Suggested Model," *Journal of Health Care Marketing* 7, 2 (June 1987): 35–44.

17 Shostack, "Service Design," p. 35.

18 Bowers, "An Exploration into New Service Development."

19 See for example a study of firms in the United Kingdom reported in Christopher J. Easingwood, "New Product Development for Service Companies," *Journal of Product Innovation Management* 4, (1986): 264–275; Eberhard E. Scheuing and Eugene M. Johnson, "New Product Management in Service Industries: An Early Assessment," in *Add Value to Your Service,* ed. Carol Surprenant (Chicago: American Marketing Association, 1987), pp. 91–95; and Shostack, "Service Design."

20 Cooper, *Winning at New Products.*

21 The service blueprinting section of the chapter draws from the pioneering works in this area: G. Lynn Shostack, "Designing Services That Deliver," *Harvard Business Review,* January–February 1984, pp. 133–139; G. Lynn Shostack, "Service Positioning Through Structural Change," *Journal of Marketing* 51 (January 1987): 34–43; Jane Kingman-Brundage, "The ABC's of Service System Blueprinting," in *Designing a Winning Service Strategy,* eds. Mary Jo Bitner and Lawrence A. Crosby (Chicago: American Marketing Association, 1989), pp. 30–33.

22 Shostack, "Understanding Services through Blueprinting," pp. 75–90.

23 These key components are drawn from Kingman-Brundage, "The ABC's."

24 The text explaining Figures 10-7 and 10-8 relies on Mary Jo Bitner, "Managing the Evidence of Service," in *The Service Quality Handbook,* eds. Eberhard E. Scheuing and William F. Christopher (New York: American Management Association: 1993), pp. 358–370.

25 Shostack, "Service Design."

26 "Hospital, Heal Thyself," *Business Week,* August 27, 1990, pp. 66–68.

27 Evert Gummesson and Jane Kingman-Brundage, "Service Design and Quality: Applying Service Blueprinting and Service Mapping to Railroad Services," in *Quality Management in Services,* eds. Paul Kunst and Jos Lemmink (Assen/Maastricht, Netherlands: Van Gorcum, 1991).

28 Shostack, "Understanding Services through Blueprinting."

29 Amy R. Hubbert, Annette Garcia Sehorn, and Stephen W. Brown, "Service Expectations: The Consumer vs. The Provider," *International Journal of Service Industry Management,* 6, 1 (1995), 6–21.

30 Kent Dorwin, "Repositioning a Leading Stockbroker," *Long Range Planning* 21 (November–December, 1988): 13–19.

31 Valarie Zeithaml, L. Berry, and A. Parasuraman, "The Nature and Determinants of Customer Expectations of Service," Marketing Science Institute Working Paper, Cambridge, Mass., 1990.

32 Michael R. Solomon, "Packaging the Service Provider," *The Services Industries Journal* 5 (July 1985): 64–71.

33 Shostack, "Service Positioning through Structural Change."

34 Ibid.

PART FIVE

DELIVERING AND PERFORMING SERVICE

11

EMPLOYEES' ROLES IN SERVICE DELIVERY

Consider the following true stories:

- *When a Xerox service engineer delivered a Xerox copier to a customer, the engineer discovered that the customer needed a table to support it. Although the table had not been ordered, the service engineer drove to a local department store and purchased an appropriate table for $65. The customer was delighted, and the service engineer felt great as well.*[1]

- *A mother terminated a nine-year relationship with her children's pediatrician because the pediatrician refused to prescribe developmental physical therapy for her son. The physician did not "believe in" the therapy and would not even discuss his reasons with the family. The family established an ongoing relationship with another pediatrician, even though they would have preferred not to switch.*

- *A phone associate at AT&T's Universal Card Services received a call from a husband whose wife, suffering from Alzheimer's disease, had vanished. The husband hoped that he could find his wife through tracing her use of her Universal Card. The phone associate placed a hold on the card and arranged to be called personally the moment there was any activity on the card. When it happened, about a week later, the associate contacted the husband, the doctor, and the police, who were then able to assist the missing woman and get her home.*[2]

- *At the Fairmont Hotel in San Francisco a computer programmer made a room reservation for a discounted price of $100. On arrival he discovered that all rooms were filled. The front desk clerk responded by sending him to the Sheraton and picking up his room charge of $250 at that hotel. He also paid for the guest's parking fee at the Fairmont and taxi fare to the new hotel, and threw in a free meal at the Fairmont as well.*[3]

These stories illustrate the important roles played by service employees in creating satisfied customers and in building customer relationships. The front-line service providers in each example are enormously important to the success of the organizations they represent. They are responsible for understanding customer needs and for interpreting customer requirements in real time.

At many companies, the critical role of contact employees is recognized and capitalized on. At Universal Card Services, phone associates hold the premier jobs in the business and are treated accordingly.[4] Only 1 in 10 applicants makes it through the screening and hiring process, and post-hiring training is extensive. Employees are given the opportunity to expand their knowledge and skills constantly through ongoing training, and are empowered to take whatever actions are needed to help card members. Measures of quality are documented daily, and each person at UCS receives a bonus equal to 12 percent of daily salary for each day the UCS team jointly achieves quality targets. Monthly customer surveys and other forms of customer information as well as internal suggestions from employees fuel the focus on quality by all employees. UCS employees are also supported off the job with tuition reimbursement programs, quality child care alternatives, and an on-site health club for employees and spouses.

In this chapter we focus on service employees and human resource practices that facilitate delivery of quality services. The assumption is that even when customer expectations are well understood (GAP 1) and services have been designed and specified to conform to those expectations (GAP 2), there may still be discontinuities in service quality when the service is not delivered as specified. These discontinuities are labeled GAP 3—the service performance gap (Figure 11-1)—in the service quality framework. Because employees frequently deliver or perform the service, human resource issues are a major cause of GAP 3. By focusing on the critical role of service employees, and by develop-

FIGURE 11-1   Provider GAP 3.

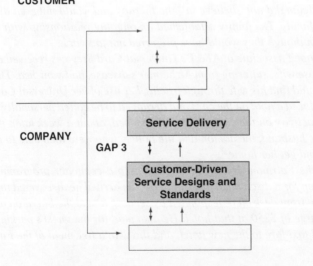

ing strategies that will lead to effective customer-oriented service delivery, organizations can begin to close GAP 3.

Figure 11-2 illustrates the factors contributing to GAP 3 that we will focus on in this chapter. The failure to deliver services as designed and specified can result from a number of employee and human-performance factors: ineffective recruitment of service-oriented employees, role ambiguity and role conflict among contact employees, poor employee-technology-job fit, inappropriate evaluation and compensation systems, and lack of empowerment, perceived control, and teamwork. The chapter will give you an understanding of these factors and strategies for overcoming them.

The objectives of this chapter are to:

1 Illustrate the critical importance of service employees in creating customer satisfaction and service quality.

2 Demonstrate the challenges inherent in boundary-spanning roles.

3 Provide examples of strategies for creating customer-oriented service delivery through: hiring the right people, developing employees to deliver service quality, providing needed support systems, and retaining the best service employees.

4 Show how the strategies can support a service culture where providing excellent service to both internal and external customers is a way of life.

THE CRITICAL IMPORTANCE OF SERVICE EMPLOYEES

An often-heard quote about service organizations goes like this: *"In a service organization, if you're not serving the customer, you'd better be serving someone who is."*[5] Peo-

FIGURE 11-2   Key reasons for provider GAP 3.

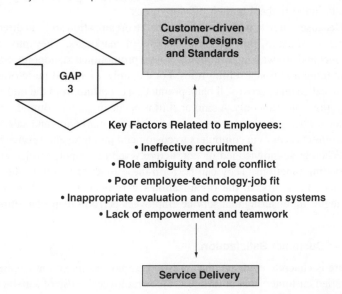

Customer-driven
Service Designs
and Standards

GAP
3

Key Factors Related to Employees:

• Ineffective recruitment
• Role ambiguity and role conflict
• Poor employee-technology-job fit
• Inappropriate evaluation and compensation systems
• Lack of empowerment and teamwork

Service Delivery

ple—front-line employees and those supporting them from behind the scenes—are critical to the success of any service organization. The importance of people in the marketing of services is captured in the *people* element of the services marketing mix, which we described in chapter 1 as *all of the human actors who play a part in service delivery and thus influence the buyer's perceptions; namely the firm's personnel, the customer, and other customers in the service environment.*

In this chapter we focus on service employees because:

- They *are* the service.
- They *are* the organization in the customer's eyes.
- They *are* marketers.

In many cases, the contact employee is the service—there is nothing else. For example, in most personal services (e.g., haircutting, physical trainers, child care, cleaning/maintenance, limousine services, counseling, legal services) the contact employee provides the entire service singlehandedly. The offering *is* the employee. Thus, investing in the employee to improve the service parallels making a direct investment in the improvement of a manufactured product.

Even if the contact employee doesn't perform the service entirely, he or she may still personify the firm in the customer's eyes. All of the employees of a law firm or health clinic—from the professionals who provide the service to the receptionists and office staff—represent the firm to the client, and everything these individuals do or say can influence perceptions of the organization. Even off-duty employees, such as flight attendants or restaurant employees on a break, reflect on the organizations they represent. If they are unprofessional or make rude remarks about or to customers, customers' perceptions of the organization will suffer even though the employee is not on duty. This is why the Disney Corporation insists that its employees maintain "onstage" attitudes and behaviors whenever they are in front of the public, and that they relax these behaviors only when they are truly behind the scenes or "backstage" in underground tunnels where guests can't see them in their off-duty times.

Because contact employees represent the organization and can directly influence customer satisfaction, they perform the role of marketers. They physically embody the product and are walking billboards from a promotional standpoint. Some may also perform more traditional selling roles. For example, more and more often bank tellers are being called on to cross-sell bank products, a departure from the traditional teller role of operations function only. A similar shift is occurring in telecommunications, where customer service personnel are asked to assist with marketing and sales activities through their direct access via computers to customers' purchase and service records.

Whether acknowledged or not, actively selling or not, service employees perform marketing functions. They can perform these functions well, to the organization's advantage, or poorly, to the organization's detriment. In this chapter we will examine strategies for ensuring that service employees perform their marketing functions well.

Employee Satisfaction ↔ Customer Satisfaction

There is concrete evidence that satisfied employees make for satisfied customers (and satisfied customers can in turn reinforce employees' sense of satisfaction in their jobs).

Some have even gone so far as to suggest that unless service employees are happy in their jobs, customer satisfaction will be difficult to achieve.[6]

Through their research with customers and employees in 28 different bank branches, Benjamin Schneider and David Bowen have shown that both a *climate for service* and a *climate for employee well-being* are highly correlated with overall customer perceptions of service quality.[7] That is, both service climate and human resource management experiences that *employees* have within their organizations are reflected in how *customers* experience the service. Table 11-1 shows the correlations between elements of climate for service and for employee well-being and customer perceptions of overall service quality of the bank. The highest correlation is found for employee perceptions of the overall quality of the company's human resource management practices.

In a similar vein, Sears found customer satisfaction to be strongly related to employee turnover. In their stores with the highest customer satisfaction, employee turnover was 54 percent, whereas in stores with the lowest customer satisfaction, turnover was 83 percent. Studies by Ryder Truck demonstrated that when the company put pressure on employees through certain negative human resource practices, employees reacted with low motivation and dissatisfaction. Ultimately there is a connection between employee tension levels, poorer quality service, and negative customer reactions.[8]

The underlying logic connecting employee satisfaction and loyalty to customer satisfaction was shown as a figure in chapter 7 and is repeated here as Figure 11-3. In the earlier chapter we focused on customer retention issues; in this chapter we will focus on employee issues. The figure illustrates how employee satisfaction, customer satisfaction, and customer loyalty reinforce each other over time.

TABLE 11-1   CORRELATIONS BETWEEN EMPLOYEE PERCEPTIONS OF SERVICE CLIMATE AND HUMAN RESOURCE MANAGEMENT (HRM) PRACTICES AND CUSTOMER PERCEPTIONS OF OVERALL QUALITY*

	Customer perceptions of overall quality
Employee perceptions of service climate	
Managerial behavior	.53
Systems support	.58
Customer attention/retention	.37
Logistics support	.36
Employee perceptions of HRM practices	
Work facilitation	.42
Supervision	.51
Organizational career facilitation	.35
Organizational status	.56
New employee socialization	.30
Overall quality	.63

Source: Schneider and Bowen, 1993. Reprinted by permission of publisher from *Organizational Dynamics,* Spring 1993, © 1993. American Management Association, New York. All rights reserved.

*Correlations reflect the relationship between the specific factor in the column and customer perceptions of overall quality, and can range from 0 to 1. The closer the correlation is to 1, the stronger the relationship. All correlations in the table are statistically significant at $p < .05$.

FIGURE 11-3 Underlying logic of relationships between customer satisfaction and employee satisfaction.

Service Quality Dimensions Are Driven by Employee Behaviors

All of the five dimensions of service quality (reliability, responsiveness, assurance, empathy, tangibles) can be influenced directly by service employees.

Delivering the service as promised—*reliability*—is often totally within the control of front-line employees. Even in the case of automated services (such as ATMs, automated ticketing machines, or self-serve and pay gasoline pumps), behind-the-scenes employees are critical for making sure all of the systems are working properly. When services fail or errors are made, employees are essential for setting things right and using their judgment to determine the best course of action for service recovery.

Front-line employees often directly influence customer perceptions of *responsiveness* through their personal willingness to help and their promptness in serving customers. Consider the range of responses you receive from different retail store clerks when you need help finding a particular item of clothing. One employee may ignore your presence, while another offers to help you search and calls other stores to locate the item. One may help you immediately and efficiently, while another may move slowly in accommodating even the simplest request.

The *assurance* dimension of service quality is highly dependent on employees' ability to communicate their credibility and to inspire trust and confidence. The reputation of the organization will help, but in the end, individual employees with whom the customer interacts confirm and build trust in the organization or detract from its reputation and ultimately destroy trust. For start-up or relatively unknown organizations, credibility, trust, and confidence will be tied totally to employee actions.

It is difficult to imagine how an organization would deliver "caring, individualized attention" to customers independent of its employees. *Empathy* implies that employees will pay attention, listen, adapt, and be flexible in delivering what individual customers need. Organizations that leave this quality dimension to chance are likely to find extreme variation on this dimension across employees and customer experiences.

Employee appearance and dress are important aspects of the *tangibles* dimension of quality, along with many other factors that are independent of service employees (e.g., the service facility, decor, brochures, signage).

BOUNDARY-SPANNING ROLES

Our focus in this chapter is on front-line service employees who interact directly with customers, although much of what is described and recommended can be applied to internal service employees as well. The front-line service employees are referred to as *boundary spanners* because they operate at the organization's boundary. As indicated in Figure 11-4, boundary spanners provide a link between the external customer and environment and the internal operations of the organization. They serve a critical function in understanding, filtering, and interpreting information and resources to and from the organization and its external constituencies.

Who are these boundary spanners? What types of people and positions comprise critical boundary-spanning roles? Their skills and experience cover the full spectrum of jobs and careers. In industries such as fast food, hotels, telecommunication, and retail, the boundary spanners are the least skilled, lowest paid employees in the organization. They are order takers, front desk employees, telephone operators, store clerks, truck drivers, and delivery people. In other industries, boundary spanners are well-paid, highly educated professionals, for example, doctors, lawyers, accountants, consultants, architects, and teachers.

No matter what the level of skill or pay, boundary-spanning positions are often high-stress jobs. In addition to mental and physical skills, these positions require extraordinary levels of emotional labor, frequently demand an ability to handle interpersonal and interorganizational conflict, and call on the employee to make real-time trade-offs between quality and productivity on the job. Sometimes these stresses and trade-offs result in a failure to deliver services as specified, which widens GAP 3.

Emotional Labor

The term *emotional labor* was coined by Arlie Hochschild to refer to the labor that goes beyond the physical or mental skills needed to deliver quality service.[9] It means delivering smiles, making eye contact, showing sincere interest, and engaging in friendly conversation with people who are essentially strangers and who may or may not ever be seen again. Friendliness, courtesy, empathy, and responsiveness directed toward customers all require huge amounts of emotional labor from the front-line employees who shoulder this responsibility for the organization. Emotional labor draws on people's feel-

FIGURE 11-4   Role of boundary spanners.

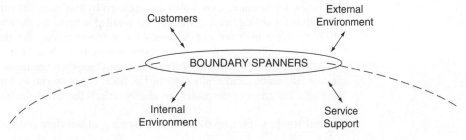

ings (often requiring them to suppress their true feelings) to be effective in their jobs. A front-line service employee who is having a bad day or isn't feeling just right is still expected to put on the face of the organization when dealing with customers. One of the clearest examples of emotional labor is the story (probably apocryphal) of the flight attendant who was approached by a businessman who said, "Let's have a smile." "Okay," she replied, "I'll tell you what, first you smile and then I'll smile, okay?" He smiled. "Good," she said. "Now hold that for fifteen hours," and walked away.[10]

Many of the strategies we'll discuss later in the chapter can help organizations and employees deal with the realities of emotional labor on the job. For the organization such strategies include carefully selecting people who can handle emotional stress, training them in needed skills (e.g., listening skills, problem solving), and teaching or giving them coping abilities and strategies (e.g., job rotation, scheduled breaks, teamwork). Delta Airlines puts prospective employees through simulated customer-contact exercises to see the kind of friendliness and warmth they naturally communicate.[11] Other companies train employees in how *not* to absorb a customer's bad mood, by having them spend hours role playing to suppress the natural reaction to return an insult with an insult.[12] Providing good physical working conditions and allowing employees to take scheduled breaks, to rely on each other for support, and to rotate positions among the most demanding front-line jobs also help to reduce the stress of excessive emotional labor.

Sources of Conflict

Front-line employees often face interpersonal and interorganizational conflicts on the job. Because they represent the customer to the organization and often need to manage a number of customers simultaneously, front liners inevitably have to deal with conflicts, including person/role conflicts, organization/client conflicts, and interclient conflicts.[13]

Person/Role Conflicts In some situations, boundary spanners feel conflicts between what they are asked to do and their own personalities, orientations, or values. In a society such as the United States, where equality and individualism are highly valued, service workers may feel role conflict when they are required to subordinate their feelings or beliefs, as when they are asked to live by the motto "The customer is always right—even when he is wrong." Sometimes there is a conflict between role requirements and the self-image or self-esteem of the employee. An Israeli service expert tells an example from that culture.

> In Israel, for instance, most buses are operated by one man, the driver, who is also responsible for selling tickets. No trays are installed in buses for the transferring of bus fare from passenger to driver, and the money is transferred directly. Bus drivers often complain about the humiliating experience of having to stretch out their hands like beggars in order to collect the fare. Another typical case in Israeli buses is when money changes hands and a coin falls down accidentally onto the bus floor. The question, who will bend down to lift the coin, the driver or the passenger, clearly reflects the driver's role conflict.[14]

Whoever stoops to pick up the coin is indicating subservient status.

Person/role conflict also arises when employees are required to wear clothing or change some aspect of their appearance to conform to the job requirements. A young lawyer, just out of school, may feel an internal conflict with his new role when his employer requires him to cut his long hair and trade his casual clothes for a three-piece suit. Another source of role conflict is the employee's relative inability to control the relationship she has with the customer: the customer largely determines when the interaction will begin and when it will end. In naturally occurring relationships both parties share the right to begin and end the interaction.

Organization/Client Conflict   A more salient type of conflict for most front-line service employees is the conflict between their two bosses, the organization and the individual customer. Service employees are typically rewarded for following certain standards, rules, and procedures. Ideally these rules and standards are customer based, as described in chapter 8. When they are not, or when a customer makes excessive demands, the employee has to choose whether to follow the rules or satisfy the demands. The conflict is greatest when the employee believes the organization is wrong in its policies and must decide whether to accommodate the client and risk losing her job or follow the policies. These conflicts are especially severe when service employees depend directly on the customer for income. For example, employees who depend on tips or commissions are likely to face greater levels of organization/client conflict because they have even greater incentives to identify with the customer.

Interclient Conflict   Sometimes conflict occurs for boundary spanners when there are incompatible expectations and requirements from two or more customers. This occurs most often when the service provider is serving customers in turn (e.g., a bank teller, a ticketing agent, a doctor) or is serving many customers simultaneously (e.g., teachers, entertainers).

In the case of serving customers in turn, the provider may satisfy one customer by spending additional time, customizing the service, and being very flexible in meeting the customer's needs. Meanwhile, waiting customers are becoming dissatisfied because their needs are not being met in a timely way. Beyond the timing issue, different clients may prefer different modes of service delivery. Having to serve one client who prefers personal recognition and a degree of familiarity in the presence of another client who is all business and would prefer little interpersonal interaction can also create conflict for the employee.

In the case of serving many customers at the same time, it is often difficult or impossible to serve the full range of needs of a group of heterogeneous customers simultaneously. This type of conflict is readily apparent in any college classroom where the instructor must meet a multitude of expectations and different preferences for formats and style. Some students prefer lectures, others prefer class discussions, others prefer projects, and still others prefer learning through reading. Some students expect familiarity and openness in the classroom; others expect formality and a businesslike environment. Trying to satisfy all of these needs results in conflict for the instructor.

Quality/Productivity Trade-offs

Front-line service workers are asked to be both effective and efficient: they are expected to deliver satisfying service to customers and at the same time to be cost effective and productive in what they do. A physician in an HMO, for example, is expected to deliver caring, quality, individualized service to her patients but at the same time to serve a certain number of patients within a specified time frame. A checker at a grocery store is expected to know his customers and to be polite and courteous, yet also to process the groceries accurately and move people through the line quickly. An architectural draftsperson is expected to create quality drawings, yet to produce a required quantity of drawings in a given period of time. These essential trade-offs between quality and quantity, and between maximum effectiveness and efficiency, place real-time demands and pressures on service employees.

Peter Drucker suggests that productive performance in all service jobs will combine both quality and quantity objectives.[15] For some jobs, such as that of a research scientist, quality is really all that matters—the number of results, or quantity, is quite secondary. If a scientist can develop one new drug with the potential of saving millions of lives and generating substantial revenues for a company, that one quality result is invaluable. At the other extreme, there are service jobs that are almost totally quantity dominated, for example, filing papers, processing claims, cleaning rooms, serving fast food. In these jobs, once certain customer-based standards are set and systems are in place to ensure conformance, the measure of performance is largely that of how much the worker can accomplish in a certain period of time. Most service jobs fall somewhere between that of the research scientist and that of the claims processor. Most require a balance of quality and quantity, as in the case of the physician, grocery clerk, and draftsperson already described, and often the worker himself is faced with making the trade-off.

Evidence of the pressure placed on employees in making quality and quantity trade-offs is apparent in changes taking place at UPS. UPS has a reputation for a high level of productivity, and its delivery people are highly efficient. "The company knows exactly how many workers it needs to deliver its 10 million packages a day. It tells drivers how fast to walk (3 feet per second), how many packages to pick up and deliver a day (400, on average), even how to hold the keys (teeth up, third finger)."[16] Faced with increasing competition, UPS has introduced a variety of new services that drivers must understand and be able to communicate to customers. They have had to become experts on 20 new services and products, whereas the company used to have just one. They are also being asked to scout out users of Federal Express and other competitors and to pass on sales leads. In other words, they are being asked to focus on customizing services, accommodating customers, and developing sales opportunities, while at the same time they must adhere to efficiency and delivery quotas. A quote from one of their drivers captures the conflict felt by these employees: "It's tough to make all your deliveries when they got us doing all these show-and-tells."[17]

In some cases technology can be used to balance the quality/quantity trade-off to increase productivity of service workers and at the same time free them to provide higher quality service for the customer. At AT&T's customer sales and service centers, workers

TECHNOLOGY SPOTLIGHT

IMAGING SYSTEM INCREASES PRODUCTIVITY AND CUSTOMER SERVICE

United Services Automobile Association, an insurance company located in San Antonio, Texas, provides insurance for military officers and their families. USAA is unique in the insurance industry in its ability to provide true real-time service to its customers. Almost all of the company's transactions take place over the phone or through the mail. Yet at USAA it takes only a few seconds to locate a customer's file, and if the same customer calls back a few minutes later, the same file is instantaneously available to any of the more than 2,500 customer-service representatives in the company. This speed of service is the result of USAA becoming a truly paperless office environment where all customer documents and correspondence are stored electronically in customers' files.

Twenty years ago the USAA began its effort to eliminate paper in the workplace, using microfilm. In the late 1980s, working with IBM, it developed the archetype of large-scale, sophisticated imaging systems to allow scanning of all incoming mail and automatic filing into the appropriate customer file. The imaging system is able to store policy files of all of the company's members. Every day approximately 125,000 pieces of mail are received, sorted, and examined by mail analysts; scanned into the system; and electronically filed.

Customer-service representatives have immediate access to this information and no longer need to search for lost files or delay responding to customers because an important piece of information hasn't moved from the mail room to the customer's file. Each representative is able to be efficient and productive and at the same time offer superior customer service.

Customers benefit through speed of processing of their claims, inquiries, and policy changes, and little chance for error. They also benefit in that any representative who answers the phone has immediate access to their up-to-date file, resulting in few transfers and little need for call backs.

Positive results of the imaging and electronic filing system are seen in increased productivity, cost savings, higher employee job satisfaction, and increased levels of customer service.

Sources: Ken Graham, "Image Systems Expand beyond Service," *Best's Review* 94, 1, (1993) 79–80+; Barry Rabkin, "Winners Will Deliver Real-Time Customer Service," *National Underwriter,* October 3, 1994, pp. 51–52.

are given immediate access via their computer screen to information and tools they need to serve the customer efficiently. Immediately when a customer calls, the representative can view on the screen the customer's account records and any notes from previous phone calls from the customer. The representatives also have at their fingertips rate information, other relevant data, and information on commonly asked questions. Through the use of technology the phone representatives are relieved of many of the basic technical demands of their job, thus being freed to provide courteous and empathetic interaction with the customer. They avoid trading off quality and quantity—technology allows them to do both. Our Technology Spotlight features another company that has effectively used advanced technology to increase productivity and customer service simultaneously.

Given the demands, conflicts, and pressures of service jobs, how can organizations ensure efficiency and effectiveness and maintain a service-oriented work force? The next sections of the chapter outline strategies to answer this question.

STRATEGIES FOR CLOSING GAP 3

A complex combination of strategies is needed to ensure that service employees are willing and able to deliver quality services and that they stay motivated to perform in customer-oriented, service-minded ways. As described in chapter 1, we are focusing on strategies for ensuring that service promises can be kept. These strategies for enabling service promises are often referred to as internal marketing, as shown on the left side of Figure 1-5 in chapter 1.[18] By approaching human resource decisions and strategies from the point of view that the primary goal is to motivate and enable employees to deliver customer-oriented promises successfully, an organization will move toward closing GAP 3.

The strategies presented here are organized around four basic themes. To build a customer-oriented, service-minded work force, an organization must: (1) hire the right people, (2) develop people to deliver service quality, (3) provide the needed support systems, and (4) retain the best people. Within each of these basic strategies are a number of specific substrategies for accomplishing the goal, as shown in Figure 11-5.

FIGURE 11-5   Human resource strategies for closing GAP 3.

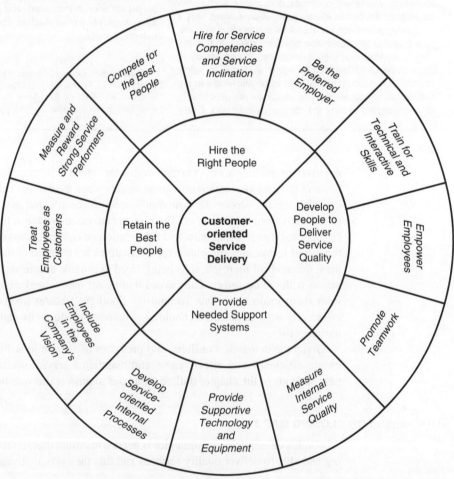

Hire the Right People

One of the best ways to close GAP 3 is to start with the right service delivery people from the beginning. This implies that considerable attention should be focused on hiring and recruiting service personnel. Such attention is contrary to traditional practices in many service industries, where service personnel are the lowest on the corporate ladder and work for minimum wage. The traditional approach in industries such as fast food, hospitality, maintenance, and some retail is to "make the jobs 'idiot proof.' . . . We'll treat them just like a piece of equipment. When they stop being productive, we'll just bring in somebody new."[19] But even in these industries, managers are beginning to focus on more effective recruitment practices. At the other end of the spectrum, in the professional services, the most important recruiting criteria are typically technical training, certifications, and expertise. However, here too many organizations are looking above and beyond the technical qualifications of applicants to assess their customer and service orientation as well. Figure 11-5 shows a number of ways to improve service employee recruitment efforts to get the right people from the beginning.

Compete for the Best People   To get the best people, an organization needs to identify who the best people are and compete with other organizations to hire them. Leonard Berry and A. Parasuraman refer to this as "competing for talent market share."[20] They suggest that firms act like marketers in their pursuit of the best employees, just as they use their marketing expertise to compete for customers. This means using a variety of methods to recruit employees, beyond just advertising in the newspaper. Ideas include communicating with prospective employees through appropriate media such as university campus publications, career fairs, and organizations and using incentives to encourage current employees to recruit potential employees. Thinking of recruiting as a marketing activity results in addressing issues of market (employee) segmentation, product (job) design, and promotion of job availability in ways that attract potential long-term employees. By competing for employees using the strategies it uses to compete for customers, the organization essentially is creating a marketing plan directed at identifiable employee market segments.

A complementary strategy is to interview multiple employees for every position. At Southwest Airlines, the People Department (the name Southwest has given to what others call the human resource, or personnel, department) is relentless in its pursuit of talented employees. A quote from Southwest's president, Herb Kelleher, illustrates the point: "The People Department came to me one day and said, 'We've interviewed 34 people for this ramp agent's position, and we're getting a little worried about the time and effort and cost that's going into it.' And I said if you have to interview 154 people to get the right person, do it."[21]

Another way to compete for the best people is to raise what might be unnecessarily low standards in order to identify more qualified employees. Sometimes these potential recruits may be found in unlikely places, and among untraditional populations. Women and minorities are increasingly represented in the labor pool in the United States, as are senior citizens, recent immigrants, and disabled persons. Many of the potentially best employees are likely to be represented in these groups, and firms that ignore them are missing real opportunities. Developing a diverse employee base can have an added benefit of complementing the increasingly diverse customer base that most service organizations are experiencing.

Hire for Service Competencies and Service Inclination   Once potential employees have been identified, organizations need to be conscientious in interviewing and screening to truly identify the best people from the pool of candidates. It has been suggested that service employees need two complementary capacities: they need both *service competencies* and *service inclination.*[22]

Service competencies are the skills and knowledge necessary to do the job. In many cases, competencies are validated by achieving particular degrees and certifications, such as attaining a doctor of law (JD) degree and passing the relevant state bar examination for lawyers. Similar rites of passage are required of doctors, airline pilots, university professors, teachers, and many other job seekers before they are ever interviewed for a service job in their field. Applicants for these professional occupations must possess minimum credentials, and those who have the best credentials (e.g., degrees from prestigious schools, professional accomplishments in their fields) will be more competitive for the top positions. In other cases, service competencies may not be degree related, but may instead relate to basic intelligence or physical requirements. A retail clerk, for example, must possess basic math skills and the potential to operate a cash register. An airport shuttle driver must be able to drive a large van and be physically capable of loading and unloading heavy luggage. In a typical applicant pool for a service job, service competencies vary widely.

Given the multidimensional nature of service quality—quality service is reliable, responsive, empathetic—service employees should be screened for more than their service competencies. They must also be screened for *service inclination*—their interest in doing service-related work—which is reflected in their attitudes toward service and orientation toward serving customers and others on the job. Self-selection suggests that most service jobs will draw applicants with some level of service inclination, and that most employees in service organizations are inclined toward service. However, some employees clearly have a greater service inclination than others. Research has shown that service effectiveness is correlated with having service-oriented personality characteristics such as helpfulness, thoughtfulness, and sociability.[23] This same research defines service orientation as a syndrome containing elements of good adjustment, likability, social skill, and willingness to follow rules.

An ideal selection process for service employees assesses both service competencies and service inclination, resulting in employee hires who are high on both dimensions.[24] Depending on the nature of the job, the assessment of competencies and inclinations will include a variety of tests and interviewing formats. It may include testing for basic competencies (e.g., reading, math, computer skills) or the requirement that the employee has completed a particular degree or certification program. The process will also likely include an in-depth, structured interview to assess service inclination. The key to a successful interviewing procedure is to determine in advance specifically what the organization is looking for in terms of skills and inclination, to develop structured questions to learn the needed information, and to train interviewers thoroughly.

In addition to the interview, many firms use innovative approaches to assessing service inclination and other personal characteristics that fit the organization's needs. Southwest Airlines looks for people who are compassionate and who have common sense, a sense of humor, a "can do" attitude, and an egalitarian sense of themselves (they think in terms of "we" rather than "me"). One way the company assesses these service inclinations is by interviewing potential flight attendants in groups to see how they interact with each other. Pilots are also interviewed in groups to assess their teamwork skills, a critical factor above and beyond the essential technical skills they are required to possess.

In many cases a component of the selection process will include a form of work simulation that allows employees to demonstrate how they would actually perform on the job. A simulation may take the form of a series of exercises that parallel the demands of the job and thus allow applicants to demonstrate their skills and competencies without actually having the specific knowledge needed to do the job. Box 11-1 gives examples of three exercises used to assess potential applicants for a telephone sales and service job. Role playing is another form of simulation that can be used effectively in assessing service skills and inclination. In addition to being a good way to assess potential employee abilities, simulations can give the potential hire a better view of what the job is actually like. Those who don't like what they experience can then select out of the applicant pool before being hired and finding out the job isn't what they had expected.

Be the Preferred Employer   One way to attract the best people is to be known as the preferred employer in a particular industry or in a particular location. In San Antonio and in the insurance industry at large, USAA enjoys being a preferred employer for

---

BOX 11-1

WORK SIMULATION EXERCISES FOR TELEPHONE SALES AND SERVICE

The following exercises were designed in support of a multifaceted recruitment process to hire telephone sales and service people in an insurance context. Before the exercises, each candidate read and studied an instruction manual describing the basic rules and guidelines for the job. Each exercise represented an actual phone call that the job candidate was asked to respond to in a role-play context. The specific skills assessed by the exercises were: *persuasion, clerical speed and accuracy, social sensitivity, dealing with pressure, comprehension, memory, understandability.* The relevant skill being assessed is shown in parentheses within the text of the exercise.

Exercise 1   A simple sales call in which the candidate must persuade callers to purchase more than they initially ask for (*persuasion*) and must accurately complete a series of forms summarizing the sale (*clerical speed and accuracy*).

Exercise 2   A call by a person who is unknowledgeable, uncooperative, and eventually abusive, who wishes to make a purchase (assessment of the candidate's *social sensitivity* and ability to *deal with pressure*). In addition, because paperwork is needed for this call, clerical assessments are possible (*clerical speed and accuracy*).

Exercise 3   A service call requiring the candidate to resolve a dispute over a late payment fee. The caller is an established customer who moved and received his or her statement late, eventually causing a bill for a late payment fee (*comprehension, memory*). The customer argues it was not his or her fault, and the candidate needs to handle the issue (*social sensitivity*). One part of the exercise requires the candidate to write a memo to his or her supervisor about the incident (*understandability*).

Source: Schneider and Schechter, 1991. Reprinted with permission of Lexington Books, an imprint of The Free Press, a division of Simon & Schuster, from *Service Quality: Multidisciplinary and Multinational Perspectives,* eds. Stephen W. Brown, Evert Gummesson, Bo Edvardsson, and BengtOve Gustavsson. Copyright © 1991 by Lexington Books.

many reasons. In addition to having superb technical support (see the Technology Spotlight earlier in this chapter), people who work there feel they are part of a family, despite the fact that USAA's headquarters is the largest private office building in the world. As one employee said, "At USAA they keep telling me that I'm important in various ways—through benefits and all the different kinds of communications. And my boss is just there all the time. For a place this size, it's remarkable to me that you feel like you're part of a family." Promotions are common at USAA, and training is ingrained at all levels—and not just training in insurance-related topics. In addition to employing 159 full-time trainers and spending approximately $19 million on career training, USAA also puts a lot of money into tuition reimbursement so employees can get college degrees.[25] In 1991 USAA ended the year with 30,341 applications or resumes on file, and a 37:1 applicant/hire ratio that allows the company to maintain an outstanding work force.[26]

Rosenbluth International, headquartered in Philadelphia, is another company that enjoys a reputation as a preferred employer. With close to six hundred offices in 48 states, London, and Tokyo, Rosenbluth is the fourth largest travel agency in the United States. The company's president, Hal Rosenbluth, has gone so far as to say "We don't believe that the customer can come first unless our people come first. If our people don't come first, then they're not free to focus on our clients; they're worrying about other kinds of things."[27]

Being a preferred employer involves a variety of strategies, many of which revolve around treating employees as whole people and addressing their personal as well as work needs. Companies like Duke Power in North Carolina are trying to create environments where people want to work, recognizing that "people have lives." By banishing swing shifts, working to build child care and fitness centers for employees, and providing greater flexibility in work schedules, the company has created an atmosphere within Duke Power Company's customer service area where the 500-member staff can handle family and personal matters more easily. The result has been increased productivity and reduced attrition.[28]

Other strategies that support a goal of being the preferred employer include providing extensive training, career and advancement opportunities, excellent internal support, and attractive incentives, and offering quality goods and services that employees are proud to be associated with.

Develop People to Deliver Service Quality

To grow and maintain a work force that is customer oriented and focused on delivering quality, an organization must develop its employees to deliver service quality. That is, once it has hired the right employees, the organization must train and work with these individuals to ensure service performance.

Train for Technical and Interactive Skills To provide quality service, employees need ongoing training in the necessary technical skills and knowledge and in process or interactive skills.[29] Examples of technical skills and knowledge are working with accounting systems in hotels, cash machine procedures in a retail store, underwriting procedures in an insurance company, and any operational rules the company has for running its business. Most service organizations are quite conscious of and relatively effective at training employees in technical skills. These skills may be taught through formal education, as is the case at McDonald's "Hamburger University." Additionally, technical skills are often taught through on-the-job training, as when education majors work with experienced teachers in internship programs, or when telephone service trainees listen in on the conversations of experienced employees. Recently, companies are increasing their use of information technologies to train employees in the technical skills and knowledge needed on the job. This is the case at Federal Express, where at least once a year each of its 40,000 couriers and customer service agents plugs into an interactive personal computer that tests their job knowledge.[30] If couriers specialize in hazardous goods, for example, they must update their knowledge every six months through the computer training to stay abreast of government regulations and company policies. Through the computer-based training, employees take exams (approximately two hours long) to pinpoint where they need help.

In addition to the type of technical skills and knowledge training just described, service employees need training in interactive skills that allow them to provide courteous, caring, responsive, and empathetic service. Through interactive skills training employees learn listening, problem-solving, communication, and interpersonal skills. To be a truly excellent service-oriented employee, these process skills are essential. Since 1989 Target Stores, a division of Dayton Hudson, has used training to enhance the service orientation of its contact employees.[31] Every time the company opens a new store, it sets up a portable "Target University" to train new employees. One of the first things employees learn is to refer to shoppers as "guests." Employees also go through four hours of role playing to learn how to deal with different types of difficult customers. They learn how to "schmooze with your guests, and compliment them on their clothing. If they're buying pet food, talk to them about their dog."[32] The training has had a tremendous impact on employee turnover (dropping from 89% in 1989 to 59% in 1992), and customer service ratings have steadily improved. Box 11-2 explains how the Tokyo Imperial Hotel in Japan effectively combines service employee training in both the technical and interactive skills needed to provide quality service.

It isn't just front-line service personnel who need this combination of service skills and interactive training. Support staff, supervisors, and managers need service training as well. Unless contact employees experience the same values and behaviors from their supervisors, they are unlikely to deliver high-quality service to customers. Scandinavian Airline Systems, a highly regarded international carrier, applied this logic in its dramatic turnaround in 1981 and again in a move to "reinvent" the company in the early 1990s. At both times it started with service training for top management and then worked through the organization to supervisors and contact employees, giving everyone a shared vision and perspective on service.

It is important that training be ongoing, not just something offered to new employees. This is even more true today than it was in the past, with available job-related information increasing daily and continuous process improvement being the goal in many organizations. Companies that recognize the importance of ongoing training invest heavily in it both in terms of dollars and employee time. For example, Motorola, a company that employs approximately 107,000 people worldwide, invested 3.6 percent of

---

BOX 11-2

TRAINING AT TOKYO'S IMPERIAL HOTEL

Tokyo's Imperial Hotel provides an excellent example of training for both knowledge and skills as well as interactive service quality. The hotel's "Capability Development Program" consists of training in "occupational abilities and knowledge" (technical skills) as well as "service manners training" (interactive skills). The first type of training involves on-the-job apprenticing, rotations through all of the major departments within the hotel, visitations and inspection tours of comparable hotels in other countries, and focused study tours (for example Imperial Hotel's senior waiters and sommeliers might tour famous wineries in California and France every three years). In addition, employees get specialized skills training through independent educational organizations on needed topics ranging from management strategy decision-making to food hygiene to presentation know-how.

The second part of the training, the "service manners training" focuses on the etiquette and psychology of guest contact and attitudes of service. Proper etiquette is taught via role playing and videotaping (to critique appearance, mannerisms, and personal idiosyncrasies). The way the staff should appear to hotel guests is stressed and demonstrated, with emphasis placed on cleanliness, a sense of understated elegance, and good taste. Guest psychology is discussed, emphasizing the following six main points:

1 Imperial Hotel patrons, given the rank and reputation of the hotel, expect that you will consider them your most important priority, the center of your attention.

2 Guests do not want to suffer losses of any kind while in the hotel.

3 Guests expect to be received in a warm, welcoming fashion.

4 A guest does not want to be extended a level of treatment that is in any way inferior to that provided to other guests of the hotel.

5 Guests wish to experience an appropriate feeling of prestige or superiority, purely by virtue of their using what is commonly evaluated as a deluxe enterprise.

6 Guests enjoy feeling possessive about the hotel's facilities and services, and expect exclusive attention.

Finally, the basic principles of nonverbal communication and body language are discussed. Demonstrations and detailed explanations of appropriate behaviors are given, covering such points as: facial expressions, appearance, and posture when standing; pleasing, attractive ways of talking and carriage; proper posture; and courtesy when escorting guests within the hotel premises. Because the bow is used regardless of the national origin of the guest, considerable time is spent on the intricacies of proper bowing. A bow of welcome involves a 15-degree angle, a bow of gratitude is 30 degrees, and a bow of apology is a full 45 degrees from the normal straight standing position. The remainder of the service manners training concentrates on the complexities of the Japanese language and the appropriate applications for hotel service. Trainees are instructed in some 25 common daily expressions, learning their politest forms as well as the English equivalents.

Ongoing training and service improvement programs at all levels are part of the hotel's total operations strategy.

Source: Adapted, with permission of the publisher, from M. Ignatius Cronin, 3rd, "Staff Training Delivers Quality Service at Tokyo's Imperial Hotel," in The Service Quality Handbook, eds. Eberhard E. Scheuing and William F. Christopher, © 1993, AMACOM, a division of the American Management Association. All rights reserved.

---

payroll in 1992 in training, requiring an average of thirty-six hours per year from each of its employees. Federal Express, with 93,000 employees worldwide, invested 4.5 percent of its payroll in training during 1992, which translated into twenty-seven hours per employee on average. Anderson Consulting invested 6.8 percent of its payroll and required 109 hours of training for each of its 26,700 employees in 1992.[33] While training takes a variety of forms in these organizations, all view it as an important investment for future success.

Empower Employees   Many organizations have discovered that to be truly responsive to customer needs, front-line providers need to be empowered to accommodate customer requests and to recover on the spot when things go wrong. *Empowerment* *means giving employees the desire, skills, tools, and authority to serve the customer.* While the key to empowerment is giving employees authority to make decisions on the customer's behalf, authority alone is not enough. Employees need the knowledge and tools to be able to make these decisions, and they need incentives that will encourage them to make the right decisions. Organizations do not succeed in empowering their employees if they simply tell them, "You now have the authority to do whatever it takes to satisfy the customer." First, employees often don't believe this, particularly if the organization has functioned hierarchically or bureaucratically in the past. Second, employees often don't know what it means to "do whatever it takes" if they have not received training, guidelines, and the tools needed to make such decisions.

There are many reasons why empowerment works, however, when implemented appropriately. First, most service workers don't want to be robots. They like to serve people, and would like to make decisions about how to do that best. Too many rules and volumes of rule books are overwhelming to employees and may inhibit their judgment. If they can't find the answer in the rule book, they don't know what to do. Thus, one of the hallmarks of an empowering organization is a relatively thin employee rule book. Nordstrom, an upscale retailer in the United States, has probably the best known example of an extremely thin employee handbook and a highly empowered work force. The entire Nordstrom employee handbook is shown in Exhibit 11-1.

Clearly, not all organizations will have such a short list of rules as Nordstrom. The point is that an empowered work force needs only as many rules and guidelines as are essential. Scandinavian Airline Systems severely reduced the size of its employee manuals when it went through a restructuring in the early 1980s. Although the safety rules and procedures airlines must adhere to require a considerable number of pages to describe, it was determined, for example, that the pages from the old manual that instructed flight attendants in how to hold a baby for a passenger needing such assistance could be eliminated!

Another hallmark of empowerment is that it pushes decision-making down into the organization and encourages people to think and use judgment. Frequently an empowered front-line employee will be making decisions that were relegated to his or her supervisor in the past.

EXHIBIT 11-1   NORDSTROM EMPLOYEE HANDBOOK

WELCOME TO NORDSTROM

We're glad to have you with our Company.
Our number one goal is to provide outstanding customer service.
Set both your personal and professional goals high.
We have great confidence in your ability to achieve them.

Nordstrom Rules:

Rule #1: Use your good judgment in all situations.
There will be no additional rules.
Please feel free to ask your department manager, store manager, or division general manager any question at any time.

Source: Reprinted with permission of Nordstrom.

EXHIBIT 11-2   POTENTIAL COSTS AND BENEFITS OF EMPOWERMENT

BENEFITS

Quicker on-line responses to customer needs during service delivery: Employees who are allowed to make decisions on behalf of the customer can make decisions more quickly, bypassing what in the past might have meant a long chain of command, or at least a discussion with an immediate supervisor.

Quicker on-line responses to dissatisfied customers during service recovery: When there are failures in the delivery system, customers hope for an immediate recovery effort on the part of the organization. Empowered employees can recover on the spot, and a dissatisfied customer can potentially be turned into a satisfied, even loyal one.

Employees feel better about their jobs and themselves: Giving employees control and authority to make decisions makes them feel responsible and gives them ownership for the customer's satisfaction. Decades of job design research suggest that when employees have a sense of control and of doing meaningful work, they are more satisfied. The result is lower turnover and less absenteeism.

Employees will interact with customers with more warmth and enthusiasm: Because they feel better about themselves and their work, these feelings will spill over into their feelings about customers and will be reflected in their interactions.

Empowered employees are a great source of service ideas: When employees are empowered, they feel responsible for the service outcome and they will be excellent sources of ideas about new services or how to improve current offerings.

Great word-of-mouth advertising from customers: Empowered employees do special and unique things that customers will remember and tell their friends, family, and associates about.

COSTS

A potentially greater dollar investment in selection and training: To find employees who will work well in an empowered environment requires creative, potentially more costly selection procedures. Training will also be more expensive in general since employees need more knowledge about the company, its products, and how to work in flexible ways with customers.

Higher labor costs: The organization may not be able to use as many part-time or seasonal employees, and it may need to pay more for asking employees to assume responsibility.

Potentially slower or inconsistent service delivery: If empowered employees spend more time with all, or even some, customers, then service overall may take longer. This may annoy customers who are waiting. Empowerment also means that customers will get what they need or request. When decisions regarding customer satisfaction are left to the discretion of employees, there may be inconsistency in the level of service delivered.

May violate customers' perceptions of fair play: Customers may perceive that sticking to procedures with every customer is fair. Thus, if they see that customers are receiving different levels of service or that employees are cutting special deals with some customers, they may believe that the organization is not fair.

Employees may "give away the store" or make bad decisions: Many people fear that empowered employees will make costly decisions that the organization cannot afford. While this can happen, good training and appropriate guidelines will help.

While the benefits of empowerment are many, there are also potential costs. Exhibit 11-2 enumerates both the costs and benefits as documented by David Bowen and Edward Lawler, experts on this subject.[34] These authors suggest that firms should employ a contingency view of empowerment, meaning that while empowerment has many benefits, it may be more or less appropriate under certain circumstances. They contrast an *empowerment approach* to a *production line approach* for managing services. An empowered organization is characterized by flexibility, quick decisions, and authority given to front-line people, whereas a production line organization is characterized by standardization and little decision-making latitude or authority given to front-line employees.

Federal Express, a company referred to throughout this text, is an excellent example of an empowered organization; McDonalds is a good example of a company that operates successfully using a production line approach to service. Workers at McDonalds are taught how to greet customers, how to take their orders, and how to assemble an order, place items on the tray, ring up the order, and hand the tray to the customer. There is a script for almost every step, and little variability in the process.

Table 11-2 shows contingency trade-offs for the two approaches to service. Organizations that score high on the contingencies will be better suited for empowerment. That is, organizations well suited to empowerment strategies are ones in which (1) the business strategy is one of differentiation and customization, (2) customers are long-term relationship customers, (3) technology is nonroutine or complex, (4) the business environment is unpredictable, and (5) managers and employees have high growth and social needs and strong interpersonal skills. Service organizations that score lower on these contingencies, or have the opposite characteristics, will favor the production line approach.

Promote Teamwork   The nature of many service jobs suggests that customer satisfaction will be enhanced when employees work as teams. Because service jobs are frequently frustrating, demanding, and challenging, a teamwork environment will help to alleviate some of the stresses and strains. Employees who feel supported and that they have a team backing them up will be better able to maintain their enthusiasm and provide quality service. "An interactive community of coworkers who help each other, com-

TABLE 11-2   THE CONTINGENCIES OF EMPOWERMENT

Contingency	Production line approach		Empowerment
Basic business strategy	Low cost, high volume	1 2 3 4 5	Differentiation, customized, personalized
Tie to customer	Transaction, short time period	1 2 3 4 5	Relationship, long time period
Technology	Routine, simple	1 2 3 4 5	Nonroutine, complex
Business environment	Predictable, few surprises	1 2 3 4 5	Unpredictable, many surprises
Types of people	Theory X managers; employees with low growth needs, low social needs, and weak interpersonal skills	1 2 3 4 5	Theory Y managers; employees with high growth needs, high social needs, and strong interpersonal skills

Source: Reprinted from Bowen and Lawler III, 1992, by permission of publisher. Copyright 1992 by the Sloan Management Review Association. All rights reserved.

miserate, and achieve together is a powerful antidote to service burnout,"[35] and, we would add, an important ingredient for service quality. By promoting teamwork an organization can enhance the employees' *abilities* to deliver excellent service, while at the same time the camaraderie and support enhance their *inclination* to be excellent service providers.

One way of promoting teamwork is to encourage the attitude that "everyone has a customer." That is, even when employees are not directly responsible or in direct interaction with the final customer, they need to know who they do serve directly and how the role they play in the total service picture is essential to the final delivery of quality service. If each employee can see how he or she is somehow integral in delivering quality to the final customer, and if each employee knows who he or she must support to make service quality a reality, teamwork will be enhanced. Service blueprints, described in chapter 10, can serve as useful tools to illustrate for employees their integral roles in delivering service quality to the ultimate customer. Team goals and rewards will also promote teamwork. When teams of individuals are given rewards, rather than all rewards being based on individual achievements and performance, team efforts and team spirit will be encouraged.

The effective promotion of teamwork may require restructuring around market-based groupings rather than along traditional functional lines. This means that all people who impact the customer (or a particular customer segment) will work together as a team to coordinate their efforts, regardless of their functional affiliations. On the other hand, when functionalism dominates in an organization, the operations, marketing, and human resources groups may work at cross-purposes almost unknowingly, and as a result inhibit teamwork directed at satisfying the customer. Creating teams and supporting effective teamwork, especially across functions, is no small task, and there are many barriers and obstacles to overcome in implementing such strategies in most traditional organizational structures.[36] When done well, however, the benefits for both customers and employees can be tremendous.

Provide Needed Support Systems

To be efficient and effective in their jobs, service workers require internal support systems that are aligned with their need to be customer focused. This point cannot be overemphasized. In fact, without customer-focused internal support and customer-oriented systems, it is nearly impossible for employees to deliver quality service no matter how much they want to. For example, to be effective a patient-focused doctor requires that the hospital have internal systems that allow her to get access to patient information, modern surgical and testing equipment, and staff who share her commitment to patient satisfaction. Similarly, a bank teller who is rewarded for customer satisfaction as well as for accuracy in bank transactions needs easy access to up-to-date customer records, a well-staffed branch (so that he isn't constantly facing a long line of impatient customers), and supportive customer-oriented supervisors and back-office staff. These internal support systems can be as critical as the skills and competencies of contact employees in creating customer satisfaction. The following sections suggest strategies for ensuring customer-oriented internal support.

Measure Internal Service Quality One way to encourage supportive internal service relationships is to measure and reward internal service. By first acknowledging that everyone in the organization has a customer and then measuring customer perceptions of internal service quality, an organization can begin to develop an internal quality culture. This is what happened at San Diego Gas and Electric, a company in which internal service survey results are now tied to managers' salary increases and where internal service is one of the company's key strategic goals.[37] San Diego Gas and Electric measures internal service using an 11-question survey that is applicable to any department, from purchasing to fleet maintenance, and is intended to measure four key service dimensions: customer service attitude, skills and ability, the responsiveness of processes, and quality of the final product (see Exhibit 11-3). All employees get the survey and are asked to choose which departments or areas they will evaluate based on which (of the 124 areas surveyed) they've dealt with over the past year. Results are reported to department managers, and the top four or five areas are publicized by name only, not by

---

EXHIBIT 11-3   SAN DIEGO GAS AND ELECTRIC'S INTERNAL SERVICE SURVEY FORM

SDG&E's Internal Service Survey Form

Scale:	1 = Strongly Agree	3 = Tend to Disagree	5 = Don't Know/Not Applicable
	2 = Tend to Agree	4 = Strongly Disagree	

	Dept. Name	Dept. Name
During the past 12 months, approximately how many contacts have you had with this area (circle one)?	# Contacts 1 to 5 6 to 20 21 or more	#Contacts 1 to 5 6 to 20 21 or more

Evaluation (using 1–5 scale above)

1. When I contact them, the first person I talk to helps me or refers me to someone who can help. _____ _____
2. They have the knowledge and skills to give me what I need. _____ _____
3. Overall, the people are easy to work with. _____ _____
4. They meet my requests on time or ahead of schedule. _____ _____
5. They respond promptly to my phone calls and messages. _____ _____
6. They make an effort to find out what I really need. _____ _____
7. I am satisfied with the turnaround time for my requests. _____ _____
8. They keep me adequately informed about the status of my order/request. _____ _____
9. They show a sincere desire to help. _____ _____
10. They provide high quality services/products. _____ _____
11. Overall, I am satisfied with the end product/service they provide. _____ _____

Source: "Internal Service: How One Company Uses Pay Incentives to Create Enduring Change." Reprinted with permission from the June 1993 issue of *The Service Edge,* Lakewood Publications, 50 South Ninth Street, Minneapolis, Minnesota. All rights reserved.

actual scores, since the internal quality measures are intended as a tool to help people improve. In many departments, a manager's salary is now tied directly to the change in the department's service score from the previous year.

Provide Supportive Technology and Equipment   When employees don't have the right equipment, or their equipment fails them, they can be easily frustrated in their desire to deliver quality service. To do their jobs effectively and efficiently, service employees need the right equipment and technology. Our Technology Spotlight presented earlier showed how USAA's customer service phone representatives are able to be extremely customer focused because they have immediate access to customer files on their computer screens. These files have up-to-date information in them since every piece of relevant mail and other documentation has been electronically scanned into the file on receipt.

Having the right technology and equipment can extend into strategies regarding work place and work station design. For example, in designing their corporate headquarters offices, Scandinavian Airline Systems identified particular service-oriented goals that it wished to achieve, among them teamwork and open and frequent communication among managers. An office environment was designed with open spaces, to encourage meetings, and internal windows in offices, to encourage frequent interactions. In this way the work space facilitated the internal service orientation.

Develop Service-oriented Internal Processes   To best support service personnel in their delivery of quality service on the front line, an organization's internal processes should be designed with customer value and customer satisfaction in mind. In other words, internal procedures must support quality service performance.

To illustrate, at Banca di America e di Italia in Italy, retail banking support systems allow tellers to service customers effectively and quickly, while at the same time providing them with detailed information for cross-selling. The teller handles a check only twice, and because of technological support requires no human back-office assistance. This efficient system came about as a result of a decision in 1988 to cut costs and simultaneously improve customer service. To achieve these goals, all retail banking transactions were broken down into 10 "families" (e.g., payments, deposits, withdrawals, etc.). Then each type of transaction was redesigned to make it more customer-service oriented and to eliminate unnecessary steps that created no value for the customer. For example, the checking deposit transaction previously required 64 activities, nine forms, and 14 accounts. After redesign it needed 25 activities, two forms, and two accounts. The result for BAI has been increased efficiency, reduced costs, greater customer satisfaction, and profitable growth (revenue doubled between 1987 and 1992).[38]

In many companies internal processes are driven by bureaucratic rules, tradition, cost efficiencies, or the needs of internal employees. Providing service- and customer-oriented internal processes can therefore imply a need for total redesign of systems, similar to the changes implemented by BAI. This kind of wholesale redesign of systems and processes has become known as "process reengineering," a concept presented in chapter 9. While developing service-oriented internal processes through reengineering sounds sensible, it is probably one of the most difficult strategies to implement, especially in organizations that are steeped in tradition.

Retain the Best People

An organization that hires the right people, trains and develops them to deliver service quality, and provides the needed support must also work to retain the best ones. Employee turnover, especially when the best service employees are the ones leaving, can be very detrimental to customer satisfaction, employee morale, and overall service quality. And, just as they do with customers, some firms spend a lot of time attracting employees but then tend to take them for granted (or even worse), causing these good employees to search for job alternatives. Whereas all of the strategies noted in the internal marketing wheel (Figure 11-5) will support the retention of the best employees, here we will focus on some strategies that are particularly aimed at this goal.

Include Employees in the Company's Vision   For employees to remain motivated and interested in sticking with the organization and supporting its goals, they need to share an understanding of the organization's vision. People who deliver service day in and day out need to understand how their work fits into the big picture of the organization and its goals. They will be motivated to some extent by their paychecks and other benefits, but the best employees will be attracted away to other opportunities if they aren't committed to the vision of the organization. And they can't be committed to the vision if that vision is kept secret from them. What this means in practice is that the vision is communicated to employees frequently, and that it is communicated by top managers, often by the CEO. In chapter 9 we provided a number of examples of CEOs who are known for their visionary qualities and abilities to communicate the vision to employees.

Treat Employees as Customers   If employees feel valued and their needs are taken care of, they are more likely to stay with the organization. An extreme example of this view is provided by this quotation from Hal Rosenbluth, CEO of Rosenbluth Travel:

> As I watched people knocking themselves out for Rosenbluth Travel, I suddenly realized that it was my responsibility to make their lives more pleasant. In simple terms, that meant giving people the right working environment, the right tools, and the right leadership. It meant eliminating fear, frustration, bureaucracy, and politics. Of course, it meant decent compensation—and bonuses when the company did well—but it also meant helping people develop as human beings.[39]

Many companies have adopted the idea that employees are also customers of the organization, and that basic marketing strategies can be directed at them.[40] The product that the organization has to offer its employees is a job (with assorted benefits), and quality of work life. To determine whether the job and work-life needs of employees are being met, organizations conduct periodic internal marketing research to assess employee satisfaction and needs. For example, within American Express Travel Related Services, the Travelers Check Group (TCG) had a goal of "Becoming the Best Place to Work" by doing the following:[41]

- Treating employees as customers
- Using employee input and a fact-based approach for decision-making in the design and implementation of human resources policies, programs, and processes

- Measuring employee satisfaction and trying to continuously improve the workplace environment
- Benchmarking and incorporating best practices

TCG developed an integrated employee survey program that included assessment of employee satisfaction, an evaluation of how well the organization was doing in living up to its basic values, and an assessment from the viewpoint of its employees on how well the company was doing in progressing toward its quality goals. These surveys are combined with companywide internal work force profiles and work and family surveys to assess employee needs. On the basis of all of the research, a number of initiatives to benefit employees were launched, including: an expanded employee assistance program; child care resource and referral service; adoption assistance; health care and dependent care reimbursement plans; family leave; family sick days; flexible returns; sabbaticals; improved part-time employee benefits; flexible benefits; and work place flexibility initiatives including job-sharing, flexplace, flextime scheduling. What American Express and many other companies are finding is that to ensure employee satisfaction, productivity, and retention they are getting more and more involved in the private lives and family support of their workers.[42]

In addition to basic internal research, organizations can apply other marketing strategies to their management of employees. For example, segmentation of the employee population is apparent in many of the flexible benefit plans and career path choices now available to employees. Because not all employees are homogeneous and their needs will change over time, employees will have different insurance, work-scheduling, and family needs. Organizations that are set up to meet the needs of specific segments and to adjust as people proceed through their lives will benefit from increased employee loyalty.

Advertising and other forms of communication directed at employees can also serve to increase their sense of value and enhance their commitment to the organization. A public thank-you letter from the president of First Interstate Bank of Arizona published in a local newspaper reflects this type of communication. The full-page ad thanked employees for their dedication to, commitment, and support of First Interstate Bank's Extra Mile Service Guarantee Program. The letter shown in the ad concluded with "My confidence in you is well placed. Thank you. Your efforts are appreciated and recognized. Keep up the good work," and was signed by then president and CEO, Williams S. Randall. Organizations also use their employees in their TV and print advertisements with the idea that employees are a secondary (sometimes even primary) target for the advertisement.

Measure and Reward Strong Service Performers   If a company wants the strongest service performers to stay with the organization, it must reward and promote them. This may seem obvious, but often the reward systems in organizations are not set up to reward service excellence. Reward systems may value productivity, quantity, sales, or some other dimension that can potentially work *against* good service. Even those service workers who are intrinsically motivated to deliver high service quality will become discouraged at some point and start looking elsewhere if their efforts are not recognized and rewarded. Alternatively, they may stop providing high levels of service and simply sink to meet the service performance of the lowest common denominator.

Reward systems need to be linked to the organization's vision and to outcomes that are truly important. For instance, if customer retention is viewed as a critical outcome, service behaviors that increase retention need to be recognized and rewarded. This is the case at Toronto-based Cadet Uniform Services, a uniform rental company (featured in our chapter 1 discussion of the services marketing triangle).[43] Cadet employs 35 delivery route drivers (called customer service representatives, or CSRs), 50 to 60 percent of whose pay is based on customer retention levels. Reductions in pay are made for every customer that is lost for controllable reasons. (Situations *not* within the control of the CSR include a business closing, bankruptcy, or nonpayment cancellation.) Another 28 percent of CSR pay is based on direct customer satisfaction input obtained in face-to-face interviews conducted by a five-person team. Ninety-five percent of Cadet's drivers are college graduates, and their annual pay far exceeds industry averages. In determining whether this large investment in employee rewards is worthwhile, the company can point to the following statistics: Turnover among employees is close to 0 percent, customer retention (excluding customers who leave for uncontrollable reasons) is close to 99 percent, sales continue to grow, and for the past eighteen years average compounded growth for the company has been 22 to 23 percent annually.

In companies where customer satisfaction in every service encounter is a goal, there is often a need to adjust the criteria by which employee performance is judged. In some cases this means shifting from a total emphasis on productivity data and hard numbers to other means of assessment. This was the case at US WEST. Its 4,000 customer service phone representatives and credit consultants had been reviewed every month on how well they performed on various productivity measures such as the number of customer calls taken per day and the length of call.[44] The performance appraisal system was driving employees to meet and achieve better productivity numbers rather than focusing on customer satisfaction. To address this issue, service executives and union representatives began working toward a system that would more fully reward employees for customer satisfaction by developing a variety of alternatives as ways of gathering customer input for employee appraisals. Some of the alternatives now used by the company include: employees asking to have survey postcards sent to customers they've dealt with in the past month (average 10 surveys per month); team analysis of complaint data; and internal feedback by employees to their supervisors assessing how well they are doing in supporting the cultural change toward a focus on customer satisfaction.

The US WEST example suggests just how difficult it can be to implement new reward systems to recognize customer-based standards and encourage customer focus and orientation. Frequently these new reward structures are very difficult for managers to accept because they may not be linked to hard data and thus may appear more subjective. In fact, many companies are still struggling with this piece of the internal marketing puzzle, and many find it the most difficult of all. Reward systems are usually well entrenched, and employees have learned over time how they need to perform within the old structures. Change is difficult both for the managers who may have created and still may believe in the old systems and for employees who are not sure what they need to do to succeed under the new rules.

In developing new systems and structures to recognize customer focus and customer satisfaction, organizations have turned to a variety of types of rewards. Traditional approaches such as higher pay, promotions, and one-time monetary awards or prizes can be linked to service performance. In some organizations employees are encouraged to recognize each other by personally giving a "peer award" to an employee they believe has excelled in providing service to the customer. This type of award was known as the "Groo" award among employees of the Ochoco National Forest in central Oregon. The award was named after Tyler Groo, a forestry technician, who came up with the idea that each employee within the Forest Service should have one award per year to be given to another employee to recognize excellent service. Employees proudly display their "Groo" awards as an important reminder of their achievements.[45]

Other types of rewards include special organizational and team celebrations for achieving improved customer satisfaction or for attaining customer retention goals. In most service organizations it is not only the major accomplishments but the daily perseverance and attention to detail that moves the organization forward, so recognition of the "small wins" is also important.

SERVICE CULTURE

Most of this chapter has focused on strategies for enabling customer-oriented service delivery. Looking at the bigger picture, beyond the specific strategies, it is apparent that the behavior of employees in an organization will be heavily influenced by the culture of the organization, or the pervasive norms and values that shape individual and group behavior. Corporate culture has been defined as *"the pattern of shared values and beliefs that give the members of an organization meaning, and provide them with the rules for behavior in the organization."*[46] Culture has been defined more informally as "what we do around here," or "organizational glue," or "central themes."

Piglet in *Winnie the Pooh* might refer to culture as one of those things we sense "in an underneath sort of way." To understand at a personal level what corporate culture is, think of different places you've worked or organizations you've been a member of such as churches, fraternities, schools, or associations. Your behavior and the behaviors of others were no doubt influenced by the underlying values, norms, and culture of the organization. Even when you first interview for a new job, you can begin to get a sense of the culture through talking to a number of employees and observing behavior. Once on the job your formal training as well as informal observation of behavior will work together to give you a better picture of the organization's culture.

Experts have suggested that a customer-oriented, service-oriented organization will have at its heart a "service culture" defined as *"a culture where an appreciation for good service exists, and where giving good service to internal as well as ultimate, external customers is considered a natural way of life and one of the most important norms by everyone."*[47] This is a very rich definition with many implications for employee behaviors. First, a service culture exists if there is an "appreciation for good service." This doesn't mean that the company has an advertising campaign that stresses the importance of service, but that "in that underneath sort of way" people know that good service is appreciated and valued. A second important point in this definition is that good service is

---

BOX 11-3

SERVICE CULTURE: A PASSION FOR SERVICE

Benjamin Schneider, an authority on service and culture, emphasizes the importance of developing a "culture for service" in stating that if employees are going to behave in customer-oriented, service-oriented ways, they need to be supported by a culture that treats them in these same ways. Schneider and his colleagues have conducted research that aims to understand the elements of organizational culture that add up to a shared passion for customer service across the organization. Their research was conducted through 97 focus groups with employees in three different financial services companies. The central question of interest was: "When employees have a positive passion for service, what are the other kinds of themes for which they have passion?" Passion for service was defined as employee perceptions about the service orientation of their organizations, measured by how frequently and how positively the employee spoke about

service. Service passion was significantly correlated with a number of other organizational themes. Most notably, the research found that when service passion is high, employees speak frequently and favorably about the service delivery process, the product offered to the consumer, and how responsive the unit is to customer opinions. When service passion is high, employees also speak favorably and frequently about various human resource issues like performance feedback, internal compensation equity, training, staff quality, and most significantly, hiring practices. When service passion is high, other resources such as office conditions and facilities and automation systems are also mentioned positively and frequently.

Sources: Benjamin Schneider, "Notes on Climate and Culture," in *Creativity in Services Marketing,* eds. M. Venkatesan, Diane M. Schmalensee, and Claudia Marshall (Chicago: American Marketing Association, 1986), pp. 63–67; Benjamin Schneider, Jill K. Wheeler, and Jonathan F. Cox, "A Passion for Service:

---

given to internal as well as external customers. It is not enough to promise excellent service to final customers; all people within the organization deserve the same kind of service. Finally, in a service culture good service is "a way of life" and it comes naturally because it is an important norm of the organization.

This last point suggests why a service culture cannot be developed quickly and why there is no magic answer for how to develop a service culture. The human resource, internal marketing practices illustrated by the strategies wheel in Figure 11-5 will support the development of a service culture over time. If, however, an organization has a culture that is rooted in nonservice-oriented traditions, no single strategy will change it overnight. Research by Benjamin Schneider, noted expert on service culture, and his colleagues confirms this conclusion from the point of view of service employees (see Box 11-3).

SUMMARY

Because many services are delivered by people to people in real time, closing the service performance gap is heavily dependent on human resource strategies. Often service employees *are* the service, and in all cases they represent the organization in customers' eyes. They impact service quality perceptions to a large degree through their influence on the five dimensions of service quality: reliability, responsiveness, empathy, assurance, and tangibles. It is essential to match what the customer wants and needs with service employees' abilities to deliver.

In this chapter we have focused on service employees to provide understanding of the critical nature of their roles and appreciation of the inherent stresses and conflicts they face. You learned that front-line service jobs demand significant investments of emotional labor and that employees confront a variety of on-the-job conflicts. Sometimes service employees are personally uncomfortable with the roles they are asked to play; other times the requirements of the organization may conflict with client expectations and employees must resolve the dilemma on the spot. Sometimes there are conflicting needs among customers who are being served in turn (e.g., a bank teller line), or among customers being served simultaneously (e.g., a college classroom). At other times a front-line employee may be faced with a decision regarding satisfying a customer versus meeting productivity targets (e.g., an HMO physician who is required to see a certain number of patients in a defined period of time).

Grounded in this understanding of the importance of service employees and the nature of their roles in the organization, the chapter focused on strategies for integrating appropriate human resource practices into service firms. The strategies are aimed at allowing employees to be effective in satisfying customers as well as efficient and productive in their jobs. The strategies were organized around four major human resource goals in service organizations: to hire the right people, to develop people to deliver service quality, to provide needed support systems, and to retain the best people.

By focusing on these goals and developing practices to support them, an organization can move toward a true service culture where "an appreciation for good service exists, and where giving good service to internal as well as ultimate, external customers is considered a natural way of life and one of the most important norms by everyone."[48] A company that works toward implementing the strategies is certain to diminish GAP 3 as well.

DISCUSSION QUESTIONS

1 Why are service employees critical to the success of any service organization? Why do we include an entire chapter on service employees in a marketing course?

2 What is emotional labor? How can it be differentiated from physical or mental labor?

3 Reflect on your own role as a front-line service provider, whether in a current job or in any full- or part-time service job you've had in the past. Did you experience the kinds of conflicts described in the boundary-spanning roles section of the chapter? Be prepared with some concrete examples for class discussion.

4 Select a service provider (your dentist, doctor, lawyer, hair stylist) with whom you are familiar and discuss ways this person could positively influence the five dimensions of service quality in the context of delivering his or her services. Do the same for yourself (if you are currently a service provider).

5 Describe the four basic human resource strategy themes and why each plays an important role in building a customer-oriented organization.

6 What is the difference between technical and interactive service skills? Provide examples (preferably from your own work context, or from another context with which you are familiar). Why do service employees need training in both?

7 Is empowerment always the best approach for effective service delivery? Why is employee empowerment so controversial?

8 Define service culture. Can a manufacturing firm have a service culture? Why or why not?

EXERCISES

1 Review the section of the chapter on boundary-spanning roles. Interview at least two front-line service personnel regarding the stresses they experience in their jobs. How do the examples they provide relate to the sources of conflict and trade-offs described in the text?

2 Assume that you are the manager of a crew of front-line customer-service employees in a credit-card company. Assume that these employees do their work over the phone and that they deal primarily with customer requests, questions, and complaints. In this specific context: (a) Define what is meant by "boundary-spanning roles" and discuss the basic purposes or functions that participants in these roles perform. (b) Discuss two of the potential conflicts that your employees may face on the basis of their roles as boundary spanners. (c) Discuss how you, as their supervisor, might deal with these conflicts based on what you have learned.

3 Choose one or more of the human resource strategy themes (hire the right people, develop people to deliver service quality, provide needed support systems, retain the best people). Interview a manager in a service organization of your choice regarding his or her current practices within the theme you have chosen. Describe the current practices and recommend any appropriate changes for improving them.

NOTES

1 John Swaim, "Customer Obsession: Xerox's Source of Competitive Advantage," in *Advances in Services Marketing and Management: Research and Practice,* eds. Teresa A. Swartz, David E. Bowen, and Stephen W. Brown, Vol. 2 (Greenwich, Conn.: JAI Press, 1993), pp. 109–129.

2 Peter Gallagher, "Getting It Right from the Start," *Journal of Retail Banking* 15, 1 (Spring 1993): 39–41.

3 James S. Hirsch, "Now Hotel Clerks Provide More than Keys," *Wall Street Journal,* March 5, 1993, p. B1.

4 Gallagher, "Getting It Right."

5 This quote is most frequently attributed to Jan Carlzon of Scandinavian Airline Systems.

6 See, for example, Hal Rosenbluth, "Tales from a Nonconformist Company," *Harvard Business Review,* July–August 1991, pp. 26–36; and Leonard A. Schlesinger and James L. Heskett, "The Service-driven Service Company," *Harvard Business Review,* September–October 1991, pp. 71–81.

7 Benjamin Schneider and David E. Bowen, "The Service Organization: Human Resources Management Is Crucial," *Organizational Dynamics,* Spring 1993, pp. 39–52.

8 Ibid.

9 Arlie Hochschild, *The Managed Heart, Commercialization of Human Feeling* (Berkeley: University of California Press, 1983).

10 Arlie Hochschild, "Emotional Labor in the Friendly Skies," *Psychology Today,* June 1982, pp. 13–15.

11 Jolie Solomon, "Trying to Be Nice Is No Labor of Love," *Wall Street Journal,* November 29, 1990, p. B1.

12 Ibid.

13 Boas Shamir, "Between Service and Servility: Role Conflict in Subordinate Service Roles," *Human Relations* 33, 10 (1980): 741–756.

14 Ibid., p. 744–745.

15 Peter F. Drucker, "The New Productivity Challenge," *Harvard Business Review,* November–December 1991, pp. 69–79.
16 Robert Frank, "As UPS Tries to Deliver More to Its Customers, Labor Problems Grow," *Wall Street Journal,* May 23, 1994, p. A1.
17 Ibid.
18 For discussions of internal marketing see Leonard L. Berry and A. Parasuraman, "Marketing to Employees," chapter 9 in *Marketing Services* (New York: Free Press, 1991); Christian Gronroos, "Managing Internal Marketing—a Prerequisite for Successful External Marketing," chapter 10 in *Service Management and Marketing* (Lexington, Mass.: Lexington Books, 1990).
19 Jolie Solomon, "Managers Focus on Low-Wage Workers," *Wall Street Journal,* May 9, 1989, p. B1.
20 Berry and Parasuraman, "Marketing to Employees," p. 153.
21 Tim W. Ferguson, "Airline Asks Government for Room to Keep Rising," *Wall Street Journal,* March 9, 1993, p. A17.
22 This section on hiring for service competencies and service inclination draws from work by Benjamin Schneider and colleagues, specifically: Benjamin Schneider and Daniel Schechter, "Development of a Personnel Selection System for Service Jobs," in *Service Quality, Multidisciplinary and Multinational Perspectives,* eds. Stephen W. Brown, Evert Gummesson, Bo Edvardsson, and BengtOve Gustavsson (Lexington, Mass.: Lexington Books, 1991), pp. 217–236.
23 Joyce Hogan, Robert Hogan, and Catherine M. Busch, "How to Measure Service Orientation," *Journal of Applied Psychology* 69, 1 (1984): 167–173.
24 For a detailed description of a model selection system for telephone sales and service people see Schneider and Schechter, "Development of a Personnel Selection System."
25 Robert Levering and Milton Moskowitz, *100 Best Companies to Work For in America* (New York: Penguin Group, 1994), p. 457.
26 Antonio T. Rivera, "Selecting and Developing the Right People to Sustain Competitive Advantage," in *The Service Quality Handbook,* eds. Eberhard E. Scheuing and William F. Christopher (1993) (New York: American Management Association), pp. 233–247.
27 Levering and Moskowitz, *100 Best Companies,* p. 398.
28 Chuck Hawkins, "We Had to Recognize that People Have Lives," insert in *Business Week,* cover story on "Work and Family," June 28, 1993, pp. 80–88.
29 Richard Normann, "Getting People to Grow," *Service Management* (John Wiley, 1984), pp. 44–50.
30 Ronald Henkoff, "Companies that Train Best," *Fortune,* March 22, 1993, pp. 62–75.
31 Ibid.
32 Ibid., p. 73.
33 Ibid., p. 64.
34 David E. Bowen and Edward E. Lawler III, "The Empowerment of Service Workers: What, Why, How, and When," *Sloan Management Review,* Spring 1992, pp. 31–39.
35 Berry and Parasuraman, "Marketing to Employees," p. 162.
36 It is beyond the scope of this book to discuss all of the issues and pros and cons of team-based service delivery. For a discussion of team issues in the context of creative decision-making see Peter R. Dickson, *Marketing Management* (Fort Worth, Tex.: Dryden Press, 1994), appendix 1.
37 "Internal Service: How One Company Uses Pay Incentives to Create Enduring Change," *The Service Edge* 6, 6 (June 1993): 1–2.

38 Gene Hall, Jim Rosenthal, and Judy Wade, "How to Make Reengineering Really Work," *Harvard Business Review,* November–December 1993, pp. 119–131.

39 Hal Rosenbluth, "Tales from a Nonconformist Company," *Harvard Business Review,* July–August 1991, p. 33.

40 Leonard L. Berry, "The Employee as Customer," *Journal of Retail Banking* 3, 1 (March 1981): 33–40.

41 Carmen Hegge-Kleiser, "American Express Travel Related Services: A Human Resources Approach to Managing Quality," in *Managing Quality in America's Most Admired Companies,* ed. Jay W. Spechler (San Francisco: Berrett-Koehler Publishers, 1993), pp. 205–212.

42 Amanda Bennett, "As Pool of Skilled Help Tightens, Firms Move to Broaden Their Role," *Wall Street Journal,* May 8, 1989, p. 1.

43 "How to Keep Customers for Life: Some Clues for Putting Theory into Practice," *The Service Edge* 5, 9 (1992): 1–2.

44 "US WEST Abolishes Performance Appraisals to Shift Focus to Customers," *The Service Edge* 6, 6 (June 1993): 5.

45 Tom Peters, "Excellence in the Public Sector," video broadcast on Public TV, 1989.

46 S. M. Davis, *Managing Corporate Culture* (Cambridge, Mass.: Ballinger, 1985).

47 Gronroos, *Service Management and Marketing,* p. 244.

48 Ibid.

12

DELIVERING SERVICE THROUGH INTERMEDIARIES

MOVE OVER ATM, HERE COMES BANKING ON THE INTERNET[1]

Banking by automatic teller machines (ATM) is so natural to customers today that bank employees are the only people who regularly see bank interiors. But back in 1966, when the first prototypes of ATMs were developed, the idea caught on very slowly. In fact, by 1980, many small banks were convinced by market research that customers would never accept the technology, and so the banks did not adopt the machines. A full fifteen years later, however, virtually all successful banks distribute their services (and the customer's money) through ATMs. It appears that consumers do not always embrace technology quickly, even when it provides more convenient ways of doing business.

Many banking experts predict that ATMs were just the first step, with home banking and on-line banking poised to replace most traditional banking. One banker forecasts that:

The knowledge and information revolution will either destroy or fundamentally change financial institutions that have existed for the last 100 years . . . Banks are waking up to the fact that this is a major game, and they need to be in it.

Banking in cyberspace may sound new, but much of the technology for home banking has been available since the early 1980s. At that time, the market for home banking didn't develop as expected, largely because the penetration of home computers in U.S. households was low. By early 1990, only 1% of U.S. households banked by computer.

By 1995, however, the penetration of computers, on-line services, and the Internet were growing rapidly. To respond to those changes, virtually all large banks—including

BankAmerica, NationsBank, Chemical Bank, and Citicorp—are offering or contemplating updated home-banking services, most of them aligned with Microsoft Money or Quicken personal-finance software.

While only fifteen North American banks had registered addresses on the Internet in 1993, sixty-one went on-line in 1994, and more than 300 were projected for 1995. Using their PCs, consumers can track accounts, apply for loans and credit cards, make transfers and pay bills electronically to anyone with a bank account number. Internet users will also be able to buy goods and services and have the costs deducted from their accounts. In fact, the only banking services that cannot be distributed electronically are withdrawing and depositing cash. For that, perhaps we'll need to keep a few of the ATMs around for a while, at least until and unless we have a cashless society.

Due to the inseparability of production and consumption in service, providers must either be present themselves when customers receive service or find ways to involve others in distribution. Involving others can be problematic, because quality in service occurs in the service encounter between company and customer. Unless the service distributor is willing and able to perform in the service encounter as the service principal would, the value of the offering decreases and the reputation of the original service may be damaged. Chapter 11 points out the challenges of controlling encounters within service organizations themselves, but most service (and many manufacturing) companies face an even more formidable task: attaining service excellence and consistency when intermediaries represent them to customers. This chapter discusses both the challenges of delivering service through intermediaries and approaches that engender alignment with the goals of the service provider.

Two services marketers are involved in delivering service through intermediaries: the *service principal,* or originator, and the *service deliverer,* or intermediary. The service principal is the entity that creates the service concept (whose counterpart is the manufacturer of physical goods) and the service deliverer is the entity that interacts with the customer in the actual execution of the service (whose counterpart is the distributor or wholesaler of physical goods). Because both the service supplier and the service deliverer are potential roles that you may play in your career, we will examine the issues surrounding distribution of services from both perspectives.

Service intermediaries perform many important functions for the service principal. First, they often co-produce the service, fulfilling service principals' promises to customers. Franchise services such as haircutting, key-making, and dry cleaning are produced by the intermediary (the franchisee) using a process developed by the service principal (hence the phrase "co-producer"). Service intermediaries also make services locally available, providing time and place convenience for the customer. Because they represent multiple service principals, such intermediaries as travel and insurance agents provide a retailing function for customers, gathering together in one place a variety of choices. And in many financial or professional services, intermediaries function as the glue between the brand or company name and the customer by building the trusting relationship required in these complex and expert offerings.

In contrast to channels for products, channels for services are almost always direct, if not to the customer then to the intermediary that sells to the customer. Because services cannot be owned, there are no titles or rights to most services that can be passed along a delivery channel. Because services are intangible and perishable, inventories cannot exist, making warehousing a dispensable function. In general, because services can't be produced, warehoused, and then retailed as goods can, many channels available to goods producers are not feasible for service firms. Many of the primary functions distribution channels serve—inventorying, securing, and taking title to goods—have no meaning in services. The focus in service distribution is on identifying ways to bring the customer and principal or its representative together. The options for doing so are limited to franchisees, agents, brokers, and electronic channels (Figure 12-3).

We do not include retailers in our short list of service intermediaries because most retailers—from department stores to discount stores—are channels for delivering physical goods rather than services. Retailers that sell only services (movie theaters, film-processing kiosks, restaurants), or retail services that support physical products (automobile dealers, gas stations), can also be described as dealers or franchises. For our purposes in this chapter they are grouped into the franchise category, for they possess the same characteristics, strengths, and weakness as franchises.

Goods retailers, by the way, are service organizations themselves, making them intermediaries for goods if not services. Manufacturing companies depend on retailers to represent, explain, promote, and assure their products—all presale services. They also need retailers to return, exchange, support, and service products—all postsale services. These roles are increasingly critical as products become more complex, technical, and expensive. For example, camera and computer firms rely on retailers carrying their products to understand and communicate highly technical information so that customers choose products that fit their needs. A retailer that leads the customer to the wrong product choice or that inadequately instructs on how to use it creates service problems that strongly influence the manufacturer's reputation.

Service principals depend on their intermediaries to deliver service to their specifications. It is in the execution by the intermediary that the customer evaluates the quality of the company. When a McDonald's franchisee cooks the McNuggets too short a time, the customer's perception of the company—and of other McDonald's franchisees—is tarnished. When one Holiday Inn franchisee has unsanitary conditions, it reflects on all others and on the Holiday Inn brand itself. Unless service providers ensure that the intermediary's goals, incentives, and motives are consistent with their own, they lose control over the service encounters between the customer and the intermediary. When someone other than the service principal is critical to the fulfillment of quality service, a firm must develop ways to either control or motivate these intermediaries to meet company goals and standards. This chapter describes the types and roles of service intermediaries.

Specific objectives of the chapter are to:

1 Articulate the reasons for Provider GAP 3 that relate to intermediaries.
2 Identify the primary channels through which services are delivered to end-customers.

3 Provide examples of each of the key service intermediaries.

4 View delivery of service from two perspectives—the service provider and the service deliverer.

5 Identify the benefits and challenges of each method of service delivery.

6 Outline the strategies that are used to manage service delivery through intermediaries.

INTERMEDIARIES AND THE GAPS MODEL

Primarily, intermediaries are a force in the service performance gap (Provider GAP 3, Figure 12-1), the difference between service quality standards (as set by management of the company) and delivery to customers (as executed by employees, franchisees, agents, and anyone else involved in service encounters with the customer). Service principals design the systems and standards for delivery to be executed by the intermediaries. The gap occurs when delivery does not meet the specifications of the principal.

Intermediaries also play a role in other gaps, particularly GAP 1. Because intermediaries are contact personnel, they have a strong role in facilitating communication between the customer and the service principal to ensure that policy about service meets customer expectations. Since the service principal does not interact directly with customers in the course of doing business, it depends on information from intermediaries about what the customer expects. Intermediaries also influence GAP 2 by setting customer-defined standards to meet the expectations of customers, and GAP 4 by making realistic promises in external communication. In summary, intermediaries can play a role in all gaps, although here we will discuss in detail their role in GAP 3.

FIGURE 12-1   Provider GAP 3.

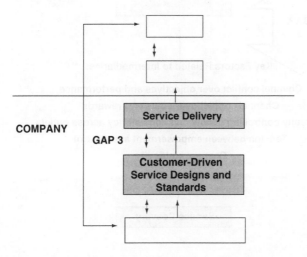

Reasons for GAP 3 Involving Intermediaries

The reasons for GAP 3 that involve intermediaries include conflict over objectives and performance, conflict over costs and rewards, difficulty controlling quality and consistency across outlets, tension between empowerment and control, and channel ambiguity (Figure 12-2).

Channel Conflict over Objectives and Performance   The parties involved in delivering services are not always in agreement about the way the channel should operate. Channel conflict can occur between the service provider and the service intermediary, among intermediaries in a given area, and between different types of channels used by a service provider (for example, when a service principal has its own outlets as well as franchised outlets). The conflict most often centers on the parties having different goals, competing roles and rights, and conflicting views of the way the channel is performing. Sometimes the conflict occurs because the service principal and its intermediaries are too dependent on each other.

Channel Conflict over Costs and Rewards   The monetary arrangement between those who create the service and those who deliver it is a pivotal issue of contention. Nowhere was this type of conflict better demonstrated than when major airlines in 1995 surprised their major distribution channel (travel agencies) with caps on fees. Instead of the traditional 10-percent commission on total airfare, Delta pioneered a $50-or-less fee per ticket, unilaterally and dramatically altering the compensation arrangement. The manner in which the airlines made the change so infuriated travel agencies that they

FIGURE 12-2   Key reasons for provider GAP 3.

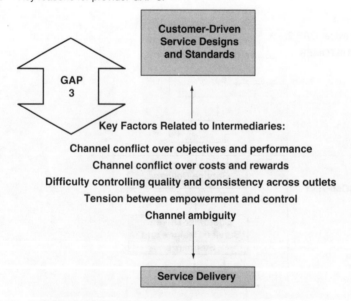

struck back against the airlines through such strategies as teaching consumers how to buy cheap tickets without staying over a Saturday night, purchasing wholesale tickets, and recommending small, discount carriers.

Difficulty Controlling Quality and Consistency across Outlets   One of the biggest difficulties for both principals and their intermediaries involves the inconsistency and lack of uniform quality that result when multiple outlets deliver services. When shoddy performance occurs, even at a single outlet, the service principal suffers because the entire brand and reputation are jeopardized, and other intermediaries endure negative attributions to their outlets. The problem is particularly acute in highly specialized services such as management consulting or architecture, where execution of the complex offering may be difficult to deliver to the standards of the principal. Intermediaries in any service must be selected, motivated, rewarded, and trained carefully to align their performance level with that of the principal. Technical quality inconsistency has led some states to create laws governing who can legally distribute services (e.g., banking).

Tension between Empowerment and Control   McDonald's and other successful service businesses were founded on the principle of performance consistency. Both they and their intermediaries attained profits and longevity by the company's controlling virtually every aspect of their intermediaries' businesses. McDonald's, for example, is famous for its demanding and rigid service standards (such as "turn, never flip, hamburgers on the grill"), carefully specified supplies, and performance monitoring. The strategy makes sense, for unless an intermediary delivers service exactly the same way the successful company outlets provide it, the service may not be as desirable to customers. From the principal's point of view, its name and reputation are on the line in each outlet, making careful control a necessity.

Control, however, can have negative ramifications within intermediaries. Many service franchisees, for example, are entrepreneurial by nature and select service franchising because they can own and operate their own business. If they are to deliver according to consistent standards, their independent ideas must be integrated into and often subsumed by the practices and policies of the service principal. In these situations they often feel like automatons with less freedom than they had in corporate jobs. And nowhere is this diminished perception of control more apparent than in the hordes of ex-corporate executives, many of them downsized out, who used to have autonomy and power in their jobs. For this reason, service principals have tested approaches that involve empowerment rather than control strategies. The upside is greater satisfaction and freedom of movement, but the downside—lower consistency and potentially lower revenues—must be weighed.

Channel Ambiguity   When empowerment is the chosen strategy, doubt exists about the roles of the company and the intermediary. Who will undertake market research to identify customer requirements, the company or an intermediary? Who owns the results and in what way are they to be used? Who determines the standards for service delivery, the franchiser or the franchisee? Who should train a dealer's customer-service representatives, the company or the dealer? In these and other situations, the roles of the principal and its intermediaries are unclear, leading to confusion and conflict.

KEY INTERMEDIARIES FOR SERVICE DELIVERY

One way to organize the discussion of delivering service through intermediaries is to describe the primary channels of service distribution. As shown in Figure 12-3, services can be distributed to the end-customer through franchisees, electronic channels, and agents and brokers. *Franchisees* are service outlets licensed by a principal to deliver a unique service concept it has created or popularized. Examples include fast-food chains (McDonald's, Burger King), video stores (Blockbuster's), automobile repair services (Jiffy Lube), and hotels (Holiday Inn). *Electronic Media* include all forms of service provision through television, telephone, interactive multimedia, and computers. Many financial and information services are currently distributed through electronic media: banking, bill paying, education. *Agents and brokers* are representatives who distribute and sell the services of one or more service suppliers. Examples include insurance (Paul Revere Insurance Company), financial services (Oppenheimer mutual funds), and travel services (American Express).

Exhibit 12-1 reviews basic principles about distribution, for your information.

Franchising

Franchising is the most common type of distribution in services and accounts for most retail sales.[2] The practice is large and growing rapidly—312,800 franchises in 1987; 424,500 in 1992. In this chapter we will use the broadest possible definition of franchising and incorporate three other types of intermediaries in the category: retailers, dealers, and bottlers. Retailers are outlets authorized to distribute products and services to end-customers. Because this chapter is about distributing services rather than products, we will discuss only those retailers that distribute services, such as film-processing companies, restaurants, dry cleaners, and distributors of movies. When we narrow the

FIGURE 12-3   Major types of intermediaries used in distributing services.

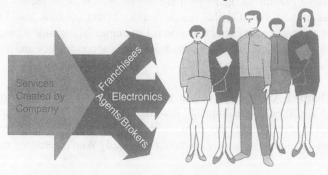

EXHIBIT 12-1 REVIEWING THE BASICS ABOUT DISTRIBUTION FROM MARKETING PRINCIPLES

Rather than reiterate topics covered in your marketing principles course and textbook, we list and briefly summarize below the basics about distribution. Knowing these basics allows you to step right into our chapter's discussion of service intermediaries.

Basic channel functions

1 *Decreasing the cost of delivering products and services to customers.* Because the channel allows specialization, all parties can concentrate on what they do best, thereby lowering cost.
2 *Regrouping activities.* Intermediaries are charged with sorting out, accumulating, allocating, and assorting products and services.
3 *Standardizing transactions.* Intermediaries deliver products or services in consistent form, based on the needs of the buyer and the supply of the seller.
4 *Matching buyers and sellers.* Intermediaries spend time in the market, learning about customers and about what sellers have to offer them.
5 *Provide customer service and support.* Intermediaries provide various services including technical support, delivery, transportation, and education.

Types of intermediaries

Retailers: intermediaries who sell directly to end customers. They may be retail stores, mail order, door-to-door, even vending machines.
Wholesalers: organizations that buy from producers and sell to retailers and organizational customers.

Number of intermediaries

Three strategies are available for distribution of products and services:

Intensive distribution: Locating the offering in numerous outlets
Selective distribution: Use of more than one but less than all intermediaries who are willing.
Exclusive distribution: Limiting the number of intermediaries to one per given area.

Criteria for evaluating the channel alternatives

Economic criteria: the sales expected and costs associated with the channel
Control criteria: the degree to which the service provider can expect to have its policies and procedures adhered to in the relationship
Adaptive criteria: the extent to which the type of channel is able to change and be flexible when desired by the service provider

"Push" versus "Pull" strategies

"Push" strategy involves companies aggressively promoting their products to intermediaries through personal selling, trade advertising, and trade incentives.
"Pull" strategy consists of building a reputation with customers through direct advertising and branding, creating a desire for the manufacturer's brand which is then pulled through the channel of distribution.

Source: Basics from Courtland L. Bovee and John V. Thill, Marketing (New York: McGraw-Hill, 1992), pp. 389–392.

list of retailers to services, most are operated as franchises and are subject to the same advantages and challenges.

Disagreement also exists about whether to distinguish franchising from automobile dealers, gasoline stations, and soft-drink bottlers.[3] Called *trade-name franchising,* these three categories account for more than half of all franchise sales, according to the director of the Small Business Development Center. Because the licensing of these products and services is subject to the same regulations and possesses similar strengths and weaknesses, we will discuss them as part of franchising. Dealers are representatives authorized to provide maintenance or repair services that accompany physical products such as cars, computers, and business equipment. Dealers of tangible products, such as automobiles and appliances, are responsible not just for selling the products but also for servicing them.

The other major type of franchise is *business format franchises,* in which the franchiser's requirements and specifications rule nearly every aspect of the enterprise, from the appearance of a facility to worker training. Business format franchises range from services targeted at individual consumers, including fast food and haircutting, to those targeted primarily at business customers, such as print shops and bookkeeping services.[4]

Franchising works well with services that can be standardized and virtually duplicated, typically through the delivery process, service policies, warranties, guarantees, promotion, and branding. Jiffy Lube, H&R Block tax services, and Red Roof Inns are examples of companies that are ideal for franchise operations. The more complex and professional the service, such as with internal medicine or business consulting, the less likely it is that services will be duplicated exactly the way the franchiser desires. At its best, franchising refers to a relationship or partnership in which the service provider—the franchiser—develops and optimizes a service format that it licenses for delivery by other parties—the franchisees. Both parties agree on how profits and risks will be determined (see Exhibit 12-2). A more formal definition of franchising, established by the industry association, the International Franchise Association, states that it is

[A] contractual relationship between the [two parties] in which the franchiser offers or is obliged to maintain a continuing interest in the business of the franchisee in such areas as know-how and training; wherein the franchise operates under a common trade name, format or procedure owned by or controlled by the franchiser, and in which the franchisee has made or will make a substantial capital investment in his business from his own resources.[5]

EXHIBIT 12-2   ELEMENTS OF A FRANCHISE AGREEMENT

Agreements and contracts are essential in franchising. Service companies have found that a franchise agreement should describe virtually all of the following aspects of the partnership:

- The nature of the service to be supplied by the franchisee
- The geographic territory in which the franchisee can offer the service
- How much of the revenue generated by the franchisee must be paid to the franchiser
- The length of the agreement (usually 5–10 years with options to renew)
- The up-front fee for the franchise
- The instructions by which the franchisee agrees to operate and deliver service (price, reliability of service, advertising)

- The promise that the franchisee will not act as an intermediary for any other service firm in the same industry (which is what technically distinguishes franchisees from dealers and agents)
- The promotional support to be given to the franchisee to improve the value of the franchised brands
- The administrative and technical support provided by the franchiser
- The way that the franchise agreement can be terminated

As you may have guessed, these are the issues that create misunderstanding and conflict between franchisees and franchisers—the reasons for channel conflict and channel ambiguity, as well as tension between control and empowerment. The principal appears to have the upper hand because it is the entity drawing up the contracts and selecting franchisees, but franchising has benefits and challenges for all parties involved.

The Franchiser (Service Principal) Perspective   More than 2,500 U.S. franchisers license their brand names, business processes or formats, unique products, services, or reputations in return for fees and royalties from franchisees. Examples of industries where franchising is prevalent, and the reasons they are desirable to franchisees, include (1) fast foods, with unique cooking or delivery processes and brand names; (2) health and fitness centers, with established formats for marketing to customers and pricing as well as hiring and motivating employees; (3) motels, hotels, and rental cars, founded on national names and reputations; (4) travel agencies, with ticketing and distribution processes; and (4) video stores, with unique store environments, purchasing, and computer systems. Benefits and challenges for the franchiser are discussed below and summarized in Exhibit 12-3.

Benefits of Franchising for the Franchiser
- **Leverages the business format to gain expansion and revenues.** Virtually all companies that seek to franchise their business concepts do so because they want wider distribution than they can support in company outlets. The reasons they desire wider distribution are to increase revenues, gain larger market share, obtain greater brand name recognition, or gain additional economies of scale. Even when franchisers can finance additional company-owned outlets, they may choose to minimize their investment and financial risks by sharing them with franchisees. A further motivation may be to reduce the number and complexity of operational and human resource tasks to be provided by the company itself.
- **Maintains consistency in outlets.** When franchisers have strong contracts and unique business formats, they can require franchisees to deliver services according to their specifications. The franchiser can stipulate virtually all aspects, from hiring and training practices to prices to store design.
- **Gains knowledge of local markets.** National chains are unlikely to understand local markets as well as the business people who live in the markets. With franchising, the company obtains personnel knowledgeable and connected in the local markets.
- **Shares financial risk and frees up capital.** Franchisees must contribute their own capital for equipment and personnel, thereby bearing part of the risk of doing business. Rather than investing the bulk of money in distribution, having franchisees allows service principals to invest in core service production facilities.

Challenges of Franchising for the Franchiser
- **Difficulty in maintaining and motivating franchisees.** The ability to motivate internal employees is difficult enough. But motivating independent operators to price, deliver, promote, and hire according to standards the principal establishes is a difficult job. When business is down, franchisees may be hard to maintain. Most franchising contracts are for five to ten years, after which the franchisee can renew.
- **Highly publicized disputes between franchisees and franchisers.** Because they are gaining more economic clout, franchisees are organizing, then hiring lobbyists and lawyers to press their cause. Many states and even the federal government have implemented legislation boosting franchisees' rights, especially the right to renew and to transfer the franchise when desired.
- **Inconsistent quality that can undermine the company name.** In instances

---

EXHIBIT 12-3 SUMMARY OF BENEFITS AND CHALLENGES FOR FRANCHISERS OF SERVICE

Benefits	Challenges
• Leverages the business format to gain expansion and revenues	• Difficulty in maintaining and motivating franchisees
• Maintains consistency in outlets	• Highly publicized disputes and conflict
• Gains knowledge of local markets	• Possibility of inconsistent quality that can undermine the company name
• Shares financial risk and frees up capital	• Control of customer relationship by intermediary

---

where quality varies, the principal may find that the company's reputation is being damaged by low-performing franchisees. One of the three big automotive companies had a dealer in the mid-Atlantic area who performed well in selling but whose customer satisfaction ratings were considerably below those of other dealerships. Even though the company was making money from the errant dealer, it recognized that the impact on its customer-service image was eroding future business. For a time the company was unable to influence the dealership to change. Only a threatened lawsuit motivated the dealer to improve practices to satisfy customers.

• **Customer relationships controlled by the intermediary rather than the service principal.** The closer a service company is to the customer, the better able it is to listen to that customer's concerns and ideas. When franchisees are involved, a relationship forms between the customer and the franchise, rather than between the customer and the service principal. All customer information, including identifying demographics, purchase history, and preferences are in the hands of the intermediary rather than the principal.

The Franchisee's View   Generalizing about franchising can be difficult because more than 65 types of businesses exist, which generate more than $800 billion in sales each year. Some franchises are highly desirable and lucrative, such as soda bottlers and beer distributors (although these forms are largely unavailable to new franchisees because they have reached capacity). Others are less certain, including convenience marts and auto-service shops. Many are transient operations that are underfinanced and inadequately supported, and can disappoint the independent operators who purchase them.

Benefits of Franchising for Franchisees
• **Obtaining an established business format on which to base a business.** This is one of the primary benefits to the franchisee. One expert has defined franchising as an "entrepreneur in a prepackaged box, a super-efficient distributor of services and goods through a decentralized web."[6] Franchisees sign on because the franchisers have created businesses that work, that already have strong images and track records, and that have been tested for effectiveness.
• **Receiving national or regional brand marketing.** One of the biggest advantages comes from the brand name and marketing the franchisee obtains. Franchisees expect—

and usually receive—advertising and other marketing expertise as well as a reputation that they do not need to build themselves.
- **Minimizing the risks of starting a business.** One of the biggest selling points of franchising is the claim of diminished risk of purchasing a franchise over initiating one's own business. The U.S. Small Business Administration claims that whereas 63 percent of new businesses fail within six years, only 5 percent of new franchises fail. For small-business owners, franchising also offers an alternative way of raising capital that speeds growth.[7]

Challenges of Franchising for the Franchisee
- **Disappointing profits and revenues.** A recent report on franchising suggests: "For all their past successes, previous few systems are minting money for franchisees today. Most markets are crowded, and expenses are rising."[8] Nearly 9 of 10 franchisers are cutting up only about a quarter of every dollar of sales. "Most people think of franchising as some kind of bonanza . . . the reality is if you get a solid operation, work damn hard, and if you're making $40,000 a year after four years, that's good."[9]

Since the mid-1980s, the number of U.S. franchisers and franchised outlets has only matched or lagged behind the rise in GNP, according to an expert. Established franchisers like PepsiCo (which owns KFC, Pizza Hut, and Taco Bell) are opening new franchises in other countries but not in the United States.[10]
- **Encroachment and franchise saturation.** Most lawsuits by franchisees involve encroachment of existing stores—the opening of new units within 3 miles of existing ones without compensation to the existing franchisee. When encroachment occurs, potential revenues are diminished, and franchisers often will not offer the encroaching franchise to the franchisee in the local area, believing that the competition between franchisees will increase revenues. Franchisees are sometimes bitter, believing that service principals are selfishly trying to maximize their revenues by saturating markets with competing stores. Another resentment involves the shift toward franchiser-owned "distribution points" such as self-contained kiosks from Taco Bell and Pizza Hut. Any type of outlet encroaches on the markets of the franchisees.
- **High failure rates and unfair terminations.** Earlier in this chapter we stated that the International Franchise Association claims that less than 5 percent of franchises are terminated on an annual basis. Others dispute this figure, maintaining that it is based on old studies by the Department of Commerce that surveyed franchisers, not franchisees, and scored a franchisee as a failure only if a store was closed, not if the franchisee quit the business. Several new academic studies poke giant holes in the franchise association's claims. One study found that almost 35 percent of franchises failed by 1991 versus 28 percent for other small businesses. Another showed that both small businesses and franchises have roughly equal and high failure rates. In the words of the study's author, "I think the golden era of franchising might be over. Buying a McDonalds 20 years ago was a great business. Buying a Subway today is nowhere near as attractive."[11]
- **Lack of perceived control.** About one third of new franchisees are ex-employees of large companies, up from 24 percent in 1992. These are people who once exerted a great deal of control over their jobs, something that changes quickly when a franchise operation is purchased. One indicator of the perceived lack of control is that since 1990,

franchisee complaints filed against parent companies with the Federal Trade Commission have been growing at a greater than 50-percent annual rate.

Efforts are being made by the International Franchise Association to resolve disputes between franchisees and franchisers in part to avoid government regulators becoming involved with the problems. Among the strategies they are implementing are dispute-resolution programs (established in 1993), a franchisee advisory council, and allowing franchisees to become members of the association.

• **High fees and rigid contracts.** Franchisees typically pay between $5,000 and $35,000 in up-front fees to acquire a franchise. They are also required to buy equipment, pay for training, and secure a mortgage or lease. On top of these fixed charges, monthly royalties are 2 to 8 percent of gross sales, even without advertising fees.[12] Franchisees of one company, Little Caesars Enterprises Inc., say they are forced to buy ingredients and paper from a company-owned distributor, paying up to 15 percent more than rivals for identical items.[13] A lawyer for the trade group of franchisees, the American Association of Franchisees and Dealers, claims that, "Most [franchisers] treat franchisees like indentured servants. They have fewer rights than employees."[14]

The franchising contract, drafted by the franchiser, usually stipulates that franchisees must arbitrate in the franchisers' home state, refrain from leaving the system or selling a store without the franchiser's agreement, avoid competing with the franchiser, purchase supplies and equipment from the franchiser, and forfeit key assets (such as a client list and equipment) in the event of termination. These contracts can be lengthy, often totaling 50 pages, and feature all the things the franchisee must do to maintain the franchise. They sometimes also allow the franchiser to raise fees and use judgment in all matters. One customer, burned by the experience, claims, "Franchise contracts are inordinately one-sided. I'd never sign one again unless I could make major revisions."

• **Unrealistic expectations.**[15] Some of what creates problems for franchisees involves approaching the agreement with expectations about revenues and profits that are unrealistic. Franchisers are partly responsible for the elevated expectations because they attract and sign new franchisees with promises that they can achieve the performance of their star franchises. More than one service principal has been found guilty of over-promising. Another area in which expectations are unrealistic involves the time commitment the franchisee must make to achieve success.

Franchising that Works The leading franchises of the past are easy to enumerate and have been mentioned already in this chapter. Here we provide fresh examples of service delivery that are successful from the perspective of both franchiser and franchisee. (See also Figure 12-4.)

• **Takeout Taxi.** This is a service franchise that delivers food to busy professionals who are more than willing to pay full price plus a $3 to $4 delivery charge. By negotiating discounts with participating restaurants, Taxi earns a margin on the meals plus the delivery fee. The staff consists of dispatchers, customer reps, and drivers and is very popular because of the extra service the company provides.[16]

• **Taco Johns.** Taco Johns has become the number 2 Mexican fast-food chain by tak-

HERTZ RENT A CAR

PARENT COMPANY: Hertz Corp.

BIGGEST OUTLET: Los Angeles International Airport

SIZE INDICATOR: Most rentals a day

EXPLANATION: Nine counters in seven terminals serve customers round-the-clock at the West Coast's busiest airport. Daily rentals average 2,000. In the first half of 1992, the facility grossed $37 million. Hertz parking lots, maintenance facilities and offices cover 36 acres. The operation pumps more than one million gallons of gasoline a year. Seventeen buses shuttle customers to and from vehicles. Most popular car: Ford Taurus. Five percent of airport rentals are convertibles. Hertz's staff at the airport numbers 300. The size of the operation multiplies problems, such as a flight delaying fog. "If we make a mistake we can upset several hundred customers at a time," says Charles Shafer, division vice-president.

FTD FLORAL DELIVERY

PARENT COMPANY: Florists' Transworld Delivery Association

BIGGEST OUTLET: McShan Florist Inc., Dallas

SIZE INDICATOR: Most flowers-by-wire orders in U.S.

EXPLANATION: Serving Dallas but not neighboring Fort Worth, the florist typically fills 1,100 FTD orders a week; an arrangement averages $38. McShan employs 150, has more than two dozen phone lines, a 27,000-square-foot store and 50 delivery trucks, but no greenhouse. Neiman Marcus is a major local customer. Obituary-page ads read, "We don't sell flowers, we sell love." Dallas literally grew up to McShan's door. Once surrounded by cotton fields, the store now is ringed by homes, many of which it landscaped. The business hasn't branched out because, says president Bruce McShan, "We prefer to have one big headache instead of a lot of little ones."

MCDONALD'S

PARENT COMPANY: McDonald's Corp.

BIGGEST OUTLET: On turnpike near Darien, Conn.

SIZE INDICATOR: Most McDonald's customers served in U.S.

EXPLANATION: Near the New York-Connecticut border on Interstate 95, this round-the-clock McDonald's serves nearly three million travelers a year. On average, the franchise sells 8,000 meals daily. Everything about the store is mammoth. 19 cash registers, including portables for overflow crowds, a 12-foot fry grill, 32 telephones. Employees work in teams. One directs traffic, another operates a yogurt bar. Retirees pass out maps in a tourist center equipped with an automatic teller machine. Owner-operator George Michell says the busiest days of the year are Thanksgiving weekend.

FEDERAL EXPRESS

PARENT COMPANY: Federal Express Corp.

BIGGEST OUTLET: Center at 525 Seventh Ave., New York City

SIZE INDICATOR: Handles most packages and documents daily.

EXPLANATION: Located in the heart of New York City's Garment Center, between 38th and 39th streets. This is the busiest of Federal Express's 434 U.S. service centers; its daily volume of 1,000 items is three times the average. Proximity to Penn Station is a traffic booster. Major customers include dressmakers and fashion-design houses as well as neighborhood department stores. "Many parcels are boxes you couldn't carry home," says manager Valerie Blanchard. The center also handles a heavy volume of tickets for travel agents. Seven full-time employees staff the facility, which is open until 9:30 p.m. weekdays and 7 p.m. on Saturdays.

H&R BLOCK

PARENT COMPANY: H&R Block Inc.

BIGGEST OUTLET: Downtown Stamford, Conn.

SIZE INDICATOR: Most clients served

EXPLANATION: The office handled more than 8,000 returns last year—almost twice the next-busiest office. Why? "It's a mystery to me," says district manager Jack Marvill. The volume was so large that two more Stamford outlets recently opened. The downtown office doesn't offer unusual services, and its clientele is described as a typical mixture of commercial and individual taxpayers. The facility has 19 tax-preparation stations and employs about 50.

HILTON HOTELS

PARENT COMPANY: Hilton Hotels Corp.

BIGGEST OUTLET: Flamingo Hotel, Las Vegas

SIZE INDICATOR: Most rooms

EXPLANATION: This 3,530-room hotel, built by gangster Bugsy Siegel in the 1940s, is popular with tourists; the nearby 3,200-room Las Vegas Hilton caters to high rollers and conventioneers. With single rooms priced at under $50, the Flamingo averages a 90% occupancy rate and is Hilton's most profitable, says vice president Marc Grossman. Located at one of the busiest "Strip" intersections, the hotel is staffed by nearly 4,000 employees. Its 27 stories include a casino, two grand ballrooms, eight restaurants, three lounges, 55 elevators, parking for 2,830 and a furrier. A $100 million expansion will add a tower and waterfalls.

FIGURE 12-4   What makes a franchise or retail store a star?

A *Wall Street Journal* reporter answered this question by locating the biggest U.S. outlet for 20 big brands, among them many service businesses. He concluded that location, luck, and service determine the winners. Here are several of the star franchisees that won.

Source: Richard Gibson, "Location, Luck, Service Can Make a Store Top Star," *Wall Street Journal*, February 1, 1993, p. B1.

ing steps to improve the relationship between franchisees and franchisers. It redrafted its partnership agreements to protect franchisees from encroachment and unjust termination, resulting in greater "peace, harmony, and profits." One franchisee, Bill Miller in Missoula, Montana, owns four Taco Johns, thereby minimizing his risk of encroachment and leveraging his assets and time. His biggest challenge: learning to work with his taco-stuffing crew. "At a big company, you can yell and scream but in a restaurant your hourlies would quit, and you'd be stuck."[17]

- **Blimpie.** Blimpie was a successful sandwich shop franchise until Subway entered the market. The firm wisely decided it had to be more competitive in its franchises, and turned the company around with its changes. Since 1987, Blimpie's systemwide sales have jumped 38 percent, the number of stores exploded from 149 to 570, and store failures decreased from 10 to 3 percent.[18] How did the company do it? First, it hired a consultant to evaluate Blimpie and learned that franchisee trust was low and eroding effectiveness. Blimpie's cofounder Conza opened communication, flying to stores in more than 75 cities to meet the owners. He formed a franchisee advisory council to get their input on key issues, including new products and pricing. He also published a newsletter and an 800 number to give tips to franchisees, and awarded them more control over their own advertising through regional advertising co-ops.

- **American Health Care Groups.** One final innovative approach to service franchising involves the purchasing and coordination of individual physicians' private practices into chains. Changes in health care fuel this innovation, allowing doctors to focus on medicine while the chain provides the business, operations, and marketing processes around the practice. A start-up company called American Health Care Groups took the approach one step further by building new practices from scratch, recruiting doctors to be part of the franchises. By collecting a management fee equal to about 7 percent of revenue, these firms provide administration, purchasing, accounting, and solicitation of clients in blocks of business.[19]

Agents and Brokers

In common terminology, an agent is an intermediary who acts on behalf of a service principal (such as a brokerage firm or a popular sports figure) and is authorized to make agreements between customers and those principals. Agents and brokers do not take title to services but instead deliver the rights to them. They have legal authority to market services as well as to perform other marketing functions on behalf of producers. The two forms of intermediaries perform many of the same functions but are distinct from each other in some ways.

Types of Agents   Agents generally work for principals continuously, rather than for a single deal. Consider the agent who works for a film star, an athlete, a public speaker. During the 1994 Winter Olympics, women's figure skating silver medalist Nancy Kerrigan became so popular that she brought her agent, Jerry Solomon of Pro-Serve, with her to Lilihammer to handle media requests for her time, offers for commercial endorsements, and opportunities for television specials and movies. His role, like that of all agents, is to facilitate buying or selling (or both), for which he is paid a commission. Most agents receive commissions equaling 2 to 6 percent of selling price.

Selling agents, of which Pro-Serve's Jerry Solomon is one, have contractual authority to sell a service principal's output (which can be anything from an athlete's time to insurance or financial services), usually because the principal is not interested, feels unqualified, or lacks the resources to do so. Nancy Kerrigan needed to focus on her skating and knew little about negotiation and contracts, so she hired Pro-Serve to represent her and handle all business aspects for her. Selling agents act as a sales force with a difference: Because they know the market better than the service principal, they are typically entrusted with influence over prices, terms, and conditions of sale. Unlike a sales force, the selling agent normally has no territorial limits but represents the service principal in all areas.

Purchasing agents also have long-term relationships with buyers, evaluating and making purchases for them. They are knowledgeable and provide helpful market information to clients as well as obtaining the best services and prices available. Purchasing agents are frequently hired by companies and individuals to find art, antiques, and rare jewelry. *Facilitating agents* help with the marketing process by adding expertise or support such as financial services, risk taking, or transportation.

Types of Brokers   Brokers bring buyers and sellers together while assisting in negotiation. They are paid by the party who hired them, rarely become involved in financing or assuming risk, and are not long-term representatives of buyers or sellers.[31] The most familiar examples are real-estate brokers, insurance brokers, and security brokers.

Benefits and challenges in using agents and brokers are summarized in Exhibit 12-4.

Benefits of Agents and Brokers   The travel industry provides an example of both agents and brokers. As shown in Figure 12-5, three main categories of travel intermediaries exist: tour packagers, retail travel agents, and specialty channelers (including incentive travel firms, meeting and convention planners, hotel representatives, association

---

**EXHIBIT 12-4   SUMMARY OF BENEFITS AND CHALLENGES
IN DISTRIBUTING SERVICES THROUGH AGENTS AND BROKERS**

Benefits	Challenges
• Reduced selling and distribution costs	• Loss of control over pricing and other aspects of marketing
• Intermediary's possession of special skills and knowledge	• Representation of multiple service principals
• Wide representation	
• Knowledge of local markets	
• Customer choice	

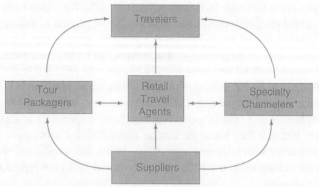

FIGURE 12-5 The distribution system for travel services.

*Incentive travel firms, business meeting and convention planners, corporate travel offices, association executives, hotel representatives, and supplier sales offices.
Source: Mary Jo Bitner and Bernard H. Booms, "Trends in Travel and Tourism Marketing: The Changing Structure of Distribution Channels," *Journal of Travel Research,* Spring 1982, pp. 39–44.

executives, and corporate travel offices). You are likely to be most familiar with retail travel agents. Industry convention terms the travel companies as brokers and the individuals who work for them as travel agents or sales associates. We will illustrate some of the benefits and challenges of agents and brokers using this industry.

Reduced Selling and Distribution Costs If an airline or resort hotel needed to contact every potential traveler to promote its offerings, costs would be exorbitant. Because most travel services are transactional rather than long-term in nature, travelers would need to expend tremendous effort to find services that meet their needs. Travel agents and brokers accomplish the intermediary role by assembling information from travel suppliers and offering it to travelers.

Possession of Special Skills and Knowledge Each of the three intermediaries in Figure 12-5 have special knowledge and skills in their area. The retail travel agents know the industry well and know how to access the information they do not possess, often through reference materials and on-line services. Tour packagers have a more specialized role—they assemble, promote, and price bundles of travel services from travel suppliers, then offer these bundles either to travelers themselves or to retail travel agents. Specialty channelers (which we could put in the category of facilitating agents) have even more specialized roles: Some work in corporate travel offices to lend their skills to an entire corporation, others are business meeting and convention planners who act almost as tour packagers for whole companies or associations, and some are incentive travel firms that focus on travel recognition programs in corporations or associations.

Wide Representation Because agents and brokers are paid by commission rather than by salary, there is little risk or disadvantage in extending the service offerings to a wide geography. Thus, companies have representatives in many places, far more places than the company would place them if fixed costs such as buildings, equipment, and salaries were required.

Knowledge of Local Markets   Another key benefit of agents and brokers is that they become experts in the markets they serve. They know or learn the unique needs of different markets, including international markets. They understand what their clients' preferences are and how to adapt the principal's services to match the needs of clients. This benefit is particularly needed and appreciated when clients are dispersed internationally. Knowing the culture and taboos of a country is critical for successful selling. Most companies find that obtaining local representation by experts with this knowledge is necessary.

Customer Choice   Travel and insurance agents provide a retailing service for customers—they represent the services of multiple suppliers. If a traveler needed to visit six or eight different travel agencies, each of which carried the services of a single supplier, imagine the effort a customer would need to make to plan a trip! Independent insurance agents have the right to sell a wide variety of insurance, which allows them to offer customers a choice. These types of agents also are able to compare prices across suppliers and get the best prices for their clients.

Challenges of Delivering Service through Agents and Brokers

Loss of Control over Pricing and Other Aspects of Marketing   As representatives of service principals and experts on customer markets, agents and brokers are typically empowered to negotiate price, configure services, and otherwise alter the marketing of a principal's service. This issue could be particularly important—and possibly detrimental—when a service provider depends on a particular (high) price to convey a level of service quality. If the price can be changed, it might reach a level that undermines the quality image. In addition, the agent has the flexibility to give different prices to different customers. As long as the customers are geographically dispersed, this will not create a problem for the service principal; however, if buyers compare prices and realize they were given different prices, they may perceive the service principal as unfair or unethical.

Representation of Multiple Service Principals   As we have already discussed, when independent agents represent multiple suppliers they offer customer choice. From the perspective of the service principal, however, customer choice means that the agent represents—and in many cases advocates—a competitive service offering. This is the same challenge a manufacturer confronts when distributing products in a retail store. Only in rare cases are its products the only ones in a given category on the retail floor. In a service context, consider the use of independent insurance agents. These agents carry a range of insurance products from different companies, serving as a surrogate service retail store for customers. When they find a customer who needs insurance, they sell from their portfolio the offerings that best match customers' requirements.

Electronic Channels

Electronic channels are the only service distributors that do not require direct human interaction. What they do require is some predesigned service (almost always information, education, or entertainment) and an electronic vehicle to deliver it. We are all familiar with telephone and television channels, and other electronic vehicles are currently being developed. *Video dial tone* (VDT) is the term used by telecommunications companies to describe full-motion video that is delivered on a switched basis. Some of the newer ways in which sound, video, and information are transported directly to service customers are through the Internet, satellites, and computers. And the consumer and business services that will be made possible through these vehicles include movies on demand, interactive news and music, banking and financial services, multimedia libraries and data bases, distance learning, desktop video conferencing, remote health services, and interactive, network-based games.[20]

The more a service relies on technology and/or equipment for service production, and the less it relies on face-to-face contact with service providers, the less the service is characterized by inseparability and nonstandardization. As you will see in the paragraphs that follow (see also Exhibit 12-5), using electronic channels overcomes some of the problems associated with service inseparability and allows a form of standardization not previously possible in most services.

Benefits of Electronic Channels

Quality Control   In most cases, the channel in electronic distribution does not alter the service as channels with human interaction tend to do. Unlike personal delivery, electronic delivery does not interpret the service and execute it according to that interpretation. Its delivery is likely to be the same in all transmissions.

Distribution of television programming from networks through affiliate television and radio stations illustrates electronic distribution. Networks create and finance programming including shows, news, and sports and distribute them through local stations in return for fees and advertising dollars. In most cases, the local stations deliver what is fed to them through the networks. Local television stations can elect to not carry a particular show because of low ratings or lack of fit with the local market. When the situation comedy "All in the Family" was first released in the 1970s, several local television markets believed it was too controversial and did not carry it for the first year. When it became the top-rated show during that year, however, many stations reversed their decisions. Local stations can also refuse to carry advertising spots that are judged in bad taste or too controversial, such as political advertising that ranges on poor taste. Except

---

EXHIBIT 12-5   SUMMARY OF BENEFITS AND CHALLENGES IN ELECTRONIC DISTRIBUTION OF SERVICES

Benefits	Challenges
• Quality control	• Lack of control of electronic environment
• Low cost	• Inability to customize
• Customer convenience	• Customer Involvement
• Potential for wide distribution	• Security
• Customer choice	

---

for these situations, which are not common, what is distributed through electronic channels is what is sent by the service creator.

Low Cost   Electronic media offer more efficient means of delivery than does interpersonal distribution. For example, the cost of reaching buyers using a direct sales force has been estimated to exceed $100 per interaction, whereas the use of electronic media such as television or radio costs less than $20 per *thousand* interactions. Critics could rightly claim that the personal sales interaction was more powerful and effective, but with interactive media—now possible and being examined for commercial viability—service advertisers will be able to gain some of the credibility benefits (being able to answer individual questions or tailor the service for individuals) from personal interaction.

Customer Convenience   Customers are able to access the services when and where they want. For the marketer this allows access to a large group of customers who would otherwise be unavailable to them because their schedules do not allow them to visit service outlets.

Wide Distribution   Electronic channels do more than allow the service provider to interact with a large number of end-users. They also allow the service provider to interact (often simultaneously) with a large number of intermediaries. The costs and effort to inform, select, and motivate nonelectronic channels are higher than the costs for electronic channels.

Customer Choice   Consider the options that will be available in movies and videos to customers who use video-on-demand services. Among the many services being piloted today, one from Southern New England Telephone offers a package of 40 broadcast and cable channels, 18 traditional pay-per-view choices, and about 1,300 video-on-demand movies and special interest videos.[21] While customers will not be able to fast-forward or rewind the video choices, they will have available in their homes a wealth of viewing choices. The customer will be in control of the process.

Challenges in Distributing Services through Electronic Channels

Lack of Control of the Electronic Environment   It did not take long for the Internet to face the challenges of unregulated media. As soon as the network became popular, pornographic and other controversial material started to appear. When a service's advertising or information appears in proximity to such material, the result can be a negative spillover effect. It is similar to the challenge advertisers faced in using print media such as *TV Guide*—the advertiser had to be careful to separate its advertising for banking from the ever-present balding-concealment devices and quick weight loss programs. With the *TV Guide,* however, the advertiser could request or pay for the right positioning, something not possible on the Internet at this time, for there is not yet a regulator of the Internet (there are bills pending in states to introduce regulation).

Inability to Customize   Some of you have experienced learning basic college courses through large, video-transmitted courses. If you consider what you missed in learning that way compared with learning directly from a professor, you will understand this challenge. In mass sections, you cannot interact directly with the professor, ask questions, raise points for clarification, or experience the connection that you receive in person. In electronic classes—as in video conferences that are springing up in many businesses—the quality of the service can also be impeded by the way the audience reacts (or doesn't react) in those situations. People talk among themselves, leave, laugh, and criticize, among other behaviors.

Customization can be increased in these channels. In college courses, small groups of students can be led by teaching assistants to discuss the electronic lecture. Call-in questions can simulate direct interaction. Two-way video can control the behavior of receivers. In advertising on the Internet and other electronic channels, it is conjectured that personalized advertising will ultimately be developed because customers will be in control. Consumers will actively seek pertinent advertising, so marketers must develop ways to make their advertising compelling. Ad resources will shift toward supplying information the customer wants to know, rather than pitching what the company wants to sell.

Customer Involvement   Many times the customer produces the service herself using the technology. Unless the technology is highly user-friendly, customers may be reluctant to try it or to continue using it if it requires ongoing education.

Security   One issue confronting marketers using electronic channels is security of information, particularly financial information. Many marketers who advertise on the Internet will not accept credit-card orders because of potential security problems in the transactions. Hyatt Hotels, for example, requires users to call its toll-free number after becoming interested in its services on the Net.

Electronic Channels in Action   The Technology Spotlight shows one example of an electronic distribution channel. Other illustrations are discussed below.

Smart Cards   Many banks are marketing "smart cards" as a replacement for cash and checks. Customers insert cards into automatic teller machines and instruct them to transfer money electronically to a small computer chip on the card. With this transaction, the bank subtracts the money from the customer's account. Then, when the customer makes a purchase in a store, the merchant inserts the card into a computer terminal that deducts the money from the funds stored on the card. When the electronic money is depleted, the customer returns to the bank to load additional money onto the card. NationsBank and First Union Corporation of Charlotte plan to introduce smart cards in Atlanta for the 1996 Olympic games by equipping 5,000 sites in the Atlanta area with the needed technology. The prospect for success looks positive:

> Smart cards have the potential to reshape banking for consumers in the same way automatic teller machines did a generation ago. Just as ATMs liberated people from lunchtime lines in bank lobbies, so may smart cards ultimately enable people to dump cash and checks.[22]

One big question: Will customers be willing to part with the "float"—the two- to three-day loan they get between the time they write a paper check and it is deposited in the bank? The cards are already used throughout Europe in many banks, for public transit (Washington, D.C.'s subway system), and for long-distance telephone service. One of the reasons both customers and companies want to use them is safety: Because the cards can be encoded with information that identifies the owner, they will be difficult to use if stolen. Smart cards mean less fraud to the banks as well because the microchips are difficult to counterfeit.

TECHNOLOGY SPOTLIGHT

TICKETLESS AIR TRAVEL

Can you imagine flying on an airline without paper tickets to prove you have a seat? Flying without a ticket has already arrived at Southwest and ValueJet airlines. To compete effectively with low costs and ticket prices, these airlines have revolutionized the distribution of air travel.

You know the traditional drill still used by most large airlines. You purchase a ticket through a travel agent or an airline and receive paper tickets for the flight. You can't board without them. To create and distribute the paper tickets, reservation systems such as American Airlines SABRE charges a fee for every ticket (equal to about $2.25 per ticket). Southwest Airlines conceived of ticketless travel when its CEO, Herb Kelleher, became angry at the high fees, which he viewed as paying millions of dollars of "ransom" to use the computerized ticketing system.[23]

In the new system, which works the way hotels currently operate, you call the airline, pay with a credit card, and receive a reservation or confirmation number. The reservation number is all that you need to check bags and board the airline.

Using the technology, ValueJet Airlines saves by eliminating travel agency commission (not necessary because it deals directly with customers), bypassing the reservation system, and avoiding the costs of a large staff to process tickets. As a result, it is able to reduce ticket prices and still make a profit.

The technology is making it possible—and financially advantageous—for passengers and airlines to bypass traditional methods of making travel arrangements. What impact does ticketless air travel have on the travel agency business? One expert claims "Our bet is the transaction focus, where travel agencies make their money, will diminish."[24] That means that the more than 23,000 travel agencies must adapt. "They're going to be changing, either by turning into a value-added business like accountants and lawyers, or they'll be automated away."[25]

One travel agency, American Express Travel, has changed its approach. The company helps other companies manage their travel and expense budgets and is paid primarily in fees rather than commissions.

Another result may be that customers become more knowledgeable and experienced in handling their own travel with the help of stores like Travelfest in Austin, Texas. The retail store sells guidebooks, out-of-town newspapers, videos, and maps as well as luggage and travel supplies.

Selling via On-line Services and the Internet As the use of on-line services increases (from 5.2 million subscribers in 1994 to a projected 15 million households in 1998), advertisers are increasingly bringing their products and services to on-line services and the Internet.[26] More than 25 million people are using PCs connected to telephone lines to read electronic versions of magazines; obtain information about travel, entertainment, or finances; get mail; and socialize in "chat" rooms. On the World Wide Web, the international information network, they can also see, hear, and experience advertising. More than 30 companies (including Reebok International, IBM, Coors, J. C. Penney, Hyatt, MCI, MCA/Universal, and Miller Brewing Company) have already set up marketing sites on-line. American Express has its own site, called Express Net, on America Online where card members can arrange travel or review their charges. Reebok allows users to chat with professional athletes and Reebok executives. The selling of products and services, particularly information, on the Internet and on-line services promises to become more competitive and creative.

Buying via On-line Services and the Internet What would make you want to shop for services and products on the Internet? Many consumers are learning the answer to this question. It is a far different experience to use advertising in that context than in conventional media:

The Internet has its own culture. You can't broadcast ads. We keep it low-key and present a combination of commercial and educational materials. . . . As long as you observe their protocol, it's fine. But that makes it harder because you can't aggressively market to them.[27]

One particular site on the World Wide Web has DealerNet, the Virtual Showroom, where multitudes of information about cars can be accessed by buyers. The information comes in layers that can be accessed by pointing and clicking on icons. One Nissan/Volvo dealer in Seattle has sold 70 cars by this method, and is marshalling 49 car dealers representing 45 different cars from Acura, Buick, and Chrysler to Saturn, Toyota, and Volvo.[28]

Education by Modem   One of the most revolutionary services soon to be widely available to companies and customers is electronic education. To reduce costs, and to allow students and employees to be educated or trained at a time and place convenient for them, most training companies and institutes of higher learning are contemplating education via computer. Phoenix University in Arizona, an eighteen-year-old graduate program, provides a prototype of an MBA program in cyberspace. Most students are older (average graduate is 38 years old) and work full-time jobs in addition to matriculating. Courses last five or six weeks, meeting once a week for four hours at a time. The university's 2,100 professors are part-time teachers, part-time professionals, earning $1,000 to $1,200 per course. The education they provide can be absorbed anywhere there is a personal computer, typically at campus and satellite sites. Over 60,000 degrees have been awarded by Phoenix since 1976. This form of education has its critics, among them the director of accreditation at the American Assembly of Collegiate Schools of Business: "It's kind of like McEducation. I can't imagine that they could convince one of our committees that their faculty have the appropriate qualifications."[29]

Business-to-Business Video Conferencing   Rather than flying to meet in person, tomorrow's executives will meet face-to-face electronically via big-screen teleconferencing units (at a cost of $34,000 per unit) or computers (at a cost of $6,000 per unit). All of the major telephone companies are gearing up for what they believe will be the answer to escalating corporate travel costs and increasingly stressed employees. The systems have been around for years but are only now being purchased and used by companies.[30]

STRATEGIES FOR EFFECTIVE SERVICE DELIVERY THROUGH INTERMEDIARIES

Service principals, of course, want to manage their service intermediaries to improve service performance, solidify their image, and increase profits and revenues. The principal has a variety of choices, which range from strict contractual and measurement control to partnering with intermediaries in a joint effort to improve service to the customer. One of the biggest issues a principal faces is whether to view intermediaries as extensions of its company, as customers, or as partners. We will discuss three categories of intermediary-management strategies: control strategies, empowerment strategies, and partnering strategies.

Control Strategies

In this category, the service principal believes that intermediaries will perform best when it creates standards both for revenues and service performance, measures results, and compensates or rewards on the basis of performance level. To use these strategies the principal must be the most powerful participant in the channel, possessing unique services with strong consumer demand or loyalty, or other forms of economic power.

Measurement   Some franchisers maintain control of the service quality delivered by their franchisees by ongoing measurement programs that feed data back to the principal. Virtually all automobile dealers' sales and service performance is monitored regularly by the manufacturer, which creates the measurement program, administers it, and maintains control of the information. The company surveys customers at key points in the service encounter sequence: after sale, thirty days out, ninety days out, and after a year. The manufacturer designs the instruments (some of them with the assistance of dealer councils) and obtains the customer feedback directly. On the basis of this information, the manufacturer rewards and recognizes both individuals and dealerships that perform well and can potentially punish those that perform poorly. The obvious advantage to this approach is that the manufacturer retains control; however, the trust and goodwill between manufacturers and dealers can easily be eroded if dealers feel that the measurement is used to control and punish.

Review   Some franchisers control through terminations, nonrenewals, quotas, and restrictive supplier sources. Expansion and encroachment are two of the tactics being used today. Another means by which franchisers exert control over franchisees is through quotas and sales goals, typically by offering price breaks after a certain volume is attained.

Empowerment Strategies

Empowerment strategies, where the service principal allows greater flexibility to intermediaries based on the belief that their talents are best revealed in participation rather than acquiescence, are useful when the service principal is new or lacks sufficient power to govern the channel using control strategies. In empowerment strategies, the principal provides information, research, or processes to help intermediaries perform well in service.

Help the Intermediary Develop Customer-oriented Service Processes   Individual intermediaries rarely have the funds to sponsor their own customer research studies or reengineering efforts. One way for a company to improve intermediary performance is to conduct research or standard-setting studies relating to service performance, then provide them as a service to intermediaries. As an example, H&R Block amassed its customer information and codified it in a set of 10 "Ultimate Client Service" standards, which are displayed in each office. The standards include:

- No client will wait more than thirty minutes in the waiting area.
- Phone calls will be answered by the fourth ring, and no caller will be on hold for more than one minute.
- Every tax preparation client will receive a thorough interview to determine the client's lowest legal tax liability.
- Accurately prepared and checked returns will be delivered in four days or fewer.

Rather than administer this customer program from the home office, which could lead it to be perceived as a measurement "hammer," the company is asking each franchisee to devise a way to measure the standards in its own offices in 1995, then report this information to H&R Block. At the end of the year, the company will review the different measures and offer "best practice" information to all offices.

Provide Needed Support Systems   After Ford Motor Company conducted customer research and identified six sales standards and six service standards that address the most important customer expectations, it found that dealers and service centers did not possess the know-how to implement, measure, and improve service with them. For example, one of the sales standards specified that customers be approached within the first minute they enter the dealership and be offered help when and if the customer needs it. While dealers could see that this standard was desirable, they did not immediately know how to make it happen. Ford stepped in and provided the research and process support to help the dealers. As another form of support, the company created national advertising featuring dealers discussing the quality care standards.

In airlines and hotels, as well as other travel and ticketing services, the service principal's reservation system is an important support system. Holiday Inn has a franchise service delivery system that adds value to the Holiday Inn franchise and differentiates it from competitors.

Develop Intermediaries to Deliver Service Quality   In this strategy, the service originator invests in training or other forms of development to improve the skills and knowledge of intermediaries and their employees. Prudential Real Estate Associates, a national franchiser of real estate brokers, recently engaged in a companywide program of service excellence. To teach sales associates (real estate agents) about what buyers and sellers expect, the company first conducted focus group interviews with end-customers, then created a half-day training program to communicate what the research revealed. To teach brokers (the companies that employ the sales associates), the company created a highly successful operations review that examined the operational and financial aspects of the brokers, assessed their levels of effectiveness, then communicated individually with each broker about the specific issues that needed to be addressed and the approaches that would be successful in improving performance.

Change to a Cooperative Management Structure   Companies such as Taco Bell use the technique of empowerment to manage and motivate franchisees. They develop worker teams in their outlets to hire, discipline, and handle financial tasks such as deposits and audits. Taco Bell deliberately reduced levels of management (regional managers used to oversee 5 stores; now they oversee 50 stores) and report improvements in revenue, employee morale, and profits. The management structure was a marked departure from previous practices and the change reflected what one manager of the firm stated: "Sooner or later you trust your people or you don't."[31]

Partnering Strategies

The group of strategies with the highest potential for effectiveness involves partnering with intermediaries to learn together about end-customers, set specifications, improve delivery, and communicate honestly. This approach capitalizes on the skills and strengths of both principal and intermediary and engenders a sense of trust that improves the relationship.

Alignment of Goals   One of the most successful approaches to partnering involves aligning company and intermediary goals early in the process. Both the service principal and the intermediary have individual goals that they strive to achieve. If channel members can see that they benefit the ultimate consumer of services and in the process optimize their own revenues and profit, they begin the relationship with a target in mind. Sonic Corp, a drive-in hamburger chain, is attempting to retain open relationships with its franchisees, continually adapting to changing customer needs and franchisee suggestions.

Consultation and Cooperation   This strategy is not as dramatic as setting joint goals, but it does result in intermediaries participating in the decision-making process. In this approach, which could involve virtually any topic, from compensation to service quality to the service environment, the principal makes a point of consulting intermediaries and asking for their opinions and views before establishing policy. Alpha-Graphics, a franchiser of rapid printing services based in Tucson, Arizona, makes a habit of consulting its franchisees to hear how they think the operation should be run. When the franchiser found that the outlets needed greater support in promotion, the company began to make customer mailings for franchisees.[32] When the franchiser found that many franchisees were dissatisfied with the one-sided contracts they received, the principal revised contracts to make it easier for them to leave the system, changed fees to reflect a sliding scale linked to volume, and allowed franchisees to select the ways they use their royalty fees. This approach makes the franchisees feel that they have some control over the way they do business and also generates a steady stream of improvement ideas. Taco John's, the second-largest Mexican fast-food chain, has torn up its old contracts to forge a new state-of-the-art, cooperative relationship with franchisees.

SUMMARY

This chapter discussed the benefits and challenges of delivering service through intermediaries. Service intermediaries perform many important functions for the service principal—co-producing the service, making services locally available, and functioning as the bond between the principal and the customer. The focus in service distribution is on identifying ways to bring the customer and principal or its representatives together.

In contrast to channels for products, channels for services are almost always direct, if not to the customer then to the intermediary that sells to the customer. Many of the primary functions distribution channels serve—inventorying, securing, and taking title to goods—have no meaning in services because of services' intangibility. Because services cannot be owned, most have no titles or rights that can be passed along a delivery channel. Because services are intangible and perishable, inventories cannot exist, making warehousing a dispensable function. In general, because services can't be produced, warehoused, and then retailed like goods can, many channels available to goods producers are not feasible for service firms.

Three forms of distribution in service were described in the chapter: franchisees, agents/brokers, and electronic media. The benefits and challenges of each type of intermediary were discussed, and examples of firms successful in delivering services through each type were detailed. Discussion centered on strategies that could be used by service principals to improve management of intermediaries.

DISCUSSION QUESTIONS

1 In what specific ways does the distribution of services differ from the distribution of goods?

2 Which of the reasons for GAP 3 described at the beginning of this chapter is the most problematic? Why? Based on the chapter, and in particular the strategies discussed at the end of the chapter, what can be done to address the problem you selected? Rank the possible strategies from most effective to least effective.

3 List five services that could be distributed on the Internet that are not mentioned in this chapter. Why are these particular services appropriate for electronic distribution? Choose two that you particularly advocate. How would you address the challenges to electronic media discussed in this chapter?

4 List services that are sold through selling agents. Why is the use of agents the chosen method of distribution for these services? Could any be distributed in the other ways described in this chapter?

5 What are the main differences between agents and brokers?

6 What types of services are bought through purchasing agents? What qualifies a purchasing agent to represent a buyer in these transactions? Why does the buyer not engage in the purchase herself, rather than hiring someone to do so?

7 Which of the three categories of strategies for effective service delivery through intermediaries do you believe is most successful? Why? Why are the other two categories less successful?

EXERCISES

1 Develop a franchising plan for a service concept or idea that you believe could be successful. Use the elements of a franchise agreement (Exhibit 12-2) to describe and detail the plan. In your opinion, what would franchisees pay to become an affiliate of the franchiser?

2 Visit a franchisee and discuss the pros and cons of the arrangement from his or her per-

spective. How closely does this list of benefits and challenges fit the one provided in this chapter? What would you add to the chapter's list to reflect the experience of the franchisee you interviewed?

3 Select a service industry with which you are familiar. How do service principals in that industry distribute their services? Develop possible approaches to manage intermediaries using the three categories of strategies in the last section of this chapter. Which approach do you believe would be most effective? Why? Which approaches are currently used by service principals in the industry?

NOTES

1 Timothy L. O'Brien, "Home Banking: Will It Take Off This Time?" *Wall Street Journal,* June 8, 1995, pp. B1 and B7.
2 Lori Bongiorno, "Franchise Fracas," *Business Week,* March 22, 1993, p. 68.
3 Ibid.
4 Christopher H. Lovelock, *Services Marketing* (New York: Prentice-Hall, 1991), p. 231.
5 Ibid.
6 Andrew E. Serwer, "Trouble in Franchise Nation," *Fortune,* March 6, 1995, pp. 115–118.
7 Bongiorno, "Franchise Fracas," p. 68.
8 Serwer, "Trouble in Franchise Nation," p. 116.
9 Ibid.
10 Ibid.
11 Ibid.
12 Ibid.
13 Bongiorno, "Franchise Fracas," p. 68.
14 Serwer, "Trouble in Franchise Nation," p. 118.
15 Bongiorno, "Franchise Fracas," p. 68.
16 Serwer, "Trouble in Franchise Nation," p. 118.
17 Ibid.
18 Laurel Touby, "Blimpie Is Trying to Be a Hero to Franchisees Again," *Business Week,* March 22, 1993, p. 70.
19 George Anders, "McDonalds Methods Come to Medicine," *Wall Street Journal,* August 24, pp. B1 and B6.
20 Roland T. Rust and Richard W. Oliver, "Video Dial Tone: The New World of Services Marketing," *Journal of Services Marketing* 8, 3 (1994): 5–16.
21 David Lieberman, "Test Could Pave Way for More Services," *USA Today,* October 12, 1994, pp. B1–2.
22 Tim Gray, "The End of Cash?" *The Raleigh News and Observer,* Sunday, April 2, 1995, p. F1.
23 Blair S. Walker, "Southwest Innovation: No Tickets?" *USA Today,* May 9, 1994, p. 1B.
24 Bridget O'Brian, "Ticketless Plane Trips, New Technology Force Travel Agencies to Change Course," *Wall Street Journal,* September 13, 1994, p. B1+.
25 Ibid., p. B10.
26 Dottie Enrico, "High-Tech Pitches Still Face Tests," *USA Today,* March 7, 1995, p. B1.
27 Cyndee Miller, "Marketers Find It's Hip to Be on the Internet," *Marketing News,* February 27, 1995, p. 2.

28 Mike McKesson, "Car Shopping by Computer," *The Raleigh News and Observer,* Tuesday, April 11, 1995, p. 3D.

29 Steve Stecklow, "At Phoenix University, Class Can Be Anywhere—Even in Cyberspace," *Wall Street Journal,* September 12, 1994, p. A1.

30 Bart Ziegler, "Video Conference Calls Change Business," *Wall Street Journal,* October 12, 1994, p. B1.

31 Serwer, "Trouble in Franchise Nation," p. 118.

32 Jeffrey Tannenbaum, "To Pacify Irate Franchisees, Franchisers Extend Services," *Wall Street Journal,* February 24, 1995, p. B2.

CUSTOMERS' ROLES
IN SERVICE DELIVERY

IKEA of Sweden has managed to transform itself from a small mail-order furniture company into the world's largest retailer of home furnishings. In 1992 its one hundred stores around the world were visited by 96 million people, generating $4.3 billion in revenues. The company sells simple Scandinavian-design furnishings, charging 25 to 50 percent less than its competitors.[1]

A fascinating key to IKEA's spectacular success is the company's relationship to its customers. IKEA has drawn the customer into its production system: "If customers agree to take on certain key tasks traditionally done by manufacturers and retailers—the assembly of products and their delivery to customers' homes—then IKEA promises to deliver well-designed products at substantially lower prices." In effect, IKEA's customers become essential contributors to value—they create value for themselves through participating in the manufacturing and delivery process.

IKEA has made being part of the value-creation process easy, fun, and a pleasant experience for customers. The company's stores are a pleasure to shop in. Free strollers and supervised child care are provided as well as wheelchairs for those who need them. When customers enter the store they are given catalogs, tape measures, pens, and notepaper to use as they shop, allowing the customer to perform functions commonly done by salespeople. After payment, customers take their purchases to their cars on carts; if necessary they can rent or buy a roof rack to carry larger purchases. Thus, customers also provide furniture loading and delivery services for themselves.

At home, the IKEA customer takes on the role of manufacturer in assembling the new furnishings following carefully written, simple, and direct instructions. IKEA prints more than 45 million catalogs per year in 10 different languages, making its products and instructions for their use accessible worldwide.

IKEA's tremendous success is attributable in part to recognizing that customers can be part of the business system, performing roles they have never performed before. The company's implementation of this idea through clearly defining customers' new roles and making it fun to perform these roles is the genius of its strategy. Through the process, customers create and contribute to their own satisfaction.

In this chapter we will examine the unique roles played by customers in service delivery situations. Service customers are often present in the "factory" (the place the service is produced and/or consumed), interacting with employees and with other customers. For example, in a classroom or training situation, students (the customers) are sitting in the factory interacting with the instructor and other students as they consume the educational services. Because they are present during service production, customers can contribute to or detract from the successful delivery of the service and to their own satisfaction. These roles are unique to service situations. In a manufacturing context, rarely does the production facility contend with customer presence on the factory floor, nor does it rely on the customer's immediate real-time input to manufacture the product. As the example in the opening paragraphs of the chapter illustrates, service customers can actually produce the service themselves and to some extent are thus responsible for their own satisfaction. At IKEA, customers create value for themselves and in the process also reduce the prices they pay for furniture.

Since customers are participants in service delivery, they can potentially contribute to the widening of GAP 3 (Figure 13-1). That is, customers themselves can influence whether the delivered service meets customer-defined specifications. In this chapter we will examine the key factors relating to customer roles that can contribute to GAP 3, as shown in Figure 13-2.

FIGURE 13-1   Provider GAP 3.

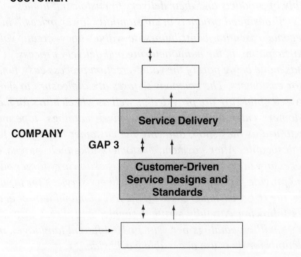

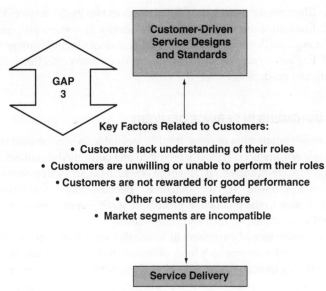

FIGURE 13-2   Key reasons for provider GAP 3.

Sometimes customers contribute to GAP 3 because they lack understanding of their roles and exactly what they should do in a given situation. This is particularly true in cases where the customer may be confronting a service concept for the first time. At other times customers may understand their roles but be unwilling or unable to perform for some reason. In a health club context, a member may understand that to get into good physical shape he must follow the workout guidelines set up by the trainer. If work schedule demands or illness keep the member from living up to his part of the guidelines, the service will not be successful due to customer inaction. In a different situation, customers may choose not to perform the roles defined for them because they are not rewarded in any way for contributing their effort. When service customers are enticed through price reductions, greater convenience, or some other tangible benefit, they are more likely to perform their roles willingly.

Finally, GAP 3 may be widened not through actions or inactions on the part of the customer, but because of what *other* customers do. Other customers who are in the service factory either receiving the service simultaneously (i.e., passengers on an airplane flight) or waiting their turn to receive the service sequentially (i.e., bank customers waiting in line, Disneyland customers waiting for one of the rides), can influence whether the service is effectively and efficiently delivered.

This chapter will focus on the roles of customers in service delivery and strategies to effectively manage customers in the production process to enhance productivity, quality, and customer satisfaction.

The objectives of the chapter are to:

1 Illustrate the importance of customers in successful service delivery

2 Enumerate the variety of roles that service customers play: productive resources for the organization; contributors to quality and satisfaction; competitors.

3 Explain strategies for involving service customers effectively to increase both quality and productivity.

THE IMPORTANCE OF CUSTOMERS IN SERVICE DELIVERY

Customer participation at some level is inevitable in service delivery. Services are actions or performances, typically produced and consumed simultaneously. In many situations employees, customers, and even others in the service environment interact to produce the ultimate service outcome. Because they participate, customers are indispensable to the production process of service organizations and they can actually control or contribute to their own satisfaction.[2]

The importance of customers in successful service delivery is obvious if one thinks of service performances as a form of drama. Based on a drama metaphor, Figure 13-3 shows the reciprocal, interactive roles of employees (actors) and customers (audience) in creating the service experience. The service actors and audience are shown surrounded by the service setting. The drama metaphor argues that the development and maintenance of an interaction (e.g., a service experience) relies on the audience's input as well as the actors' presentation. Through this metaphor, service performances or service delivery situations are viewed as tenuous, fragile processes that can be influenced by behaviors of customers as well as by employees.[3] Service performance results from actions and interactions among individuals in both groups.

Consider the services provided by a cruise ship company. The actors (ship's personnel) provide the service through interactions with their audience (the passengers) and among each other. The audience also produces elements of the service through interactions with the actors and other audience members. And, both actors and audience are sur-

FIGURE 13-3 Service performances as drama.

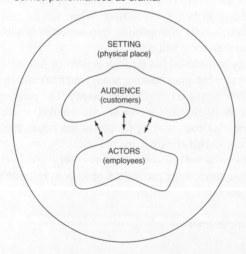

rounded by an elaborate setting (the cruise ship itself) that provides a context to facilitate the service performance. The drama metaphor provides a compelling frame of reference for recognizing the interdependent roles of actors and audience in service delivery.

Recognition of the role of customers is also reflected in the definition of the *people* element of the services marketing mix given in chapter 1: *People: all human actors who play a part in service delivery and thus influence the buyer's perceptions; namely, the firm's personnel, the customer, and other customers in the service environment.* Chapter 11 thoroughly examined the role of the firm's personnel in delivering service quality. In this chapter we focus on the customer receiving the service, and other customers in the service environment, that is, the "service audience."

Customer Receiving the Service

Because the customer receiving the service participates in the delivery process, she can contribute to GAP 3 through her own appropriate or inappropriate, effective or ineffective, productive or unproductive behaviors. The level of customer participation— low, medium, high—varies across services, as shown in Table 13-1. In some cases, all that is required is the customer's physical presence (*low level of participation*), with the employees of the firm doing all of the service production work, as in the case of a symphony concert. Symphony-goers must be present to receive the entertainment service, but little else is required once they are seated. In other cases, consumer inputs are required to aid the service organization in creating the service (*moderate level of participation*). Inputs can include information, effort, or physical possessions. All three of

TABLE 13-1   LEVELS OF CUSTOMER PARTICIPATION ACROSS DIFFERENT SERVICES

Low: Consumer presence required during service delivery	*Moderate:* Consumer inputs required for service creation	*High:* Consumers cocreate the service product
Products are standardized.	Consumer inputs customize a standard service.	Active consumer participation guides the customized service.
Service is provided regardless of any individual purchase.	Provision of service requires consumer purchase.	Service cannot be created apart from the customer's purchase and active participation.
Payment may be the only required consumer input.	Consumer inputs (information, materials) are necessary for an adequate outcome, but the service firm provides the service.	Consumer inputs are mandatory and cocreate the outcome.
Examples:	*Examples:*	*Examples:*
Airline travel	Haircut	Marriage counseling
Concert	Tax preparation	Personal training
Motel	Annual physical exam	Dissertation advising
Fast-food restaurant	Full service restaurant	Weight-reduction program

Source: Amy R. Hubbert, "Customer Co-Creation of Service Outcomes: Effects of Locus of Causality Attributions," doctoral dissertation, Arizona State University, Tempe, Arizona, 1995.

these are required for a CPA to prepare a client's tax return effectively: *information* in the form of tax history, marital status, and number of dependents; *effort* in putting the information together in a useful fashion; and *physical possessions* such as receipts and past tax returns. In some situations, customers can actually be involved in cocreating the service (*high level of participation*). For these services customers have mandatory production roles that, if not fulfilled, will affect the nature of the service outcome. All forms of education, training, and health maintenance fit this profile. Unless the customer *does* something (e.g., studies, exercises, eats the right foods), the service provider cannot effectively deliver the service outcome. Table 13-1 provides several examples of each level of participation. The effectiveness of customer involvement at all of the levels will impact organizational productivity and ultimately, quality and customer satisfaction.

Other Customers

In many service contexts, customers receive the service simultaneously with other customers or must wait their turn while other customers are being served. In both cases, "other customers" are present in the service environment and can affect the nature of the service outcome or process. Other customers can *enhance* customer satisfaction and perceptions of quality, or they can *detract* from satisfaction and quality.[4]

Some of the ways other customers can negatively affect the service experience are by exhibiting disruptive behaviors, causing delays, overusing, excessively crowding, and manifesting incompatible needs. In restaurants, hotels, airplanes, and other environments where customers are cheek to jowl as they receive the service, crying babies, smoking patrons, and loud, unruly groups can be disruptive and detract from the experiences of their fellow customers. The customer is disappointed through no direct fault of the provider. In other cases, overly demanding customers (even customers with legitimate problems) can cause a delay for others while their needs are met. This is a common occurrence in banks, post offices, and customer-service counters in retail stores. Excessive crowding or overuse of a service can also affect the nature of the customer's experience. Visiting Sea World in San Diego on the fourth of July is a very different experience from visiting the same park mid-week in February. Similarly, the quality of telecommunication services can suffer on special holidays like Christmas and Mother's Day when large numbers of customers all try to use the service at once. Finally, customers who are being served simultaneously but who have incompatible needs can negatively affect each other. This can occur in restaurants, college classrooms, hospitals, and any service establishment where multiple segments are served simultaneously.

There are just as many examples of other customers enhancing satisfaction and quality for their fellow customers as detracting from them. Sometimes the mere presence of other customers enhances the experience. This is true at sporting events, in movie theaters, and in other entertainment venues. The presence of other patrons is essential for true enjoyment of the experience. In other cases, other customers provide a positive social dimension to the service experience. At health clubs, churches, and resorts such as Club Med, other customers provide opportunities to socialize and build friendships. Long-time, established customers may also socialize new customers by teaching them

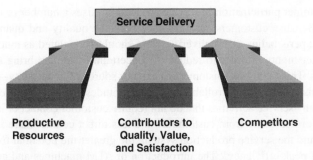

FIGURE 13-4   Three roles customers can play in service delivery.

about the service and how to use it effectively. In some situations, such as educational classrooms, group counseling, and weight-loss programs, customers may actually help each other to achieve service goals and outcomes. The success of the Weight Watchers organization, for example, depends significantly on the camaraderie and support that group members provide each other during the weight-loss process.

The following sections examine in more detail three major roles played by customers in service delivery: customers as productive resources; customers as contributors to quality, value, and satisfaction; customers as competitors (Figure 13-4).

CUSTOMERS' ROLES

Customers as Productive Resources

Service customers have been referred to as "partial employees" of the organization—human resources who contribute to the organization's productive capacity.[5] Some management experts have suggested that the organization's boundaries be expanded to consider the customer as part of the service system. In other words, if customers contribute effort, time, or other resources to the service production process, they should be considered as part of the organization. (Later in the chapter we will devote a section to defining customers' jobs and strategies for managing them effectively.)

Customer inputs can affect the organization's productivity through both the quality of what they contribute and the resulting quality and quantity of output generated. For example, in contributing information and effort in the preparation of their tax returns, clients of a CPA firm are part of the service production process. The quality of the information they provide ultimately affects the quality of the tax return. And, if they provide information in a useful form, the accountant will spend less time preparing the return, thus allowing him to produce more returns in a given time. The contributions of the client thus enhance the overall productivity of the firm in both quality and quantity of service. In a different context, Southwest Airlines depends on customers to perform critical service roles for themselves, thus increasing the overall productivity of the airline. Passengers are asked to carry their own bags when transferring to other airlines, get their own food, and seat themselves.

Customer participation in service production raises a number of issues for organizations. Because customers can influence both the quality and quantity of production, some experts believe the delivery system should be isolated as much as possible from customer inputs in order to reduce the uncertainty they can bring into the production process. This view sees customers as a major source of uncertainty—the timing of their demands, and the uncontrollability of their attitudes and actions. The logical conclusion is that any service activities that do not require customer contact or involvement should be performed away from customers—the less direct contact there is between the customer and the service production system, the greater the potential for the system to operate at peak efficiency.[6] The introduction of ATM machines and automated customer service telephone lines in the banking industry are both examples of ways to reduce direct customer contact in that industry, resulting in greater efficiencies and reduced costs. Other routine banking tasks that employees used to perform in full view of customers have also been removed to back-office locations, out of sight of customers.

Other experts believe that services can be delivered most efficiently if customers are truly viewed as partial employees and their participative roles are designed to maximize their contributions to the service creation process. The logic in this case is that organizational productivity can be increased if customers learn to perform service-related activities they currently are not doing or are educated to perform more effectively the tasks they are already doing.[7]

For example, when self-service gasoline stations first came into being, customers were asked to pump their own gas. By having customers perform this task, fewer employees were needed and the overall productivity of gas stations improved. Now many gas stations offer customers the option of paying for their gas at the pump by popping their credit card into a slot on the pump, punching a few buttons, and leaving the station without dealing directly with a cashier. This option is popular with customers because it gets them out of the station quickly, and also enhances productivity for the company by reducing reliance on cashiers. Interestingly, because of the resulting shorter lines at the cashier, some gas stations have also found that their sales of beer, soda, snacks, and other store items have actually increased.[8] Automated checkout counters and self-scanning of items are innovations evolving within the grocery industry. With this approach, customers can scan their own groceries using a hand-held scanner and then take the bill to a cashier's station to pay. This increases organizational productivity by using the customer as a resource.[9]

Customers as Contributors to Service Quality, Value, and Satisfaction

Another role customers can play in services delivery is that of contributor to their own satisfaction and the ultimate quality of the services they receive. Customers may care little that they have increased the productivity of the organization through their participation, but they likely care a great deal about whether their needs are fulfilled. Effective customer participation can increase the likelihood that needs are met and that the benefits the customer seeks are actually attained. Think about services such as health care, education, personal fitness, and weight loss, where the service outcome is highly dependent on customer participation. In these cases, unless the customer performs her role effectively, the desired service outcome is not possible. Research has shown that in education, active participation by students—as opposed to passive listening—increases learning (the desired service outcome) significantly.[10] The same is true in health care, where patient compliance in terms of taking prescribed medications or changing diet or other habits can be critical to whether the patient regains her health (the desired service outcome). In both of these examples, the customers contribute directly to the quality of the outcome and to their own satisfaction with the service.

Research suggests that customers who believe they have done their part to be effective in service interactions are more satisfied with the service. In a study done in the banking industry, bank customers were asked to rate themselves (on a scale from "strongly agree" to "strongly disagree") on questions related to their contributions to service delivery, as follows:

What they did—technical quality of customer inputs
I clearly explained what I wanted the bank employee to do.
I gave the bank employee proper information.
I tried to cooperate with the bank employee.
I understand the procedures associated with this service.
How they did it—functional quality of customer inputs
I was friendly to the bank employee.
I have a good relationship with the bank employee.
I was courteous to the bank employee.
Receiving this service was a pleasant experience.

Results of the study indicated that the customers' perceptions of both what they did and how they did it were significantly related to customers' satisfaction with the service they received from the bank.[11] That is, those customers who responded more positively to the questions were also more satisfied with the bank.

Customers contribute to quality service delivery when they ask questions, take responsibility for their own satisfaction, and complain when there is a service failure. Consider the service scenarios shown in Box 13-1.[12] The four scenarios illustrate the wide variations in customer participation that can result in equally wide variations in service quality and customer satisfaction. Customers who take responsibility, and providers who encourage their customers to become their partners in identifying and satisfying their own needs, will together produce higher levels of service quality. Our opening example of Sweden's IKEA, the world's largest retailer of home furnishings, shows how that company has creatively engaged its customers in a new role: "IKEA wants its customers to understand that their role is not to *consume* value but to *create* it."[13] The company relies on its customers to be IKEA's partners in creating value for themselves.

In addition to contributing to their own satisfaction by improving the quality of service delivered to them, some customers simply enjoy participating in service delivery. These customers find the act of participating to be intrinsically attractive.[14] They enjoy using the computer to attain airline tickets, or they may like to do all of their banking via ATMs and automated phone systems, or to pump their own gas. Often customers who like self-service in one setting (e.g., pumping their own gas) are predisposed to serving

---

BOX 13-1

HOW CUSTOMERS CONTRIBUTE TO QUALITY AND VALUE

For each scenario, ask "Which customer (A or B) will be most satisfied and receive the greatest quality and value, and why?"

Scenario 1: A major international hotel. *Guest A* called the desk right after check-in to report that his TV was not working and that the light over the bed was burned out; both problems were fixed immediately. The hotel staff exchanged his TV for one that worked and fixed the light bulb. Later they brought him a fruit plate to make up for the inconvenience. *Guest B* did not communicate to management until checkout time that his TV did not work and he could not read in his bed. His complaints were overheard by guests checking in who wondered whether they had chosen the right place to stay.

Scenario 2: Office of a professional tax preparer. *Client A* has organized into categories the information necessary to do her taxes and has provided all documents requested by the accountant. *Client B* has a box full of papers and receipts, many of which are not rele-

vant to her taxes but which she brought along "just in case."

Scenario 3: An airline flight from London to New York. *Passenger A* arrives for the flight with a portable tape player and reading material and wearing warm clothes; passenger A also called ahead to order a special meal. *Passenger B,* who arrives empty-handed, becomes annoyed when the crew runs out of blankets, complains about the magazine selection and the meal, and starts fidgeting after the movie.

Scenario 4: Architectural consultation for remodeling an office building. *Client A* has invited the architects to meet with its remodeling and design committee made up of managers, staff, and customers in order to lay the groundwork for a major remodeling job that will affect everyone who works in the building as well as customers. The committee has already formulated initial ideas and surveyed staff and customers for input. *Client B* has invited architects in following a decision the week previously to remodel the building; the design committee is two managers who are preoccupied with other more immediate tasks and have little idea what they need or what customers and staff would prefer in terms of a redesign of the office space.

---

themselves in other settings as well (e.g., carrying their own bags onto the aircraft, using the self-service vending machines as opposed to room service, purchasing travelers checks through an ATM).[15] In some cases there is a price discount advantage for self-service, but other times customers are motivated by convenience and a sense of greater control over the service outcome and timing of delivery.

Interestingly, because service customers must participate in service deliver, they frequently blame themselves (at least partially) when things go wrong. Why did it take so long to reach an accurate diagnosis of my health problem? Why was the service contract for our company's cafeteria food service full of errors? Why was the room we reserved for our meeting unavailable when we arrived? If customers believe they are partially (or totally) to blame for the failure, they will be less dissatisfied with the service provider than when they believe the provider is responsible and could have avoided the problem.[16]

Customers as Competitors

A final role played by service customers is that of potential competitors. If self-service customers can be viewed as resources of the firm, or as "partial employees," self-service customers could in some cases partially perform the service or perform the entire service for themselves and not need the provider at all. Customers thus in a sense are competitors of the companies that supply the service. Whether to produce a service for themselves (internal exchange), for example, child care, home maintenance, car repair, or have someone else provide the service for them (external exchange) is a common dilemma for consumers.[17]

Similar internal versus external exchange decisions are made by organizations. Firms frequently choose to outsource service activities such as payroll, data processing, research, accounting, maintenance, and facilities management. They find that it is advantageous to focus on their core businesses and leave these essential support services to others with greater expertise. For example, Continental Bank Corporation has contracted with other companies to provide its legal, audit, cafeteria, and mailroom services.[18] Alternatively, a firm may decide to stop purchasing services externally and bring the service production process in-house.

Whether a household or a firm chooses to produce a particular service for itself or contract externally for the service depends on a variety of factors. A proposed model of internal/external exchange suggests that such decisions depend on[19]:

Expertise Capacity: The likelihood of producing the service internally is increased if the household or firm possesses the specific skills and knowledge needed to produce it. Having the expertise will not necessarily result in internal service production, however, since other factors (e.g., available resources, and time) will also influence the decision. (For firms, making the decision to outsource is often based on recognizing that although they may have the expertise, someone else can do it better.)

Resource Capacity: To decide to produce a service internally, the household or firm must have the needed resources including people, space, money, and materials. If the resources are not available internally, external exchange is more likely.

Time Capacity: Time is a critical factor in internal/external exchange decisions. Households and firms with adequate time capacity are more likely to produce services internally than are groups with time constraints.

Economic Rewards: The economic advantages or disadvantages of a particular exchange decision will be influential in choosing between internal and external options. The actual monetary costs of the two options will be factors that sway the decision.

Psychic Rewards: Rewards of a noneconomic nature have a potentially strong influence on exchange decisions. Psychic rewards include the degree of satisfaction, enjoyment, gratification, or happiness that is associated with the external or internal exchange.

Trust: In this context trust means the degree of confidence or certainty the household or firm has in the various exchange options. The decision will depend to some extent on the level of self-trust versus trust of others in the particular context.

Control: The household or firm's desire for control over the process and outcome of the exchange will also influence the internal/external choice. Entities that desire and can implement a high degree of control over the task are more likely to engage in internal exchange.

The important thing to remember from this section is that in many service scenarios customers can and do choose to fully or partially produce the service themselves. Thus, in addition to recognizing that customers can be productive resources and cocreators of quality and value, organizations also need to recognize the customer's role as a potential competitor.

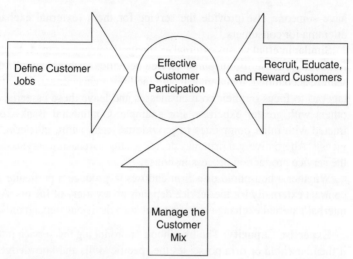

FIGURE 13-5   Strategies for enhancing customer participation.

STRATEGIES FOR ENHANCING CUSTOMER PARTICIPATION

From the preceding discussion it is clear that the level and nature of customer participation in the service process are strategic decisions that can impact an organization's productivity, its positioning relative to competitors, its service quality, and its customers' satisfaction. In the following sections we'll examine the strategies captured in Figure 13-5 for involving customers effectively in the service delivery process. The overall goals of a customer participation strategy will typically be to increase productivity and customer satisfaction while simultaneously decreasing uncertainty due to unpredictable customer actions.

Define Customers' Jobs

In developing strategies for addressing customer involvement in service delivery, the organization first determines what type of participation it wants from customers, thus beginning to define the customer's "job." Identifying the current level of customer participation can serve as a starting point. Customers' roles may be partially predetermined by the nature of the service, as suggested earlier in Table 13-1. It may be that the service requires only the customer's presence (e.g., a concert, airline travel), or it may require moderate levels of input from the customer in the form of effort or information (e.g., haircut, tax preparation), or it may require the customer to actually cocreate the service outcome (e.g., fitness training, marriage counseling).

The organization may decide that it is satisfied with the existing level of participation it requires from customers but wants to make the participation more effective. For example, Charles Schwab has always positioned itself as a company whose customers are highly involved in their personal investment decisions. Over time this position has been implemented in different ways. Currently the company's positioning tag line, "Helping Investors Help Themselves," is epitomized in its StreetSmart software that allows customers to do all their own investing and trading via computer. Advances in technology have allowed Charles Schwab to solidify its position as *the* investment company for independent investors, as shown in the Technology Spotlight.

Alternatively, the organization may choose to increase the level of customer participation, which may reposition the service in the customer's eyes. Experts have suggested that higher levels of customer participation are strategically advisable when: service production and delivery are inseparable; marketing benefits (cross-selling, building loyalty) can be enhanced by on-site contact with the customer; customers can supplement for the labor and information provided by employees.[20]

In health care, researchers and providers are working on ways to gain more active customer participation in treatment decisions. By viewing videotapes that combine scientific data, candid patient interviews, and descriptions of the risks and benefits of different treatment options, patients can be better educated and able to participate in their own treatment decisions. By actively involving patients in treatment decisions and other issues relevant to their own health, a particular health care organization (or perhaps eventually the whole industry) might reposition itself and in effect "democratize the doctor-patient relationship."[21] In addition to causing a shift in the roles of patients and providers, videos and other similar practices could have a profound effect on the industry. At Kaiser Permanente Medical Group in Denver, the rate of prostate surgery among its members plunged 44 percent in the first year after doctors began showing patients a video on benign prostate disease. The video made patients more aware of alternative treatments and the pros and cons of surgery. At Group Health of Puget Sound, a health maintenance organization in Washington state, surgery rates dropped 60 percent after patients viewed the prostate disease video.[22]

Finally, the organization may decide it wants to reduce customer participation due to all the uncertainties it causes. In such situations the strategy may be to isolate all but the essential tasks, keeping customers away from the service facility and employees as much as possible.[23] Mail order is an extreme example of this form of service. Customers are in contact with the organization by telephone, never see the organization's facility, and have limited employee interactions. The customer's role is thus extremely limited and can interfere very little with the service delivery process.

Once the desired level of participation is clear, the organization can define more specifically what the customer's "job" entails.[24] The customer's "job description" will vary with the type of service and the organization's desired position within its industry.

The Customer's Job: Helping Himself   In many cases the organization may decide to increase the level of customer involvement in service delivery through active participation. In such situations the customer becomes a productive resource, performing aspects of the service heretofore performed by employees or others. Many of the examples presented in this chapter are illustrations of customers "helping themselves" (e.g., IKEA of Sweden, Charles Schwab, Kaiser Permanente, Group Health of Puget Sound). In each of these cases, the customer has particular tasks that must be performed

TECHNOLOGY SPOTLIGHT

AT CHARLES SCHWAB INVESTORS WATCH THE MARKET THEMSELVES

Charles Schwab & Co. relies on technology to make its services totally accessible to its customers. Through StreetSmart, its trademarked investing software for Windows, Charles Schwab customers are able to: watch the market, review their portfolios, buy and sell, get real-time quotes, and read analysts' opinions. In a real sense, customers are acting as their own broker, essentially producing the service for themselves. The software epitomizes the company's positioning tag line, "Helping Investors Help Themselves," by involving customers in the production of the service and giving them a large degree of control over quality and their own satisfaction.

to fulfill his or her role. The result may be increased productivity for the firm and/or increased value, quality, and satisfaction for the customer.

The Customer's Job: Helping Others   Sometimes the customer may be called on to help others who are experiencing the service. A child at a day care center might be appointed "buddy of the day" to help a new child acclimate into the environment. Long-time residents of retirement communities often assume comparable roles to welcome new residents. Many universities have established mentoring programs, particularly for students from minority groups, in which experienced students with similar backgrounds help newcomers adjust and learn the system. Many membership organizations (e.g., health clubs, churches, social organizations) also rely heavily, although often informally, on current members to help orient new members and make them feel welcome. In performing these types of roles, customers are again performing productive functions for the organization, increasing customer satisfaction and retention. Acting as a mentor or facilitator can have very positive effects on the person performing the role and is likely to increase his or her loyalty as well.

The Customer's Job: Promoting the Company   In some cases the customer's job may include a sales or promotional element. As you know from previous chapters, service customers rely heavily on word-of-mouth endorsements in deciding which providers to try. They are more comfortable getting a recommendation from someone who has actually experienced the service than from advertising alone. A positive recommendation from a friend, relative, colleague, or even an acquaintance can pave the way for a positive service experience. Many service organizations have been very imaginative in getting their current customers to work as promoters or salespeople, as shown in Exhibit 13-1.

Individual Differences: Not Everyone Wants to Participate   In defining customers' jobs it is important to remember that not everyone will want to participate.[25] Some customer segments enjoy self-service, whereas others prefer to have the service performed entirely for them. In banking, one customer may prefer that a human teller complete all of her transactions, whereas another much prefers the ATM and automated banking via touch-tone phone. Companies that provide education and training services

---

EXHIBIT 13-1   CUSTOMERS AS SERVICE PROMOTERS

Organizations often encourage their customers to help promote the organization's services through word of mouth. Here we share a variety of examples from different industry contexts:

A *dental practice* encourages referrals by sending flowers, candy, or tickets to a local sports event to its patients whose names appear frequently in their "who referred you?" data base.

A *bowling alley* holds a drawing for one of its regular patrons. The person whose name is drawn is given a party at the bowling alley to which he or she can invite friends for free bowling. This effectively creates a "word-of-mouth champion" who brings new people into the establishment.

A *chiropractor* gives a free next exam to people who refer new patients. Patients who make referrals have their names listed on a board in office waiting area.

To increase membership, a *credit union* published a member referral coupon in its newsletter. Those who referred new members were then given $5.

A *credit card* that gives customers frequent flyer points every time they use their credit card, offers 10,000 free miles to those who can solicit a new credit card customer.

A *nightclub* holds regular drawings (using business cards left by its patrons). Those whose names are drawn get a free party (no entry charge) for as many of their friends as they want to invite.

An express *contact lens company* asks patrons to list friends' names on a card. For each friend who buys, the original patron gets $15 or a free pair of disposable contacts.

to organizations know that there are some customers who want to be involved in designing the training and perhaps in delivering it to their employees. Other companies want to hand over the entire training design and delivery to the consulting organization, staying at arms length with little of their own time and energy invested in the service. In health care, it is clear that some patients want lots of information and want to be involved in their own diagnosis and treatment decisions. Others simply want the doctor to tell them what to do.

Often an organization can customize its services to fit the needs of these different segments—those who want to participate and those who prefer little involvement. Banks typically do this by offering both automated self-service options and high-touch, human delivery options. At other times, as in the case of Charles Schwab in our Technology Spotlight or IKEA in our chapter opening example, the organization can effectively position itself to specifically serve only segments of customers who want to participate by designing its services to require customer independence and involvement.

Recruit, Educate, and Reward Customers

Once the customer's role is clearly defined, the organization can think in terms of facilitating that role. In a sense, the customer becomes a "partial employee" of the organization at some level, and strategies for managing customer behavior in service production and delivery can mimic to some degree the efforts aimed at service employees discussed in chapter 11. General models of employee behavior suggest that behavior is determined by role clarity, ability to perform, and motivation to perform. Similarly, customer behavior in a service production and delivery situation will be facilitated when (1) customers understand their roles and how they are expected to perform, (2) customers are able to perform as expected, and (3) there are valued rewards for performing as expected.[26] Through these means, the organization will also reduce the inherent uncertainty associated with the unpredictable quality and timing of customer participation.

Recruit the Right Customers Before the company begins the process of educating and socializing customers for their roles, it must attract the right customers to fill those roles. The organization should seek to attract customers who will be comfortable with the roles. To do this, it should clearly communicate the expected roles and responsibilities in advertising, personal selling, and other company messages. By previewing their roles and what is required of them in the service process, customers can self-select into (or out of) the relationship. Self-selection should result in enhanced perceptions of service quality from the customer's point of view and reduced uncertainty for the organization.

To illustrate, a child care center that requires parent participation on the site at least one-half day per week needs to communicate that expectation before it enrolls any child in its program. For some families, this level of participation will not be possible or desirable, thus precluding them from enrolling in the center. Another center could choose to have a variety of options available for families ranging from no on-site participation to daily participation. Whatever the case, the expected level of participation needs to be communicated clearly in order to attract customers who are ready and willing to perform their roles. In a sense this is similar to a manufacturing firm exercising control over the quality of inputs into the production process.[27]

Educate and Train Customers to Perform Effectively   Customers need to be educated, or in essence "socialized" so that they can perform their roles effectively. Through the socialization process, it is possible for service customers to gain an appreciation of specific organizational values, develop the abilities necessary to function within a specific context, understand what is expected of them, and acquire the skills and knowledge to interact with employees and other customers.[28] Customer education programs can take the form of formal orientation programs, written literature provided to customers, directional cues and signage in the service environment, and learning from employees and other customers. Each of these forms of education are discussed further in the following paragraphs.

Many services offer "customer orientation" programs to assist customers in understanding their roles and what to expect from the process before experiencing it. Universities offer orientation programs for new students, and often for their parents as well, to preview the culture, university procedures, and expectations of students. Similarly, health clubs use formal training programs to educate customers on how to use the facilities and equipment. When customers begin the Weight Watchers program their first group meeting includes a thorough orientation to the program and their responsibilities, as described in Box 13-2.

In a mammography screen context, research has found that orientation and formal education of customers can relieve customer fears and perceptions of risk and ultimately increase customer satisfaction (see Box 13-3).

Customer education can also be partially accomplished through written literature and customer "handbooks" that describe customers' roles and responsibilities. Many hospitals have developed patient handbooks, very similar in appearance to employee hand-

---

BOX 13-2

WEIGHT WATCHERS EDUCATES AND ORIENTS NEW MEMBERS

When new members first join Weight Watchers, one of the largest and most successful commercial weight-loss organizations in the world, they are thoroughly educated regarding the program and their responsibilities. For example, when a new member attends her first meeting at a local chapter of Weight Watchers of Arizona, she watches a video that tells about the program and reviews how the food plan works. New members are also given a booklet entitled "Welcome to Weight Watchers" that covers topics such as: *Welcome to Weight Watchers, Weight Loss Consumer Bill of Rights, Here Are the Facts, What Should I Know Before I Begin the Program?,* *Important Health Notices, How Do I Qualify for Weight Watchers Membership?, What Can I Expect from the Weight Watchers Program?, Nutritional Content of the Food Plan, Activity Plan, Behavioral Support, Maintenance Plan,* and others. In addition to the video, the booklet, and a discussion of all topics led by the group leader, the new member also receives a "Program Planner and Tracker." This form is used by the member to record daily food selections and physical activity. Weight Watchers knows that its business can succeed only if members do their part in following the weight-loss plan. Through the orientation, the booklets, and the food and activity forms, the organization clearly defines the member's responsibilities and makes the plan as easy as possible to follow.

BOX 13-3

REALISTIC SERVICE PREVIEWS REDUCE CUSTOMER ANXIETY AND IMPROVE SATISFACTION

Research in a mammography screening context found that if potential patients are oriented through a realistic preview of the process, patient anxiety is reduced and ultimate satisfaction increased. An experiment was conducted that involved 134 women who had never experienced a mammogram and who had little knowledge about the procedure. Half of the women were given a realistic preview of the process, while the others received no preview. The preview consisted of written information about mammography including sections on: what is a mammogram, how the procedure works, instructions to follow before mammography, what happens during mammography, after the examination, the role of mammography, and some common misconceptions. The realistic preview also included a seven-minute videotape illustrating the entire procedure. The written materials and the videotape both helped to dispel overly pessimistic expectations as well as to guard against overly positive ideas the potential patients may have had.

After the preview (or no preview), women in the experiment answered questions that assessed the accuracy of their expectations, their sense of control, and their level of anxiety relative to mammography. The women then read one of three versions of an actual mammography experience and were asked to imagine themselves as the woman in the story. One version of the story followed the realistic preview exactly, another version included several blunders on the part of the fictitious provider, and the final version enhanced the service experience, making it even better than the realistic preview. After reading the story, and imagining that the events had actually happened to them, the women responded to questions regarding their satisfaction with the mammography screening process.

Results of the study showed that those women who had been oriented through the realistic preview did indeed have more realistic and accurate expectations for the mammography experience than did those who had no preview. Second, the women who saw the preview reported significantly less anxiety and significantly greater perceptions of control over the process than did women who had no preview. Finally, across all of the different scenarios, women who received the preview were more satisfied with the actual service experience. The realistic preview thus affected potential mammography patients' preservice feelings (anxiety and control), as well as their satisfaction with the service.

Source: William T. Faranda, "Customer Participation in Service Production: An Empirical Assessment of the Influence of Realistic Service Previews," doctoral dissertation, Arizona State University, Tempe, Arizona, 1994.

books, to describe what the patient should do in preparation for arrival at the hospital, what will happen when he or she arrives, and policies regarding visiting hours and billing procedures. The handbook may even describe the roles and responsibilities of family members.

While formal training and written information are usually provided in advance of the service experience, other strategies can be employed for continuing the customer socialization process during the experience itself. On site, customers require two kinds of orientation: *"place orientation"* ("where am I?" and "how do I get from here to there?"), and *"function orientation"* ("how does this organization work?" and "what am I supposed to do?").[29] Signage, the layout of the service facility, and other orientation aids can help customers to answer these questions, allowing them to perform their roles more effectively. No doubt you have had the experience of deplaning in an unfamiliar airport where signage is poor and you are frustrated by your inability to get to baggage claim or a connecting gate. On the other hand, an airport with large, easily read signage and well-designed foot traffic patterns can allow you to perform your role with ease, increasing your satisfaction with the experience. Orientation aids can also take the form of rules that define customer behavior for safety (airlines, health clubs), for appropriate dress (restaurants, entertainment venues), and noise levels (hotels, classrooms, theaters). Before showing a movie, many theaters now flash a sign on the screen that says "Please, no talking, or crying babies."

Customers are also socialized to their expected roles through information provided by employees and by observing other customers. It has been said that when McDonalds first went to England, the British customers were not accustomed to bussing their own trays. They quickly learned, however, by observing the customers McDonalds had hired to "demonstrate" appropriate bussing behavior. These customers were hired to sit in the restaurants and at predictable intervals to carry a dirty tray over to the trash can and dispose of it.

Reward Customers for Their Contributions   Customers are more likely to perform their roles effectively, or to participate actively, if they are rewarded for doing so. Rewards are likely to come in the form of increased control over the delivery process, time savings, monetary savings, and psychological or physical benefits. For instance, some CPA firms provide clients with extensive forms to complete before they meet with their accountant. If the forms are completed, the CPA will have less work to do and the client will be rewarded with fewer billable hours. Those clients who choose not to perform the requested role will pay a higher price for the service. ATM customers who perform banking services for themselves are also rewarded, through greater access to their bank, both in terms of locations and times. In health care contexts, patients who perform their roles effectively are likely to be rewarded with better health or quicker recovery.

Customers may not realize the benefits or rewards of effective participation unless the organization makes the benefits apparent to them. In other words, the organization needs to clarify the performance-contingent benefits that can accrue to customers just as it defines these types of benefits to employees. The organization also should recognize that not all customers are motivated by the same types of rewards. Some may value the increased access and time savings they can gain by performing their service roles effectively. Others may value the monetary savings. Still others may be looking for greater personal control over the service outcome.

Avoid Negative Outcomes of Inappropriate Customer Participation   If customers are not effectively socialized, the organization runs the risk that inappropriate customer behaviors will result in negative outcomes:[30]

1 Customers who do not understand the service system or the process of delivery may slow down the service process and negatively affect their own as well as other customers' outcomes. In a rental car context, customers who do not understand the reservation process, the information needed from them, insurance coverage issues, and the pick-up and drop-off procedures can slow the flow for employees and other customers, negatively affecting both productivity and quality of service.

2 If customers don't perform their roles effectively, it may not be possible for employees to provide the levels of technical and process quality promised by the organization. For example, in a management consulting practice, clients who do not provide the level of information and cooperation needed by the consultants will likely receive inferior service both in terms of the usefulness of the management report and the timeliness of the delivery.

3 If customers are frustrated because of their own inadequacies and incompetencies, employees are likely to suffer emotionally and be less able to deliver quality service. For example, if customers routinely enter the service delivery process with little knowledge of how the system works and their role in it, they are likely to take out their frustrations on front-line employees. This negative impact on individual employees can take its toll on the organization in the form of turnover and decreased motivation to serve.

Manage the Customer Mix

Because customers frequently interact with each other in the process of service delivery and consumption, another important strategic objective is the effective management of the mix of customers who simultaneously experience the service. If a restaurant chooses to serve two segments during the dinner hour that are incompatible with each other—for example, single college students who want to party and families with small children who want quiet—it may find that the two groups do not merge well. Of course it is possible to manage these segments so that they do not interact with each other by seating them in separate sections or by attracting the two segments at different times of day. Smokers and nonsmokers are often incompatible segments that a service firm must manage if it wants to serve both segments well. Major tourism attractions around the world are faced with the challenge of accommodating visitor segments who differ in the languages they speak, the foods they want to eat, their values, and their perceptions of appropriate behaviors. Sometimes these visitors can clash when they do not understand and appreciate each other.

The process of managing multiple and sometimes conflicting segments is known as *compatibility management,* broadly defined as *"a process of first attracting homogeneous consumers to the service environment, then actively managing both the physical environment and customer-to-customer encounters in such a way as to enhance satisfying encounters and minimize dissatisfying encounters."*[31] Compatibility management will be critically important for some businesses (e.g., health clubs, public transportation, hospitals) and less important for others. Table 13-2 lists seven interrelated characteristics of service businesses that will increase the importance of compatibility management.

To manage multiple (and sometimes conflicting) segments, organizations rely on a variety of strategies. Attracting maximally homogeneous groups of customers through careful positioning and segmentation strategies is one approach. This is the strategy used by the Ritz Carlton Hotel Company, for which upscale travelers are the primary target segment. The Ritz Carlton is positioned to communicate that message to the marketplace, and customers self-select into the hotel. However, even in that context there are potential conflicts, for example when the hotel is simultaneously hosting a large business convention and serving individual business travelers. A second strategy is often used in such cases. Compatible customers are grouped together physically so that the

TABLE 13-2 CHARACTERISTICS OF SERVICE THAT INCREASE THE IMPORTANCE OF COMPATIBLE SEGMENTS

Characteristic	Explanation	Examples
Customers are in close physical proximity to each other.	Customers will more often notice each other and be influenced by each other's behavior when they are in close physical proximity.	Airplane flights Entertainment events Sports events
There is verbal interaction among customers.	Conversation (or lack thereof) can be a component of both satisfying and dissatisfying encounters with fellow patrons.	Full service restaurants Cocktail lounges Educational settings
Customers are engaged in numerous and varied activities.	When a service facility supports varied activities all going on at the same time, the activities themselves may not be compatible.	Libraries Health clubs Resort hotels
The service environment attracts a heterogeneous customer mix.	Many service environments, particularly those open to the public, will attract a variety of customer segments.	Public parks Public transportation Open-enrollment colleges
The core service is compatibility.	The core service is to arrange and nurture compatible relationships between customers.	Big Brothers/Big Sisters Weight-loss group programs Mental health support groups
Customers must occasionally wait for the service.	Waiting in line for service can be monotonous or anxiety producing. The boredom or stress can be magnified or lessened by other customers depending on their compatibility.	Medical clinics Tourist attractions Restaurants
Customers are expected to share time, space, or service utensils with each other.	The need to share space, time, and other service factors is common in many services, but may become a problem if segments are not comfortable with sharing or with each other or when the need to share is intensified due to capacity constraints.	Golf courses Hospitals Retirement communities Airplanes

Source: Adapted from Martin and Pranter, "Compatibility Management."

segments are less likely to interact directly with each other. The Ritz Carlton keeps meetings and large group events separated from the areas of the hotel used by individual business people. As much as possible, sleeping rooms can be assigned on the same basis.

Other strategies for enhancing customer compatibility include customer "codes of conduct" such as the regulation of smoking behavior and dress codes. Clearly such codes of conduct may vary from one service establishment to another. Finally, training employees to observe customer-to-customer interactions and to be sensitive to potential conflicts is another strategy for increasing compatibility among segments. Employees can also be trained to recognize opportunities to foster positive encounters among customers in certain types of service environments.

SUMMARY

This chapter has focused on the role of customers in service delivery. The customer receiving the service and the other customers in the service environment can all potentially cause a widening of GAP 3 if they fail to perform their roles effectively. Figure 13-2 suggested a number of reasons why customers may cause a widening of the service delivery gap: customers lack understanding of their roles; customers are unwilling or unable to perform their roles; customers are not rewarded for good performance; other customers interfere; market segments are incompatible.

The challenge of managing customers in the process of service delivery is unique to service firms. While manufacturers are not concerned with customer participation in the manufacturing process, service managers are constantly faced with this issue, for their customers are often present and active partners in service production. As participants in service production and delivery, customers can perform three primary roles, discussed and illustrated in the chapter. They can be: *productive resources* for the organization; *contributors* to service quality, satisfaction, and value; *competitors* in performing the service for themselves.

Through understanding the importance of customers in service delivery and identifying the roles being played by the customer in a particular context, managers can develop strategies to enhance customer participation. Strategies discussed in the text include: defining the customers' roles and jobs; recruiting customers who match the customer profile in terms of desired level of participation; educating customers so they are able to perform their roles effectively; rewarding customers for their contributions; and managing the customer mix to enhance the experiences of all segments. By implementing these strategies, organizations should see a reduction in GAP 3 due to effective and efficient customer contributions to service delivery.

DISCUSSION QUESTIONS

1 Discuss the general importance of customers in the successful delivery of service using your own personal examples.

2 Why might customer actions and attitudes cause GAP 3 to occur? Use your own examples to illustrate your understanding.

3 Use the elements of the drama metaphor (actors, audience, setting) to describe airline services. What insights can you gain by thinking of the service in this way?

4 Using Table 13-1, think of specific services you have experienced that fall within each of the three levels of customer participation: low, medium, high. Describe specifically what you did as a customer in each case. How did your involvement vary across the three types of service situations?

5 Describe a time when your satisfaction in a particular situation was *increased* because of something another customer did. Could (or does) the organization do anything to ensure that this happens routinely? What do they do? Should they try to make this a routine occurrence?

6 Describe a time when your satisfaction in a particular situation was *decreased* because of something another customer did. Could the organization have done anything to manage this situation more effectively? What?

7 Discuss the customer's role as a *productive resource* for the firm. Describe a time when

you played this role. What did you do and how did you feel? Did the firm help you to perform your role effectively? How?

8 Discuss the customer's role as a *contributor to service quality, satisfaction, and value.* Describe a time when you played this role. What did you do and how did you feel? Did the firm help you to perform your role effectively? How?

9 Discuss the customer's role as a potential *competitor.* Describe a time when you chose to provide a service for yourself rather than pay someone to provide the service for you. Why did you decide to perform the service yourself? What could have changed your mind, causing you to contract with someone else to provide the service?

EXERCISES

1 Visit a service establishment where customers can influence each other (e.g., a theme park, entertainment establishment, resort, shopping mall, restaurant, airline, school, hospital). Observe (or interview) customers and record cases of positive and negative customer influence. Discuss how you would manage the situation to increase overall customer satisfaction.

2 Interview someone regarding his or her decision to outsource a service, for example, legal services, payroll, maintenance in a company; cleaning, child care, pet care in a household. Use the criteria for internal v. external exchange described in the text to analyze the decisions to outsource.

3 Think of a service where a high level of customer participation is necessary for the service to be successful (e.g., health club, weight loss, educational setting, health care, golf lessons). Interview a service provider in such an organization to find out what strategies the provider uses to encourage effective customer participation.

4 Visit a service setting where multiple types of customer segments use the service at the same time. Observe (or interview the manager about) the organization's strategies to manage these segments effectively. Would you do anything differently if you were in charge?

NOTES

1 The information on IKEA was reported in Richard Normann and Rafael Ramirez, "From Value Chain to Value Constellation: Designing Interactive Strategy," *Harvard Business Review,* July–August 1993, pp. 65–77.

2 Peter K. Mills and James H. Morris, "Clients as 'Partial' Employees: Role Development in Client Participation," *Academy of Management Review* 11, 4 (1986): 726–735; Christopher H. Lovelock and Robert F. Young, "Look to Customers to Increase Productivity," *Harvard Business Review,* Summer 1979, pp. 9–20.

3 Stephen J. Grove, Raymond P. Fisk, and Mary Jo Bitner, "Dramatizing the Service Experience: A Managerial Approach," in *Advances in Services Marketing and Management,* eds. Teresa A. Swartz, David E. Bowen, and Stephen W. Brown, Vol. 1 (Greenwich, Conn.: JAI Press, 1992), pp. 91–122.

4 Charles I. Martin and Charles A. Pranter, "Compatibility Management: Customer-to-Customer Relationships in Service Environments," *Journal of Services Marketing* 3, 3 (Summer 1989): 5–15.

5 See Peter K. Mills, Richard B. Chase, and Newton Margulies, "Motivating the Client/Employee System as a Service Production Strategy," *Academy of Management Review* 8, 2 (1983): 301–310; David E. Bowen, "Managing Customers as Human Re-

sources in Service Organizations," *Human Resource Management* 25, 3 (1986): 371–383; and Mills and Morris, "Clients as 'Partial' Employees."

6 Richard B. Chase, "Where Does the Customer Fit in a Service Operation," *Harvard Business Review* November–December 1978, pp. 137–142.

7 Mills, Chase, and Margulies, "Motivating the Client/Employee System."

8 Caleb Solomon, "Self-Service at Gas Stations Includes Paying," *Wall Street Journal,* August 4, 1993, p. B1.

9 "Do-It-Yourself Grocery Checkout," *Wall Street Journal,* January 30, 1994, p. B1.

10 See David W. Johnson, Roger T. Johnson, and Karl A. Smith, *Active Learning: Cooperation in the College Classroom* (Edina, Minn.: Interaction Book Company, 1991).

11 Scott W. Kelley, Steven J. Skinner, and James H. Donnelly, Jr., "Organizational Socialization of Service Customers," *Journal of Business Research* 25 (1992): 197–214.

12 Several of the scenarios are adapted from Cathy Goodwin, " 'I Can Do It Myself': Training the Service Consumer to Contribute to Service Productivity," *Journal of Services Marketing* 2, 4 (Fall 1988): 71–78.

13 Richard Normann and Rafael Ramirez, "From Value Chain to Value Constellation: Designing Interactive Strategy," *Harvard Business Review,* July–August 1993, pp. 65–77.

14 John E. G. Bateson, "The Self-Service Customer—Empirical Findings," in *Emerging Perspectives in Services Marketing,* eds. Leonard L. Berry, G. Lynn Shostack, and Gregory D. Upah (Chicago: American Marketing Association, 1983), pp. 50–53.

15 Ibid.

16 Valerie S. Folkes, "Recent Attribution Research in Consumer Behavior: A Review and New Directions," *Journal of Consumer Research* 14 (March 1988): 548–565; Mary Jo Bitner, "Evaluating Service Encounters: The Effects of Physical Surroundings and Employee Responses," *Journal of Marketing* 54 (April 1990): 69–82.

17 Robert F. Lusch, Stephen W. Brown, and Gary J. Brunswick, "A General Framework for Explaining Internal vs. External Exchange," *Journal of the Academy of Marketing Science* 10, 2 (Spring 1992): 119–134.

18 *Business Week,* special report on "Rethinking Work," October 17, 1994, pp. 74–117.

19 Lusch, Brown, and Brunswick, "A General Framework."

20 Bowen, "Managing Customers as Human Resources."

21 Ron Winslow, "Videos, Questionnaires Aim to Expand Role of Patients in Treatment Decisions," *Wall Street Journal,* February 25, 1992, p. B1.

22 Ibid.

23 Chase, "Where Does the Customer Fit."

24 The four job descriptions in this section are adapted from Michael R. Bowers, Charles L. Martin, and Alan Luker, "Trading Places, Employees as Customers, Customers as Employees," *Journal of Services Marketing* 4, (Spring 1990): 56–69.

25 Bateson, "The Self-Service Customer."

26 Bowen, "Managing Customers as Human Resources."

27 Cathy Goodwin and Russell Radford, "Models of Service Delivery: An Integrative Perspective," in *Advances in Services Marketing and Management,* eds. Swartz, Bowen and Brown, CT: pp. 231–252.

28 Scott W. Kelley, James H. Donnelly, Jr., and Steven J. Skinner, "Customer Participation in Service Production and Delivery," *Journal of Retailing* 66, 3 (Fall 1990): 315–335.

29 Bowen, "Managing Customers as Human Resources."

30 Ibid.

31 Martin and Pranter, "Compatibility Management" pp. 5–15.

14

MANAGING DEMAND AND CAPACITY

The Ritz Carlton Hotel in Phoenix, Arizona, is an upscale hotel in the center of a met-
ropolitan area of approximately two million people. The hotel has 281 luxury rooms, two
restaurants, beautiful pools, and spacious meeting and conference facilities. These
restaurants and meeting facilities are available to guests 365 days and nights of the year.
Yet natural demand for them varies tremendously. During the tourist season from No-
vember through mid-April, demand for rooms is high, often exceeding available space.
During the summer season from mid-May through September, however, when tempera-
tures regularly exceed 100 degrees Fahrenheit, demand for rooms drops considerably.
Because the hotel caters to business travelers and business meetings, demand has a
weekly cycle in addition to the seasonal fluctuations. Business travelers don't stay over
weekends. Thus, demand for rooms from the hotel's primary market segment drops pre-
cipitously on Friday and Saturday nights.

To smooth the peaks and valleys of demand for its facilities, the Ritz Carlton in
Phoenix employs a variety of strategies. Group business (primarily business confer-
ences) is pursued throughout the year to fill the lower demand periods from Thursday
through Sunday. The timing works well for many groups who can also take advantage
of the lower air fares available for staying over Saturday night. During the hot summer
months the hotel encourages local Phoenix and Tucson residents to experience the lux-
ury of the hotel on weekends by creating an attractively priced package that includes a
Friday or Saturday night stay at the hotel combined with a "progressive dinner" at
nearby restaurants. The progressive dinner starts with a reception in the hotel, a walk
to one restaurant for appetizers, followed by dinner at a second restaurant. The evening
is finished with champagne and dessert in the guests' room. By encouraging local peo-

ple to use the hotel, the hotel increases its weekend occupancy while residents of the community get a chance to enjoy an experience they probably wouldn't be able to afford during the high season.

Most downtown hotels face the same weekly demand fluctuations that the Phoenix Ritz Carlton deals with, and many have found a partial solution by catering to families and children on the weekends.[1] For many dual-career couples, weekend getaways are a primary form of relaxation and vacation. And with discounted air fares for Saturday-night stays, many families can afford to travel on weekends. The downtown hotels cater to these couples and families by offering discounted room rates, child-oriented activities and amenities, and an environment where families feel comfortable. For example, at the Costa Mesa Marriott Suites in Orange County, California, employees dress casually on the weekend and toasters are put on the breakfast buffet, just for kids. The Hyatt Regency Reston in Reston, Virginia, rents its 21 executive suites for kids' slumber parties on the weekend. The Chicago Hilton initiated a "Vacation Station" program in 1991 that includes gifts and games for kids, plenty of cribs in inventory, and gummi bears in the minibars. The result for the Chicago Hilton is that Saturday nights are usually sold out and Friday nights average 80 percent occupancy, higher than its weekday occupancy levels.

For the Ritz Carlton Hotel in Phoenix and the other hotels just mentioned, managing demand and utilizing the hotel's fixed capacity of rooms, restaurants, and meeting facilities can be a seasonal, weekly, and even daily challenge. While the hotel industry epitomizes the challenges of demand and capacity management, many service providers are faced with similar problems. For example, tax accountants and air-conditioning maintenance services face seasonal demand fluctuations, while services like commuter trains and restaurants face weekly and even hourly variations in customer demand. Sometimes there is too much demand for the existing capacity and sometimes capacity sits idle.

Overuse or underuse of a service can directly contribute to GAP 3—failure to deliver what was designed and specified (Figure 14-1). For example, when demand for services exceeds maximum capacity, the quality of service may drop because staff and facilities are overtaxed. And some customers may be turned away, not receiving the service at all. During periods of slow demand it may be necessary to reduce prices or cut service amenities, changing the makeup of the clientele and the nature of the service and thus running the risk of not delivering what customers expect. At the Chicago Hilton mentioned in the vignette, older travelers or business groups who are in the hotel on a weekend may resent the invasion of families and children because it changes the nature of the service they expected. At the pool, for example, collisions can occur between adults trying to swim laps and children playing water games.[2]

In this chapter we will focus on the challenges of matching supply and demand in capacity-constrained services. As indicated in Figure 14-2, GAP 3 can occur when organizations: fail to smooth the peaks and valleys of demand, overuse their capacities, attract an inappropriate customer mix in their efforts to build demand, or rely too much on price in smoothing demand. The chapter will give you an understanding of these issues and strategies for addressing them. The effective use of capacity is frequently a key success factor for service organizations.

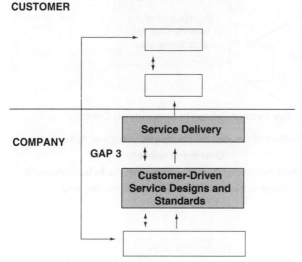

FIGURE 14-1   Provider GAP 3.

The objectives of the chapter are to:

1 Explain:

- The underlying issue for capacity-constrained services: lack of inventory capability.
- The implications of capacity constraints in the form of time, labor, equipment, and facilities.
- The implications of different types of demand patterns on matching supply and demand.

2 Lay out strategies for matching supply and demand through *(a)* shifting demand to match capacity or *(b)* flexing capacity to meet demand.

3 Demonstrate the benefits and risks of yield management strategies in forging a balance among capacity utilization, pricing, market segmentation, and financial return.

4 Provide strategies for managing waiting lines for times when capacity and demand cannot be aligned.

THE UNDERLYING ISSUE: LACK OF INVENTORY CAPABILITY

The fundamental issue underlying supply and demand management in services is the lack of inventory capability. Unlike manufacturing firms, service firms cannot build up inventories during periods of slow demand to use later when demand increases. This lack of inventory capability is due to the perishability of services and their simultaneous production and consumption. An airline seat that is not sold on a given flight cannot be resold the following day: the productive capacity of that seat has perished. Similarly, an

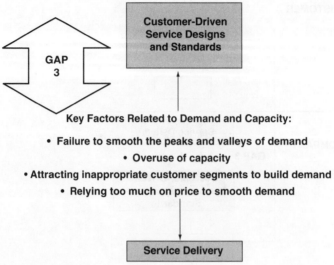

FIGURE 14-2 Key reasons for provider GAP 3.

hour of a lawyer's billable time cannot be saved from one day to the next. Services also cannot be transported from one place to another or transferred from person to person. Thus the Ritz Carlton's services cannot be moved to an alternative location in the summer months—say to the Pacific Coast where summers are ideal for tourists and demand for hotel rooms is high.

The lack of inventory capability leads to four possible scenarios at any given time (see Figure 14-3):[3]

1 Excess demand. The level of demand exceeds maximum capacity. In this situation, some customers will be turned away, resulting in lost business opportunities. For the customers who do receive the service, its quality may not match what was promised due to crowding or overtaxing of staff and facilities.

2 Demand exceeds optimum capacity. No one is being turned away but the quality of service may still suffer due to overuse, crowding, or staff being pushed beyond their abilities to deliver consistent quality.

3 Demand and supply are balanced at the level of optimum capacity. Staff and facilities are occupied at an ideal level. No one is overworked, facilities can be maintained, and customers are receiving quality service without undesirable delays.

4 Excess capacity. Demand is below optimum capacity. Productive resources in the form of labor, equipment, and facilities are underutilized, resulting in lost productivity and lower profits. Customers may receive excellent quality on an individual level because they have the full use of the facilities, no waiting, and complete attention from the staff. If, however, service quality depends on the presence of other customers, customers may be disappointed or may worry that they have chosen an inferior service provider.

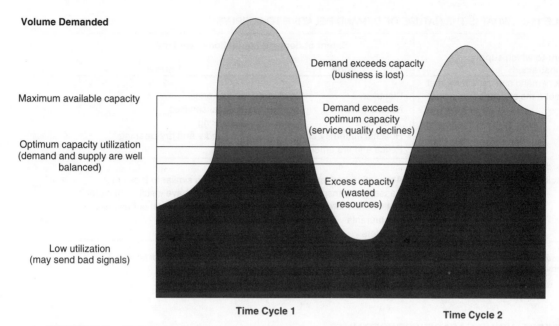

Volume Demanded

Maximum available capacity

Demand exceeds capacity
(business is lost)

Demand exceeds
optimum capacity
(service quality declines)

Optimum capacity utilization
(demand and supply are well
balanced)

Excess capacity
(wasted
resources)

Low utilization
(may send bad signals)

Time Cycle 1   **Time Cycle 2**

FIGURE 14-3   Variations in demand relative to capacity.

Source: Lovelock, "Getting the Most Out of Your Productive Capacity," p. 241.

Not all firms will be challenged equally in terms of managing supply and demand. The seriousness of the problem will depend on the *extent of demand fluctuations over time,* and the *extent to which supply is constrained* (Table 14-1).[4] Some types of organizations will experience wide fluctuations in demand (e.g., telecommunications, hospitals, transportation, restaurants) while others will have narrower fluctuations (e.g., insurance, laundry, banking). For some, peak demand can usually be met even when demand fluctuates (e.g., electricity, telephone), while for others peak demand may frequently exceed capacity (e.g., theaters, restaurants, hotels). Those firms with wide variations in demand (cells 1 and 4 in Table 14-1), and particularly those with wide fluctuations and demand that regularly exceeds capacity (cell 4), will find the issues and strategies in this chapter particularly important to their success. Those firms that find themselves in cell 3 are in need of a "one-time-fix" to expand their capacity to match regular patterns of excessive demand. The example industries in Table 14-1 are provided to illustrate where *most* firms in those industries would likely be classified. In reality, an individual firm from any industry could find itself in any of the four cells, depending on its immediate circumstances.

To identify effective strategies for managing supply and demand fluctuations, an organization needs a clear understanding of the constraints on its capacity and the underlying demand patterns.

TABLE 14-1   WHAT IS THE NATURE OF DEMAND RELATIVE TO SUPPLY?

Extent to which supply is constrained	Extent of demand fluctuations over time	
	Wide	Narrow
Peak demand can usually be met without a major delay	1 Electricity Natural gas Telephone Hospital maternity unit Police and fire emergencies	2 Insurance Legal services Banking Laundry and dry cleaning
Peak demand regularly exceeds capacity	4 Accounting and tax preparation Passenger transportation Hotels and motels Restaurants Theaters	3 Services similar to those in 2 but which have insufficient capacity for their base level of business

Source: Christopher H. Lovelock, "Classifying Services to Gain Strategic Marketing Insights," *Journal of Marketing,* 47, 3 (Summer 1983): 17.

UNDERSTANDING CAPACITY CONSTRAINTS

As we will see later in the chapter, there are some creative ways to expand and contract capacity in the short and long term, but at a given point in time we can assume service capacity is fixed. Depending on the type of service, critical fixed-capacity factors can be time, labor, equipment, facilities, or (in many cases) a combination of these.

Time, Labor, Equipment, Facilities

For some service businesses, the primary constraint on service production is *time.* For example, a lawyer, a consultant, a hairdresser, and a psychological counselor all primarily sell their time. If their time is not used productively, profits are lost. If there is excess demand, time cannot be created to satisfy it. From the point of view of the individual service provider, time is the constraint.

From the point of view of a firm that employs a large number of service providers, *labor* or staffing levels can be the primary capacity constraint. A law firm, a university department, a consulting firm, a tax accounting firm, and a repair and maintenance contractor may all face the reality that at certain times demand for their organizations' services cannot be met because the staff is already operating at peak capacity. However, it doesn't always make sense to hire additional service providers if low demand is a reality at other times.

In other cases, *equipment* may be the critical constraint. For trucking or air-freight delivery services, the trucks or airplanes needed to service demand may be the capacity limitation. During the Christmas holidays, UPS, Federal Express, and other delivery service providers are faced with this issue. Health clubs also deal with this limitation, particularly at certain times of the day (before work, during lunch hours, after work) and in certain months of the year. Telecommunication companies face equipment constraints when everyone wants to use the telephone lines during prime hours on holidays.

Finally, many service firms are faced with restrictions brought about by their limited *facilities*. Hotels have only a certain number of rooms to sell, airlines are limited by the number of seats on the aircraft, educational institutions are constrained by the number of rooms and the number of seats in each classroom, and restaurant capacity is restricted to the number of tables and seats available.

Understanding the primary capacity constraint, or the combination of factors that restricts capacity, is a first step in designing strategies to deal with supply and demand issues (Table 14-2).

Optimal versus Maximal Use of Capacity

To fully understand capacity issues, it is important to know the difference between optimal and maximal use of capacity. As suggested earlier in Figure 14-3, optimum and maximum capacity may not be the same. Using capacity at an optimum level means that resources are fully employed but not overused, and that customers are receiving quality service in a timely manner. Maximum capacity, on the other hand, represents the absolute limit of service availability. In the case of a football game, optimum and maximum capacity may be the same. The entertainment value of the game is enhanced for

TABLE 14-2   WHAT IS THE CONSTRAINT ON CAPACITY?

Nature of the constraint	Type of service*
Time	Legal Consulting Accounting Medical
Labor	Law firm Accounting firm Consulting firm Health clinic
Equipment	Delivery services Telecommunication Utilities Health club
Facilities	Hotels Restaurants Hospitals Airlines Schools Theaters Churches

*The examples illustrate the most common capacity constraint for each type of service. In reality, any of the service organizations listed can be operating under multiple constraints. For example, a law firm may be operating under constrained labor capacity (too few attorneys) and facilities constraints (not enough office space) at the same time.

customers when every single seat is filled, and obviously the profitability for the team is greatest under these circumstances. On the other hand, in a university classroom it is usually not desirable for students or faculty to have every seat filled. In this case, optimal use of capacity is less than the maximum. In some cases, maximum use of capacity may result in excessive waiting by customers, as in a popular restaurant. From the perspective of customer satisfaction, optimum use of the restaurant's capacity will again be less than maximum use.

In the case of equipment or facilities constraints, the maximum capacity at any given time is obvious. There are only a certain number of weight machines in the health club, a certain number of seats in the airplane, and a limited amount of space in a cargo carrier. In the case of a bottling plant, when maximum capacity on the assembly line is exceeded, bottles begin to break and the system shuts down. Thus, it is relatively easy to observe the effects of exceeding maximum equipment capacity.

When the limitation is people's time or labor, maximum capacity is harder to specify, since people are in a sense more flexible than facilities and equipment. When an individual service provider's maximum capacity has been exceeded, the result is likely to be decreased quality, customer dissatisfaction, and employee burnout and turnover, but these outcomes may not be immediately observable even to the employee herself. It is often easy for a consulting firm to take on one more assignment, taxing its employees beyond their maximum capacity, or for an HMO clinic to schedule a few more appointments in a day, stretching its staff and physicians beyond their maximum capacity. Given the potential costs in terms of reduced quality and customer and employee dissatisfaction, it is critical for the firm to know optimum and maximum human capacity limits.

UNDERSTANDING DEMAND PATTERNS[5]

To manage fluctuating demand in a service business, it is necessary to have a clear understanding of demand patterns, why they vary, and the market segments that comprise demand at different points in time. A number of questions need to be answered regarding the predictability and underlying causes of demand.

Charting Demand Patterns

First, the organization needs to chart the level of demand over relevant time periods. Organizations that have good computerized customer information systems can do this very accurately. Others may need to chart demand patterns more informally. Daily, weekly, and monthly demand levels should be followed, and if seasonality is a suspected problem, graphing should be done for data from at least the past year. In some services, such as restaurants or health care, hourly fluctuations within a day may also be relevant. Sometimes demand patterns are intuitively obvious; in other cases patterns may not reveal themselves until the data are charted.

Predictable Cycles

In looking at the graphic representation of demand levels, is there a predictable cycle daily (variations occur by hours), weekly (variations occur by day), monthly (variations occur by day or week), and/or yearly (variations occur according to months or seasons)? In some cases, predictable patterns may occur at all periods. For example, in the restaurant industry, especially in seasonal tourist settings, demand can vary by month, by week, by day, and by hour.

If there is a predictable cycle, what are the underlying causes? The Ritz Carlton in Phoenix knows that demand cycles are based on seasonal weather patterns and that weekly variations are based on the work week (business travelers don't stay at the hotel over the weekend). Tax accountants can predict demand based on when taxes are due, quarterly and annually. Services catering to children and families respond to variations in school hours and vacations. Retail and telecommunication services have peak periods at certain holidays and times of the week and day. When predictable patterns exist, generally one or more causes can be identified.

Random Demand Fluctuations

Sometimes the patterns of demand appear to be random—there is no apparent predictable cycle. Yet even in this case, causes can often be identified. For example, day-to-day changes in the weather may affect use of recreational, shopping, or entertainment facilities. While the weather cannot be predicted far in advance, it may be possible to anticipate demand a day or two ahead. Health-related events also cannot be predicted. Accidents, heart attacks, and births all increase demand for hospital services, but the level of demand cannot generally be determined in advance. Natural disasters such as floods, fires, and hurricanes can dramatically increase the need for such services as insurance, telecommunication, and health care.

AT&T was faced with a sudden increase in demand for services to the military during the Gulf War in 1990–1991. During this period, 500,000 U.S. troops were deployed to the Middle East, many without advance warning. Before their deployment these men and women had little time to attend to personal business, and all of them left behind concerned family and friends. With mail delivery between the United States and the Middle East taking more than six weeks, troops needed a quick way to communicate with their families and to handle personal business. Communications with home were determined by the military to be essential to troop morale. AT&T's ingenuity, responsiveness, and capacities were challenged to meet this unanticipated communication need. During and after the Gulf War crisis more than 2.5 million calls were placed over temporary public phone installations, and AT&T sent more than 1.2 million free faxes to family and friends of service men and women.[6]

Demand Patterns by Market Segment

If an organization has detailed records on customer transactions, it may be able to disaggregate demand by market segment, revealing patterns within patterns. Or the analysis may reveal that demand from one segment is predictable while demand from another segment is relatively random. For example, for a bank, the visits from its commercial accounts may occur daily at a predictable time, whereas personal account holders may visit the bank at seemingly random intervals. Health clinics often notice that walk-in or "care needed today" patients tend to concentrate their arrivals on Monday, with fewer numbers needing immediate attention on other days of the week. Knowing that this pattern exists, some clinics schedule more future appointments (which they can control) for later days of the week, leaving more of Monday available for same-day appointments and walk-ins.

STRATEGIES FOR MATCHING CAPACITY AND DEMAND

When an organization has a clear grasp of its capacity constraints and an understanding of demand patterns, it is in a good position to develop strategies for matching supply and demand. There are two general approaches for accomplishing this match. The first is to smooth the demand fluctuations themselves by shifting demand to match existing supply. This implies that the peaks and valleys of the demand curve (Figure 14-3) will be flattened to match as closely as possible the horizontal optimum capacity line. The second general strategy is to adjust capacity to match fluctuations in demand. This implies moving the horizontal capacity lines shown in Figure 14-3 to match the ups and downs of the demand curve. Each of these two basic strategies will be described next with specific examples.

Shifting Demand to Match Capacity

With this strategy an organization seeks to shift customers away from periods in which demand exceeds capacity, perhaps by convincing them to use the service during periods of slow demand. This may be possible for some customers, but not for others. For example, many business travelers are not able to shift their needs for airline, car rental, and hotel services; pleasure travelers, on the other hand, can often shift the timing of their trips. Those who can't shift and can't be accommodated will represent lost business for the firm.

During periods of slow demand, the organization will seek to attract more and/or different customers to utilize its productive capacity. A variety of approaches, detailed in the following sections, can be used to shift or increase demand to match capacity. Frequently a firm will use a combination of approaches. Ideas for how to shift demand during both slow and peak periods are shown in Figure 14-4.

Vary the Service Offering   One approach is to change the nature of the service offering, depending on the season of the year, day of the week, or time of day. For example, Whistler Mountain, a ski resort in Vancouver, Canada, offers its facilities for executive development and training programs during the summer when snow skiing is not possible. A hospital in the Los Angeles area rents use of its facilities to film production crews who need realistic hospital settings for movies or TV shows. Accounting firms focus on tax preparation late in the year and until April 15, when federal taxes are due in the United States. During other times of the year they can focus on audits and general consulting activities. Airlines even change the configuration of their plane seating to match the demand from different market segments. In some planes there may be no first-class section at all. On routes with a large demand for first-class seating, a significant

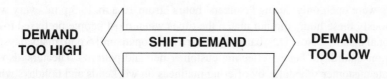

FIGURE 14-4 Strategies for *shifting demand* to match capacity.

- Use signage to communicate busy days and times
- Offer incentives to customers for usage during nonpeak times
- Take care of loyal or "regular" customers first
- Advertise peak useage times and benefits of nonpeak use
- Charge full price for the service—no discounts

- Use sales and advertising to increase business from current market segments
- Modify the service offering to appeal to new market segments
- Offer discounts or price reductions
- Modify hours of operation
- Bring the service to the customer

proportion of seats may be placed in first class. Our opening example featured ways in which downtown hotels have changed their offerings to appeal to the family market segment on weekends. In all of these examples, the service offering and associated benefits are changed to smooth customer demand for the organization's resources.

Care should be exercised in implementing strategies to change the service offering, since such changes may easily imply and require alterations in other marketing-mix variables—such as promotion, pricing, and staffing—to match the new offering. Unless these additional mix variables are altered effectively to support the offering, the strategy may not work. Even when done well, the downside of such changes can be a confusion in the organization's image from the customers' perspective, or a loss of strategic focus for the organization and its employees.

Communicate with Customers   Another approach for shifting demand is to communicate with customers, letting them know the times of peak demand periods so they can choose to use the service at alternative times and avoid crowding or delays. For example, signs in banks and post offices that let customers know their busiest hours and busiest days of the week can serve as a warning, allowing customers to shift their demand to another time if possible. Forewarning customers about busy times and possible waits can have added benefits. Research in a bank context found that customers who were forewarned about the bank's busiest hours were more satisfied even when they had to wait than were customers who were not forewarned.[7]

In addition to signage being used to communicate peak demand times to customers, advertising and other forms of promotion can be used to emphasize different service benefits during peak and slow periods. Advertising and sales messages can also be used to remind customers about peak demand times.

Modify Timing and Location of Service Delivery   Some firms adjust their hours and days of service delivery to more directly reflect customer demand. Historically, U.S.

banks were open only during "bankers' hours" from 10 a.m. to 3 p.m. every weekday. Obviously these hours did not match the times when most people preferred to do their personal banking. Now U.S. banks open early, stay open until 6 p.m. many days, and are open on Saturdays, better reflecting customer demand patterns. Theaters also accommodate customer schedules by offering matinees on weekends and holidays when people are free during the day for entertainment. Movie theaters are sometimes rented during weekdays by business groups—an example of varying the service offering during a period of low demand.

Another strategy may involve moving the service to a new location to meet customer demand, or even bringing the service to customers. Mobile training facilities, libraries, and blood donation facilities are examples of services that physically follow customers. Mobile Psychological Services (MPS) in New York is a unique example of this type of strategy. MPS is a mobile counseling service that picks clients up in a specially appointed, unmarked van and drives them wherever they need to go, providing therapy en route.[8] The service caters primarily to Wall Street clients who need to fit therapy into their busy daily schedules.

Differentiate on Price A common response during periods of slow demand is to discount the price of the service. This strategy relies on basic economics of supply and demand. To be effective, however, a price differentiation strategy depends on solid understanding of customer price sensitivity and demand curves. For example, business travelers are far less price sensitive than are families traveling for pleasure. For the Ritz Carlton in Phoenix (our opening example), lowering prices during the slow summer months is not likely to increase bookings from business travelers dramatically. However, the lower summer prices will attract considerable numbers of families and local guests who want an opportunity to experience a luxury hotel but are not able to afford the rooms during peak season.

For any hotel, airline, restaurant, or other service establishment, all of the capacity could be filled with customers if the price were low enough. But the goal is always to ensure the highest level of capacity utilization without sacrificing profits. We will explore this complex relationship between price, market segments, capacity utilization, and profitability later in the chapter in the section on yield management.

Heavy use of price differentiation to smooth demand can be a risky strategy. Overreliance on price can result in price wars in an industry where eventually all competitors suffer. Price wars are well known in the airline industry, where total industry profits have suffered as a result of airlines simultaneously trying to attract customers through price discounting. Another risk of relying on price is that customers grow accustomed to the lower price and expect to get the same deal the next time they use the service. If communications with customers are unclear, customers may not understand the reasons for the discounts and will expect to pay the same during peak demand periods. Overuse or exclusive use of price as a strategy for smoothing demand is also risky due to potential impact on the organization's image and the possibility of attracting undesired market segments.

Flexing Capacity to Meet Demand

A second strategic approach to matching supply and demand focuses on adjusting or flexing capacity. The fundamental idea here is to adjust, stretch, and align capacity to match customer demand (rather than working on shifting demand to match capacity as just described.) During periods of peak demand the organization will seek to stretch or expand its capacity as much as possible. During periods of slow demand it will try to shrink capacity so as not to waste resources. General strategies for flexing the four primary service resources (time, people, equipment, and facilities) are discussed next. Specific ideas for adjusting capacity during periods of peak and slow demand are summarized in Figure 14-5. Often a number of different strategies will be used simultaneously.

Stretch Existing Capacity   The existing capacity of service resources can often be expanded temporarily to match demand. In such cases no new resources are added but rather people, facilities, and equipment are asked to work perhaps harder and longer to meet demand.

Stretch Time   It may be possible to extend the hours of service temporarily to accommodate demand. A health clinic might stay open longer during flu season, retailers are open longer hours during the Christmas shopping season, and accountants have extended appointment hours (evenings and Saturdays) before tax deadlines.

Stretch Labor   In many service organizations, employees are asked to work longer and harder during periods of peak demand. For example, consulting organizations face extensive peaks and valleys with respect to demand for their services. During periods of peak demand, associates are asked to take on additional projects and work longer hours. And front-line service personnel in banks, tourist attractions, restaurants, and telecommunication companies are asked to serve more customers per hour during busy times than during hours or days when demand is low.

Stretch Facilities   Theaters, restaurants, meeting facilities, and classrooms can sometimes be expanded on a temporary basis by the addition of tables, chairs, or other

FIGURE 14-5   Strategies for *flexing capacity* to match demand.

DEMAND TOO HIGH   **FLEX CAPACITY**   **DEMAND TOO LOW**

- Stretch time, labor, facilities, and equipment
- Cross-train employees
- Hire part-time employees
- Request overtime work from employees
- Rent or share facilities
- Rent or share equipment
- Subcontract or outsource activities

- Perform, maintenance, renovations
- Schedule vacations
- Schedule employee training
- Lay off employees

equipment needed by customers. Or, as in the case of a commuter train, a car can hold a number of people seated comfortably or can "expand" by accommodating standing-room-only passengers.

Stretch Equipment   Computers, telephone lines, and maintenance equipment can often be stretched beyond what would be considered the maximum capacity for short periods to accommodate peak demand.

In using these types of "stretch" strategies, the organization needs to recognize the wear and tear on resources and the potential for inferior quality of service that may go with the use. These strategies should thus be used for relatively short periods in order to allow later for maintenance of the facilities and equipment and refreshment of the people who are asked to exceed their usual capacity. As noted earlier, sometimes it is difficult to know in advance, particularly in the case of human resources, when capacity has been stretched too far.

Align Capacity with Demand Fluctuations   This basic strategy is sometimes known as a "chase demand" strategy. By adjusting service resources creatively, organizations can in effect chase the demand curves to match capacity with customer demand patterns. Time, labor, facilities, and equipment are again the focus, this time with an eye toward adjusting the basic mix and use of these resources. Specific actions might include the following.[9]

Use Part-Time Employees   In this case the organization's labor resource is being aligned with demand. Retailers hire part-time employees during the holiday rush, tax accountants engage temporary help during tax season, tourist resorts bring in extra workers during peak season. Restaurants often ask employees to work split shifts (e.g., work the lunch shift, leave for a few hours, and come back for the dinner rush) during peak mealtime hours.

Rent or Share Facilities or Equipment   For some organizations it is best to rent additional equipment or facilities during periods of peak demand. For example, express mail delivery services rent or lease trucks during the peak holiday delivery season. It would not make sense to buy trucks that would sit idle during the rest of the year. Sometimes organizations with complementary demand patterns can share facilities. An example is a church that shares its facilities during the week with a Montessori preschool. The school needs the facilities Monday through Friday during the day; the church needs the facilities evenings and on the weekend.

Schedule Down Time during Periods of Low Demand   If people, equipment, and facilities are being used at maximum capacity during peak periods, then it is imperative to schedule repair, maintenance, and renovations during off-peak periods. This will ensure that the resources are in top condition when they are most needed. With regard to employees, this means that vacations and training would also be scheduled during slow demand periods.

Cross-train Employees   If employees are cross-trained, they can shift among tasks, filling in where they are most needed. This will increase the efficiency of the whole system and avoid underutilizing employees in some areas while others are being overtaxed. Many airlines cross-train their employees to move from ticketing to working the gate counters to assisting with baggage if needed. In some fast-food restaurants, employees specialize in one task (e.g., making french fries) during busy hours, and the team of specialists may number 10 people. During slow hours the team may shrink to three, with each person performing a variety of functions. Grocery stores also use this strategy, with most employees being able to move as needed from cashiering to stocking shelves to bagging groceries.

Modify or Move Facilities and Equipment   Sometimes it is possible to adjust, move, or creatively modify existing capacity to meet demand fluctuations. Hotels accomplish this by reconfiguring rooms—two rooms with a locked door between can be rented to two different parties in high demand times or turned into a suite during slow demand. The airline industry offers dramatic examples of this type of strategy. Using an approach known as "demand driven dispatch," airlines have begun to experiment with methods that assign airplanes to flight schedules on the basis of fluctuating market needs.[10] The method depends on accurate knowledge of demand and the ability to quickly move airplanes with different seating capacities to flight assignments that match their capacity. The new Boeing 777 aircraft is so flexible that it can be reconfigured within hours to vary the number of seats allocated to one, two, or three classes.[11] The plane can thus be quickly modified to match demand from different market segments, essentially molding capacity to fit demand.

YIELD MANAGEMENT: BALANCING CAPACITY UTILIZATION, PRICING, MARKET SEGMENTATION, AND FINANCIAL RETURN

Yield management is a term that has become attached to a variety of methods, some very sophisticated, matching demand and supply in capacity-constrained services. Using yield management models, organizations find the best balance at a particular point in time among the prices charged, the segments sold to, and the capacity used. The goal of yield management is to produce the best possible financial return from a limited available capacity. Specifically, yield management has been defined as "the process of allocating the right type of capacity to the right kind of customer at the right price so as to maximize revenue or yield."[12]

Although the implementation of yield management can involve complex mathematical models and computer programs, the underlying effectiveness measure is the ratio of actual revenue to potential revenue for a particular measurement period:

$$\text{Yield} = \frac{\text{Actual revenue}}{\text{Potential revenue}}$$

where

Actual revenue   = Actual capacity used × average actual price
Potential revenue = Total capacity × maximum price

The equations indicate that yield is a function of price and capacity used. Recall that capacity constraints can be in the form of time, labor, equipment, or facilities. Yield is essentially a measure of the extent to which an organization's resources (or capacities) are achieving their full revenue-generating potential. Yield can be raised by increasing capacity used or by increasing price, and the trade-offs are immediately apparent.

Take for example a hotel that has 200 rooms that it can rent at a rate of $100 per night (potential revenue of $20,000). One night it rents all of the rooms at a reduced rate of $50 per night, yielding a revenue of $10,000. Although capacity was used to the maximum level that night, yield was only 50 percent ($10,000/$20,000). If, on the other hand, the hotel had charged its full rate it might have sold only 40 percent of its rooms due to customer price sensitivity. The yield under these circumstances would have been 40 percent ($8,000/$20,000). At the $100 rate the hotel may thus be maximizing the per-room price but not the potential yield—or revenue generation—for the entire hotel. Perhaps a combination of the two room rates would be the best solution. If the hotel could fill 40 percent of the rooms at $100 per night and the other 60 percent at $50, the revenue would be $14,000, resulting in a yield of 70 percent ($14,000/$20,000), clearly better than the other two alternatives.

In a different context, a law firm could determine the best mix of business for using its labor capacity to yield the highest returns. For example, if one attorney has 40 potential billable hours in a given week and her rate is $200 per hour for private corporate clients, then maximum revenue generation by that attorney in a week is $8,000. Assume her rate for public and nonprofit clients is $100 per hour. As in the preceding hotel example, if the attorney could bill out all of her hours in a week to public clients at the $100 rate, yield would be 50 percent. If she were to hold out for private corporate clients, she might be able to sell only 30 percent of her available time (12 hours), resulting in a yield of 30 percent ($2,400/$8,000). By combining the two strategies the attorney could possibly sell 30 percent of her time at $200 per hour to private corporate clients and the remaining 70 percent to public clients for $100 per hour, resulting in a yield of 65 percent ($5,200/$8,000), clearly better than the other two alternatives.

Yield management attempts to manage demand to meet capacity (fixed number of rooms or fixed number of hours in these examples) by deciding what amount of capacity to offer at what price to what market segments in order to maximize revenues over a particular period. It forces recognition of the trade-offs inherent in serving a lower-paying market segment to fill capacity when there may be some demand from higher-paying clientele.

To implement a yield management system, an organization needs detailed data on past demand patterns by market segment as well as methods of projecting current market demand. The data can be combined through mathematical programming models, threshold analysis, or use of expert systems to project the best allocation of limited capacity at a particular point in time.[13] Allocations of capacity for specific market segments can then be communicated to sales representatives or reservations staff as targets for selling rooms, seats, time, or other limited resources. Sometimes the allocations, once determined, remain fixed. At other times allocations change weekly or even daily in response to new information. Passenger airlines are the most sophisticated and longtime users of technology-assisted yield management systems. Probably the most experienced is American Airlines, which has been using the techniques since the 1980s to juggle the timing and allotment of discount tickets with potential sales from higher-paying travelers. Decisions are made daily on how many seats to allocate to discount travelers, how many to groups, and how many to hold for last-minute full-fare customers. The percentage of seats that should be overbooked to handle "no shows" is also factored into the decisions.

Our Technology Spotlight illustrates how the shipping industry is applying the experience of the passenger airline industry in making use of sophisticated computer programs and decision-support systems to assist with yield management, load planning, routing, and driver dispatch.

Challenges and Risks in Using Yield Management

There is evidence that yield management programs can significantly improve revenues. However, while yield management may appear to be an ideal solution to the problem of matching supply and demand, it is not without risks. By becoming focused on maximizing financial returns through differential capacity allocation and pricing, an organization may find that it risks:[14]

Loss of competitive focus. Yield management may result in overfocusing on profit maximization and inadvertent neglect of aspects of the service that provide long-term competitive success.

TECHNOLOGY SPOTLIGHT

SHIPPERS TURN TO COMPUTER TECHNOLOGY TO ASSIST WITH YIELD MANAGEMENT

Major carriers such as Yellow Freight System, Inc., Northwest Airlines cargo division, North American Van Lines, Sea-Land Service, and Union Pacific Railroad are turning to computerized decision-support systems to help them with yield management, customer-based pricing, load planning, routing, and driver dispatch. The ability of cargo carriers to use such systems is a direct result of computerization and the almost immediate accessibility of complex traffic-flow data. Use of these systems aids the carriers in finding the best use of their relatively fixed capacity (e.g., trucks, containers, railroad cars, drivers) by aligning capacity with appropriate customer segments, load configurations, and pricing strategies.

Researchers at the Center for Transportation Studies at the Massachusetts Institute of Technology are working with software designers to build a package for truckload carriers that includes driver selection, profitability analysis, load acceptance, and load solicitation. A complementary system recommends the best time and place for refueling. The ability of such computerized systems to make real-time, daily decisions is likely to minimize the future reliance on human dispatchers.

At Yellow Freight System, Inc., one of the three largest carriers in the United States, automated decision-support systems are used to achieve the optimal mix of low overhead and high service quality. The systems also allow the company to more fully understand the actual costs of shipping for individual customers so that individualized prices can be more reflective of actual costs. In making an optimal routing and pricing decision, more is involved than simply finding the nearest driver and piece of equipment and quoting a standard price. The automated systems can consider such subtle factors as equipment type and the skills of a particular driver, and can match hundreds of drivers with loads in fractions of seconds to make the best dispatch and driver decisions. By tracking a particular customer's shipping patterns and needs, the company can also quote individualized prices that closely reflect the actual costs of service.

Sources: John H. Perser, "Carriers Turning to 'Smart' Computers to Assist in Yield Management, Other Business Decisions," *Traffic World,* July 18, 1994, pp. 20–22; John D. Schulz, "Computer-assisted Cost Tracking Enables Carriers to Hone Pricing Skills," *Traffic World,* June 14, 1993, pp. 7–8; Tom McNiff, "Airlines' Yield-Management Techniques Being Adopted, Slowly, By Freight Carriers," *Traffic World,* March 8, 1993, pp. 13–15.

Customer alienation. If customers learn that they are paying a higher price for service than someone else, they may perceive the pricing as unfair, particularly if they don't understand the reasons. Customer education is thus essential in an effective yield management program. Customers can be further alienated if they fall victim (and are not compensated adequately) to overbooking practices that are often necessary to make yield management systems work effectively.

Employee morale problems. Yield management systems take much guesswork and judgment away from sales and reservations people. While some employees may appreciate the guidance, others may resent the rules and restrictions on their own discretion.

Incompatible incentive and reward systems. Employees may resent yield management systems if these don't match incentive structures. For example, many managers are rewarded on the basis of capacity utilization *or* average rate charged, whereas yield management balances the two factors.

Lack of employee training. Extensive training is required to make a yield management system work. Employees need to understand its purpose, how it works, how they should make decisions, and how the system will affect their jobs.

Inappropriate organization of the yield management function. To be most effective with yield management, an organization must have centralized reservations. While airlines and some large hotel chains and shipping companies do have such centralization, other smaller organizations may have decentralized reservations systems and thus find it difficult to operate a yield management system effectively.

WAITING LINE STRATEGIES: WHEN DEMAND AND CAPACITY CANNOT BE ALIGNED

Sometimes it is not possible to manage capacity to match demand, or vice versa. It may be too costly—for example, for most health clinics it would not be economically feasible to add additional facilities or physicians to handle peaks in demand during the winter flu season; patients usually simply have to wait to be seen. Or demand may be very unpredictable and the service capacity very inflexible (it can't be easily stretched to match unpredictable peaks in demand). Sometimes waits may occur when demand backs up due to variability in length of time for service. For example, even though patients are scheduled by appointments in a physician's office, frequently there is a wait because some patients take longer to serve than the time allotted to them.

For most service organizations, waiting customers are a fact of life at some point. Waiting can occur on the telephone—customers put on hold when they call in to ask for information, order something, or make a complaint—and waiting can occur in person—customers waiting in line at the bank, post office, at Disney Land, or at a physician's office. Waiting can occur even with service transactions through the mail—delays in mail order delivery, or backlogs of correspondence on a manager's desk.

In today's fast-paced society, waiting is not something most people tolerate well. As people work longer hours, individuals have less leisure, and families have fewer hours together, the pressure on people's time is greater than ever. In this environment, customers are looking for efficient, quick service with no wait. Organizations that make customers wait take the chance that they will lose business or at the very least that customers will be dissatisfied.[15]

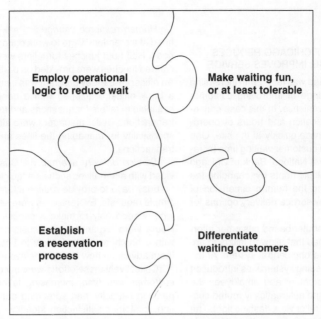

FIGURE 14-6   Waiting line strategies.

To deal effectively with the inevitability of waits, organizations employ a variety of strategies, described next and illustrated in Figure 14-6.

Employ Operational Logic

If customer waits are common, a first step is to analyze the operational processes to remove any inefficiencies. It may be possible to redesign the system to move customers along more quickly. Modifications in the operational system were part of the solution employed by the First National Bank of Chicago in its efforts to reduce customer waiting and improve service (see Box 14-1).

In introducing its express check-in, Marriott Hotels used an operations-based modification to eliminate much of the waiting previously experienced by its guests. Guests who use a credit card and preregister can avoid waiting in line at the hotel front desk altogether. The guest can make it from the curb outside the hotel to his or her room in as little as three minutes when escorted by a "guest service associate" who checks the guest into the hotel, picks up keys and paperwork from a rack in the lobby, and then escorts the guest directly to the room.[16]

When queues are inevitable, the organization faces the operational decision of what kind of queuing system to use, or how to configure the queue. Queue configuration refers to the number of queues, their locations, their spatial requirement, and their effect on customer behavior.[17] Several possibilities exist, as shown in Figure 14-7. In the multiple-queue alternative, the customer arrives at the service facility and must decide

BOX 14-1

FIRST NATIONAL BANK OF CHICAGO REDUCES
CUSTOMER WAITING TIME, IMPROVES SERVICE

First National Bank of Chicago was faced with increasing
competition and the challenge of improving customer
service through added convenience. In this case convenience meant more than location and hours of operation—it meant providing service quickly at the site. One
major hurdle was to shorten customer waiting time by reducing teller-line delays. First National Bank of Chicago
tackled this problem on multiple fronts by: changing the
operating system; improving the human dimension of
service; and introducing new service delivery options for
the customer.

System changes. A computer-based customer information system was developed that allowed tellers to answer questions quickly using one central system. At the
same time, an electronic queuing system was introduced
that displayed for both customers and employees the
current length of wait time and automatically routed customers to the next available teller via a flashing light. The
system also projected staffing requirements on the basis
of demand patterns. Automated cash-dispatch machines
were introduced that saved about thirty seconds per
transaction and physically removed many customers
from the teller line.

Human resource changes. "Peak-time" tellers were
hired at a premium wage to work during high demand periods. Half-hour lunches for tellers were introduced, and
catered lunches were provided on particularly busy days.
An officer-of-the-day program was instituted to designate
a bank officer, equipped with a beeper, to be quickly
available to tellers for questions and to assist with longer
transactions. Teller managers were also given a new responsibility for managing the lines and facilitating quick
transactions.

Service delivery alternatives. Customers were provided with alternatives such as a "quick drop" desk set up
on busy days to provide routine information and handle
simple requests. Express lines were set up for customers
who needed only to make a deposit or cash a check.
Hours were expanded, and customers were provided
with a brochure entitled "How to Lose Wait" that gave
them advice on how to avoid delays at the bank.

Collectively these efforts were successful in reducing
customer wait time, increasing teller productivity, expanding capacity, and spreading out demand. In addition, customer satisfaction steadily improved following
the changes.

Source: Leonard L. Berry and Linda R. Cooper, "Competing
with Time-saving Service," *Business,* April–June 1990, pp. 3–7.

which queue to join, and whether to switch later if the wait appears to be shorter in another line. In the single-queue alternative, fairness of waiting time is ensured in that the
first-come, first-served rule applies to everyone; the system can also reduce the average
time customers spend waiting overall. However, customers may leave if they perceive
the line is too long, or there is no opportunity to select a particular service provider. The
last option shown in Figure 14-7 is the take-a-number option, where arriving customers
take a number to indicate line position. Advantages are similar to the single-queue alternative with the additional benefit that customers are able to mill about, browse, and
talk to each other. The disadvantage is that customers must be on the alert to hear their
number when it is called.

Establish a Reservation Process

When waiting cannot be avoided, a reservation system can help to spread demand.
Restaurants, transportation companies, theaters, physicians, and many other service
providers use reservation systems to alleviate long waits. The idea behind a reservation
system is to guarantee that the service will be available when the customer arrives. Beyond simply reducing waiting time, a reservation system has the added benefit of po-

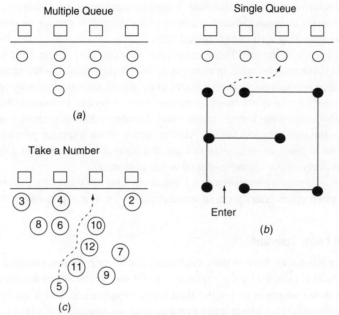

FIGURE 14-7   Waiting line configurations.

Source: Fitzsimmons and Fitzsimmons, *Service Management for Competitive Advantage,* p. 280.

tentially shifting demand to less desirable time periods. A challenge inherent in reservation systems, however, is what to do about "no shows." Inevitably there will be customers who reserve a time but do not show up. Some organizations deal with this by overbooking their service capacity on the basis of past records of no-show percentages. If the predictions are accurate, overbooking is a good solution. When predictions are inaccurate, however, customers may still have to wait and sometimes may not be served at all, as when airlines overbook the number of seats available on a flight. Victims of overbooking may be compensated for their inconvenience in such cases. To minimize the no-show problem, some organizations (e.g., hotels, airlines, conferences/training programs, theaters) charge customers who fail to show up or cancel their reservations within a certain time frame.

Differentiate Waiting Customers

Not all customers necessarily need to wait the same length of time for service. On the basis of need or customer priority, some organizations differentiate among customers, allowing some to experience shorter waits for service than others. Known as "queue discipline," such differentiation reflects management policies regarding who to select next for service.[18] The most popular discipline is first-come, first-served. However, other rules may apply. Differentiation can be based on factors such as:[19]

Importance of the customer. Frequent customers or customers who spend large amounts with the organization can be given priority in service by providing them with a special waiting area or segregated lines.

Urgency of the job. Those customers with the most urgent need may be served first. This is the strategy used in emergency health care. It is also the strategy used by maintenance services such as air-conditioning repair who give priority to customers whose air conditioning is not functioning over those who call for routine maintenance.

Duration of the service transaction. In many situations, shorter service jobs get priority through "express lanes." At other times, when a service provider sees that a transaction is going to require extra time, the customer is referred to a designated provider who deals only with these special needs customers.

Payment of a premium price. Customers who pay extra (e.g., first class on an airline) are often given priority via separate check-in lines or express systems.

Make Waiting Fun, or at Least Tolerable

Even when they have to wait, customers can be more or less satisfied depending on how the wait is handled by the organization. Of course the actual length of the wait will affect how customers feel about their service experience. But it isn't just the actual time spent waiting that has an impact on customer satisfaction—it's how customers feel about the wait and their perceptions during it. In a classic article entitled "The Psychology of Waiting Lines," David Maister proposes several principles regarding waiting, each of which has implications for how organizations can make waiting more pleasurable, or at least tolerable.[20]

Unoccupied Time Feels Longer than Occupied Time When customers are unoccupied they will likely be bored and will notice the passage of time more than when they have something to do. Providing something for waiting customers to do, particularly if the activity offers a benefit in and of itself or is related in some way to the service, can improve the customer's experience and may benefit the organization as well. Examples include giving customers menus to look at while waiting in a restaurant, providing interesting information to read in a dentist's office, or playing entertaining programs over the phone while customers are on hold. At Macy's in New York, children waiting to see Santa Claus wend their way through displays of dancing teddy bears, elves, and electric trains that become part of the total service adventure.[21]

Preprocess Waits Feel Longer than In-process Waits If wait time is occupied with activities that relate to the upcoming service, customers may perceive that the service has started and they are no longer actually waiting. This in-process activity will make the length of the wait seem shorter and will also benefit the service provider by making the customer better prepared when the service actually does begin. Filling out medical information while waiting to see the physician, reading a menu while waiting to be seated in a restaurant, and watching a videotape of the upcoming service event are all activities that can at the same time educate the customer and reduce perceptions of waiting. Research in a restaurant context found that customers reacted less negatively to in-process waits than to either preprocess or postprocess waits.[22]

Anxiety Makes Waits Seem Longer   When customers fear that they have been forgotten or don't know how long they'll have to wait, they become anxious, and this anxiety can increase the negative impact of waiting. Anxiety also results when customers are forced to choose in a multiple-line situation and they discover they have chosen the "wrong line." To combat waiting line anxiety, organizations can provide information on the length of the wait. This is what Disney does at its theme parks: It uses signs at intervals along the line that let customers know how long the wait will be from that point on. Using a single-line strategy also alleviates customer anxiety over having chosen the wrong line. Explanations and reassurances that no one has forgotten them alleviate customer anxiety by taking away their cause for worry. At the Omni Park Central Hotel in New York, when the line exceeds a certain length assistant managers bring orange and grapefruit juice to serve to those waiting.[23] The customers know they have not been forgotten.

Uncertain Waits Are Longer than Known, Finite Waits   Anxiety is intensified when customers don't know how long they'll have to wait. Health care providers combat this by letting customers know when they check in how far behind the physician is that day. Some patients resolve this uncertainty themselves by calling ahead to ask. Maister provides an interesting example of the role of uncertainty, which he terms the "appointment syndrome." Customers who arrive early for an appointment will wait patiently until the scheduled time, even if they arrive very early. However, once the expected appointment time has passed, customers grow increasingly anxious. Before the appointment time the wait time is known; after that, the length of the wait is not known. Research in an airline context has suggested that as uncertainty about the wait increases, customers become more angry, and their anger in turn results in greater dissatisfaction.[24]

Unexplained Waits Are Longer than Explained Waits   When people understand the causes for waiting, they frequently have greater patience and are less anxious, particularly when the wait is justifiable. Being provided with an explanation can reduce customer uncertainty and may help customers to make at least a ballpark estimate of how long they'll be delayed. Customers who don't know the reason for a wait begin to feel powerless and irritated.

Unfair Waits Are Longer than Equitable Waits   When customers perceive that they are waiting while others who arrived after them have already been served, the apparent inequity will make the wait seem even longer. This can easily occur when there is no apparent order in the waiting area and many customers are trying to be served. Queuing systems that work on a first-come, first-served rule are best at combatting perceived unfairness. However, as pointed out earlier, there may be reasons for the use of other approaches in determining who is to be served next. For example, in an emergency medical care situation, the most seriously ill or injured patients would be seen first.

When customers understand the priorities and the rules are clearly communicated and enforced, fairness of waiting time should not be an issue.

The More Valuable the Service, the Longer the Customer Will Wait   Customers who have substantial purchases or who are waiting for a high-value service will be more tolerant of long wait times and may even expect to wait longer. For example, in a supermarket, customers who have a full cart of groceries will generally wait longer than customers who have only a few items and expect to be checked through quickly. And we expect to wait longer for service in an expensive restaurant than we do when eating at a "greasy spoon."

Solo Waits Feel Longer than Group Waits   People will wait longer when they are in a group than when they are alone due to the distractions provided by other members of the group. There is also comfort in waiting with a group rather than alone. In some group waiting situations, such as at Disneyland or when patrons are waiting in long lines to purchase concert tickets, customers who are strangers begin to talk to each other and the waiting experience can actually become fun and a part of the total service experience.

SUMMARY

Because service organizations lack the ability to inventory their products, the effective use of capacity can be critical to success. Idle capacity in the form of unused time, labor, facilities, or equipment represents a direct drain on bottom-line profitability. When the capacity represents a major investment, for example, airplanes, expensive medical imaging equipment, or lawyers and physicians paid on a salary, the losses associated with underuse of capacity are even more accentuated. Overused capacity is also a problem. People, facilities, and equipment can become worn out over time when used beyond optimum capacity constraints. People can quit, facilities become run down, and equipment can break. From the customer's perspective, service quality also deteriorates. For organizations focused on delivering quality service, therefore, there is a natural drive to balance capacity utilization and demand at an optimum level in order to meet customer expectations.

This chapter has provided you an understanding of the underlying issues of managing supply and demand in capacity-constrained services by exploring the lack of inventory capability, the nature of service constraints (time, labor, equipment, facilities), the differences in optimal versus maximum use of capacity, and the causes of fluctuating demand.

Based on grounding in the fundamental issues, the chapter presented a variety of strategies for matching supply and demand. The basic strategies fall under two headings: *demand strategies* (shifting demand to match capacity) and *supply strategies* (flexing capacity to meet demand). Demand strategies seek to flatten the peaks and valleys of demand to match the flat capacity constraint, whereas supply strategies seek to align, flex, or stretch the fixed capacity to match the peaks and valleys of demand. Organizations frequently employ several strategies simultaneously to solve the complex problem of balancing supply and demand.

Yield management was presented as a sophisticated form of supply and demand management that balances capacity utilization, pricing, market segmentation, and financial return. Long practiced by the passenger airline industry, this strategy is growing in use by hotel, shipping, car rental, and other capacity-constrained industries where bookings are made in advance. Essentially, yield management allows organizations to decide on a monthly, weekly, daily, or even hourly basis to whom they want to sell their service capacity at what price.

All strategies for aligning capacity and demand need to be approached with caution. Any one of the strategies is likely to imply changes in multiple marketing-mix elements to support the strategy. Whenever such changes are made, even if done well, there is a risk of the firm losing focus or inadvertently altering its image in pursuit of increased revenues. While this is not necessarily bad, the potential strategic impact on the total organization should definitely be considered.

The last section of the chapter discussed situations where it is not possible to align supply and demand. In these unresolved capacity-utilization situations, the inevitable result is customer waiting. Strategies for effectively managing waiting lines were described such as: employ operational logic; establish a reservation process; differentiate waiting customers; and make waiting fun, or at least tolerable.

DISCUSSION QUESTIONS

1 Why do service organizations lack the capability to inventory their services? Compare a car repair and maintenance service with an automobile manufacturer/dealer in terms of inventory capability.

2 Discuss the four scenarios presented in Figure 14-3 and presented in the text (excess demand, demand exceeds optimum capacity, demand and supply are balanced, excess capacity) in the context of a basketball team selling seats for its games. What are the challenges for management under each scenario?

3 Discuss the four common types of constraints (time, labor, equipment, facilities) facing service businesses and give an example of each (real or hypothetical).

4 How does optimal capacity utilization differ from maximal capacity utilization? Give an example of a case where the two might be the same, and an example of where they are different.

5 Choose a local restaurant or some other type of service with fluctuating demand. What is the likely underlying pattern of demand? What causes the pattern? Is it predictable or random?

6 Describe the two basic strategies for matching supply and demand and give at least two specific examples of each.

7 What is yield management? Discuss the risks in adopting a yield management strategy.

8 How might yield management apply in the management of: a Broadway theater? A consulting firm? A commuter train?

9 Describe the four basic waiting line strategies, and give an example of each one, preferably based on your own experiences as a consumer.

EXERCISES

1 Choose a local service organization that is challenged by fixed capacity and fluctuating demand. Interview the marketing manager (or other knowledgeable person) to learn: (a) in what ways capacity is constrained; (b) the basic patterns of demand; (c) strategies the organization has used to align supply and demand. Write up the answers to these questions and make your own recommendations regarding other strategies the organization might use.

2 Assume you manage a winter ski resort in Colorado or Banff, Canada. (a) Explain the underlying pattern of demand fluctuation that is likely to occur at your resort and the challenges it would present to you as a manager. Is the pattern of demand predictable or random? (b) Explain and give examples of how you might use both demand-oriented and supply-oriented strategies to smooth the peaks and valleys of demand during peak and slow periods.

3 Choose a local organization where you know people have to wait in line for service. Design a waiting line strategy for the organization.

NOTES

1 James S. Hirsch, "Vacationing Families Head Downtown to Welcoming Arms of Business Hotels," *Wall Street Journal,* June 13, 1994, p. B1.
2 Ibid.
3 Christopher Lovelock, chap. 16, "Getting the Most Out of Your Productive Capacity," in *Product Plus* (Boston: McGraw-Hill, 1994).
4 Christopher H. Lovelock, "Classifying Services to Gain Strategic Marketing Insights," *Journal of Marketing* 47, 3 (Summer 1983): 9–20.
5 Portions of this section are based on Christopher H. Lovelock, "Strategies for Managing Capacity-Constrained Service Organizations," in *Managing Services: Marketing, Operations, and Human Resources,* 2d ed. (Englewood Cliffs, N.J.: Prentice Hall, 1992), pp. 154–168.
6 Deanna Kenny, Helen McGrath, Thomas J. Olsen, Brian Sullivan, Merrill R. Tutton, and Steve Yusko, "Service Quality under Crisis . . . AT&T Serving the Service—a Case Study," in *Advances in Services Marketing and Management,* Vol. 1, eds. Teresa A. Swartz, David E. Bowen, and Stephen W. Brown (Greenwich, Conn.: JAI Press Inc., 1992), pp. 229–246.
7 Elizabeth C. Clemmer and Benjamin Schneider, "Toward Understanding and Controlling Customer Dissatisfaction with Waiting during Peak Demand Times," in *Designing a Winning Service Strategy,* eds. Mary Jo Bitner and Lawrence A. Crosby (Chicago: American Marketing Association, 1989), pp. 87–91.
8 Mark D. Fefer, "This Will Drive You Healthy," *Fortune,* September 5, 1994, p. 16.
9 Lovelock, "Getting the Most Out of Your Productive Capacity."
10 Matthew E. Berge and Craig A. Hopperstad, "Demand Driven Dispatch: A Method for Dynamic Aircraft Capacity Assignment, Models and Algorithms," *Operations Research* 41, 1 (January–February 1993): 153–168.
11 Lovelock, "Getting the Most Our of Your Productive Capacity."
12 Sheryl E. Kimes, "Yield Management: A Tool for Capacity-constrained Service Firms," *Journal of Operations Management* 8, 4 (October 1989): 348–363.
13 Ibid.
14 Ibid.

15 For research supporting the relationship between longer waits and decreased satisfaction and quality evaluations see Clemmer and Schneider, "Toward Understanding and Controlling Customer Dissatisfaction"; Shirley Taylor, "Waiting for Service: The Relationship between Delays and Evaluations of Service," *Journal of Marketing* 58 (April 1994): 56–69; Karen L. Katz, Blaire M. Larson, and Richard C. Larson, "Prescription for the Waiting-in-Line Blues: Entertain, Enlighten, and Engage," *Sloan Management Review,* Winter 1991, pp. 44–53.

16 Ronald Henkoff, "Finding, Training and Keeping the Best Service Workers," *Fortune,* October 3, 1994, pp. 110–122.

17 James A. Fitzsimmons and Mona J. Fitzsimmons, *Service Management for Competitive Advantage* (New York: McGraw-Hill, 1994), chap. 11.

18 Ibid.

19 Lovelock, "Getting the Most Out of Your Productive Capacity."

20 David A. Maister, "The Psychology of Waiting Lines," in *The Service Encounter,* eds. John A. Czepiel, Michael R. Solomon, and Carol F. Surprenant (Lexington, Mass.: Lexington Books, 1985), pp. 113–123.

21 Amanda Bennett, "Their Business Is on the Line," *Wall Street Journal,* December 7, 1990, p. B1.

22 Laurette Dube-Rioux, Bernd H. Schmitt, and France Leclerc, "Consumer's Reactions to Waiting: When Delays Affect the Perception of Service Quality," in *Advances in Consumer Research,* Vol. 16, ed. T. Srull (Provo, Utah: Association for Consumer Research, 1988), pp. 59–63.

23 Ibid.

24 Taylor, "Waiting for Service."

15

INTERNATIONAL SERVICES MARKETING

Undoubtedly, the greatest gap between customer expectations and service delivery exists when Japanese meet Russians. In Japan the customer is more than king. When patrons walk into the largest department stores in Tokyo, sales personnel bow! In the old command economy of the Soviet Union, products were usually scarce, so suppliers ruled. Sellers decided who got what—the concept of customer service was literally nonsense.

According to the International Herald Tribune,[1] *Japanese customers have problems getting along even when shopping in "civilized" Britain: "Hideo Majima, 57, a Japanese tourist, looked puzzled and annoyed. He was standing in a London department store while two shop assistants conversed instead of serving him. He left without buying anything."*

Now try to imagine how our friend, Majima-san, might feel about dining in a fine Russian restaurant in 1992: "Excuse the waiters at the Izmailova Hotel if they're too busy to serve you: They're playing chess. 'Can't you see we're one move away from checkmate?,' yelled waiter Oleg Shamov, surrounded by six other waiters in a restaurant back room. The match kept customers waiting for 40 minutes."[2] The reader should note that free enterprise is apparently having strong effects in the former Soviet Union. Professor Peter Shikhirev at the Graduate School of International Business in Moscow assures us that as of 1995, many Russian restaurants are now providing service comparable to fine American restaurants. However, we're still not convinced that even that level of customer service would "delight" Japanese customers!

Cultural gaps such as that in the vignette are the primary topic of this chapter. The other set of factors that makes the marketing of services across cultures and borders difficult

414

CUSTOMER

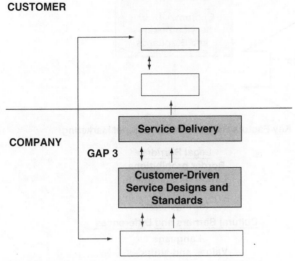

COMPANY

GAP 3

FIGURE 15-1   Provider GAP 3.

is legal restrictions. Moreover, both cultures and legal systems are dynamic, which can make yesterday's advice obsolete today. However, such complexities and barriers also create opportunities for creative services marketers in both international and domestic markets.

Although international differences can serve to widen all of the gaps that have been described in previous chapters, the main effects will be seen in GAP 3 (Figure 15-1). Legal barriers and cultural factors (particularly difficulties in managing customers' and employees' behaviors and adapting the marketing mix) will impede the efficient delivery of services in foreign countries, widening GAP 3 (Figure 15-2). Cultural barriers also can secondarily widen GAP 1 in several ways, but primarily because consumers from different countries have different expectations about the qualities of services. A good example is the difficulties international airlines often have in serving passengers from several countries. One airline reports that Japanese passengers consistently express lower levels of satisfaction than do groups of passengers from any other country in surveys of all aspects of in-flight services. Certainty their "disappointment" reflects the uniquely high level of personal service they are accustomed to in their home country. Because Japanese expectations are generally higher than those of other fliers, airlines' customer satisfaction levels will be commensurably lower if adaptations are not made in the service provided.

Different from cultural barriers, legal barriers have more to do with widening GAP 3 by not allowing marketers to deliver the kinds of services customers prefer or need. Going back to our "underserved" Japanese airline passengers, all the air carriers know Japanese passengers would like to smoke during transcontinental U.S. flights. However, American laws preclude their doing so. During the aftermath of the 1995 Kobe earthquake, Japanese laws precluded American physicians from providing life-saving treatments to disaster victims.[3]

FIGURE 15-2   Key reasons for provider GAP 3.

In this chapter we will acquaint the reader with the importance of cultural and legal barriers encountered in marketing services in a global environment. Although we will most often be taking the perspective of U.S. service providers, our U.S. readers should appreciate what those from other countries already know, which is that the United States also poses both cultural and legal barriers to entry. Further, although almost all of the examples in this chapter come from an international context, much of this information can also inform the marketing of services in the cultural mosaic of the United States.

The objectives of this chapter are to:

1 Examine the legal restrictions to trade in services and their changing importance in view of the global spread of free trade agreements.

2 Identify cultural barriers, including their effects on management of both customers and employees in the international context.

3 Discuss reasons for optimism about the burgeoning opportunities associated with the current and future globalism of commerce and smart managers' abilities to close the "international" gaps between expectations and perceptions, thereby increasing services' customer satisfaction worldwide.

CHALLENGES IN THE GLOBAL MARKET

Opportunities for the export of services are great and growing. However, because trade creates jobs and holds the key to economic growth, all the world wants a share of the growing global services sector. Global competition will continue to increase, necessitating better understanding of international services concepts, issues, and challenges.[4] These issues will be discussed in the remainder of the chapter in the context of legal and cultural barriers.

Legal Barriers to Services Marketing

Because the production and marketing of services are closely intertwined with the societies being served, often the barriers associated with trade in services are even more restrictive than those associated with trade in merchandise. The creativity of regulators is best illustrated by considering the plethora of legal restrictions facing marketers of services in the global marketplace. An interesting example is the South Korean government's ban of Japanese movies—Godzilla has never treaded the streets or silver screens of Seoul.[5] The new paradox facing the regulators in Seoul is the acquisition of Columbia Pictures by Sony. Does that make "Ghostbusters II" or "When Harry Met Sally" Japanese films, and thus subject to the ban? If these two, filmed in the United States with American actors, are allowed, what should the regulators do about "Black Rain," starring Michael Douglas but filmed in large part in Japan using many Japanese actors?

The ban of Japanese movies in South Korea is an unusual example because the motivation behind the ban is cultural preservation stemming from Japan's colonization of Korea before World War II. While we see other similarly motivated restrictions around the world, the purposes behind most legal barriers are economic protection of domestic service industries and workers. Such barriers usually fall into four main categories: (1) quantitative or qualitative border prohibitions and restrictions, (2) laws and regulations discriminating against foreign firms, (3) direct and indirect subsidies to local firms, and (4) infringement of international copyright and trademark laws (and intellectual property rights). Each will be discussed in some detail in the following. But readers should appreciate that our descriptions represent only a tiny fraction of the dynamic environment of restrictions in place around the world. A brief sampling of just a few countries' regulations regarding one area, the international marketing of accounting services, makes this last point. Argentina has required that audits be supervised by locally registered and qualified accountants; Belgium has required that a foreigner can practice accounting only after passing a special exam; Brazil has required that accountants have the requisite degree from a Brazilian university; France has pressured for majority domestic ownership of accounting firms; Japan has required that audits be signed by local firms if the audits are publicly registered locally.[6]

Border Restrictions Perhaps the simplest forms of restrictions are those that affect firms at the time their operations cross borders. For example, tariffs (taxes) are often assessed by one country when advertisements or computer services are produced in another country. Tariff rates seem to change almost on a monthly basis. Quotas are another common form of border restriction. For example, to protect local film and TV producers, the European Community (EC) authorities have proposed restrictions on the percentage of air time allotted to U.S.-produced programs such as "Dallas."[7] Of course, one can easily imagine an element of cultural protection behind such restrictions. Likewise, in the United States the Federal Communication Commission restricts ownership of some print and broadcast media to citizens. Many countries have erected barriers to entry of foreign banks and insurance firms; France has prohibited the latter. Finally, almost all countries restrict the marketing of services by controlling work permits. Since 1992, EuroDisney can hire workers from any EC country without their having to obtain a work permit, but American managers must receive work permission from the French immigration authorities to oversee the company's substantial investments outside of Paris.

Discriminatory Laws A second common approach to protecting domestic firms from foreign competition is to let foreign firms in, but then discriminantly restrict their operations. Perhaps the best examples occur in the international banking and insurance industries. In Indonesia, foreign banks have been allowed to operate only in Jakarta, with limits on import financing. In Malaysia, foreign banks have had to meet racial employment quotas. Belgium has required non-European Community insurance companies to have higher solvency margins, thus reducing their flexibility. In the EC, only the United Kingdom has no restrictions on foreign insurance companies.[8] Even in the United States, some in Congress have advocated higher taxes on subsidiaries of foreign firms.

Subsidies A more subtle form of protection from outside competition is government subsidies of domestic workers and industries. Subsidies to agriculture are the most well known, but local services industries are commonly supported financially by governments as well. For example, most countries around the world subsidize to some degree their local telecommunications companies. Likewise, most countries give their national airlines concessional loans, fare subsidies, and other financial assistance. In the Philippines, only national flagships have been allowed to carry "government-sponsored" imports and exports.[9]

Intellectual Property Rights This last category is perhaps the most important from the perspective of American industry. The main thing the United States has to offer in trade to the rest of the world is technology. This often takes the form of ideas and innovations that are quite easily copied. Foreign governments' lack of laws about intellectual property or lack of enforcement of laws serves to protect their own domestic industries and limits the profitability of U.S. exports. An egregious example of this problem is the recent release of a pirated video version of "True Lies," the Arnold Schwarzenegger action thriller, in Russia *before* it was shown in American theaters! The

Peoples Republic of China is the number-one problem country on the U.S. trade representative's list. The political power and intransigence of the PRC has made progress on adequate enforcement of intellectual property rights so far unacceptable. Advertising agencies in China feel quite free to copy campaigns successful in the United States—one candy "knock-off" is W&W chocolates, whose advertising promises, "Melts in your mouth, not in your hands!" The U.S. government estimates that such piracy of American creativity worldwide costs American firms some $60 billion per year. Unfortunately, some of America's most important high-technology firms have recently been forced to use attorneys as "marketers." That is, sales increases have resulted from aggressive enforcement of intellectual property rights against some of the firms' best foreign customers!

As we mentioned at the outset of this section, our descriptions here are exemplary. Complexity and dynamism are the key terms characterizing the legal context of international marketing of services. Yes, our account of present circumstances is depressingly daunting. As tough as the legal barriers appear to be, however, at least the laws are written down somewhere. Certainly enforcement of those laws is still a key area of ambiguity. But it is important to recognize that the most difficult part of marketing services in other countries has to do with cultural barriers, which we address next. And there is some good news—in terms of legal restrictions on the international marketing of services, things are getting simpler with the passage of regional and global trade agreements, and we consider those remarkable achievements later in the chapter.

Cultural Barriers to Services Marketing

Because trade in services frequently involves people-to-people contact, culture plays a much bigger role in such trade than in merchandise trade. Many a successful domestic marketer has come away from a foreign market "adventure" wondering what went wrong. A case in point is an American health care provider attempting to market birthing services in Japan. Preliminary economic and legal analyses predicted a large potential market. Appropriately, a joint venture partner was selected and proposals were made. The Japanese partner gave no response, and after one year of "courtship" in Tokyo, costing about $100,000, the American firm gave up. On the basis of what we heard from the executives involved, the failure might be attributed to any of three kinds of cultural barriers. First, the consumers themselves may have rejected the service innovations—no Japanese women were directly contacted during the preliminary research. Second, the very conservative Japanese physicians and health care system may have been the obstacle. Third, the American executives making the proposals may never have established the kind of close personal relationships with their Japanese counterparts on which all commercial relationships in Japan are based. Indeed, it's quite likely that all three cultural obstacles played a role in the demise of an otherwise economically viable venture.

The very concept of what service is depends on cultural context. Good service at Kentucky Fried Chicken in the United States means orders are filled accurately and quickly. At KFC in Japan, accuracy and speed are likewise important, but good service also means that the customer is handed his or her order by the clerk "with two hands," demonstrating the respect the customer deserves. The British are notorious for tolerating bad service. A recent *Wall Street Journal* article attributes part of the blame to the remnants of the British class system, under which only servants served. "Waiters, busboys and salesmen like to remind customers that they are *not* servants. A little rudeness proves the point."[10] In Eastern European countries service is even worse. The notion of catering to the customer's wishes is so incongruous in those countries that "customer service" has no linguistic equivalent in most.[11]

It is useful to consider important dimensions of culture and the ways in which culture can affect services buyers, services providers, and the implementation of entry strategies in international markets. We begin by examining how culture is defined.

What Is Culture?   Over forty years ago, A. Kroeber and C. Kluckhohn[12] identified more than 160 ways to define culture, although most of these coalesce around modes of behavior or modes of thought. Culture is learned, shared, and transmitted from one generation to the next, and is multidimensional. Culture is important in international services marketing because of its effects on the ways companies and their customers interact and on the behavior of employees. Unfortunately, human nature dictates that we tend to view other cultures through the often cluttered lens of our own.[13] Edward T. Hall[14] observed that, at least in the United States, people tend to view foreigners as "underdeveloped Americans." Geert Hofstede[15] sums up the message of one of his books as follows:

> Everybody looks at the world from behind the windows of a cultural home and everybody prefers to act as if people from other countries have something special about them (a national character) but home is normal. Unfortunately, there is no normal position in cultural matters. (p. 235)

Definitions of the elements of culture vary, but a simple list of the major areas would include: (1) language (both verbal and nonverbal), (2) values and attitudes, (3) manners and customs, (4) material culture, (5) aesthetics, and (6) education and social institutions.[16] These "cultural universals" are manifestations of the way of life of any group of people. Services marketers must be particularly sensitive to culture because of customer contact and interaction with employees. Each of these elements of culture is discussed here in the context of services marketing. The purpose of this section is to sensitize you to the importance of cultural differences. Management implications are specifically addressed in the subsequent section.

Language   Language is an obvious difference between cultures. It reflects cultural values in its lexicon, form, and structure. Communication is an essential part of the marketing task; therefore services marketers must communicate in the language of the market. Adaptation is needed in advertising and personal selling and in market research, which is often accomplished using national employees, distributors, and advertising agencies. As demonstrated by the chapter opening vignette, when service provider and service customer are of different cultural backgrounds, sensitivity is especially needed to ensure a satisfactory service encounter.

Many business blunders result from simple errors in translation. Figure 15-3 illustrates some translation errors in service contexts.[17]

The role of language has influence beyond that of a medium of direct communica-

In a Bucharest hotel lobby:
The lift is being fixed for the next day. During that time we regret that you will be unbearable.

In a Yugoslavian hotel:
The flattening of underwear with pleasure is the job of the chambermaid.

On the menu of a Swiss restaurant:
Our wines leave you nothing to hope for.

In an advertisement by a Hong Kong dentist:
Teeth extracted by the latest Methodists.

In a Czechoslovakian tourist agency:
Take one of our horse-driven city tours—we guarantee no miscarriages.

In a Copenhagen airline ticket office:
We take your bags and send them in all directions.

On the door of a Moscow hotel room.
If this is your first visit to the USSR, you are welcome to it.

From a brochure of a car rental firm in Tokyo:
When passenger of foot heave in sight, tootle the horn. Trumpet him melodiously at first, but if he still obstacles your passage then tootle him with vigor.

FIGURE 15-3   International blunders in translation around the world.

tion. SPRINT Canada ran into difficulties in using spokeswoman Candice Bergen in its ad campaign. Response to commercials for discount long-distance services in Quebec has lagged behind that of English-speaking Canada. Ms. Bergen, who speaks French, filmed ads in the language. However, the actress' popular show "Murphy Brown" is dubbed into French before it is aired in Quebec, and therefore the voice that viewers associate with Candice Bergen is not her real voice. Further, the colloquialisms used in the ad copy, such as "Tigidou, mon minou" ("OK, my pussycat"), are not the type of expressions used by the Quebecois.[18]

K-Mart upset its clerks in Prague when it required them to wear name tags stating, "I am here for you." The salesclerks insisted that the tags be changed to read, "*We* are here for you," which a sentiment more consistent with familiar Communist-era practices.[19]

Another language issue is what language to use in providing services. Obviously the native language of the customer is most appropriate. Mistakes made in this area can have serious repercussions, particularly when one cultural group feels threatened by another.

As reported in the *Los Angeles Times,* language problems in service encounters can get ugly very quickly, even in the United States:

> The front line is the polished burger counter where high school history teacher Roger Hughes said he felt hot fury when the clerk inquired pleasantly in Spanish: "May I help you?"
>
> "I said, 'Wait a minute, you're in America now.' They said, 'Excuse me, what would you like?' " said Hughes. "That's a social insult. I'm a customer. I don't speak Spanish. They should be conducting their business in English. If you want to conduct it in Spanish, then I say move back to Mexico."[20]

Finally, nonverbal behaviors can speak quite loudly in cross-cultural interactions. John Gumperz, an anthropologist at Berkeley reports:

> . . . in a staff cafeteria of a major London airport, newly hired Indian and Pakistani women were perceived as surly and uncooperative by their supervisors as well as by the cargo handlers they served. Observation revealed that while relatively few words were exchanged, the intonation and manner in which their words were pronounced were interpreted negatively. For example, a person who had chosen meat would have to be asked whether he wanted gravy. A British attendant would ask by saying "Gravy?" using rising intonation. The Indian women, on the other hand, would say the word using falling intonation: "Gravy."

It was learned that "gravy" said with a falling intonation was interpreted as an announcement rather than an offer by the British customers served. This misinterpretation led to unanticipated and unfriendly responses from the customers and associated claims of ethnic discrimination by the Indian women.[21]

Values and Attitudes　These help to determine what members of a culture think is right, important, and/or desirable. Because behaviors, including consumer behaviors, flow from values and attitudes, services marketers who want their services adopted cross-culturally must understand these differences.

While American brands often have an "exotic" appeal in other countries, U.S. firms should not count on this as a long-term strategy. Wal-Mart has found that the cachet of U.S. brands is fading in Mexico. The Mexican news media have been alerting consumers to shoddy foreign goods, and some Wal-Mart customers are turning to a spirit of nationalism. The retailer is responding with an "Hecho en Mexico" program similar to the "Made in the U.S.A." program that has been successful here. And in some cases it is more than a case of nationalism. In some situations brand attitudes are negatively influenced by specific prejudices toward "dominating" cultures. The aforementioned Korean ban on Japanese movies and the French phobia about EuroDisney are good examples of the latter.[22]

Manners and Customs　These represent a culture's views of appropriate ways of behaving. It is important to monitor differences in manners and customs, as these can have a direct impact on the service encounter. Central and Eastern Europeans are perplexed by Western expectations that unhappy workers put on a "happy face" when dealing with customers. As an example, McDonald's requires Polish employees to smile whenever they interact with customers. Such a requirement strikes many employees as artificial and insincere. The fast-food giant has learned to encourage managers in Poland to probe employee problems and to assign troubled workers to the kitchen rather than to the food counter.[23]

Material Culture   Material culture consists of the tangible products of culture, or as comedian George Carlin puts it, "the stuff we own." What people own and how they use and display material possessions varies around the world. Cars, houses, clothes, and furniture are examples of material culture.

The majority of Mexicans do not own cars, limiting retailers' geographic reach. Further, most Mexicans own small refrigerators and have limited incomes, which limit the amount of groceries they can purchase at one time. Instead of the once-per-week shopping trip typical in the United States, Mexicans make frequent smaller trips. Promotional programs are also constrained by the availability of media. Ownership of televisions and radios affects the ability of services marketers to reach target audiences.

Zoos as entertainment represent an interesting reflection of culture's influence. Any American visiting the Tokyo Zoo is impressed by two things—of course the fine collection of animals, but also the small cages in which the animals are kept. To the Japanese who live in one of the most crowded countries in the world and own relatively small houses, the small cages seem appropriate, whereas to the American eye the animals may be perceived as being mistreated.

Aesthetics   Aesthetics refers to cultural ideas about beauty and good taste. These are reflected in music, art, drama, and dance, as well as the appreciation of color and form.

Perhaps Madonna and MTV sell well internationally (please see Technology Spotlight),[24] but even so the adage, "There's no accounting for taste," still rings quite true with most consumers around the world. A summer stroll through one of Madrid's important tourist attractions, Parque de Retiro, provides a simple but memorable lesson in how aesthetics vary across cultures. There are trash cans everywhere, but somehow the refuse doesn't seem to make it into them. Spaniards litter. From the American perspective, the litter detracts from the otherwise beautiful park. German tourists, used to the clean organization of their own fastidiously tidy forests, react with disgust. Or consider the earth tones in the decor of Japanese restaurants around the word vis-à-vis the glossy reds evident in their Chinese competitors' establishments.

Educational and Social Institutions   Both kinds of institutions are affected by, and are transmission agents of, culture. Education includes the process of transmitting skills and knowledge, and thus may take place in schools and in less formal "training" circumstances. The structure and functioning of each are heavily influenced by culture. Culture manifests itself most dramatically in the people-to-people contact of our social institutions. Notice if the student from Japan sitting next to you in class ever verbally disagrees with your instructor. Classroom interactions vary substantially around the world. Japanese students are used to listening to lectures, taking notes, and asking questions only after class, if then. In Japan the idea of grading class participation is nonsense. Alternatively, because Spaniards are used to huge undergraduate classes (hundreds rather than dozens), they tend to talk to their friends even when the instructor is talking.

Likewise, health care delivery systems and doctor/patient interactions also reflect cultural differences. Americans ask questions and get second opinions. Innovative health care services are developed on the basis of extensive marketing research. Alternatively, the social hierarchy is heavily reflected in the Japanese health care system, but

**TECHNOLOGY SPOTLIGHT:
INTERNATIONALIZING THE AIRWAVES**

It has been said that the only pan-European culture is the American culture. That is, Europeans' exposure to things American, such as blue jeans, hamburgers, and movies, has been greater than their exposure to any European culture other than their own. Satellite TV technology offers tremendous opportunities for U.S. exports of entertainment and new services.

One of the most successful cable TV stations in Europe is MTV Europe, a joint venture between U.S. and European partners. MTV president Tom Freston has said, "Music crosses borders very easily, and the lingua franca of rock n' roll is English. Rock is an Anglo-American form. German rock bands sing in English; Swedish rock banks sing in English."

The key to cross-national entertainment and news is language. When people seek entertainment, they rarely choose a foreign language medium. As a contrast to MTV's success, SuperChannel, an English-based satellite station, lost money until it changed its format to sports, where language is less important.

But U.S. companies aren't the only ones interested in the opportunities provided by satellite TV. For the majority of its fourteen years, Cable News Network (CNN) has enjoyed a dominant position in the business of televising twenty-four-hour-a-day global news. CNN's main subscriber growth comes from CNN International, whose content is 80 percent foreign news. But now the business has turned competitive, with players from around the world. The British Broadcasting Corporation (BBC) is the latest entrant, offering a twenty-four-hour news channel in the United States to compete directly with CNN, in addition to a separate twenty-four-hour station geared to European viewers. National Broadcasting Corporation plans an overnight business news broadcast in Asia as a part of Australia Broadcasting Corporation's twenty-four-hour Asia-news channel. With many nations opening their airwaves to satellite and cable, and with more households in developing countries able to afford televisions, media executives believe that there is pent-up demand just waiting to be filled.

instead of customers (i.e., patients) being on top, it's the doctors who command deference. Thus, the Japanese health care system, while delivering the best longevity statistics of any country, is quite unresponsive to concerns of consumers.

What Japan lacks in terms of customer orientation in health care innovations it more than makes up for in funeral services. The millennia of crowding has forced the mortuary industry in Japan to use cremation almost exclusively. There simply is no room for all the dead bodies. But according to *Business Week,*[25] the ash-filled urns can get a real send-off, including ceremonies with synthesized music, pink and green laser lights, and dry-ice smoke.

Culture's Effects on Customer Behavior   Given all the kinds of cultural differences associated with the delivery and marketing of services, it's a wonder that some firms are so successful in international markets. That is, efficient delivery of services and customer satisfaction almost always require that customers cooperate in the transaction. Thus, part of that success depends on the firms' abilities to manage behaviors of customers. For example, customer complaints are a key source of information regarding satisfaction and potential innovations. While we have seen no systematic cross-cultural comparisons of complainant behavior, on the basis of anecdotal evidence and one study about American and Dutch attitudes about complaining[26] we conclude that Americans are quite good about expressing dissatisfaction with bad service. In the Netherlands consumers don't complain because they doubt its efficacy. In other countries already mentioned (England and Russia, for example), in part because expectations are low, consumers may have to be encouraged to complain. Mexico's Grupo Posadas, Latin America's largest hotel operator, has found it useful to amplify the voice of the consumer by requiring each hotel's managing director to start every morning by reading every customer complaint regarding all operations.[27]

Given culture's pervasive influence on consumer preferences and expectations, how can services marketers narrow the gaps culture creates so that they can maximize customer satisfaction in the international context? We provide answers to this key question in a later section. There we discuss the management of customer and employee behavior and the adaptation of the marketing mix in international markets.

OPPORTUNITIES IN INTERNATIONAL SERVICES

As we pointed out in chapter 1, the fastest growing segment of the U.S. economy is services. Services dominate the economies of other developed nations as well. As countries develop, the role of agriculture in the economy declines as that of services rises. In countries in the OECD (Organization for Economic Cooperation and Development),[28] services employ more than half of the labor force and produce more than half of GDP.[29] Table 15-1 shows the role of services in employment and GDP in selected countries from all areas of the world. Highly developed countries all have more than 50 percent of GDP and employment derived from services. The world market for services has grown at a faster rate (16%) than that for merchandise trade (7%).[30]

The dynamism and competitiveness of American services industries ensures that innovations will continue to emanate from U.S. firms. More than products, what the United States has to offer the rest of the world is new ideas, expressed, of course, in high-

TABLE 15-1   SERVICES AS A PERCENTAGE OF GDP AND LABOR FORCE IN SELECTED COUNTRIES

Country	Percent of GDP (1988)	Percent of labor (1987)
China	13.8	10.2
Poland	26.3	32.6
India	39.5	15.7
Nigeria	40.5	20.2
Indonesia	40.8	35.6
Hungary	42.1	40.8
South Africa	53.6	42.1
Egypt	55.5	34.1
Mexico	55.6	24.0
Japan	56.8	55.9
Brazil	57.5	46.0
Spain	57.5	46.0
Canada	62.0	68.8
United Kingdom	62.9	59.6
France	64.3	55.0
United States	72.3	67.7

Source: The Economist Book of Vital World Statistics, 1990.

technology products, but even more importantly in engineering and architectural services, in software and entertainment, in medical procedures and efficient marketing services and so on. While some lament the marginalization (i.e., declining importance) of manufacturing in the United States, others celebrate the growing emphasis on high-quality service industries. In fact, Professor Carlton Scott of the University of California at Irvine predicts that U.S. manufacturing in the 1990s will go the same way agriculture did in the 1940s.[31] The opportunities for American service providers in world markets will explode during the next decade.

Fortune magazine annually compiles a ranking of the world's leading service companies, separated into eight categories: diversified services, commercial banks, diversified financials, savings institutions, life insurance, retailers, transportation, and utilities. In 1994 Japan led the list with 140 service firms, compared with 136 U.S. firms (Figure 15-4). This was the first year in which Japan edged past the United States to become the number-one country. Japan also had the largest service firms in five of the eight categories (diversified services, commercial banking, life insurance, transportation, and utilities); the United States led in only two categories (diversified financial services and retailers).[32]

U.S. Exports of Services

Business people who have entered international markets say exporting is a logical step for U.S. companies, as the greatest potential for growth is clearly outside U.S. borders. Wallace O. Stephens, chairman and CEO of Stephens Engineering, which has performed projects worldwide for a number of U.S. agencies, stated, "Here in the U.S. we're competing for only 20 percent of the world's economic pie."[33]

The international selling of services has represented major growth opportunities for many U.S. firms. For example, the Big Six accounting firms receive almost half their revenues from outside the United States. Similarly, over half the billings of the top 10 U.S. advertising agencies are from overseas trade. A total of 65 percent of Citibank's revenues are from operations abroad.[34]

U.S. exports of services have increased substantially, from almost $86 billion in 1987 to $173 billion in 1993 (Figure 15-5). The United States is the world's leading producer and exporter of services. Services exports have traditionally made a significant contribution to the U.S. balance of trade. Over 40 percent of the 1993 goods trade deficit of $132.6 billion was offset by the $56.9 billion surplus in service trade (see Figure 15-6). For many years, growth in services trade enabled the United States to maintain a favorable trade balance, despite a deficit in goods trade. (Although the services trade balance remains a large surplus, it can no longer offset the merchandise deficit.[35]) Figure 15-7 lists the top 10 U.S. service industry exports in 1992. It shows the wide variety of services involved.

Free Trade Agreements

Addressing foreign market barriers to services exports has been one focus of U.S. government negotiations with foreign powers. Recent successful trade agreements have po-

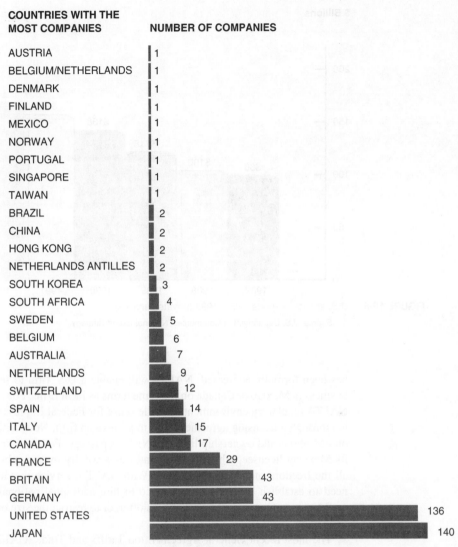

COUNTRIES WITH THE MOST COMPANIES	NUMBER OF COMPANIES
AUSTRIA	1
BELGIUM/NETHERLANDS	1
DENMARK	1
FINLAND	1
MEXICO	1
NORWAY	1
PORTUGAL	1
SINGAPORE	1
TAIWAN	1
BRAZIL	2
CHINA	2
HONG KONG	2
NETHERLANDS ANTILLES	2
SOUTH KOREA	3
SOUTH AFRICA	4
SWEDEN	5
BELGIUM	6
AUSTRALIA	7
NETHERLANDS	9
SWITZERLAND	12
SPAIN	14
ITALY	15
CANADA	17
FRANCE	29
BRITAIN	43
GERMANY	43
UNITED STATES	136
JAPAN	140

FIGURE 15-4   The world's largest service corporations and countries where they are located.
Source: Fortune, August 22, 1994.

tentially far-reaching positive impacts on services exporters. Indeed, as the services sector begins to dominate world trade in the next decades, even more attention of regulators and negotiators will be focused on allowing markets to work efficiently.

The North American Free Trade Agreement (NAFTA) has the effect of opening many markets for services. For the first time, the need for the protection of trade secrets and coordinated standards to facilitate trade between the United States, Canada, and Mexico

$ Billions

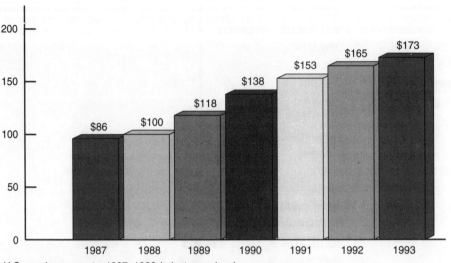

FIGURE 15-5   U.S. services exports, 1987–1993 (private services).

Source: U.S. Department of Commerce, "National Export Strategy."

has been formally addressed. NAFTA will enable a U.S. firm to set up and operate a business in Mexico or Canada on the same terms as local firms. For example, in the pre-NAFTA regulatory environment, it made sense for Federal Express to operate in Mexico through a licensing agreement sold to a Mexican firm. Now, with many restrictions on operations and ownership lifted by NAFTA passage, Federal Express has purchased its Mexican licensee, which now operates as a wholly owned subsidiary with almost all the freedom of a local company.[36] With NAFTA, service providers will no longer need to establish themselves in Mexico to hire additional nationals, to accept limits on the range of services they are able to offer, or to restrict the size of the affiliated firm in Mexico.

The most recent General Agreement on Tariffs and Trade (GATT), signed in 1994, provides for most-favored-nation treatment, national treatment, market access, transparency (in legislation and enforcement), and the free flow of payments and transfers. Specific rules in the framework deal with issues affecting financial services, movement of persons, and basic telecommunications services. For example, the Mexican telephone company, Telmex, changed its operations substantially (reduced tariffs on telecommunications equipment and services) when it joined the earlier General Agreement on Tariffs and Trade (GATT) in 1986, and with the new agreement, American firms will see new opportunities in places like Mexico.[37]

The Trade Related Intellectual Property Rights (TRIPs) part of the GATT agreement obligates all member nations signing on to GATT to provide strong protection for copy-

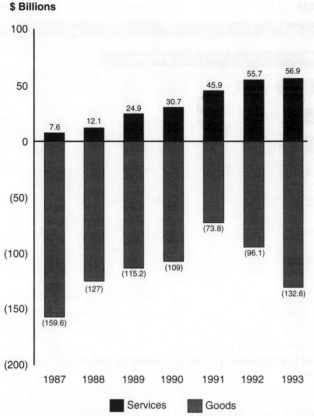

FIGURE 15-6   U.S. trade balance, 1987–1993.

Source: U.S. Department of Commerce, "National Export Strategy."

right and related rights, patents, trademarks, trade secrets, industrial designs, geographic indications, and layout designs for integrated circuits. Such intellectual property protection has tremendous implications for the U.S. export of many high-technology services, such as custom software, as well as entertainment services.[38] Indeed, in previous GATT agreements, services were given little attention, but in the 1994 GATT, issues related to free trade in services and the reduction of barriers have taken center stage.

Another controversial issue is the right of "nonestablishment," which is increasing in importance as more service firms are able to deliver their services electronically or through the mails without ever being physically present in a country. Such regulations govern the conditions under which a company can be said to have established a presence in a foreign market, which will affect whether the company qualifies for domestic firm status. Establishing a domestic presence is frequently necessary to qualify for protection under the laws for intellectual property rights in a particular country.[39]

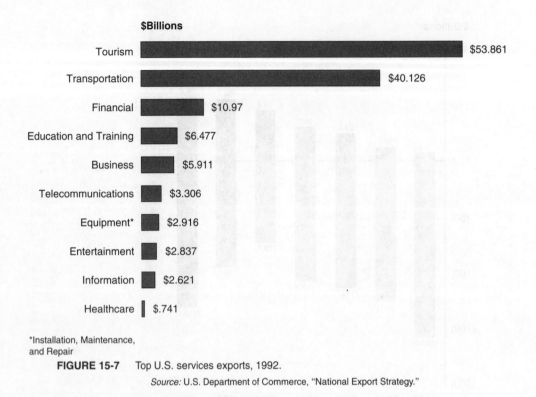

$Billions

Tourism	$53.861
Transportation	$40.126
Financial	$10.97
Education and Training	$6.477
Business	$5.911
Telecommunications	$3.306
Equipment*	$2.916
Entertainment	$2.837
Information	$2.621
Healthcare	$.741

*Installation, Maintenance,
and Repair

FIGURE 15-7   Top U.S. services exports, 1992.

Source: U.S. Department of Commerce, "National Export Strategy."

OPPORTUNITIES IN INTERNATIONAL MARKETS

International transactions take place under the following conditions: (1) selling abroad from home, (2) selling in the home market to visiting foreign citizens, and (3) selling abroad through a company's foreign representative.[40] Experience has taught that because services are intangible, exporting them is often infeasible without also exporting the personnel to provide them. Hence direct investment in foreign countries, licensing and franchising to foreign firms, and joint ventures with foreign partners are common vehicles for exporting services.[41] For U.S. multinational companies, the overwhelming majority of sales abroad are made through the use of such affiliates. In 1991, approximately 85 percent of sales to foreign customers were accomplished through affiliates, with only 15 percent being direct exports.[42]

Selling Services Internationally the Easy Way, at Home

It is not necessary to go abroad to market services internationally. International tourism is the largest business services export in the United States, and the third largest export overall, ranking behind only capital goods and industrial supplies. Projections indicate that the number of travelers to the United States will continue to grow, keeping international tourism as a top U.S. export well into the twenty-first century.[43] Spending by foreign visitors on such services as hotel rooms, restaurant meals, and air fares generated one third of the U.S. international services trade surplus in 1992. Also, foreign enrollment in U.S. universities totals more than 400,000 students and represents $5 billion in export revenues.[44]

The tourist business worldwide is dominated by OECD countries, which make up more than 80 percent of spending and almost 75 percent of receipts. Many developing countries have targeted tourism as a means of increasing exports, helping to balance other services imports and create jobs. But in practice, benefits rarely live up to expectations, as earnings often go to foreign airlines or hotel management firms. Also, the demands of pampered, wealthy tourists can serve to put a strain on scarce resources.[45]

Trade Creates Service Demand

In addition to the growth in demand for services worldwide, the increase in international trade has itself spurred demand for specialized services for exporters. A number of U.S. consulting firms are seeing their influence expand as large companies demand their expertise on how to manage globally and build worldwide networks of information technology. Coopers and Lybrand consultants are traversing China to find appropriate locations for Burger King, while AT&T has retained McKinsey & Co. to help it find strategic partners abroad. Table 15-2 provides information on the activities and range of services of the 10 leading U.S. global consulting firms.[46] For many of these, revenues from outside the United States represent more than half their total revenues.

As Japanese firms expanded operations globally, they encountered various problems requiring the assistance of lawyers experienced in transborder disputes. The legal services provided by domestic firms were limited primarily to courtroom activities. The growing new demand for attorneys experienced in a broader range of international financial negotiations, projects, and contracts forced Japanese firms to import legal services during the 1970s. The Japanese bar is quite restrictive, and initially this new demand was handled by allowing American lawyers to work as "trainees" in Japanese firms. Then in 1986 the Japanese government for the first time permitted American firms to provide legal advice to Japanese firms as it pertained to their international ventures. Now several American firms have opened offices in Tokyo. Indeed, the burgeoning growth in international trade has initiated the spread of U.S. legal services worldwide (see Figure 15-8).[47] This enormous growth has occurred in both developed (e.g., Japan) and developing (e.g., Poland) nations.

Increased global trade also creates demand for distributors. For example, InterForward in Germany handles European distribution for Harley-Davidson, the U.S. motorcycle manufacturer, as well as for Denon, the Japanese stereo-speaker maker. The company takes responsibility for preparing customers' products to meet the specifications of the various countries, distributes JIT (just-in-time) to retailers, and offers maintenance services to end-users. Such services are necessary only because of international distribution needs.[48]

Other firms have developed services to meet the needs of international travelers. Sprink's Insurance maintains an extensive data base, which is made available to its customers in France through the electronic Minitel network. If clients are planning foreign travel, the data base can tell them, for example, which vaccinations are needed, what dis-

TABLE 15-2 TEN LEADING GLOBAL CONSULTING FIRMS

Firm	1993 revenues* (millions)	Percent revenues outside U.S.	No. of professionals	Highlights
Andersen Consulting, Chicago	$2,876	51	24,598	Now boasts 150 offices in 46 countries; hottest region is Asia/Pacific, where revenues jumped 24% in 1993 to $259.4 million
Arthur D. Little, Cambridge, Mass.	385	50	1,579	Has 36 offices in 23 countries, with newest opening in Korea; in a typical year, firm undertakes assignments in some 60 nations
A. T. Kearney, Chicago	278	53	950	One of fastest growing U.S. firms, recognized as an authority in both operations and logistics
Booz, Allen & Hamilton, New York	800	30	4,600	Staff boasts 73 nationalities serving clients in more than 75 countries, from helping east Germany privatize companies to reshaping Australia's Broken Hill Proprietary
Boston Consulting Group, Boston	340	63	1,250	Half of staff is based in Europe where revenues nearly equal those in the U.S.; Asia and Far East now represent 12% of revenues
Coopers & Lybrand, New York	1,050	52	7,650	Envisions major growth in Asian and Latin American markets; will triple 35-person Eastern European privatization practice
Ernst & Young, New York	922	42	7,200	Former CEO of a leading Australian company now heads consulting services; he alone directed projects in 20 nations
Gemini Consulting, Morristown, N.J.	516	49	1,700	Has landed major assignments with many multinationals, from British Telecom to DuPont; aggressively expanding in all markets
McKinsey, New York	1,274	60	3,100	Arguably the most global of all firms, with 29 nationalities represented among some 500 partners; 63 offices in 32 countries
Price Waterhouse, New York	995	55	7,200	Boasts network of more than 400 offices in 118 nations and territories worldwide; high growth in Asia, India, and Latin America

Source: "Hired Guns Packing High-powered Knowhow," p. 94.

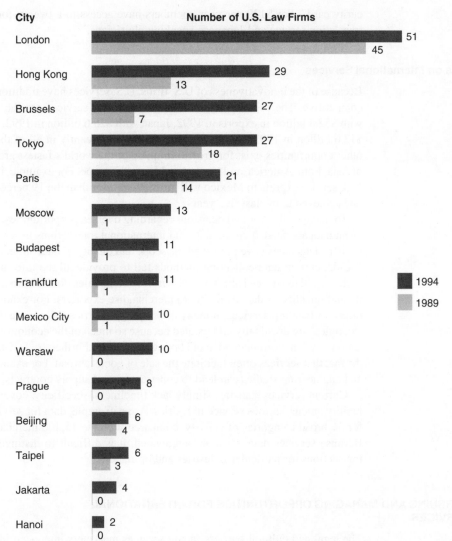

City   **Number of U.S. Law Firms**

London   51
                                                                      45

Hong Kong   29
                                        13

Brussels   27
                              7

Tokyo   27
                                   18

Paris   21
                                   14

Moscow   13
                       1

Budapest   11
                      1

Frankfurt   11
                      1

Mexico City   10
                      1

Warsaw   10
                   0

Prague   8
                  0

Beijing   6
                     4

Taipei   6
                   3

Jakarta   4
                  0

Hanoi   2
               0

■ 1994
▨ 1989

FIGURE 15-8   Expansion of U.S. law firms abroad. Going Global Over the past five years, law firms expanded overseas. As a result, the number of branch offices of U.S. firms in may foreign cities rose sharply.

Source: Data From *National Law Journal,* as published in Schmitt, "The Business of Law."

eases are potentially problematic and how to protect against them, what visas are required, and what laws pertain to currency, accidents, and so on.[49]

Closer to home, Intersec taps into Japanese parents' fears about their children studying in the United States. For $3,000 a year plus expenses, the company both counsels and monitors Japanese exchange students and makes reports to parents. The Japanese Assistance Network has signed up over 1,300 Japanese residents and students for a "security card." For $120 per year, members have access to a twenty-four-hour Japanese translation service and Japanese-speaking physicians.[50]

Data on International Services

Because of the innovativeness of U.S. firms, U.S. services have traditionally been highly competitive. The primary international markets for services are the European Union with $52.4 billion in exports in 1992, Japan with $25.6 billion in 1992, and Canada with $17.6 billion in 1992. Service exports are up significantly in all of these markets, and other opportunities exist for growth in many of the world's fastest growing economies of Asia, Latin America, and Central and Eastern Europe. For example, it is predicted that U.S. service exports to Mexico will grow even faster than the 19 percent annual growth rate achieved in the last five years.[51]

To make well-informed decisions regarding overseas opportunities, accurate and relevant data are needed on markets and international transactions in services. While U.S. statistical agencies have improved the scope and quality of data on services over the last decade, current data collection methods fail to provide all the information service exporters need to succeed abroad. U.S. services companies do not have access to the quality and quantity of data available to merchandise exporters. For example, the opportunities for banking services in many developing countries (Mexico and Russia are good examples) are drastically understated because so much of the economy (monetary transactions) is "underground" to avoid taxing authorities. Further, trade data fail to highlight the fact that services often facilitate the sale of goods abroad. For example, architectural and engineering studies can lead to construction and supply contracts.

Current services statistics simply lack timeliness, specificity, coverage, and comparability among various service industries. As an example, data for services are available for 31 broad categories of activity, compared with the 15,400 merchandise categories. Because services data are more aggregated, it is difficult to distinguish international transactions for particular industries and/or markets.[52]

PURSUING AND MANAGING OPPORTUNITIES FOR INTERNATIONAL SERVICES

The legal and cultural barriers facing services marketers interested in pursuing export opportunities are indeed daunting. One or both types of barriers spring up during the planning of export activities. While some have argued for global standardized products, service companies will be most successful when they adapt offerings in international markets. It will be important to consider all aspects of the marketing mix, from adapting the service itself to making changes in strategy and implementation. The most important aspects of these marketing decisions are discussed in this section.

Adapting the Service Itself

Even the most mundane financial services require special attention in foreign markets. Bank branches in Spain, compared with branches in many other European countries, have traditionally been unusually small and numerous. Spaniards like to use and therefore be close to their cash. They seem to have an aversion to checks and credit cards because, according to some, both instruments create transaction records that can be tracked by tax authorities. So walking-distance convenience is a key attribute of banking services in Spain. Meanwhile, in Mexico with interest rates of over 30 percent and credit purchases representing few sales, customers need access to cash. One reason for K-Mart's greater success in Mexico compared with Wal-Mart is its decision to place a bank branch inside the store to facilitate customers' cash access.[53]

Terms of mortgages are another interesting area of cross-cultural differences in financial services. The typical mortgage in the United States is for thirty years. In Mexico, most people pay cash for houses because mortgages are virtually unavailable. And in Japan, one-hundred-year mortgages are quite common. Indeed, there the mortgage is often passed along with the house or flat to the next generation.

Finally, the travel industry has been responsive to the special preferences of big-spending Japanese tourists. Because Japanese take few long vacations—seven to ten days is the norm—vacation packages are unusually crammed with activities. Rome, Geneva, Paris, and London in ten days is representative.[54] The Four Seasons Hotel chain provides special pillows, kimonos, slippers, and teas for Japanese guests. Virgin Atlantic Airways and other long-haul carriers will soon have available interactive screens for each passenger, allowing viewing of Japanese (or American, French, etc.) movies, TV, and even gambling if regulators approve.

Adapting Promotion and Distribution

According to Hans-Gunther Meissner at Dortmund University in Germany,[55] Japanese and German passengers differ substantially in what they value regarding airline services. German patrons are most interested in getting there on time, and Lufthansa advertising and in-flight services such as passenger loading procedures reflect this emphasis. Japanese patrons, on the other hand, are most interested in the comfort of the flight (in Professor Meissner's words, "the process of consumption, not the outcome"), and Japan Airlines advertisements and in-flight services reflect this different approach.

Some of our own work indicates that sales strategies must be adapted to fit culturally determined search patterns for industrial services. In Figure 15-9 we compare the word-of-mouth networks employed by managers of (1) a small American firm and (2) a small Japanese firm in choosing a variety of industrial service vendors in the United States. As evident from the figure, word-of-mouth referrals are much more important to the more collectivistic Japanese manager (that is, the network is more complex and involves more indirect contacts to vendors) than his more individualistic American counterpart. Our continuing research well demonstrates the representativeness of these two examples. The implications for marketers of such services to Japanese clients here or in Japan is to emphasize promotion via the opinion leaders.[56]

An unusual problem has cropped up in trying to expand catalog sales in the burgeoning Brazilian market. Because in the past the economic system in Brazil has been unreliable, Brazilian catalog customers get very uncomfortable when shipments are delayed even one day. They expect delivery on or before the deduction occurs in their credit-card account. This special Brazilian "delivery anxiety" requires extra staff to handle the frequent postpurchase calls.[57]

AMERICAN COMPANY

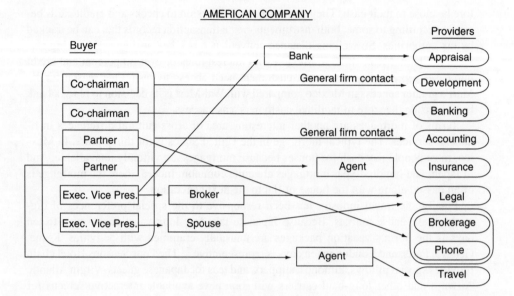

JAPANESE COMPANY

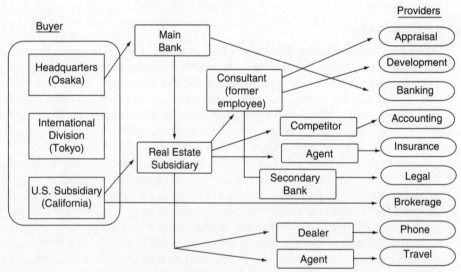

FIGURE 15-9 Examples of actual referral networks (from an exploratory study—two California real estate companies).

The marketing of health care services to Asian immigrants in the Los Angeles area is made somewhat more complicated by the necessity of health care outstations in addition to the more traditional free-standing clinics. And the ideal location of outstations depends on the specific group served and the ailments targeted—churches for Tongans, private homes for Filipinos, and schools for Vietnamese seem to work well. Also, food (and the homey ambiance and social interaction connoted by its presence) has been found to be a key promotional device for many of the Asian groups studied.[58]

Adapting Entry Modes

Common strategies that are often appropriate for the international marketing of merchandise such as selling to an exporter in the United States or to an importer or distributor in the target country are unusable for services trade. Rather, franchising, joint ventures, and ownership with local management are the principal entry strategies for the sale of services in other countries, because of the importance of people and personal contact in the marketing and delivery of services. All of these strategies depend on the availability of qualified managers if such foreign ventures are to succeed. American managers must have as a minimum cultural sensitivity. Ideally they will know at least a second language and have experience living in a foreign culture. Of course it would be best if the language skills and cultural knowledge pertained to the specific target country. But we should expect that in the growing global business environment, American managers will manage operations and negotiate with business partners in several countries during their careers.

The other kind of person that is essential for the success of an excursion into a foreign market is a local informant. Ideally, that will be someone who understands American culture and the American business system. This informant can be a consultant, but a long-term relationship is to be preferred. A better informant might be a franchisee, a partner, or an employee, the last given great latitude to manage the operation after an initial setup period. Indeed, the comments of Wallace Doolin of TGI Fridays in Figure 15-10 are most insightful in this regard.

Finally, by far the most important thing we have to say in this chapter is *listen to and believe your local manager or partner.* It is quite natural for Americans to consider American ways as best. But the best approaches will usually result from a creative blending of ideas and practices. It will take managers' conscious and continuous efforts to avoid the pitfalls of underestimating the importance of cultural differences.

A stepwise entry is another useful concept. Recall our earlier description of Federal Express's strategies in Mexico, starting with a license agreement. As the firm's experience in Mexico increased and the regulatory environment relaxed with NAFTA, the shift to a wholly owned subsidiary (by purchase of its licensee) made sense.[59]

Finally, one way to sell a foreign client is to first approach that client's U.S. subsidiary. But even this preliminary "domestic" sale requires adaptation. For example, AT&T has found it useful to reorganize its sales strategies when subsidiaries of Japanese firms in the United States are targeted. In Japan, two different sales representatives would call on Toyota and Nissan because the two customer firms are in different, very competitive industrial groups (*kieretsu*). Thus, in the Los Angeles area, even though American employees of Japanese subsidiaries make the purchasing decision, it is still

Manager's Journal

By Wallace Doolin

A few months ago, a competitor of TGI Friday's called me for advice on opening restaurants overseas. Although he asked all the right questions, I sensed that the call was a formality. His attitude seemed to say, "It's just another restaurant. How hard can it be?"

What may seem self-evident can't be over-emphasized: While you have to modify certain strategies and procedures when you open for business abroad, you must protect the unique identity, quality of product and standards of service that made your business a success at home.

To transport your personal identity into a foreign setting, it usually is advisable to take on a development partner—in our case, a franchisee or joint-venture partner—who knows how to conduct business in Europe, Asia, or whichever market you want to enter. A strong partner can help you negotiate government obstacles, labor unions, hiring practices and other hurdles that are unique to various parts of the world.

In interviewing prospective partners, we make a point of visiting their offices or the facilities they manage to watch the interaction between supervisors and employees. If we observe an attitude of casual respect and openness, rather than trepidation, we know we've found a partner who appreciates our style of business. A partner who doesn't share your philosophy might ask you to compromise your principles and style.

In the early years of our international expansion, one of our development partners told us we would never find the kind of outgoing, enthusiastic employees in Europe that we hire in the U.S. For example, in Britain, we were told the waiters don't sing "Happy Birthday" to customers.

This created a dilemma. We had to ask ourselves whether we should introduce our traditional standards to customer service abroad, or adjust our standards to the local market. We decided that a restaurant without our brand of service would be a "TGI Friday's" in name only. So with our partners we developed a new approach to hiring that suited our style of business.

When we look for employees outside the U.S., we hold auditions instead of traditional job interviews. We rent a theater or set up a stage, and ask our job candidates to sing, dance or tell a joke—anything that will show us their fun side. There are outgoing people in every culture; once we find them, we can give them the necessary job training.

Choosing good partners and hiring good employees are among the biggest challenges you will encounter overseas. But our international ventures have taught us other lessons, such as:

• *You can't overlook market research.* Preliminary research might have saved us the expense of putting kimchi on the menu in South Korea. Kimchi, a kind of pickled cabbage, is a staple in Korean restaurants, and we assumed customers would look for it on our menu as well. We were wrong. It seems that customers in an American restaurant want only American food.

• *You may have to modify your research methods in a foreign market.* We discovered that there is no word in Spanish that means "value" as we define it here. So in Spain, we ask our guests such questions as "Do you think the quality of the food was equal to the price you paid?" It's all a matter of thinking about the kind of information you want, then figuring out ways of obtaining it.

• *You can't take little things for granted.* In certain countries, the supplies and materials you need to run your business may be unavailable or unbelievably expensive. In Malaysia, for instance, sour cream costs $16 a pound. We found it was cheaper for us to make our own sour cream to serve with baked potatoes and potato skins.

We encountered an even more difficult problem in London. We assumed that one potato is pretty much like another, so we went about making french fries the same way that we make them at home. What we got was a greasy mess. It seems that English potatoes have a different texture and sugar content than Idaho potatoes. So we had to develop an entirely new procedure to make fries in London.

• *You can't rush it.* Opening for business abroad takes two to three times longer than you would expect. Finding the right locations and securing development permits are only part of it. Training also takes longer, partly because of language barriers, but mainly because your way of doing business is literally foreign to most people outside the U.S.

• *Eventually, you have to let go.* I played a lead role in opening some of our first overseas restaurants. After months of scouting locations, hiring managers and training employees, it was hard to pull back and let the local crew take over. But you can't open a restaurant in Germany or the Philippines and expect to run the place as if it were in Dallas or Detroit.

Your U.S. staff can see a new operation through its start-up period, but then you must turn it over to those who truly understand the culture of the home country. Once you entrust your overseas partners and employees with your business philosophy, they must carry it forward.

We seek out foreign nationals who may be on assignment or pursuing higher education in the U.S. and offer them an opportunity to return home. These individuals already understand U.S. business and service standards. But just as important, they are experts in the traditions, ethics and ways of life of the customers we want to serve in foreign markets.

Opening for business abroad requires a substantial investment—in capital and in human resources. With a knowledgeable partner and a commitment to understanding your new customers, you can transcend virtually any cultural barrier.

Mr. Doolin is president and chief executive officer of TGI Friday's, Inc., in Dallas.

FIGURE 15-10   On taking your business on the road abroad.

Source: Doolin, "Taking Your Business on the Road Abroad," *Wall Street Journal,* July 25, 1994, p. A12.

wise for companies like AT&T to have different representatives call on the two companies. When it comes to servicing Japanese accounts, much care must be taken about crossing industrial group lines, even in the United States.

Adapting Communication

Communication across cultures, whether in the office, at the service counter, or over the telephone or fax machine, is fraught with potential disasters. Communications researchers point to a hierarchy of four kinds of potential problems: differences in (1) language, (2) nonverbal behaviors, (3) values, and (4) thinking processes. The order of the list is important. Problems starting at (1) are more obvious and therefore more easily corrected. As you go down the list the problems are more subtle, more difficult to diagnose, and consequently harder to fix. If the person behind the counter speaks only Spanish and the customer only English, the problem is obvious. However, if those same two people value time differently, the cause of the resulting ill feelings when one party is "late" is less obvious. Examples of all four types of problems are in the following sections.

Language differences cause problems in service encounters. In many parts of the United States, consumer service providers are frequently recent immigrants. In some of its southern California stores, Del Taco has tried using a recorded greeting in the drive-through speaker to reduce the extent of this language problem. Some customers, however, express irritation with the depersonalization of the greeting (aren't greetings supposed to be personal?) and the mix of recorded and real people.

In the international context, language skills are crucial. Many American multinationals such as Citibank and McKinsey specifically recruit foreigners with American MBAs to work in their foreign offices. It is not simply an issue of higher costs associated with compensation packages for American expatriates. On the contrary, the key issue is the efficient delivery of banking and consulting services to the foreign customers. Moreover, it's not just the language skills that are valuable, it's the cultural cross-training of foreigners with an understanding of the American business system that commands the attention of recruiters.

Finally, Americans with language skills and overseas living experiences will be required in increasing numbers if U.S. service firms are to achieve their potential sales in global markets. True, English is the international language of commerce. But until an American has struggled to learn a second language, he or she cannot possibly appreciate the advantages afforded multilingual competitors or dangers of communicating across cultures.

Nonverbal behaviors also affect service encounters. As alluded to in a previous section, communication is not accomplished by words alone. We all take in and give off all kinds of nonverbal cues, and these cues provide information principally about the way we feel. In service transactions, how customers feel is key information. In cross-cultural situations, such nonverbal cues are usually hard to read and easy to misinterpret. Smiles, frowns, silent periods, interruptions, tone of voice, passing a tray with two hands—all of these nonverbal behaviors can speak paragraphs about relationships between service providers and customers. But the meaning of such cues varies substantially across cultures. When the Japanese consulting client turns silent, it does not necessarily mean the American consultant should speak. The Japanese may just need some "thinking space," not more information. A Brazilian passenger's interruption of her American flight attendant should be interpreted as enthusiasm, not pushiness.

Training in this area is crucial for the efficient delivery of services and maximization of customer satisfaction. Obviously, service providers cannot be taught the complete nonverbal "lexicon" of customers, but key, recurring problems can be identified and appropriate management strategies and training programs can be developed.

Adapting Work Force Management

Culture's Effects on Employee Behavior　Managing a global work force is certainly no simple task. Just ask the folks at UPS:

> Some of the surprises UPS ran into: indignation in France, when drivers were told they couldn't have wine with lunch; protests in Britain, when drivers' dogs were banned from delivery trucks; dismay in Spain, when it was found that the brown UPS trucks resembled the local hearses; and shock in Germany, when brown shirts were required for the first time since 1945.[60]

Brown shirts aside, the primary difference between domestic and international marketing is that the latter activity *always* includes an interaction across cultures. When merchandise is marketed, the main interaction may be between a product made in one country and a consumer in another country. Even in this relatively simple transaction, however, at some point professionals from one country talk to those in another country. For example, American headquarters personnel deal with local sales representatives, or American sales representatives sell to buyers representing local retailers. The case of services marketing can be even more complicated because frequently an American service provider may interact directly with the foreign customer. American flight attendants serving European passengers, or Japanese bankers calling on American executives, are good examples of this latter case.

Adapting Service Employee Incentives　In the United States, the probability that good service will be provided is increased when financial incentives are directly tied to performance and customer satisfaction. Tips, commissions, bonuses, and compensation packages are designed to motivate workers. Simply stated, money talks loudest in America.

People in other cultures are motivated by other things. Thus we see substantial differences in tipping behavior around the world. According to *CultureGrams,* published by Brigham Young University, restaurant tips should be at least 15 percent in the United States and Canada, rounded to the next deutsche mark in Germany, and considered an insult in China. In Japan, incentives based on individual performance, such as tips and commissions, are not used to motivate workers. Instead, a strong corporate culture and frequent interactions with fellow workers are used in a spirit of collective effort.[61] Compensation schemes must be designed with consideration of such cultural differences.

Adapting Service Standards for International Service Delivery　Value differences impact the delivery of quality service internationally. Americans are known around the world for their wristwatches—not for making them, just for looking at them. However, time is not money everywhere in the world. What may seem efficient service to the American provider may come across as pushiness to foreign customers. For example, in restaurants in Madrid, the waiter will never bring you the check until you ask for it, Many a hungry American has been frustrated by the careful wrapping, boxing, bagging, and two-handed delivery of pastries in Japanese bakeries.

Perhaps the most serious cross-cultural conflict in values for Americans has to do with the importance of personal relationships in business transactions. Anyone in the consulting business will tell you that in the United States the personal relationship between consultant and client is crucial to both diagnosing problems and implementing the advice provided. Such personal relationships are even *more* important in almost all other countries. In this country, we depend on our legal system to resolve conflicts between business partners. In almost all other countries, trusting, personal relationships are invested in and depended on to serve the same purpose. Brazilians and Japanese won't even talk business until they feel comfortable with the American calling on them, perhaps not until the second or third meeting.[62] Finally, we hope it is obvious that the same kinds of problems can also cause friction between American managers and their local employees.

Differences in thinking processes and decision-making processes are the most subtle problem area. American managers are taught to think in a sequential way, reducing problems to their component parts. Consider the approach to case analysis you've been taught to use in your business classes: problem definition, listing of alternatives, analysis, and recommendations for action. Or consider sales training in the United States: determine the customer's needs, make the offer, handle objections, close the sale. All these thinking processes, which Americans take for granted, may cause all kinds of problems with foreign clients. Asian clients may not think in the same linear fashion. Discussions, presentations, their questions and objections, may appear to the "linear-thinking" American as disorganized and yielding little progress. As you are listing alternatives, your Korean counterpart may be redefining the problem. The typical sales presentation in Japan is front loaded with copious background and detailed information, because once the offer is made and the buyer has decided, there is no opportunity for sellers to handle objections. In Japan, sellers never challenge buyers.[63]

Again, training programs that raise the awareness level of client contact people will be crucial. Native employees and partners will be important assets and *must be* listened to and depended on.

Adapting Marketing Research Internationally

Marketing research in the international context is generally a daunting task because of cultural influences in response behavior.[64] In many cultures, survey research is seen as an invasion of privacy, even more so than in the United States. Indeed, American consumers are perhaps the most responsive of all consumers. In many cultures (Mexico and Japan are good examples), research respondents are even more likely than people here to give socially acceptable answers to questions rather than expressing their true feelings. Special approaches may be necessary to hear the voice of the consumer accurately. Less direct measurement techniques such as projective methods, conjoint analysis, gap analysis, and data analysis methods such as partial least squares may be more appropriate.

Some consumers may even have to be taught how to consume new (to them) services. Indeed, one of EuroDisney's greatest challenges is to manage cultural differences in the queuing behavior of its European patrons. Perhaps half the typical August day for customers at EuroDisney is spent standing in line. The British and Germans are quite good about queuing up in an orderly manner. Conversely, Spaniards and Italians are quite adept at squeezing to the front of lines. Such differences among patrons can seriously affect the consumption experiences of some, and if not effectively managed by the host firm, can result in high levels of dissatisfaction.

CONCLUSION

The legal and cultural barriers to the international marketing of services are substantial. But so are the opportunities for smart services marketers.

Current research reports that achieving high customer satisfaction is more difficult in the services business than in the merchandise business. On a 100-point consumer satisfaction scale, Americans rate nondurable products available in the United States at 82, durables at 80, retailing at 76, and services at 74. A comparable nationally representative sample of Swedish consumers rates nondurables available in Sweden at 72, durables at 70, retailing at 65, and services at 64. So services seems to be a tougher business in both countries.[65] The consistently higher satisfaction levels in the United States are attributed not to Americans' lower standards or cultural response biases, but rather to greater choices available at lower prices. This latter finding bodes well for American exports to Sweden, and indeed to the rest of the world.

Finally, free trade is spreading fast around the world. GATT and NAFTA appear to be only the beginning of government actions that will render American service firms even more competitive in the global marketplace in the years to come. As legal barriers and national borders continue to dissolve, the management of cultural factors will become a much stronger determinant of survival and success in the global marketplace. American firms have the advantage of superior technology and a remarkable innovativeness. But we must also recognize the natural weaknesses associated with existing in the largest and most dynamic national market. American managers and firms must fight the natural tendency toward ethnocentricity. Marketing services in the global market demands that attention be paid to cultural differences, because they widen the gap between customer expectations and perceptions of service quality.[66]

DISCUSSION QUESTIONS

1   Why are cultural factors more important in services than in product marketing?
2   Describe cross-cultural service encounters you have had and discuss in detail possible cross-cultural communication problems experienced.
3   List and discuss the difficulties of marketing services in other countries.
4   Is it getting easier or harder to market services abroad? Explain.
5   What language should Disney use in its attractions at EuroDisney? Why?
6   Why is the United States a leader in global services? What factors may affect this leadership role in the future?
7   Why are services marketing problems caused by cultural differences more vexing than legal barriers to marketing?
8   If you have been to a U.S. service provider in a foreign country (e.g., American Express, McDonald's), describe how the service was different from the service you receive from the same company in the United States. How was it the same?

9 Think of a nonprofit organization that offers services abroad (e.g., Peace Corps, Red Cross). What problems might such organizations face in "marketing" their services in other countries that for-profit organizations would not face?

10 As pointed out in this chapter, many U.S. consulting firms derive a large percentage of their revenues from foreign customers. List and describe problems consultants would face at every step of service provision, from getting the job to presenting the results.

EXERCISES

1 Find a foreign student and interview him or her about what is different (better or worse) regarding services in the United States than in his or her own country. List three examples and associated reasons.

2 Interview a person who has traveled extensively in other countries and make a list of aspects of customer services that are different from those in the United States. Conjecture as to why.

3 Invite a foreign student out for a typical "business lunch." Ask the student how this ritual/activity might vary in his or her country.

4 Visit authentic Chinese, Japanese, and Italian restaurants. Note differences in service and ambiance. Explain.

5 Rent or go see a foreign film (in a modern setting). Describe any service encounters in the film and how they are different or similar to those in the United States.

NOTES

1 "Japanese Put Tourism on a Higher Plane," *International Herald Tribune,* February 3, 1992, p. 8.

2 Jack Kelley, "Service without a Smile, Russians Find a Friendly Face Works Better," *USA Today,* January 22, 1992, p. 1.

3 "Japan Relaxes Rule, Lets Foreign Doctors Treat Victims," *The Orange County Register,* January 25, 1995, p. 9.

4 Vinay Kothari, "Strategic Dimensions of Global Marketing of Services," *Journal of Professional Services Marketing* 3 (1988): 209–220.

5 Teresa Watanabe, "The Collision of Two Cultures," *Los Angeles Times,* June 3, 1994, pp. A1, A6, A7.

6 U.S. Trade Representative Computer Group, 1992, Office of U.S. Trade Association, Washington, D.C.

7 "Battling for the Box," *Economist,* April 9, 1994, p. 32.

8 Jean Waelbroeck, Peter Praet, and Hans Christopher Rieger, eds., *ASEAN-EEC Trade in Services* (Singapore: ASEAN Economic Research Unit, Institute for Southeast Asian Studies, 1985).

9 Ibid.

10 Dana Milbank, "Service Economy Seems Rather Creaky in Britain Just Now," *Wall Street Journal,* December 7, 1993, pp. A1, A12.

11 Dean E. Murphy, "New East Europe Retailers Told to Put on a Happy Face," *Los Angeles Times,* November 26, 1994, pp. A1, A18.

12 A. Kroeber and C. Kluckhohn, "Culture: A Critical Review of Concepts and Definitions," Papers of Peabody Museum of American Archaeology and Ethnology, Harvard University, 1952, pp. 1–223.

13 R. Bruce Money and Mary C. Gilly, "The Effects of Culture on Word-of-Mouth Referral Behavior in the Buying of Industrial Services: The Case of the U.S. and Japan," Working Paper, University of California, Irvine, 1995.

14 Edward T. Hall, *Silent Language* (Garden City, N.Y.: Anchor Press/Doubleday, 1959).

15 Geert Hofstede, *Culture and Organizations, Software of the Mind* (London: McGraw-Hill, 1991).

16 Michael R. Czinkota and Ilkka A. Ronkainen, *International Marketing* (Chicago: Dryden Press, 1988).

17 Anne Helming, "Culture Shocks," *Advertising Age,* May 17, 1982, pp. M-8, M-9 (illustrations by Gary Giani).

18 Solange DeSantis, " 'Murphy Brown Goes to Canad,' or, 'Parlez-Vous Long Distance?' " *Wall Street Journal,* November 25, 1994, p. B1.

19 Murphy, "Put on a Happy Face."

20 Doreen Carvajal, "When Languages Collide," *Los Angeles Times,* December 19, 1993, pp. A1, A52.

21 John J. Gumperz, "Sociocultural Knowledge in Conversational Inference," *28th Annual Roundtable Monograph Series in Language and Linguistics,* Georgetown University, Washington, D.C., 1979.

22 Christina A. Roemer and John L. Graham, "Intercultural Prejudice and Brand Equity: An Eastern German Example," Working Paper, University of California, Irvine, 1995.

23 Murphy, "Put on a Happy Face."

24 Vern Terpstra and Ravi Sarathy, *International Marketing,* 6th ed. (Fort Worth, Tex.: Dryden Press, 1994).

25 Karen Lowry Miller, "Rest in Peace . . . with Lasers, Smoke, and Synthesizer Music," *Business Week,* September 16, 1991, p. 48.

26 Commission of the European Community, *European Consumers: Their Interests, Aspirations and Knowledge on Consumer Affairs* (Brussels: European Community, 1976).

27 Joachim Bamrud, "Hotel Boom," *U.S./Latin Trade,* March 1995, p. 32.

28 The OECD is the Paris-based "rich countries' club" which was established in 1961 to promote the expansion of world trade and economic growth in member countries. Members include Australia, Austria, Belgium, Canada, Denmark, Finland, France, West Germany, Greece, Iceland, Ireland, Italy, Japan, Luxembourg, Netherlands, New Zealand, Norway, Portugal, Spain, Sweden, Switzerland, Turkey, United Kingdom, and United States.

29 *The Economist Book of Vital World Statistics* (London: Hutchinson Business Books, 1990).

30 Czinkota and Ronkainen, *International Marketing.*

31 Carlton Scott, personal communication, 1995.

32 Rajiv Rao, "The Year of Mixed Results: The World's Largest Service Corporations," *Fortune,* August 22, 1994, pp. 180–208.

33 Martha M. Hamilton, "The Service Trade," *The Washington Post,* July 18, 1994, pp. 1, 12.

34 Czinkota and Ronkainen, *International Marketing.*

35 U.S. Department of Commerce, "National Export Strategy," *Business America,* October, 1994.

36 Gary Newman and Anne Szterenfeld, *Guide to Doing Business in Mexico* (New York: McGraw-Hill, 1993).

37 Ibid.

38 U.S. Department of Commerce, "National Export Strategy."

39 Terpstra and Sarathy, *International Marketing.*

40 Kothari, "Strategic Dimensions."

41 Terpstra and Sarathy, *International Marketing.*

42 U.S. Department of Commerce, "National Export Strategy."

43 Ibid.

44 Ralph T. King, Jr., "U.S. Service Exports Are Growing Rapidly, but Almost Unnoticed," *Wall Street Journal,* April 21, 1993, pp. A1, A6.

45 *The Economist Book of Vital World Statistics.*

46 "Hired Guns Packing High-powered Knowhow," *Business Week,* special 1994 bonus issue, pp. 92–96.

47 Richard B. Schmitt, "The Business of Law," *Wall Street Journal,* January 13, 1995, p. B12.

48 Sandra Vandermerwe, *From Tin Soldiers to Russian Dolls: Creating Added Value through Services* (Oxford: Butterworth-Heinemann, 1993).

49 Ibid.

50 Sarah Lusman, "Firm Taps into Japanese Parents' Fears," *Wall Street Journal,* September 1, 1994, pp. B1, B2.

51 U.S. Department of Commerce, "National Export Strategy."

52 Ibid.

53 Bob Ortega, "Wal-Mart Is Slowed by Problems of Price and Culture in Mexico," *Wall Street Journal,* July 29, 1994, pp. A1, A4.

54 "Japanese Put Tourism on a Higher Plane."

55 Hans-Gunther Meissner, "A Structural Comparison of Japanese and German Marketing Strategies," *Irish Marketing Review,* Spring 1986, pp. 66–78.

56 Money and Gilly, "The Effects of Culture."

57 James Bruce, "Catalog Time in Brazil," *U.S./Latin Trade,* October, 1994, pp. 30, 32.

58 Rika Houston, "The Role of Culture in Health Care Consumption: Asian Immigrants as Consumers," Working Paper, University of California, Irvine.

59 Newman and Szterenfeld, *Guide to Doing Business in Mexico.*

60 Dana Milbank, "Can Europe Deliver?" *Wall Street Journal,* September 30, 1994, pp. R15, R23.

61 Grant Paul Skabelund, ed., *CultureGrams,* (Provo, Utah: David M. Kennedy Center for International Studies Publication Series, Brigham Young University, 1994).

62 John L. Graham and Roy A. Herberger, "Negotiators Abroad, Don't Shoot from the Hip," *Harvard Business Review,* July-August, 1983, pp. 160–168.

63 John L. Graham and Yoshiro Sano, *Smart Bargaining, Doing Business with the Japanese* (New York: Harper, 1989).

64 Susan P. Douglas and C. Samuel Craig, *International Marketing Research* (Englewood Cliffs, N.J.: Prentice Hall, 1983).

65 Claes Fornell, "1994 American Customer Satisfaction Index, Baseline Results Summary," University of Michigan Business School pamphlet, 1994.

66 Terpstra and Sarathy, *International Marketing.*

PART **SIX**

MANAGING SERVICE PROMISES

16

THE ROLE OF ADVERTISING, PERSONAL SELLING, AND OTHER COMMUNICATION

WE GUARANTEE YOUR SATISFACTION

How many times have you heard a company guarantee your satisfaction? Because customers want reliable service, many companies promise to provide it. But 100 percent reliable performance is difficult to achieve for a service organization, and many promises of satisfaction are not fulfilled. A true service guarantee is a vow that service delivery will meet company promises or the company will make it up to the customer.

Here are two guarantees that are well constructed and implemented, giving the companies that make them solid competitive advantages.

HAMPTON INN. In 1989, Hampton Inn offered a 100-percent Satisfaction Guarantee to any customer who didn't receive "high quality accommodations, friendly and efficient service, and clean, comfortable surroundings,"[1] in short, any customer dissatisfied for any reason (Figure 16-1). To back up the guarantee, any hotel employee—whether the front-desk clerk, a housekeeper, or a maintenance man—has the authority to do whatever is necessary to satisfy any customer. If the customer can't be satisfied, the employee can personally refund the customer's money without getting permission from a manager or supervisor. As you might imagine, both customers and employees benefit—customers by being satisfied or compensated, and employees by feeling personally empowered to please them. What may not be as obvious are the financial returns to the company. While refunds to guests totaled $1.1 million in 1993, the program brought in $11 million in additional revenue from repeat business of the compensated guests. Guest and employee surveys show that customers are persuaded and that employees have higher morale. Employee turnover has been reduced to 50 percent from a high of 117 percent three years ago.[2]

"BUGS" BURGER BUG KILLERS (BBBK). This pest-extermination company in Miami instituted the following four-part service guarantee:

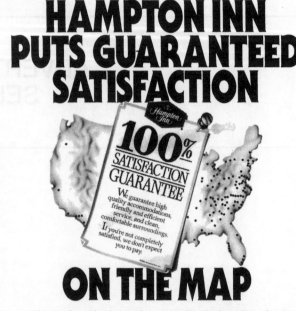

FIGURE 16-1   Example of a true service guarantee.

Source: This ad was used in October 1989 to announce the launch of Hampton Inn's "100% Satisfaction Guarantee."

1 You don't owe one penny until all pests on your premises have been eradicated.

2 If you are ever dissatisfied with BBBK's service, you will receive a refund of up to 12 months of the company's services—plus fees for another exterminator of your choice for the next year.

3 If a guest spots a pest on your premises, BBBK will pay for the guest's meal or room, send a letter of apology, and pay for a future meal or stay.

4 If your facility is closed down due to the presence of roaches or rodents, BBBK will pay any fines, as well as all lost profits, plus $5,000.[3]

To back up the guarantee the company uses complex preparation, cleaning, and checkup procedures; spends more on pesticides than competitors do; and compensates employees with higher-than-average pay. BBBK charges up to 10 times more than com-

petitors yet has a high market share in its operating areas. "Many restaurants and hotels are willing to pay BBBK's higher prices because to them it's ultimately cheaper: the costs of 'errors' (guests spotting roaches or ants) is higher than the cost of error prevention."[4]

Al Burger works to eliminate all obstacles to service quality. After discovering that clients' poor cleaning and storage practices are one of these obstacles, BBBK requires customers to maintain sanitary practices and in some cases even makes physical changes to their property. These and other activities result in quality so outstanding that the company rarely needs to make good on its guarantee. In one year it paid out only $120,000 on sales of $33 million. The company performs at levels other companies cannot match. According to the owner of a competing pest-control company, BBBK "is number one. There is no number two."[5]

A major cause of poor perceived service is the gap between what a firm promises about a service and what it actually delivers. As we discussed in chapter 4, customer expectations are shaped by both uncontrollable and company-controlled factors. Word-of-mouth communication, customer experience with other service providers, and customer needs are key factors that influence consumer expectations but are rarely controllable by the firm. However, controllable factors such as company advertising, price, personal selling, and the tangibles associated with the service also influence the expectations that customers hold for a service. In this chapter we focus on these controllable factors. Accurate and appropriate company communication—advertising, personal selling, and other messages that do not overpromise or misrepresent—is essential to delivering services that customers perceive as high in quality.

Because company communications about services promise what people do, and because people's behavior cannot be standardized the way physical goods produced by machines can be, the potential for Provider GAP 4 is high (Figure 16-2). By regulating communications within and outside the organization, companies can minimize the size of this gap.

Discrepancies between service delivery and external communications, in the form of exaggerated promises and/or the absence of information about service delivery aspects intended to serve customers well, can powerfully affect consumer perceptions of service quality. Figure 16-3 shows the factors that contribute to this gap, including (1) inadequate management of service promises; (2) overpromising in advertising and personal selling; (3) insufficient customer communication; (4) inadequate horizontal communication, particularly among operations, marketing, and human resources; and (5) differences in policies and procedures across distribution units. In this chapter we describe the problems stemming from these factors and detail strategies that firms have found useful in dealing with them to close Provider GAP 4.

The objectives of this chapter are to:

1 Discuss the key reasons for Provider GAP 4 that relate to marketing communications.

2 Present strategies for managing customer expectations.

3 Present four categories of strategies for matching service delivery with promises.

CUSTOMER

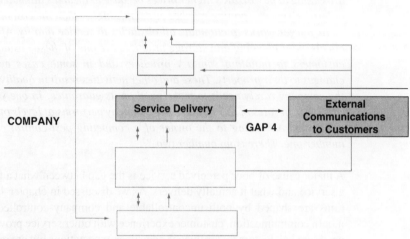

COMPANY

FIGURE 16-2   Provider GAP 4.

4 Present strategies for clear customer communication.

5 Discuss the critical requirement for horizontal communication within a service provider in order to meet or exceed customer expectations.

6 Provide perspective on the popular service objective of exceeding customer expectations.

KEY REASONS FOR GAP 4 INVOLVING COMMUNICATION

Inadequate Management of Service Promises

A discrepancy between service delivery and promises occurs when companies fail to manage service promises—the vows made by salespeople, advertising, and service personnel. One of the primary reasons for this discrepancy is that the company lacks the information and integration needed to make fulfillable promises. Salespeople often sell services, particularly new business services, before their actual availability and without having an exact date when they will be ready for market. Demand and supply variations also contribute to the problem of fulfilling service promises. They make service provision possible at some times, improbable at others, and difficult to predict. The traditional functional structure in many companies obscures the end-to-end processes that allow the company to project when work will be accomplished or whether the service to be delivered will match what is promised.

GAP 4 can also occur when companies neglect to inform customers of special efforts to ensure quality that are not visible to customers. Customer are not always aware of everything done behind the scenes to serve them well or to fulfill what they expect. In this situation, communication about customer needs or actions to address those needs are lost in the complex network of employee interactions with customers.

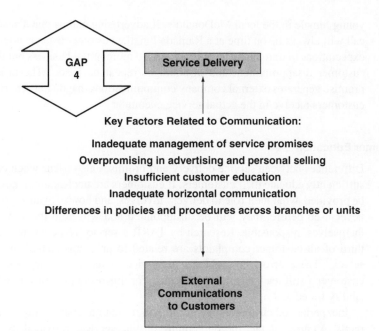

FIGURE 16-3   Key reasons for provider GAP 4.

Overpromising in Advertising and Personal Selling

Appropriate and accurate communication about services is the responsibility of both marketing and operations: Marketing must accurately (if compellingly) reflect what happens in actual service encounters; operations must deliver what is promised in communications. For example, when a management consulting firm introduces a new offering such as return-on-quality analysis, the marketing and sales departments must make the offering appealing enough to be viewed as superior to competing services. In promoting and differentiating the service, however, the company cannot afford to raise expectations above the level at which its consultants can consistently perform. If advertising, personal selling, or any other external communication sets up unrealistic expectations, actual encounters will disappoint customers.

Because of increasing deregulation and intensifying competition in the services sector, many service firms feel more pressure than ever before to acquire new business and to meet or beat competition. To accomplish these ends, service firms often overpromise in selling, advertising, and other company communications. In the airline industry, advertising is a constant battlefield of competing offers and price reductions to gain the patronage of customers. The greater the extent to which a service firm feels pressured to generate new customers, and perceives that the industry norm is to overpromise ("everyone else in our industry overpromises"), the greater is the firm's propensity to overpromise.

If advertising shows a smiling young female at the counter in a McDonald's commercial, the customer expects that, at least most of the time, there will be a smiling young female in the local McDonald's. If advertising claims that a customer's wake-up call will always be on time at a Ramada Inn, the customer expects no mistakes. Raising expectations to unrealistic levels may lead to more initial business but invariably fosters customer disappointment and discourages repeat business.[6] The propensity to over-promise generates external company communications that do not accurately reflect what customers receive in the actual service encounter.

Inadequate Customer Education

Differences between service delivery and promises also occur when companies do not sufficiently educate their customers. If customers are unclear about how the service will be provided, what their role in delivery involves, and how to evaluate services they have never used before, they will be disappointed and will hold the service company, not themselves, responsible. Research by TARP, a service research firm, reveals that one-third of all customer complaints are related to problems caused by customers themselves.[7] These errors or problems in service—even when they are "caused" by the customer—still lead customers to defect. For this reason the firm must assume responsibility for educating customers.

Inexperienced customers, by definition, do not understand how to use services correctly. As an example, the burgeoning on-line services provided by America Online, Prodigy, and CompuServe have high visibility and publicity; hardly a day goes by without a story about the Internet and its special-interest bulletin boards, electronic romances, and even on-line pizza delivery. Because this service industry is very new, many customers do not realize that using the services requires payment of a monthly fee to the service, additional costs for telephone time, a computer equipped with modem and other requirements, and a great deal of patience to wade through the often user-unfriendly installation. These prerequisites are beyond the capability of many customers and the churn rate (defection of customers) is high, largely because customers are not accurately informed.

For services high in credence properties—expert services that are difficult for customers to evaluate even after they have received the services—many customers do not know criteria by which they should judge the service. Automobile repair is one example: Because the technology has improved dramatically in recent years, few customers are now knowledgeable enough to determine whether recommended repairs are justified or performed correctly. Consequently, high- or low-quality technical service may be provided without the customer recognizing or realizing it, leading in some cases to dissatisfaction and defection when service is effectively performed and in others to retention and satisfaction when the technical service is inferior.

For high-involvement services, such as long-term medical treatment or purchase of a home for the first time, customers are also unlikely to comprehend and anticipate the service process. First-time home buyers rarely understand the complex set of services (inspection, title services, insurance) and processes (securing a mortgage, offers and counteroffers, escrow) that will be involved in their purchases. Professionals and other providers of high-involvement services often forget that customers are novices who must be educated about each step in the process. They assume that an overview at the beginning of the service, or a manual or set of instructions, will equip the customer. Unfortunately this is rarely sufficient, and customers defect because they can neither understand the process nor appreciate the value received from the service.

A final condition under which customer education can be beneficial involves services where demand and supply are not synchronized as discussed in chapter 14. If the customer is not informed about peaks and valleys in demand, service overloads and failures, not to mention underutilized capacity, are likely to result. Service organizations need to advise customers about variations in demand and supply to ensure that customers will not be disappointed when they need service.

Inadequate Horizontal Communications

Another major difficulty associated with Provider GAP 4 is that multiple functions in the organization, such as marketing and operations, must be coordinated to achieve the goal of service provision. Because service advertising and personal selling promise what *people* do, frequent and effective communication across functions—horizontal communication—is critical. If *horizontal communication* is poor, perceived service quality is at risk. If company advertising and other promises are developed without input from operations, contact personnel may not be able to deliver service that matches the image portrayed in marketing efforts.

This lack of communication is illustrated by Holiday Inn's unsuccessful "No Surprises" advertising campaign. Holiday Inn's advertising agency found through consumer research that hotel customers wanted greater reliability in lodging and created a television campaign promising "no surprises" to customers. Top managers accepted the campaign in spite of skepticism of operations executives who believed that the claim would be difficult to live up to. The campaign raised consumer expectations, gave dissatisfied customers additional reasons to be angry, and had to be discontinued.[8]

Not all service organizations advertise, but all need coordination or integration across departments or functions to be able to deliver quality service. All need horizontal communication between the sales force and service providers. Unfortunately, salespeople and operations employees are often in conflict, each function believing that the other makes work difficult. Operations employees feel that salespeople constantly promise more than they can deliver in order to get or maintain the business. Salespeople believe that operations employees are unwilling to push hard enough to deliver to customer expectations. A spirit of misunderstanding and mistrust can develop, enlarging Provider GAP 4.

Horizontal communication also must occur between the human resource and marketing departments. To deliver excellent customer service, firms must be certain to inform and motivate employees to deliver what their customers expect. If those who understand customer expectations (marketing and sales personnel) do not communicate this information to contact employees through training, motivation, compensation, and recognition, the lack of knowledge will affect the quality of service that employees deliver. Breaking down the walls between functions is difficult and time consuming, but high-quality service cannot be delivered without doing so.

Differences in Policies and Procedures across Distribution Outlets

A final form of coordination central to providing service quality is consistency in policies and procedures across departments and branches. If a service organization operates many outlets under the same name, whether franchised or company owned, customers expect similar performance across those outlets. If managers of individual branches or outlets have significant autonomy in procedures and policies, customers may not receive the same level of service quality across the branches. The size of Provider GAP 4 again may increase.

A question frequently asked by companies is, "How much standardization can we achieve across branches without taking away the autonomy and perceived control of employees?" At issue is the need to ensure consistency—so that expectations set by one outlet do not interfere with perceptions of service at another—while empowering managers and employees to serve customers in their own ways. If one Supercuts hair salon provides hors d'oeuvres and wine for its customers—a touch that can make customers feel special—will customers expect hors d'oeuvres and wine at every location and be disappointed if they do not receive the special service? If one McDonald's offers a contest or sweepstakes, won't the customer expect it at every McDonald's?

Lack of consistency across outlets explains a large part of the financial and operational difficulties experienced by Jiffy Lube, the Baltimore-based franchiser of quick-lube auto centers, in the late 1980s. Despite the tremendous demand for this new service, the brilliance of the service idea (a quick, efficient, and inexpensive lube job for which the customer does not need an appointment), and herculean efforts to ensure similarity of the physical aspects of the service, service quality perceptions of the firm were low. To respond to heavy demand and to penetrate the market quickly, the company grew from 400 outlets in 1987 to over 1,000 in 1989. Practices to deliver similar service in all were encouraged, but not required, by the franchiser, and the result was noticeably uneven service. In the geographic area of one of us, for example, three Jiffy Lube franchises produce very diverse service. One site offers outstanding personal service: The service manager consults with the customer several times during service provision, shows the customer samples of the fluids to be used, asks about problems, and answers questions directly and politely. At the second outlet the service manager speaks to the customer only on the customer's arrival and when the bill is settled. In this outlet the customer must wait in the shop until service is provided and then leave the premises, because the manager does not want cars that have already been serviced taking space in the parking lot. In contrast, customers in the third outlet may leave a car for at least an hour, allowing them to run errands or attend to other business in the nearby shopping center. This inconsistency of service, even within the same geographic region, has led to poor word of mouth and customer disappointment with Jiffy Lube and has resulted in complaints and class actions suits that severely damaged the firm's image.

FOUR CATEGORIES OF STRATEGIES TO MATCH SERVICE PROMISES WITH DELIVERY

Figure 16-4 shows four categories of strategies to match or exceed service delivery with promises: (1) manage service promises, (2) reset customer expectations, (3) improve

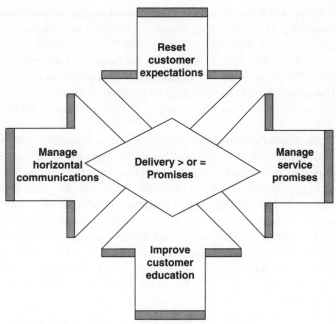

FIGURE 16-4   Approaches for matching service delivery and promises.

customer education, and (4) manage horizontal communications. Managing service promises involves coordinating the vows made by all employees in the company to ensure that they are consistent and feasible. Resetting customer expectations, a more dramatic strategy that tells customers the firm can no longer provide the level of service that it has provided in the past, is required when customer expectations must be lowered due to significant changes in the environment or company. Educating customers means providing customers with information about the service process or evaluative criteria that informs them about important aspects of service. Finally, managing horizontal communication means transmitting information across functional boundaries—between marketing and operations, human resources and finance—to align all functions with customer expectations. Strategies in each of these categories will be discussed in detail in the following sections.

Managing Service Promises

In manufacturing physical goods, the departments that make promises and those that deliver them can operate independently. Goods can be fully designed and produced and then turned over to marketing for promotion and sale. In services, however, the sales and marketing departments make promises about what other employees in the organization will fulfill. Because what employees do cannot be standardized the way physical goods produced mechanically can be, greater coordination and management of promises are required. Successful services advertising and personal selling become the responsibility of both marketing and operations: Marketing must accurately but beguilingly reflect what happens in actual service encounters and operations must deliver what is promised in advertising. If advertising or personal selling sets up unrealistic expectations for customers, the actual encounter will disappoint the customer. In a similar way, operations must cooperate with advertising to carry out themes of courtesy, responsiveness, and reliability that are presented in advertising. Interdependence exists, making cooperation and communication between these two functions critical.

Figure 16-5 shows specific strategies that are effective in managing promises.

Make Realistic Promises   The expectations customers bring to the service affect their evaluations of its quality: the higher the expectation, the higher the delivered service must be to be perceived as high quality. Therefore, promising reliability in advertising is appropriate only when reliability is actually delivered. Promising no surprises at a hotel, as Holiday Inn did, is disastrous if what actually happens in the delivery process includes many surprises. It is essential for the marketing or sales department to understand the actual levels of service delivery (e.g., percentage of times the service is provided correctly, percentage and number of problems that arise) before making promises about reliability. To be appropriate and effective, communications about service quality must accurately reflect what the customer will actually receive in the service encounter.

Offer Service Guarantees   Service guarantees are formal promises made to customers about aspects of the service they will receive. While many services carry implicit service satisfaction guarantees, the true benefits from them—an increase in the likelihood of a customer choosing or remaining with the company—come only when the customer knows that guarantees exist and trusts that the company will stand behind them. Among the most well-known service guarantees are those from Domino's Pizza (thirty-minute delivery), L.L. Bean (100% customer satisfaction), Bennigan's (fifteen-minute

FIGURE 16-5   Approaches for managing service promises.

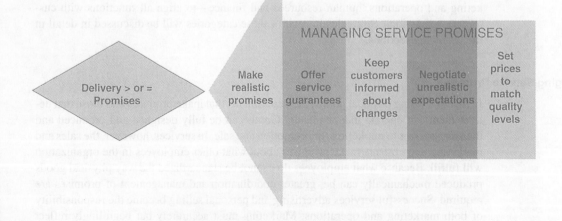

service), the U.S. Postal Service (two days for $2.90), and Hampton Inn's (100% customer satisfaction). As we shall see later in this chapter, some of these guarantees are more effective than others.

Service guarantees work when they promise customers that service will be more consistent than is typically true in services, and that if customers are dissatisfied they will receive compensation and restitution. Guarantees also help solidify and sharpen the firm's promise to customers. They have internal benefits as well: They focus employee efforts on customer priorities and provide clear standards for employee performance. Another benefit of a guarantee is that it generates feedback to the company about how well it is performing on its promises. Guarantee lapses—the number of times customers invoke a service guarantee—give the firm a hard operational measure for how well the company is doing in the areas important to customers.

One example of a service guarantee used to improve service performance was adopted by the cable industry when it felt the pressure of impending competition from telephone and wireless companies on the information highway. Three decades of cable monopoly had allowed service in the industry to be dismal, exemplified best by failed promises to install and fix cable problems. In an unprecedented move, an industrywide guarantee was offered on March 1, 1995, that pledged on-time service calls and installation. When pledges are not met, customers receive a month of free cable service. To communicate the guarantee to customers, the industry financed advertising, outreach programs, and a television special about cable technology and programming. Several of the 11,000 individual cable systems nationwide had tested the guarantee before it was implemented in the industry. Time Warner, for example, promised a free month of service if a cable appointment was broken. To introduce the guarantee, it featured a green alien sitting on the New York subway while a voice-over stated, "It takes a hell of a lot to surprise New Yorkers. And that's exactly what we're prepared to do."[9]

Christopher Hart, a former Harvard professor and acknowledged expert on service guarantees, claims that an effective service guarantee is unconditional, easy to understand and communicate, meaningful, easy to invoke, and easy and quick to collect on.[10] *Unconditional* means that no exceptions are built into the promise; the guarantee should cover either all elements of service or all elements that the firm can control. *Ease of understanding and communication* means that the guarantee should be simple and pinpoint the promise enough to tell employees what to do and customers what to expect. Guarantees should also be *meaningful,* both by covering service aspects that are important to customers and by providing significant payout when the promise is not kept. A guarantee of service within twenty-four hours will not be meaningful if the customer really wants service at a preappointed time. Finally, guarantees should also be *easy to invoke* (i.e., activated without hassle) and the monetary compensation for the broken promise *easy to collect.*[11]

Service guarantees are not appropriate for all services; they make the most sense under the following conditions: (1) the price for the service is high, (2) the negative impact of unsolved problems is high, (3) the customer's ego is on the line, (4) buyer resistance is high, (5) customer expertise with the service is low, (6) the industry has a bad image for service quality, (7) the company depends on frequent customer purchases, and

(8) the company's business is affected deeply by word of mouth.[12] Many business-to-business, personal, and professional services meet many of these criteria.

Exhibit 16-1 gives examples of successful and not-so-successful guarantees.

Keep Customers Informed about Provider Availability   Responsiveness and access are important aspects of service quality. Being able to reach a person who can help immediately or who can confirm a time by which help will arrive can be comforting to customers, particularly when they are experiencing service interruptions. Yet anyone who has ever worked in a service organization knows that 100-percent availability is unlikely to occur.

Voice mail—which initially seemed to inhibit access to company personnel—can be a useful tool to communicate availability. One large business-to-business manufacturer found that by requiring the date, availability of employee, and a promised callback time (e.g., eight hours) on all voice-mail messages, customers felt that unavailable service providers were more accessible. Meeting the callback commitment, or even exceeding it, then created a perception of responsiveness on the part of the customer.

Keep Customers Informed about Changes to Schedules and Offerings   More than anything, service quality means keeping promises. We all know this is true and yet we also realize that situations do arise when promises can't be met. In airline service, the weather sometimes prohibits takeoffs. In software service, problems in the program are discovered after the introduction of the software. In professional services such as medical services, a delayed test from the lab makes the doctor's diagnosis late. The reasons for unmet promises may involve the company, the customer, or other parties. In any case, the question arises: How soon do we let the customer know about the delay? Do we wait until we are sure there are no further delays/problems/issues or do we inform the customer quickly?

While the answer to this question may depend on individual customers' priorities, in general it is best to inform the customer immediately and keep her or him informed throughout the process. American Airlines pilots and crew are trained to inform customers immediately when delays occur, and to keep customers advised at regular intervals about changes. American's policy for informing customers involves telling customers throughout the flight what is coming up, whether it is as planned, and what will happen in the case of changes. Flight attendants inform flyers of scheduled departure time and often must ask passengers to stow their luggage quickly so that they do not hold up the plane's pushing back from the gate. As soon as the flight is aloft, passengers are told what type of service will be offered in the cabin. Next, the pilot addresses passengers stating the status of on-time arrival. Any change that occurs mid-flight, such as a revision to the routing or a slowdown near the destination, will be communicated to passengers.

This approach is particularly relevant to business-to-business services that are customized, such as marketing research, consulting, and computer programming services. In these and all industries that perform project work for other companies, schedules often slip because of the unpredictability of the creative work and because customers themselves change requirements for the projects along the way. In these cases, service

---

EXHIBIT 16-1   SERVICE GUARANTEES THAT WORKED . . . AND DIDN'T WORK

Successful Guarantees

Domino's Pizza's thirty-minute service guarantees was wildly successful for many years in gaining market share by meeting two primary customer needs: home delivery and fast food. The guarantee was a strong tool against rivals such as Pizza Hut. The payout was adjusted over the years from a free pizza to $3 off when the company found that some customers believed a free pizza was too much compensation for late arrival. (See last paragraph for the latest on Domino's guarantee).

Xerox Business Services vows in writing that all services provided by the Xerox Business Services division will completely satisfy customer expectations for performance. For facilities management, XBS commits in writing to:

Set performance standards based on specific customer requirements;

Promptly correct, at no cost to the customer, all work that does not meet requirements;

Provide qualified, trained personnel, with a specific clause in the agreement to promptly correct performance standards if they fall below the agreed-upon performance expectations;

Provide Xerox equipment that is covered by the Xerox Total Satisfaction guarantee for equipment; and

Provide timely management reports with specific recommendations to improve a customer's on-site operation.[13]

If the company does not perform to the guarantee, customers get a penalty-free cancellation of the contract. One potent aspect of this guarantee is that standards are tailored to requirements of each customer.

Metropolitan Life Insurance uses customized business-to-business service guarantees, such as a promise to American Airlines that customer calls would be answered within sixty seconds or it would forfeit its fees. Because of the service commitment, AA switched to Met Life.[14]

Satisfaction Guaranteed Eateries, Inc., a five-restaurant chain, implemented an unconditional service guarantee program.[15] One of the benefits of the guarantee was that it exposed process problems involved in service. For example, the company found that the wait-staff never checked to see if they had accurately entered meals into the computer. When they corrected these process problems, they eliminated expense and errors.

Not-So-Successful Guarantees

Bank of America in 1986 offered customers a choice of free checks or six months of retroactive free checking if they were dissatisfied with their checking account. "Cashing in" on the guarantee was a problem, however, because customers had to close their accounts to do so. When the bank realized that it was inconveniencing customers *and* losing business—many customers closed the accounts and went elsewhere!—it dropped the guarantee. In essence, the guarantee was an incentive for customers to find failures and leave the bank.[16]

Domino's Pizza's thirty-minute delivery guarantee was revoked in 1993 after a St. Louis jury awarded $79 million to Jean Kinder, injured by an 18-year-old Domino's driver who ran a red light. Other injuries, and even a few deaths (including a woman who died after a Domino's truck hit her), had been blamed on the guarantee. While the company defended itself, citing the good driving records of its employees, it recognized that the publicity was harmful to the company and discontinued the thirty-minute promise.[17]

---

providers need to inform clients of departures from the schedule as soon as possible and as often as the changes are made.

Negotiate Unrealistic Expectations   Sometimes customers express service requests like they would their lowest bid at a swap meet. The service they request for the price they are willing to pay is unrealistic; they know it and the firm knows it. It is, in effect, a starting point for discussion, not the expected end point. In these situations (common in business-to-business services when the purchasing agent, who is promoted and compensated on the basis of the low prices he or she negotiates, is the buyer), service providers must learn to present their offerings in terms of value and not price alone. They also must be aware of these practices and be prepared to negotiate more realistic expectations. If they do not, they may find themselves losing money in serving the client.

A large information technology services company often faced this challenge when purchasing agents were the buyers and executives were the decision-makers. The company made a wise decision that it would seek business only where it could cover costs and make a certain amount of profit. It advised purchasing agents of this decision and refused to compete on price alone. It also forged bonds with decision-makers in client organizations to whom it emphasized the value-add provided by the firm.

Set Prices to Match Quality Levels   One of the primary indicators of service level is price. We will discuss this topic in greater detail in chapter 17, but for now it is important to recognize that price establishes an expectation for the service level. Companies thus need to be cautious in setting their prices. A price that is too low relative to competitors' prices may signal an inferior level of quality and may actually deter customers from trying or adopting the service. A too-high price may lead customers to expect a level of service considerably higher than competing services priced lower.

Exhibit 16-2 mentions additional strategies for managing service promises.

Resetting Customer Expectations

In the 1990s era of downsizing and cost cutting, product and service companies often find themselves in the position of having to tell customers that service previously provided will be discontinued or available only at a higher price. Service from large computer companies, such as IBM and DEC, typically included salespeople who interacted with customers in person. This level of service attention was deemed necessary (because without it customers comprehended neither the options nor their needs adequately) and worthwhile (because almost all customers were perceived to be potentially large customers for computers). When demand for computers shifted from mainframes to PCs, the personal attention provided by direct salespeople was no longer necessary or cost effective. Instead of the traditional face-to-face service, the companies shifted to telephone interaction alone, a distinct—and for many customers disappointing—departure from the past. Credit-card companies that offered multiple value-added services when interest rates were high also found they needed to withdraw these services when interest rates dropped.

Service delivery has been cut back in many service industries, but few as dramatically as in the health care industry. Hospital patients now experience far shorter stays and less complex diagnostic procedures. Patients requiring psychotherapy are limited to six visits unless their doctors can substantiate in writing the need for more. Alcohol treatment is handled on an out-patient rather than in-patient basis.

EXHIBIT 16-2   EFFECTIVE ADVERTISING OF SERVICES

In addition to the suggestions made in this chapter about the use of advertising to manage promises and demand, other recommendations have been made by experts concerning what makes effective service advertising. These suggestions include the following.

Focus on the Evidence

Because services are performances and cannot be seen, touched, or otherwise sensed like products can be, tangibles associated with the service provide clues about its nature and quality.[18] Tangibles provide vivid information, information that creates a strong or clear impression on the senses and produces a distinct mental picture.[19] Using vivid information cues is particularly desirable when advertising services are highly intangible and complex. One way that advertisers can incorporate vivid information is to feature the tangibles, as in showing the bank's marble columns or gold credit card.[20] Another way is to feature related tangibles, such as Quantas Airline's use of the koala bear. Advertisers

can also evoke strong emotion, such as in AT&T's successful "Reach Out and Touch Someone" campaign.

Feature Service Employees in Advertising

Customer-contact personnel are an important second audience for services advertising.[21] Featuring actual employees doing their jobs or explaining their service in advertising is an effective way to communicate to employees that they are important. The featured employee also becomes a standard for other employees in the company by modeling high performance. In featuring employees, the marketing department must interact with at least some of the people in operations. Therefore, the communication and coordination needed to create the advertising results in closing the gap between external communications and delivery.

Focus on Primary Quality Determinants

Communicating service quality begins with an understanding of the aspects of service quality that are most important to customers. Isolating quality dimensions pivotal to customers provides a focus for advertising efforts.[22]

How can a company gracefully give the customer news that service will be cut back? Figure 16-6 summarizes four possible strategies.

Offer Choices   One way to reset expectations is to provide the customer with options. The options can deal with any aspects of service that are meaningful, such as time and cost. A clinical psychologist charging $100 per hour, for example, might offer clients the choice between a price increase of $10 per hour or a reduction in the number of minutes comprising the hour (e.g., fifty minutes). With the choice, clients can select the aspect of the trade-off (time or money) that is most meaningful to them. Making the choice serves to solidify the client's expectations of service.

This strategy is effective in business-to-business situations, particularly in terms of speed versus quality. Customers who are time conscious often want reports or proposals or other written documents quickly. When asked to provide a 10-page proposal for a project within three days, an architectural firm responded that it could provide either a 2-page proposal in three days *or* a 10-page proposal in a week. Its customer selected the latter option, recognizing in so doing that the deadline could be extended. In most business-to-business services, speed is often essential but threatens performance. If customers understand this trade-off and are asked to make a choice, they are likely to be more satisfied because their service expectations for each option become more realistic.

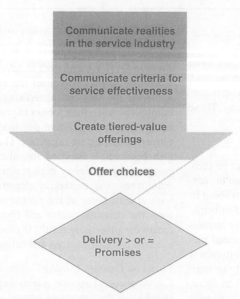

FIGURE 16-6   Approaches for resetting customer expectations.

Create Tiered-Value Service Offerings   Product companies are accustomed to offering different versions of their products with prices commensurate with the value customers perceive. Automobiles with different configurations of extras carry with them price tags that match not their cost to provide but instead their perceived value to the customer. This same type of formal bundling and pricing can be accomplished in services, with the extra benefit of managing expectations.

WordPerfect created tiered-value offerings for its help-line support. A customer with low need for support (or a tight budget) can sign up for minimum service. Another with higher need for support and willingness to pay can buy a slightly higher support plan. And the customer with a need for immediate and ongoing support can purchase the most expensive service package.

Credit-card companies offer similar tiered-value offerings. American Express has multiple levels based on type of service provided: The traditional green card offers basic service features, the Gold Card additional benefits, and the Platinum Card still more. Two of the advantages to the firm of tiered offerings are (1) the practice puts the burden of choosing the service level on the customer, thereby familiarizing the customer with specific service expectations, and (2) the company can identify quite simply which customers are willing to pay higher prices for higher service levels.

The opportunity to set expectations accurately is present when the customer makes the decision up front and can be reminded of the terms of the agreement when support is requested that is above the level in the contract.

Communicate the Criteria and Levels of Service Effectiveness   At times companies have the opportunity to establish the criteria by which customers assess service.

Consider a business customer who is purchasing market research services for the first time. Because market research is an expert service, it is high in credence properties that are hard for customers to judge. Moreover, the effectiveness of this type of service differs depending on the objectives the client brings to the service. In this situation, a service provider has the opportunity to teach the customer the criteria by which the service can be evaluated. The provider who teaches the customer in a credible manner will have an advantage in shaping the evaluation process.

As an example, consider research company A that communicates the following criteria to the customer: (1) a low price signals low quality, (2) reputation of the firm is critical, and (3) person-to-person interviews are the only type of customer feedback that will provide accurate information. A customer who accepts these criteria will evaluate all other suppliers using them. If research company B had talked to the customer first, consider these (very different!) criteria and their impact on the buyer: (1) market research companies with good reputations are charging for their reputation, not their skill, (2) telephone interviews have been found to work as well as person-to-person interviews, and (3) price is not indicative of quality level.

The same approach can be used with service *levels* rather than evaluative criteria. If research company B tells the customer that it can provide four-day turnaround on the results of the data analysis, this sets the customer's expectation level for all other suppliers.

Communicate Realities in the Industry   How can companies lower expectations without losing business to a competitor that is inflating promises? This question is particularly difficult when an industry as a whole is suffering from a poor image. Airlines were faced with difficult service delivery problems when the industry was deregulated: Overcrowded airports, intense price and route competition, and scheduling problems led to poor service and declining customer perceptions. Airlines knew that reliability—getting to the destination on time safely—was the most important dimension of airline service, but also realized that this was never more difficult to deliver than during the intensely confusing and competitive postderegulation era. Developing an advertising campaign that did not overpromise but that engendered awareness and positive perceptions toward a firm was a major challenge.

American Airlines ran an advertisement that identified with customer frustrations and explained the key uncontrollable industry reasons for the problems. At the same time, the airline described efforts it was taking to improve the situation. American was comfortable with such claims because it had already documented that its on-time service was better than that of any of its competitors. Because American's reliability was the highest in the industry, the advertisement was believable and did not stimulate unrealistic expectations. Soon after, American was awarded top billing in service performance by a frequent flyer survey in North America. Later advertisements in the campaign made explicit reliability claims about American's service.

Improving Customer Education

As discussed in chapter 13, customers must perform their roles properly for many services to be effective. If the customer forgets to perform this role, or performs it improp-

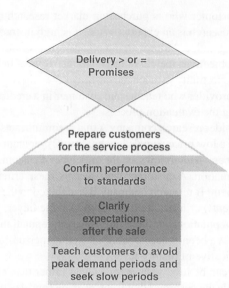

FIGURE 16-7   Approaches for educating customers.

erly, disappointment may result. For this reason, communication to customers can take the form of customer education. Figure 16-7 shows several types of customer education that can help match promises with delivery.

Prepare Customers for the Service Process   One of us, on a return trip from Singapore on Singapore Airlines, neglected to heed the airline's warning that return flights to the United States must be confirmed twenty-four hours in advance. On arrival at the airport to return home, her seat had been given to another customer (who *had* conformed to the airline's request for confirmation). Depending on the perspective taken, one could argue that either the company or the customer was right in this situation. Whose responsibility is it to make sure that the customer performs her role properly?

Companies can avoid this situation by preparing customers for the service process. And they may need to prepare the customer often, even every step of the way, for the subsequent actions the customer needs to take. A business-to-business example will help illustrate this strategy.

Customers of management consulting services purchase intangible benefits: reengineered processes, marketing effectiveness, motivated work forces, downsizing. The very fact that companies purchase these services usually indicates that they do not know how to perform them alone. Many customers will also not know what to look for along the way to judge progress. In management consulting and other complex service situations, the provider must prepare the customer for the service process and may even need to create structure for the customer. At the beginning of the "engagement," the management consulting firm often establishes "checkpoints" throughout the process, at which times progress will be evaluated, and also leads the customer to establish objectives for project completion. Because customers do not know what that progress will look like, the consulting firm takes the lead in setting goals or criteria to be examined at those times.

A similar approach is sometimes necessary and effective with individual service customers. Do you remember registration at the beginning of your first college semester or quarter? How aware were you of the steps in the process? Where to go after each step? It is unlikely that printed directions, even in great detail, made you feel confident and competent in the new service experience. You may have required step-by-step—"next call this telephone number or go to table B"—guidance.

As these and other examples show, any time a customer is inexperienced or a service process is new or unique, education about what to expect is essential.

Confirm Performance to Standards and Expectations   Service providers sometimes provide service, even explicitly requested service, yet fail to communicate to the customer that it has been accomplished. Providers sometimes stop short of getting credit for their actions when they do not reinforce their actions with appropriate communication about their fulfillment of the request. This may happen under one or more of the following conditions: (1) The customer cannot evaluate the effectiveness of a service, (2) the decision-maker in the service purchase is a person different from the users of the service, (3) the service is invisible, and (4) the provider depends on others to perform some of the actions to fulfill customer expectations.

When the customer cannot evaluate service effectiveness, usually because he is inexperienced or the service is technical, the provider may fail to communicate specific actions that address client concerns because the actions seem too complex for the customer to comprehend. In this situation the service provider needs to be able to translate the actions into customer-friendly terms. A personal injury lawyer who executes activities to aid a client with the medical and financial implications of an accident needs to be able to tell the client that these activities have been performed, in language the customer can understand.

When the decision-maker in service purchases is a person different from the users of the service, the provider has insufficient contact with the decision-maker and frequent contact with users. It is not unusual in these (typically) business-to-business situations for a wide discrepancy in satisfaction to exist between decision-makers and users. An example is in the purchase of information technology products and services in a company. The decision-maker—the manager of information technology or someone in a similar position—makes purchase decisions but interacts with the service provider only during the decision process and rarely during usage. Providers must make a special effort to keep these customers informed about performance to expectations.

Customers are not always aware of everything done behind the scenes to serve them well. Most services have invisible support processes. For instance, physicians frequently request diagnostic tests to rule out possible causes for illness. When these tests come back negative, the doctors may neglect to inform patients. Many hair-styling firms have guarantees that ensure customer satisfaction with haircuts, permanents, and color treatments. However, only a few of them actively communicate these guarantees in advertising because they assume customers know about them. The firm that explicitly communicates the guarantee may be selected over others by a customer who is uncertain about the quality of the service. Even though many competitors provide the same service, the firm that communicates it to customers will be the one chosen on that attribute. Making customers aware of standards or efforts to improve service that are not readily apparent can improve service quality perceptions.

Clarify Expectations after the Sale   When service involves a hand-off between sales and operations, as it does in most companies, clarifying expectations helps the service delivery arm of the company to align with customer expectations. Salespeople are motivated and compensated to raise customer expectations—at least to the point of making the sale—rather than to communicate realistically what the company can provide. In these situations, service providers can avoid future disappointment by clarifying what was promised as soon as the hand-off is made.

Teach Customers to Avoid Peak Demand Periods and Seek Slow Demand Periods   Few customers want to face lines or delays in receiving services. In the words of two researchers, "At best, waiting takes their time, and at worst, they may experience a range of unpleasant reactions—feeling trapped, tired, bored, angry or demeaned."[23] In a bank setting, researchers tested three strategies for dealing with customer waits: (1) giving customers prior notice of busy times, (2) having employees apologize for the delays, and (3) assigning all visible employees to serving customers. Only the first strategy focuses on educating customers; the other two involve managing employees. Researchers expected—and confirmed—that customers warned ahead of time of a wait in line tended to minimize the negative effects of waiting to justify their decision to seek service at peak times. In general, customers given a card listing the branch's busiest and slowest times to customers were more satisfied with the banking service. The other two strategies, apology and all-tellers-serving, showed no effects on satisfaction.[24]

Educating customers to avoid peak times benefits both customers (through faster service) and companies (by easing the problem of overdemand). This strategy may require frequent messages about peak and slow times. Companies may also want to reinforce the communication with cheaper prices at slow times—a strategy that airlines and telecommunications companies have found effective in managing demand.

Managing Horizontal Communications

To close Provider GAP 4, horizontal communication—communication across functional boundaries in an organization—must be facilitated. This is a difficult task because functions typically differ in goals, philosophies, outlook, and view of the customer, but the payoff is high. Coordination between marketing and operations can result in communication that accurately reflects service delivery, thus reducing the gap between customer expectations and actual service delivery. Integration of effort between marketing and human resources can improve the ability of each employee to become a better marketer. Coordination between finance and marketing can create prices that accurately reflect the customer's evaluation of a service. In service firms, these functions need to be integrated to produce consistent messages and to narrow the service quality gaps (Figure 16-8).

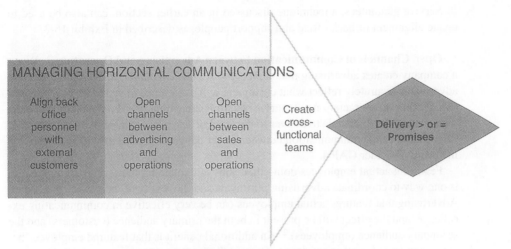

MANAGING HORIZONTAL COMMUNICATIONS

| Align back office personnel with external customers | Open channels between advertising and operations | Open channels between sales and operations | Create cross-functional teams | Delivery > or = Promises |

FIGURE 16-8   Approaches for managing horizontal communications.

Align Back Office and Support Personnel with External Customers through Interaction or Measurement   As companies become increasingly customer focused, front-line personnel develop improved skills in discerning what customers require. As they become more knowledgeable about and empathetic toward external customers, they also experience intrinsic rewards for satisfying customers. Back office or support personnel, who typically do not interact directly with external customers, miss out on this bonding and, as a consequence, fail to gain the skills and rewards associated with it.

Interaction   Companies are creating ways to facilitate the interaction between back office and support personnel and external customers. Xerox, for example, created a program called "Adopt A District" to allow employees to meet and build relationships with particular customers. Weyerhaeuser sends hourly employees to customers' plants to better understand their needs. When actual interaction is difficult or impossible, some companies have videotaped customers in their service facilities during the purchase and consumption process to vividly portray needs and requirements of customers and to show personnel the support front-line people need to deliver to those expectations.

Measurement   When company measurement systems are established, internal employees are sometimes judged on the basis of how they perform for the next internal customer in the chain. While this approach provides feedback in terms of how well the employees are serving the internal customer, it lacks the motivation and reward that come from seeing their efforts affect the end-customer. Federal Express is one company that has aligned internal personnel with the external customer using measurement. As we discussed in chapter 8, FedEx's service quality indicator (SQI) computes on a daily basis the number of companywide service failures. To clearly communicate customer fail points to internal employees, the company created linking measures to trace the causes to each internal department. For example, the company's information technology department affects 8 of the 12 SQI measurements and therefore has submeasures that provide feedback on how the department's work is affecting the SQI.

Service guarantees, a technique discussed in an earlier section, can also be used to create alignment of back office and support people, as described in Exhibit 16-3.

Open Channels of Communication between Advertising and Operations   When a company creates advertising that depicts the service encounter, it is essential that the advertising accurately reflect what customers will experience in actual service encounters. Puffery or exaggeration puts service quality perceptions at risk, especially when the firm is consistently unable to deliver to the level of service portrayed in the advertising. Coordination and communication between advertising and service providers are pivotal in closing Provider GAP 4.

Featuring actual employees doing their jobs or explaining the services they provide is one way to coordinate advertising portrayals and the reality of the service encounter. Advertising that features actual employees can be very effective in communicating excellence, and the effect will be present in both the primary audience (customers) and the secondary audience (employees).[25] An additional benefit is that featured employees become standards for other employees by modeling good performance.

In featuring employees, the advertising department must interact directly with service providers, facilitating horizontal communication. Similar benefits can be achieved using other forms of advertising if employees are included in the advertising process in other ways. A common frustration of service employees is that companies run advertisements promising services or benefits before employees are told about the advertisements and sometimes before they are told about the services! Customers come to them asking for the services and they feel uninformed, left out, and helpless.[26] This problem can be avoided by requesting input or opinions from operations employees during the planning stages in advertising.

When advertising and operations personnel talk to each other, especially when contact personnel provide input to the advertising department about the feasibility of what is being promised in advertising, customers are led to expect what contact personnel can deliver. Service providers also need to preview advertising campaigns to prepare themselves for the service customers will expect them to perform; they must be motivated to carry out themes of courtesy, responsiveness, and reliability that are presented in advertising. In both these strategies, marketing reflects a full and accurate understanding of the operations function—how long it takes to accomplish a project, how successfully the company delivers, how often mistakes occur. This communication bridge between marketing and operations is essential in closing the promises-delivery gap.

Open Channels of Communication between Sales and Operations   Mechanisms for opening channels of communication between sales and operations employees can take many forms, both formal and informal. Annual planning meetings, retreats, team meetings, or workshops where the departments interact can clarify the issues and allow each department to understand the goals, capabilities, and constraints of the other. Some companies hold "gap workshops" at which employees from both functions meet for a day or two to try to understand the difficulties in matching promises made through selling with delivery accomplished by operations personnel.[27]

Involving the operations staff in face-to-face meetings with external customers is also

EXHIBIT 16-3   HOW A SERVICE GUARANTEE HELPED HORIZONTAL COMMUNICATION AT DELTA DENTAL PLAN

Delta Dental Plan, a managed-care insurance company that insures 600,000 people, instituted a powerful service guarantee that helped sales and new business as well as stimulating employees to higher levels of participation and productivity. Specific steps the company took in the process contributed to the success, including:

1 *Commitment to Employee Participation.* At the outset, the company had every employee read about service guarantees and discuss them in management-facilitated discussion groups.

2 *Employee Task-Force Evaluation of Guarantee Type.* After the discussion groups and brainstorming ended, 15 potential guarantees and payouts and company requirements for them (e.g., training, timing, and advertising) were examined. Independent market research also investigated the meaningfulness of different guarantees to customers.

3 *Decision Based on Employee and Research Input.* On the basis of both employee and external customer input, the firm decided on seven services that it now guarantees, including "no hassle" customer relations, accurate and quick turnaround of ID cards, and

minimum 10-percent savings on claims paid to its participating dentists.

4 *Communications Campaign Focused on All Stakeholders.*

5 *Clear Refund Policies.* Delta Dental paid out $36,007 to compensate customers for service failures involving 238 accounts.

6 *Formation of an Independent Quality Group of Nonmanagement Employees.* The purpose of this group was to provide ongoing feedback to claims-processing operators and analysts to eliminate rework.

7 *Internal and External Customer Satisfaction Surveys.* These kept a finger on the pulse of the customer.

8 *Attention to the Educational and Training Needs of Employees.*

9 *Organization Designed to Support the Guarantee.*

10 *Test of Service Capacity before External Rollout.*

Among the successes of the program were the signing up of seven major new accounts, addition of 20,000 subscribers, increase in revenues by 15 percent, improvement in account retention rate from 95 to 97.1 percent, and increase in sales leads by 50 percent.

Source: Robert E. Hunder and Thomas Raffio, "Implementing Service Guarantees—the Delta Dental Plan Story," *Sloan Management Review,* Spring 1992, pp. 21–22.

a strategy that allows operations personnel to more readily understand the salesperson's role and the needs and desires of customers. Rather than filtering customers' needs through the sales force, operations employees can witness firsthand the pressures and demands of customers. A frequent and desirable result is better service to the internal customer—the salesperson—from the operations staff as they become aware of their own roles in satisfying both external and internal customers.

Create Cross-functional Teams   Another approach to improving horizontal communications to better serve customers is to involve employees in cross-functional teams to align their jobs with end-customer requirements. For example, if a team of telephone operators (contact personnel) was working to improve interaction with customers, back office people such as computer technicians or training personnel could become part of the team. The team could learn requirements and set goals for achieving them together, an approach that directly creates communications across the functions.

An advertising agency is a context in which the cross-functional team approach can be understood. The individual in an advertising agency who typically interacts directly with the client is the account executive (often called a "suit" by the creative staff). In the traditional agency, the account executive visits the client, elicits client expectations, and then interacts with the various departments in the agency (art, copywriting, production, traffic, and media buying) that will perform the work. All functions are specialized and, in the extreme case, get direction for their portion of the work directly from the account executive. A cross-functional team approach would involve having representatives from all of the areas meet together with the account executive, even the client, and collectively discuss the account and approaches to address client needs. Each brings his or her function's perspectives and opens communication. All members can then understand the constraints and schedules of the other groups.

Our Technology Spotlight illustrates how computer networking can aid cross-functional team communication.

EXCEEDING CUSTOMER EXPECTATIONS: CAVEATS AND STRATEGIES

An increasingly popular service maxim urges companies to "exceed customer expectations"—to delight, excite, surprise, and otherwise amaze. According to this credo, which we briefly discussed in chapter 4, merely *meeting* customer expectations is not enough; a company must *exceed* them to retain customers. While this is an appealing slogan as well as one that sets a high performance standard for employees, it holds the potential to overpromise not only to customers but also to employees. In attempting to exceed customer expectations, a company must understand (1) what type of expectations can and should be exceeded, (2) what customer group or segment is to be targeted, and (3) the impact exceeding expectations has on future expectations of customers.

In chapter 4 we distinguished between types of service expectations including *desired service,* the level the customer hopes to receive, and *adequate service,* the minimum acceptable level of service. When service research has viewed expectations as desired service, perceptions of performance rarely *meet* customer expectations, and almost always produce a negative gap between expectations and perceptions.[28] When focusing on desired service, it appears extremely difficult to exceed expectations. On the other hand, adequate service is not only feasible but also required for a company to remain viable. In research that included both desired and adequate service, three of four companies' services were perceived as being higher than the adequate service level whereas they almost never met or exceeded desired service level.[29]

These results suggest that a company's ability to exceed expectations depends on the type of customer expectation: Surpassing the desired service level on an ongoing basis may be infeasible, while exceeding the adequate service level is possible yet unimpressive. In essence, the goal of exceeding desired service may be too high and that of performing higher than adequate service may be too low. Setting a goal of exceeding desired service may frustrate employees and set the company up for overpromising. But exceeding adequate expectations is unlikely to produce "delight" in customers.

Another important issue involves actively deciding whether all customers' expectations should be exceeded or those of only certain segments of customers. Exceeding the expectations of poor relationship customers (from chapter 7), those a firm is not making

---

TECHNOLOGY SPOTLIGHT

HOW COMPUTER NETWORKING REVOLUTIONIZES HORIZONTAL COMMUNICATION

As we have emphasized in this chapter, one of the strategies companies need to manage customer expectations is horizontal communication among the different functions in the organization. Horizontal communication used to be inhibited by "the vertical processing of information—up the chain, across . . . and down again . . . from me up to my boss and then hers, then down to your boss and to you—to pass directly between us."[30] Susan Falzon of CSC Research and Advisory Services, who studied networks in more than 75 companies, commented: "When work is carried out through networks, an organization's structure changes whether you want it to or not. I can't find a single case where it doesn't happen."[31]

Computer networks and technology such as E-mail, teleconferencing, and groupware revolutionize communication and participation among employees. Lotus Notes, the dominant software for working in groups (termed "groupware") allows people working on a project all over the world to access files, work on them, and update the files immediately in all locations. Hewlett-Packard illustrates the impact this can have on customer service and the way its 1,900 technical support staff works:

When a customer reports a problem, the call (or electronic message) goes automatically to one of four hubs around the world, depending on the time of day. Operators get a description of the problem and its ur-

gency, typing the information into a database and zapping the file to one of 27 centers where it might be picked up by a team specializing in, say, operating system foul-ups. The database is shared by all the centers and is "live"—that is, whenever an employee works in a file, it is instantly updated, so every center has identical information about each job at all times. If the first center can't solve a problem quickly, it follows the sun: At 6 p.m. in California, for example, the action shifts to Australia, to be picked up by a crew a third of a world away. The file, of course, is already there.[32]

Customer service advantages of networks include speed of communication, time savings, cost savings, and quality of personnel that can be brought to the task. However, its ability to envision its markets and customers more clearly is perhaps the most critical benefit in serving customers. Rather than allowing the bureaucracy to process and dehumanize information about the customer, networks allow everyone to get direct information. Lotus avails itself of this benefit:

. . . 4 million phone calls a year go straight into a Notes database, available on demand. Anyone with access to the data can search according to his needs, rather than accept someone else's idea of what numbers to crunch. Interdepartmental problem-solving teams form spontaneously. Best of all, about 500 customer companies can enter the database directly and share solutions. Fully half of Lotus's technical support is now handled on-line. Net result: Many more employees watch the market from front-row seats.[33]

---

money from or who are difficult to do business with, will only exacerbate the negative impact of these customers. There are many cases when sound business decisions need to be made about the desirability of some customer segments. Another issue of customer selection involves the customer groups within companies that business-to-business service providers focus on, among them decision-makers, users, and influencers. To exceed the expectations of all of these groups simultaneously would be overwhelming to employees and financially prohibitive.

Another intriguing question about customer delight is whether delight is possible on a consistent basis. By most definitions, delight occurs when the customer is pleasantly surprised by an unexpected level of service provision. L. L. Bean accepts the return of a boot purchased ten years ago, Nordstrom salespeople dash from the store to accessorize a customer's wardrobe from competing retailers, Hampton Inn housekeepers refund money because guest room temperature is to high or too low—all of these pleasantly surprise customers. A company's best chances to delight are when expected service is low to mediocre. But after the customer is delighted the first time, do his or her expectations rise, thereby making it ever more difficult to exceed them in the future? Are higher and higher levels of service required to continue the delight?

Examining service from companies that appear to exceed expectations over the long term may help us understand how to achieve continuing delight. One of the most visible examples of a company that succeeds by continuing to delight customers is AT&T's Universal Card Service. From the conception of this service, the company vowed to create the most comprehensive set of competitive services and then monitor continuously to pursue improvements. The UCS card is now the second largest in the industry and won a Malcolm Baldrige National Quality Award in 1992. The company continues to "stay ahead of customer expectations"—to anticipate where customer requirements are moving, constantly seeking new ways to delight. Similarly, British Airways recently began offering first-class travelers who must fly at night the option of dinner on the ground in the first-class lounge, after finding that some passengers prefer that to in-flight meals. Another extra that customers are not likely to receive on other flights: British Airways pajamas![34]

No matter how much a company might intend to meet customer needs, it may be unwilling or unable to do so at times. Customers sometimes expect more and higher levels of service than can be effectively or efficiently delivered by the firm. The customer may want a repairperson to come to his home to fix a broken appliance within an hour of the telephone call requesting service. A business telecommunications customer may want to cut her budget but increase service levels because her company is focusing on value while downsizing. A software firm may plan the introduction of a new product two months after a large customer needs the software. A gynecologist may have no free appointments for the next six months. In all of these cases, despite good intentions the company will not be able to exceed or even meet expectations.

The argument is that companies can aim for delight where and when it is appropriate and possible. Strategies for bypassing the pitfalls discussed here and reaching service goals include demonstrating understanding of customer expectations, leveraging the delivery dimensions, exceeding expectations of selected customers, underpromising and overdelivering, and positioning unusual service as unique.

Demonstrate Understanding of Customer Expectations

At the foundation of all strategies for meeting and exceeding customer expectations is the need to know and communicate back to the customer what his or her expectations are. Sometimes just the simple act of trying to understand expectations exceeds them— customers familiar with uncaring, indifferent service workers can be very impressed when someone actually listens to them. The action itself, at least in the short term, delights customers. An example is USAA, one of the most profitable insurance and financial firms in the world.

United Services Automobile Association, along with other insurance companies, had long grappled with a way to provide personal service for its member customers. The company sells and services only by telephone, virtually guaranteeing impersonal service. To avoid this, the company instituted an imaging system that allowed all correspondence with customers to be immediately input into the computer system as it enters the firm, making complete histories of customers easily accessible to all service workers who may talk with each customer. (See Technology Spotlight in chapter 11.)

There is another, more basic, reason to understand and demonstrate understanding of customer expectations. Unless a company grasps what the customer expects, meeting requirements is random and unfocused. Company effort is wasted on service issues that are unimportant to the customer, and critical requirements may be overlooked altogether.

Leverage the Delivery Dimensions

Customers judge four of the service quality dimensions (responsiveness, assurance, empathy, and tangibles) primarily during the service delivery process. These four dimensions could aptly be called delivery or process dimensions. Reliability, which is judged for the most part following the service, could be called an outcome dimension. Although reliability is the most important dimension in meeting customers' service expectations, companies are supposed to be reliable—to provide the service they promise to deliver. Thus, it is difficult for firms to exceed customers' expectations by being reliable. The delivery dimensions—especially assurance, responsiveness, and empathy—are pivotal in exceeding them.[35]

The best opportunity for surprising customers is when service providers and customers interact during delivery. It is during delivery, when customers directly experience providers' service skills and "tone," that firms are best able to augment the service core of reliability in ways that differentiate. These delivery dimensions play a role different from the outcome dimension of reliability. Companies must be reliable simply to compete. If they also do well on the process dimensions, they have a chance to dominate the competition.[36]

Leveraging the delivery dimensions is especially important when service failures occur. Customers' expectations are higher for both reliability and the delivery dimensions during recovery service, and the opportunity for recovery is greater with the delivery dimensions because of lower expectations and a larger zone of tolerance. Yet many service firms do not turn service failures into satisfactory experiences. Researchers, using the critical incidents research technique we discussed in chapter 5, found that a large percentage of unsatisfactory service encounters (42.9% of all unsatisfactory encounters in their study) were related to employees' inability or unwillingness to respond effectively to service failure situations. They refer to service recovery failures as a "double deviation" from customer expectations.[37]

Leveraging the delivery dimensions involves a wide span of actions that enhance employees' willingness and ability to be effective. LaSalle Steel Company in Indiana is in an industry that many consider a commodity, yet by focusing on customer service as its top objective it exceeded customer expectations. It started by requesting feedback from all 1,000 of its business customers, an action that by itself delighted them—for this was the first time any supplier had asked their ideas about how to improve their relationships.

Perhaps the most effective outcome was the establishment of an "Adopt-A-Customer" program in which middle managers became champions of accounts, opening direct lines of communication and anticipating customer needs.[38]

In business-to-business situations, companies can act as partners rather than vendors, understand and solve a customer's business problems, and strengthen communication links, among other strategies.

Exceed Expectations of Selected Customers

One reason many companies have difficulty meeting, much less exceeding, customer expectations is that they do not distinguish among groups of customers to be served. Except for public and nonprofit firms that must treat all customers equally, nearly all service companies have some customers that are more important than others, as we described earlier in chapter 7. In fact, customers can be tiered from most important (the A group in Figure 16-9) to least desirable (the D group). Reasons why one group is preferred over others may vary: They may pay higher fees, generate higher profits, have a longer history with the company, make fewer demands on employee time, spread positive word-of-mouth advertising, or interact with the firm in positive ways.

The age-old adage that 20 percent of a firm's customers account for 50 to 80 percent of the profits needs to be reexamined in service firms, for all customers are not equally important to the company. Baxter HealthCare, a supplier of products and services for hospitals, has found that 80 percent of its incremental sales are from large customers with already established relationships.[39] Companies that can distinguish among tiers of customers have more precise knowledge of their customer needs. And while not all customers' expectations can be met or exceeded, if effort is focused on the most important tiers the most important customers' expectations can be met and perhaps exceeded.

An example of tiering is evident with airlines. Most airlines know who their best customers are, typically business travelers who fly the most miles on (and therefore provide the most revenue to) the company. By identifying and capturing these customers in the upper levels of their frequent flier programs, airlines are able to ensure that this group's expectations can be met. In a general sense, any company with a clear understanding of the importance of different customer groups can selectively reward customers in ways that could surprise and delight them. Automatic upgrades to first class, special meals, champagne, fresh-baked cookies, and early boarding are all special services provided for elite airline customers.

While airlines, hotels, and car rental firms acknowledge customer tiers, virtually all service companies other than nonprofit or public service firms (that usually cannot deny service to any qualified customer) could benefit from this approach. Bank One, in Columbus, Ohio, now watches balances in its customers' checking accounts to increase what it calls "depth of relationship."[40] When an account reaches a predetermined level, the customer receives some form of contact from the bank that demonstrates other ways the bank might provide service to her.

Explicitly developing customer tiers can also help the company meet its standards during peak season. Tax accountants and preparers face heavy demand in January-February and March-April. During these times employees must scramble to keep to the stan-

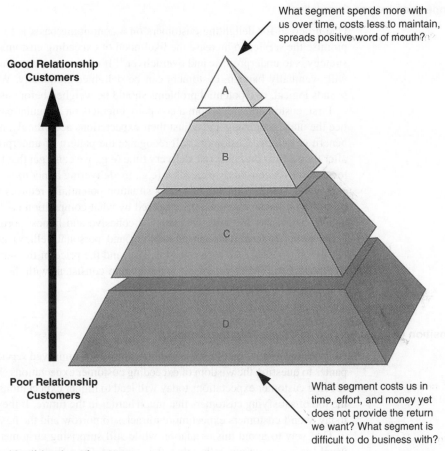

What segment spends more with us over time, costs less to maintain, spreads positive word of mouth?

Good Relationship Customers

A

B

C

D

Poor Relationship Customers

What segment costs us in time, effort, and money yet does not provide the return we want? What segment is difficult to do business with?

FIGURE 16-9   Identifying tiers of customers.

dards they are able to achieve easily at other times of the year. Unfortunately, customers' requirements tend to be high during these peak times because they have their own (and the IRS's) demands to meet. Employees become overwhelmed trying to do it all for all customers. In this and other situations, identifying customer tiers, perhaps by differentially priced services or other criteria (such as whether a customer is regular versus transient), can help the company and employees decide how to allocate their time.

If service or product firms have ways to identify tiers of customers, they can selectively meet the expectations of the most important customers in the upper tiers. Long-term patients should get preference over new patients when a doctor's practice is overbooked during a flu epidemic. Seniors should get priority over freshmen in courses they must complete to graduate. Regular customers ought to be able to get a table in a crowded restaurant. Once identified, customers in the lower tiers can be the focus of company efforts to manage their expectations downward, particularly during peak times.

Underpromise and Overdeliver

One proposal for delighting customers on a continuing basis is to deliberately under-promise the service to increase the likelihood of exceeding customer expectations. The strategy is to underpromise and overdeliver.[41] If every service promise is less than what will eventually happen, customers can be delighted frequently. While this reasoning sounds logical, two potential problems should be weighed before using this strategy.

First, customers with whom a company interacts on a regular basis are likely to no-tice the underpromising and adjust their expectations accordingly, negating the desired benefit of delight. Customers will recognize the pattern of underpromising when time after time a firm promises one delivery time (e.g., we can't get that to you before 5 p.m. tomorrow) yet constantly exceeds it (e.g., by delivering at noon).

Second, underpromising in a sales situation potentially reduces the competitive ap-peal of an offering and must be tempered by what competition is offering. When com-petitive pressures are high, presenting a cohesive and honest portrayal of the service both explicitly (e.g., through advertising and personal selling) and implicitly (e.g., through the appearance of service facilities and the price of the service) may be wiser. Controlling the firm's promises, making them consistent with the deliverable service, may be a better approach.

Position Unusual Service as Unique, Not the Standard

At times the escalation of expectations as a result of improved service leads some com-panies to question the wisdom of exceeding customer expectations. They reason that ex-ceeding customer expectations today will lead to higher expectations tomorrow, making the job of satisfying customers that much harder in the future. If they perform a miracle today, won't customers expect more miracles tomorrow and the next day?

One way to avoid this escalation while still surprising customers is to position un-usual service as unique rather than the standard. On a flight between Raleigh-Durham and Charlotte, North Carolina, one of us experienced an example of this strategy. The flight is extremely short, less than half an hour, and typically too brief for beverage ser-vice. On the night in question, a crew member announced over the intercom that an un-usually ambitious crew wanted to try to serve beverages anyway. He warned passengers that the crew may not get to all of them, and positioned the service as unique by im-ploring passengers not to expect beverage service on other flights. In this scenario, pas-sengers seemed delighted but their expectations for regular service were not heightened by the action. (To this day, we have never received beverage service on that route, but are really not expecting it!).

SUMMARY

Discrepancies between service delivery and external communications have a strong im-pact on customer perceptions of service quality. In this chapter we discussed the factors affecting the size of Provider GAP 4, the gap between service promises and delivery. We defined these factors, described the problems they create in organizations, and offered suggestions for dealing with them to close the gap.

DISCUSSION QUESTIONS

1 What makes Provider GAP 4 different from the other provider gaps?
2 Which of the key reasons for Provider GAP 4 discussed in this chapter do you think is the easiest to address in a company? Which is the hardest to address? Why?
3 Which of the four categories of strategies to match service promises with delivery do you believe costs the most within an organization? Which costs the least?
4 Describe three service guarantees that are currently offered by companies or organizations in addition to the ones already presented in the chapter. Are these good or poor guarantees on the basis of the criteria described in the chapter?
5 Find five service advertisements that you consider strong and five that you consider weak. Why do you consider them strong (weak)?
6 Using the section on resetting customer expectations, put yourself in the position of your professor who must reduce the amount of "service" provided to the students in your class. Give an example of each strategy in this context. Which of the strategies would work best with you (the student) in managing your expectations? Why?
7 Consider a complex service provided where you live or go to school. How could you prepare customers for the service process so that their expectations would be managed?
8 Managing horizontal communications was described in the chapter as sharing information across functions in an organization. Which functions in an organization do you believe have the most difficulty in communicating? Why?

EXERCISES

1 Choose a service with which you are familiar. Explain the service offered and develop a good service guarantee for it. Discuss why your guarantee is a good one, and the benefits to the company of implementing it.
2 Debate the issue of exceeding customer expectations with another person or group in the class. One of the groups or individuals should be *for* establishing a company goal of exceeding customer expectations and one should be *against* establishing such a goal. What company evidence can you provide for your side of the argument?

NOTES

1 Rob Martin and Larry Meltzer, "Hampton Inn Establishes Hotel Industry First with 100 Percent Satisfaction Guarantee," *Hampton Inn News,* October 16, 1989, p. 1.
2 David Greising, "Quality: How to Make it Pay," *Business Week,* August 8, 1994.
3 Christopher W. L. Hart, "The Power of Unconditional Service Guarantees," *Harvard Business Review,* July–August 1988, pp. 54–62.
4 Ibid., p. 60.
5 Ibid., p. 61.
6 William R. George and Leonard L. Berry, "Guidelines for the Advertising of Services," *Business Horizons,* May–June 1981, pp. 52–56.
7 K. Anderson and Ron Zemke, *Delivering Knock Your Socks Off Services* (New York: AMACOM, 1991).
8 George and Berry, "Guidelines for the Advertising of Services."
9 James Overstreet, "Cable Installers Guarantee Service," *USA Today,* December 2, 1994, p. B1.
10 Hart, "The Power of Unconditional Service Guarantees."

11 Ibid.

12 Christopher W. L. Hart, Leonard A. Schlesinger, and Dan Maher, "Guarantees Come to Professional Service Firms, *Sloan Management Review,* Spring 1992.

13 "Xerox Business Services Introduces Written Guarantee to Assure Customer Satisfaction," *Executive Report on Customer Satisfaction,* November 15, 1993, pp. 3–4.

14 Michael Schachner, "Clients Ask TPAs to Guarantee Their Work," *Business Insurance,* January 29, 1990, pp. 20–21.

15 Timothy W. Firmstahl, "My Employees Are My Service Guarantee," *Harvard Business Review,* July–August 1988, p. 60.

16 Christopher W. L. Hart, "An Objective Look at Unconditional Service Guarantees," *Bankers Magazine,* November–December 1990, pp. 80–83.

17 Michael Clements, "Dominos Detours 30-Minute Guarantee," *USA Today,* December 22, 1993, p. A1.

18 G. Lynn Shostack, "Breaking Free from Product Marketing," *Journal of Marketing* 41 (April 1977): 73–80; Leonard L. Berry and Terry Clark, "Four Ways to Make Services More Tangible," *Business,* 36 (October–December 1986): 53–54.

19 Donna Legg and Julie Baker, "Advertising Strategies for Service Firms," in *Services Marketing* (New Jersey: Prentice Hall 1991), pp. 282–291.

20 Leonard L. Berry and Terry Clark, "Four Ways to Make Services More Tangible."

21 George and Berry, "Guidelines for the Advertising of Services."

22 Ibid.

23 Elizabeth C. Clemmer and Benjamin Schneider, "Managing Customer Dissatisfaction with Waiting: Applying Social-Psychological Theory in a Service Setting," in *Advances in Services Marketing and Management,* Vol. 2, Teresa Schwartz, David E. Bowen and Stephen W. Brown, eds. (Greenwich, CT: JAI Press, 1993) 213–229.

24 Ibid.

25 George and Berry, "Guidelines for the Advertising of Services."

26 Leonard L. Berry, Valarie A. Zeithaml, and A. Parasuraman, "Quality Counts in Services, Too," *Business Horizons,* May–June 1985, pp. 44–52.

27 Valarie A. Zeithaml, A. Parasuraman, and Leonard L. Berry, *Delivering Quality Service: Balancing Customer Perceptions and Expectations* (New York: Free Press, 1990), p. 120.

28 Zeithaml, Parasuraman, and Berry.

29 Parsu Parasuraman, Valarie A. Zeithaml, and Leonard L. Berry, "Alternative Scales for Measuring Service Quality: A Comparative Assessment Based on Psychometric and Diagnostic Criteria," *Journal of Retailing,* 70, 3, pp. 193–199.

30 Thomas A. Stewart, "Managing in a Wired Company," *Fortune,* July 11, 1994, p. 46.

31 Ibid., p. 44.

32 Ibid., p. 46.

33 Ibid., p. 47.

34 Rahul Jacob, "Why Some Customers Are More Equal than Others," *Fortune,* September 19, 1994, pp. 215–224.

35 Leonard L. Berry, A. Parasuraman, and Valarie A. Zeithaml, "Improving Service Quality in America: Lessons Learned," *Academy of Management Executive,* 8, 2, 1994, pp. 32–48.

36 A. Parasuraman, Leonard L. Berry, and Valarie A. Zeithaml, "Understanding Customer Expectations of Service," *Sloan Management Review,* 32, 3 (Spring 1991): pp. 39–48.

37 Mary Jo Bitner, Bernard L. Booms and Mary S. Tetrault, "The Service Encounter: Diagnosing Favorable and Unfavorable Incidents," *Journal of Marketing* (January 1990): pp. 71–84.

38 Bob Allen, "An Extra Effort in Servicing the Customer," *American Metal Market,* December 2, 1991.

39 Jacob, "Why Some Customers Are More Equal than Others."

40 Ibid.

41 Davidow and Uttal.

17

PRICING OF SERVICES

WHEN IS PRICING A CAR A SERVICE?

Ten years ago, purchasing an automobile was a complex and stressful transaction for most customers. Buyers entered showrooms and examined price lists on cars, only to find that the prices were considerably higher than the actual price that could be negotiated. Dickering with salespeople was expected, and most customers, confused and uncertain about the real price of the automobile, spent several hours haggling. The customer with the best negotiation skills got the cheapest car, all else being equal.

Those of you who purchased a car within the last few years may not have experienced this hassle in the showroom because 40 percent of new cars are now purchased some way other than the traditional shop-haggle-buy-on-credit approach.[1] Some dealerships offer a one-price policy, avoiding price negotiation altogether and setting lower, nonnegotiable prices. One-price dealerships now account for an estimated 9 percent of all automobile dealerships. J.D. Power and Associates, an automotive market research firm in California, estimated that 2,265 dealers tried one-price selling in 1994, up from 1,655 in 1993.[2]

Consumers today have choices when buying an automobile. The way that price is presented and processed actually becomes part of the service the dealerships offer. Good service in the sales encounter means making the process simpler and less financially risky. If you have not yet purchased your first car, you may want to know what these choices are.

ONE-PRICE POLICY   When the Saturn automobile was developed by General Motors, one of the early decisions was to price the cars in a customer-friendly way: a single, no-dicker price rather than a negotiated price. Automobile manufacturers were aware that customers wanted the one-price option, but resisted changing the way cars were sold because their dealers preferred the conventional policy. Saturn's pricing policy was followed by other automobile manufacturers. Oldsmobile offered "Oldsmobile

Simplified Pricing"—no haggling, no complicated option packages, no rebates. Recent research indicates that the proportion of the car-buying public desiring the new pricing policy ranges anywhere from 34 to 68 percent.[3]

TRADITIONAL DICKERING   The majority of dealerships still expect you to haggle over prices. One survey examining the desirability of single-price policies found that 29 percent of the customers interviewed would rather haggle because it helped them get a good deal, 8 percent simply liked to haggle, and 17 percent felt that not negotiating prices was a clear customer disadvantage.[4]

DEALER LEASING   Nearly one-third of all cars and trucks sold last year were under lease. If you want lower monthly payments, no down payment, little risk, and the ability to turn in your two-year-old car for a new one, leasing might be for you. Ford and other automobile companies (predominantly in North America, although Germany leases 20% of its cars; other European countries like Britain require value-added taxes on them, cutting down on their desirability) now offer cut-rate, short-term leases. The surge in leases is due in part to the "stark reality" that many consumers can't afford today's cars at an average price of $18,100.[5] In one year, Ford priced two years of use of a $19,825 Taurus for $279 a month, less than the $378 monthly payment it would take to buy the car over four years. More than 40 percent of Oldsmobiles were also moved on short-term lease contracts that year.[6]

CREDIT UNIONS AND WAL-MART   Brokers and price clubs such as credit unions and Wal-Mart serve as buying organizations for members and customers by prenegotiating prices with dealers. By representing groups of customers, they are able to command a lower and perhaps fixed price similar to that available to many corporations. Members can save as much as $1,800 and hours of hassle buying this way instead of through traditional buying methods.

CONSUMER REPORTS   Sources of buyer information such as Consumer Reports *and* Car and Driver *publish price guides and data on reliability and repairs. They also offer 900 numbers that consumers can call to get information. These savings, according to some sources, fall about $800 short of the lowest negotiated price for a Ford Taurus or Olds Cutlass.[7]*

ELECTRONIC PRICE GUIDES   Kevin King, a former car salesman, now runs a service business called 1-900-Autofax, Inc., which lists prices dealers pay for cars and various options, giving buyers an idea of how much they can negotiate off the sticker price. For $29.95, the service allows buyers to compare prices and options on more than two hundred models. Dozens of other on-line services, including AutoVantage or CompuServe's New Car-Truck Showroom, offer up-to-date price guides from $7 to more than $20.

Which approach sounds best to you? Which will you use when you purchase your next car?

According to one of the leading experts on pricing, most service organizations use a "naive and unsophisticated approach to pricing without regard to underlying shifts in demand, the rate that supply can be expanded, prices of available substitutes, consideration of the price-volume relationship, or the availability of future substitutes."[8] What makes the pricing of services more difficult than pricing of goods? What approaches work well in the context of services?

This chapter builds on three key differences between customer evaluation of pricing for services and goods: (1) customers often have inaccurate or limited reference prices for services, (2) price is a key signal to quality in services, and (3) monetary price is not the only relevant price to service customers. As we will demonstrate, these three differences can have profound impact on the strategies companies use to set and administer prices for services.

The chapter also discusses common pricing structures including (1) cost based, (2) competition based, and (3) demand based. One of the most important aspects of demand-based pricing is perceived value, which must be understood by service providers so that they price in line with offerings and customer expectations. For that reason we will also describe how customers define value and discuss pricing strategies in the context of value.

The objectives of this chapter are to:

1 Discuss three major ways that service prices differ from goods prices for customers.

2 Demonstrate what value means to customers and the role that price plays in value.

3 Articulate the key ways that pricing of services differs from pricing of goods.

4 Delineate strategies that companies use to price services.

5 Give examples of pricing strategy in action.

THE ROLE OF PRICE AND VALUE IN PROVIDER GAP 4

As we explained in chapter 16, discrepancies between service delivery and external communications cause Provider GAP 4 (Figure 17-1). One of the important types of external communications in services is the price of the service. Price sends a critical sig-

FIGURE 17-1 Provider GAP 4.

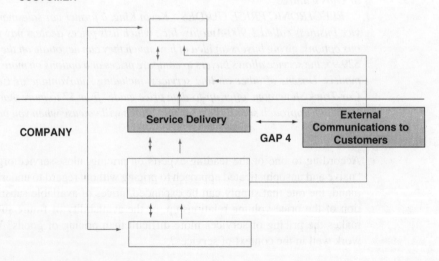

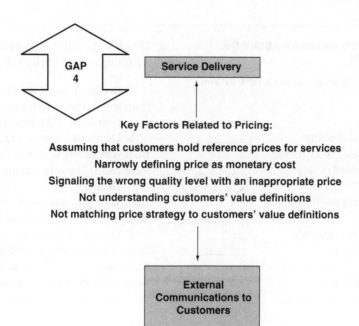

FIGURE 17-2   Key reasons for provider GAP 4.

nal about the service and must therefore be considered carefully. Figure 17-2 shows the pricing and value factors that contribute to GAP 4, including (1) assuming that customers hold reference prices for services, (2) narrowly defining price as monetary cost, (3) signaling the wrong quality level with an inappropriate price, (4) not understanding customer value definitions, and (5) not matching price strategy to customer value definitions. In this chapter we describe these problems and offer strategies that service firms have found useful in dealing with them to close Provider GAP 4.

THREE KEY WAYS SERVICE PRICES ARE DIFFERENT FOR CONSUMERS

What role does price play in consumer decisions about services? How important is price to potential buyers compared with other factors and service features? Service companies must understand how pricing works, but first they must understand how customers perceive prices and price changes. The three sections that follow describe what we know about the ways customers perceive services, and each is central to effective pricing.

Customer Knowledge of Service Prices

To what extent do customers use price as a criterion in selecting services? How much do consumers know about the costs of services? Before you answer these questions, take the services quiz in Exhibit 17-1. Were you able to fill in a price for each of the services listed? If you were able to answer the questions on the basis of memory, you have inter-

EXHIBIT 17-1   WHAT DO YOU KNOW ABOUT THE PRICES OF SERVICES?

1. What do the following services cost in your hometown?

Dental checkup   _____

General medical checkup   _____

Legal help with a DWI (driving
    while intoxicated) charge   _____

Dental braces   _____

Rental of a videocassette
    for one night   _____

One hour of housecleaning   _____

Room at the Hilton   _____

Haircut   _____

Oil change and lube   _____

2. Which of the following would you select if you needed a filling replaced in a tooth?

a. Dentist A—cost is $25, located 15 miles from your home, wait is three weeks for an appointment and 1 1/2 hours in waiting room

b. Dentist B—cost is $35, located 15 miles from your home, wait is one week for appointment and 1/2 hour in waiting room

c. Dentist C—cost is $75, located 3 miles from your job, wait is one week for appointment and no time in waiting room

d. Dentist D—cost is $75, located 3 miles from your job, wait is one week for appointment and no time in waiting room, nitrous oxide used so no pain is involved

nal *reference prices* for the services. A reference price is *a price point in memory for a good or a service,* and can consist of the price last paid, the price most frequently paid, or the average of all prices customers have paid for similar offerings.[9]

To see how accurate your reference prices for services are, you can compare them with the actual price of these services from the providers in your home town. If you are like many consumers, you feel quite uncertain about your knowledge of the prices of services, and the reference prices you hold in memory for services are not as accurate as those you hold for goods. There are many reasons for this difference.

Because services are intangible and are not created on a factory assembly line, service firms have great flexibility in the configurations of services they offer. Firms can conceivably offer an infinite variety of combinations and permutations, leading to complex and complicated pricing structures. As an example, consider how difficult it is to get comparable price quotes when buying life insurance. With the multitude of types (e.g., whole life versus term), features (different deductibles), variations associated with customers (age, health risk, smoking or nonsmoking), few insurance companies offer exactly the same features and the same prices. Only an expert customer, one who knows enough about insurance to completely specify the options across providers, is likely to find prices that are directly comparable.

Another reason customers lack accurate reference prices for services is that many providers are unable or unwilling to estimate price in advance. Consider most medical or legal services. Rarely are legal or medical service providers willing—or even able—to estimate a price in advance. The fundamental reason in many cases is that they do not know themselves what the services will involve until they have fully examined the patient or the client's situation or until the process of service delivery (such as an operation in a hospital or a trial) unfolds. In a business-to-business context, companies will obtain bids or estimates for complex services such as consulting or construction, but this type of price estimation is typically not undertaken with end-consumers; therefore, they often buy without advance knowledge about the final price of the service.

How did you answer the questions about prices for a medical checkup? If you are like most consumers, you probably wanted more information before you offered a reference price. You probably wanted to know what type of checkup the physician is providing. Does it include X-rays and other diagnostic tests? What types of tests? How long does it take? What is its purpose? If the checkup is undertaken simply to get a signature on a health form or a marriage certificate, the doctor may conduct a brief medical history, listen for a heart beat, and take the blood pressure. If, however, the check-up is to monitor a chronic ailment such as diabetes or high blood pressure, the doctor may be more thorough. The point we want to illustrate here is that a high degree of variability often exists across providers of services. Not every physician defines a checkup the same way. You may have found it easier to estimate dental services than medical services. Dental checkups are likely to be more standardized than medical services, consisting of two basic types: with X-rays and without.

Another factor that results in the inaccuracy of reference prices is that individual customer needs vary. Some hair stylists' service prices vary across customers on the basis of length of hair, type of haircut, and whether a conditioning treatment and style are included. Therefore, if you were to ask a friend what a cut costs from a particular stylist, chances are that your cut from the same stylist may be a different price. In a similar vein, a service as simple as a hotel room will have prices that vary greatly: by size of room, time of year, type of room availability, and individual versus group rate. These two examples are for very simple services. Now consider a service purchase as idiosyncratic as braces from a dentist or help from a lawyer. In these and many other services, customer differences in need will play a strong role in the price of the service.

Still another reason customers lack accurate reference prices for services is that customers feel overwhelmed with the information they need to gather. With most goods, retail stores display the products by category to allow customers to compare and contrast the prices of different brands and sizes. Rarely is there a similar display of services in a single outlet. If customers want to compare prices (for example, for dry cleaning), they must drive to or call individual outlets.

One final price test about reference prices. Earlier in this textbook we discussed several novel services being offered to help the time-deficient customer cope. See if you have reference prices for the unusual services of these providers: wedding adviser, pet nutritionist and therapist, baby-proofing expert, and executive organizer. We expect that your reference prices—if you can even come up with some—are even more uncertain and less accurate than for the services in the price quiz in Exhibit 17-1.

Here are estimates from actual consultants: $3,500 for a wedding adviser's attention to all details, $75 to $125 a visit for depressed pets, $200 to $300 to protect a house for and from baby, and $1,000 for four hours of executive organization.[10]

The fact that consumers often possess inaccurate reference prices for services has several important managerial implications. First, promotional pricing (as in couponing or special pricing) may be less meaningful for services, for which price anchors do not exist, than for goods, for which they do. Perhaps that is why price is not featured in service advertising as much as it is featured in advertising for goods. Promotional pricing may also create problems if the promotional price (such as a $50 permanent special from a salon) is the only one customers see in advertising, for it could become the customer's anchor price, making the regular price of $75 for a future purchase seem high by comparison.

The absence of accurate reference prices also suggests that advertising actual prices for services the customer is not used to purchasing may reduce uncertainty and overcome a customer's inflated price expectations for some services. For example, a marketing research firm's advertising citing the price for a simple study (such as $10,000) would be informative to business customers who are not familiar with the costs of research studies and therefore would be guessing at the cost. By featuring price in advertising, the company overcomes the fear of high cost by giving readers a price anchor.

One requirement for the existence of customer reference prices is *price visibility*—the price cannot be a hidden or implicit price. In many services, particularly financial services, most customers know only about the rate of return and not the costs they pay in the form of fund and insurance fees. IDS Financial Services recently discovered how little customers know about prices of the company's services.[11] After being told by the independent agents who sell their services to customers that IDS was priced too high, the company did a research study to find out how much customers know about what they pay for financial services and how much price factors into customer value assessments.

The study surprised the company by revealing that customers knew even less than expected: Not only did they not understand *what* they were paying for many of their services, very few consumers understood *how* they pay for financial services in general. Only for financial products where price was visible—such as with securities and term life—were customers aware of fees. When price was invisible, such as in certificates, whole-life insurance, and annuities (which have rear-load charges), customers didn't know how they were charged and what they paid. Further, when customers were asked to indicate how important 10 factors (including price) were, price ranked seventh. Finally, the company found that shopping behavior in the category of financial services was extremely limited. Fifty to sixty percent of customers bought financial products from the very first person they talked to.

For all of the reasons just listed, many customers don't see the price at all until *after* they receive certain services. Of course in situations of urgency, such as in accident or illness, customers must make the decision to purchase without respect to cost at all. And if cost is not known to the customer before purchase, it cannot be used as a key criterion for purchase as it often is for goods. Price is likely to be an important criterion in *repurchase,* however. Furthermore, in repurchase monetary price may be an even more important criterion than in initial purchase.

Because many customers do not possess accurate reference prices for services, services marketers are more likely than product marketers to use the strategy of *price framing.*[12] This means that the way service providers organize the information for customers has a major impact on how they perceive it. Later in this chapter we will discuss this and other strategies that are highly important in the pricing of services. Customers naturally look for anchors, and if they accept the anchors they will view the price favorably.

The Role of Nonmonetary Costs

In recent years economists have recognized that monetary price is not the only sacrifice consumers make to obtain products and services. Demand, therefore, is not just a function of monetary price but is influenced by other costs as well. Nonmonetary costs represent other sources of sacrifice perceived by consumers when buying and using a service. Time costs, search costs, and psychic costs often enter into the evaluation of whether to buy or rebuy a service, and may at times be more important concerns than monetary price.

Most services require direct participation of the consumer and thus consume real time: time waiting as well as time when the customer interacts with the service provider. Consider the investment you make to exercise, see a physician, or get through the crowds to watch a concert or baseball game. Not only are you paying money to receive these services; you're also expending time. Time becomes a sacrifice made to receive service in multiple ways. First, because service providers cannot completely control the number of customers or the length of time it will take for each customer to be serviced, service customers are likely to expend time waiting to receive the service. The average waiting time in physicians' offices is 20.6 minutes, according to the American Medical Association, with 22 minutes for family practice doctors and 23 minutes for pediatricians, orthopedic surgeons, and gynecologists.[13] Waiting time for a service is virtually always longer and less predictable than waiting time to buy goods. Second, customers often wait for an available appointment from a service provider (in the price quiz, dentist A required a three-week wait while dentist D required only one week). Virtually all of us have expended waiting time to receive services.

Search costs—the effort invested to identify and select among services you desire—are also higher for services than for physical goods. Prices for services are rarely displayed on shelves of service establishments for customers to examine as they shop, so these prices are often known only when a customer has decided to experience the service. As an example, how well did you estimate the costs of an hour of housecleaning in the price quiz? As a student, it is unlikely that you regularly purchase housecleaning, and you probably have not seen the price of an hour displayed in any retail store. Another factor that increases search costs is that each service establishment typically offers only one "brand" of a service (with the exception of brokers in insurance or financial services), so a customer must initiate contact with several different companies to get information across sellers.

There are also convenience (or perhaps more accurately nonconvenience) costs of services. If customers have to travel to a service, they incur a cost, and the cost becomes greater when travel is difficult, as it is for elderly persons. Further, if service hours do not coincide with the customer's available time, she must arrange her schedule to correspond to the company's schedule. And if a consumer has to expend effort and time to prepare to receive a service (such as removing all food from kitchen cabinets in preparation for an exterminator's spraying), he makes an additional sacrifice.

Often the most painful nonmonetary costs are the psychic costs incurred in receiving some services. Fear of not understanding (insurance), fear of rejection (bank loans), fear of uncertainty (including fear of high cost)—all of these constitute psychic costs that customers experience as sacrifices when purchasing and using services. All change, even positive change, brings about psychic costs that consumers factor into the purchase of services. When banks first introduced ATMs, customer resistance was significant, particularly to the idea of putting money into a machine: customers felt uncomfortable with the idea of letting go of their checks and bank cards. Direct deposit, a clear improvement in banking service for the elderly with limited mobility, was looked on with suspicion until the level of comfort improved. And consider how many customers rejected voice mail when it was first developed.

You can assess your own priorities on these nonmonetary cost components—time, effort, search, psychic—by thinking about your answer to question 2 in the price quiz. If you chose dentist A, you are probably most concerned about monetary costs—you are willing to accept a wait for an appointment and in the waiting room of the dentist's office. If you chose dentist B over dentist A, your time and convenience costs are slightly more important than your monetary costs, for you are willing to pay $10 more to reduce the waiting time. If you chose dentist C, you are much more sensitive to time and convenience costs, including travel time, than to monetary costs—you are willing to pay three times what you would pay for dentist A to avoid the other nonmonetary costs. And if you chose dentist D, you are someone who wants to minimize psychic costs as well, in this case fear and pain!

The managerial implications of these other sources of sacrifice are compelling. First, a service firm may be able to increase monetary price by reducing time and other costs. For example, a services marketer can reduce the perceptions of time and convenience costs when use of the service is embedded in other activities (such as when a convenience store cashes checks, sell stamps, and serves coffee along with selling products). Second, customers may be willing to pay to avoid the other costs. Many customers willingly pay extra to have items delivered to their home—including restaurant meals—rather than transporting the services and products themselves. Some customers also pay a premium for fast check-in and checkout (as in joining the Hertz #1 club), for reduced waiting time in a professional's office (as in so-called executive appointments where, for a premium price, a busy executive comes early in the morning and does not have to wait), and to avoid doing the work themselves (such as paying one and one-half times the price per gallon to avoid having to put gas in a rental car before returning it). If time or other costs are pivotal for a given service, the company's advertising could effectively emphasize these savings rather than monetary savings.

Many other services save time, thus actually allowing the customer to "buy" time. Household cleaning services, lawn care, baby-sitting, interactive cable shopping, personal shopper service, home banking, home delivery of groceries, painting, and carpet cleaning—all of these represent net gains in the discretionary time of consumers and could effectively be marketed that way. Services that allow the customer to buy time are likely to have monetary value for busy consumers.

Price as an Indicator of Service Quality

One of the intriguing aspects of pricing is that buyers are likely to use price as an indicator of both service costs and service quality—price is at once an attraction variable and a repellent.[14] Customers' use of price as an indicator of quality depends on several factors, one of which is the other information available to them. When service cues to quality are readily accessible, when brand names provide evidence of a company's reputation, or when level of advertising communicates the company's belief in the brand, customers may prefer to use those cues instead of price. In other situations, however, such as when quality is hard to detect or when quality or price varies a great deal within a class of services, consumers may believe that price is the best indicator of quality. Many of these conditions typify situations that face consumers when purchasing services.[15] Another factor that increases the dependence on price as a quality indicator is the risk associated with the service purchase. In high-risk situations, many of which involve credence services such as medical treatment or management consulting, the customer will look to price as a surrogate for quality.

Because customers depend on price as a cue to quality and because price sets expectations of quality, service prices must be determined carefully. In addition to being chosen to cover costs or match competitors, prices must be chosen to convey the appropriate quality signal. Pricing too low can lead to inaccurate inferences about the quality of the service. Pricing too high can set expectations that may be difficult to match in service delivery.

Because goods are dominated by search properties, price is not used to judge quality as often as it is in services, where experience and credence properties dominate. Any services marketer must be aware of the signals that price conveys about its offerings.

APPROACHES TO PRICING SERVICES

Exhibit 17-2 briefly reviews some key concepts about pricing that apply equally to goods and services. Rather than repeat what you learned about pricing in your marketing principles class, we want to emphasize in this chapter the way that services prices and pricing differ from both the customer's and the company's perspective. We will discuss these differences in the context of the three pricing structures typically used to set prices: (1) cost based, (2) competition based, and (3) demand based. These categories, as shown in Figure 17-3, are the same bases on which goods prices are set, but adaptations must be made in services. The figure shows the three structures interrelating, because companies need to consider each of the three to some extent in setting prices. In the following sections we will describe in general each basis for pricing and discuss differences that occur when the approach is used in services pricing. Figure 17-3 summarizes those differences.

Cost-based Pricing

In cost-based pricing, a company determines expenses from raw materials and labor, adds amounts or percentages for overhead and profit, and thereby arrives at the price. This method is widely used by industries such as utilities, contracting, wholesaling, and advertising. The basic formula for cost-based pricing is:

$$Price = Direct\ costs + overhead\ costs + profit\ margin$$

EXHIBIT 17-2   REVIEW OF MARKETING PRINCIPLES ABOUT PRICING

Many of the aspects of pricing of services are the same as pricing of goods. A very brief summary of the basics is provided here. For more details, return to your basic marketing textbook or to *Marketing Management: Analysis, Planning, Implementation and Control* by Philip Kotler, the text from which we excerpted these fundamental points about pricing.

1 The firm must consider many factors in setting its pricing policy, including: selecting the pricing objective, determining demand, estimating costs, analyzing competitors' prices and offers, selecting a pricing method, and selecting the final price.

2 Companies do not always seek to maximize profits through pricing. Other objectives they may have include survival, maximizing current revenue, maximizing sales growth, maximizing market skimming, and product/quality leadership.

3 Marketers need to understand how responsive demand would be to a change in price. To evaluate this important criterion of price sensitivity, marketers can calculate the price elasticity of demand, which is expressed as:

$$\text{Elasticity} = \frac{\text{Percent change in quantity purchased}}{\text{Percent change in price}}$$

4 Various types of costs must be considered in setting prices, including direct and indirect costs, fixed and variable costs, indirect traceable costs, and allocated costs. If a product or service is to be profitable for a company, price must cover all costs and include a markup as well.

5 Competitors' prices will affect the desirability of a company's offerings and must be considered in establishing prices.

6 A variety of pricing methods exist including markup, target return, perceived-value, going-rate, sealed-bid, and psychological.

7 After setting a price structure, companies adapt prices using geographic pricing, price discounts and allowances, promotional pricing, discriminatory pricing, and product-mix pricing.

Source: Philip Kotler, "Designing Pricing Strategies and Programs," in *Marketing Management: Analysis, Planning, Implementation and Control*, 7th ed. (New York: Prentice-Hall, 1991), chap. 18.

Direct costs involve materials and labor that are associated with the service, overhead costs are a share of fixed costs, and the profit margin is a percent of full costs (direct + overhead).

Special Problems in Cost-based Pricing for Services   One of the major difficulties in cost-based pricing involves defining the units in which a service is purchased. Thus the price per unit—a well-understood concept in pricing of manufactured goods—is a vague entity. For this reason many services are sold in terms of input units rather than units of measured output. For example, most professional services (such as consulting, engineering, architecture, psychotherapy, and tutoring) are sold by the hour.

What is unique about services when using cost-based approaches to pricing? First, costs are difficult to trace or calculate in services businesses, particularly where multiple services are provided by the firm.[16] Consider how difficult it must be for a bank to allocate teller time accurately across its checking, savings, and money market accounts in order to decide what to charge for the services. Second, a major component of cost is employee time rather than materials, and the value of people's time, particularly nonprofessional time, is not easy to calculate or estimate.

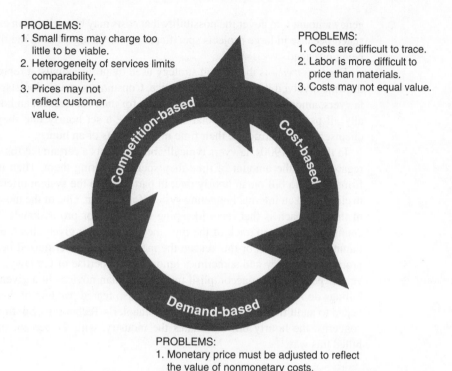

PROBLEMS:
1. Small firms may charge too little to be viable.
2. Heterogeneity of services limits comparability.
3. Prices may not reflect customer value.

PROBLEMS:
1. Costs are difficult to trace.
2. Labor is more difficult to price than materials.
3. Costs may not equal value.

PROBLEMS:
1. Monetary price must be adjusted to reflect the value of nonmonetary costs.
2. Information on service costs is less available to customers, hence price may not be a central factor.

FIGURE 17-3   Three basic marketing price structures and difficulties associated with their use for services.

An added difficulty is that actual service costs may underrepresent the value of the service to the customer. A tailor located in the home town of one of us charges $10 for taking in a seam on a $350 ladies suit jacket and an equal $10 for taking in a seam on a pair of $14 sweat shorts. The tailor's rationale is that both jobs require the same amount of time. What she neglects to see is that the customer would pay a higher price—and might even be happier about the alterations—for the expensive suit jacket, and that $10 is too high a price for the sweat shorts.

Examples of Cost-based Pricing Strategies Used in Services   *Cost-plus pricing* is a commonly used approach in which component costs are calculated and a markup added. In product pricing this approach is quite simple; in service industries, however, it is complicated because the tracking and identification of costs are difficult. The approach is typically used in industries where cost must be estimated in advance, such as construction, engineering, and advertising. In construction or engineering, bids are solicited by clients on the basis of the description of the service desired. Using their knowledge of the costs of the components of the service (including the raw materials such as masonry and lumber), labor (including both professional and unskilled), and margin, the company estimates and presents to the client a price for the finished service. A contingency amount—to cover the possibility that costs may be higher than estimated—is also stated because in large projects specifications can change during the time the service is being provided.

Fee for service is the pricing strategy used by professionals; it represents the cost of the time involved in providing the service. Consultants, psychologists, accountants, and lawyers, among other professionals, charge for their services on an hourly basis. Virtually all psychologists and social workers have a set hourly rate they charge to their clients, and most structure their time in increments of an hour.

In the early 1900s, lawyers typically billed clients a certain fee for services rendered regardless of the amount of time they spent delivering them. Then in the 1970s, law firms began to bill on an hourly rate, in part because the system offered accountability to clients and an internal budgeting system for the firm. One of the most difficult aspects of this approach is that record-keeping is tedious for professionals. Lawyers and accountants must keep track of the time they spend for a given client, often down to 10-minute increments. For this reason the method has been criticized because it does not promote efficiency and sometimes ignores the expertise of the lawyers (those who are very experienced can accomplish much more than novices in a given time period, yet billings do not always reflect this). Clients also feared padding of their legal bills, and began to audit them, as discussed in this chapter's Technology Spotlight. Despite these concerns, the hourly bill dominates the industry, with 77 percent of revenues being billed this way.[17]

Competition-based Pricing

This approach focuses on the prices charged by other firms in the same industry or market. Competition-based pricing does not always imply charging the identical rate others charge but rather using others' prices as an anchor for the firm's price. This approach is used predominantly in two situations: (1) when services are standard across providers, such as in the dry cleaning industry, and (2) in oligopolies where there is a small number of large service providers, such as in the airline or rental car industry. Difficulties involved in provision of services sometimes make competition-based pricing less simple than it is in goods industries.

Special Problems in Competition-based Pricing for Services   Small firms may charge too little and not make margins high enough to remain in business. Many mom-and-pop service establishments—dry cleaning, retail, and tax accounting, among others—cannot deliver services at the low prices charged by chain stores.

Further, the heterogeneity of services across and within providers makes this approach complicated. Bank services illustrate the wide disparity in service prices. Customers buying checking accounts, money orders, or foreign currency, to name a few services, will find prices are rarely similar across providers. For example, at one point NationsBank charged $5 for a money order when the Postal Service charged $0.75 and 7-Eleven stores charged $1.09.[18] Compare these prices for having a check drawn on foreign currency: Bank of America, $20; Thomas Cook, Inc., $7; and Citibank, $15. And fees for cashier's checks ranged from $10 to no charge, with a nationwide average of

TECHNOLOGY SPOTLIGHT

ON-LINE LEGAL FEES

Corporate America is striking back at what it perceives to be unreasonable legal fees: Companies are requiring law firms to give them on-line access to billing computers so that they can track legal fees day in and day out. Clients are "now reading over their lawyers' shoulders, with the ability to question each charge almost as soon as it's incurred."[19]

One of the legal firms that is allowing client perusal of its fees is Bullivant, Houser, Bailey, Pendergrass and Hoffman of Portland, Oregon. The firm began the practice to build trust among customers: "To be candid, the level of trust isn't as high as it used to be. . . . This is a way, if you will, that you don't have to trust your law firm, because you can see in real time exactly what we've put on the books, with real numbers, real hours, real people and real dollars."[20] The system places entries from individual lawyers about their time into a central file once a day, then transmits the file to client computers.

One of the clients now entitled to the computer service is Dow Chemical. According to one of the company's systems specialists, the computer "looks for people billing who were approved to work on the case, looks for hourly rates that weren't consistent and looks for duplicate billing." Rejected entries automatically return to the law firm for explanation.

As you might expect, many law firms resist sharing their billings with clients. One concern is that adjustments to time sheets are sometimes made before bills are mailed to clients. Access will make these adjustments very noticeable. Others fear that access will allow clients to snoop into other clients' information.

Clients like the new practice so much that they are asking the software developers to take it one step further and develop programs to pick up on billing abnormalities so that they won't need to pore over the detailed fees.

Source: Stevens, "Clients Second-Guess Legal Fees On-line."

$2.69.[21] Banks claim that they set fees high enough to cover the costs of these services; the wide disparity in prices probably reflects the bank's difficulty in determining prices as well as their belief that financial customers find it difficult to shop around and discern the differences (if any) among offerings from different providers. A banking expert makes the point that "It's not like buying a quart of milk . . . Prices aren't standardized."[22] Only in very standardized services (such as dry cleaning) are prices likely to be remembered and compared.

Examples of Competition-based Pricing in Services Industries   *Price signaling* occurs in markets with a high concentration of sellers. In this type of market, any price offered by one company will be matched by competitors to avoid giving a low-cost seller a distinct advantage. The airline industry exemplifies price signaling in services. When any competitor drops the price of routes, others match the lowered price almost immediately. In the period between 1994 and 1995, for example, Continental created "Continental Lite" flights with prices designed to match Southwest Airlines' low prices. Other airlines flying those routes dropped prices to meet Continental's prices.

Focusing on competitors when setting services prices can create strange prices in the airline industry. The cost for a one-way fare between Newark, New Jersey, and Raleigh-Durham, North Carolina, was $299 when Continental Lite entered the market and dropped prices between Newark and Greensboro, North Carolina, to $99 one way. American did not have direct service from New York to Greensboro but did match the fare: $99 one way with a stop in Raleigh-Durham. Many fare-wise travelers purchased the $99 fare on American and did not fly the leg to Greensboro, giving them a $200 discount to Raleigh-Durham. Flyers using this strategy, called "hidden-city ticketing," are taking advantage of the complex, arcane, and competitor-focused system of pricing used by the airline industry.

Going-rate pricing involves charging the most prevalent price in the market. Rental car pricing is an illustration of this technique (and also an illustration of price signaling, since the rental car market is dominated by a small number of large companies). For years, the prices set by one company (Hertz) have been followed by the other companies. When Hertz instituted a new pricing plan that involved "no mileage charges, ever," other rental car companies imitated the policy, constraining themselves to depending on other variables for their prices. Those variables include base rates, size and type of car, daily or weekly rates, and drop-off charges. Prices in different geographic markets, even cities, depend on the going rate in that location, and customers often pay different rates in contiguous cities in the same state. The newsletter *Consumer Reports Travel Letter* advises customers that the national toll-free reservation lines offer better rates than are obtained calling local rental car companies in cities, perhaps because those rates are less influenced by the going rates in a particular area.[23]

Demand-based Pricing

The two approaches to pricing just described are based on the company and its competitors rather than on customers. Neither approach takes into consideration that customers may lack reference prices, may be sensitive to nonmonetary prices, and may judge quality on the basis of price. All of these factors can and should be accounted for in a company's pricing decisions. The third major approach to pricing, *demand-based pricing,* involves setting prices consistent with customer perceptions of value: prices are based on what customers will pay for the services provided.

Special Problems in Demand-based Pricing for Services

One of the major ways that pricing of services differs from pricing of goods in demand-based pricing is that nonmonetary costs and benefits must be factored into the calculation of perceived value to the customer. When services require time, inconvenience, and psychic and search costs, the monetary price must be adjusted to compensate. And when services save time, inconvenience, and psychic and search costs, the customer is likely to be willing to pay a higher monetary price. The challenge is to determine the value to customers of each of the nonmonetary aspects involved.

Another way services and goods differ with respect to this form of pricing is that information on service costs may be less available to customers, making monetary price not as large or salient a factor in initial service selection as it is in goods purchasing.

Four Meanings of Perceived Value

One of the most appropriate ways that companies price their services is basing the price on the perceived value of the service to customers. Among the questions a services marketer needs to ask are the following: What do consumers mean by value? How can we quantify perceived value in dollars so that we can set appropriate prices for our services? Is the meaning of value similar across consumers and services? How can value perceptions be influenced? To fully understand demand-based pricing approaches, we must fully understand what value means to customers.

This is not a simple task. When consumers discuss *value,* they use the term in many different ways and talk about a myriad of attributes or components. What constitutes value, even in a single service category, appears to be highly personal and idiosyncratic. Customers define value in four ways: (1) Value is low price. (2) Value is whatever I want in a product or service. (3) Value is the quality I get for the price I pay. (4) Value is what I get for what I give (Figure 17-4).[24] Let's take a look at each of these definitions more carefully.

Value Is Low Price   Some consumers equate value with low price, indicating that what they have to give up in terms of money is most salient in their perceptions of value, as typified in these representative comments from customers:

For dry cleaning: "Value means the lowest price."
For carpet steam cleaning: "Value is price—which one is on sale."
For a fast-food restaurant: "When I can use coupons, I feel that the service is a value."
For airline travel: "Value is when airline tickets are discounted."[25]

Value Is Whatever I Want in a Product or Service   Rather than focusing on the money given up, some consumers emphasize the benefits they receive from a service or product as the most important component of value. In this value definition, price is far less important than the quality or features that match what the consumer wants. In the telephone industry, for example, business customers strongly value the reliability of the systems, and are very willing to pay for the safety and confidentiality of the telephone lines. Service customers describe this definition of value as follows:

For an MBA degree: "Value is the very best education I can get."
For medical services: "Value is high quality."
For a social club: "Value is what makes me look good to my friends and family."
For a rock or country music concert: "Value is the best performance."

Value Is the Quality I Get for the Price I Pay   Other consumers see value as a trade-off between the money they give up and the quality they receive.

FIGURE 17-4   Four customer definitions of value.

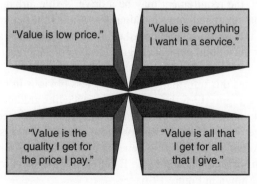

For a hotel for vacation: "Value is price first and quality second."

For a hotel for business travel. "Value is the lowest price for a quality brand."

For a computer services contract: "Value is the same as quality. No—value is affordable quality."

Value Is What I Get for What I Give   Finally, some consumers consider all the benefits they receive as well as all sacrifice components (money, time, effort) when describing value.

For a housekeeping service: "Value is how many rooms I can get cleaned for what the price is."

For a hair stylist: "Value is what I pay in cost and time for the look I get."

For executive education: "Value is getting a good educational experience in the shortest time possible."

The four consumer expressions of value can be captured in one overall definition consistent with the concept of utility in economics: *Perceived value is the consumer's overall assessment of the utility of a service based on perceptions of what is received and what is given.* While what is received varies across consumers (e.g., some may want volume, others high quality, still others convenience), as does what is given (e.g., some are concerned only with money expended, others with time and effort), value represents a trade-off of the give and get components. Customers will make a purchase decision on the basis of perceived value, not solely to minimize the price paid. These definitions are the first step in identifying the elements that must be quantified in setting prices for services. We provide in the following a framework for breaking the give and get components of value into manageable pieces that can be useful in quantifying value.

Integrating Framework for Customer Perceptions of Value   One way to view the information consumers hold about products and services is to picture it as occurring at a series of levels. As shown in Figures 17-5 and 17-6, the lowest, simplest, and most concrete level is a product or service feature. The highest, most abstract, and most complex level is the payoff of the service to the customer in terms of benefits. For a good such as an automobile, for example, one of the most abstract customer requirements (and hence the "highest" in Figure 17-5) might be safety or protection of the family. The lower we go in the figure, the more specific the requirements become. At the lowest, most specific level, the requirement may be a driver's-side airbag. Manufacturers use this type of information in building cars; after determining the central customer benefits (i.e., the payoff to the customer) they translate these into concrete, specific engineering attributes that they must build into cars to give customers their desired benefits and perceptions of value.

Intangibility makes this information hierarchy less obvious in services, but the central idea is the same. Figure 17-6 shows that in a service like graduate education, the student customer seeks abstract benefits such as knowledge, experience, and skill development. As we move lower in the hierarchy, these abstract benefits are translated into specifics. The corollary to engineering benefits in products are *service features* or *behaviors and actions of contact employees.* Examples of the specific levels for graduate education are also shown in Figure 17-6.

Abstract	Reliability	Performance	Durability	Prestige
	Has a good service record	Gives a smooth ride Provides safety	Lasts a long time	Impresses my friends and neighbors
	Starts on cold mornings	Has comfortable interior	Does not rust	Looks stylish
Concrete	Is rated #1 in J. D. Powers survey	Has driver-side airbags	Still runs after 250,000 miles	Has lots of chrome and leather

FIGURE 17-5   Means-ends depiction of consumer requirements in automobiles.

Understanding these levels and their linkages reveals how service features or employee behaviors are interpreted by consumers and then used in making decisions about service purchases or repurchases. These approaches—called *means-end chains*—describe how concrete attributes relate to higher level abstract concepts such as quality and value.[26] Figure 17-7 is a means-ends conceptual framework representing service information at different levels of abstraction. The "means" in means-ends models are the

FIGURE 17-6   Means-ends depiction of consumer requirements in graduate education.

Abstract	Knowledge	Experience	Skill Development	Personal Development
	Professor is competent	Professor talks about her experiences	Classes are rigorous	Professor gives me full attention
	Professor is good teacher	Professor gives real-world examples	Professor assigns useful and challenging projects	Professor listens to me
Concrete	Assigned books are informative	Professor has enough office hrs/week to help me with projects	Papers have many comments from professor	Professor calls me by my name

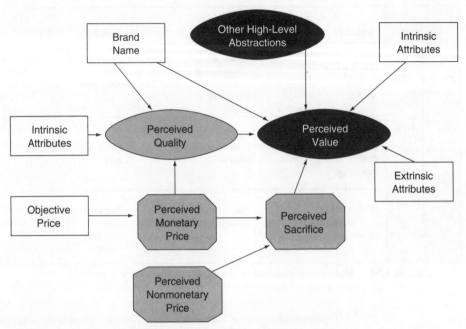

FIGURE 17-7   Means-ends model relating price, perceived quality, and perceived value.

Source: Zeithaml, "Consumer Perceptions of Price, Quality and Value: A Means-End Model & Synthesis of Evidence," 1988.

paths by which the service is linked by the customer through a chain of benefits, the "ends."

The most concrete and specific means in Figure 17-7 are shown as rectangles without shading. The more abstract the concept, and the closer to the ends, the darker the shading. Understanding how consumers organize information about services, and how they make the leaps from specific attributes to quality and value, is extremely helpful to marketers in pricing services to match customers' own configurations of value. The elements of the model are described in more detail below.

Service Features or Cues   These are the simplest, most concrete elements of the model (shown in rectangular boxes). Many of these cues are *intrinsic attributes,* specific features of the service itself such as duration of the service, times of availability, and types. For example, intrinsic attributes of insurance would include the type of insurance (whole life or term), the coverage amounts ($200,000 or $500,000), the date of policy initiation, and the payment method. Intrinsic attributes of physicians would include the types of diagnostic tests performed, the hours they are available, and the school from which the doctor received her degree. Intrinsic attributes of a pet grooming service would include the hours the service is available and the types of services offered (shampoo, cut, style, etc.). Intrinsic attributes cannot be changed without altering the nature of the service itself and are consumed as the service is consumed.[27]

The other category of service features is *extrinsic attributes* (such as price, brand name, and level of advertising) that consumers associate with the service. Extrinsic attributes are not an inherent part of the service. *Objective price* and *brand name,* two of the most frequently used extrinsic attributes, are therefore shown in separate boxes in the model.

Perceived Monetary Price This is the price the customer perceives the service to be, whereas *objective price* is the actual price. As we discussed earlier, many consumers do not attend to, know, and remember actual prices of services. Instead, they reframe prices in ways that are meaningful to them. Some consumers may notice that the price of dry cleaning a shirt is $1.69. Others may perceive and remember the price only as "expensive" or "cheap." Still others may not pay any attention to the price.

Perceived Nonmonetary Price This price represents the other costs we discussed earlier in this chapter that are perceived by consumers when buying and using a service: time costs, search costs, and psychic costs.

Perceived Sacrifice *Perceived sacrifice* includes all that the customer perceives has to be given up to obtain a service. All forms of price discussed above—monetary and nonmonetary—feed into this perceptual concept.

Perceived Quality *Perceived quality* is defined as the consumer's judgment about a service's overall superiority or excellence. This judgment is an abstract assessment and combines multiple service dimensions (such as reliability and responsiveness), which in turn are signaled by a combination of service features, behaviors, or actions.

Perceived Value *Perceived value* is defined as the consumer's overall assessment of the utility of a service based on perceptions of what is received and what is given.

Other Higher-level Abstractions Abstractions other than quality or value that are related to the product or customer also influence perceptions of value. For example, the high-level abstractions for graduate education in Figure 17-6 were knowledge, maturity, and skill development. If the marketer (in this case a university) understands these requirements and can link them to specific behaviors and attributes of service providers, their services should meet the customer's requirements.

Incorporating Perceived Value into Service Pricing It is the buyers' perception of total value that prompts the willingness to pay a particular price for a service. To translate the customer's value perceptions into an appropriate price for a specific service offering, the marketer must answer a number of questions. What benefits does the service provide? How important is each of these benefits to the others? How much is it worth to the customer to receive a particular benefit in a service? At what price will the service be economically acceptable to potential buyers? In what context is the customer purchasing the service?

The most important thing a company must do—and often a difficult thing—is to estimate the value to customers of the company's services. Value may be perceived differently by consumers because of idiosyncratic tastes, knowledge about the service, buying power, and ability to pay. In this type of pricing, what the consumer values—not what he pays—forms the basis for pricing. Therefore its effectiveness rests solely on accurately determining what the market perceives the service to be worth. To do so, the following steps must take place:

1 Elicit customer definitions of value in their own words and terms, allowing for the full range of components.

2 Help customers articulate their expressions of value by identifying their value definition, key abstract benefits sought, and abstract dimensions of quality that are relevant to them.

3 Capture requirements information at the concrete level—intrinsic and extrinsic attributes—linking them with the key benefits they indicate—so that the definition becomes actionable.

4 Quantify the monetary and nonmonetary value to customers.

5 Establish a price based on the value of the service to customers.

When the services are for the end-consumer, most often service providers will decide that they cannot afford to give each individual exactly the bundle of attributes he or she values (some firms do practice mass customization, described in chapter 7). They will, however, attempt to find one or more bundles that address segments of the market. On the other hand, when services are sold to businesses (or to end-customers in the case of high-end services), the company can understand and deliver different bundles to each customer. Johnson and Johnson Hospital Services has developed a prototype process for executing these steps in the hospital market, where its customers are materials managers (see Exhibit 17-3).

One of the most complex and difficult tasks of services marketers is setting prices internationally. If services marketers price on the basis of perceived value, and if perceived value and willingness to pay differ across countries (which they do for the most part), then services marketers may provide essentially the same service but charge different prices in different countries. Here, as in pricing domestically, the challenge is to determine the perceived value not just to different customers but to different customers in different parts of the world. Pricing in Europe provides one of the most compelling examples of the pricing challenges marketers face internationally.

Historically, Europe was considered to be a loosely aligned group of more than 12 separate countries, and a services marketer could have as many different pricing approaches as it had countries in which it offered the services. While pricing was complex to administer, the marketer had full flexibility in pricing and could seek the profit-maximizing price in each country. Prices across countries tended to vary widely, both in services and in products: "In most markets, [there are] still enormous price differentials between countries. For identical consumer products, prices show typical deviations ranging between 30–150%—for example 115% for chocolate, 65% for tomato ketchup and up to 155% for beer in Europe."[28] In the early 1990s, however, the European Community created a single internal market, holding the potential to simplify marketing in the area but also creating grave concerns about pricing. The largest concern is that marketers will be required to offer all services at a single European price—the lowest price offered in any European country—which could dramatically reduce revenues and profits.

Pricing Strategies that Link to the Four Value Definitions   The four customer value definitions that we have discussed can be positioned in the framework of the model, detailing the segments and showing the paths among the concepts that are most salient for each of the value segments. A clear understanding of these paths help services marketers price services in ways that align with the customer segments' meanings of

EXHIBIT 17-3

DELIVERED VALUE ANALYSIS (SM) BY JOHNSON AND JOHNSON HOSPITAL SERVICES

While the role of perceived value in developing and strengthening strategic relationships between customers and service companies has been well documented, *delivering* value is often hindered by difficulties in assessing the meaning of value to customers. As we discussed in this chapter, the difficulty is that customers vary in the ways they define perceived value: some consider monetary price the key driver, others emphasize service attributes without reference to price, still others carefully weigh the "give" and "get" aspects of an offering. Most companies need—yet few possess—a way to assess, discuss, and quantify the requirements that constitute value to individual business service customers.

Johnson and Johnson Hospital Services (JJHS) created a process for understanding and calibrating its customers' (who are materials managers in hospitals) perceptions of value. Its process and software—called Delivered Value Analysis (SM)—was designed to (1) capture individual business customer's meanings of value, (2) assist customers in articulating their own meanings and monetary worth of the different value components, and (3) quantitatively assess and document the monetary value of its services to customers. Delivered Value Analysis (SM) was developed through

interviews with customers, was tested and validated with customers, and is part of the J&J companies' efforts to strengthen strategic relationships.

As JJHS' former vice president, Nino Pionati, stated, "In the context of a total customer relationship it is our responsibility to provide both the quality products and responsive services to help our customers achieve improved clinical outcomes. We must do that with every customer, and we must do it in a way that is measurable against their performance criteria."[29] Materials managers' needs generally fell into three categories: information, assessment, and solutions. Information needs include current industry and product data to facilitate decision-making or training programs. Assessment needs involve product evaluations or analysis of processes or business functions that save time. Solution needs include specific business or patient-care problems and cross-functional processes to achieve improved efficiency or cost-effectiveness.[30]

Delivered Value Analysis (SM) is also an interactive software decision support tool that allows customers to quantify the value of their relationship with J&J on the basis of the criteria they select. It helps J&J better serve its customers by jointly identifying and quantifying the activities they value most.[31] A JJHS representative works with each client individually to evoke both the meaning of value and the monetary worth of products and services provided by J&J companies.

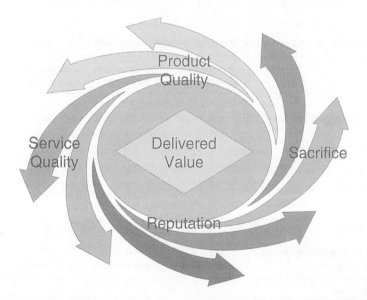

EXHIBIT 17-4

PRICING RESEARCH FOR DECISION-MAKING[32]

In addition to the methods and strategies of pricing that are discussed in this chapter, there are other research approaches that marketers can use to help them set prices and understand the impact of those prices. Four basic research methods exist for setting prices, each with its strengths and its limitations. They include purchase simulation, historical data modeling, trade-off analysis, and controlled market test.

Purchase simulation is a controlled simulated test where the researcher systematically varies aspects of pricing in order to study their impact on sales and revenue. Marketers select respondents who represent the ultimate customers of the product or service being studied, bring them to an interview location with different service or product displays, and give them 10 poker chips to place in front of the display to represent their next 10 service purchases. Respondents repeat the chip allocation exercise with different pricing approaches. The marketer then compares the purchasing behavior in the different price approaches. *Strengths:* inexpensive, quick, realistic, provides information about market segments, easy to understand/communicate, applicable to new products, appropriate for simple, low-risk questions. *Limitations:* artificial consumer behavior tasks, does not identify optimal price points (because it does

not examine all possible prices), does not measure the impact of price change on demand for other products and services.

In the **historical data modeling** approach, researchers look at past buying patterns using a statistical approach such as regression analysis. The impact of different marketing variables, including price, are examined for trends in past data. *Strengths:* enables "what if" scenarios, uses real consumer data, finds optimal historical price points, is supported by personal software, and is based on well-developed statistical tools. *Limitations:* rarely identifies price points for different market segments, is limited to data within historical data ranges, requires researcher expertise, is not applicable to new products, and is the most cumbersome method.

Trade-off analysis includes two approaches: conjoint measurement and discrete choice modeling. Conjoint measurement asks respondents to choose what they prefer in a series of price/service combinations (groups of specific services with prices). Discrete choice modeling derives measures of importance that reflect the market's value system of preferences. *Strengths:* allows playing "what if" games, achieves all pricing research objectives, is the most flexible method, analyzes market segments, is supported by PC software, measures interaction effects, is applicable to new products, and is the least costly method when studying multiple issues. *Limitations:* is based on simulated con-

A SELECTED COMPARISON OF WHEN TO USE VARIOUS PRICING RESEARCH METHODS

Criteria	Purchase simulation*	Historical data modeling	Trade-off analysis	Controlled market test
Decision issue:				
• Pricing strategies for existing product mix	2	3	4	5
• Price gap analysis	1	4	5	3
• Optimal pricing points	1	3	5	1
• Pricing new products	2	0	5	4
• Product switching patterns	3	2	4	5
• Value for product attributes	0	0	5	0
• Price promotion assessment	1	5	4	1
Cost	3	4	4	5
Statistical expertise required	2	5	4	3
Accuracy	2	4	4	5
Difficulty of understanding/interpreting results	2	4	5	3
Time horizon for implementation	1–4 weeks	1–4 weeks	1–2 months	1–2 months

*Ratings: 0=lowest; 5=highest.
Source: Mohn, "Pricing Research for Decision Making."

sumer tasks, is the most complex task for respondents, few researchers have expertise, and assumes "all else equal."

In the **controlled market test** approach, marketers select sample locations that are then divided into two groups: a control group and a test group. In the control group, prices do not change. In the test group, there is first a period with prices the same as in the control group and then a period with test pricing. Sales activity and profitability are monitored in both the control and test groups. Identifying changes in the test group compared with the control group gives the marketer a measure of the impact of the new pricing approach. *Strengths:* examines behavior in the real marketplace, tests specific price strategies, is appropriate for new

products, and is the best approach for high-risk questions. *Limitations:* is unable to examine many alternative price scenarios, is expensive, other variables in the market are hard to control, takes the longest to conduct, alerts competitors to what is being planned, does not measure cross-price elasticities, and is difficult to secure sample location cooperation.

Which approach is best to use? That depends on the decision issue, cost, statistical expertise required, accuracy, difficulty of understanding results, and time horizon for implementation. The preceding table rates each of the four pricing research methods on these criteria from 0 (lowest) to 5 (highest).

Source: Mohn, "Pricing Research for Decision Making."

---

value, thus making the offerings more viable in the marketplace. In the next section we describe the approaches to services pricing that are particularly suited to each of these value definitions. Exhibit 17-4 presents research approaches to setting prices.

Pricing Strategies When the Customer Means "Value Is Low Price" When monetary price is the most important determinant of value to a customer, the company focuses mainly on path A shown in Figure 17-8. This does not mean that the quality level and intrinsic attributes are always irrelevant, just that monetary price dominates in importance. To establish a service price in this definition of value, the marketer must understand and incorporate each of the highlighted boxes in the figure into the decision. The marketer must understand to what extent customers know the objective prices of services in this category, how they interpret various prices, and how much is too much of a perceived sacrifice. These are best understood when the service provider also knows the relative dollar size of the purchase, the frequency of past price changes, and the range of acceptable prices for the service. Some of the specific pricing approaches appropriate when customers define value as low price include discounting, odd pricing, synchropricing, and penetration pricing (Figure 17-9).

Discounting Service providers offer discounts or price cuts to communicate to price-sensitive buyers that they are receiving value. Colleges are now providing many forms of discounting to attract students. Lehigh University allows top students to get a fifth year of undergraduate or graduate education free, and also offers scholarships based on criteria other than financial need. The business school also cut tuition 22 percent for its master's program and allows graduates to take two-thirds off the regular tuition price.[33] Discount pricing has become a creative art at other educational institutions. The University of Rochester offered a $5,000 grant to all New York State residents enrolling as freshmen in 1995. Susquehanna University in Pennsylvania and Clarkson University in upstate New York are offering four-year degrees for the price of three. And Stevens Institute of Technology in New Jersey and Clark University in Massachusetts offer a no-tuition fifth year.[34]

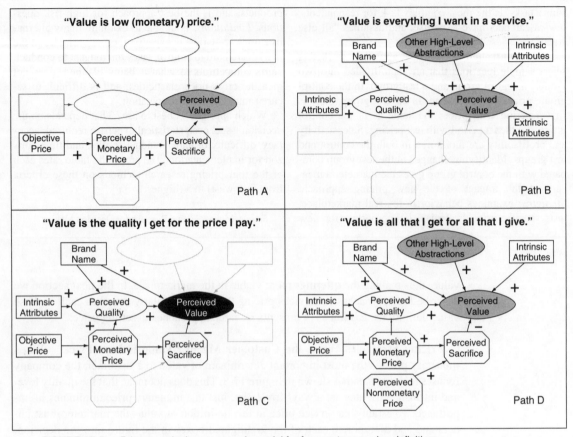

FIGURE 17-8   Primary paths in means-ends model for four customer value definitions.

Odd Pricing   This is the practice of pricing services just below the exact dollar amount to make buyers perceive that they are getting a lower price. Dry cleaners charge $2.98 for a shirt rather than $3.00, health clubs have dues priced at $33.90 per month rather than $34, and haircuts are $9.50 rather than $10.00. Odd prices suggest discounting and bargains and are appealing to customers for whom value means low price.

Synchro-pricing   Synchro-pricing is the use of price to manage demand for a service by using customer sensitivity to prices. Certain services, such as tax preparation, passenger transportation, long-distance telephone, hotels, and theaters have demand that fluctuates over time as well as constrained supply at peak times. For companies in these and other industries, setting a price that provides a profit over time can be difficult. Pricing can, however, play a role in smoothing demand and synchronizing demand and supply. Time, place, quantity, and incentive differentials have all been used effectively by service firms.

Place differentials are used for services where customers have a sensitivity to location. The front row at concerts, the 50-yard line in football, center court in tennis or bas-

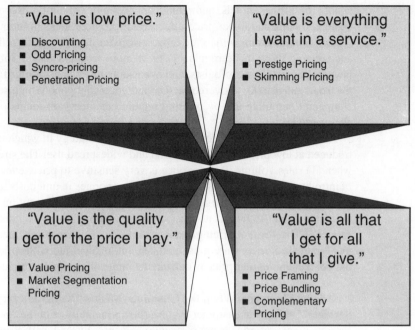

FIGURE 17-9   Summary of service pricing strategies for four customer definitions of value.

ketball, ocean-side rooms in resort hotels—all these represent place differentials that are meaningful to customers and that therefore command higher prices.

Time differentials involve price variations that depend on when the service is consumed. Telephone service after 11 p.m., hospital rooms on weekends, airline tickets that include a Saturday night stay, and health spas in the off season are time differentials that reflect slow periods of service. By offering lower prices for underused time periods, a service company can smooth demand and also gain incremental revenue.

After decades of cryptic time differentials that were hard for customers to understand, the long-distance telephone industry had its pricing structure overhauled by Sprint. In 1995, Sprint introduced Sprint Sense, a residential pan with a simple price structure for domestic long-distance calls: 22 cents a minute for calls made from 7 a.m. to 7 p.m. Customers making less than $25 worth of calls would pay a $3 per month fee for the service. Those making more than $25 worth would not pay a fee. One of the most interesting aspects of this plan is that the prices it creates are so different from those of other long-distance offerings that consumers will have difficulty comparing prices across companies.

Quantity differential are usually price decreases given for volume purchasing. This pricing structure allows a service company to predict future demand for its services. Customers who buy a booklet of coupons for a tanning salon or facial, a quantity of tokens for public bridges, or packages of advertising spots on radio or television are all responding to price incentives achieved by committing to future services. Corporate discounts for airlines, hotels, and rental cars exemplify quantity discounts in the business context; by offering lower prices, the service provider locks in future business.

Differentials as incentives are lower prices for new or existing clients in the hope of encouraging them to be regular users or more frequent users. Some professionals—lawyers, dentists, electrologists, and even some physicians—offer free consultations at the front end, usually to overcome fear and uncertainty about high service prices. Other companies stimulate use by offering regular customers discounts or premiums during slow periods.

Penetration Pricing   Penetration pricing is a strategy in which new services are introduced at low prices to stimulate trial and widespread use. The strategy is appropriate when (1) sales volume of the service is very sensitive to price, even in the early stages of introduction; (2) it is possible to achieve economies in unit costs by operating at large volumes; (3) a service faces threats of strong potential competition very soon after introduction; and (4) there is no class of buyers willing to pay a higher price to obtain the service.[35] This form of pricing can lead to problems when companies then select a "regular" increased price. Care must be taken not to penetrate with so low a price that customers feel the regular price is outside the range of acceptable prices.

Pricing Strategies When the Customer Means "Value Is Everything I Want in a Service"   When the customer is concerned principally with the "get" components of a service, monetary price is not of primary concern. Instead, path B in Figure 17-8 represents the criteria considered. Each of the linkages between boxes shows a positive association—the more plus paths a given service possesses, the more highly valued the service is likely to be and the higher the price the marketer can set.

Prestige Pricing   This is a special form of demand-based pricing by service marketers who offer high-quality or status services. For certain services—restaurants, health clubs, airlines, and hotels—a higher price is charged for the luxury end of the business. Some customers of service companies who use this approach may actually value the high price because it represents prestige or a quality image. Others prefer purchasing at the high end because they are given preference in seating or accommodations and are entitled to other special benefits. In prestige pricing, demand may actually increase as price increases because the costlier service has more value in reflecting quality or prestige.

Skimming Pricing   This is a strategy in which new services are introduced at high prices with large promotional expenditures. It is an effective approach when services are major improvements over past services. In this situation many customers are more concerned about obtaining the service than about the cost of the service, allowing service providers to skim the customers most willing to pay the highest prices.

Pricing Strategies When the Customer Means "Value Is the Quality I Get for the Price I Pay"   Path C in Figure 17-8 shows the elements that constitute value when the customer primarily considers quality and monetary price. The task of the marketer is to understand what quality means to the customer (or segments of customers) and then to match quality level with price level.

"Value Pricing"   This widely used term has come to mean "giving more for less."

In current usage it involves assembling a bundle of services that are desirable to a wide group of customers and then pricing them lower than they would cost alone. Taco Bell pioneered value pricing in 1988 with a $0.59 Value Menu. After sales at the chain rose 50 percent in two years to $2.4 billion, McDonald's and Burger King adopted the value pricing practice. The menu at Taco Bell has since been reconfigured to emphasize plain tacos and burritos (which are easier and faster for the chain to make) for less than a dollar. Southwest Airlines also offers value pricing in its airline service: a low cost for a bundle of desirable service attributes like frequent departures, friendly and funny employees, and on-time arrival. The airline offers consistently low fares with bare-bones service.

Market Segmentation Pricing   In this form of pricing, a service marketer charges different prices to groups of customers for what are perceived to be different quality levels of service, even though there may not be corresponding differences in the costs of providing the service to each of these groups. This pricing is based on the premise that different segments show different price elasticities of demand and desire different quality levels.

Some services marketers price by *client category,* based on the recognition that some groups find it difficult to pay a recommended price. Health clubs located in college communities will typically offer student memberships, recognizing that this segment of customers has limited ability to pay full price. Accompanying the lower price, student memberships may also carry with them reduced hours of use, particularly in peak-use times. The same line of reasoning leads to memberships for "seniors," who are less able to pay full price and also are willing to patronize the clubs during daytime hours when most full-price members are working.

Companies also use market segmentation by *service version,* recognizing that not all segments want the basic level of service at the lowest price. When they can identify a bundle of attributes that are desirable enough for another segment of customers, they can charge a higher price for that bundle. Companies can configure service bundles that reflect price and service points appealing to different groups in the market. Hotels, for example, offer standard rooms at a basic rate but then combine amenities and tangibles related to the room to attract customers willing to pay more for the concierge level, jacuzzis, additional beds, and sitting areas.

Pricing Strategies When the Customer Means "Value Is All that I Get for All that I Give"

Price Framing   Because many customers do not possess accurate reference prices for services, services marketers are more likely than product marketers to organize the price information for customers so they know how to view it. Customers naturally look for price anchors, as well as familiar services against which to judge focal services. If they accept the anchors, they will view the price and service package favorably. Gerald Smith, a professor at Boston College, provided an enlightening example of the way price framing could have improved sales of the 1994 Olympic TripleCast, minute-by-minute coverage of different Olympic arenas that was a well-documented failure because few customers were willing to pay the price of $130. He suggested that if CBS had segmented the market, isolated meaningful packages of sports, and framed them in a way that was familiar to customers, the service might have been successful. He proposed a boxing package for $24.95, a skating package for $24.95 (which might have been underpriced given the high demand to see Tonya Harding and Nancy Kerrigan!), and equestrian and wrestling packages for $19.95. In each case the service could be framed in an appropriate price context. For example, boxing at $24.95 is priced somewhere between attending a boxing match and watching it on pay-per-view. Boxing afficionados would recognize the price for the full package of matches as a value.[36]

Price Bundling Some services are consumed more effectively in conjunction with other services; other services accompany the products they support (e.g., extended service warranties, training, and expedited delivery). When customers find value in a package of services that are interrelated, price bundling is an appropriate strategy. Bundling, which means pricing and selling services as a group rather than individually, has benefits to both customers and service companies. Customers find that bundling simplifies their purchase and payment, and companies find that the approach stimulates demand for the firm's service line, thereby achieving cost economies for the operations as a whole while increasing net contributions.[37] Bundling also allows the customer to pay less than she would in purchasing each of the services individually, which contributes to perceptions of value.

The effectiveness of price bundling depends on how well the service firm understands the bundles of value that customers or segments perceive, and on the complementarity of demand for these services. Effectiveness also depends on the right choice of services from the firm's point of view. Since the firm's objective is to increase overall sales, the services selected for bundling should be those with a relatively small sales volume without the bundling to minimize revenue loss from discounting a service that already has a high sales volume.

Approaches to bundling include mixed bundling, mixed-leader bundling, and mixed-joint bundling.[38] In *mixed bundling,* the customer can purchase the services individually or as a package, but a price incentive is offered for purchasing the package. As an example, a health club customer may be able to contract for aerobics classes at $10 per month, weight machines at $15, and pool privileges at $15—or the group of three services for $27 (a price incentive of $8 per month).[39] In *mixed-leader bundling,* the price of one service is discounted if the first service is purchased at full price. For example, if cable TV customers buy one premium channel at full price, they can acquire a second premium channel at a reduced monthly rate. The objective is to use a price reduction in the higher-volume service to generate an increase in its volume that "pulls" an increase in demand for a lower volume but higher contribution margin service. In *mixed-joint bundling,* a single price is formed for the combined set of services with the objective to increase demand for both services by packaging them together.

Complementary Pricing This pricing includes three related strategies—captive pricing, two-part pricing, and loss leadership.[40] Services that are highly interrelated can be leveraged by using one of these forms of pricing. In captive pricing, the firm offers a base service or product and then provides the supplies or peripheral services needed to continue using the service. In this situation the company could off-load some part of the price for the basic service to the peripherals. For example, cable services often drop the price for installation to a very low level, then compensate by charging enough for the peripheral services to make up for the loss in revenue. With service firms, this strategy is often called "two-part pricing" because the service price is broken into a fixed fee plus variable usage fees (also found in telephone services, health clubs, and commercial services such as rentals). *Loss leadership* is the term typically used in retail stores when providers place a familiar service on special largely to draw the customer to the store and then reveal other levels of service available at higher prices.

Results-based Pricing   In service industries in which outcome is very important but uncertainty is high, the most relevant aspect of value is the *result* of the service. In personal injury law suits, for example, clients value the settlement they receive at the conclusion of the service. From tax accountants, clients value cost savings. From trade schools, students most value getting a job upon graduation. From Hollywood stars, production companies value high grosses. In these and other situations, an appropriate value-based pricing strategy is to price on the basis of results or outcome of the service.

Two simple examples, one for a consumer service and one for a business-to-business service, will illustrate how results-based pricing reduces risk for customers. Boens-Aloisi, a small advertising agency in Pennsylvania, used this approach by drawing up contracts with its clients to receive the full fee if sales rise 10 percent, half fee if sales rise only 5 percent, and no fee if sales are under 5 percent increase. At the Windows restaurant in Rosslyn, Virginia, customers order from a menu without any prices. After the meal they pay what they decide the food is worth. Most people pay as much, if not more, than the regular individual prices.[41] Obviously, the service provider in each of these illustrations must feel confident that its services will provide high value to customers, for its sales and margins depend on it.

Contingency Pricing   The most commonly known form of results-based pricing is a practice called contingency pricing used by lawyers. Contingency pricing is the major way that personal injury and certain consumer cases are billed; it accounts for 12 percent of commercial law billings.[42] In this approach, lawyers do not receive fees or payment until the case is settled, when they are paid a percentage of the money that the client receives. Therefore, only an outcome in the client's favor is compensated. From the client's point of view, the pricing makes sense in part because most clients in these cases are unfamiliar with and possibly intimidated by law firms. Their biggest fears are high fees for a case that may take years to settle. By using contingency pricing, clients are assured that they pay no fees until they receive a settlement.

In these and other instances of contingency pricing, the economic value of the service is hard to determine before the service, and providers develop a price that allows them to share the risks and rewards of delivering value to the buyer. Partial contingency pricing, now being used in commercial law cases, is a version in which the client pays a lower fee than usual but offers a bonus if the settlement exceeds a certain level. Bickel and Brewer, a commercial law firm, agreed to cap fees for legal work at $800,000 but to split with its client, Prentiss Properties Ltd. any judgment over $10 million. When the federal judge awarded Prentiss $100 million in settlement, the law firm walked away with $45 million more in payment for taking the risk.

Sealed Bid Contingency Pricing   Companies wishing to gain the most value from their services purchases are increasingly turning to a form of results-based pricing that involves sealed bids guaranteeing results. Consider the challenge of a school district with energy bills (including heating oil, gas, and electricity) so high that money was diverted from its primary mission of educating students. In its most recent year, costs for energy were $775,000 and the proposed budget for the coming year was $810,000. The school board wanted a long-term solution to the problem, desiring to expend less of their budget on energy and more on direct education expenses. The EMS Company, an engineering firm providing services to control and reduce energy use in large buildings, was one of three companies submitting bids to the school district. EMS's proposal provided for a computer-controlled system that monitored energy use and operated on/off valves for all energy-using systems. The proposal specified a five-year contract with a fixed price of $254,500 per year, with the additional guarantee that the school district would save at least that amount of money each year or EMS would refund the difference. Included in the proposal was a plan to take into account energy prices, hours the buildings were in use, and degree days so as to provide a basis of calculating the actual savings occurring. After five years the school district would own the system with the option of purchasing a management operating service for an annual fee of $50,000.[43]

Although two other firms submitted lower multiyear bids of $190,000 and $215,000 annually, neither bid provided any guarantee for energy savings. The school board was intrigued by the EMS approach, because at worst the cost of the service was zero. EMS was awarded the bid. During the first year, actual calculated savings exceeded $300,000. A cost-plus bid by EMS would have been priced at $130,000 per year. The use of contingency pricing by EMS removed the risk from the school board's decision and added additional profit contribution to EMS.[44]

Money Back Guarantees   Vocational colleges offer one major promise: to get students jobs upon graduation. So many schools commit to this promise—often blatantly in television advertising—that prospective students have come to distrust all promises from these colleges. To give substance to its promise, Brown-MacKenzie College, a for-profit vocational college, offered a tuition-back guarantee to any graduate who, after due effort, failed to obtain a suitable position within ninety days of program completion. While other educational institutions cannot do this, largely because the results desired do not often arrive within a ninety-day period, other results-based plans are taking shape. A future-income-dependent payment plan has been considered by many schools. Under such a plan, a student would receive a full scholarship and, after graduation, pay a fixed percentage of salary for a set time period—for example, 5 percent of salary for twenty years. Under this plan, the more "value added" by education and the more money-oriented the student, the more the student and the institution would benefit financially.[45]

Commission   Many services providers—including real estate agents, travel agents, and advertising agencies—earn their fees through commissions based on a percentage of the selling price. In these and other industries, the convention is for commission to be paid by the supplier rather than the buyer. Travel agents were traditionally compensated 10 percent by the airlines, not by the traveler. Advertising agencies are paid 15 percent commission by the print and broadcast media (e.g., newspaper, radio, TV, and magazines) for the amount they place with them, not by their clients.

The commission approach to services pricing is compelling in that agents are compensated most when they find the highest rates and fares. It would seem that agents have an underlying motivation to avoid the lowest fares and rates for their clients. In fact, commission pricing in the travel industry may be phased out because of discounted, low-priced airline tickets. American Express has recently introduced charges of $5 to $25 to book airline tickets that cost less than $100. Roger Ballou, president of the division that runs American Express's travel agency business, stated, "We'll lose some business, but it's going to be the kind that was costing us money."[46] Other agencies, such as Davidson Travel in Phoenix, provide new customers with a listing of a dozen fees for "everything from Visa processing to dinner reservations." Travelers who want a long trip, for example, must put down a $100 deposit, which is nonrefundable if the trip isn't taken.

SUMMARY

This chapter began with three key differences between customer evaluation of pricing for services and goods: (1) customers often have inaccurate or limited reference prices for services, (2) price is a key signal to quality in services, and (3) monetary price is not the only relevant price to service customers. These three differences can have profound impact on the strategies companies use to set and administer prices for services. The chapter also discussed common pricing structures including (1) cost based; (2) competition based; and (3) demand based. Central to the discussion were the specific difficulties in each of these structures and the services pricing techniques that have emerged in practice.

The chapter also defined customer perceptions of value and suggested appropriate pricing strategies that match each customer definition.

DISCUSSION QUESTIONS

1 Which approach to pricing (cost based, competition based, or demand based) is the most fair to customers? Why?

2 Is it possible to use all three approaches simultaneously when pricing services? If you answer yes, describe a service that is priced this way.

3 For what consumer services do you have reference prices? What makes these services different from others for which you lack reference prices?

4 Name three services you purchase in which price is a signal to quality. Do you believe that there are true differences across services that are priced high and those that are priced low? Why or why not?

5 Identify additional service examples of cost-, competition-, and demand-based pricing.

6 Describe the nonmonetary costs involved in the following services: having a will prepared, getting an automobile loan, belonging to a health club, having allergies diagnosed and treated, attending an executive education class, and buying life insurance.

7 Consider the specific pricing strategies for each of the four customer value definitions. Which of these strategies could be adapted and used with another value definition?

8 Consider the service of graduate education. Using the means-ends model shown in Figure 17-7, indicate your particular value aspects (including intrinsic and extrinsic attributes, abstract dimensions, and high-level abstractions).

EXERCISES

1 List five services for which you have no reference price. Now put yourself in the role of the service providers for two of those services and develop pricing strategies. Be sure to include in your description which of the value definitions you believe customers will possess and what types of strategies would be appropriate given those definitions.

2 In the next week, find five price lists for services. Identify the pricing base and the strategy used in each of them. If some approaches do not fit into one of the categories in this chapter, how would you describe them? What would you call them?

3 Consider that you are the owner of a new private college and can prepare a value/price package that is appealing to students. Describe your approach. How does it differ from existing offerings?

NOTES

1 Douglas Lavin and Krystal Miller, "Goodbye to Haggling: Savvy Consumers Are Buying Their Cars Like Refrigerators," *Wall Street Journal,* August 20, 1993, p. B1.

2 Ibid.

3 Ibid.

4 Ibid.

5 David Woodruff, "Leasing Fever: Why the Car Business Will Never Be the Same," *Business Week,* February 7, 1994, pp. 92–97.

6 Lavin and Miller, "Goodbye to Haggling."

7 David Germain, "Dial 900 for Help in Buying Auto," *The News and Observer,* Raleigh, N.C., November 26, 1993, p. 10C.

8 Kent Monroe, "The Pricing of Services," *Handbook of Services Marketing,* eds. Carole A. Congram and Margaret L. Friedman (New York: AMACOM, 1989), pp. 20–31.

9 Ibid.

10 "Pet Depressed? Call Us," *Newsweek,* May 22, 1989, p. 60.

11 Mark A. Ernst, "Price Visibility and Its Implications for Financial Services," presentation at the Effective Pricing Strategies for Service Providers Conference, Institute for International Research, Boston, October 1994.

12 Gerald E. Smith, "Framing and Customers' Perceptions of Price and Value in Service-oriented Businesses," presentation at the Effective Pricing Strategies for Service Providers Conference, Institute for International Research, Boston, October 1994.

13 Marilyn Chase, "Whose Time Is Worth More: Yours or the Doctor's," *Wall Street Journal,* October 24, 1994, p. B1.

14 Monroe, "The Pricing of Services."

15 Valarie A. Zeithaml, "The Acquisition, Meaning, and Use of Price Information by Consumers of Professional Services," in *Marketing Theory: Philosophy of Science Perspectives,* eds. R. Bush and S. Hunt (Chicago: American Marketing Association, 1982), pp. 237–241.

16 Christopher H. Lovelock, "Understanding Costs and Developing Pricing Strategies," *Services Marketing* (New York, NY: Prentice Hall, 1991), pp. 236–246.

17 Amy Stevens, "Firms Try More Lucrative Ways of Charging for Legal Services," *Wall Street Journal,* November 25, 1994, p. B1+.

18 Kenneth H. Bacon, "Banks' Services Grow Costlier for Consumers," *Wall Street Journal,* November 18, 1993, p. B1.

19 Amy Stevens, "Clients Second-Guess Legal Fees On-line," *Wall Street Journal,* January 6, 1995, pp. B1, B6.

20 Ibid., p. B6.

21 Ibid.

22 Janet L. Fix, "Consumers Are Snarling over Charges," *USA Today,* August 2, 1994, pp. B1–B2.

23 Cathy Lynn Grossman, "The Driving Forces behind Rental Car Costs," *USA Today,* October 25, 1994, p. 50.

24 Valarie A. Zeithaml, "Consumer Perceptions of Price, Quality, and Value: A Means-End Model and Synthesis of Evidence," *Journal of Marketing* 52 (July 1988): 2–22.

25 All comments from these four sections are based on those from ibid., pp. 13–14.

26 James H. Myers and Allan D. Shocker, "The Nature of Product-related Attributes," in *Research in Marketing,* Vol. 5 (Greenwich, Conn.: JAI Press, 1981), pp. 211–236. See also Jerry Olson and Thomas J. Reynolds, "Understanding Consumers' Cognitive Structures: Implications for Advertising Strategy," in *Advertising and Consumer Psychology,* eds. L. Percy and A. Woodside (Lexington, Mass.: Lexington Books, 1983).

27 J. Jacoby and Jerry C. Olson, "Consumer Response to Price: An Attitudinal, Information Processing Perspective," in *Moving Ahead with Attitude Research,* eds. Y. Wind and P. Greenberg (Chicago: American Marketing Association, 1977), pp. 73–86.

28 William R. Deeter, "Johnson and Johnson Sets New Standard for Supplier Performance," News Release, August 1994.

29 Ibid., p. 3.

30 Ibid., p. 5.

31 Hermann Simon, "If the Price Isn't Right," *World Link,* September–October 1994.

32 N. Carroll Mohn, "Pricing Research for Decision Making," *Marketing Research: A Magazine of Management and Applications,* 7, 1 (Winter 1995): 10–19.

33 "Colleges Get Creative in Price-cutting," *St. Petersburg Times,* December 27, 1994, pp. B1, B6.

34 Ibid., p. B6.

35 Monroe, "The Pricing of Services."

36 Smith, "Framing and Customers' Perceptions."

37 Monroe, "The Pricing of Services."

38 Ibid.

39 Joseph P. Guiltinan, "The Price Bundling of Services: A Normative Framework," *Journal of Marketing* 51 (April 1987): 74–85.

40 Gerard J. Tellis, "Beyond the Many Faces of Price: An Integration of Pricing Strategies," *Journal of Marketing,* 50 (October 1986), pp. 146–60.

41 "Paying What You Like," *New York Times,* August 3, 1988.

42 Stevens, "Clients Second-Guess Legal Fees."

43 Example adapted from Peter J. LaPlaca, "Pricing that Is Contingent on Value Delivered," given at the First Annual Pricing Conference, The Pricing Institute, New York, December 3, 4, 1987, and described in Monroe, "The Pricing of Services," p. 23.

44 Ibid.

45 Karen Fox, *Service Marketing Newsletter,* American Marketing Association, Chicago, 1984, pp. 1–2.

46 Jonathan Dahl, "Agents Ask Travelers to Start Paying Fees," *Wall Street Journal,* December 20, 1994, p. B1.

18

THE PHYSICAL EVIDENCE OF SERVICE

When Speedi-Lube opened its doors in Seattle, Washington, it was one of the first ten-minute oil and lubrication services ever introduced. Now there are hundreds of such outlets, but fifteen years ago the concept was totally new. The idea was to offer an alternative to corner gas stations for basic car lubrication service, quickly (within 10 minutes), with no appointment necessary. Because the concept was unknown to consumers at the time, the owners of Speedi-Lube needed to communicate and position the service clearly so that consumers would form accurate expectations. And because car maintenance is highly intangible and consumers often don't understand what is actually done to their cars, the owners relied heavily on tangible physical evidence to communicate the concept both before, during, and after the sale.

To communicate an image of fast, efficient service, Speedi-Lube relied on straightforward, to-the-point advertising using clean, crisp letters. For example, a large billboard read in large blue and white letters: SPEEDI-LUBE, 10-MINUTE OIL CHANGE, NO APPOINTMENT, OPEN 7 DAYS, 9 TO 6. The very buildings where the service was performed communicated the efficiency theme clearly. In fact, the exteriors of some of the first Speedi-Lube facilities had the look of a fast-food restaurant, not inconsistent with the intended image of speed, efficiency, and predictability. Entrance and exit signs were clearly displayed so that customers coming to Speedi-Lube for the first time would know exactly where to drive their cars.

On driving into the service bay the customer was greeted with additional physical evidence that clearly differentiated Speedi-Lube from its competitors at that time. The service bay was very neat and brightly painted, with a professional-appearing service counter in the bay where the customer filled out paperwork to get the service. Service personnel in professional uniforms helped with the paperwork and the customer was in-

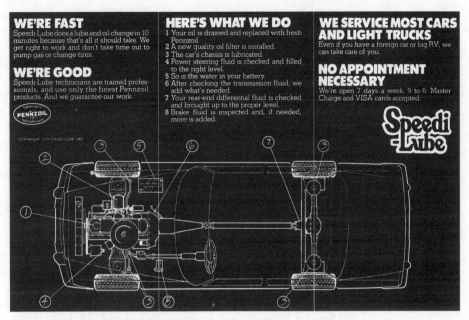

WE'RE FAST
Speedi-Lube does a lube and oil change in 10 minutes because that's all it should take. We get right to work and don't take time out to pump gas or change tires.

WE'RE GOOD
Speedi-Lube technicians are trained professionals, and use only the finest Pennzoil products. And we guarantee our work.

HERE'S WHAT WE DO
1 Your oil is drained and replaced with fresh Pennzoil.
2 A new quality oil filter is installed.
3 The car's chassis is lubricated.
4 Power steering fluid is checked and filled to the right level.
5 So is the water in your battery.
6 After checking the transmission fluid, we add what's needed.
7 Your rear-end differential fluid is checked and brought up to the proper level.
8 Brake fluid is inspected and, if needed, more is added.

WE SERVICE MOST CARS AND LIGHT TRUCKS
Even if you have a foreign car or big RV, we can take care of you.

NO APPOINTMENT NECESSARY
We're open 7 days a week, 9 to 6. Master Charge and VISA cards accepted.

FIGURE 18-1   Speedi-Lube spells out the service offering.

vited to wait in a clean and functional waiting area where coffee and magazines were provided. (Alternatively, customers were welcome to stay in the service area to observe the work on their cars.) On one of the waiting-room walls was displayed a large schematic that showed the underside of an automobile and identified all of the lubrication points and exactly what was being done to the car (Figure 18-1). This form of evidence informed customers and gave them confidence in what was being done.

On completion, the customer was given a checklist itemizing the lubrication services provided. As a finishing touch, the employee would then lubricate the door locks on the car to indicate that nothing had been overlooked. Three months later Speedi-Lube would mail a reminder postcard suggesting that it was time for another oil change.

It is difficult to imagine a time when ten-minute oil and lubrication services didn't exist on every street corner in U.S. cities. Yet when Speedi-Lube was established the quick oil change concept was totally unknown to consumers. Speedi-Lube was dealing with both a totally new concept and an industry in which services are generally high in credence attributes. The company used physical evidence very effectively to communicate the new concept and to make elements of the process itself very concrete. The schematic on the waiting-room wall detailing what the service entailed as well as the checklist showing exactly what had been done were ways the company tried to make credence attributes more tangible.

In this chapter we explore the importance of physical evidence for communicating service quality attributes and creating the service experience. As defined in chapter 1 when we introduced the expanded marketing mix for services, *physical evidence is the environment in which the service is delivered and where the firm and the customer interact; and any tangible commodities that facilitate performance or communication of the service.* The first part of this definition encompasses the actual physical facility where the service is performed, delivered, and consumed; throughout this chapter the physical facility is referred to as the *servicescape.*[1]

Physical evidence is particularly important for communicating about credence services (such as auto repair), but it is also important for services such as hotels, hospitals, and theme parks that are dominated by experience attributes. Think of how effectively Disney uses the physical evidence of its service to excite its customers. The brightly colored displays, the music, the fantastic rides, and the costumed characters all reinforce the feelings of fun and excitement that Disney seeks to generate in its customers. Think also of how effective Disney is in portraying consistent physical evidence that is compatible with its goals. The physical evidence and servicescape, or the "stage" in Disney's terms, is always stimulating to the extreme, is always clean, is always in top repair, and never fails to deliver what it has promised to consumers, and more. In this chapter we will see many examples of how physical evidence communicates with customers and how it can play a role in creating the service experience, in satisfying customers, and in enhancing customers' perceptions of quality.

Physical evidence that is inconsistent with service delivery or that overpromises what the firm can do will contribute to a widening of GAP 4 (Figure 18-2). The chapter will focus on the roles and functions of physical evidence and strategies that will close GAP 4. The key factors contributing to GAP 4 that will be emphasized in this chapter are: incompatible or inconsistent physical evidence; overpromising through physical evidence; and lack of physical evidence strategy (Figure 18-3). (As we progress through the chapter it will also be apparent that effective physical evidence strategies can play a role in reducing the size of GAPS 2 and 3.)

FIGURE 18-2   Provider GAP 4.

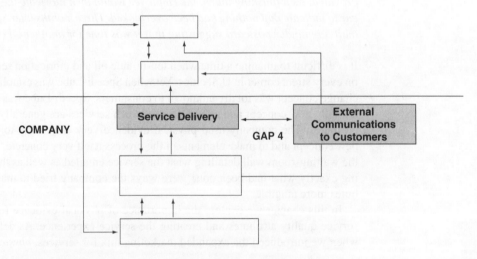

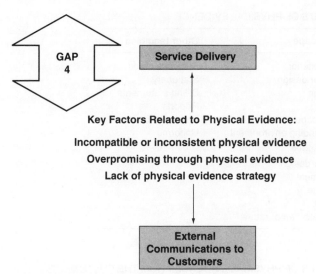

FIGURE 18-3   Key factors leading to provider GAP 4.

The objectives of this chapter are to:

1 Explain the impact on customer perceptions of physical evidence, particularly the servicescape.

2 Illustrate differences in types of servicescapes, the roles played by the servicescape, and the implications for strategy.

3 Explain why the servicescape affects employee and customer behavior, using a framework based in marketing, organizational behavior, and environmental psychology.

4 Analyze four different approaches for understanding the effects of physical evidence and servicescapes, namely environmental surveys, direct observation, experiments, and photographic blueprints.

5 Present elements of an effective physical evidence strategy.

PHYSICAL EVIDENCE—WHAT IS IT?

Because services are intangible, customers often rely on *tangible cues,* or *physical evidence,* to evaluate the service before its purchase and to assess their satisfaction with the service during and after consumption.

General elements of physical evidence are shown in Table 18-1. They include all aspects of the organization's physical facility (the servicescape) as well as other forms of tangible communication. Elements of the servicescape that affect customers include both exterior attributes (such as signage, parking, landscape) and interior attributes (such as design, layout, equipment, decor). Physical evidence examples from different service contexts are given in Table 18-2. It is apparent that some services communicate *heavily* through physical evidence (e.g., hospitals, resorts, child care), while others provide limited physical evidence (e.g., insurance, express mail). All of the elements of ev-

TABLE 18-1   ELEMENTS OF PHYSICAL EVIDENCE

Servicescape	Other tangibles
Facility exterior	Business cards
Exterior design	Stationery
Signage	Billing statements
Parking	Reports
Landscape	Employee dress
Surrounding environment	Uniforms
Facility interior	Brochures
Interior design	
Equipment	
Signage	
Layout	
Air quality/temperature	

TABLE 18-2   EXAMPLES OF PHYSICAL EVIDENCE FROM THE CUSTOMER'S
POINT OF VIEW

Service	Physical evidence	
	Servicescape	Other tangibles
Insurance	Not applicable	Policy itself
		Billing statements
		Periodic updates
		Company brochure
		Letters/cards
Hospital	Building exterior	Uniforms
	Parking	Reports/stationery
	Signs	Billing statements
	Waiting areas	
	Admissions office	
	Patient care room	
	Medical equipment	
	Recovery room	
Airline	Airline gate area	Tickets
	Airplane exterior	Food
	Airplane interior	Uniforms
	(decor, seats,	
	air quality)	
Express mail	Not applicable	Packaging
		Trucks
		Uniforms
		Computers
Child care center	Building exterior	Brochures
	Parking	Billing statements
	Signs and layout	Food
	Hallways, rooms	
	Equipment	
	Decor, air quality	

idence listed for each service *communicate* something about the service to consumers and/or *facilitate* performance of the service. While we focus in this chapter primarily on the servicescape and its effects, keep in mind that what is said applies to the other forms of evidence as well.

Consumer researchers know that the design of the servicescape can influence customer choices, expectations, satisfaction, and other behaviors. For example, retailers know that customers are influenced by smell, decor, music, and store layout. Furthermore, because services generally are purchased and consumed simultaneously, employees and customers will interact with each other in the servicescape. Thus, the same physical setting that communicates with and influences customers will also affect employees of the firm.[2] On the basis of a totally separate area of research, we know that the design of work environments can affect employees' productivity, motivation, and satisfaction.[3] The challenge in many service settings is to design the physical space and evidence so that it can support the needs and preferences of both customers and employees simultaneously. For example, in a study of employee and customer preferences in a bank environment, customers tended to agree that "A bank should not look like too much money was spent on the decor," while employees tended not to agree.[4] Customers may perceive that they are paying for expensive decor. Employees, on the other hand, may perceive an investment in the environment as an indication of management's concern for their feelings of job satisfaction.

In this chapter we will explain the roles played by the servicescape and how it affects employees and customers and their interactions. The chapter relies heavily on ideas and concepts from environmental psychology, a field that encompasses the study of human beings and their relationships with built (man-made), natural, and social environments.[5]

TYPES OF SERVICESCAPES

As is true of any marketing variable, the importance of the physical setting for customers and/or employees depends on both the nature of the service work and the service consumption experience. That is, the physical setting may be more or less important in achieving the organization's marketing and other goals depending on certain factors. Table 18-3 is a framework for categorizing service organizations on two dimensions that capture some of the key differences that will impact the management of the servicescape. Organizations that share a cell in the matrix will face similar issues and decisions regarding their physical spaces.

Servicescape Use

First, organizations differ in terms of *who* the servicescape will actually have an effect on. That is, who actually comes into the service facility and thus is potentially influenced by its design—customers, employees, or both groups? The first column of Table 18-3 suggests three types of service organizations that differ on this dimension. At one extreme is the *self-service* environment where the customer performs most of the activities and few if any employees are involved. Examples of self-service environments include ATMs, movie theaters, express-mail drop-off facilities, and self-service entertainment such as golf and theme parks. In these primarily self-service environments the organi-

TABLE 18-3   TYPOLOGY OF SERVICE ORGANIZATIONS BASED ON VARIATIONS IN FORM AND USE OF THE SERVICESCAPE

Servicescape usage	Complexity of the servicescape	
	Elaborate	Lean
Self-service (customer only)	Golf Land Surf 'n Splash	ATM Ticketron Post office kiosk Movie theater Express mail drop-off
Interpersonal services (both customer and employee)	Hotels Restaurants Health clinic Hospital Bank Airline School	Dry cleaner Hot dog stand Hair salon
Remote service (employee only)	Telephone company Insurance company Utility Many professional services	Telephone mail-order desk Automated voice-messaging-based services

Source: Bitner, "Servicescapes." Reprinted with permission of the American Marketing Association.

zation can plan the facility focusing exclusively on marketing goals such as attracting the right market segment and making the facility pleasing and easy to use. Creative use of physical design supports positioning and segmentation strategies as well.

At the other extreme of the use dimension is the *remote service* where there is little or no customer involvement with the servicescape. Telecommunication, utilities, financial consultants, editorial, and mail-order services are examples of services that can be provided without the customer ever seeing the service facility. In fact, the facility may be in a different state or a different country. To illustrate, all of AT&T's customer service calls are handled out of a small number of call centers located throughout the United States. A person calling in from New York in the middle of the night is likely to talk to a service representative in Arizona. In these remote services, decisions about how the facility should be designed can focus on the employees' needs and preferences almost exclusively. The place can be set up to keep employees motivated and to facilitate productivity, teamwork, operational efficiency, or whatever organizational behavior goal is desired without any consideration of customers, since they will never need to see the servicescape.

In Table 18-3, *interpersonal services* are placed between the two extremes and represent situations where both the customer and the employee must be present in the servicescape. Examples abound such as hotels, restaurants, hospitals, educational settings, and banks. In these cases the servicescape must be planned to attract, satisfy, and facilitate the activities of both customers and employees simultaneously. Special attention must also be given to how the servicescape affects the nature and quality of the social interactions between and among customers and employees. A cruise ship provides a good example of a service setting where the servicescape must support customers and the employees who work there and also facilitate interactions between the two groups.

Complexity of the Servicescape

The horizontal dimension of Table 18-3 suggests another factor that will influence servicescape management. Some service environments are very simple, with few elements, few spaces, and few pieces of equipment. Such environments are termed *lean.* Ticketron outlets and Federal Express drop-off kiosks would be considered lean environments, as both provide service from one simple structure. For lean servicescapes, design decisions are relatively straightforward, especially in self-service or remote service situations in which there is no interaction among employees and customers.

Other servicescapes are very complicated, with many elements and many forms. They are termed *elaborate* environments. An example is a hospital with its many floors, rooms, sophisticated equipment, and complex variability in functions performed within the physical facility. In such an elaborate environment, the full range of marketing and organizational objectives theoretically can be approached through careful management of the servicescape. For example, a patient's hospital room can be designed to enhance patient comfort and satisfaction while simultaneously facilitating employee productivity. Firms such as hospitals that are positioned in the elaborate interpersonal service cell face the most complex servicescape decisions.

Typology Implications

By locating itself in the appropriate cell of the typology, an organization can start to answer the following questions:

1 *Who should be consulted in making servicescape and other evidence decisions?* If an organization finds itself in the self-service cell, it can focus on the needs and preferences of customers. If in the remote service cell, it can focus on employees. If, however, the organization finds itself in one of the interpersonal service cells, it will know that decisions about the servicescape can potentially impact both customers and employees, as well as their interactions. Thus, both groups' needs and preferences should be considered, suggesting a more difficult decision process.

2 *What organizational goals might be targeted through servicescape design?* For self-service firms, the focus can be on marketing goals such as customer attraction and customer satisfaction. For remote service firms, priority can be given to work-group needs and employee motivation, productivity, and satisfaction in designing the service facility. For interpersonal services, both marketing and organizational goals could potentially be targeted, with the understanding that the solutions for one set of goals may not be compatible with the other set.

3 *How complex is the set of decisions regarding the servicescape?* Decisions will clearly be more complex for elaborate than for lean service environments. The more elaborate the servicescape in terms of spaces, equipment, and diversity of services de-livered, the more complex will be decisions about its design. Added complexity will also require more resources in terms of time, money, and people involvement in design de-cisions. The most complex servicescape decisions will be in the elaborate, interpersonal services cell where multiple needs (employees, customers, and their interactions) will be considered as well.

ROLES OF THE SERVICESCAPE

Within the cells of the typology, the servicescape can play many roles simultaneously. An examination of the variety of roles and how they interact makes clear how strategi-cally important it is to provide appropriate physical evidence of the service.

Package

Similar to a tangible product's *package,* the servicescape and other elements of physical evidence essentially "wrap" the service and convey an external image of what is "in-side" to consumers. Product packages are designed to portray a particular image as well as to evoke a particular sensory or emotional reaction. The physical setting of a service does the same thing through the interaction of many complex stimuli. The servicescape is the outward appearance of the organization and thus can be critical in forming initial impressions or setting up customer expectations—it is a visual metaphor for the intan-gible service. This packaging role is particularly important in creating expectations for new customers and for newly established service organizations that are trying to build a particular image. The physical surroundings offer an organization the opportunity to convey an image in a way not unlike the way an individual chooses to "dress for suc-cess." Interestingly, the same care and resource expenditures given to package design in product marketing are not generally provided for services, even though the service pack-age serves a variety of important roles.

Facilitator

The servicescape can also serve as a *facilitator* in aiding the performances of persons in the environment. How the setting is designed can enhance or inhibit the efficient flow of activities in the service setting, making it easier or harder for customers and employ-ees to accomplish their goals. A well-designed, functional facility can make the service a pleasure to experience from the customer's point of view and a pleasure to perform from the employee's. On the other hand, poor and inefficient design may frustrate both customers and employees. For example, an international air traveler who finds himself in a poorly designed airport with few signs, poor ventilation, and few places to sit or eat will find the experience quite dissatisfying, and employees who work there will proba-bly be unmotivated as well. The same international traveler will appreciate seats on the airplane that are conducive to work and sleep, as illustrated in the KLM/Northwest World Business Class ad shown in Figure 18-4. In this case the seating itself, part of the physical surroundings of the service, has been improved over the years to better facili-tate travelers' needs to sleep. The ad copy focuses on other improved elements of the

FIGURE 18-4   The servicescape can facilitate
service delivery.

Source: Northwest Airlines,
reprinted with permission.

physical surroundings: personal video system, 50 percent more leg room, and more
space overall. All of these factors emphasize the facilitator role of the servicescape.

Socializer

The design of the servicescape aids in the *socialization* of both employees and customers in the sense that it helps to convey expected roles, behaviors, and relationships.
For example, a new employee in a professional services firm would come to understand
her position in the hierarchy partially through noting her office assignment, the quality
of her office furnishings, and her location relative to others in the organization. The design of the facility can also suggest to customers what their role is relative to employees, what parts of the servicescape they are welcome in and which are for employees
only, how they should behave while in the environment, and what types of interactions
are encouraged.

Differentiator

The design of the physical facility can differentiate a firm from its competitors and signal the market segment the service is intended for. Given its power as a *differentiator,* changes in the physical environment can be used to reposition a firm and/or to attract new market segments. In shopping malls the signage, colors used in decor and displays, and type of music wafting from a store signal the intended market segment. In another context, the servicescape of a store-front legal services clinic located in a strip development differentiates it from corporate law firms located in downtown high rises. The design of a physical setting can also differentiate one area of a service organization from another. This is commonly the case in the hotel industry where one large hotel may have several levels of dining possibilities, each signaled by differences in design. Price differentiation is also often partially achieved through variations in physical setting. Bigger rooms with more physical amenities cost more, just as larger seats with more leg room (generally in first class) are more expensive on an airplane.

While it is useful from a strategic point of view to think about the multiple roles of the servicescape and how they interact, making actual decisions about servicescape design requires an understanding of why the effects occur and how to manage them. The next sections of the chapter present a framework or model of environment and behavior relationships in service settings.

FRAMEWORK FOR UNDERSTANDING SERVICESCAPE EFFECTS ON BEHAVIOR

The Underlying Framework

The framework for understanding servicescape effects on behavior follows from basic "stimulus-organism-response" (SOR) theory. In the framework the multidimensional environment is the *stimulus,* consumers and employees are the *organisms* that respond to the stimuli, and behaviors directed at the environment are the *responses,* as shown in Figure 18-5. The assumptions are that dimensions of the servicescape will impact customers and employees and they will behave in certain ways depending on their internal reactions to the servicescape.

Let's focus on a particular example. Assume there is a cookie cart that is parked outside the student union on campus. The cart is colorful and playful in design and an aroma of baking cookies wafts from it. The design and the aroma are two elements of the servicescape that will impact customers in some way. Now assume you are a hungry student, just out of class, strolling across campus. The fun design of the cart attracts your attention, and simultaneously you smell baking cookies. The fun design and the delicious smell cause you to feel happy, relaxed, and hungry at the same time. You are attracted to the cart and decide to buy a cookie, since you have another class to attend before you can break for lunch. The movement toward the cart and the purchase of a cookie are behaviors directed at the servicescape. Depending on how much time you have, you may even choose to get into a conversation with the vendor or other customers standing around munching cookies, other forms of behavior directed at the servicescape.

The framework shown in Figure 18-6 will be detailed and developed in the next sec-

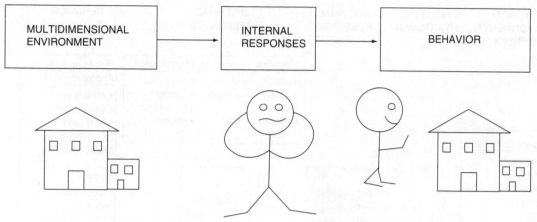

FIGURE 18-5   Stimulus-organism-response model.

tions. It represents a comprehensive stimulus-organism-response model that recognizes complex dimensions of the environment, impacts on multiple parties (customers, employees, and their interactions), multiple types of internal responses (cognitive, emotional, and physiological), and a variety of individual and social behaviors that can result. If the framework seems complex at times, refer back to the basic SOR model and the simple cookie cart example to re-identify the key features and elements.

Our discussion of the framework will begin on the right side of the model with *behaviors*—"response" in the SOR model. Next we will explain and develop the *internal responses* and *response moderators* portions of the model, corresponding to the "organism" in the SOR model. Finally we will turn to the *dimensions* of the environment and the holistic perception of the environment, which correspond to the "stimulus" in the SOR model.

Behaviors in the Servicescape

That human behavior is influenced by the physical setting in which it occurs is essentially a truism. Interestingly, however, until the 1960s psychologists largely ignored the effects of physical setting in their attempts to predict and explain behavior. Since that time, a large and steadily growing body of literature within the field of environmental psychology has addressed the relationships between human beings and their built environments.

Individual Behaviors   Environmental psychologists suggest that individuals react to places with two general, and opposite, forms of behavior: approach and avoidance. Approach behaviors include all positive behaviors that might be directed at a particular place, such as desire to stay, explore, work, and affiliate.[6] Avoidance behaviors reflect the opposite—a desire not to stay, to explore, to work, or to affiliate. In a study of consumers in retail environments, researchers found that approach behaviors (including shopping enjoyment, returning, attraction and friendliness toward others, spending

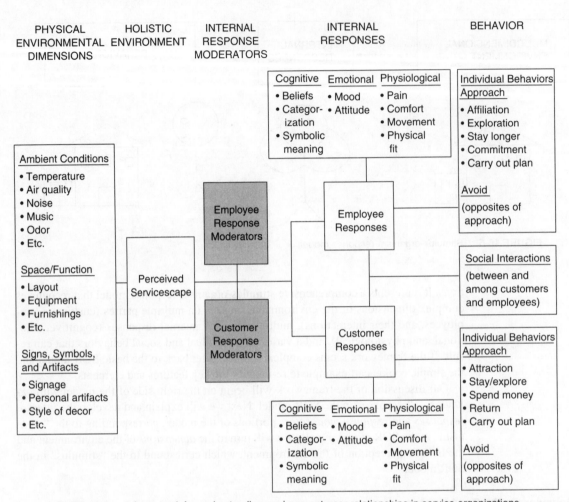

PHYSICAL ENVIRONMENTAL DIMENSIONS · HOLISTIC ENVIRONMENT · INTERNAL RESPONSE MODERATORS · INTERNAL RESPONSES · BEHAVIOR

FIGURE 18-6   A framework for understanding environment-user relationships in service organizations.
Source: Mary J. Bitner, "Servicescapes." Reprinted with permission of the American Marketing Association.

money, time spent browsing, and exploration of the store) were influenced by perceptions of the environment.[7] Other examples are abundant. At one 7-Eleven store the owners played "elevator music" to drive away the youthful market segment that was detracting from the store's image and keeping customers who would spend more from coming in. And the cookie cart example just given is reminiscent of cinnamon roll bakeries in malls that attract patrons through the power of smell.

In addition to attracting or deterring entry, the servicescape can actually influence the degree of success consumers and employees experience in executing their plans once inside. Each individual comes to a particular service organization with a goal or purpose that may be aided or hindered by the setting. NBA basketball fans are aided in their enjoyment of the game by adequate, easy-access parking; clear signage directing them to their seats; efficient food service; and clean rest rooms. The ability of employees to do their jobs effectively is also influenced by the servicescape. Adequate space, proper equipment, and comfortable temperature and air quality all contribute to an employee's comfort and job satisfaction, causing him or her to be more productive, stay longer, and affiliate positively with co-workers.

Clearly firms will want to encourage approach behaviors and the ability of customers and employees to carry out their plans and at the same time discourage avoidance behaviors. As Figure 18-6 indicates, the approach/avoidance behaviors of employees and customers are determined largely by individual internal responses, which we will discuss in a later section.

Social Interactions   In addition to its effects on their individual behaviors, the servicescape influences the nature and quality of customer and employee interactions, most directly in interpersonal services. It has been stated that "all social interaction is affected by the physical container in which it occurs."[8] The "physical container" can affect the nature of social interaction in terms of the duration of interaction and the actual progression of events. In many service situations, a firm may want to ensure a particular progression of events (a "standard script") and limit the duration of the service. Environmental variables such as physical proximity, seating arrangements, size, and flexibility can define the possibilities and limits of social episodes such as those occurring between customers and employees, or customers and other customers. The Carnival Cruise Line photo shown in Figure 18-7 illustrates how the design of the servicescape can help to define the social rules, conventions, and expectations in force in a given setting, thus serving to define the nature of social interaction.[9] The close physical proximity of passengers on the sunbathing deck will in and of itself prescribe certain patterns of behavior. This is not a vacation designed for a social recluse! Others have implied that recurring social behavior patterns are associated with particular physical settings and that when people encounter typical settings, their social behaviors can be predicted.[10]

Research confirms the impact of physical setting on the nature of social interactions. Behaviors such as small-group interaction, friendship formation, participation, aggression, withdrawal, and helping have all been shown to be influenced by environmental conditions. Similarly, in studies of workplace design, researchers have found that communication patterns, group cohesion, and the formation of friendships and small groups can be influenced by the physical setting.[11]

Examples are again abundant in actual service settings. Even casual observation of a Club Med facility confirms that the highly complex setting is designed to encourage social interaction among and between guests and employees. Seating arrangements and the food preparation process at Benihana restaurants similarly encourage interactions among total strangers, as well as contact between patrons and the Japanese chef who prepares their meals in full view. In most airports, in contrast, research suggests that the arrangement of seating typically *discourages* comfortable conversation among travelers and their companions.

One of the challenges in designing environments to enhance individual approach behaviors and encourage the appropriate social interactions is that the best design for one person or group may not be the best design for others. Research in a bank setting suggests, for example, that employees and customers have different needs and desires for their physical surroundings while in the bank.[12] Similarly, an environment that is con-

FIGURE 18-7   Social interactions are defined partially by the configuration of the servicescape.
Source: Carnival Cruise Lines, Miami, reprinted by permission.

ducive to an employee's individual work needs may not enhance the employee's ability to converse and interact interpersonally with customers.

Managerial Issues   The typology presented in Table 18-3 provides a structure for beginning to isolate relevant behavioral issues. Self-service firms will be most interested in predicting and managing *customer* behaviors (e.g., coming in, exploration, staying) in the physical setting and the potential achievement of marketing objectives such as customer attraction, satisfaction, and retention. In contrast, firms that operate remote services will focus on *employee* behaviors (e.g., productivity, affiliation with co-workers) and the achievement of organizational goals such as teamwork, productivity, and innovation. Organizations that are positioned in the interpersonal service cell will be concerned with both customer and employee behaviors as well as the effects of physical setting on the *interactions* between and among customers and employees.

Once behaviors most likely to be influenced by the servicescape are identified, challenging questions emerge: What causes these behaviors to occur, and how should the environment be configured to bring about desired responses?

Internal Responses to the Servicescape

Employees and customers respond to dimensions of their physical surroundings cognitively, emotionally, and physiologically, and those responses are what influence their be-

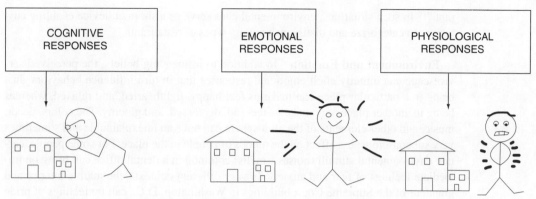

FIGURE 18-8   Internal responses to the servicescape.

haviors in the environment. In other words, the perceived servicescape does not directly *cause* people to behave in certain ways. As Figure 18-8 shows, perceptions of the servicescape lead to certain emotions, beliefs, and physiological sensations, which in turn influence behaviors. Though the internal responses are discussed independently here, they are clearly interdependent: a person's beliefs about a place, a cognitive response, may well influence the person's emotional response, and vice versa. For example, patients who come into a dentist's office that is designed to calm and sooth their anxieties (emotional responses), may believe as a result that the dentist is caring and competent (cognitive responses).

Environment and Cognition   The perceived servicescape can have an effect on people's beliefs about a place and their beliefs about the people and products found in that place. In a sense the servicescape can be viewed as a form of nonverbal communication, imparting meaning through what is called "object language."[13] For example, particular environmental cues such as the type of office furniture and decor and the apparel worn by the lawyer may influence a potential client's beliefs about whether the lawyer is successful or not successful, expensive or not expensive, and trustworthy or not trustworthy. In a consumer study, variations in descriptions of store atmospheres were found to alter beliefs about a product (perfume) sold in the store.[14] Another study showed that a travel agent's office decor affected customer attributions and beliefs about the travel agent's behavior.[15] Travel agents whose facilities were more organized and professional were viewed more positively than were those whose facilities were disorganized and unprofessional.

In other cases, perceptions of the servicescape may simply help people to distinguish a firm by influencing how it is categorized. Categorization is the process by which people assign a label to an object; when people see a feathered animal flying through the air they categorize it as a "bird" and not a "fish." Similarly, the overall perception of the servicescape enables the consumer or employee to categorize the firm mentally. Research shows that in the restaurant industry a particular configuration of environmental cues suggests "fast food" whereas another configuration suggests "elegant sit-down restaurant."[16] In such situations, environmental cues serve as a shortcut device enabling customers to categorize and distinguish among types of restaurants.

Environment and Emotion   In addition to influencing beliefs, the perceived servicescape can directly elicit emotional responses that in turn influence behaviors. Just being in a particular place can make us feel happy, lighthearted, and relaxed, whereas being in another place may make us feel sad, depressed, and gloomy. The colors, decor, music, and other elements of the atmosphere can have an unexplainable and sometimes very subconsciousness effect on the moods of people in the place. For some people, certain environmental stimuli (noises, smells) common in a dental office can bring on immediate feelings of fear and anxiety. In very different contexts, the marble interior and grandeur of the Supreme Court buildings in Washington, D.C., call up feelings of pride and awe and respect for many; lively music and bright decor in a local night spot may cause people to feel excited and happy. In all of these examples, the response from the consumer probably doesn't involve thinking, but rather is just an unexplained feeling. The Game Keeper store exterior shown in Figure 18-9 is intended to instill a lighthearted, fun feeling.

Environmental psychologists have researched people's emotional responses to physical settings.[17] They have concluded that any environment, whether natural or manmade, will elicit emotions that can be captured by two basic dimensions: (1) pleasure/displeasure, and (2) degree of arousal (i.e., amount of stimulation or excitement).[18] Servicescapes that are both pleasant and arousing would be termed *exciting,* while those that are pleasant and nonarousing, or sleepy, would be termed *relaxing.* Unpleasant servicescapes that are arousing would be called *distressing,* while unpleasant, sleepy servicescapes would be *gloomy.* These basic emotional responses to environments can be used to begin predicting the expected behaviors of consumers and employees who find themselves in a particular type of place. Environments that elicit feelings of pleasure are likely to be ones where people want to spend time and money, whereas unpleasant environments are avoided. Similarly, arousing environments are viewed positively unless the excitement is combined with unpleasantness.[19] Unpleasant environments that are also high in arousal (lots of stimulation, noise, confusion) are particularly avoided. The Game Keeper store (Figure 18-9) would be described as exciting since it is both pleasant and arousing.

Environment and Physiology   The perceived servicescape may also affect people in purely physiological ways. Noise that is too loud may cause physical discomfort, the temperature of a room may cause people to shiver or perspire, the air quality may make it difficult to breathe, and the glare of lighting may decrease ability to see and cause physical pain. All of these physical responses may in turn directly influence whether people stay in and enjoy a particular environment. It is well known that the comfort of seating in a restaurant influences how long people stay. The hard-surface seats in a fast-food restaurant cause most people to leave within a predictable period of time. Similarly, environmental design and related physiological responses affect whether a person can perform his or her job function well.

A vast amount of research in engineering and design has addressed human physio-

FIGURE 18-9   The clever retail designs of The Game Keeper Stores in
Sacramento (*right*) and Thousand Oaks, California (*left*) reflect the playful feeling that game stores hope to evoke in
customers.

Source: The Game Keeper, reprinted with permission.

logical responses to ambient conditions as well as physiological responses to equipment
design.[20] Such research fits under the rubric of *human factors design* or *ergonomics*.
Human factors research systematically applies relevant information about human capabilities and limitations to the design of things and procedures people use. The primary
focus and application of the research has been within the military, in space programs,
and in the design of computers, automobiles, and employee work stations. There is great
potential to apply this work in the design of commercial environments, taking into account the effects of design on both customers and employees who coexist and interact
in the environment.

For example, at Choice Hotels International, the age-60-and-over segment is the
largest and fastest growing customer group. To increase its appeal to older travelers and
physically challenged individuals, Choice began an effort to redesign its rooms to better meet their physiologically determined needs.[21] Special rooms will have telephones
and TV remote controls with large buttons and numbers, and wall switches will have
lights so they can be found easily at night. To help people with arthritis, doors will have
lever handles instead of knobs so that every door and every drawer in the room can be
opened with a fist rather than requiring hand and wrist dexterity.

Internal Response Moderators

In general, people respond to environment in the ways just described—cognitively,
emotionally, physiologically—and their responses influence how they behave in the environment. However, the response will not be the same for every individual, every time.

In the model shown earlier in Figure 18-6, "internal response moderators" refer to factors that may cause one individual to respond to the same servicescape differently from other individuals. Personality differences as well as temporary conditions such as moods or the purpose for being there can cause variations in how people respond to the servicescape.[22]

One personality trait that has been shown to affect how people respond to environments is "arousal seeking." Arousal seekers enjoy and look for high levels of stimulation, whereas arousal avoiders prefer lower levels of stimulation. Thus, an arousal avoider who found himself in a loud, bright disco with flashing neon might show strong dislike for the environment, whereas an arousal seeker would be very happy. In a related vein, it has been suggested that some people are better screeners of environmental stimuli than others.[23] Screeners of stimuli would be able to experience a high level of stimulation but not be affected by it. Nonscreeners would be highly affected and might exhibit extreme responses even to low levels of stimulation.

The particular purpose for being in a servicescape can also affect a person's response to it. A person who is on an airplane for a one-hour flight will likely be less affected by the atmosphere on the plane than will the traveler who is embarking on a ten-hour overseas flight. Similarly, a day-surgery hospital patient will likely be less sensitive and demanding of her environment than would a patient who is spending two weeks in the hospital. And a person who is staying at a resort hotel for a business meeting will respond differently to the environment than a couple who is there for their honeymoon.

Temporary mood states can also cause people to respond differently to environmental stimuli. A person who is feeling frustrated and fatigued after a long day at work is likely to be affected differently by a highly arousing restaurant than the person would be after a relaxing three-day weekend. Similarly, people who are in a hurry are likely to be more sensitive to elements of the environment such as crowding than they would be on a different day when they were not under time pressure.

The important thing to remember is that not every person will always respond in the same way to the environment—individual moods, purposes, and expectations may influence the response. And common personality characteristics (e.g., arousal seeking, environment screening) may cause certain groups of people to respond in predictably similar ways. The environmental dimensions (discussed next) will pass through these individual filters, or moderators, causing some variability in internal responses.

Environmental Dimensions of the Servicescape

The preceding sections have described customer and employee behaviors in the servicescape and the three primary responses—cognitive, emotional, and physiological—that lead to those behaviors. In this section we turn to the complex mix of environmental features that influence these responses and behaviors (the left portion of Figure 18-6). Specifically, environmental dimensions of the physical surroundings can include all of the objective physical factors that can be controlled by the firm to enhance (or constrain) employee and customer actions. There is an endless list of possibilities—lighting, color, signage, textures, quality of materials, style of furnishings, layout, wall decor, temperature, and so on. In the figure and in the discussion that follows here, the hundreds of potential elements have been categorized into three composite dimensions: *ambient conditions, spatial layout and functionality,* and *signs, symbols, and artifacts.*

While these three dimensions will be discussed separately, we know from environmental psychology that people respond to their environments holistically. That is, though individuals perceive discrete stimuli (e.g., they can perceive noise level, color, decor as distinct elements), it is the total configuration of stimuli that determines their reaction to the place. Hence, though the dimensions of the environment are defined independently below, it is important to recognize that they are perceived by employees and customers as a holistic pattern of interdependent stimuli. The holistic response is shown in Figure 18-6 as the "perceived servicescape."

Ambient Conditions   Ambient conditions include background characteristics of the environment such as temperature, lighting, noise, music, scent, and color. All of these factors can profoundly affect how people feel, think, and respond to a particular service establishment. For example, a nursing home chain discovered that in its facilities "the best odor was no odor." Patients and their families believed that unpleasant odors signified an unclean facility, while the odor of cleaning solvents signified that unpleasant odors were being covered up. Other ambient conditions similarly affect people's beliefs and feelings about a place.

As a general rule, ambient conditions affect the five senses. Sometimes such dimensions may be totally imperceptible (gases, chemicals, infrasound) yet have profound effects particularly on employees who spend long hours in the environment.

The effects of ambient conditions are especially noticeable when they are extreme. For example, people attending a symphony in a hall where the air conditioning has failed and the air is hot and stuffy will be uncomfortable, and their discomfort will be reflected in how they feel about the concert. If the temperature and air quality were within a comfort tolerance zone, these ambient factors would probably go unnoticed.

Ambient conditions also have a greater effect when the customer or employee spends considerable time in the servicescape. The impact of temperature, music, odors, and colors builds over time. Thus the air quality and noise levels in a hotel room will be more critical for customers than would the air quality and noise levels in a dry-cleaning establishment where most customers spend only a few minutes. Since employees often spend many more hours in the servicescape than do customers, ambient conditions are very important in creating a satisfying work environment.

Another instance in which ambient conditions will be particularly influential is when they conflict with what the customer or employee expects. If a potential client were greeted with loud rock music on entering a law office, she might decide to go elsewhere.

Spatial Layout and Functionality   Because service environments generally exist to fulfill specific purposes or needs of customers, spatial layout and functionality of the physical surroundings are particularly important. Spatial layout refers to the ways in which machinery, equipment, and furnishings are arranged, the size and shape of those items, and the spatial relationships among them. Functionality refers to the ability of the same items to facilitate the accomplishment of customer and employee goals. Previous examples in this chapter illustrate the layout and functionality dimensions of the servicescape: the airplane seating improvements illustrated in the KLM Northwest ad in Figure 18-4; Choice Hotels International's room adaptations for senior citizens; and work-station layout for service employees.

The spatial layout and functionality of the environment are particularly important for customers in self-service environments where they must perform the service on their own and cannot rely on employees to assist them. Thus, the functionality of an ATM machine and of self-serve restaurants, gasoline pumps, and computer-assisted retail shopping is critical to success and customer satisfaction.

Layout and functionality increase in importance when the tasks to be completed are complex and when either the employees or customers are under time pressure. Think of an airport where people come and go, often under extreme time pressure to make a connecting flight. If the airport is laid out in ways that make identification of gates easy and facilitate easy movement to, from, and between gates, travelers will be satisfied. If, on the other hand, connecting gates are located great distances apart, signage is poor, and there are no moving sidewalks or other means of moving quickly through the airport, travelers will be frustrated.

Signs, Symbols, and Artifacts   Many items in the physical environment serve as explicit or implicit signals that communicate about the place to its users. Signs displayed on the exterior and interior of a structure are examples of explicit communicators. They can be used as labels (e.g., name of company, name of department), for directional purposes (e.g., entrances, exits), and to communicate rules of behavior (e.g., no smoking, children must be accompanied by an adult). Adequate signs have even been shown to reduce perceived crowding and stress.

Other environmental symbols and artifacts may communicate less directly than signs, giving implicit cues to users about the meaning of the place and norms and expectations for behavior in the place. Quality materials used in construction, artwork, presence of certificates and photographs on walls, floor coverings, and personal objects displayed in the environment can all communicate symbolic meaning and create an overall aesthetic impression. Restaurant managers, for example, know that white tablecloths and subdued lighting symbolically convey full service and relatively high prices, whereas counter service, plastic furnishings, and bright lighting symbolize the opposite. In office environments, certain cues such as desk size and placement symbolize status and may be used to reinforce professional image.[24]

Signs, symbols, and artifacts are particularly important in forming first impressions of customers and for communicating new service concepts. When customers are unfamiliar with a particular service establishment, they will look for environmental cues to help them categorize the place and begin to form their quality expectations. In a study of dentists' offices it was found that consumers use the environment, in particular its style of decoration and level of quality, as a cue to the competence and manner of the service provider.[25]

Signs, symbols, and artifacts can also be important for repositioning and differentiating a service. When Skippers Seafood and Chowder House repositioned itself away from the fast-food dining segment and into the family dining segment it used a variety of physical evidence cues to do so. Everything from changing the exterior and interior colors and decor from red, white, and blue to more natural tones, to adding nautical photographs as wall decor, and to changing its serving implements from styrofoam to plastic and glass, was done to aid in the repositioning. Because Skippers served beer and wine and featured fresh seafood cooked to order, the existing food offerings already reflected family dining and it wasn't necessary to change the menu. Skippers simply needed to match its servicescape evidence to other strategic elements to be successful in repositioning itself in customers' minds.[26]

APPROACHES FOR UNDERSTANDING SERVICESCAPE EFFECTS

It is obvious from the framework, theories, and research results discussed thus far in this chapter that the servicescape can have profound effects on both customers and employees in service settings. To design environments that work from both a marketing and an organizational behavior perspective firms need to research environmental decisions and plan them strategically. The needs of ultimate users and the requirements of various functional units must be incorporated into environmental design decisions.

In this section we will look at various means whereby an organization can learn about users' reactions to and preferences for different types of environments. We discuss these approaches here because often it is very challenging to capture the true importance of physical evidence. Each of the approaches shown in Figure 18-10 has advantages and disadvantages. The four approaches are: environmental surveys, direct observation, experiments, and photographic blueprints.

FIGURE 18-10   Approaches for understanding servicescape effects.

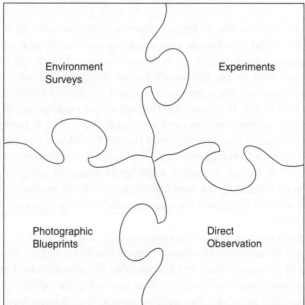

Environment Surveys

Experiments

Photographic Blueprints

Direct Observation

Environment Surveys

An environment survey asks people (either customers or employees) to express their needs and preferences for different environmental configurations by answering predetermined questions in a questionnaire format.

This is the type of research conducted in a retail bank setting that was designed to measure the importance of different environmental dimensions and elicit user expectations about bank facilities.[27] The study surveyed 3,000 bank customers and 2,000 bank employees about 32 environmental variables organized into five categories: ambient conditions, aesthetics, privacy, efficiency/convenience, and social conditions. Across the categories, employees and customers often had different expectations for the bank facility.

The advantages of surveys are the ease of administration and interpretation of results. Usually the data are collected via standardized questions and the results can be entered into a computer and easily interpreted. Thousands of questionnaires can be sent out or administered over the phone, so sample sizes can be very large and many environmental variables can be explored simultaneously. Depending on the decisions being made, surveys can at times be completely adequate for the task. Surveys are also less time consuming than the other approaches.

The primary disadvantage of an environmental survey is that sometimes the results may be less valid than results from other methods—that is, the answers to the survey questions may not truly reflect how people feel or how they will behave. This can occur when the dimensions of the servicescape affect people subconsciously or through complex interrelationships of dimensions, and people cannot accurately express these effects through paper and pencil surveys.

Direct Observation

Using observation methods, trained observers make detailed accounts of environmental conditions and dimensions, also observing and recording the reactions and behaviors of customers and employees in the servicescape. Essentially the observer attempts to fill in the boxes in the framework shown in Figure 18-6 with details for a specific setting by observing that setting over a period of time. An example of such a study was done in a retail gift shop context. Through direct observation, depth interviews, and photography, researchers compared detailed accounts of gift giving as it was observed and experienced in two separate retail stores: The Mouse House and Baubles.[28] Over time and extended involvement with the stores, the researchers were able to explore settings, actors, events, processes, and objects related to gift giving. Exhibit 18-1 provides excerpts regarding the store ambience taken from the study's field notes and journals. The kind of detailed information available using direct observation is apparent from the exhibit.

The advantages of direct observation, when done by highly trained and skilled observers, are the depth of information acquired and its accuracy. The interrelationship of elements of the environment and the reactions and interactions of participants in the environment can be unobtrusively recorded, increasing the validity of the findings beyond what is typically found in a standardized survey. The findings could be very useful in re-

EXHIBIT 18-1   A COMPARISON OF TWO GIFT STORES

The Mouse House

Tucked away near the corner of a festively lighted concourse of a very upscale suburban retail strip, nestled among restaurants, doctors' offices, specialty food stores, boutiques, spas and beauty parlors, is a quaint little gift shop called "The Mouse House." The shop takes its name from a once popular children's novel, and both the physical structure and ambience of its setting heighten the nostalgic storybook quality of the store. Every aspect of the Mouse House seems to invite the consumer's participation. . .

This invited participation is enhanced as the customer moves further into the store. The modest size of the store (a roughly trapezoidal 450 square feet) is a structural asset. Rustic barrel tables and containers, nonlocking glass cabinets and shelving units of various construction crowd the aisles of the shop. Walls and ceiling beams hold merchandise. Hutches, chairs and couches are similarly laden with goods. Walkways are narrow, and the displays cornucopic, forcing browsers to slow their pace in order to avoid upsetting or overlooking items. Nowhere is there displayed a sign requesting browsers to refrain from handling the often fragile and costly items. In fact, such handling is expected and encouraged. Such design creates the impression that the store is on the verge of bursting with its contents, overflowing with treasures of every description. Thus displayed, the merchandise seems quite accessible and familiar.

This cornucopic effect is enhanced by the owner's practice of rearranging merchandise periodically, highlighting the formerly hidden and downplaying the familiar; the appearance of added abundance is achieved with no additional stock. Yet at no time does the store display appear chaotic or haphazard, despite the high traffic of the holidays.

Baubles

Baubles is located in the downtown area of an older suburb of a major midwestern city . . . It is nested among and affiliated with a neighborhood business cooperative. . . The surrounding member stores, specializing in gourmet bakery items, handmade jewelry, imported children's toys, fireplace equipment, women's clothing, and original artworks in paper, metal and glass are relatively expensive small shops.

[Baubles] may be classified as small by modern retailing standards, with 1,100 square feet for receiving, administration and storage. . . The merchandise is displayed on several pieces of furniture (a canvas chair and loveseat, a cushioned loveseat and chaise lounge with frames constructed of natural willow branches, some still sprouting leaves), a pine table, white formica tables and cubes, an antique hutch and a carved oak fireplace mantel. These display pieces vary greatly in size, shape and texture, and all are for sale. The furnishings convey an aura of hominess and hospitality, but due to the vast accumulation of merchandise which they hold, they cannot be used for repose. Store merchandise is also hung on the walls, or from cross pieces in the ceiling. Items hung from the ceiling by nylon filament appear to be floating in space. . .

The owners and employees continually rearrange merchandise in the course of a selling day. The owners "totally take apart" the entire store every two weeks, moving the display pieces into different areas, and constructing new displays. . . One of the owners characterizes the atmosphere of the store as "fragile, but deliberate." She is initially reluctant to allow the researcher to question customers because they might get "a strange or pushy view of the store." Appropriate customer interactions are carefully planned to reinforce the themes of "fun" and illusion. Each customer is usually greeted at the door by an owner or salesperson."

Source: Sherry, Jr., and McGrath, "Unpacking the Holiday Presence," adapted with permission.

designing the servicescape or in comparing different facilities. Direct observation can also be useful when there is a very specific servicescape question that needs answering, for example, "What are the foot traffic flow patterns in the mall during peak business hours, and are the new signs effective in directing people?"

The disadvantages of direct observation are primarily related to time and dollar costs. First, the researchers who observe the servicescape must be highly trained and skilled in ethnographic methods, which makes data collection expensive. Second, they must be allowed to observe for some period of time, and the interpretation of their detailed records can be very labor intensive. Unlike the survey method, the data cannot as a rule be entered into a computer and analyzed with nice, clean quantitative results.

Experiments

Experimental methods are one of the best ways to assess specific customer and employee reactions to environmental changes or alternatives when it is important to know their true reactions and preferences. Experiments involve exposing groups of customers to different environmental configurations and measuring their reactions. For example, one experiment asked travelers to imagine that they had not received the cheapest air fare as requested from their travel agent.[29] Half of the travelers were shown a photo of an organized travel agency while the others saw a photo of a disorganized agency (see Figure 18-11). Results of the experiment showed that subjects exposed to the organized travel agency were more satisfied and more forgiving of the agent's error than were subjects exposed to the disorganized agency. In two other studies, background music type and tempo have been varied in grocery stores and restaurants and the effect on traffic pace, sales, and other variables has been measured.[30] In both cases, the type of music played had an effect on sales. Yet it is unlikely that shoppers would be conscious of this effect, nor would they be able to predict that they would buy more when a certain type of music is playing, if asked such a question on a survey.

The advantages of experiments lie primarily in the validity of the results; that is, if the experiment is carefully done, you can believe and rely on the results. Because envi-

FIGURE 18-11   Photos used in travel agency experiment: organized versus disorganized environments.

ronmental dimensions often affect people subconsciously and the multitude of dimensions interact to form a composite impression, it is difficult to get accurate responses to questions about the environment in the absence of actual experience. By controlling the environmental conditions experimentally and then measuring consumers' responses, there is a certainty that the environment and not something else actually was the cause of the internal response or the behavior. Further, different dimensions can be varied systematically to assess the independent impact of factors such as music, color, layout. The interactions among the dimensions can also be assessed systematically. Experiments also overcome the disadvantage of surveys in which people respond to questions in one way but actually behave differently in the real situation.

As with direct observation methods, the disadvantages of experiments relate primarily to costs and time. Ideally, actual servicescape prototypes would be designed and various groups of consumers would respond to the alternatives. Marriott Hotels has used this approach in designing its hotel rooms. However, because of the expense involved in constructing actual servicescapes, some form of simulation (verbal descriptions, photos/slides, scale models, videos, computer simulations) will likely be used. Environmental psychologists and marketers have shown that simulated environments can work well in achieving results similar to what would be found in actual, constructed environments.[31] Our Technology Spotlight shows how advances in computer technology can be used to employ "virtual reality" for effective environmental simulation.

Another disadvantage of experimental research is that only a few dimensions can be varied in any given experiment. If only one or two dimensions are of interest, such as

---

TECHNOLOGY SPOTLIGHT

VIRTUAL REALITY: SIMULATING SERVICE ENVIRONMENTS

Virtual reality is a term that encompasses a wide variety of computer technology applications allowing people to experience places and react to them without actually being there. Two characteristics of VR are that it conveys multiple sensory information and that it is interactive, allowing the viewer to in some way interact with the environment. The technology offers tremendous potential for the effective design and marketing of servicescapes.

As an example, urban planners in Los Angeles built an 80-block-by-80-block virtual model of renovation plans for riot-damaged areas. Because it is difficult for average citizens to read blueprints, and scale models are expensive, the VR rendition of the area gives residents and other interested parties a chance to react to the design and aid in its development. Residents use a computer mouse to guide themselves on the computer screen through the streets of Los Angeles as if they were in a helicopter. Designers can choose to put in a store or

a park, delete a gas station, or do whatever else they choose, to test residents' suggestions and determine preferences.

In addition to its usefulness as a service environment design tool, VR has been used to create simulated environments for consumers (or service providers) and bring them into artificial servicescapes where they actually "experience" the service. This is what theme parks and other entertainment centers are doing in creating fantastic, stomach-churning thrill rides using motion simulators and big-screen video. Other entertainment forms ask customers to don special headgear allowing them to play and participate in games, and tour retail shops and restaurants. In a totally different context, VR has been used to help surgeons plan surgeries or assist in surgeries taking place miles away by simulating the actual service delivery environment.

Sources: "Virtual Reality: How a Computer-generated World Could Change the Real World," cover story, *Business Week*, October 5, 1992, pp. 97–105; James R. Norman and Nikhil Hutheesing, "Hang On to Your Hats—and Wallets," *Forbes*, November 22, 1993, pp. 90–98.

music or color, then an experiment will be quite reasonable in terms of cost and time. However, multiple factors and combinations of factors are often under consideration. Thus it may take considerable time and multiple experiments to test systematically the effects of these numerous factors.

Photographic Blueprints

In chapter 10 we briefly introduced the idea of photographic blueprints in the general discussion of service blueprints. A photographic blueprint essentially provides a visualization of the service at each customer action step. The visual can be a slide, a photograph, or the entire service process as videotaped from the customer's point of view. By combining a service blueprint with photos, managers and other service employees can see the evidence of service from the customer's point of view. The photographic blueprint can provide a powerful analytic tool to begin assessing the service process. A photographic blueprint of the "Overnight Hotel Stay" in chapter 10 would include the blueprint as shown in Figure 10-8 together with photos or videotape of all of the evidence shown across the top of the blueprint.

Photographic blueprints are extremely useful in providing clear and logical documentation of the physical evidence as it currently exists in a given service situation. Before changes can be made, the current state of physical evidence should be made apparent to all concerned. The photos and/or videotapes give more depth to the process blueprint and the blueprint forces a certain logic on the analysis of the physical evidence. The photographic blueprint can give a vivid picture of how things are. The main disadvantage of a photographic blueprint is that it is just a starting point. In and of itself it doesn't answer any questions, but many questions can be asked of it. In and of itself it doesn't give any clues as to customer and employee preferences and needs; it could, however, be used as a catalyst for gathering customer and employee opinions.

GUIDELINES FOR PHYSICAL EVIDENCE STRATEGY[32]

Given the relative intangibility of most services, the strategy for managing physical evidence of service is critical. And customers will react to the company's evidence whether or not an evidence strategy exists. That is, the tangible evidence of service will communicate to customers whether or not its power to do so is recognized and planned. Unplanned, inconsistent, and incompatible physical evidence can contribute to a widening of GAP 4 (as suggested in Figure 18-3 at the beginning of this chapter), since physical evidence plays an important role in communicating promises and creating customer expectations. (From our discussion it is also apparent that poor design of physical evidence, particularly the servicescape, can contribute to a widening of GAP 2 or GAP 3 as well).

To this point in the chapter we have presented ideas, frameworks, psychological models, and research approaches for understanding the effects of physical evidence, and most specifically the effects of the physical facility or servicescape. In this section we will suggest some general guidelines for an effective physical evidence strategy.

Recognize the Strategic Impact of Physical Evidence

Physical evidence can play a prominent role in determining service quality expectations and perceptions. For some organizations, just acknowledging the impact of physical evidence is a major first step. After this step they can take advantage of the potential of physical evidence and plan strategically.

For an evidence strategy to be effective it must be linked clearly to the organization's overall goals and vision. Thus, planners must know what those goals are and then determine how the evidence strategy can support them. At a minimum, the basic service concept must be defined, the target markets (both internal and external) identified, and the firm's broad vision of its future known. Because many evidence decisions are relatively permanent and costly (particularly servicescape decisions), they must be planned and executed deliberately.

Map the Physical Evidence of Service

The next step is to map the service. Everyone should be able to *see* the service process and the existing elements of physical evidence. An effective way to depict service evidence is through the service map, or blueprint. (Service blueprinting was presented in detail in chapter 10.) While service maps clearly have multiple purposes, they can be particularly useful in visually capturing physical evidence opportunities. People, process, and physical evidence can be seen in the service map. From the map one can read the actions involved in service delivery, the complexity of the process, the points of human interaction that provide evidence opportunities, and the tangible representations present at each step. To make the map even more useful, photographs or videotape of the process can be added to develop a photographic blueprint, as described in the preceding section.

Clarify Roles of the Servicescape

Early in the chapter we discussed the varying roles played by the servicescape and how firms could locate themselves in the typology shown in Table 18-3 to begin to identify those roles in their particular cases. For example, a child care company would locate itself in the "elaborate, interpersonal" cell of the matrix and quickly see that its servicescape decisions would be relatively complex and that the servicescape strategy would have to consider the needs of both the children and the service providers and could impact marketing, organizational behavior, and consumer satisfaction goals.

Sometimes the servicescape may have no role in service delivery or marketing from the customer's point of view. This is essentially the case for telecommunication services or express mail services. Clarifying the roles played by the servicescape in a particular situation will aid in identifying opportunities and deciding just who needs to be consulted in making facility design decisions.

Assess and Identify Physical Evidence Opportunities

Once the current forms of evidence and the roles of the servicescape are understood, possible changes and improvements can be identified. One question to ask is: Are there missed opportunities to provide service evidence? The service map of an insurance or utility service may show that little if any evidence of service is ever provided to the customer. A strategy might then be developed to provide more evidence of service to show customers exactly what they are paying for. Speedi-Lube, our opening example, effectively used this approach in providing multiple forms of evidence to make car maintenance service more tangible to the consumer.

Or it may be discovered that the evidence provided is sending messages that don't serve to enhance the firm's image or goals. For example, a restaurant might find that its high-price cue is not consistent with the design of the restaurant, which suggests "family dining" to its intended market segment. Either the pricing or the facility design would need to be changed, depending on the restaurant's overall strategy.

Another set of questions to address concerns whether the current physical evidence of service suits the needs and preferences of the target market. To begin answering such questions, the framework for understanding environment-user relationships (Figure 18-6) and the research approaches suggested in this chapter could be employed. And finally, does the evidence strategy take into account the needs (sometimes incompatible) of both customers and employees? This question is particularly relevant in making decisions regarding the servicescape.

Be Prepared to Update and Modernize the Evidence

Some aspects of the evidence, particularly the servicescape, require frequent or at least periodic updating and modernizing. Even if the vision, goals, and objectives of the company don't change, time itself takes a toll on physical evidence, necessitating change and modernization. There is clearly an element of fashion involved, and over time different colors, designs, and styles may come to communicate different messages. Organizations obviously understand this when it comes to advertising strategy, but sometimes they overlook other elements of physical evidence.

Work Cross-functionally

In presenting itself to the consumer, a service firm is concerned with communicating a desired image, with sending consistent and compatible messages through all forms of evidence, and with providing the type of service evidence the target customers want and can understand. Frequently, however, evidence decisions are made over time and by various functions within the organization. For example, decisions regarding employee uniforms may be made by the human resources area, servicescape design decisions may be made by the facilities management group, process design decisions are most frequently made by operations managers, and advertising and pricing decisions may be made by the marketing department. Thus it is not surprising that the physical evidence of service may at times be less than consistent. Service mapping, or blueprinting, can be a valuable tool for communicating within the firm, identifying existing service evidence, and providing a springboard for changing or providing new forms of physical evidence.

A multifunction team approach to physical evidence strategy is often necessary, particularly for making decisions about the servicescape. It has been said that "Facility planning and management . . . is a problem-solving activity that lies on the boundaries between architecture, interior space planning and product design, organizational [and consumer] behavior, planning and environmental psychology."[33]

SUMMARY

In this chapter we have explored the roles of physical evidence in forming customer and employee perceptions. Because services are intangible and because they are often produced and consumed at the same time, they can be difficult to comprehend or evaluate before their purchase. The physical evidence of the service thus serves as a primary cue for setting customer expectations before purchase. These tangible cues, particularly the servicescape, can also influence customers' responses as they experience the service. Because customers and employees often interact in the servicescape, the physical surroundings also influence employees and the nature of employee/customer interactions.

The chapter focused primarily on the servicescape—the physical surroundings or the physical facility where the service is produced, delivered, and consumed. A typology of servicescapes was presented that illustrated its range of complexity and usage. By locating itself in the appropriate cell of the typology an organization can quickly see who needs to be consulted regarding servicescape decisions, what objectives might be achieved through careful design of the facility, and how complex the decisions are likely to be. General roles of the servicescape were also described. The servicescape can serve as a package (a "visual metaphor" for the service itself), a facilitator in aiding the accomplishment of customer and employee goals, a socializer in prescribing behaviors in the environment, and a differentiator to distinguish the organization from its competitors.

Given this grounding in the importance of physical evidence, in particular the servicescape, the chapter presented a general framework for understanding servicescape effects on employee and customer behaviors. The servicescape can affect the approach and avoidance behaviors of individual customers and employees as well as their social interactions. These behavioral responses come about because the physical environment influences (1) people's beliefs or cognitions about the service organization, (2) their feelings or emotions in response to the place, and (3) their actual physiological reactions while in the physical facility. The chapter also pointed out that individuals may respond differently to the servicescape depending on their personality traits, the mood they are in, or the goals they are trying to accomplish.

Three categories of environmental dimensions were presented to capture the complex nature of the servicescape: ambient conditions; spatial layout and functionality; and signs, symbols, and artifacts. It is these dimensions that affect people's beliefs, emotions, and physical responses, causing them to behave in certain ways while in the servicescape.

Given the importance of physical evidence and its potentially powerful influence on both customers and employees, it is important for firms to think strategically about the management of the tangible evidence of service. This means that the impact of physical evidence and customer-employee-oriented design decisions need to be researched and planned as part of the marketing strategy.

The chapter concluded with a discussion of four different research approaches for understanding servicescapes—environmental surveys, direct observation, experiments, photographic blueprints—and specific guidelines for evidence strategy. Such research can form the base on which strategic decisions can be made. If physical evidence is researched, planned, and implemented effectively, key problems leading to service quality shortcomings can be avoided. Through research and careful thinking about physical evidence decisions, an organization can avoid miscommunicating to customers via incompatible or inconsistent evidence or overpromising and raising customer expectations unrealistically. Beyond its role in helping to avoid these negative outcomes, an effective physical evidence strategy can play a critically important role in communicating to customers and in guiding them in understanding the firm's offerings and setting up accurate expectations. During the service experience, physical evidence can be part of an effective delivery strategy as well.

DISCUSSION QUESTIONS

1 What is physical evidence and why do we have a whole chapter devoted to it in a marketing text?

2 Describe and give an example of how servicescapes play each of the following roles: package, facilitator, socializer, and differentiator.

3 Imagine that you are the owner of an independent copying and printing shop (similar to Kinko's). Where (in which cell) would you locate your business in the typology of servicescapes shown in Table 18-3? What are the implications for designing your physical facility?

4 How can an effective physical evidence strategy help to close Provider GAP 4? Could such a strategy also help close Provider GAPS 2 and 3? Explain.

5 Explain the underlying stimulus-organism-response theory and how it relates to the effects of the servicescape on customers and employees.

6 Why are both customers and employees included in the framework for understanding servicescape effects on behavior (Figure 18-6)? What types of behaviors are influenced by the servicescape according to the framework? Think of examples.

7 Using your own experiences, give examples of times when you have been affected cognitively, emotionally, and physiologically by elements of the servicescape (in any service context).

8 Why is everyone not affected in exactly the same way by the servicescape?

9 Describe the physical environment of your favorite restaurant in terms of the three categories of servicescape dimensions: ambient conditions, spatial layout and functionality, and signs, symbols, and artifacts.

10 Imagine that you are serving as a consultant to a local health club. How would you ad-

vise the health club to begin the process of developing an effective physical evidence strategy?

EXERCISES

1 Choose two very different firms (different market segments or service levels) in the same industry. Observe both establishments. Describe the service "package" in both cases. How does the package help to distinguish the two firms? Do you believe the package sets accurate expectations for what the firm delivers? Is either firm overpromising through the manner in which its servicescape (or other types of physical evidence) communicates with customers?

2 Think of a particular service organization (it can be your project company, the company you work for, or some other organization) where you believe physical evidence is particularly important in communicating with and satisfying customers. Prepare the text of a presentation you would give to the manager of that organization to convince him or her of the importance of physical evidence in the organization's marketing strategy.

3 Create a photographic blueprint for a service of your choice.

4 Choose a service organization and collect all forms of physical evidence that the organization uses to communicate with its customers. If customers see the firm's facility, also take a photo of the servicescape. Analyze the evidence in terms of compatibility, consistency, and whether it overpromises or underpromises what the firm can deliver.

NOTES

1 The term *servicescape* used throughout this chapter, and much of the content of this chapter, are based, with permission, on Mary Jo Bitner, "Servicescapes: The Impact of Physical Surroundings on Customers and Employees," *Journal of Marketing,* 56 (April 1992): 57–71.

2 Julie Baker, Leonard L. Berry, and A. Parasuraman, "The Marketing Impact of Branch Facility Design," *Journal of Retail Banking* 10, 2 (1988): 33–42.

3 See, for example, Eric Sundstrom and Irwin Altman, "Physical Environments and Work-Group Effectiveness," *Research in Organizational Behavior* 11 (1989): 175–209; or Eric Sundstrom and Mary Graehl Sundstrom, *Work Places* (Cambridge: Cambridge University Press, 1986).

4 Baker, Berry, and Parasuraman, "Marketing Impact."

5 For reviews of environmental psychology, see Daniel Stokols and Irwin Altman, *Handbook of Environmental Psychology* (New York: John Wiley, 1987); and James A. Russell and Lawrence M. Ward, "Environmental Psychology," *Annual Review of Psychology* (1982): 651–688.

6 Albert Mehrabian and James A. Russell, *An Approach to Environmental Psychology* (Cambridge: Massachusetts Institute of Technology, 1974).

7 Robert Donovan and John Rossiter, "Store Atmosphere: An Environmental Psychology Approach," *Journal of Retailing* 58 (Spring 1982): 34–57.

8 David J. Bennett and Judith D. Bennett, "Making the Scene," in *Social Psychology Through Symbolic Interactionism,* eds. G. Stone and H. Farberman (Waltham, Mass.: Ginn-Blaisdell, 1970), pp. 190–196.

9 Joseph P. Forgas, *Social Episodes* (London: Academic Press, 1979).

10 Roger G. Barker, *Ecological Psychology* (Stanford, Calif.: Stanford University Press, 1968).

11 Sundstrom and Sundstrom, *Work Places,* part III.

12 Baker, Berry, and Parasuraman, "Marketing Impact."

13 Amos Rapoport, *The Meaning of the Built Environment* (Beverly Hills, Calif.: Sage Publications, 1982); Reginald G. Golledge, "Environmental Cognition," in *Handbook of Environmental Psychology,* Vol. 1, eds. Daniel Stokols and Irwin Altman (New York: John Wiley, 1987), pp. 131–174.

14 Meryl P. Gardner and George Siomkos, "Toward a Methodology for Assessing Effects of In-store Atmospherics," in *Advances in Consumer Research,* Vol. 13, ed., Richard J. Lutz (Ann Arbor, Mich.: Association for Consumer Research, 1986), pp. 27–31.

15 Mary Jo Bitner, "Evaluating Service Encounters: The Effects of Physical Surroundings and Employee Responses," *Journal of Marketing* 54 (April, 1990): 69–82.

16 James C. Ward, Mary Jo Bitner, and John Barnes, "Measuring the Prototypicality and Meaning of Retail Environments," *Journal of Retailing* 69, 2 (1992): 194–220.

17 See for example: Mehrabian and Russell, *Environmental Psychology;* James A. Russell and U. F. Lanius, "Adaptation Level and the Affective Appraisal of Environments," *Journal of Environmental Psychology* 4, 2 (1984): 199–235; James A. Russell and Geraldine Pratt, "A Description of the Affective Quality Attributed to Environments," *Journal of Personality and Social Psychology* 38, 2 (1980): 311–322; James A. Russell and Jacalyn Snodgrass, "Emotion and the Environment," in *Handbook of Environmental Psychology,* Vol. 1, eds., Stokols and Altman, pp. 245–281.

18 James A. Russell, Lawrence M. Ward, and Geraldine Pratt, "Affective Quality Attributed to Environments," *Environment and Behavior* 13, 3 (May 1981): 259–288.

19 Mehrabian and Russell, *Environmental Psychology.*

20 See for example: Mark S. Sanders and Ernest J. McCormick, *Human Factors in Engineering and Design* (New York: McGraw-Hill, 1987); David J. Osborne, *Ergonomics at Work,* 2d ed. (New York: John Wiley, 1987).

21 *Wall Street Journal,* "Lodging Chain to Give Older Guests a Choice," February 19, 1993, p. B1.

22 Mehrabian and Russell, *Environmental Psychology;* Russell and Snodgrass, "Emotion and the Environment."

23 Albert Mehrabian, "Individual Differences in Stimulus Screening and Arousability," *Journal of Personality* 45, 2 (1977): 237–250.

24 Tim R. V. Davis, "The Influence of the Physical Environment in Offices," *Academy of Management Review* 9, 2 (1984): 271–283.

25 James C. Ward and John P. Eaton, "Service Environments: The Effect of Quality and Decorative Style on Emotions, Expectations, and Attributions," in *Proceedings of the American Marketing Association Summer Educators' Conference,* eds. Ravi Achrol and Andrew Mitchell (Chicago: 1994), pp. 333–334.

26 Robin Ashton, "Skipper's Pipes a New Tune," *Institutions* 86, 7 (April 1, 1980): 47–49.

27 Baker, Berry, and Parasuraman, "Marketing Impact of Branch Facility Design."

28 John F. Sherry, Jr., and Mary Ann McGrath, "Unpacking the Holiday Presence: A Comparative Ethnography of Two Gift Stores," in *Interpretive Consumer Research,* ed. Elizabeth C. Hirschman (Provo, Utah: Association for Consumer Research, 1989), pp. 148–167.

29 Bitner, "Evaluating Service Encounters."

30 Ronald Milliman, "Using Background Music to Affect the Behavior of Supermarket Shoppers," *Journal of Marketing,* 46 (Summer 1982), pp. 86–91; Ronald Milliman,

"The Influence of Background Music on the Behavior of Restaurant Patrons," *Journal of Consumer Research,* 13 (September 1986), pp. 286–289.

31 See John E. G. Bateson and Michael Hui, "The Ecological Validity of Photographic Slides and Videotapes in Simulating the Service Setting," *Journal of Consumer Research,* September 1992, pp. 271–281; and Jack L. Nasar, "Perception, Cognition, and Evaluation of Urban Places," in *Public Places and Spaces,* eds., Irwin Altman and Ervin H. Zube (New York: Plenum Press, 1989), pp. 31–56.

32 This section is adapted from Mary Jo Bitner, "Managing the Evidence of Service," in *The Service Quality Handbook,* eds. Eberhard E. Scheuing and William F. Christopher (New York: AMACOM, 1993), pp. 358–370.

33 Franklin D. Becker, *Workspace* (New York: Praeger, 1981).

THE CHARTERED BANK
OF CANADA

Ken Powell, manager of the Cambridge Street branch of the Chartered Bank of Canada, looked up in response to the knock on his door. Dale Beeler, newly appointed assistant administrative officer, hesitantly entered Ken's office. This was the first transaction Dale had had to refer to her manager. A long time customer of the branch, Mrs. Terwilliger, had an out-of-town cheque she needed to cash but the funds in her account were insufficient to cover it if it bounced. Ken listened to Dale's problem, then initialled the cheque and sent her on her way. Dale was amazed.

Dale returned to Ken's office later to ask him how he could approve the cheque so easily when everything Dale had learned from the bank's manual of operating procedures said that a 'hold' should have been put on the funds until the cheque cleared. Ken explained:

> Mrs. Terwilliger brings in those cheques fairly often. They're from her sister in Toronto. She needs the money to tide her over 'til her pension cheque comes in next week. She's a good old girl and I don't mind giving her a little slack.

Dale looked quizzical and asked for clarification. Ken explained:

Richard Dean and Koren Volk prepared this case under the supervision of Professor John Haywood-Farmer solely to provide material for class discussion. The case is not intended to illustrate either effective or ineffective treatment of a managerial decision. The authors may have disguised certain names and other identifying information to protect confidentiality. The University prohibits any reproduction, in any form, of the material in this case without written consent from the School. © 1988 The University of Western Ontario   94.01.11.

Well Dale, sometimes you just have to take the risk to give good service. Let's look at some of the decisions we've faced recently and see what you would have done with them.

GENERAL ENVIRONMENT

The spring of 1988 was full of promise, with the Canadian dollar appreciating against the U.S. dollar and the Bank of Canada promising to keep interest rates high enough to curb inflation but low enough not to retard growth. Economists had been predicting a recession for late 1987, following the major stock market correction of October 19th, 1987, but to date there had been no significant indication of any recessionary trends.

THE BANKING INDUSTRY

The retail banking industry in Canada was fiercely competitive. The Schedule A banks competed among themselves and with the major Canadian trust companies for a share of the domestic market. Although globalization and deregulation of the financial services industry worldwide allowed the international expansion of the banks, many, faced with large third world loan losses, were returning to the domestic market as their primary source of revenue.

Each financial institution could offer a wide range of personal banking products to the customer. Institutions constantly introduced innovative products as well as longer hours, competitive interest rates, and higher levels of service to secure additional market share. However, these products could not provide a sustainable competitive advantage because competitors could easily duplicate most of them.

THE CHARTERED BANK OF CANADA

The Chartered Bank of Canada (CBC) was one of the nation's leading Schedule A banks. It operated through a network of over 1,500 branches across Canada and also had offices in another 23 countries. In addition, the CBC had a large Automated Teller Machine (ATM) network of over 600 units which was in turn connected to a shared Canada-wide network of over 3,000 more machines.

The bank had reorganized its corporate structure in 1984 to improve service by focusing on customer groups. The bank's annual report acknowledged the central role of customer service to success in the industry. The bank had centralized major commercial accounts at commercial branches and separated the personal banking component of the bank's business from the rest of the bank on a corporate level. Over the past five years net income had been increasing at about 5% per year. Income other than interest income had been increasing at about 18% per year and, by 1988, made up about 25% of all income. Personal banking as measured by mortgages, loans, and deposits had been increasing slightly faster than their non-personal counterparts. Annual loan losses were almost twice as large as net income.

Training and Evaluation   Formal training at the CBC was primarily technical or product knowledge in nature. This training was supported by:

- Personnel and Product Development departments
- regional training centres
- videos and other training aids
- the Manual of Routine Operating Procedures (a weighty tome of the bank's rules and procedures).

The bank provided this level of technical training so that it could offer standardized products throughout its large branch network, because the Bank Act stipulated legal requirements for many of the services provided by the bank, and to ensure that each employee would provide a minimum acceptable level of customer service. Supervisors and peers guided each employee through the customer service aspects of each successive position.

The bank evaluated staff on customer service, which ranged from 5% to 50% of the evaluation, and which was measured by a combination of qualitative and (increasingly) quantitative techniques. Customer service had a higher weight for staff with high degrees of contact with the public.

Promotion depended on staff ability to master the requirements of successive positions or levels of responsibility. These requirements included both technical and customer service competence.

The bank evaluated branch managers on the following criteria which it considered to be of approximately equal importance:

- achievement of revenue and profit goals
- attainment of satisfactory ratings in branch inspections
- provision of supplementary information by customer complaints or other sources
- development of subordinates.

THE CAMBRIDGE STREET BRANCH OF THE CBC

The CBC branch on Cambridge Street was situated on a corner of a busy intersection just outside the downtown core of Greenlands, Ontario. Two competitors had branches at the same intersection. A large general hospital and a major university were nearby.

With the restructuring of the CBC on the basis of commercial and retail banking, the bank designated the Cambridge Street branch a consumer branch, and transferred its medium-to-large commercial accounts to a main branch in downtown Greenlands. *Exhibit 1* gives some summary statistics on the branch's accounts and services offered. The branch retained its small commercial accounts, which included professional offices and small businesses. Additionally, the branch retained responsibility for negotiating student loans secured by the Canadian government.

The branch was open to the public from 9 am to 4:30 pm Monday through Thursday and from 9 am to 6 pm on Friday. The branch had only recently begun to open before 10 am in response to the early hours begun recently by the other two banks at the intersec-

EXHIBIT 1   DATA ON THE CAMBRIDGE STREET BRANCH'S ACCOUNTS AND SERVICES

Account Numbers

Type of Account	Number
Chequing	3,730
Savings	2,761
Business	810
Chequing/savings	486
Term deposits	145
Total	7,932

Client Base

	Accounts	Transactions	Average Balance
Professionals	20%	15%	$10,000
Students	15	5	1,000
Small businesses	25	40	10,000
Others	40	40	5,000

Negotiable Instruments

Travellers' cheques	Canadian	U.S.	Sterling	D.M.
Money orders	Canadian	U.S.		
Drafts	Canadian	U.S.	Sterling	Sundry

Accounts

Chequing	Chequing—seniors
Daily interest chequing	Daily interest chequing—seniors
Chequing savings	Under-18 account
Savings	Savings—seniors
Daily interest savings	Daily interest savings—seniors
Investment rate account	Investment rate account—seniors
Non-personal accounts	Non-resident accounts
U.S. dollar accounts	
Guaranteed investment certificates	
Term deposits	

Sundry Services

ATM cards and PINs*	Safety deposit boxes
Telephone transfers	Telex
Collections	Foreign exchange transactions
VISA cash advances	

Seasonal Services

Registered retirement savings plans   Student loans—federal and provincial
Canada savings bonds

* Personal identification numbers.

Source: Branch records.

tion. Two ATMs on the branch's exterior allowed customers to have access to their accounts outside of normal business hours.

The branch was staffed by an authorized complement of 27 full time and five part time employees. The average length of service of these employees was significantly above that of a typical branch. Turnover was low.

In addition to the base of typical bank customers, the Cambridge Street branch possessed three somewhat unique and distinct groups—professionals, students and small businesses (see *Exhibit 1*).

Professionals (doctors, lawyers, accountants, etc.) had very special needs in areas such as flexible financing, foreign exchange and specific types of accounts. Bank staff required a good deal of technical knowledge to satisfy these needs. Satisfied professionals were likely to refer their colleagues to their bank branch. Furthermore, professionals had connections with many non-professional clients and were never hesitant to recommend a good service.

Students were quite different. In dealing with this segment the emphasis was on the future. The challenge was to educate them about the bank and to provide them with a level of service which would keep them as customers once they began a career. Students required such special services as student loans, access to ATMs, and negotiation of out-of-town cheques (often from out-of-town parents).

Small businesses needed special care. Their needs changed as they grew and became successful, at which point the branch transferred them to a commercial branch. Financing and account management and advice were often the services most important to these customers. Professional customers often referred small business customers to the branch.

Ken Powell and Branch Performance   Ken Powell was a career banker who had just celebrated his twenty-fifth year with the bank, and his seventh as manager of the Cambridge Street branch. He was very pleased with his success in turning the branch around and he attributed a great deal of this success to his philosophy of banking.

Under Ken the branch had become a consistent top-five-performer in the region. Profits, as measured by net operating results, had increased over 400% in the last five years. Even in the face of growing automation the increased business at the branch justified doubling the authorized staff complement. Though the branch had lost all of its major business accounts to the commercial branch three years previously, the dollar amount of business loans outstanding was even higher in 1988, thanks to the active solicitation of small business accounts. Ken's performance had been acknowledged by the upgrading of his own position to a higher management level.

Ken's role, as he saw it, was to oversee operations in the branch, to ensure that his management team was in tune with his ideas and goals, and to see that these ideas trickled down to the staff. He was concerned with maintaining and constantly improving the level of service in the branch. Ken was the final authority in the branch's chain of referral for situations requiring management judgement. As a result, he could keep in tune with the day to day functioning of the branch and keep in touch with the customers.

Ken's Concept of Customer Service   Ken recognized that customer service in the branch was his primary source of competitive advantage. He firmly believed that it was this service which had enabled the branch to grow so rapidly during his tenure.

I want every customer who comes in here to feel wanted, and to feel respected. I want each person to leave saying: "this is *my* bank." If we achieve that sort of recognition in the community then growth becomes much easier.

When asked to describe his approach to customer service, Ken replied:

I believe in the common sense approach to banking. The keys are judgement and flexibility, not just rules and regulations. Sometimes you have to take a calculated risk in order to provide the best customer service you can. Customers can be lost so easily through poor service: you always have to be aware of their needs, and you have to show them you care. There's more to banking than just black and white, yes or no decision making. It's how you handle the grey areas that will make or break you. I'll admit it, I'm a risk taker as far as bankers go, but you just can't paint everyone with the same brush, especially in this branch where we have customers with special needs that we have to satisfy if we want to keep them around.

I try to instill this feeling in my staff. We are a team. We are a family. I have regular weekly meetings to keep the information flowing and I have just begun a series of personal interviews with each of my staff so that I know what's going on with them—not just from a banking viewpoint, but how their life is going in general, their kids, their spouse, their last vacation. It's all very important in understanding your staff, maintaining those lines of communication, and constantly improving your customer service. We can't afford to lose our edge.

BRANCH ORGANIZATION

The branch itself had four functional areas: commercial loans, consumer loans, tellers and deposit accounting, and the back counter (*Exhibit 2*).

Commercial Loans   An assistant manager of commercial credit headed the commercial loans department which consisted of a credit officer, a credit clerk, a discount clerk, and a typist. This department focused on the credit needs of small businesses through personal service and the structuring of each loan to the customer's requirements.

Consumer Loans   The consumer loan department, staffed by an assistant manager of consumer credit, two loans officers, and a clerk/typist, handled the credit needs of individuals. Car loans were the most typical of the products offered. The service was individualized, as in commercial loans, but in most cases the branch achieved a greater degree of standardization due to the less complex nature of consumer credit requests.

Tellers and Deposit Accounting   The teller department was certainly the most visible of the areas of service within the branch. There, ten tellers, half of them full time, completed transactions for customers. They emphasized processing speed and accuracy, and on serving the customer in a friendly manner. Most of the clerical positions in the

EXHIBIT 2   CAMBRIDGE STREET BRANCH ORGANIZATION CHART

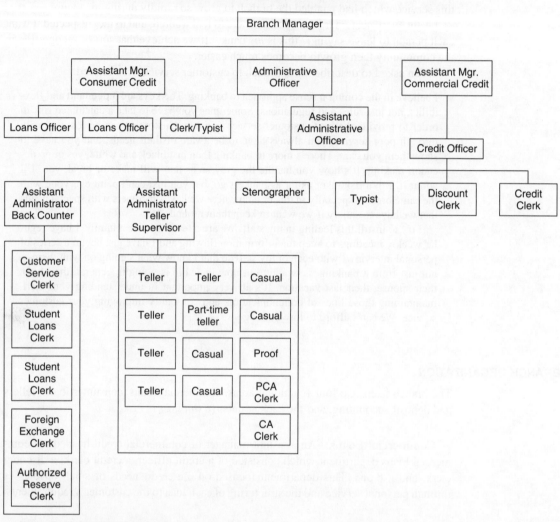

Source: The Cambridge Street Branch.

branch were filled by promotion from the teller line. Two ledger clerks, one for individual and one for business accounts, were responsible for ensuring the correct maintenance of accounts. These individuals also dealt with customer problems specifically relating to bookkeeping, such as unintentional overdrafts and uncleared cheques.

Back Counter Services   The catch-all of customer service in the branch, the back counter, under the supervision of an assistant administrator, was responsible for a wide variety of services and duties. A foreign exchange clerk, a customer service clerk, two student loan clerks, and an authorized reserve clerk each had specific desk and customer service duties to perform. The staff generally accomplished the balancing required to complete these tasks in a cooperative atmosphere.

The service at the back counter was generally more personalized and time consuming than on the teller line, but could have far more variety. An idea of the wide variety of services offered can be gathered from *Exhibit 1*. In addition to these normal services, the back counter was the most likely contact point for customers with special circumstances—complaints, cheque cashing, unusual or exceptional requests. Furthermore, as new accounts were opened almost solely at the back counter, customers often received their first real contact with the branch's customer service personnel there.

The back counter employees were the most important representatives of the manager's concept of service. They were all highly experienced and each very knowledgeable in his or her own specialized area. They had established relationships with many customers who would request them specifically when in need of service at the counter.

The foreign exchange clerk who claimed to spend over 50% of her time on customer service explained her tactics for customer satisfaction: "You've got to zero in on people's needs. If you really listen you can learn a lot."

One student loan officer stated: "I like customers, and I will work to midnight as long as the customer gets served."

The other student loan officer quipped: "Your day starts the same and ends the same but you never know what that next person is going to ask you. That's what I love about this job. You have to enjoy people," she continued, "if you don't want to meet a stranger, you shouldn't be working at the counter."

The authorized reserve clerk, whose position entailed covering for almost any other clerical position in the branch, sometimes on very little notice, summed it up best:

> Service is what we're here for. If I don't do that I'm not doing my job. If we aren't servicing the customer then we are handing them to the competition. Your workload is something you have to do and if that means working an extra 15 or 20 minutes, then so be it. If you see someone coming to the counter you should be there. I don't believe in making people wait. I wouldn't want to be standing there ignored.

SITUATIONS

Offering his assistant administrative officer a seat, Ken proffered: "OK Dale, let's start with some of the more common decisions that we have recently faced around here."

1. The Teller Line Complaint   It is noon on Friday and from your office you can see that the teller line has almost extended to the front door of the bank. A customer pops his head in the door and asks: "How come you've only got two tellers?"

"I don't know. Let's have a look!" you reply, and join the customer outside your office. You look over to the teller counter and see only two tellers at their wickets. However, with a brief glance around the bank, you see three other tellers: one with the administrative officer, one with the teller supervisor, and a third on the phone. "You see," exhorts the customer, "just two tellers. That's a hell of a way to run a bank!"

2. The Last Minute Cheque   It is five minutes before closing on Friday. An attractive young woman, neatly dressed, but obviously flustered, rushes into your branch. "Can you cash this for me?" she asks. "I didn't realize that my bank closes at 5:30 on Friday! I need some money over the weekend."

She has a personal cheque drawn on her own account at a competitor's bank for $150. "I've only just moved to Greenlands," she adds when your teller asks her for some identification. She produces several pieces of identification, but none of them has the same address that appears on the personal cheque. You do not know if there are funds in her account at the other bank. You do not even know the customer. Bank policy clearly would advise against the request.

3. Paula Simpson's Request   Paula Simpson is out front. She has a cheque for $1,000 made payable to her from her father. The cheque is drawn on a bank in Ottawa. She wants $1,000 in travellers' cheques before she leaves on her holiday tomorrow. I've checked Paula's account balance. She has $37.50, total, in her account. What should I do?

You remember that Paula is a medical student at the local university. She must be in her fourth year by now. She's always appeared bright and cheerful. She also has student loans through your branch. However, the bank's policy requires that you put a hold on all or part of the funds until the cheque from her father has cleared.

4. Myrna Saunders' Loan   Myrna Saunders, from Saunders Hardware, has just asked to see you. She appears somewhat distraught as she states her concern. "I recently applied for a business loan from your branch. Your credit officer has just informed me that the application has been refused. Mr. Belcher, my accountant, told me to come to this branch because you give such good service. He said this loan wouldn't be any trouble. I want to know why I was refused."

You recall that Pat Belcher has his business account at your branch. You also know little about the loan application itself as Vera Lee, your credit officer, was handling the matter.

Ken shifted to a more comfortable position in his chair and continued: "Now let's consider some of the more unusual circumstances that can come up."

5. Dan Logan's Overdraft   Kimberly Paige, a teller, approaches you. "Guess who just walked into the bank? Dan Logan!" Dan's account has been overdrawn to the tune of $127 for several weeks and you have been trying unsuccessfully to reach him. You feel that Dan may have been deliberately avoiding you.

You look over the teller line and Kimberly identifies Dan Logan as the large (2 metre, 115 kilogram) young man with hair past his shoulders and wearing a leather jacket decorated with the crest of a local bike gang. It appears that he has his unemployment cheque in his hand; you assume he probably wants to cash it.

6. Harry and Ona Perkins   You have agreed to see Ona Perkins, and while she is being shown to your office, you recall that Ona's brother, Harry, has been a customer at your bank for over 20 years.

"I'm so sorry to bother you," begins an obviously upset Ona Perkins, "but I don't know what to do. Harry got very sick last Wednesday, and I had to take him to the hospital. They admitted him, and the doctor thinks he may be in the hospital for a long time yet. They don't seem to know what's wrong with him. But he's unconscious most of the time."

"But the last few days these bills have been coming for Harry," she continues as she digs a handful of bills from her purse and pushes them towards you. "Harry has always looked after me. He always pays all the bills and looks after the money. And now, I'm running out of money. Harry always gives me $50 every week. And Harry should have a little money at the hospital. I don't know what to do!"

You check Harry Perkins' account and signature card and notice that the signing authority is only in Harry's name. Ona Perkins does not have an account in her name. The bills amount to about $150 and Ona wants $100 in cash. The account balance is well over $5,000.

7. Counterfeit Lira? Rose, the customer service clerk, catches your attention and signals you to the customer service counter. She introduces you to the tiny dishevelled gentleman standing at the back counter. "This is Mr. Biagio D'Angelo. He has a bit of a problem. If you could tell us your problem again, Mr. D'Angelo?"

In his broken English, Biagio D'Angelo begins. "I have just arrived in your country yesterday from my home in Italy. I have lots of money, but people here tell me my money is no good. They say I have to get some Canadian money. They told me to come to the bank and that you would give me some Canadian money." At this point, Mr. D'Angelo pulls an envelope from inside his coat. The envelope contains currency which appears to be Italian Lira. After examining it, you estimate it to be the equivalent of $75,000 Canadian. You have no way of knowing if the currency is legitimate, and Mr. D'Angelo's identification, including a passport, is all from Italy. From the bank's perspective, because Mr. D'Angelo has no collateral for a loan and no identified source of income, he would not normally qualify for credit.

"Well, Mr. D'Angelo," you begin, "we could exchange this money for you, but this branch does not handle foreign currencies other than US dollars, Deutsche Marks and Pounds Sterling. I would have to send the lira on collection to Toronto to be verified. The process would take about two weeks."

"Two weeks!" exclaims Mr. D'Angelo. "How am I going to live for the next two weeks? My wife and I, we have to eat, and we have to have a place to live! You have to give me some money now!"

8. "I've Never Trusted the Banks" An elderly man, looking about 75 years old, has just entered your branch. He is dirty and unkempt and is carrying two large glass jars of what appear to be melted and charred coins.

"My name is Nick Green. I live, or used to live, out on Governor Road. My house burnt down last night. I just never understood or trusted the banks and I've always kept all my money in my house." Mr. Green's voice is beginning to crack, but he continues: "I don't have any insurance. I have never trusted those guys either. All I've got left are these." With that he pushes the two jars of coins across the counter towards you. Although some of the coins are merely dirty, most of them are unrecognizable. "Can you help me?" he asks.

9. The Lawyer   "Michael Falcon, the lawyer, is at the counter," Diane, the foreign exchange clerk, informs you. "He has a power of attorney for Mrs. Vivian Douglas. Her current address on this account is the Sunset Retirement Home. Mr. Falcon is requesting that Mrs. Douglas' Canada Savings Bonds be redeemed. The power of attorney gives him signing authority on all of Mrs. Douglas' accounts. But, the proceeds are to be issued in a cheque, made payable to Mrs. Sheila Falcon, Michael Falcon's wife. When I asked him why the cheque was being made out to his wife, he said Mrs. Douglas wanted him to invest her money in something that would give her a better return on her investment. Therefore, he's going to invest her money in a second mortgage on his house. Doesn't that sound a bit unusual to you? I sure don't feel right about this one, but everything appears to be in order. What should I do?"

10. The Bank Inspector Fraud   There has been a recent ring of thieves operating in your banking community. Just this morning you received a warning circular from your Regional Office. The thieves pose as bank inspectors and approach unsuspecting senior citizens, requesting them to withdraw all their funds from their account and bring it back to them so that the 'inspector' can verify the transaction. The 'inspector' tells the victim that there have been complaints of tellers stealing by deliberately short changing the customers of this bank. When the victim returns from the bank, the 'inspector' then steals the money. You circulated the memo to your staff.

"I'm really worried," Judy, one of the clerks at the back counter, says. "Mrs. Vera Harris wants to withdraw $5,000 cash from her savings account—virtually the entire balance. I know her pretty well and I've tried to get her to tell me why she wants so much money, and why in cash, but she keeps saying that it's none of my business. I'm afraid that it could be a fake inspector, like in the memo this morning. What do I do?"

Ken leaned back from the desk and said: "Well Dale, those are some of the decisions I have had to make recently. Based on them, what do you think it takes to give good service in a branch bank?"

ROSCOE NONDESTRUCTIVE TESTING (A)

After nine months, Grover Porter, president of Roscoe Nondestructive Testing, Inc. (Roscoe) was beginning to question the success of his new quality improvement program (QIP). Initiated in March 1991, the QIP had produced substantial increases in recent customer satisfaction surveys; however, none of that satisfaction seemed to be fueling a return to growth in either revenue or number of clients. Porter anticipated Roscoe's second down year in a row as the company continued to lose major customers, and he was eager to re-establish the growth that had preceded the last two years of decline.

It was hard to believe that the cyclical downturn in the pulp and paper industry had pushed the boiler inspection business to competing solely on price. Porter still felt that there was room in the industry for a quality service at a fair price, but the ineffectiveness of the QIP had prompted Porter to reconsider adjusting Roscoe's pricing structure.

THE NONDESTRUCTIVE TESTING INDUSTRY

Nondestructive testing (NDT) involves the examination of materials to discover microscopic cracks, corrosion, or malformation, using inspection techniques that do not damage the material under scrutiny. Common inspection techniques include the use of x-rays, ultrasonics, and electrical eddy currents.

This case was prepared by Brian Wansink and Eric Cannell as the basis for class discussion rather than to illustrate either effective or ineffective handling of an administrative situation.

NDT is used in a wide variety of applications, including the examination of aircraft parts, tanks and vessels of various shapes and sizes, and welds of all kinds. Roscoe primarily uses ultrasonic thickness measuring devices to determine the thickness of metal plating.

NDT technicians are certified by area of expertise (e.g., ultrasonic) and accumulated skill and experience (Levels I–III). Technicians certified in more than one inspection technique are a treasured resource in most firms. They were generally employed by four types of companies:

1 Mom and pop labs usually employ fewer than 25 people and provide a single type of inspection service to a small number of customers. These firms are the low-cost providers and are quite willing to bid at cost, simply to keep busy. Many are often tied to a single client who wields considerable control over pricing and delivery.

2 Nation-wide companies have labs around the country and a high degree of name recognition. These firms also provide inspection services to a large number of different industries; however, individual offices usually serve a narrow segment of the market.

3 Specialty firms target very narrow market segments that have specific needs. These firms make large capital investments in the latest inspection equipment and employ the highest skilled technicians. Barriers to entry into these specialized markets are high, so specialty firms have traditionally achieved high levels of profitability.

4 While much larger than the mom and pop labs, *regional* firms lack the name recognition and market strength of the nation-wide companies. These firms employ up to 150 technicians and have the resources to tackle the largest inspection jobs. Roscoe is a regional firm, operating primarily in the central southern part of the United States.

All in all, management of NDT firms has been historically uninspired, driven mainly by owner-operators who managed to survive the lean years.

HISTORY OF ROSCOE

Roscoe was founded in 1973 by Hans Norregaard, in Roscoe, Louisiana. After 30 years as an NDT technician, Norregaard decided to set up shop for himself amidst many of the pulp and paper mills located in western Louisiana. Roscoe focused on the inspection of large boilers, a service designed to monitor the corrosion of the boiler walls. Inspections conducted every two to three years provided mills with sufficient warning to replace weakened, corroded plates in boiler walls before a catastrophic accident occurred.

In 1980, Norregaard sold the company to National Inspection Services (NIS) for $1.75 million. NIS was a subsidiary of Swanson Industries, a large diversified holding company. At that time, NIS brought in Chad Huerlmann (a Harvard MBA) to manage the company. Huerlmann was eager to run a small business and viewed the Roscoe acquisition as a great opportunity.

The company continued well for four years, until the pulp and paper industry bottomed out again. Hampered by misguided directives and burdened by corporate overhead, Roscoe's low cost position no longer protected it from the growing price pressure facing NDT companies in the pulp and paper industry. Also, Huerlmann failed to establish an effective relationship with the technicians in the company and many resigned or left the NDT industry altogether. By 1984, Swanson Industries decided to divest of NIS completely and Roscoe was once again up for sale.

At that time, Hans Norregaard and a long-time business associate, Grover Porter, decided to get back into the NDT business. Together they bought back Roscoe for about 35 cents on the dollar. They were convinced that by offering an improved inspection service for a fair price, they could rebuild the company's reputation and good fortunes.

After dismissing Huerlmann, Hans and Grover began building a new management team for Roscoe. A new controller, Jane Bottensak, was hired away from MQS Inspection. Ted Witkowski, a staff Professional Engineer (PE) out of Texas A&M, who had previously worked for Exxon, was also taken on. Both men thought Ted would bring some much-needed technical backbone to the company. Also, long-time technician, Ed Brown, was promoted to operations manager. Finally, Roscoe began recruiting technicians from the best vocational tech schools in the country.

In 1987, Hans Norregaard retired and Grover Porter became president. Roscoe was back on track.

In 1990, Roscoe encountered a downturn in both revenues and customers. Many mills simply decided not to release bids as often as they used to. While Roscoe always lost some contracts to lower bidders, Porter felt the recent slowdown in the pulp and paper industry exacerbated Roscoe's situation by forcing mills to be more cost conscious. Still, Porter felt that there must be room for the services that Roscoe offered:

> Hans and I have put together a great management team over the last three years and our technicians are some of the best in the industry. Roscoe offers an efficient, quality inspection service and we feel that we can price accordingly.

However, the recent loss of established customers caused Grover Porter to question the validity of Roscoe's purported "high quality" service.

CUSTOMER PROFILES

Although boiler inspections in pulp and paper mills have been standard practice for many years, mills differed widely on the representative who interacted with Roscoe's inspection team. This contact could be almost anyone from the plant manager down to a purchasing agent. The following descriptions illustrate many of the problems that have plagued Roscoe recently.

George McDonald at the Franklin Paper Company was a typical plant manager who reigned over his plant like a king over his castle. Like any other plant manager, McDonald was primarily concerned about controlling costs and was hostile to the idea of boiler inspections in general. Since inspections could only be conducted during plant shut downs. McDonald was unhappy about the lost production time:

> Besides the $85,000 inspection fee, my plant is idle during the two days it takes your team to complete the job. At 750 tons per day, I pay an additional opportunity cost of over $330,000 every day you are in my plant. A boiler will last 20 years without exploding and if it wasn't for corporate HQ, I would never bother with the inspections. Besides, the only thing that I ever get out of it is an "OK" and a pile of figures that I can't make head nor tail of.

International Paper's plant in Longview, Texas, was one of the few clients that maintained their own NDT department. As with other mills, the department consisted of only one retired NDT technician who interacted with service providers like Roscoe. Bob Kapala typified the kind of NDT person often found in paper mills. He was friendly and eager to help, but was actually often more of a hindrance. The last thing a technician wanted was someone looking over his shoulder all the time.

After the inspection was completed, Bob would combine the recent inspection data with a pile of past data and attempt to find trends in corrosion patterns. The fact that different inspection firms provided data in different formats complicated Bob's task.

Jim Bulgrin at the Rockton Paper Mill in Texarcana, Texas, presented a different problem. Bulgrin, a recent graduate of Georgia Tech, had been hired into the mill's engineering services department seven months ago. As one of Roscoe's team supervisors described him, Bulgrin was "as wet behind the ears as a new born calf." But he was eager to learn and was on top of every detail.

Problems arose when Jim noticed that thickness readings on one section of a boiler were considerably greater than when inspected two years before. After confronting the technicians, who ended up getting very angry, Jim eagerly reported the discrepancy to his boss. It was later discovered that a new plate had been welded onto the boiler in that area, but Roscoe lost the contract with Rockton.

Pulp mill supervisors, like Billy Dunlap at the Lufkin Pulp Mill, were Roscoe's most common contact inside a mill. Dunlap has been cajoling his boiler along for the last 15 years and did not take easily to anyone mistreating his "baby."

Finally, the inevitable contact is the purchasing representative who files the paperwork with accounting. Lucy Boyle in purchasing at Lufkin was never happy about processing paperwork relating to inspection services:

> Corporate headquarters requires us to file additional paperwork for one time expenses greater than $50,000. With inspection fees well over $75,000, I end up processing over three times more paperwork than normal. My life doesn't return to normal until the mill goes back on-line.

A PRELUDE TO ACTION

In January 1991, while attending the Nondestructive Testing Managers Association meeting in Las Vegas, Grover Porter was still struggling with the question of what defined a quality service. As it turned out, one of the speakers in the New Business Segment of the conference presented a talk on the components of service quality. And in that same month, a number of articles describing quality improvement programs at major aerospace inspection firms ran in both the ASNT and AWS Journals.[1]

At the monthly staff meeting in February, Porter discussed his concerns regarding the level of service provided by Roscoe:

> As you all know, we've lost a bunch of accounts in the last few months. I suspect our service quality is not what it should be, and I've been thinking about a quality improvement program. If we don't do something soon, we may be forced to reduce our fees.

[1] Trade journals of the American Society of Nondestructive Testing and the American Welding Society.

Bottensak, the controller, nodded her head in agreement and commented that something had to be done:

Let's go for it! None of us needs reminding that 1990 was a bad year, but it looks like this year will be even worse. That's not great for our bonuses!

Ted Witkowski, the staff PE, and Ed Brown, the operations manager, were extremely skeptical. Ted explained:

Look, we have the best trained technicians out there with top of the line equipment. They make some mistakes now and then, but when a boiler inspection requires 20,000 readings, that will happen. Besides, the mill has to look at the readings over an entire area and not just a single point. It's not reasonable to inspect every point twice. The mills couldn't afford the cost or the downtime.

After further discussion, Porter suggested that they first conduct a short customer survey to determine if there were any areas for improvement. No one resisted the idea so Porter spent the weekend composing the survey, and Bottensak pulled together a mailing list of Roscoe customers from the last five years. On Monday morning 357 surveys were dropped in the mail.

THE SURVEY RESULTS

By the first week of March, Porter had collected 82 responses. With only three responses returned in the last four days, Porter felt his sample was as big as it was going to get and asked Jane Bottensak to aggregate the results into a single report (Exhibit 1). The next morning, Jane walked into Porter's office with a grin:

Grover, look's like we got something here. I ignored 11 of the responses since they obviously knew nothing about our work. I reckon those surveys didn't even reach the right contact in the mills. Anyway, that left 71 responses. I pulled all the results together to determine the frequency distributions and from what I can see it seems our people skills need work. Even our office staff could use some improvement.

Porter was surprised that the accuracy of inspection data and time to completion rated so highly, considering that business was so tough these last months. But then he recalled that the speaker at the NDTMA Conference last month emphasized the importance of the people aspect in service quality.

Unfortunately, Roscoe did not attract the type of people blessed with an abundance of social grace. The environment around a boiler is not pleasant. There is constant noise, grime, and heat. And if there was a reason to climb inside the boiler, the technician found himself struggling through cramped areas with his equipment and his flashlight. Once out, his clothing and equipment were coated with a black muck that not even *Ultra Tide* could remove. Thus, while technicians survived the conditions on-site, they did not necessarily do so quietly.

At the March staff meeting, Porter announced his plans for Roscoe's Quality Improvement Program.

EXHIBIT 1   ROSCOE CUSTOMER SATISFACTION SURVEY (MARCH 1991)[2]

Dear Roscoe Customer,

In an effort to provide you with the best inspection service possible, we would like your opinion of Roscoe and the people who work for us. Simply check the appropriate column on the survey and drop it in the mail within the enclosed stamped envelope. Your cooperation is truly appreciated.

Grover Porter
President

Questions	Poor	Below Average	Average	Above Average	Excellent
On-Site Inspection Team					
Accuracy of inspection data	1.3%	5.9%	15.3%	34.7%	42.8%
Time to complete inspection	2.9	4.8	8.4	45.6	38.3
Knowledge of technicians	1.5	11.5	25.6	33.3	28.1
Willingness to make an extra effort	24.6	26.0	23.6	13.5	12.3
Courtesy of technicians	26.1	30.3	18.7	16.2	8.7
Degree of individualized attention	17.6	29.6	38.2	9.9	4.7
Conveys trust and confidence	9.2	28.3	34.7	23.8	4.0
Organization of team supervisor	4.2	25.6	37.2	29.9	3.1
Accounting Department					
Accuracy of billing	3.4	8.3	16.1	55.8	16.4
Promptness of billing	9.8	43.9	21.7	16.5	8.1
Courtesy of staff	6.9	24.7	38.6	13.5	16.3
Willingness to help	22.7	25.6	38.1	8.9	4.7
Overall Performance of Roscoe					
Ability to deliver the promised service	2.7	15.6	18.5	39.4	23.8
Variety of services that meet your needs	2.3	13.2	48.8	26.5	9.2
Overall service value for your money	12.7	34.1	43.2	7.8	2.2

[2] Recorded percentages are the frequency distribution of 71 responses compiled by Jane Bottensak, RNDT's controller. An average was taken for respondents who checked adjacent ratings (i.e., poor and below average).

THE QUALITY IMPROVEMENT PROGRAM

The three elements that Porter decided to include in the QIP were initial training, a bonus reward system, and customer surveys at the conclusion of every job. He recognized that the QIP had to be more than a one shot deal to be successful and felt that the proposed combination of training, surveys, and bonuses would establish the lasting, fundamental changes Roscoe needed.

Training was provided by ABS Consultants of Madison, Wisconsin, who specialized in teaching customer contact skills for industrial service companies. Training consisted of guided round table discussions and role playing, through which technicians and office staff explored not only customers' perceptions of Roscoe, but also their perceptions of the customers as well.

ABS also had Ed Brown put together some service guidelines that went beyond the traditional level of service. Brown explained one aspect of the guidelines:

> For example, while on-site, we need to emphasize constant visual inspection of the customer's plant and equipment. If a technician see some insulation hanging off a section of piping, we expect that person to make a note in his report to the client. It doesn't take much time and our customers appreciate the extra effort.

Technicians also earned bonus points that were cashed out at the end of the year for $25 per point. Every time a client requested a particular technician to be part of the on-site inspection team, that person received a bonus point. Also, after each job, the client filled out a customer satisfaction survey. At the end of the year, the surveys were ranked and for each instance that a technician's team was in the top 5%, that technician received a bonus point.

Porter also gave a cash bonus to technicians who passed their certification tests and advanced a level. Achieving Level II earned a $150 cash bonus, while reaching Level III earned $500, as this was the most difficult level to achieve. Finally, the customer satisfaction surveys were compiled monthly and the statistics displayed in the shop area.

ANOTHER DISAPPOINTING YEAR

Jane Bottensak wrapped up her part of the December staff meeting:

> Well, as I predicted, 1991 is going to be a disappointing year. Revenues were down again and profits were negligible. However, our performance wasn't as bad as I expected, so maybe the quality improvement program was more successful than I thought. But, I think we will still need to re-evaluate our fee structure for the coming year.

Ted Witkowski agreed that the program was a success and commented that Roscoe had a record number of technicians certified at Levels II and III.

Even Ed Brown conceded that customer satisfaction ratings had improved dramatically over the second half of 1991 (Exhibit 2):

> Most of the experienced technicians are excited about the program. They have been around Roscoe a number of years and have established their families in the area. On the other hand, some of the younger folks have not committed as easily. Part of that is the fact that less experienced workers get smaller bonuses, on average. But, also, the younger technicians are more mobile and easily move from company to company. Overall, our work force is providing a better service to the customer.

However, regardless of how well the quality improvement program increased customer satisfaction, unless it could support new growth in the company, Grover Porter could only deem the program a failure.

In light of the continued downturn in the pulp and paper industry, Porter felt resigned to restructure the company's pricing policies. And that would mean big changes for Roscoe.

EXHIBIT 2   ROSCOE CUSTOMER SATISFACTION SURVEYS (NOVEMBER 1991)[3]

Questions	Poor	Below Average	Average	Above Average	Excellent
On-Site Inspection Team					
Accuracy of inspection data	1.0%	4.2%	2.1%	24.8%	55.9%
Time to complete inspection	1.4	6.3	7.1	60.0	25.2
Knowledge of technicians	0.9	12.1	20.5	37.4	29.1
Willingness to make an extra effort	11.9	18.2	36.5	27.8	5.6
Courtesy of technicians	9.3	8.9	55.3	16.3	10.2
Degree of individualized attention	2.1	16.7	45.9	30.1	5.2
Conveys trust and confidence	3.8	22.7	39.8	30.6	3.1
Organization of team supervisor	0.0	11.9	31.8	44.7	11.6
Accounting Department					
Accuracy of billing	1.5	10.4	19.6	44.2	24.3
Promptness of billing	13.5	33.4	25.6	18.5	9.0
Courtesy of staff	7.9	17.8	33.4	35.1	5.8
Willingness to help	8.6	29.4	30.3	24.6	7.1
Overall Performance of Roscoe					
Ability to deliver the promised service	0.0	13.2	23.1	44.2	19.5
Variety of services that meet your needs	7.4	13.5	56.1	15.3	7.7
Overall service value for your money	10.2	31.2	47.1	11.5	0.0

[3] Compilation of 17 customer satisfaction surveys for inspections completed during November 1991. An average was taken for those respondents who checked adjacent ratings.

THE LAUNCH OF CLASSIC FM

On Thursday 4th July 1991 the British radio industry regulator, the Radio Authority, announced that Showtime Radio had been awarded Britain's first independent national radio (INR) franchise. Showtime planned to offer its listeners a musical diet of film and television theme tunes together with songs from hit musicals. The new station, backed by a group of private investors and chaired by former British Rail chairman Sir Peter Parker, would broadcast from Chiltern Radio's studios in Milton Keynes. Showtime had been awarded the first of three new national commercial radio licences; the only one of the three that would be broadcasting on a high quality FM waveband.

In the camp of rival bidders, classical music station Classic FM, there was a mixture of acute disappointment and disbelief. Disappointment because after a succession of near misses with bids for the new London FM franchises, Classic had been determined to secure this national franchise. The inferior sound quality offered by the remaining two AM frequencies ruled out any possibility of a classical music station bidding for the remaining INRs. The disbelief related to the size of the Showtime bid, a staggering £14m, almost triple Classic's own offer and five times the sum bid by the third contestant, the Hanson Trust/Radio Clyde consortium. Could a station like Showtime—aimed at a predominately middle aged, female audience—ever really attract enough advertising revenue to cover its estimated £8m per year overheads? Classic FM decided to bide its time and wait and see.

This case was prepared by Helen Peck, Cranfield School of Management, as a basis for class discussion rather than to illustrate effective or ineffective handling of an administrative situation. April 1994. © Copyright Cranfield University.

INDUSTRY BACKGROUND

Since the formative years of British broadcasting, the radio industry in the UK had been dominated by the BBC. The BBC was born in November 1922 when three fledgling radio stations—Marconi's 2LO, Metropolitan Vickers' Manchester based 2ZY, and Western Electric's 2WP—merged to form the British Broadcasting Company. In January 1923 the BBC emerged as the country's sole broadcaster following the closure of its only remaining competitor, the pioneering 2MT. In 1927 the company became a corporation on receipt of a Royal Charter, guaranteeing the BBC a right to broadcast for the next 70 years. For four decades the BBC's national radio networks enjoyed a near monopoly, challenged only by overseas commercial broadcasters like Radio Luxembourg, or the off-shore pirate, Radio Caroline.

Local radio made its British debut in 1967, with the launch of eight experimental local BBC stations. Six years later London Broadcasting, Britain's first legal, on-shore, independent local radio station, went on air. Within days a second London commercial station, Capital Radio, joined the fray. By the late 1980s, 49 independent local radio (ILR) contractors were broadcasting under the jurisdiction of the Independent Broadcasting Authority (IBA). The ILRs competed for commercial funding with a handful of off-shore terrestrial broadcasters, and a host of unlicensed pirates. Meanwhile, the BBC's radio services—four national networks (Radios 1,2,3, and 4) and 36 local stations—continued to be funded through the licence fee, a grant-in-aid from the Treasury, and the sale of programmes or other merchandise. But Charter renewal was on the horizon, and change was in the air.

POLITICS AND THE BROADCASTING BILL

Following the re-election of Conservative Prime Minister Margaret Thatcher in 1983, the British Government was avidly pursuing a programme of market deregulation and the privatisation of public sector enterprises. In July 1986 the controversial 'Peacock Report' recommended that Radios 1 and 2, and possibly BBC local radio services, should be privatised (see Exhibit 1 for details of BBC radio services). A few months later the Government published a Green Paper putting forward an altogether different course of action. Instead of a partial privatisation of existing BBC services, the Green Paper advocated a wholesale expansion of the industry. The proposal went on to become the foundation of the Broadcasting Bill. The Bill allowed for the creation of a new tier of 'incremental' local or community radio stations, a clutch of new regional stations, and three new independent national networks.

The new stations should complement existing BBC and ILR services; they would be contracted and regulated by the Independent Broadcasting Authority (or by its successor the Radio Authority), and funded through advertising. The Government believed that several hundred new commercial radio stations could be funded and licensed in this way. The British economy was booming at the time, media space was in short supply, and commercial radio was flourishing. Bloated advertising budgets had created a seemingly insatiable demand for new promotional opportunities.

The incremental contracts were to be awarded on the grounds of "local relevance, and suitability for the community," whereas the new national franchises would be sold to the

EXHIBIT 1   BBC RADIO SERVICES (1991), UK ONLY

Radio 1

A rock and pop station, catering for all tastes from the charts to new music, classic hits, heavy metal, dance, and world music. Supplemented by music documentaries, news programmes, and social action campaigns. Costs per hour £3,800.

Radio 2

A 24-hour entertainment network. A daytime mix of popular music and conversation is complemented in the evenings and at weekends by jazz, big band, light classical, country, and folk music, interspersed with comedy and quizzes. Costs per hour £5,200.

Radio 3

Mainly classical music, but jazz traditional works from around the world are also broadcast. The network draws on the resources of the BBC's 5 symphony orchestras, commissions over 30 new works each year, and broadcasts many live concerts. Speech programmes include drama, documentaries, science, and news about the arts. Costs per hour £6,700.

Radio 4

The main speech network. News and current affairs programmes, with conversation, and series on medicine, science, religion, law, natural history, books, money, and gardening, as well as programmes for people with disabilities. There are a dozen dramas every week, and humour with situation comedies, quizzes, and satire. Costs per hour £8,400.

Radio 5 (introduced August 1990)

A network carrying sport, education, programmes for young people, and some elements of the BBC's World Service. Costs per hour £5,500.

BBC Regional

Radio Scotland, Radio Ulster, Radio Wales, and Radio Cymru (Welsh language), are community stations to serve the interests of local audiences, providing regional listeners with 'opt-outs' from the national networks.

BBC Local Radio

Local radio stations carrying news and information as well as reflecting important local issues. The local radio stations play an important role in the BBC's national and international news gathering operation.

---

highest bidder. Home Secretary Douglas Hurd announced that "the key test stations will have to pass to obtain a licence to broadcast is that of widening the range of consumer choice." There was to be minimal control of content or format and the new stations would be excused all public service broadcasting requirements. The expansion of the industry would create new revenue streams for the exchequer, while neatly avoiding much of the "hands off the BBC" opposition encountered by the Peacock Report. The availability of frequencies was a limiting factor at this point, so it was decided that the BBC and some of the ILRs—currently transmitting on more than one waveband—would surrender some of their frequencies to make room for the newcomers.

LONDON INCREMENTAL FRANCHISES

In November 1988, the Government announced its intent to release the first 20 incremental franchises early the following year. The contracts were open to all comers, including existing ILR contractors. Pirate operators were offered a short amnesty to get off the air and apply for a licence. Only cross-holdings with newspapers and television were restricted. A total of 26 venues for the new local services were on offer, mostly in urban areas. Seven of the sites were reserved for services to ethnic minorities, and an additional contract was to be available for an information service for London's Heathrow and Gatwick airports.

A total of 163 applications for the incremental franchises were received by the IBA, almost a third related to the two London contracts. The London ethnic contract (to broadcast on AM) attracted 18 bidders; but it was the vaguely defined "community of interest" FM franchise which was most hotly contended, with 32 applications. The London contracts were effectively regional radio franchises, covering roughly the area encircled by the M25 motorway, with a listening audience of 6.5 million adults. The high proportion of young, single professionals made Greater London a uniquely attractive advertising market, and the London FM franchise potentially one of the most profitable in the industry.

A CLASSICAL CONTENDER

The IBA had specified that the new London FM station should cater for tastes not covered elsewhere on commercial radio. Among the first to register an interest was Classic FM, a consortium chaired by David Astor from the radio holding company Golden Rose Broadcasting. Astor's colleague David Maker was appointed as chief executive. Further financial backing for Classic came from composer Andrew Lloyd Webber's Really Useful Group, and from LBC. Programme advisors included such luminaries as conductor Andre Previn, Dame Kiri Te Kanawa, Lady Christie (director of Glyndebourne), and Mr. Henry Wrong, (director of London's Barbican Centre). The consortium planned to launch Britain's first commercially funded classical music station since the 1920s. More specifically, Classic proposed to offer Londoners popular classical music presented in a light and friendly manner. For the first time lovers of classical music could have an alternative to the BBC's worthy, but intimidatingly elitist, Radio 3.

Classic claimed that its proposed programme mix—80% popular classical music interspersed with news, financial reports, and arts reviews—would attract an audience of one million listeners. A large proportion of these would be from the high earning professional and managerial classes, the AB audience so sought after by advertisers. The ABs were notoriously light commercial television viewers, displaying highly selective viewing patterns. The evening news and a small number of other programmes did attract ABs in reasonably large numbers, but related advertising slots were often prohibitively expensive. Advertisers wishing to address the ABs usually turned instead to the quality press and special interest magazines.

Some media analysts and advertising executives believed that a classical music station, with the right presentation, could pull around 10% of radio listeners in the London area. Many others, mindful of Radio 3's minute market share and cripplingly high overheads, remained sceptical about the financial viability of a commercial classical music station.

PARADISE LOST

The IBA quickly narrowed down the London FM bids, producing a short list of about a dozen serious contenders. Classic FM was one of eight short listed bidders offering a variation on the same popular classical theme, most backed by equally impressive rolls of the great and the good. Other contenders proposed jazz, rock, dance, or easy listening music stations to complement the news and pop output of London's existing ILR contractors, LBC and Capital Radio. As the announcement of the franchise award grew closer, media pundits were certain that Classic FM would be awarded the contract. However, lobbying was intense and supporters of proposals favouring other musical genres argued that a classical music station was sure to get one of the new national franchises, so the ILR contract should be awarded elsewhere.

When the announcement came on July 12th 1989, it was Jazz FM—a specialist station supported by jazz singer Cleo Laine, four Members of Parliament, an Earl, and a Bishop—that emerged triumphant. However, the IBA quickly announced that due to the enormous interest in the franchise, two further London FM contracts would soon be made available. Unsuccessful bidders were urged to reapply. Once more it seemed certain that Classic FM would be awarded a contract. Again it was disappointed. The franchises were awarded to Kiss FM—a former pirate station with record industry support—and to Melody Radio, owned by Lord Hanson of Hanson Trust. Kiss had a distinguished three and a half year track record and a loyal, predominantly male, following among London's young club-goers. During its days as a pirate, Kiss had already won awards for its energetic mix of dance, reggae, soul, bhangra, and Latin music. Melody was aiming for the other end of the age range with its proposal for a presenterless, non-stop, easy listening station. Kiss FM was a popular choice with media commentators, but the award of a franchise to Melody was less well received. Critics argued that the speechless format would not appeal to an older audience, which already had an easy listening option with BBC Radio 2. Worse still, they argued, it left Radio 3 without a competitor.

NATIONAL FRANCHISES

By early 1990 the radio industry had focused its attention on the forthcoming auction of the three new national licences, to be advertised early the following year. One of the licenses would be awarded to a speech-based service; one would be reserved for a non-pop service; and one would be unrestricted. No announcement had been made as to which format would be specified for FM or AM frequencies, or in which order the franchises would be sold.

The IBA (and its imminent successor the shadow Radio Authority) were expecting around 50 bids for the new licenses, even though the sums of money involved in securing an INR franchise were expected to be far in excess of the average £4m raised by bidders for the London FM contracts. In August 1990, Classic FM announced its intention to bid for the only FM franchise, so did a number of well financed pop and rock consortia. Heavyweight backers were needed just to stay in contention, but Classic soon managed to recruit the *Daily Telegraph,* Time Warner, Carlton Communications, and N.M. Rothschild to fortify its bid. Meanwhile influential supporters lobbied the Government to restrict bidders for the FM franchise to non-pop formats.

Eventually the Radio Authority revealed that it had received a total of 39 letters of intent regarding the INR franchises. Adult rock station Rock FM was now hotly tipped as the main contender for the FM franchise, but much still rested on whether the FM waveband would be reserved for a non-pop station. All but four of the would-be bidders intended to try for the FM license, although 19 said that they would also be interested in an AM franchise. Most of the proposals were from rock or pop stations intent on securing the FM licence. On the 30th of October 1990, their plans were torpedoed by arts minister David Mellor's announcement that the FM franchise, the first to be auctioned, would be reserved for music other than pop. In the outcry that followed, consortia planning rock music stations accused the Radio Authority of ignoring market forces. They believed that the Authority was trying to protect existing local radio stations, most of which operated pop-based services. The rock contenders argued that the Treasury's income from the sale, and from future advertising revenue, would be drastically reduced if the Radio Authority ignored popular demand for an FM rock station.

To avoid further squabbles with the rock music lobby, the Radio Authority set down an official definition of pop music. They concluded that pop music was post-1960 music with "a strong rhythmical element and a reliance on electronic amplification for its performance." The definition eliminated most modern rock music, but left plenty of scope for 'golden oldies.' Suddenly a golden oldie/easy listening station (like the one Hanson was rumoured to be planning with assistance from established ILR operators, Radio Clyde) looked like a realistic proposition. Even this option was undermined though when the Radio Authority subsequently revised its definition of pop, to exclude all chart singles since the arbitrary dateline of January 1st 1960.

CLASSICAL MUSIC: DEMAND AND VIABILITY

By mid-1990 though, the economic tide had turned and advertising budgets became early casualties as the British economy sank into recession. The advertising industry—paymaster of the new national franchises—was overwhelmingly in favour of an adult-orientated rock station on FM, playing mostly tracks from albums by well known artists. The format was known to appeal to males, in their 20s and 30s, with money to spend. The industry as a whole still nurtured serious doubts as to whether a non-pop INR station would ever get off the ground, let alone survive its first year. Analysts pointed once again to the track record of Radio 3 which, despite its £44m annual funding, still only managed to appeal to a tiny (but steadfastly loyal) 2% of the population.

Astor was undeterred, citing the popularity of Pavarotti's Nessum Dorma (used as the theme tune for the 1990 soccer World Cup), and to the fact that 20% of all compact disc sales were of classical music, as evidence of an upswell in demand. Then of course there was Inspector Morse, Central Television's enigmatic police inspector with a passion for classical music. Morse solved countless murders among Oxford's dreaming spires, to the accompaniment of Brahms, Handel, or Beethoven. After the screening of each episode Central's switchboard would be besieged by telephone calls from viewers asking for the details of "the music in the background, when Morse discovered the second corpse." Central eventually supplied its telephonists with details of the music ahead of every screening. Astor was convinced that he could unlock this wider but latent demand for accessible classical music.

In spite of the prophets of doom, it emerged that Astor's optimism was not unfounded. Independent research undertaken by the government-funded Broadcasting Research Unit (BRU) indicated that a classical music station could be popular. A quarter of all people questioned in a recent BRU study had said they liked classical music, and a third wanted more of it on the radio. BRU researchers felt that it was Radio 3's presentation, and its fondness for impenetrable or avant garde material, that was responsible for the poor ratings. The station's high costs were largely attributable to live coverage of major musical events from around the world, specially commissioned concerts of works by obscure composers, and the expense of supporting five orchestras. A commercial radio station would not be expected to fulfil the role of patron of the arts.

RADIO ADVERTISING IN THE UK

Commercially funded classical music stations in the US had been very successful, but North American perceptions of radio as an advertising medium were very different from those of their transatlantic cousins. In the US, radio attracts over 7% of advertising spending. In the UK, where commercial radio has distinctly down-market connotations (a medium for those who can't afford a television campaign), that figure had never climbed higher than 2.8%.

Advertising agencies, gatekeepers to the juicy advertising budgets of their blue-chip clients, had shown little enthusiasm for radio as belts began to tighten. They quickly retreated back to the visual forms of media long favoured by agency creatives. The creative limitations of radio did little to fire agency imaginations, but there were other problems too. Many believed that radio was less effective for the client and that it provided lower commissions for the buyer than other forms of media. The fragmented nature of the commercial radio industry was another drawback; buying radio time was believed to be inconvenient, despite the emergence of sales houses. These problems were compounded by the industry's poor research image. Buyers, accustomed to constantly updated programme-by-programme television viewing figures, felt that radio research was inaccessible and inadequate. They were unimpressed by the intermittent nature of the listening surveys produced by JICRAR (the Joint Industry Committee for Radio Audience Research), a reputable research body founded and funded by the industry itself. At the root of the research problem though was the fact that the JICRAR figures excluded the mighty BBC, and were incompatible with the BBC's own Listener Research (a continuous consumption survey of its services dating back to the 1930s). Agency prejudices were further reinforced by a substantial body of market research showing that a large proportion of people in the UK disliked advertising on the radio. Listeners felt that commercials were often unimaginative, repetitive, and ill-suited to the surrounding programming.

The downmarket overtones were also echoed by market research into radio listening habits which consistently demonstrated that, in the UK, upmarket audiences favoured the BBC while commercial radio was popular with lower earning C2DE socio-economic groups (see Exhibit 2). The ABs in particular showed a marked preference for the BBC, and a penchant for ruinously expensive speech-based programming (see Exhibit 3). High brand loyalty is a feature of the radio industry as a whole, so prising listeners away from established stations is never easy. Radio listeners tend to listen to only one or two stations and are not given to exploring the airwaves in the same way that television viewers channel-hop.

Some of the more open-minded analysts did believe that Classic could possibly deliver the elusive ABs, but noted that even if agencies did overcome their prejudice to the

EXHIBIT 2   RADIO LISTENING BEHAVIOUR BY SOCIO-ECONOMIC GROUP, UK, 1990

	All	AB	C1	C2	D	E
Base: Radio Listeners	1,280	209	315	370	219	167
Listen only to the BBC	24%	37%	22%	18%	21%	27%
Listen mainly to the BBC	25	27	29	24	24	18
Listen only to commercial radio	10	9	9	10	11	11
Listen mainly to commercial radio	11	4	13	13	12	12
Listen to both equally	22	20	20	28	20	15
Listen to whatever is on	7	3	6	6	9	12
Unsure	1	—	1	1	3	5
Total	100	100	100	100	100	100

Source: BMRB/Mintel 1991.

medium, it would require a major effort on their behalf to adapt commercials for a classical format. Their clients would need to be re-educated too.

BAD NEWS FROM THE ILRS

While the pundits had been speculating on the viability and recession resistance of the various INR contenders, the ILRs had been experiencing the problem firsthand. From

EXHIBIT 3   BBC RADIO AUDIENCE PROFILES 1990

	Sex (%)		Age (%)					Social grade (%)		Share (%) all radio listening
	M	F	4–15	16–24	25–44	45–64	65+	ABC1	C2DE	
UK population aged 4+	48	52	17	14	30	23	16	42	58	—
Radio 1	57	43	6	30	53	9	2	36	64	24
Radio 2	47	53	1	1	11	49	38	43	57	15
Radio 3	62	38	1	2	23	42	32	73	27	2
Radio 4	44	56	1	2	31	37	29	69	31	11
Radio 5	77	23	6	5	35	31	23	47	53	1
BBC Local	46	54	1	3	21	43	32	32	68	12*

*Includes BBC regional.
N.B. The same source lists commercial radio's share of listening as 35%.

Source: BBC 1991.

EXHIBIT 4   COMMERCIAL RADIO ADVERTISING REVENUES AND PROLIFERATION OF SERVICES

Year	Advertising revenues £m*	No. of services†	Coverage of UK population (%)	Commercial radio share of listening
1985	72.0	49	87.1	—
1986	79.0	49	87.1	27.9
1987	99.4	50	89.5	28.3
1988	125.0	60	90.0	30.8
1989	145.0	76	92.0	—
1990	143.4	106	93.0	33.4

*Excludes revenues from promotions and sponsorship.
†Number of services broadcasting at year end, including split services.

Source: AIRC/JICRAR.

1986–1989 commercial radio had been the beneficiary of spectacular year-on-year gains in advertising expenditure, but in 1990 revenues stalled (see Exhibit 4). For many operators this could not have come at a worse time. Up until 1988, ILR contractors had been offering listeners the same service on both AM and FM frequencies but, prompted by the imminent arrival of the new incremental stations, many decided to split their frequencies, broadcasting separate services on the two wavelengths. Moving to split frequency broadcasting had a number of advantages: programmers no longer had to settle for pleasing all of the people some of the time, instead they could select strong formats that appealed to certain sections of their audience. This in turn would allow advertisers to use the medium more effectively. Moreover, delivering two separate services prevented the confiscation of one of the frequencies and reduced the likelihood of the Radio Authority licensing a direct competitor in the same area. It also increased overheads dramatically.

By the end of 1990 around 30 ILR contractors had split their frequencies. Almost without exception they chose to offer chart based pop music services on the FM frequencies, with 'gold' on the lower quality AM. As a result most of the split frequency broadcasters had increased their reach,[1] a few had also achieved an increase in average listening hours, but for the industry as a whole the results were disappointing (see Exhibit 4). The Radio Authority continued to issue new licenses (on single frequencies) to fill the remaining 'white space' between existing franchises. Where possible, established contractors extended their spheres of influence by underwriting neighbouring bids. The ILRs were heavily dependent on local or regional advertisers: only in the very largest conurbations such as London, Manchester, or Glasgow could commercial radio hope to attract more than 50% of revenues from national advertisers, the most active of which were likely to be stores and record labels.

[1] "Reach" refers to the total number of people who listen to the service at some time during the given period.

By January 1991 the recession had deepened and a dearth of advertising was turning into a famine. Worst affected was the South East of England, the epicentre of the collapsing property market, where revenues for 1990/91 were almost a quarter down from the previous year. In February 1991 the airport information service for Heathrow and Gatwick vanished from the airwaves. Reports were also coming through of redundancies at Kiss FM, together with murmurings of difficulties at Jazz FM.

AWARD OF THE NATIONAL FM FRANCHISE

On the eve of the formal invitation to bid for the national FM franchise, the Radio Authority finally announced the level of additional charges that would be incurred on top of the cash bid (estimated to be between £8–9m) to secure the eight year tenure. Firstly, all bidders would pay £10,000 for the right to bid. The successful applicant would pay an annual license fee of £1m to the Authority, and a 4% levy on its advertising revenue to the Treasury. The invitation to tender was issued, but as the April deadline for applications approached, it became clear that all was not well. The anticipated deluge of tenders had not materialised, so the deadline was extended by another month. Would-be bidders were getting cold feet.

Classic was among the many consortia which announced it could no longer afford to bid. Backers Carlton Communications and the *Daily Telegraph* were no longer prepared to finance such a high-risk venture. Astor made feverish attempts to find new sources of finance. At the eleventh hour, and with new backers—radio group GWR and Sir Peter Michael of Cray Electronics—in tow, Classic submitted a £5.3m bid for the franchise.

When bidding finally closed on May 24th 1991, Classic's efforts appeared once more to have been to no avail. Showtime Radio's bid dwarfed those of the other two contenders. The Showtime consortium had convinced the Radio Authority that it could pull an audience of 4–5 million listeners and was confident that it could attract the necessary revenue to support itself. In fact Showtime's management believed that by positioning the station as "the radio equivalent of *The Daily Mail* or *Hello* magazine" it could match Capital's revenues of £37m within four years. The proposed mix of show business music was to be supplemented with a little easy listening pop music, together with news and reports from Hollywood or London's West End. Showtime's target market was officially described as "housewives in their 20s upwards," an audience which appeared to be underserved by existing broadcasters. In fact recently conducted independent market research had suggested that to increase the radio audience by winning over non-listeners, radio should be seeking to attract primarily women, people over 35 in general and those over 65 in particular, as well as those in the C2DE socio-economic groups."[2] Media watchers were not optimistic; commenting that the downmarket, predominately female audience was one that mass-market advertisers were already reaching effectively through television.

Showtime had six weeks to finalise the £15.7m of funding pledged earlier by City backers. When the time came most of the would-be financiers had suddenly gone on holiday—without their portable telephones. Only £12m was raised by the August 16th

---

[2] Mintel, Leisure Intelligence, Vol. 2, 1991.

deadline. Three days later the franchise was awarded by default to the next highest bidder. Classic FM's tenacity had finally paid off.

Meanwhile, Astor and Maker had attempted to persuade Classic's backers to finance a bid for the troubled Jazz FM, but the financiers refused. In doing so, they destroyed Astor's and Maker's plan to establish a new radio empire. Their intention had been to have Classic and Jazz FM both broadcasting from Jazz's London premises and to bring the administration of Golden Rose's Birmingham-based Buzz FM in under the same roof. Classic's majority share holders, GWR, vetoed the proposal, prompting Astor's and Maker's immediate resignations from Classic FM. Henry Meakin, chairman of GWR, was appointed chairman of Classic's newly reconstructed board and the search for a new chief executive commenced. In March 1992, John Spearman took up the post. Spearman had no previous experience in radio, but had a long track record in the advertising industry as director of Laser (a television advertising sales agency) and as former chairman of advertising agency Collet Dickenson Pearce. In Spearman's opinion Classic FM was not just another radio station, it was "a new national advertising medium." There then followed a scramble to get Classic FM on air.

PUTTING CLASSIC ON AIR

Broadcasting would commence later the following summer from studios in a converted boiler room in North London. In the meantime experienced BBC broadcaster Robin Ray was contracted to develop a play list of 10,000 listener-friendly classical pieces. Market research was commissioned to improve programme planning and to define further the target market for advertising. A range of possible formats were tested out with the help of 2,000 potential listeners (all drawn from the target ABC1 audience) in six English and Scottish cities. From the results of the market reserch, programme controller Michael Bukht concluded that the original ILR format should be given a slightly more populist slant. New features were to be added to the popular classical core, news, concert listings, and arts reviews. Listeners would be able to use a 'Hum Line' to identify pieces of music by humming the tune down the phone to one of Classic's presenters. There would also be racing tips and competitions with prizes ranging from bottles of champagne to "Inspector Morse Weekends." Bukht aimed to deliver "classical music dressed by Benetton" to affluent 25–54 year olds.

Presenters were picked for their broadcasting experience rather than their knowledge of the music. Henry Kelly, Margaret Howard, Susannah Simons, and Adrian Love were among the well-known names (often with BBC Radio 4 and 2 backgrounds) who were signed up by Classic. The team would introduce musical excerpts lasting from between 90 seconds and 90 minutes. Short movements would be played during the early morning and early evening 'drive-times,' with longer pieces in the mid mornings and afternoons. A whole concert would be aired every weekday evening at 8:00 p.m. News would be on the hour; with weather, financial and traffic reports concentrated around early morning and evening 'drive times.' To make commercials as unobtrusive as possible, Classic planned to limit them to 3 slots per hour with a high proportion of sponsored programmes. Sponsorship was already commonplace in the concert halls, and sat easily with Classic's programming objectives.

To sell the new medium to national advertisers, a well-known commercial radio in-

---

EXHIBIT 5   PERFORMANCE COMPARISON: CLASSIC FM PILOT AUDIENCE AND QUALITY DAILY NEWSPAPERS

	Cost (mono page/ 50% rate card)	Reach
Daily Telegraph	£16,750	1,984,000
Financial Times	£13,440	518,000
Times	£7,500	816,000
Guardian	£7,750	972,000
Independent	£7,000	861,000
	Cost (28 spots @ £2.50 ABC1 cpt*)	Reach
Classic FM	£7,627	1,263,000

*Cost per thousand.

Source: Classic FM.

---

dustry insider, Nigel Reeve, was appointed to the key post of sales director. To distance Classic from commercial radio's traditional image, sales would not be handled by an agency, but a small, dedicated, in-house sales force operating from the station's Camden base. In the run-up to launch, Reeve and his colleagues made presentations to 215 advertising agencies and to 410 of their clients. Classic's own market research (based on a six-month long test transmission) was offered as evidence that it could supply a 25–45 ABC1 audience, at a significantly lower cost to advertisers than similarly targeted newspapers (see Exhibit 5). The socioeconomic data was supplemented by information about the pilot audience's consumption of certain categories of goods and services including audio consumer durables, air travel, new cars, and financial services (see Exhibit 6.) Through the presentations Reeve hoped to build up a client list of around 30 blue-chip clients in the first year, all of which would be new to radio. In financial terms the Classic team was hoping to pull in around £10m in advertising and sponsorship revenues during the first year, £15m in its second year, building up to around £30m by 1998. Classic's first advertising rate card was published and circulated in June 1992.

Revenue to the tune of £1.3m was secured ahead of launch, with high street retailer WH Smith, and financial services companies such as Barclays Bank, Commercial Union, the Woolwich Building Society, among the first to sign advertising or sponsorship deals. Joint promotions with *Esquire* magazine and *The Guardian* were also arranged.

By July 1992, Classic FM was in the final stage of its preparations for launch. The press had hitherto assumed that Classic FM would be battling for listeners with Radio 3. But with only weeks to go before launch, Michael Bukht revealed that Classic's audience was far more likely to be made up of defectors from Radio 4 and the upwardly mobile element of Radio 1's audience. It was anticipated that a smaller proportion of listeners would be drawn from Radios 3 and 2. This was a direct contradiction of the BBC's

EXHIBIT 6   CLASSIC FM PILOT AUDIENCE: VITAL STATISTICS

98%	of the pilot audience would listen once a week+
28%	of them would listen every day

Motoring

37%	of pilot audience had 2+ cars
34%	bought a new car in the last 3 years
82%	were responsible/partly responsible for deciding the type of car
62%	travelled to work by car

Air Travel

59%	of pilot audience have flown in the last year
52%	flew on holiday/for pleasure
21%	flew on business
35%	flew on business 4+ times in the last year

Audio/Durables

	Ownership	Intend to purchase in next year
Camcorder	12%	10%
CD Player	52%	15%
Mobile Phone	12%	3%
Home Computer	44%	7%
NICAM Stereo TV	17%	6%

41%	bought 3+ CDs in the last 6 months
19%	bought 3+ prerecorded videos in the last 6 months

Financial

41%	have a bank deposit account
51%	have a building society savings account
15%	have unit trusts (UK adults = 7%)
42%	have stocks and shares (UK adults = 24%)

Press Readership

	Classic FM Audience*	UK ABC1[†]
Times	22%	8%
Daily Telegraph	22%	19%
Independent	23%	11%
Financial Times	13%	6%
Guardian	24%	10%
Sunday Times	31%	14%
Sunday Telegraph	10%	7%
Observer	18%	7%
Independent on Sun.	16%	5%

*Proportion of Classic's pilot audience who read this newspaper.
[†]Proportion of UK ABC1s who read this newspaper.

own market research findings. Bukht stressed that Classic would also be targeting the non-radio listening public.

When fully operational Classic's not-quite-national network of transmitters would only cover around 86% of the UK's population. From this potential audience Classic aimed to achieve a minimum weekly reach of 8% of available adults, each listening for around eight hours per week. Put another way, that equated to 3.5 million adults listening for a combined total of 28 million hours per week—an audience share of just over 3%. The target weekly reach was similar in size to that of Radio 3, but Classic was hoping that listeners would be tuning in to Classic for longer, i.e., eight hours per week compared with Radio 3's current average of five hours per week.

Test transmissions began six weeks prior to launch, using a tape of morning birdsong and animal noises. To the surprise of all, the birdsong acquired a cult following. As launch date approached a number of listeners, currently detained at Her Majesty's pleasure, wrote to Classic requesting copies of the tapes and pleading for the birds to be included in the daily programming. The possibility was considered but rejected. To promote the station to a more liberated audience Classic invested in a sponsorship deal with Queens Park Rangers Football Club. The aim of sponsoring a Premier League soccer team was to reaffirm Classic's populist stance and dispel any lingering suspicions of elitism. From the birth of the Classic consortium, relationships with the press had been cultivated assiduously, and a full press and poster campaign was mounted to announce the station's imminent launch.

In the meantime, Radio 3—while stating that it did not view Classic FM as a serious competitor—was preparing a pre-emptive strike. A month before Classic's launch, Radio 3 rescheduled, replacing its heavy duty concerts at breakfast time with a lighter selection of shorter pieces and news reports. Soon afterwards, Radio 3's own sophisticated poster campaign hit the hoardings, and the ever popular Tchaikovsky was lined up as 'Composer of the Week' for the day of Classic's launch.

At 6:00 a.m. on Monday 7th September 1992, Classic FM went live. A rendering of Handel's 'Zadok the Priest' was followed by other samples of "the world's most beautiful music" and a tasteful commercial for Barclay's Bank. Then more music, news, commercials, and all the other features as promised by the prelaunch publicity. The day went well, barring a few hiccups. The telephonists were unable to connect listeners to the Hum Line, one of the presenters got confused and introduced the wrong piece of music, and some composers' names were mispronounced; but, next morning the press reviews were encouraging. The technical hitches continued, and so did the occasional mismatches between the music and composer, but there were remarkably few complaints. Classic was soon receiving 2,000 pieces of mail each day, much of it complimentary. A new member of staff was hired simply to answer the flood of musical enquiries. It would be over four months before the size and nature of the audience could be independently confirmed, but early indications suggested that Classic had indeed tapped into a rich vein of appreciative listeners.

THE FUTURE?

Classic's reign as the UK's only independent national radio station was to be short-lived. INR2, in the form of Virgin Radio, was due on air in March 1993. Virgin Radio—backed by music and airline industry tycoon Richard Branson, and deposed breakfast television franchise holders, TV-a.m.—would be providing the one-stop, adult-orientated rock station, long awaited by advertisers. With more local and regional stations and a third INR still to come, together with new news and sports initiatives from the BBC, competition within the industry could only increase. Nevertheless, as 1992 drew to a close, Classic FM was anticipating a promising future and a prosperous New Year.

CEDARBRAE VOLKSWAGEN— QUALITY OF SERVICE

> I never really paid very much attention
> to the customer satisfaction index while
> I was in the middle of the pack, because
> it did not affect me one way or another.
> When I found out my index score had fallen
> into the bottom twenty dealers in Canada,
> my first reaction was disbelief.

Herbert Boehm, owner and general manager of the Cedarbrae Volkswagen dealership located in Scarborough, Ontario, was recalling the events of past months. As an "I Care" dealer for several years, Herb had been shocked to receive a letter from Volkswagen Canada (VWC) in October, indicating that he was a "less than satisfactory" dealer. Herb was dedicated to his business and his customers and could not understand how his index could have fallen to such a great extent.

This case was prepared by Rhonda English under the supervision of Randolph Kudar, and funded by the Society of Management Accountants of Ontario, for the sole purpose of providing material for class discussion at the Western Business School. Certain names and other identifying information may have been disguised to protect confidentiality. It is not intended to illustrate either effective or ineffective handling of a managerial situation. Any reproduction, in any form, of the material in this case is prohibited except with the written consent of the School. Copyright 1989 © The University of Western Ontario.   03/20/92

This material is not covered under authorization from CanCopy or any Reproduction Rights Organization. Permission to reproduce or copies may be obtained by contacting Case and Publication Services, Western Business School, London, Ontario, N6A 3K7.

VOLKSWAGEN CANADA INC.

Volkswagen Canada Inc., a wholly-owned subsidiary of Volkswagen AG, operated approximately two hundred dealerships in Canada in four main regions. The Quebec region was the largest contributor to Volkswagen Canada's national volume, the Central zone (Saskatchewan, Manitoba, Ontario) the second largest, Western (Alberta, British Columbia) the third, and Atlantic accounted for the smallest volume. Toronto alone made up more than half of the total Central zone volume.

Dealerships were categorized in one of three volume groups. Volume Group I represented the largest dealers with new car sales in excess of 500 vehicles per year. Volume Group II dealers had annual sales in the range of 200 to 500 vehicles, and Group III consisted of dealers selling fewer than 200 automobiles per year. Each year, the dealers were placed in one of the volume groups based on their Annual Planning Volume (APV) for the upcoming year. The APV was estimated by the dealers and submitted to VWC for review. VWC had the final say on APV figures and sometimes adjusted the figure developed by the dealers. Although anticipated volume was fairly speculative, it was a very important figure for the dealers since it was used as a basis for a number of decisions. Car deliveries from the factory for the upcoming year were based on APVs, bonuses and trips were rewarded to the dealers contingent on meeting projected volumes, and common expenses from head office were allocated to dealers based on APVs.

Various VW dealerships offered a number of different services to customers. In terms of types of new cars, dealers could sell Volkswagens, Audis, or Porsches solely, or any combination of the three makes. Depending upon location, some dealers received significant fleet sale business, where a leasing company would purchase a number of vehicles and subsequently lease them to third parties. As well, a number of dealers operated their own leasing businesses, dealing directly with the end customer. Other services offered at various dealerships included used car sales and body shops.

VWC had in place, dealer councils, through which dealer concerns and ideas could be voiced. Each of the four zones (Atlantic, Central, Quebec, Western) was divided into districts, with a district covering anywhere from six to seventeen individual dealers, depending upon geographic location. The four Zone Councils then, were made up of one representative from each of their respective districts. Each council met separately, semi-annually with VWC, and dealt primarily with issues of specific concern to the particular zone. A chairman of each zone was elected annually, who also served as a representative of the National Council. The National Dealer Council term was two years, and therefore each zone was represented by two dealers (current chairman and past chairman). As well, the past president remained a member of National Council for one year subsequent to holding the president position, resulting in a total of nine dealers at the National level. This Council officially met four times per year. Two of the four meetings (spring and fall) focused primarily on dealer concerns, a third (normally held in January) was devoted to "product and research development," and the fourth, usually held at Volkswagen AG in Germany, discussed more global areas of importance.

VWC believed that customer satisfaction had become an increasingly significant competitive factor. The conditions of the cyclical nature of the car industry and production overcapacity had created a buyer's market. As a result, emphasis on the treatment of customers had taken on major importance. If automobile manufacturers and their dealers hoped to sustain themselves through the downturns, a strong and loyal customer base needed to be established. Thus VWC had, over the years, turned its attention towards customer satisfaction and evaluation of dealers on that basis.

CEDARBRAE OPERATIONS

Cedarbrae Volkswagen employed fifty-five full-time workers—nine in sales, eighteen in service, ten in paint and body, twelve in administration, and six in parts. As well, six part-time employees worked in various administrative positions such as night cashiers and telephone follow-up clerks. Cedarbrae was involved in Audi and Volkswagen new car sales, used car sales, leasing, fleet sales, body shop work, and service work.

New Vehicles

Typically, new vehicles were received in bulk from the factory at specified times throughout the year. Each new car had to be thoroughly inspected before being sold. This Pre Delivery Inspection (PDI) consisted of a six-page list covering under hood, under vehicle, vehicle exterior and interior, road test, and after road test checks (see Exhibit 1). The service department was responsible for the initial inspection and it usually required about an hour and a half to perform. The salesperson was then responsible for making a first check of selected items and reporting any items needing adjustment back to the service department. A final check was then made by the salesperson. When a shipment of new cars arrived at the dealership, any sold cars were inspected first. The remaining vehicles were subsequently inspected during slow times in the service department. Herb preferred the cars to be checked in an organized fashion so that rush jobs were reduced and better quality inspections were performed.

When a car was sold, the salesperson was required to thoroughly explain the operation of the vehicle (e.g., control panel, seats, trunk latch, etc.) to the customer. This explanation typically took about half an hour and any questions the customer might have were answered during this time. In addition, the "I Care" philosophy of Volkswagen was outlined to the new owner in the sales office. The buyer was informed of the PDI completed by the service department, the checks done by the salesperson, and the availability of the salesperson if the customer had any problems. VWC was attempting to eliminate the customer belief that once a sale was finalized, the salesperson no longer cared about the customer.

The "I Care" certificate (see Exhibit 2) was subsequently presented to the new owner. This certificate was signed by the salesperson and guaranteed that the PDI checks had been conducted. The final step in the sale of a new vehicle was a telephone follow-up made by the salesperson, usually within seven days of the sale. The telephone call simply ensured that the customer was satisfied with the new vehicle. If repairs or adjustments were necessary, the salesperson would coodinate the activity for the car owner.

Herb had developed a new car survey exclusive to Cedarbrae, which was mailed out to all new vehicle buyers. The survey (see Exhibit 3) enabled Herb to follow up on the results since names and addresses were identified on each.

EXHIBIT 1   VW NEW VEHICLE DELIVERY INSPECTION—SERVICE AND SALES CHECKLIST

VIN _____

Items O.K. mark ✔

Purchased by: _____

Mechanic's Name/No. _____

Work Order No: _____

This checklist only identifies the components which require checking. Ensure that each component is checked (if applicable) over the whole range of its function and rectified if necessary.

	Model Year 1989										
	FOX	GOLF/GTI	ALL JETTAS	CABRIOLET	SCIROCCO	ALL TYPE 2	GOLF	JETTA	JETTA TURBO	SERVICE	SALES
	GASOLINE						DIESEL				

UNDER HOOD CHECKS

	FOX	GOLF/GTI	ALL JETTAS	CABRIOLET	SCIROCCO	ALL TYPE 2	GOLF	JETTA	JETTA TURBO
• Engine Oil Level: Check	x	x	x	x	x	x	x	x	x
• Coolant Level: Check anti-freeze concentration	x	x	x	x	x	x	x	x	x
• Brake Fluid Level: Check	x	x	x	x	x	x	x	x	x
• Battery Electrolyte Level: Check	x	x	x	x	x	x	x	x	x
• Battery: Check voltage with engine off, if less than 12.2 volts, recharge. Note: Remove surface charge by turning on headlights for sixty (60) seconds prior to voltage check	x	—	x	x	x	x	—	x	x
• Battery: Check hydrometer eye for state of battery charge, if other than green, add water or recharge per instructions on battery	—	x	—	—	—	—	x	—	—
• Windshield Washer Fluid Level Front and Rear: Check	x	x	x	x	x	x	x	x	x
• V-Belt(s) Tension: Check	x	x	x	x	x	x	x	x	x

EXHIBIT 1   (Continued)

NEW VEHICLE DELIVERY INSPECTION	FOX	GOLF/GTI	ALL JETTAS	CABRIOLET	SCIROCCO	ALL TYPE 2	GOLF	JETTA	JETTA TURBO	SERVICE	SALES
			GASOLINE					DIESEL			
• Cooling System: Check for tightness and leaks	x	–	–	–	–	–	–	–	–		
• A/C Compressor Belt Tension: Check	x	x	x	x	x	x	x	x	x		
• Lambda System Thermo Switch: Connect wires and remove "Caution" label from wires	x	x	x	x	x	x	–	–	–		
UNDER VEHICLE CHECKS											
• Water Separator Hand Wheel and Drain Hose: Remove protector tape	–	–	–	–	–	–	–	x	x		
• Standard Transmission: Check oil level	x	x	x	x	x	x	x	x	x		
• Standard Transmission: Check for leaks	x	–	–	–	–	–	–	–	–		
• Automatic Transmission Final Drive: Check oil level	–	x	x	x	x	x	–	–	–		
• Brake System: Check all brake lines and hoses	x	x	x	x	x	x	x	x	x		
• Steering Components, Lock Plates, Linkage and Cotter Pins: Check	x	x	x	x	x	x	x	x	x		
• Tie Rod Ends and Tie Rods: Check	x	x	x	x	x	x	x	x	x		
• Exhaust System: Check for damage and leaks	x	–	–	–	–	–	–	–	–		
VEHICLE EXTERIOR CHECKS											
• Wheel Mounting Bolts: Check torque	x	x	x	x	x	x	x	x	x		
• Tire Pressure Including Spare Tire: Correct to specifications	x	x	x	x	x	x	x	x	x		
• Hub Caps/Wheel/Lug Nut Covers: Check retention	x	x	x	x	x	x	x	x	x		
• Front License Plate Bracket: Install	x	x	x	x	x	x	x	x	x		

EXHIBIT 1 **(Continued)**

NEW VEHICLE DELIVERY INSPECTION	FOX	GOLF/GTI	ALL JETTAS	CABRIOLET	SCIROCCO	ALL TYPE 2	GOLF	JETTA	JETTA TURBO	SERVICE	SALES
			GASOLINE				DIESEL				
VEHICLE EXTERIOR CHECKS CONTD.											
• Headlights: Check function and adjustment	x	x	x	x	x	x	x	x	x		
• Parking Lights: Check	x	x	x	x	x	x	x	x	x		
• Side Marker Lights: Check	x	x	x	x	x	x	x	x	x		
• Turn Signals/Indicators: Check	x	x	x	x	x	x	x	x	x		
• Emergency Flashers/Indicators: Check	x	x	x	x	x	x	x	x	x		
• Windshield Wipers/Washer: Check and adjust if necessary	x	x	x	x	x	x	x	x	x		
• Windshield Wiper Arms: Torque retaining nut to 12–15 Nm	–	x	x	–	–	–	x	x	x		
• Tail Lights: Check	x	x	x	x	x	x	x	x	x		
• Brake Lights: Check	x	x	x	x	x	x	x	x	x		
• License Plate Lights: Check	x	x	x	x	x	x	x	x	x		
• Back Up Lights: Check	x	x	x	x	x	x	x	x	x		
• Gas Cap Lock and Door: Check	x	x	x	x	x	x	x	x	x		
• Rear Wiper/Washer: Check adjustment	x	x	–	–	x	x	x	–	–		
• Doors and Lids opening and closing (Including safety catches): Check	x	x	x	x	x	x	x	x	x		
• Trunk Light: Check	x	x	x	x	x	x	x	x	x		
• Spare Tire, Jack, and Tools secured: Check	x	x	x	x	x	x	x	x	x		
• Front Spoiler: Install (where applicable)	–	x	x	–	–	–	–	–	–		
• Antenna: Install mast	x	–	–	–	–	–	–	–	–		

EXHIBIT 1 (Continued)

NEW VEHICLE DELIVERY INSPECTION	FOX	GOLF/GTI	ALL JETTAS	CABRIOLET	SCIROCCO	ALL TYPE 2	GOLF	JETTA	JETTA TURBO	SERVICE	SALES
	GASOLINE						DIESEL				

VEHICLE INTERIOR CHECKS CONTD.

	FOX	GOLF/GTI	ALL JETTAS	CABRIOLET	SCIROCCO	ALL TYPE 2	GOLF	JETTA	JETTA TURBO
• Fuse: Install fuse for dome light, luggage compartment light, radio and multi function indicator. Fuse located in plastic bag in Owner's Manual or in glove box.	x	x	–	–	–	–	x	–	–
• Fuse for Auxilliary Heater: Install	–	–	–	–	–	x	–	–	–
• Fuse for Camping Equipment: Install	–	–	–	–	–	x	–	–	–
• Ignition Lock: Check	x	x	x	x	x	x	x	x	x
• Warning Lights: Check	x	x	x	x	x	x	x	x	x
• Glove Compartment Light: Check	x	x	x	x	x	–	x	x	x
• Clock Operation: Check, set correct time	x	x	x	x	x	x	x	x	x
• Cigarette Lighters: Check	x	x	x	x	x	x	x	x	x
• Heater/Air Conditioner Controls: Check	x	x	x	x	x	x	x	x	x
• Instrument Lights: Check, including rheostat	x	x	x	x	x	x	x	x	x
• Horn: Check	x	x	x	x	x	x	x	x	x
• Rear Window Defogger/Indicator: Check	x	x	x	x	x	x	x	x	x
• Door Locks and Trunk Lock: Check operation (Power Locks where appl.)	x	x	x	x	x	x	x	x	x
• Sound System Wiring: Check with tester and correct if necessary*	x	x	x	x	x	x	x	x	x
• Radio: Write chassis number onto serial number stickers, attach sticker to radio, warranty book and dealership record, install radio*	x	x	x	x	x	x	x	x	x
• Radio, Antenna, Cassette Player: (Key-in radio security code) check operation and select stations*	x	x	x	x	x	x	x	x	x

EXHIBIT 1   (Continued)

NEW VEHICLE DELIVERY INSPECTION	FOX	GOLF/GTI	ALL JETTAS	CABRIOLET	SCIROCCO	ALL TYPE 2	GOLF	JETTA	JETTA TURBO	SERVICE	SALES
	GASOLINE						DIESEL				
• Radio Control Layout Card: Attach to mirror*	x	x	x	x	x	x	x	x	x		
• ESC Warning Stickers: Attach to door windows or locations chosen by customer*	x	x	x	x	x	x	x	x	x		
• Interior Lights: Check	x	x	x	x	x	x	x	x	x		
• Mirrors: Check	x	x	x	x	x	x	x	x	x		
• Door Windows: Check	x	x	x	x	x	x	x	x	x		
• Seats, Front: Check	x	x	x	x	x	x	x	x	x		
• Seats, Rear: Check folding mechanism	x	x	–	x	x	x	x	–	–		
• Sunroof: Check	–	x	x	–	x	x	x	x	x		
• Convertible Top: Check	–	–	–	x	–	–	–	–	–		
• Vanity Mirror Light: Check	–	x	x	x	x	x	x	x	x		
• Sun Visors: Check	x	x	x	x	x	x	x	x	x		
ROAD TEST CHECKS											
• Engine Starting, Idle and Performance: Check	x	x	x	x	x	x	x	x	x		
• Seat Belts: Check	x	x	x	x	x	x	x	x	x		
• Brake System including Parking Brake: Check	x	x	x	x	x	x	x	x	x		
• Clutch and Gearshift Mechanism: Check	x	x	x	x	x	x	x	x	x		
• Differential Lock on Syncro Model: Check	–	–	–	–	–	x	–	–	–		
• Instruments: Check	x	x	x	x	x	x	x	x	x		
• Automatic Transmission including Kickdown: Check	–	x	x	x	x	x	–	–	–		

* Only required on dealer installed security coded radios

EXHIBIT 1   (Continued)

NEW VEHICLE DELIVERY INSPECTION

	FOX	GOLF/GTI	ALL JETTAS	CABRIOLET	SCIROCCO	ALL TYPE 2	GOLF	JETTA	JETTA TURBO	SERVICE	SALES
			GASOLINE					DIESEL			
• Cruise Control: Check	–	x	x	x	x	x	x	x	x		
• Multifunction Indicator: Check	–	x	x	x	x	–	–	–	–		
• Heating/Ventilation/Air conditioning System: Check	x	x	x	x	x	x	x	x	x		

AFTER ROAD TEST CHECKS

	FOX	GOLF/GTI	ALL JETTAS	CABRIOLET	SCIROCCO	ALL TYPE 2	GOLF	JETTA	JETTA TURBO	SERVICE	SALES
• Automatic Transmission Fluid Level: Check	–	x	x	x	x	x	–	–	–		
• Power Steering Fluid Level: Check	–	x	x	x	x	x	x	x	x		
• Fluid/Oil Leaks: Check	x	x	x	x	x	x	x	x	x		
• Fuel Level: Check and add if necessary	x	x	x	x	x	x	x	x	x		
• Interior Cleanliness: Check	x	x	x	x	x	x	x	x	x		
• Exterior Body Integrity/Cleanliness, All wax removed: Check	x	x	x	x	x	x	x	x	x		
• Owners/Radio Manuals and Warranty/Maintenance Booklets, completed as required; (Theft Protection Warning Stickers installed; Radio Security Code Card in glove box): Check	x	x	x	x	x	x	x	x	x		
• Radio Serial Number Stickers Completed and Affix to Vehicle Warranty Book and Dealership Record: Check	x	x	x	x	x	x	x	x	x		
• Radio Control Layout Card Attached to Mirror: Check	x	x	x	x	x	x	x	x	x		

All items have been completed, checked and/or rectified.   _____

Date   Service

_____

Date   Sales

August 26, 1988   English   41N-1359E
HW: je 1330F   French   41N-1359F

EXHIBIT 2   PRE-DELIVERY QUALITY SERVICE CERTIFICATE

"I Care" Pre-delivery *Quality Service* Certificate 	**Certificat de** Service pré-livraison de *QUALITÉ:* j'y vois

Name of Customer/Nom du client

Vehicle Identification Number/N° d'identification de véhicule

As part of this dealership's and my commitment to "I Care" Quality Service, I have personally checked the items listed on the back of this card. I have found everything to be in order. If you have any reason not to agree, please call me.

Comme nous faisons ici partie du programme "La qualité: j'y vois". J'ai personnellement vérifié les points indiqués au verso de la présente carte. J'ai constaté que tout est en bon état. Toutelois, si pour une raison quelconque, vous n'étiez pas satisfait, n'hésitez pas à m'appeler.

Name of Sales Representative/Nom du Vendeur

Telephone No. N° de téléphone	Date	Signature	Dealer Stamp/Timbre du concessionnaire
			VWC-41-025

Appearance Exterior	Is the car clean, its protective coating removed? Is it free of dents and surface blemishes?	Apparence extérieure	La voiture est-elle propre? Sa couche de protection a-t-elle enlevée? Est-elle sans bosseiures et imperfections de surface?
Appearance Interior	Are seats, carpet and headliner clean? Are shipping labels removed? Is the cigarette lighter working? Are the ashtrays spotless?	Apparence intérieure	Les sièges, le tapis et al doublure de plafond sont-ils propres? Les étiquettes d'expédition ont-elles été enlevés? L'allume-cigarette fonctionne-t-il? Les cendriers sont-ils impeccables?
Power Equipment	Do the following items function properly? • Power Windows • Power Door Locks • Power Mirrors • Power Sunroof • Power Antenna • Power Seats and Seat Memory • Seat Heating Elements	Equipement servocommandé	Les éléments suivants fonctionnent-ils convenablement? • Léve-glaces électriques • Verrouillage électrique de portes • Rétroviseurs électriques • Toit ouvrant électrique • Antenne électrique • Sièges à réglaçe électrique et mémoire des sièges • Eléments de chauilage des sièges
Auto Check System	Does system signal "OK"?	Systéme global de contróle	Le symbols "OK" s'allume-t-il?
Climate Control	Does system operate properly? Set system on "auto" and with warm engine check through several temperature selections.	Climatisation	Le système fonctionne-t-il convenablement? Règlèz le système sur "auto" et le moteur élant à chaud, vériliez plusieurs sèlections de température.
Interior Lights	Do the switches work? Are they set to go on when the door opens?	Éclairage intérieur	Les interrupteurs fonctionnent-ils? Sont-lis règlés de laçon à provoquer l'allumage à l'ouverture de la porte?
Wipers-Washer	Do window wipers work? Are washer jets aimed? Washer container(s) filled? Do wipers park when switched off?	Essulié-glaces et lave-glace	Les essuie-glaces fonctionnent-ils? Les jets de lave-glace sont-ils bien dirigés? Le(s) rèservoir(s) de lave-glace est (sont)-il(s) rempli(s)? Les essuie-glaces reviennent-ils à la position de repos à l'arrêt?
Fuel Quantity	Does the fuel guage work? Does it read out of the red reserve area?	Jauge à essence	La jauge fonctionne-t-elle? Donne-t-elle une indication en dehors de la zone rouge de réserve?
Sound System	Does the radio work? AM, FM, FM-stereo, cassette and speaker volume control? Are pre-select buttons set to local stations?	Systéme stéréo	La radio fonctionne-t-elle? En particulier les commandes de volume, AM, FM, FM stéréo et le lecteur de cassettes? Les boutons de présélection sont-ils règls pour les stations locales?
Accessories	Are they properly installed and operational?	Accessoires	Les accessoires sont-ils installés correctement et fonctionnent-ils?
Clock	Does the clock work? Is it set to the correct local time?	Montre	La montre fonctionne-t-elle? Est-elle règls à l'heure locale?
Literature	Are all the necessary booklets in the glove compartment: Owners Manual, Warranty & Maintenance Booklets and Radio Operating Manual.	Documentation	Toute la documentation nécessaire se trouve-t-elle dans la boite à gants: Manuel du propriétaire, Guide de garantie et d'entretien, Guide de l'utilisation de la radio?
Starting and Idle	Does the engine turn over and start easily? Is the engine running smoothly?	Démarrage et raienu	Le moteur démarre-t-il facilement? Le raienu est-il régulier?
Tires and Tools	Is the spare tire secure in its recess? Are the tool kit and jack neatly in place? Are the front and rear tires at correct pressure?	Pneus et outils	La roue de secours est-elle solidement dans son logement? La trousse d'outils et le cric sont-ils bien en place? La pression de gonilage des pneus avant et arrière est-elle correcte?

EXHIBIT 3 CEDARBRAE VOLKSWAGEN CUSTOMER QUESTIONNAIRE

Cedarbrae Volkswagen (1981) Ltd.

666 Markham Road
Scarborough, Ont.
M1H 2A7

Telephone (416) 438-1900

Mr. Bob Smith
240 Duncan Road
Scarborough, Ontario
M1B 1R6

Dear Mr Smith:

Cedarbrae Volkswagen is committed to providing you with the best possible service. In order to help us meet that high goal, I ask you to take a moment to fill out this questionnaire.

1. *Is the owner information (name, address, etc.) correct?
    If not, please correct us:*

    change area code to M1B 1R8

2. *How satisfied are you with your new vehicle,
    i.e., very satisfied, somewhat satisfied, satisfied, unsatisfied?*

    Satisfied

3. *How satisfied are you with the service provided to you thus far?*

    Very satisfied

4. *Were the facts of your transaction properly recorded and explained to you
    by your sales representative?* PAUL MACINNIS
    YES __✓__ NO _____

5. *At the time of delivery, was the condition and performance of your
    car satisfactory?*   YES _____ NO __✓__
    If no, what was unsatisfactory?

    scratch marks on the front hood

6. *Was the operation of your vehicle sufficiently explained to you at the time
    of delivery?*   YES __✓__ NO _____

7. *Did you receive an "I Care" Certificate from your sales rep?
    Was "I Care" Quality Service explained to you?* YES __✓__ NO _____

8. *What was your main reason for purchasing your vehicle from
    Cedarbrae?* _____
    Satisfactory deal (money wise)

Thank you for helping us improve our services.

*Herb Boehm
General Manager*

"I Care"
Quality
Service

Service Department

When a customer brought a vehicle in for servicing, the service advisor would discuss the problems with the car owner and write up a work order. The work orders were sent to the Dispatch Office, located in the service area, where the shop foreman scheduled and distributed them to the mechanics. The mechanics were expected not only to fix the items indicated on the work order, but also to do a thorough check for other items that needed repair. If additional problems were discovered, a service advisor would contact the customer to see if he/she wanted the extra repairs done. When a mechanic finished working on a vehicle, a time card was punched and the service advisor completed the bill. The service department processed about seventy to eighty work orders per day, of which approximately a third were warranty repairs.

It was the service advisor's responsibility to make a visual inspection for cleanliness of all vehicles after repair, and to hang a quality control certificate (see Exhibit 4) in each car after inspection. Due to the volume of daily work orders, however, only a sampling of cars were actually test-driven after repair. The vehicles tested were selected based on the type of problem that was fixed, the particular mechanic working on the car (some had higher comeback rates so their vehicles were tested more frequently), or simply at random.

When customers picked up their vehicle, they were charged $45 per hour for labour, plus parts on a marked up basis. If the repairs were covered under warranty, Cedarbrae submitted the work order to VWC where clerks checked and authorized the work before reimbursement was made to the dealer. Compensation from VWC for warranty work was issued at a fixed multiple of the mechanic's rate of approximately $15 per hour (before benefits, pensions, etc.) for labour, and at cost plus, for parts.

One copy of all work orders processed on a given day was compiled and used as a record for telephone follow-ups. The service telephone calls were made by two part-time employees, two nights per week and on Saturdays. On average, two calls per customer were necessary to reach a car owner. Cedarbrae attempted to call customers within a week of the repair work and usually averaged about four days between the work and the call. All telephone follow-ups were recorded on a follow-up sheet (see Exhibit 5) which outlined the customer's name, repair date and order number, questions asked, and any further work necessary.

In Herb's opinion, quality of service meant getting the job done right the first time, in a reasonable amount of time, in a friendly manner. The service manager had to be a "people person" more importantly than a great mechanic. The customers had to feel like they were well taken care of and considered important to the dealership.

INDEX DEVELOPMENT

Volkswagen Canada began measuring customer satisfaction in 1982 in the form of Pre Delivery Inspection for new car sales. A customer survey was mailed out to new vehicle owners inquiring about such things as working order of the car when received, and how well the vehicle operation had been explained. The survey accounted for 60% of a dealer's score, while the remaining 40% was derived through field force input from visits to the dealership.

EXHIBIT 4   QUALITY CONTROL CERTIFICATE

VWC-41-008

PRINTED IN CANADA

Please detach

Quality Control Certificate

Name

Invoice Number

I have personally inspected your vehicle and checked that we have carried out the work you requested.

If you have any questions or are not completely satisfied please call me.

CEDARBRAE VOLKSWAGEN (1981) LTD.
(416) 438-1900

"I Care"

QualityService

Keep this for reference

EXHIBIT 5   TELEPHONE FOLLOW-UP SHEET

"I Care"
Quality
Service

DATE ....19 ....

Repair Date	Repair Order #	Customer's Name	Telephone Number(s)	Satisfied Yes/No	Finished On Time	Condition Of Vehicle	Price As Expected	General Remarks	Service Manager's Follow Up

VOLKSWAGEN CANADA INC.

Listed by _____   Called by _____   _____   _____

Dealer   Service Manager

Printed in Canada 41-99-90332

In 1985, VWC introduced Service as an element of the customer satisfaction index. This new element measured quality of service of warranty repair work at the dealerships, through mailed customer surveys. Each area was worth a maximum of one hundred points of the total two hundred point index. Field force input was eliminated in the dealership index measurement in 1986 due to bias—all dealers were receiving between thirty-five and forty out of a possible forty points. Thus, as of 1986, index scores were based totally on customer survey feedback.

EXHIBIT 6   VWC KUNDENDIENST INDEX

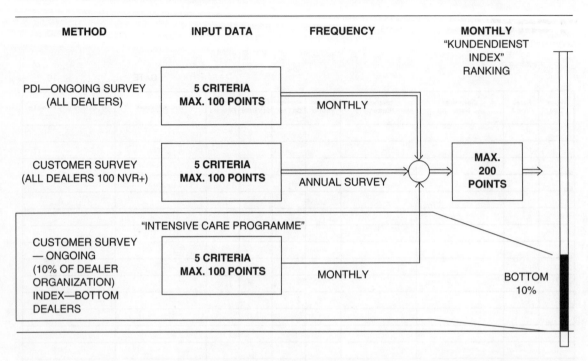

As of 1987, dealers whose scores fell among the top 90% of all dealers in Canada were considered "I Care" dealers, while the bottom 10% of scores indicated "Intensive Care" dealerships. For "I Care" dealers, PDI was measured monthly and Service annually. Intensive Care dealers were also measured monthly for PDI, but the frequency of Service measurement was increased from annually to monthly to offer more timely feedback (see Exhibit 6).

The Kundendienst Index, which roughly translates into "customer satisfaction" index, measured ten specific items; five for PDI and five for Service. Each item had been assigned relative importance through a weighting designation (see Exhibit 7). These weightings had been developed through customer focus groups and managerial input in the early eighties. The PDI survey (see Exhibit 8), in addition to covering the five areas measured in the index, included two questions concerning leased vehicles and an area for further comments by the customer. If a car owner indicated that his/her vehicle was leased, VWC did not incorporate the PDI results in the dealership index calculation since, in the case of fleet sales, the dealership would not necessarily have had any direct contact with the customer. PDI surveys were mailed to all new car owners with approximately a 15% response rate.

To calculate the PDI portion of the Kundendienst Index, the percentage of "yes" responses in each of the five areas measured was multiplied by the weighting assigned to

EXHIBIT 7   "I CARE" CRITERIA

"I CARE" PDI — CUSTOMER INPUT					POINTS
PDI OK %	VEHICLE OPERATION EXPLANATION, %	TELEPHONE FOLLOW-UP %	"I CARE" EXPLANATION %	PDI CERTIFICATE PRESENTED %	
Weight 30	Weight 25	Weight 20	Weight 15	Weight 10	100

"I CARE" SERVICE SURVEY — CUSTOMER INPUT					
REPAIRS DONE RIGHT FIRST TIME %	BASED ON SERVICE, WOULD BUY ANOTHER CAR, %	AFTER-SALES SERVICE SATISFACTION %	QUALITY CONTROL CERTIFICATE %	TELEPHONE FOLLOW-UP %	
Weight 30	Weight 24	Weight 19	Weight 15	Weight 12	100

MAXIMUM POINTS	200

each area, and then summed. For example, referring to Exhibit 9, the current PDI points of 95.00 were arrived at as follows:

	Positive Response		Weighting		Score
1. Condition OK	83.33%	×	30%	=	25.00
2. Vehicle Operation Explained	100.00%	×	25%	=	25.00
3. I Care Certificate	100.00%	×	20%	=	20.00
4. I Care Explained	100.00%	×	15%	=	15.00
5. Telephone Follow-up	100.00%	×	10%	=	10.00
Total PDI Points Current Month					**95.00**

The actual PDI cards returned to VWC were sent to the individual dealers monthly. As well, a Kundendienst Index Report (Exhibit 9) was forwarded to each dealer monthly. This report summarized year-to-date and monthly results in the five areas of PDI, and gave the dealer year-to-date total points for PDI and Service.

The Service survey was more detailed and asked a number of questions, the results of which were not actually measured (see Exhibit 10). These surveys were sent out on an ongoing basis to a maximum of eighty randomly chosen warranty repair work orders per month per dealer, with approximately a 20 to 25% response. Only dealers with greater than one hundred annual vehicle sales were measured on Service. The dealers

EXHIBIT 8 PDI SURVEY

Dear Volkswagen Owner:

Volkswagen Canada Inc. and your Volkswagen Dealer are interested in your satisfaction at the time you took delivery of your new Volkswagen. Please answer these few questions, and mail this questionnaire in the pre-stamped envelope provided.

Name of Dealer ___*Cederbrae*___

City or Town ___*Toronto*___ Province ___*Ont*___

1. ON THE DAY OF DELIVERY was the condition and performance of your car satisfactory? .... ☑ Yes ☐ No

2. IF NO, what was unsatisfactory? — vehicle interior .... ☐
   — vehicle exterior .... ☐
   — mechanical and/or electrical .... ☐

3. Was operation of the car sufficiently explained to you at the time of delivery? .... ☑ Yes ☐ No

4. Did you receive an "I Care" Certificate from your Sales Representative? .... ☑ Yes ☐ No

5. Was "I Care" Quality Service explained to you by your Sales Representative? .... ☑ Yes ☐ No

6. Did you receive a follow-up phone call from your dealer after car was delivered? .... ☐ Yes ☑ No

7. Do you lease your car? .... ☐ Yes ☑ No

8. What car did you own/lease before this one?

   North ☑ American 1   ☐ VW 2   ☐ Japanese 3   Other ☐ Import 4

9. Please use this space to make any further comments about your purchase.

_____

_____

_____

_____

_____

_____

_____

EXHIBIT 9   VWC DEALER'S KUNDENDIENST INDEX REPORT

YTD Including the Month of June

Current PDI Points	YTD PDI Points	Annual 'I Care' Customer Survey Points	Total Points
95.00	84.57	74.34	158.91

PDI	Total Cards	Condition OK	Vehicle Operation Explained	'I Care' Certificate Given	'I Care' Program Explained	Telephone Follow-Up
Current month	6%	83.33%	100.00%	100.00%	100.00%	100.00%
YTD	100	87.00	92.00	93.00	85.00	67.00
Zone 2 Average YTD	87.96	96.61	92.69	88.36	76.34	
National Average YTD	86.93	96.70	91.73	86.99	74.43	

did not receive from VWC the actual surveys completed by the customers. Instead, they received a three-page summary of the Service survey results (see Exhibit 11) in the form of overall performance in each category and individual results for Volkswagen and Audi (Porsche was measured under a different system) in the five areas. Of the five Service criteria (Exhibit 7), the first, fourth, and fifth were "yes or no" questions and calculations of the index were done as explained under PDI. The second criteria, "based on service, would you buy another car?," offered the customer "yes, maybe, or no" responses. The yes and maybe answers were considered positive and determined the percentage to be applied to the 24% weighting. The third criteria, "after-sales service satisfaction," was measured using a scale question, where the top three responses (extremely satisfied, somewhat satisfied, neutral) were used to determine the percentage of positive answers to be applied to the 19% weighting.

Exhibit 12 illustrates a summary of the Kundendienst Index Status Year-To-Date for October 1987. The top five dealerships in each volume group and the top and bottom twenty dealers in Canada were reported. About fifteen of the bottom twenty dealers were in Volume Group I, three in Volume Group II, and two in Volume Group III. The overall index scores were based on a twelve month revolving system. That is, October-1986 scores would be dropped and October 1987 scores added. The Service portion of the index remained unchanged for a twelve month period, while the PDI was revised monthly. Index scores were measured and reported formally, every six months.

Those dealers in the Intensive Care Program represented approximately 25% of annual new vehicle sales volume, 25% of annual repair orders, and 25% of annual parts sales for VWC. For these dealers, VWC measured Service monthly and adjusted both PDI and Service indexes each month. Six months was the minimum time a dealer could be in Intensive Care given the formal reporting system.

EXHIBIT 10   SERVICE SURVEY

Volkswagen Canada

Volkswagen Canada Inc.
1940 Eglinton Avenue East
Scarborough, Ontario
M1L 2M2

Telephone (416) 288-3000
Telex 06-963588
Fax (416) 288-3298

Dear Customer:

Our aim is to serve you better. May we ask you to assist us in our effort?

Our records indicate that you are the owner of an Audi or Volkswagen serviced recently by one of our franchised Dealers.

We would appreciate it if you could take a few minutes to complete this questionnaire.

When completed, please mail it in the prepaid envelope provided.

Thank you very much for assisting us.

K. Luttmann
Service Organization Manager

EXHIBIT 10   (Continued)

GENERAL INFORMATION AND PRODUCT

_ _ _ _ _
QUESTIONNAIRE NO.

___ __ __ __ __
MAKE   DEALER NO.   VG

1. Did you buy your car new or used?   NEW ☐   USED ☐

2. How satisfied are you with the car so far?

EXTREMELY SATISFIED	SATISFIED	NEUTRAL	DISSATISFIED	EXTREMELY DISSATISFIED
☐	☐	☐	☐	☐

3. How many kilometers do you usually drive your car in a 12 month period?

UNDER 10,000 KM	10,000– 20,000 KM	20,000– 30,000 KM	30,000– 40,000 KM	OVER 40,000 KM

4. a) How many times during the last 12 months was your car serviced and/or repaired? ☐

   b) How many of these service/repairs were performed at each of the following:

AUDI/VW DEALER	INDEPENDENT WORK SHOP	DO-IT YOURSELF	OTHER
☐	☐	☐	☐

DEALERSHIP SELECTION

5. Why did you select this dealer for service? (Check as many as apply)

   a) Bought the car from this dealer.   ☐   d) Had previous work done here and   ☐
                                                                was satisfied.

   b) Referred by friends/associates.   ☐   e) Nearest place to get the work done. ☐

   c) Was not satisfied with work done at
      another dealer.   ☐

   (Name of previous dealer) _____

CUSTOMER CONTACT PERSONNEL

6. In terms of the level of courtesy that you would have expected, how satisfied were you
   with the people you dealt with in the dealership?

   a) Telephone Receptionist

EXTREMELY SATISFIED	SATISFIED	NEUTRAL	DISSATISFIED	EXTREMELY DISSATISFIED
☐	☐	☐	☐	☐

   b) Service Adviser–on phone

EXTREMELY SATISFIED	SATISFIED	NEUTRAL	DISSATISFIED	EXTREMELY DISSATISFIED
☐	☐	☐	☐	☐

   c) Service Adviser–when car was taken in

EXTREMELY SATISFIED	SATISFIED	NEUTRAL	DISSATISFIED	EXTREMELY DISSATISFIED
☐	☐	☐	☐	☐

EXHIBIT 10   (Continued)

d) Cashier

EXTREMELY SATISFIED	SATISFIED	NEUTRAL	DISSATISFIED	EXTREMELY DISSATISFIED
☐	☐	☐	☐	☐

e) Other person(s)

EXTREMELY SATISFIED	SATISFIED	NEUTRAL	DISSATISFIED	EXTREMELY DISSATISFIED
☐	☐	☐	☐	☐

(please specify) _____

YOUR MOST RECENT SERVICE VISIT

Thinking back to the service/repair done at the Audi/Volkswagen Dealership, please tell us:

7. Was the job done right the first time?   YES ☐   NO ☐

8. Was the car ready when promised?   YES ☐   NO ☐

9. Were there any delays caused by: YES ☐   NO ☐
    a) Parts not available?   YES ☐   NO ☐
    b) Service Department too busy?   YES ☐   NO ☐

10. Was the work explained to your satisfaction?   YES ☐   NO ☐

11. Was the car clean?   YES ☐   NO ☐

12. Did you find an "I Care" Repair Quality Control Certificate in your car showing that their work was checked before you got the car back?   YES ☐   NO ☐

13. Did you receive a telephone call from the Dealership 2 or 3 days after the repair to enquire if you were satisfied?   YES ☐   NO ☐

YOUR GENERAL EXPECTATIONS

14. Please tell us how well your Servicing Audi/Volkswagen Dealer meets your expectations in the following categories:

	EXTREMELY SATISFIED	SATISFIED	NEUTRAL	DISSATISFIED	EXTREMELY DISSATISFIED
a) Repairs are done right first time:	☐	☐	☐		☐
b) Appointments are scheduled promptly:	☐	☐	☐	☐	☐
c) Minimum wait at reception counter:	☐	☐	☐	☐	☐
d) Courteous treatment:	☐	☐	☐	☐	☐
e) Loaner or Rental cars are available:	☐	☐	☐	☐	☐

EXHIBIT 10   (Continued)

	EXTREMELY SATISFIED	SATISFIED	NEUTRAL	DISSATISFIED	EXTREMELY DISSATISFIED
f) Work is performed only with my approval:	☐	☐	☐	☐	☐
g) The nature of the problem and the work performed are explained to me:	☐	☐	☐	☐	☐
h) Repairs are not delayed because Parts are not available:	☐	☐	☐	☐	☐
i) Repairs are reasonably priced: – PARTS	☐	☐	☐	☐	☐
– LABOUR	☐	☐	☐	☐	☐
j) The car is ready when promised:	☐	☐	☐	☐	☐
k) I have confidence in their Technicians:	☐	☐	☐	☐	☐

YOUR OVERALL SATISFACTION

15. Generally speaking, how satisfied are you with the service provided by your servicing/ repairing Audi/VW dealer?

EXTREMELY SATISFIED	SATISFIED	NEUTRAL	DISSATISFIED	EXTREMELY DISSATISFIED
☐	☐	☐	☐	☐

16. Would you recommend this dealership's service department to others?   YES ☐   NO ☐

17. Based on your service experience would you buy another Audi/VW product?
    YES ☐   MAYBE ☐   NO ☐

18. Are there any other remarks that you feel you want to add, concerning the service you have been getting?:

    _____

    _____

    _____

    _____

    _____

    _____

    Please indicate here whether you want us to follow-up on the above remarks, in the interest of straightening out any problems you may be experiencing.

    Please follow-up ☐   Please do not follow-up ☐

EXHIBIT 11 "I CARE" QUALITY SERVICE SURVEY 1987

Dealer # 3005 Auto. Cedarbrae

Question	1987 Nation Total	1987 Dealer Total	1986 Dealer Total	1987 Nation Audi	1987 Dealer Audi	1986 Dealer Audi	1987 Nation VW	1987 Dealer VW	1986 Dealer VW
# Responses	13010	46	96	2268	5	0	10742	41	96
Did you buy your car									
New	89.9	87.0	87.5	82.0	60.0	0.0	91.6	90.2	87.5
Used	10.1	13.0	12.5	18.0	40.0	0.0	8.4	9.8	12.5
How satisfied with car									
Extremely sat %	58.3	48.9	54.7	52.5	20.0	0.0	59.5	52.5	54.7
Somewhat sat %	31.5	46.7	40.0	33.6	80.0	0.0	31.0	42.5	40.0
Neutral %	3.5	4.4	2.1	4.0	0.0	0.0	3.4	5.0	2.1
Somewhat dissat %	4.7	0.0	3.2	6.5	0.0	0.0	4.3	0.0	3.2
Extremely dissat %	2.1	0.0	0.0	3.4	0.0	0.0	1.8	0.0	0.0
How many repairs/services in the last 12 months									
0 %	6.8	4.4	15.6	7.3	20.0	0.0	6.6	2.5	15.6
1– 3 %	50.4	53.3	37.5	45.2	80.0	0.0	51.5	50.0	37.5
4–6 %	31.3	26.7	27.1	32.8	0.0	0.0	31.0	30.0	27.1
7–12 %	10.2	15.6	18.8	13.0	0.0	0.0	9.6	17.5	18.8
13+ %	1.4	0.0	1.0	1.6	0.0	0.0	1.3	0.0	1.0
Who performed serv/repair									
Dealer %	80.9	83.2	71.7	90.8	100.0	0.0	78.6	82.8	71.7
Independent %	9.6	12.4	6.5	5.0	0.0	0.0	10.7	12.6	6.5
Gas station %	2.3	1.7	8.9	1.2	0.0	0.0	2.5	1.7	8.9
Do it yourself %	6.3	2.3	12.4	2.3	0.0	0.0	7.3	2.3	12.4
Other %	0.9	0.6	0.5	0.7	0.0	0.0	0.9	0.6	0.5
Serviced by selling dealer									
Yes %	75.8	84.8	93.8	77.6	60.0	0.0	75.4	87.8	93.8
Done right first time									
Yes %	71.9	60.9	0.8	71.1	80.0	0.0	72.1	58.5	70.8
I care o.c. certificate									
Yes %	52.0	28.3	51.0	62.7	40.0	0.0	49.8	26.8	51.0
Received phone call									
Yes %	32.4	13.0	13.5	39.6	0.0	0.0	30.9	14.6	13.5
How does dealer meet your expectations									
A. Prompt appointment									
Excellent 1 %	53.4	52.2	54.3	61.5	20.0	0.0	51.7	56.1	54.3
2 %	27.2	34.8	28.7	23.5	80.0	0.0	27.9	29.3	28.7
3 %	11.3	8.7	12.8	9.4	0.0	0.0	11.6	9.8	12.8
4 %	4.6	2.2	3.2	3.0	0.0	0.0	5.0	2.4	3.2
Poor 5 %	3.5	2.2	1.1	2.5	0.0	0.0	3.7	2.4	1.1

EXHIBIT 11   (Continued)

Question			1987 Nation Total	1987 Dealer Total	1986 Dealer Total	1987 Nation Audi	1987 Dealer Audi	1986 Dealer Audi	1987 Nation VW	1987 Dealer VW	1986 Dealer VW
B. Min wait at reception											
Excellent	1	%	45.0	40.0	43.0	52.9	40.0	0.0	43.3	40.0	43.0
	2	%	32.1	35.6	30.1	31.0	60.0	0.0	32.4	32.5	30.1
	3	%	14.5	11.1	18.3	11.0	0.0	0.0	15.3	12.5	18.3
	4	%	5.0	6.7	5.4	3.3	0.0	0.0	5.4	7.5	5.4
Poor	5	%	3.3	6.7	3.2	1.8	0.0	0.0	3.6	7.5	3.2
C. Courteous treatment											
Excellent	1	%	63.6	56.5	59.4	69.9	40.0	0.0	62.3	58.5	59.4
	2	%	23.3	37.0	26.0	20.9	60.0	0.0	23.9	34.1	26.0
	3	%	8.0	4.3	9.4	6.6	0.0	0.0	8.5	4.9	9.4
	4	%	2.7	0.0	4.2	2.1	0.0	0.0	2.9	0.0	4.2
Poor	5	%	2.3	2.2	1.0	1.5	0.0	0.0	2.5	2.4	1.0
D. Work only with approval											
Excellent	1	%	68.4	50.0	66.3	72.7	40.0	0.0	67.4	51.2	66.3
	2	%	22.2	32.6	24.2	20.3	40.0	0.0	22.5	31.7	24.2
	3	%	5.9	8.7	5.3	4.4	0.0	0.0	6.2	9.8	5.3
	4	%	1.7	4.3	3.2	1.4	20.0	0.0	1.8	2.4	3.2
Poor	5	%	1.9	4.3	1.1	1.2	0.0	0.0	2.0	4.9	1.1
E. Defect/work explained											
Excellent	1	%	49.9	35.6	53.8	52.1	50.0	0.0	49.4	34.1	53.8
	2	%	24.5	33.3	25.8	24.0	50.0	0.0	24.6	31.7	25.8
	3	%	14.1	13.3	10.8	13.0	0.0	0.0	14.3	14.6	10.8
	4	%	6.2	8.9	5.4	5.9	0.0	0.0	6.3	9.8	5.4
Poor	5	%	5.3	8.9	4.3	5.0	0.0	0.0	5.3	9.8	4.3
F. No delay for parts											
Excellent	1	%	44.7	40.9	39.4	37.2	0.0	0.0	46.3	45.0	39.4
	2	%	26.1	36.4	26.6	27.2	75.0	0.0	25.9	32.5	26.6
	3	%	14.9	11.4	17.0	19.3	25.0	0.0	14.0	10.0	17.0
	4	%	7.2	6.8	11.7	8.4	0.0	0.0	7.0	7.5	11.7
Poor	5	%	7.1	4.5	5.3	7.9	0.0	0.0	6.9	5.0	5.3
G. Reasonable prices											
Excellent	1	%	26.1	11.4	25.3				24.5	12.5	25.3
	2	%	26.3	34.1	28.6				26.8	35.0	28.6
	3	%	26.9	31.8	35.2				27.8	30.0	35.2
	4	%	11.8	18.2	7.7				12.0	17.5	7.7
Poor	5	%	8.9	4.5	3.3				8.9	5.0	3.3

EXHIBIT 11   (Continued)

Question			1987 Nation Total	1987 Dealer Total	1986 Dealer Total	1987 Nation Audi	1987 Dealer Audi	1986 Dealer Audi	1987 Nation VW	1987 Dealer VW	1986 Dealer VW
H. Ready when promised											
Excellent	1	%	55.9	24.4	42.6				54.8	24.4	42.6
	2	%	26.6	55.6	29.8				27.0	53.7	29.8
	3	%	9.7	6.7	17.0				9.9	7.3	17.0
	4	%	4.0	6.7	7.4				4.2	7.3	7.4
Poor	5	%	3.7	6.7	3.2				4.0	7.3	3.2
I. Confidence in mechanic											
Excellent	1	%	48.8	44.2	47.9				47.8	41.0	47.9
	2	%	28.5	39.5	30.2				29.2	41.0	30.2
	3	%	12.1	9.3	18.8				12.4	10.3	18.8
	4	%	5.0	7.0	3.1				4.9	7.7	3.1
Poor	5	%	5.6	0.0	0.0				5.7	0.0	0.0
Satisfied with service											
Extremely sat		%	49.5	41.3	45.2				48.5	43.9	45.2
Somewhat sat		%	31.2	39.1	40.9				31.7	36.6	40.9
Neutral		%	7.0	10.9	4.3				7.4	9.8	4.3
Somewhat dissat		%	7.1	6.5	7.5				7.1	7.3	7.5
Extremely dissat		%	5.2	2.2	2.2				5.4	2.4	2.2
Would you recommend this dealer to others											
		Yes	79.0	71.7	0.0				78.3	73.2	0.0
		No	21.0	28.3	0.0				21.7	26.8	0.0
Based on service would you buy another											
		Yes	67.5	52.2	71.9				68.5	51.2	71.9
		Maybe	23.2	43.5	18.8				22.9	46.3	18.8

THE EVENTS

In October, as Herb was sifting through a stack of mail received from VWC over the past few days, his eyes fell upon a one-page letter. The letter had initially been included in an intercompany pouch along with various other correspondence from head office. The contents of the letter indicated that Herb's Kundendienst Index had fallen significantly and that his dealership was consequently in the Intensive Care Program. As a member of Intensive Care, Herb would not be entitled to receive money from the VP Fund or send any of his employees to company commendations. The VP Fund was a system whereby VWC gave money to dealers to do their own advertising rather than use a co-operative advertising fund to which each dealer contributed. A couple of weeks after re-

EXHIBIT 12   KUNDENDIENST INDEX STATUS YTD OCT 1987

"Top 20" Dealers

Rank		Dealer	KD—Index
1	3284	Guelph	179.96
2	1416	Prince George	179.68
3	5867	Yarmouth	178.42
4	4738	Tracy	176.82
5	5853	Middleton	176.05
6	2724	Win. St. James	175.49
7	4762	Vallee	175.23
8	1575	Red Deer	174.88
9	3112	Sault Ste. Marie	173.59
10	2906	Thunder Bay	173.46
11	2703	Win. Ft. Garry	172.66
12	3250	Ottawa Mark	172.65
13	3008	Newmarket	171.84
14	3266	Welland	171.82
15	5866	Sydney	170.87
16	3200	Oakville	170.35
17	4802	Rimouski	170.03
18	4806	New Richmond	169.95
19	1405	Campbell River	169.58
20	5856	Kentville	169.08

"Top 5" by Volume Group

Rank		Dealer	KD—Index
		Volume Group I	
1	3076	Owasco	169.02
2	4752	Blainville	163.80
3	* 4789	Charlesbourg	158.43
4	3030	Agincourt	157.17
5	3032	Tor. Thornhill	156.61
		Volume Group II	
1	2703	Win. Ft. Garry	172.66
2	5211	Dieppe	166.69
3	4711	St-Hyacinthe	166.04
4	3361	Brampton	165.65
5	* 4776	Trois Rivieres	165.64
		Volume Group III	
1	3284	Guelph	179.96
2	1416	Prince George	179.68
3	5867	Yarmouth	178.42
4	4738	Tracy	176.82
5	5853	Middleton	176.05

"Bottom 20" Dealers

	Dealer	KD—Index
* 4788	Levis	147.34
* 4348	Longueuil	147.11
1440	Burnaby	146.32
* 1506	Calgary S. Centre	146.11
1585	Edmon. Westview	146.03
4770	Place de Bleury	145.68
3005	Cedarbrae	145.61
3187	Barrie	145.03
* 4748	Ville LaSalle	144.81
* 4744	Mont. Hamer	144.18
* 3202	Queensway	141.22
3267	Burlington	141.06
3243	Pembroke	140.67
* 3023	Tor. Downtown	140.09
* 3007	Tor. Don Valley	137.62
4713	Laval	137.58
3020	Mississauga	137.36
* 4739	Mont. Nordest	136.46
4706	Mont. Popular	135.77
* 4768	Mont. Mizzi	134.84

* Currently in Intensive Care

National Avg. 158.38; W. Zone 159.53; C. Zone 158.24; Q. Zone 156.59; A. Zone 163.67

ceiving the letter, a VWC service employee, on his routine visit, removed Cedarbrae's "I Care" plaque from the dealership.

After the initial shock of the letter had subsided, Herb had become quite angry and began to question the system. During the time over which his index had fallen, many things, planned and unplanned, had happened at Cedarbrae. Of most significance were the events that had occurred in the service department. The service manager had been in the hospital for seven months due to a heart problem, a service advisor had left because of heart trouble, and a third service employee had retired. The short staff position that resulted meant that some areas of business were not given their usual attention (e.g., quality certificates in cars). Amidst the staff situation, the service department had also been undergoing renovations to improve layout and customer service.

Over the ensuing months, Herb visited some of the more successful service dealers to see how they operated. He concluded that there were no significant differences between how their service departments were operated and his own normal operations. The employee situation in the service department was gradually rectified and by the end of six months, Herb's index score had rebounded back to the "I Care" level. At that time, Herb decided to contact VWC about the events which had taken place over the last year. He was now preparing for a meeting with the VWC Service Manager and wondered if the Kundendienst Index really measured, in a meaningful way, the quality of service offered at his dealership.

BAXTER HEALTHCARE CORPORATION, SHARED SERVICES (A)

INTRODUCTION

Greg Finley, Vice President of Operations, hadn't been with Baxter for very long when he moved to New Mexico in 1988 to start up the new Shared Services operation in Albuquerque. However, Finley did bring with him extensive experience in financial operations, specifically with the shared services approach. The functions located in Albuquerque represented activities, such as cash application, credit and collection, and accounts payable, previously dispersed among Baxter's field operations offices and the corporation's headquarters. So, what was new about the operation in Albuquerque was not the work being done, but instead where and how the work was accomplished. Each function came with a history, operational objectives, and a set of long-standing internal customers. The address of the service provider may have changed, but the needs of those customers had not. But since how the service was provided did change, the transition to Albuquerque introduced a new set of variables in terms of communication and service requirements.

Measurement was set in place as each function went through the transition from decentralization to centralization. With each key operating factor measured, initial indications were very positive. The functions were meeting or exceeding internally established operational targets (for quality indicators such as unit cost, accuracy, and cycle time) despite the ups and downs associated with most transition processes. However, along with the positive messages of early success, executive management was also receiving neg-

Lynn LeCropane, Baxter Healthcare Corporation, and Bernard Booms, Professor, College of Business and Economics, Seattle Center for Hotel and Restaurant Administration, Washington State University, prepared this case as a basis for class discussion rather than to illustrate either an effective or ineffective handling of an administrative situation. © 1991 International Service Quality Association.

tive feedback from the field operations. Most were in the form of complaints. And most were about service. The operational results had improved. But service had not. And according to some, the service was worse. What about service levels? Did they differ among the area field locations? Did they vary among the internal customers, perhaps among divisions? The measurement systems in place were not capturing the information to answer these questions.

In 1990, it was clear to Finley that the service issues had to be addressed, but he wondered, "How does a new operation, servicing several divisions, get a handle on service requirements and service levels?" The issues of service levels kept leading Finley to questions about measurement, "How is service measured? Issues and requirements about customer service had been measured for products, usually surveying the user or external customer. But how could the same approach be appropriately and effectively applied to **services** provided to **internal customers**?"

BAXTER HEALTHCARE CORPORATION

Baxter Healthcare Corporation, a Fortune 100 company, is a leading manufacturer and distributor of health care products, systems, and services. Headquartered in a northwest suburb of Chicago, Baxter employs approximately 62,000 employees in 33 countries, offering a product line of more than 120,000 products. In 1990, Baxter reported sales of $8.1 billion, with operating income of 4.5% of sales.

Baxter had experienced significant change and growth, especially since the 1985 merger with American Hospital Supply Corporation. The "new" Baxter had earned a leadership position in the health care market, due to the rich histories of innovation of both the former Baxter Travenol Laboratories and American Hospital Supply Corporation. The merger created a stronger, more broadly based independent supply source for hospitals and health care providers.

Baxter's contributions to medical history included the first commercially available intravenous solutions, the first product for separating plasma from whole blood, and the first commercially built disposable artificial kidney.

Baxter's mission statement reflects the fundamental values of innovation, service to customers, and leadership that exist throughout the corporation:

> We will be the leading health-care company by providing the very best products and services for our customers around the world, consistently emphasizing innovation, operational excellence, and the highest quality in everything we do.

To achieve the mission, continuous quality improvement is practiced as a strategic imperative. Baxter emphasized the commitment to quality by developing the Quality Leadership Process (QLP), a set of principles and an approach to quality improvement implemented throughout the corporation worldwide. QLP has helped drive the focus of quality at all functions and at all levels within the corporation.

SHARED SERVICES, ALBUQUERQUE

In 1987, the Baxter Finance Division adopted the theme of creating the best organization in America. Senior Vice President and Chief Financial Officer, Bob Lambrix, asked

EXHIBIT 1   TRANSITION OF FINANCIAL SERVICES TO ALBUQUERQUE

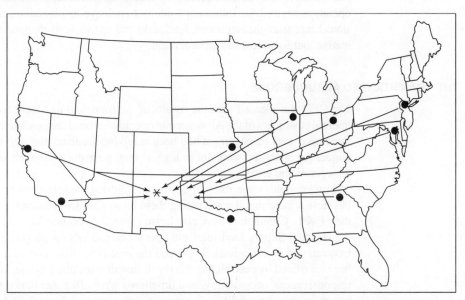

his direct reports for ideas on how the Finance Division could go about turning that goal into a reality. One recommendation suggested that the Finance organization begin employing the principles of QLP, Baxter's customized Total Quality Management process.

Each area within the Finance Division applied the tools and techniques of QLP in order to focus their efforts on becoming the best organization in America. The areas included: Shared Services, Treasury, Controller, Tax, Audit, and Financial Planning and Analysis.

The Shared Services Division, with offices at headquarters, Puerto Rico, and Albuquerque, represented activities servicing several corporate and divisional functions, such as Payroll, Leasing Services, Accounts Payable, Credit and Collection, and Cash Application. Shared Services found operational advantages from consolidating large, high-volume transactional and repetitive processes to Albuquerque, while still maintaining the capability to respond to the unique needs of specific divisions.

Among all the areas, none faced more challenging issues and rapid growth than the Albuquerque Shared Services operation. In addition, Albuquerque experienced some of the most dramatic success while being held under constant scrutiny by members of Baxter's key business units, including those Albuquerque did not serve.

Albuquerque Shared Services actually grew out of the Finance Division's use of QLP. And since then, the concepts have been adhered to even more strongly. The principles of QLP assisted the Albuquerque operation faced with the challenges that accompanied a 225% growth in employee population in 1990 due to the expansion of services provided.

The mission of the Albuquerque operation had been stated rather simply: To be the leader in quality service at the lowest cost. The objective: To continuously improve both service levels and cost efficiency by eliminating manual processes. The Albuquerque operation devised the following strategy to achieve its objective and carry out its mission: Emphasize measurement, feedback, and openness to change, in a pleasant, participative, but focused work environment.

THE TRANSITION TO ALBUQUERQUE

The CFO was pleased with the results of the transition to Albuquerque. But not all the internal customers of the Albuquerque operation shared the positive feelings of the CFO. Executive level management had been receiving feedback that service levels of the Albuquerque operation were not as high as they were prior to centralizing functions from the operational areas.

For example, some internal customers felt that the transition had put some of their business at risk, that it was costing them money, and was having a negative impact on their P & L. Complaints were also heard regarding communication issues. For instance, the Hospital Supply Division field operations and sales management felt the level and frequency of communication between the area field offices and the credit function had been sacrificed by centralizing the credit function in Albuquerque. Issues such as speed, responsiveness, accessibility, and timeliness were often mentioned by the internal customers as they described the communication elements they felt had deteriorated.

Prior to the transition, each area field office had both customer service and credit functions located on site to service the associated sales and distribution regions. Consolidating the area credit functions and locating the activity alongside the cash application function presented significant opportunities that would streamline and standardize the process. But despite the efficiencies realized by the transition, the area offices and other internal customers felt a loss of control and lack of communication that appeared to detract from the positive results documented early in the transition.

Baxter had considered several alternatives for the location of what began as a transaction processing operation. Late in 1987, after considering the various options, Baxter chose Albuquerque, New Mexico, as the site based on the quality of the workforce available, the ability to coordinate training with the local Technical and Vocational Institute, and the cost of facilities, communication systems, and labor. The transitions were set to begin in 1988.

By third quarter 1991, the Shared Services function located in Albuquerque had over 300 employees in six primary operational areas: Cash Application, Data Entry, Audit Control, Accounts Payable, Credit and Collection, and Customer Billing. Prior to the transitions, these functions were scattered throughout the U.S., located at the headquarters and the nine sales and distribution areas, and in some cases, at regional offices.

However, those functions were identified as highly repetitive, high-volume processes that also had strong crossfunctional relationships and dependencies on each other. So, along with the opportunities to increase operational efficiency, the consolidation was also seen as a way to enhance the service and communication between these highly interrelated functions. Most functions were consolidated in phases and the transitions of the various functions were spread out over the course of 3 years (Exhibit 1).

By August 1991, the operation serviced nineteen Baxter organizations, including the two largest, the Hospital Supply Division and the Scientific Products Division. Albuquerque processed payment for more than 6 million invoices, applied cash to over 9 million invoices, and processed payments for over 800,000 invoices annually.

The transition began in September 1988 by centralizing the cash application operation. The Cash Application function processes customer payments that do not automatically apply to a specific invoice. Payments, sent by customers to bank lockboxes, were first deposited by the bank to a general account and then the invoices and copies of the checks were batched, usually in groups of no more than 50 checks. The bank would then send the batches to Albuquerque daily by express mail. In addition, the bank would transmit a report for each batch that would indicate the amount and details of the deposit. The Cash Application function would use the transmission report and the batch to process the transactions, to make sure the payments were applied to the correct invoice.

In most cases, when the information contained on the check and the remittance matched, the payment would automatically apply to the correct customer invoice, through the use of an expert system. However, discrepancies such as a check paying multiple invoices, a short payment, or a missing purchase order number would prevent payments from automatically applying. The account would show that payment was made, but would not relate the payment to a specific invoice. In these situations, the cash application representative would take the role of detective to match the name and amount to Baxter's accounts receivable. Applying cash quickly and accurately was critical in order to ensure that the most accurate and up-to-date information was available to those in the credit and collection functions of each division.

In September 1989, Corporate Accounts Payable (A/P) and Data Entry moved to Albuquerque. Corporate A/P processed payments for employees such as check requests, purchase orders, and expense reports. Customers of Corporate A/P included the purchasing department, buyers, and vendors. In the case of check requests and purchase orders, the processing also meant verifying the receipt of goods. After processing, the paperwork would then be batched and sent to Data Entry, who performed the keying function. Information keyed by Data Entry included the information necessary for a check to be cut, such as price, quantity, item, and payment terms. After the information was keyed, a check would be scheduled for the appropriate check run.

The following year, September 1990, the Hospital Supply Division, Baxter's largest division, centralized its Accounts Payable, Credit and Collection, Audit Control, and Customer Billing functions in Albuquerque. Accounts Payable processed payment to vendors and worked closely with the Data Entry function. Credit and Collection was responsible for collecting the Division's receivables, as well as handling issues surrounding aged receivables (over 90 days) and bad debt. Customer Billing processed both vendor payment and customer billing, primarily dealing with shipments made directly from the vendor to the customer. In these situations, the vendor would bill Baxter and Baxter would bill the customer. Therefore a key measurement was monitoring the amount not yet billed to the customer, but paid by Baxter. The Audit Control function processed information and discrepancies regarding shipments (both to Baxter and to the customer), assisting the Distribution function with inventory control and reconciliation.

The Albuquerque operation continued to expand. Freight Processing moved to Albuquerque in January 1991. In February 1991, Physical Inventory, responsible for preparing the paperwork for inventory reconciliation, was centralized and moved to Albuquerque. Initially, with the exception of Cash Application and Corporate Accounts Payable, most of the functions serviced the Hospital Supply Division only. However, in June 1991, the second largest division within Baxter, the Scientific Products Division, announced the transition of its Accounts Payable, Inventory Control, and Customer Billing function, which began in August 1991.

OPERATIONAL EFFICIENCY

An example of the results of the transition was illustrated by the continuous improvement in the Data Entry and Cash Application functions. The role of Data Entry expanded with virtually every transition by assuming the keying responsibility associated with each process. Consequently, Data Entry had several internal customers representing most of Baxter's divisions, as well as internal customers representing almost every function located in Albuquerque.

Even after the early success of the cash application transition in 1988, the function continued to make improvements. For instance, enhancements to the expert system and expansion of Data Entry's role resulted in a dramatic increase in the automatic application rate. Before the improvements, approximately 20% of the cash received automatically applied to the correct invoice. In early 1991, about seven months after those particular system improvements, the auto-application rate rose to almost 80%. As a result, the role of the cash application representative changed and became more heavily focused on the most difficult cash to apply. The changing role required additional training in decision making and system applications.

The operation had maintained a relatively flat organization structure, consisting of only four levels of employee responsibility. The constant expansion was reflected in the fact that in the second quarter 1991, 75% of the employees in Albuquerque had been with the operation for one year or less. The growth had presented an enormous set of challenges to management in areas of recruiting, training, cross-training, and employee involvement. Management faced these challenges by applying the principles found in QLP. The Shared Services operation in Albuquerque saved 28% to 33% of baseline costs in each of the key functional areas in 1990.

QLP AT ALBUQUERQUE

Throughout the expansion, Finley stressed the ongoing use of measurement. Performance, results, and operational efficiency were quantified, each considered a critical factor to the success of the operation. In addition, Finley and the management team communicated the results and goals to all employees, keeping everyone informed regarding overall performance issues. Finley found that the methodology and principles of QLP provided the framework to support the objectives of the Albuquerque operation.

"The whole QLP approach forces you to quantify what you need in terms of quality," Finley explained. "If you do something for a living, you should be able to measure it." That philosophy was communicated even as early as on-the-job training classes provided to new employees.

"First, we told them: Here's Baxter, here's our set of values, here's QLP and customer service," said Finley. "Then, we covered the 'how-to' of the job." As a result, employees received broad-based training that went beyond the specific mechanics of the job. The approach provided the "bigger picture" essential to an environment of continuous quality improvement.

But despite the success, mentioned earlier, Finley continued to be confronted by negative feedback regarding service levels. The feedback was generally qualitative and sporadic. It was also very unclear as to whether input at any given time provided a fair representation of all the Albuquerque operation's internal customers. In addition, no system existed to verify that, in fact, the feedback provided an accurate reflection of customer satisfaction.

"How do we get a handle on determining service levels, in addition to our other performance indicators?" remained the primary question Finley wrestled with regarding service.

THE QLP STORY

Baxter formalized its quality management process, known as QLP, in 1983. Baxter's corporate-wide quality initiative resulted in Performance Management Objectives for Division Vice Presidents, as well as Directors and Managers throughout the organization. Baxter's management policies included three corporate policies regarding Quality Leadership that gave management of each business unit the following responsibilities:

• To integrate QLP into everyday management practice.
• To continually improve its capability to deliver quality service and products by increasing its ability to understand and meet customer requirements, and by improving work processes.
• To ensure that all of its employees participate in QLP by providing formal training in basic quality tools and establishing appropriate structures and channels for participation.

As a result, management supported participation of employees at all levels in an aggressive quest to continually improve the quality of their work and to strive to meet the challenges of achieving operational excellence.

Finley understood that QLP provided more than just a set of principles. Aspects of QLP were alive and well in his organization. But he also felt that to really get a handle on the customer service issue would require a more focused effort. Finley turned to the QLP Department, Baxter's internal TQM group of quality improvement professionals. QLP had researched and developed a methodology for determining customer requirements, satisfaction, and competitive gaps, referred to as Customer Requirements Research (CRR).

The method, CRR, provided management with a powerful technique that could be applied during both the design and the improvement stages of a product. In the Fall of

EXHIBIT 2   APPROACH TO IDENTIFY ACTUAL DIMENSIONS OF QUALITY—THREE PHASES

1. **Management Interviews** *(Shared Services, Albuquerque)*
   - Survey Management Team
   - Obtain Qualitative Data
   - Establish Key Customer List for Phase 2
   - Capture Specific Service Characteristics

2. **Customer Interviews** *(Area Field Operations)*
   - Small Sample
   - Customers Selected included Management and Supervisory Levels
   - Obtain Qualitative Data (specific requirements drawn from responses to Requirement Dimensions)
   - Gather Additional Names for Phase 3 Mailing List

3. **Customer Survey**
   - Significant Sample
   - Obtain Quantitative Data
   - Sample Represents All Customers Demographically (Department, Division, Region)

1990, after learning about the technique, Finley was struck by the idea that the CRR methodology may enable Albuquerque to obtain some of the same valuable information for the services they provide.

Following a series of conversations with the QLP Department, QLP decided to relocate one of its program managers to Albuquerque. Although the program manager would also service other clients, her primary focus would be on facilitating the QLP implementation and Customer Requirements Research at Albuquerque.

CUSTOMER REQUIREMENTS RESEARCH

Shared Services, Albuquerque, chose to conduct CRR to assist with four primary objectives:

- Clarify Requirements
- Measure Customer Satisfaction
- Refine Performance Indicators and Internal Measurements
- Establish Baseline Data for Future Comparison

Although the Albuquerque operation customized the CRR approach in order to meet their goals, the methodology remained fairly consistent with previous applications within Baxter, consisting of three key phases. The objectives of each phase helped focus management on achieving two goals: to identify service requirements and to measure customer satisfaction (Exhibit 2).

Shared Services Albuquerque compiled two data sets, input from internal customers and input from management and teams located in Albuquerque. The customer responses focused on the importance and assessement of specific requirements, in addition to overall satisfaction with the operation. Management input represented Albuquerque's perception of customer satisfaction. The input for both data sets was gathered using the same survey instrument. After the input was compiled, the data sets were used to identify gaps between Albuquerque's perception and actual customer response.

During the initial phases of the process, the Requirement Dimensions were used as a

EXHIBIT 3   GENERAL FRAMEWORK

REQUIREMENT DIMENSIONS

Performance: basic operational requirements that must be met

Tangibles: physical attributes such as legibility of reports and documents

Features: extras that go beyond basic performance, but are not "must have" requirements

Security: attributes related to sensitive issues, such as confidentiality and discretion

Responsiveness: requirements such as turnaround time, timeliness of delivery, and accessibility

Reliability: requirements related to consistent and dependable service

Credibility: characteristics related to confidence in the abilities and integrity of the service providers

Courtesy: attributes dealing with professionalism, i.e., treating the customer politely, with consideration and respect

---

guide to identify and describe customer requirements. The Requirement Dimensions represented fundamental quality characteristics found in most services. The dimensions were not intended to describe actual customer requirements. Instead, the dimensions provided a framework within which to work, in order to translate the service or performance characteristics into measurable requirements (Exhibit 3).

The first phase involved interviewing the managers and supervisors of the functions located in Albuquerque. The interviews focused on identifying the internal customers and gathering qualitative data describing the manager's understanding of customer expectations. Phase 1 also provided an opportunity to further educate the managers and supervisors on the method and objectives of CRR.

The information gathered during the initial phase was then used to formulate the next set of interviews conducted during phase 2. The second set of interviews were held with a small sample of field operations management, identified as key customers of the Albuquerque operation. The individuals interviewed included area field operations managers, financial managers, and customer service managers. The objective was to move from broad generalizations about customer expectations to specific, measurable requirements.

During the next stage, the results of the interviews (conducted in Phase 1 and Phase 2) were analyzed to determine the content of the customer satisfaction survey. Organizing the results of Phases 1 and 2 not only proved to be very valuable in constructing the customer survey, but also provided structure for interpreting the survey results (Exhibit 4).

Information obtained during the interviews was tabulated in order to uncover any trends in the management or customer responses. The interview results were organized in terms of frequency of a particular response or requirement, the perspective of the individual (managerial and functional level), and what Requirement Dimension was associated with a particular response. At first, tracking the responses with the associated Requirement Dimension may have appeared unnecessary. After all, the ultimate goal was to identify the specific requirements and obtain data regarding customer satisfaction.

However, understanding how the requirements clustered around a particular Requirement Dimension assisted management during the final analysis. Continuing to use the Requirement Dimensions as a guide was found to be useful when, for instance, man-

EXHIBIT 4   PRELIMINARY INTERVIEW SUMMARY FORM

Interview with: _____ Date: _____

Title: _____ Function: _____ Division: _____

Service or Product	Customer	Quality Characteristic

Interview by: _____

agement looked at what customers considered basic Performance requirements versus Features or Tangibles. In addition, the importance and level of satisfaction could then be determined for both the individual requirements and for the cluster of requirements, such as Courtesy.

Conducting the interviews and analyzing the results were essential to constructing a meaningful customer satisfaction survey. Following the CRR methodology enabled management to design a survey they were confident contained items that were *driven by the customer.* Asking the customer to rate the importance of each item, along with the satisfaction, also enabled management to verify the significance of each customer requirement (Exhibit 5).

Clarifying customer requirements was also accomplished by asking the customer to consider importance and satisfaction on two levels:

• Satisfaction with the Albuquerque operation as a whole
• Satisfaction with the services provided by specific functions

To obtain the data on both levels, the survey was divided in two sections. Section One contained items written to obtain data on the customer's perception of the Albuquerque

EXHIBIT 5   ALBUQUERQUE OPERATION

Customer Satisfaction Survey

Section I. *Overall Satisfaction—Albuquerque Operation*
Instructions: For the following items, please indicate the importance and satisfaction rating that best reflects *your overall experience* with service(s) provided by the Albuquerque operation.

	Importance	**Assessment**
Use the following scales to rate the importance of each item and how often your requirement is met.	The item is . . .	My requirement is . . .
	1—Not Important	1—Never Met
	2—Of Minor Importance	2—Seldom Met
If you feel the item does not apply to you or your area, circle **N/A** and proceed to the next item.	3—Somewhat Important	3—Usually Met
	4—Important	4—Always Met
	5—Essential	5—Exceeded

Service Characteristic	**Importance**	**Assessment**
1. Accessibility of managers	N/A 1 2 3 4 5	1 2 3 4 5
2. Accessibility of staff (reps, clerks)	N/A 1 2 3 4 5	1 2 3 4 5
3. Responsiveness to my phone calls	N/A 1 2 3 4 5	1 2 3 4 5
4. Meets deadlines/turnaround commitments	N/A 1 2 3 4 5	1 2 3 4 5
5. Understands my requirements	N/A 1 2 3 4 5	1 2 3 4 5
6. Informs me of changes in advance	N/A 1 2 3 4 5	1 2 3 4 5
7. Prepares for meetings and teleconferences	N/A 1 2 3 4 5	1 2 3 4 5
8. Connects me with the correct individual	N/A 1 2 3 4 5	1 2 3 4 5
9. Provides accurate directory of staff	N/A 1 2 3 4 5	1 2 3 4 5
10. Takes a proactive versus reactive approach	N/A 1 2 3 4 5	1 2 3 4 5
11. Applies prevention whenever possible	N/A 1 2 3 4 5	1 2 3 4 5
12. Initiates creative solutions	N/A 1 2 3 4 5	1 2 3 4 5
13. Accurate information and reports	N/A 1 2 3 4 5	1 2 3 4 5
14. Legible documents (e.g., fax, invoice)	N/A 1 2 3 4 5	1 2 3 4 5
15. Thoroughly researched information	N/A 1 2 3 4 5	1 2 3 4 5
16. Qualified and trained staff	N/A 1 2 3 4 5	1 2 3 4 5
17. Understanding of my operational issues	N/A 1 2 3 4 5	1 2 3 4 5
18. Technical knowledge of systems/procedures	N/A 1 2 3 4 5	1 2 3 4 5
19. Professionalism of staff	N/A 1 2 3 4 5	1 2 3 4 5
20. Demonstrates interest in my requirements	N/A 1 2 3 4 5	1 2 3 4 5
21. Treats me with respect	N/A 1 2 3 4 5	1 2 3 4 5
22. Resolves problems in a timely manner	N/A 1 2 3 4 5	1 2 3 4 5
23. Notifies me when a problem has been resolved	N/A 1 2 3 4 5	1 2 3 4 5
24. Keeps me informed of potential problems	N/A 1 2 3 4 5	1 2 3 4 5
25. Displays pride in work and service provided	N/A 1 2 3 4 5	1 2 3 4 5
26. Demonstrates commitment to quality	N/A 1 2 3 4 5	1 2 3 4 5
27. Maintains a customer focus	N/A 1 2 3 4 5	1 2 3 4 5
28. Overall Performance Rating for the Albuquerque Operation		**1 2 3 4 5**

Please Return Survey by July 17, 1991

EXHIBIT 5   (Continued)

Section II. *Satisfaction with Specific Functions*

Instructions: This section contains items grouped by specific functions within the Albuquerque operation. If you receive services from, or have contact with, a particular function listed below, please complete the items listed in that group. For each item, indicate the importance and satisfaction rating that best reflects your experience with that particular function.

Complete only those functions that apply to you.

For example: Complete the items listed under Customer Billing Reports (CBR) if you receive services from (or have contact with) CBR. If you do not feel you are a customer of CBR, proceed to the next group, in this example, Credit.

Use the following scales to rate the importance of each item and how often your requirement is met.

If you feel the item does not apply to you or your area, circle **N/A** and proceed to the next item.

Importance The item is . . .	**Assessment** My requirement is . . .
1—Not Important	1—Never Met
2—Of Minor Importance	2—Seldom Met
3—Somewhat Important	3—Usually Met
4—Important	4—Always Met
5—Essential	5—Exceeded

Service Characteristic	**Importance**	**Assessment**

Customer Billing Reports (CBR):

	Importance	Assessment
1. Calls before sending a second/duplicate fax	N/A 1 2 3 4 5	1 2 3 4 5
2. Allows a two-day lead for P.O. requests	N/A 1 2 3 4 5	1 2 3 4 5
3. Understands work Customer Service performs	N/A 1 2 3 4 5	1 2 3 4 5
4. Uses the ADEPT system efficiently	N/A 1 2 3 4 5	1 2 3 4 5
5. Demonstrates persistent follow-up	N/A 1 2 3 4 5	1 2 3 4 5
6. **Overall Service Level of Customer Billing Reports (CBR)**		1 2 3 4 5

7. If the customer receives merchandise on June 2, CBR in Albuquerque receives the vendor invoice on June 7, and the customer order is placed in the system on June 15 . . .

N/A   7a. When would you expect the customer to be billed? _____

   7b. Based on your experience, when would this be billed? _____

8. If the customer receives merchandise on June 2, CBR in Albuquerque receives the vendor invoice on June 7, and the customer order is placed in the system on June 3 . . .

N/A   8a. When would you expect the customer to be billed? _____

   8b. Based on your experience, when would this be billed? _____

Credit and Collection (Hospital Supply and IV Systems):

	Importance	Assessment
1. Uses ARMS, ADEPT, microfiche efficiently	N/A 1 2 3 4 5	1 2 3 4 5
2. Reviews each account's DSO & aging weekly	N/A 1 2 3 4 5	1 2 3 4 5
3. Takes initiative to keep me informed	N/A 1 2 3 4 5	1 2 3 4 5
4. Demonstrates reliable follow through	N/A 1 2 3 4 5	1 2 3 4 5

Please Return Survey by July 17, 1991

EXHIBIT 5   (Continued)

5. Provides timely delivery information	N/A	1	2	3	4	5	1	2	3	4	5
6. Remains accessible to phone calls	N/A	1	2	3	4	5	1	2	3	4	5
7. Updates bad debt status throughout month	N/A	1	2	3	4	5	1	2	3	4	5
8. Demonstrates effective interpersonal skills	N/A	1	2	3	4	5	1	2	3	4	5
9. Provides required credit memo paperwork	N/A	1	2	3	4	5	1	2	3	4	5
10. **Overall Service Level of Credit** (Hospital Supply & IV Systems)							1	2	3	4	5

Hospital Supply Accounts Payable:

1. Researches to prevent duplicate payment	N/A	1	2	3	4	5	1	2	3	4	5
2. Understands the purchasing operations	N/A	1	2	3	4	5	1	2	3	4	5
3. Processes efficiently to take discounts	N/A	1	2	3	4	5	1	2	3	4	5
4. Remains accessible to vendors	N/A	1	2	3	4	5	1	2	3	4	5
5. Remains accessible to purchasing staff	N/A	1	2	3	4	5	1	2	3	4	5
6. Responds to phone calls within 24 hours	N/A	1	2	3	4	5	1	2	3	4	5
7. Is interested in meeting my requirements	N/A	1	2	3	4	5	1	2	3	4	5
8. Processes payment documents in 7 to 10 days	N/A	1	2	3	4	5	1	2	3	4	5
9. **Overall Service Level of Hospital Supply Accounts Payable**							1	2	3	4	5

Audit Control:

1. Clears outstanding items before 60 days	N/A	1	2	3	4	5	1	2	3	4	5
2. Performs research prior to bounce	N/A	1	2	3	4	5	1	2	3	4	5
3. Keeps me informed	N/A	1	2	3	4	5	1	2	3	4	5
4. Provides accurate received-not-paid (RNP) data for manual receivings	N/A	1	2	3	4	5	1	2	3	4	5
5. Clears factory return items before 30 days	N/A	1	2	3	4	5	1	2	3	4	5
6. Provides timely information & reports	N/A	1	2	3	4	5	1	2	3	4	5
7. Accurately reconciles items on paper close	N/A	1	2	3	4	5	1	2	3	4	5
8. Provides feedback and support to field	N/A	1	2	3	4	5	1	2	3	4	5
9. **Overall Service Level of Audit Control**							1	2	3	4	5

Corporate Accounts Payable:

1. Researches to prevent duplicate payment	N/A	1	2	3	4	5	1	2	3	4	5
2. Understands the purchasing operations	N/A	1	2	3	4	5	1	2	3	4	5
3. Processes efficiently to take discounts	N/A	1	2	3	4	5	1	2	3	4	5
4. Follows preferred vendor procedures	N/A	1	2	3	4	5	1	2	3	4	5
5. Remains accessible to purchasing/vendors	N/A	1	2	3	4	5	1	2	3	4	5
6. Responds promptly to phone calls	N/A	1	2	3	4	5	1	2	3	4	5
7. Assists users with A/P Flash & APAL	N/A	1	2	3	4	5	1	2	3	4	5
8. Provides accurate, researched information	N/A	1	2	3	4	5	1	2	3	4	5
9. Processes payment documents in 7 to 10 days	N/A	1	2	3	4	5	1	2	3	4	5
10. **Overall Service Level of Corporate Accounts Payable**							1	2	3	4	5

Please Return Survey by July 17, 1991

EXHIBIT 5   (Continued)

Section II. *Satisfaction with Specific Functions (continued)*
Cash Application:

1. Provides back-up within two working days	N/A 1 2 3 4 5	1 2 3 4 5
2. Provides requested check copies within two working days	N/A 1 2 3 4 5	1 2 3 4 5
3. Specialists are accessible to me	N/A 1 2 3 4 5	1 2 3 4 5
4. Responds to phone calls with 24 hours	N/A 1 2 3 4 5	1 2 3 4 5
5. Applies cash within two working days	N/A 1 2 3 4 5	1 2 3 4 5
6. Demonstrates professionalism	N/A 1 2 3 4 5	1 2 3 4 5
7. **Overall Service Level of Cash Application**		1 2 3 4 5

8. If a check is dated Monday, May 6 in the system, received in Albuquerque on May 7 . . .   N/A   8a. When would you expect the check to be applied? _____

8b. Based on your experience, when would it be applied? _____

Section III. *Improvement Opportunities*
Instructions: Use the space below for comments and suggestions. Feel free to include improvement opportunities for the Albuquerque operation or for a specific function. Additional space is provided on the back page of this booklet.

_____
_____
_____
_____
_____
_____
_____
_____
_____

Section IV. *General Information*
Instructions: Please complete the information listed below. The information will assist us with the interpretation of the survey data. In addition, this information will help us prepare our distribution list when we begin communicating the survey results back to you.

Function: _____

Title: _____

Location: _____
_____

Division: _____

Name: _____
              (optional)

Area: (check one)
[ ] Atlanta
[ ] Chicago
[ ] Columbus
[ ] Dallas
[ ] District of Columbia
[ ] Kansas City
[ ] Los Angeles
[ ] New York
[ ] San Francisco

Thank you very much for participating in the Albuquerque Operation Customer Satisfaction Survey. We appreciate your feedback and comments!

Please Return Survey by July 17, 1991

EXHIBIT 6 INITIAL SURVEY DATA—SECTION ONE

Assessment (Means)

Survey Item Number:	1	2	3	4	5	6	7	8	9	10	11	12	13	14	15	16	17	18	19	20	21	22	23	24	25	26	27	28
Overall Customer Response	2.75	3.14	3.41	2.97	2.8	2.57	2.87	3.29	3.0	2.75	2.74	2.37	3.16	3.46	2.88	2.95	2.66	2.93	3.53	3.19	3.85	3.0	2.86	2.62	3.39	3.11	2.93	2.96
Atlanta	2.67	3.57	4.16	2.5	2.86	2.57	2.67	3.4	2.6	2.86	2.71	2.71	2.86	3.66	3.14	2.71	2.14	2.43	3.86	3.43	4.33	3.0	2.4	2.33	2.86	2.71	2.5	2.86
Chicago	2.2	2.0	2.75	2.6	3.0	2.6	2.8	3.0	3.2	2.0	2.2	2.2	3.2	3.6	2.6	3.0	2.4	3.0	2.8	2.8	3.2	2.6	2.2	2.2	3.2	3.0	2.8	3.0
Columbus	2.5	3.0	3.0	3.0	3.0	3.5	2.0	2.0	2.5	2.5	3.0	3.0	3.0	3.5	2.5	3.5	3.0	2.5	3.0	3.17	4.0	3.0	3.0	2.5	3.0	3.0	2.5	2.29
Dallas	2.75	2.83	2.75	2.5	2.5	2.4	3.0	3.82	3.3	2.8	2.6	2.0	3.27	3.27	2.82	2.9	2.3	2.73	3.46	2.73	3.73	2.5	2.55	2.82	3.27	3.0	2.9	2.5
District of Columbia	2.5	2.83	3.6	3.0	3.26	2.0	3.5	3.75	3.5	2.5	3.0	2.25	3.2	3.6	2.6	2.83	2.22	3.0	3.83	3.67	4.17	3.4	2.75	2.6	3.8	3.4	3.0	2.8
Kansas City	3.17	3.2	3.17	3.33	2.83	3.0	3.25	3.5	3.33	3.4	2.67	2.8	3.17	3.83	3.33	3.17	3.0	2.83	3.67	3.5	4.17	3.33	3.33	3.0	3.83	3.33	3.33	3.17
Los Angeles/Irvine	2.83	3.0	3.6	3.25	3.0	2.8	3.0	3.2	3.33	3.0	3.0	2.5	3.33	3.33	2.83	3.0	3.0	3.17	4.17	3.5	4.0	3.17	3.17	2.67	3.33	3.33	3.33	3.3
New York/Edison	2.2	3.0	3.33	3.17	2.8	3.4	3.0	3.0	3.0	2.2	2.4	2.0	2.83	3.67	2.8	2.83	3.0	3.2	3.67	3.17	3.83	3.0	3.0	3.0	3.4	2.8	2.8	2.67
San Francisco/Hayward	3.29	3.57	3.5	2.71	2.57	2.57	3.5	3.5	3.0	2.83	2.83	2.14	3.0	3.17	2.57	2.71	2.57	2.71	3.43	2.83	3.57	3.0	2.83	2.67	3.57	3.0	2.57	3.14
Albuquerque Perception	3.19	3.47	3.51	3.25	3.28	2.97	3.33	3.36	3.48	3.1	3.12	3.25	3.52	3.5	3.33	3.52	3.24	3.31	3.38	3.22	3.57	3.18	3.04	2.98	3.59	3.39	3.42	3.61
HS Audit Control	3.25	3.67	3.67	2.8	3.22	2.78	2.57	3.56	3.33	3.1	3.0	3.1	3.67	3.63	3.67	3.44	2.89	3.38	3.5	3.22	3.44	2.78	3.1	3.0	3.67	3.8	3.33	3.43
Cash Application	3.11	3.6	3.44	4.0	3.5	3.11	3.56	3.2	3.2	3.4	3.4	3.1	3.4	3.2	3.1	3.6	3.5	3.6	3.4	3.4	3.3	3.3	2.9	3.0	3.6	3.5	3.5	3.75
Customer Billing	3.0	3.5	3.5	3.5	3.0	2.5	3.33	3.33	3.33	3.0	3.0	3.0	3.5	3.5	3.5	3.33	2.67	2.67	2.67	3.0	3.0	3.0	3.0	2.67	2.67	2.67	3.0	3.67
Credit and Collection	3.12	3.19	2.94	2.94	3.22	3.2	3.4	3.6	3.6	3.0	2.94	3.44	3.47	3.44	3.21	3.53	3.38	3.35	3.53	3.19	3.58	3.06	3.06	3.0	3.76	3.38	3.63	3.63
HS Accounts Payable	3.5	3.75	3.33	3.33	3.0	2.75	3.5	3.5	3.5	2.75	3.0	3.0	3.0	3.25	3.5	3.75	3.25	3.0	3.0	3.0	5.0	3.5	3.25	3.0	3.25	3.25	3.0	3.5

EXHIBIT 7 INITIAL SURVEY DATA—SECTION ONE

Importance (Means)

Survey Item Number:	1	2	3	4	5	6	7	8	9	10	11	12	13	14	15	16	17	18	19	20	21	22	23	24	25	26	27
Overall Customer Response	4.08	4.48	4.27	4.49	4.44	4.03	3.81	4.0	3.85	4.28	4.15	3.97	4.54	4.18	4.9	4.64	4.31	4.39	4.2	4.12	4.05	4.45	4.08	4.13	4.26	4.43	4.37
Atlanta	3.0	4.0	4.16	4.16	4.43	4.14	3.33	3.67	3.83	4.17	4.29	3.71	4.57	4.17	4.14	4.29	4.14	4.29	3.71	4.0	3.17	4.17	4.0	4.0	4.0	4.29	4.0
Chicago	4.4	4.8	4.5	4.8	4.4	4.0	3.8	4.0	3.4	4.6	4.2	4.2	4.6	4.2	4.2	4.8	4.2	4.8	4.0	4.2	3.6	4.4	4.0	4.2	4.0	4.4	4.2
Columbus	5.0	4.5	5.0	5.0	5.0	4.5	4.5	4.5	4.5	5.0	4.0	4.0	4.5	4.5	4.5	5.0	5.0	4.5	4.5	4.0	4.0	4.5	4.1	4.0	5.0	4.5	5.0
Dallas	4.25	4.58	4.58	4.54	4.58	4.1	4.0	4.27	3.8	4.4	4.27	4.09	4.36	4.36	4.45	4.36	4.45	4.36	4.36	4.36	4.55	4.64	4.25	4.1	4.27	4.36	4.27
District of Columbia	4.5	4.83	4.75	4.75	4.5	4.8	4.5	4.5	4.5	3.0	4.5	4.5	5.0	4.4	5.0	4.83	4.6	4.83	4.3	4.17	4.17	4.3	3.83	4.25	4.0	4.8	4.6
Kansas City	4.0	4.4	4.5	4.5	4.67	4.33	4.0	4.0	3.33	4.5	4.2	3.8	4.67	3.83	4.0	4.5	4.4	4.33	4.0	4.17	4.17	4.33	4.17	4.17	5.0	4.67	4.83
Los Angeles/Irvine	3.67	4.5	4.17	4.5	4.67	4.0	2.5	3.8	3.6	4.0	3.83	3.6	4.83	4.0	4.5	4.5	3.83	4.33	4.5	4.17	4.33	4.5	4.0	4.0	4.0	4.17	4.17
New York/Edison	4.2	4.33	4.33	4.33	4.17	4.0	4.0	3.4	3.5	4.2	3.8	4.0	4.33	4.0	4.2	4.5	4.0	4.2	4.17	3.83	3.83	4.33	4.0	4.0	4.2	4.6	4.6
San Francisco/Hayward	3.57	4.14	4.17	4.29	4.43	3.86	3.33	3.67	3.5	4.43	3.86	4.0	4.57	4.17	4.57	4.86	4.43	4.83	4.0	3.57	3.86	4.29	3.57	3.71	4.29	4.43	4.29
Albuquerque Perception	4.37	4.4	4.45	4.54	4.43	4.19	4.0	4.2	4.18	4.16	4.23	4.05	4.51	4.37	4.38	4.63	4.24	4.22	4.28	3.96	4.22	4.36	3.8	3.95	4.21	4.36	4.43
HS Audit Control	4.38	4.33	4.33	4.56	4.22	4.22	4.29	4.33	4.33	4.3	4.1	4.0	4.67	4.33	4.44	4.56	4.22	4.38	4.2	4.0	4.22	4.1	4.0	3.88	4.2	4.4	4.33
Cash Application	4.33	4.4	4.56	4.4	4.4	4.22	3.56	4.1	4.2	3.7	3.9	3.7	4.4	4.2	4.2	4.8	4.3	4.2	4.1	3.9	4.0	4.5	3.2	3.78	4.4	4.5	4.5
Customer Billing	4.0	4.0	4.5	4.5	4.5	4.0	4.0	3.67	4.0	3.5	4.0	4.0	4.5	5.0	4.5	4.3	3.3	3.3	3.67	3.3	3.67	4.0	4.0	3.3	3.3	3.3	4.0
Credit and Collection	4.53	4.59	4.65	4.31	4.31	4.25	4.13	4.13	4.07	4.56	4.44	4.31	4.53	4.29	4.47	4.65	4.29	4.29	4.58	4.06	4.38	4.5	4.06	4.19	4.29	4.4	4.53
HS Accounts Payable	4.25	4.25	4.25	4.25	4.5	4.25	3.5	4.25	4.5	4.25	4.5	4.0	4.25	3.67	4.5	4.5	4.25	4.25	4.5	4.25	4.5	4.25	3.75	4.5	4.25	4.5	4.5

626

EXHIBIT 8   INITIAL SURVEY DATA—SECTIONS ONE AND TWO (MEANS)

Dimension/Item	Customer Response		Albuquerque Perception	
	Importance	Assessment	Importance	Assessment
Performance				
#4 Meets deadlines	4.49	2.97	4.54	3.25
#5 Understands requirements	4.44	2.8	4.43	3.28
#10 Takes proactive approach	4.28	2.75	4.16	3.1
#11 Applies prevention	4.15	2.74	4.23	3.12
#13 Accurate information	4.54	3.16	4.51	3.52
#22 Timely problem resolution	4.45	3.0	4.36	3.18
Responsiveness				
#1 Accessibility of managers	4.06	2.75	4.37	3.19
#2 Accessibility of staff	4.48	3.14	4.4	3.47
#3 Responsiveness of phone calls	4.27	3.41	4.45	3.51
#23 Notification of problem resolution	4.06	2.86	3.8	3.04
#27 Maintains customer focus	4.37	2.93	4.43	3.42
Credibility				
#16 Qualified and trained staff	4.64	2.95	4.63	3.52
#17 Understands operational issues	4.31	2.66	4.24	3.24
#18 Technical knowledge	4.39	2.93	4.22	3.31
#25 Displays pride in work	4.25	3.39	4.21	3.59
Reliability				
#7 Prepares for meetings	3.81	2.87	4.0	3.33
#8 Connects customer with correct staff	4.0	3.29	4.2	3.36
#24 Keeps customer informed	4.13	2.62	3.95	2.98
#26 Demonstrates commitment to quality	4.43	3.11	4.36	3.39
Courtesy				
#19 Professionalism	4.2	3.53	4.28	3.38
#20 Interest in customer requirements	4.12	3.19	3.96	3.36
#21 Treats customer with respect	4.06	3.85	4.22	3.57
Tangibles				
#14 Legible documents	4.18	3.46	4.37	3.5
#15 Thorough research	4.9	2.88	4.38	3.33
Features				
#9 Accurate directory of staff	3.85	3.0	4.18	3.48
#12 Initiates create solutions	3.97	2.37	4.05	3.25
Security				
#6 Informs customer of changes	4.03	2.57	4.18	2.97
Overall Satisfaction (#28)	**	2.96	**	3.61
Customer Billing*	**	2.78	**	4.0
Credit and Collection*	**	3.06	**	3.64
Hospital Supply Accounts Payable*	**	3.11	**	4.0
Hospital Supply Audit Control*	**	2.33	**	3.2
Cash Application*	**	3.36	**	4.36

*Response in Section Two.

**No importance for Rating Overall Satisfaction Items.

operation. Section Two contained items grouped by specific functions within Albuquerque, such as Credit and Collection, Audit Control, and Cash Application. The customer was asked to complete Section One and limit response in Section Two to only those functions from which they received services. Each function in Section Two included an item asking the customer to rate the overall satisfaction of that particular function.

THE RESULTS

The data from the customer satisfaction survey was compiled using a relatively simple database structure. Each record was differentiated by area, division, and function. The overall response rate was 45%, although the response by area varied slightly. In addition to completing the first two sections of the survey, 65% of the respondents included written comments. The comments included both positive and negative feedback, primarily referring to issues surrounding communication, procedures, and staffing.

Management began sorting the data, focusing on the responses to the items in the first section. The data was also sorted by specific requirement and examining importance ratings and assessment rating. The input obtained by management and employee teams was sorted using the same method for comparison. Although data obtained in the second section was noted and tabulated, the initial analysis focused on comparing the overall satisfaction rating of specific functions compared with the overall satisfaction rating of the Albuquerque operation. Further analysis of both the first and second sections assisted in identifying Albuquerque-wide issues versus specific functional issues (Exhibits 6-8).

WHAT NEXT?

After compiling the data and entering the numbers into the database, the means were calculated for each item, on importance and assessment, and were sorted primarily by operational area. The means of the customer responses were also compared with the means of the Albuquerque perception. Even though the initial analysis focused on only the first section of the survey, examining the data was overwhelming.

"The analysis of the customer response could be looked at in many different ways," but Finley wondered, "In order to make the best use of the data, what direction should the analysis take? What can be concluded from the data? And once we have the conclusions, who should receive the information? How should the information be communicated? And how should we use the information?"

SHOULDICE HOSPITAL LIMITED

Two shadowy figures, enrobed and in slippers, walked slowly down the semidarkened hall of the Shouldice Hospital. They didn't notice Alan O'Dell, the hospital administrator, and his guest, who had just emerged from the basement boiler room on a tour of the facility. Once they were out of earshot, O'Dell remarked good naturedly, "By the way they act, you'd think our patients own this place. And while they're here, in a way they do."

Following a visit to the five operating rooms, also located on the first of three levels, O'Dell and his visitor once again encountered the same pair of patients still engrossed in discussing their hernia operations, which had been performed the previous morning.

HISTORY

Born on a farm in Bruce County, Ontario, Dr. Earle Shouldice, who was to found the hospital bearing his name, first displayed his interest in medical research at the age of 12. He performed a postmortem on a calf that, he discovered, had died from an intestinal obstruction. After a year of following the wishes of his parents that he study for the ministry, Shouldice persuaded them to let him enroll in medicine at the University of Toronto.

Professor James L. Heskett prepared this case as a basis for class discussion rather than to illustrate either effective or ineffective handling of an administrative situation. Some of the data in this case are disguised.
Copyright © 1983 by the President and Fellows of Harvard College.

An attractive brochure that was recently printed, although neither dated nor distributed to prospective patients, described Earle Shouldice as follows:

While carrying on a private medical and surgical practice in the years between the two World Wars and holding a post as lecturer in anatomy at the University of Toronto, Dr. Shouldice continued to pursue his interest in research. He did pioneer work towards the cure of pernicious anemia, intestinal obstruction, hydrocephalic cases and other areas of advancing medical knowledge.

His interest in early ambulation stemmed, in part, from an operation he performed in 1932 to remove the appendix from a seven-year-old girl and the girl's subsequent refusal to stay quietly in bed. In spite of her activity, no harm was done, and the experience recalled to the doctor the postoperative actions of animals upon which he had performed surgery. They had all moved about freely with no ill effects. Four years later he was reminded of the child when he allowed washroom privileges immediately following the operations to four men recovering from hernia repair. All had trouble-free recovery.

By the outset of the Second World War in 1940, Shouldice had given extensive thought to several factors that contributed to early ambulation following surgery. Among them were the use of a local anesthetic, the nature of the surgical procedure itself, the design of a facility to encourage movement without unnecessarily causing discomfort, and the postoperative regimen designed and communicated by the medical team. With all of these things in mind, he had begun to develop a surgical technique for repairing hernias[1] that was superior to others. He offered his services in correcting hernias for army inductees who otherwise would not qualify for service. Because hospital beds often were not available, sometimes the surgery took place in the emergency department of the Toronto General Hospital, and the patients were transported later in the day to a medical fraternity where they were cared for by medical students for two or three days.

By the war's end, word of the Shouldice technique had spread sufficiently that 200 civilians had contacted the doctor and were awaiting surgery upon his discharge from the army. Because of the scarcity of hospital beds, particularly for an operation that was considered elective and of relatively low priority, he started his own hospital. Dr. Shouldice's medical license permitted him to operate anywhere, even on a kitchen table, and consequently he received authorization from the provincial government to open his first hospital in a six-room nursing home in downtown Toronto in July 1945. As more and more patients requested operations, Dr. Shouldice extended his facilities by buying a rambling 130-acre estate with a 17,000-square-foot main house in the suburb of Thornhill, 15 miles north of downtown Toronto. Initially, a 36-bed capacity was created in Thornhill, but after some years of planning, a large wing was added to the house to provide a total capacity of 89 beds.

---

[1]Most hernias, known as external abdominal hernias, were protrusions of some part of the abdominal contents through a hole or slit in the muscular layers of the abdominal wall which was supposed to contain them. Well over 90% of these hernias occurred in the groin area. Of these, by far the most common were inguinal hernias, many of which were caused by a slight weakness in the muscle layers brought about by the passage of the testicle in male babies through the groin area shortly before birth. Aging also caused inguinal hernias to develop. The other, much less common, external hernias were called "femoral," in which a protrusion appeared in the top inch or so of the thigh. Because of the cause of the affliction, 85% of all hernias occurred in males.

At the time of his death in 1965, Dr. Shouldice's long-time associate, Dr. Nicholas Obney, was named surgeon-in-chief and chairman of the board of Shouldice Hospital Limited, the corporation formed to operate both the hospital and clinical facilities. Under Dr. Obney's leadership, the volume of activity continued to increase, reaching a total of 6,850 operations in the 1982 calendar year.

THE SHOULDICE METHOD

Only external types of abdominal hernias were repaired at Shouldice Hospital. Internal types, such as hiatus (or diaphragmatic) hernias, were not treated. As a result, most first-time repairs (called primaries) involved straight-forward operating procedures that required about 45 minutes. Primaries represented approximately 82% of all operations performed at Shouldice in 1982. The remaining 18% involved patients suffering recurrences of hernias previously repaired elsewhere.[2]

In the Shouldice method, the muscles of the abdominal wall were arranged in three distinct layers, and the opening was repaired—each layer in turn—by overlapping its margins in much the same manner as the edges of a coat might be overlapped when buttoned. The end result was to reinforce the muscular wall of the abdomen with six rows of sutures (stitches) under the skin cover, which was then closed with clamps that were removed within 48 hours after the operation. (Other methods might not separate muscle layers, often involved fewer rows of sutures, and sometimes involved the insertion of screens or meshes under the skin.)

The typical first-time repair could be completed with the use of preoperative sedation (sleeping pill) and analgesic (pain killer) plus a local anesthetic, an injection of Novocain in the region of the incision. This allowed immediate patient ambulation and facilitated rapid recovery. Many of the recurrences and the very difficult hernia repairs, being more complex, could require up to 90 minutes and more. In some circumstances, a general anesthetic was administered.

THE PATIENTS' EXPERIENCE

It was thought that most potential Shouldice patients learned about the hospital and its methods from past patients who had already experienced them. Although over 1,000 doctors had referred patients, doctors were less likely to recommend Shouldice because of the generally regarded simplicity of the surgery, often considered a "bread and butter" operation. Typically, many patients had their problem diagnosed by a personal physician and then took the initiative to contact Shouldice. Many more made this diagnosis themselves and contacted the hospital directly.

The process experienced by Shouldice patients depended on whether or not they lived close enough to the hospital to visit the facility to obtain a diagnosis. Approxi-

---

[2]Based on a careful tracking of its patients over more than 30 years, it was estimated that the gross recurrence rate for all operations performed at Shouldice was 0.8%. Recurrence rates reported in the literature for these types of hernia varied greatly. However, one text published around that time stated, "In the United States the gross rate of recurrence for groin hernias approaches 10%."

mately 42% of all Shouldice patients came from the United States. Another 2% originated from provinces other than Ontario and from European countries. These out-of-town patients often were diagnosed by mail, using the Medical Information questionnaire shown in *Exhibit 1*.

Of every eight questionnaires sent, seven were returned to the hospital in completed form. Based on information in the questionnaire, a Shouldice surgeon would determine the type of hernia the respondent had and whether there were signs that some risk might be associated with surgery (for example, an overweight or heart condition, or a patient who had suffered a heart attack or a stroke in the past six months to a year, or whether a general or local anesthetic was required). At this point, a patient was given an operating date, the medical information was logged into a computerized data base, and the patient was sent a confirmation card; if necessary, a sheet outlining a weight-loss program prior to surgery and a brochure describing the hospital and the Shouldice method were also sent. A small proportion was refused treatment, either because they were too fat, represented an undue medical risk, or because it was determined that they did not have a hernia.

If confirmation cards were not returned by the patient three days or more prior to the scheduled operation, that patient was contacted by phone. Upon confirmation, the patient's folder was sent to the reception desk to await his or her arrival.[3]

Arriving at the clinic between 1:00 P.M. and 3:00 P.M. the day before the operation, a patient might joint up with 30 to 34 other patients and their friends and families in the waiting room. After a typical wait of about 20 minutes—depending on the availability of surgeons—a patient was examined in one of six examination rooms staffed by surgeons who had completed their operating schedules for the day. This examination required no more than 15 to 20 minutes, unless the patient needed reassurance. (Patients typically exhibited a moderate level of anxiety until their operation was completed.) At this point it occasionally was discovered that a patient had not corrected his or her weight problem; others might be found not to have a hernia after all. In either case, the patient was sent home.

Following his or her examination, a patient might experience a wait of 5 to 15 minutes to see one of two admitting personnel in the accounting office. Here, health insurance coverage was checked, and various details were discussed in a procedure that usually lasted no more than 10 minutes. Patients sometimes exhibited their nervousness by asking many questions at this point, requiring more time of the receptionist.

Patients next were sent to one of two nurses' stations where, in 5 to 10 minutes and with little wait, their hemoglobin (blood) and urine were checked. At this point, about an hour after arriving at the hospital, a patient was directed to the room number shown

---

[3]Patients living within 50 miles from the hospital (about 40% of all patients) were encouraged to come to the clinic on a walk-in basis for an examination, usually requiring no more than 15 or 20 minutes for the physical and completion of an information questionnaire. If the doctor performing the examination diagnosed the problem as an external hernia, the individual could obtain immediately a future booking for the operation. On occasion, when a previously booked patient canceled at the last minute, a walk-in patient, or one selected from a special waiting list, could be scheduled for the next day. At the time of booking, the potential patient was given a specific date for the operation, a letter estimating the total cost of the operation (as required by the Ontario provincial government for all Ontario residents), and information supplied to out-of-province patients.

EXHIBIT 1   MEDICAL INFORMATION QUESTIONNAIRE

FAMILY NAME (Last Name)	FIRST NAME	MIDDLE NAME

STREET & NUMBER (or Rural Route or P.O. Box)	Town/City	Province/State

County	Township	Zip or Postal Code	Birthdate: Month Day Year

Telephone
Home ....
Work .... If none, give
neighbour's number ....

	Married or Single	Religion

NEXT OF KIN: Name ....   Address ....   Telephone #

INSURANCE INFORMATION: Please give name of Insurance Company and Numbers.

	Date form completed

HOSPITAL INSURANCE: (Please bring hospital certificates)

OTHER HOSPITAL INSURANCE

O.H.I.P.   BLUE CROSS   Company Name
Number   Policy Number

SURGICAL INSURANCE: (Please bring hospital certificates)

OTHER SURGICAL INSURANCE

O.H.I.P.   BLUE SHIELD   Company Name
Number   Policy Number

WORKMEN'S COMPENSATION BOARD

	Approved	Social Insurance (Security) Number
Claim No.	Yes No	

Occupation ....   Name of Business ....   Are you the Owner? Yes   No   If Retired – Former Occupation

How did you hear about Shouldice Hospital? (If referred by a doctor, give name & address)

Are you a former patient of Shouldice Hospital?	Yes No	Do you smoke? Yes No

Have you ever written to Shouldice Hospital in the past?   Yes   No

What is your preferred admission date? (Please give as much advance notice as possible)

No admissions Friday, Saturday or Sunday.

FOR OFFICE USE ONLY		
Date Received	Type of Hernia	Weight Loss
		lbs.

Consent to Operate ☐	Special Instructions	Approved
Heart Report ☐		
Referring Doctor Notified		Operation Date

SHOULDICE HOSPITAL

7750 Bayview Avenue
Box 370, Thornhill, Ontario L3T 4A3 Canada
Phone (416) 889-1125

(Thornhill - One Mile North Metro Toronto)

MEDICAL INFORMATION

Patients who live at a distance often prefer their examination, admission and operation to be arranged all on a single visit – to save making two lengthy journeys. The whole purpose of this questionnaire is to make such arrangements possible, although, of course, it cannot replace the examination in any way. Its completion and return will not put you under any obligation.

Please be sure to fill in both sides.

This information will be treated as confidential.

(continued on next page)

633

EXHIBIT 1   MEDICAL INFORMATION QUESTIONNAIRE (Continued)

THIS CHART IS FOR EXPLANATION ONLY

Ordinary hernias are mostly either

at the navel ("belly-button") - or just above it

or down in the groin area on either side

An **"incisional hernia"** is one that bulges through the scar of any other **surgical operation** that has failed to hold — wherever it may be.

THIS IS YOUR CHART – PLEASE MARK IT!

(MARK THE POSITION OF EACH HERNIA YOU WANT REPAIRED WITH AN "X")

APPROXIMATE SIZE . . . .
Walnut (or less)
Hen's Egg or Lemon
Grapefruit (or more)

ESSENTIAL EXTRA INFORMATION

Use only the sections that apply to your hernias and put a √ in each box that seems appropriate

NAVEL AREA (AND JUST ABOVE NAVEL) ONLY
Is this navel (bellybutton) hernia your FIRST one?   Yes ☐   No ☐

If it's NOT your first, how many repair attempts so far? ☐

GROIN HERNIA ONLY

	RIGHT GROIN	LEFT GROIN
Is this your FIRST GROIN HERNIA ON THIS SIDE?	Yes ☐ No ☐	Yes ☐ No ☐

How many **hernia** operations in this groin already?   Right ☐   Left ☐

DATE OF LAST OPERATION [＿＿＿＿＿＿＿＿]

INCISIONAL HERNIAS ONLY (the ones bulging through previous operation scars)
Was the **original** operation for your Appendix? ☐, or Gallbladder? ☐, or Stomach? ☐, or Prostrate? ☐, or Hysterectomy? ☐, or Other? ......

How many attempts to repair the hernia have been made so far? ☐

PLEASE BE ACCURATE! Misleading figures, when checked on admission day, could mean postponement of your operation till your weight is suitable.

HEIGHT ...... ft. ...... ins.   **WEIGHT** ...... lbs. Nude   Recent gain? ...... lbs.
                                                  or just pyjamas   Recent loss? ...... lbs.

Waist (muscles relaxed) ...... ins.   **Chest** (not expanded) ...... ins.

GENERAL HEALTH

Age ...... years   Is your health now GOOD ☐, FAIR ☐, or POOR ☐

Please mention briefly any **severe past illness** – such as a "heart attack" or a "stroke", for example, from which you have now recovered (and its approximate date) ......

We need to know about other present conditions, even though your admission is NOT likely to be refused because of them.

Please tick ☑ any condition for which you are having **regular treatment:**

Blood Pressure ☐
Excess Body Fluids ☐
Chest Pain ("angina") ☐
Irregular Heartbeat ☐
Diabetes ☐
Asthma & Bronchitis ☐
Ulcers ☐
Anticoagulants ☐
(to delay blood-clotting or to "thin the blood")
Other ☐

Name of any prescribed pills, **tablets** or **capsules** you take regulary: –

Did you remember to MARK AN "X" on your body chart to show us where each of your hernias is located?

on his or her wrist band. Throughout the process, patients were asked to keep their luggage (usually light and containing only a few items suggested by the hospital) with them.

All patient rooms at the hospital were semiprivate, containing two beds. Patients with similar jobs, backgrounds, or interests were assigned to the same room to the extent possible. Upon reaching their rooms, patients busied themselves unpacking, getting acquainted with roommates, changing into pajamas, "prepping" themselves (shaving themselves in the area of the operation), and providing a urine sample.

At 5:00 P.M. a nurse's orientation provided the group of incoming patients with information about what to expect, the drugs to be administered, the need for exercise after the operation, the facility, and the daily routine. According to Alan O'Dell, "Half are so nervous they don't remember much from the orientation." Dinner was served from 5:30 to 6:00 P.M. in a 100-seat dining room on a first-come, first-served basis. Following further recreation, tea and cookies were served at 9:00 P.M. in the lounge area. Nurses emphasized the importance of attendance at that time because it provided an opportunity for preoperative patients to talk with those whose operations had been completed earlier that same day. Nearly all new patients were "tucked into bed" between 9:30 and 10:00 P.M. in preparation for an early awakening prior to their operations.

Patients to be operated on early in the day were awakened at 5:30 A.M. to be given preop sedation and to be dressed in an O.R. (operating room) gown. An attempt was made to schedule operations for roommates at approximately the same time. Patients were taken to the preoperating room where the circulating nurse administered Demerol, an analgesic, 45 minutes before surgery. A few minutes prior to the first operation at 7:30 A.M., the surgeon assigned to each patient administered Novocain, a local anesthetic. During the operation, it was the responsibility of the circulating nurse to monitor the patient's comfort, to note times at which the Novocain was administered and the operation begun, and to arrange for the administration of Demerol to the patient scheduled next on the operating table, depending on the progress of the surgery under way. This was in contrast to the typical hospital procedure in which patients were sedated in their rooms prior to being taken to the operating rooms.

Upon the completion of the operation, during which a few patients were "chatty" and fully aware of what was going on, patients were invited to get off the operating table and walk to the post-operating room with the help of their surgeons. According to Ursula Verstraete, director of nursing:

> Ninety-nine percent accept the surgeon's invitation. While we put them in wheelchairs to return them to their rooms, the walk from the operating table is for psychological as well as physiological [blood pressure, respiratory] reasons. Patients prove to themselves that they can do it, and they start their all-important exercise immediately.

Throughout the day after their operation, patients were encouraged to exercise by nurses and housekeepers alike. By 9:00 P.M. on the day of their operations, all patients were ready and able to walk down to the dining room for tea and cookies, even if it meant climbing stairs, to help indoctrinate the new "class" admitted that day.

Patients in their second or third day of recovery were awakened before 6:00 A.M. so they could loosen up for breakfast, which was served between 7:45 and 8:15 A.M. in the dining room. Good posture and exercise were thought to aid digestion and deter the buildup of gas that could prove painful. After breakfast on the first day after surgery, all of the skin clips (resembling staples) holding the skin together over the incision were loosened and some removed. The remainder were removed the next day. On the fourth morning, patients were ready for discharge.

During their stay, patients were encouraged to take advantage of the opportunity to explore the premises and make new friends. Some members of the staff felt that the patients and their attitudes were the most important element of the Shouldice program. According to Dr. Byrnes Shouldice, the 53-year-old son of the founder and vice president of the corporation—a surgeon on the staff and a 50% owner of the hospital:

> Patients sometimes ask to stay an extra day. Why? Well, think about it. They are basically well to begin with. But they arrive with a problem and a certain amount of nervousness, tension, and anxiety about their surgery. Their first morning here they're operated on and experience a sense of relief from something that's been bothering them for a long time. They are immediately able to get around, and they've got a three-day holiday ahead of them with a perfectly good reason to be away from work with no sense of guilt. They share experiences with other patients, make friends easily, and have the run of the hospital. In summer, the most common after-effect from the surgery is sunburn. They kid with the staff and make this a positive experience for all of us.

The average patient stay for comparable operations at other hospitals was thought to be five to seven or eight days, but it had been declining because of a shortage of beds and the tendency to give elective surgery a low priority for beds. Shouldice patients with jobs involving light exercise could return to work within a week after their operations, but those involved in more strenuous work, whose benefits were insured, received four weeks of benefits and recuperation. All self-employed persons returned to work much earlier. In general, typical times for recuperation from similar operations at other hospitals were two weeks for those in jobs requiring light exercise and eight weeks for those in more strenuous jobs, due largely to long-established treatment regimens.

THE NURSES' EXPERIENCE

The nursing staff comprised 22 full-time and 19 part-time members. They were divided into four groups (as shown in *Exhibit 2*), with supervisors for the hospital, operating room, laboratory, and central supply reporting to Ursula Verstraete, the director of nursing.

While the operating rooms were fully staffed from about 7 A.M. through the last operation ending in the mid- to late afternoon, the hospital was staffed with three shifts beginning at 7 A.M., 3 P.M., and 11 P.M. Even so, minimal patient needs for physical assistance allowed Shouldice to operate with a much lower nurse-to-patient ratio than the typical hospital. Shouldice nurses spent an unusually large proportion of their time in counseling activities. As one supervisor commented, "We don't use bedpans." In a typical year, Verstraete estimated that she might experience a turnover of four nurses.

EXHIBIT 2   ORGANIZATION CHART

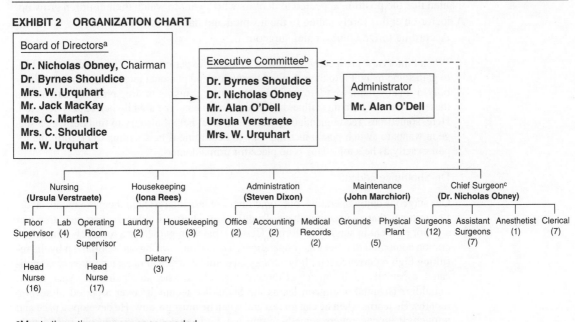

[a]Meets three times a year or as needed.
[b]Meets as needed (usually twice a month).
[c]Informally reports to Executive Committee.

THE DOCTORS' EXPERIENCE

The hospital employed 12 full-time surgeons, 7 part-time assistant surgeons, and one anesthetist. Each operating team required a surgeon, an assistant surgeon, a scrub nurse, and a circulating nurse. The operating load varied from 30 to 36 operations per day. As a result, each surgeon typically performed three or four operations each day.

A typical surgeon's day started with a *scrubbing* shortly before the first scheduled operation at 7:30 A.M. If the first operation was routine, it usually was completed by 8:15 A.M. At its conclusion, the surgical team helped the patient walk from the room and summoned the next patient. While the patient was being prepared and awaiting the full effects of the Demerol to set in, the surgeon completed the previous patient's file by dictating five or so minutes of comments concerning the operation. Postoperative instructions were routine unless specific instructions were issued by the surgeon. After scrubbing, the surgeon could be ready to operate again at 8:30 A.M.

Surgeons were advised to take a coffee break after their second or third operation. Even so, a surgeon could complete three routine operations and a fourth involving a recurrence (a 60- to 90-minute procedure) and still be finished in time for a 12:30 P.M. lunch in the staff dining room.Upon finishing lunch, as many as six of the surgeons not scheduled to operate in the afternoon moved upstairs to examine incoming patients between 1:00 and 3:00 P.M. A surgeon's day ended by 4:00 P.M. In addition, a surgeon could expect to be on call one weekday night in ten and one weekend in ten. Alan O'Dell commented that the position appealed to doctors who "want to watch their children grow up. A doctor on call is rarely called to the hospital and has regular hours."

According to Dr. Obney, chief surgeon:

When I interview prospective surgeons, I look for experience and a good education. I try to gain some insight into their domestic situation and personal interests and habits. Naturally, as in any field, we try to avoid anyone with a drinking or drug problem. Oftentimes these people can hide their illness very well and it can take a while before it is detected. Here, sometimes, recommendations can be of great help. I also try to find out why a surgeon wants to switch positions. And I try to determine if he's willing to perform the repair exactly as he's told. This is no place for prima donnas.

Dr. Shouldice added:

Our surgeons enjoy operating, but sometimes are less interested in the more mundane office routines that all vocations have. Traditionally a hernia is often the first operation that a junior resident in surgery performs. Hernia repair is regarded as a relatively simple operation compared to other major operations. This is quite wrong, as is borne out by the resulting high recurrence rate. It is a tricky anatomical area and occasionally very complicated, especially to the novice or those doing very few hernia repairs each year. But at Shouldice Hospital a surgeon learns the Shouldice technique over a period of several months. He learns when he can go fast and when he must go slow. He develops a pace and a touch. If he encounters something unusual, he is encouraged to consult immediately with other surgeons. We teach each other and try to encourage a group effort. And he learns not to take risks to achieve absolute perfection. Excellence is the enemy of good.

Dr. Obney assigned surgeons to an operating room on a daily basis by noon of the preceding day. This allowed surgeons to examine the specific patients that they were to operate on. Surgeons and assistants were rotated every few days. Scrub nurses and circulating nurses were assigned to a new operating room every two weeks and four weeks, respectively. Unless patients requested specific doctors, cases were assigned to give doctors a nonroutine operation (often involving a recurrence) several times a week. More complex procedures were assigned to more senior and experienced members of the staff, including Dr. Obney himself. Where possible, former Shouldice patients suffering recurrences were assigned to the doctor who performed the first operation "to allow the doctor to learn from his mistake."

As Dr. Obney commented:

If something goes wrong, we want to make sure that we have an experienced surgeon in charge, and we don't like surgeons who work too fast. Experience is most important. The typical general surgeon may perform 25 to 50 hernia operations per year. Ours perform 600 or more.

The 12 full-time surgeons were paid a straight salary. A typical starting salary at that time for someone with 5 to 10 years of experience was $50,000. In addition, bonuses to doctors were voted by the board of directors twice a year, depending on profit and performance. The total bonus pool paid to the surgeons in a recent year was approximately $500,000. Assisting surgeons were part-time, and they received 51% of the $60 fee that was charged to patients who received their services.

The anesthetist was hired for $300 per day from a nearby partnership. Only one was required to be on duty on any given day and could supervise all five operating rooms in addition to administering an occasional general anesthetic to a patient with a complex case or to a child.

Training in the Shouldice technique was important because the procedure could not be varied. It was accomplished through direct supervision by one or more of the senior surgeons. The rotation of teams and frequent consultations allowed for an ongoing opportunity to appraise performance and take corrective action.

According to Dr. Obney:

> We haven't had to let anyone go because they couldn't learn, or continue to adhere to, the method. However, a doctor must decide after several years whether he wants to do this for the rest of his life because, just as in other specialties—for example, radiology—he loses touch with other medical disciplines. If he stays for five years, he doesn't leave. Even among younger doctors, few elect to leave.

THE FACILITY

A tour of the facility with Alan O'Dell yielded some interesting information. The Shouldice Hospital comprised two basic facilities in one building—the hospital and the clinic.

On the first-level opening to grade at the back of the building, the hospital contained the kitchen and dining rooms as well as the office of the supervisor of housekeeping. The second level, also opening to grade but at the front of the building, contained a large, open lounge area, the admissions offices, patient rooms, and a spacious glass-covered Florida room. The third level had additional patient rooms, a large lounge, and a recreational area.

Throughout the tour, patients could be seen visiting in each others' rooms, walking up and down hallways, lounging in the sunroom, and making use of light recreational facilities ranging from a pool table to an exercycle.

Alan O'Dell pointed out some of the features of the hospital:

> The rooms contain no telephones or television sets. If a patient needs to make a call or wants to watch television, he or she has to take a walk. The steps are designed specially with a small rise to allow patients recently operated on to negotiate the stairs without undue discomfort. Every square foot of the hospital is carpeted to reduce the hospital feeling and the possibility of a fall. Carpeting also gives the place a smell other than that of disinfectant.
>
> This facility was designed by Dr. Byrnes Shouldice. He thought about it for years and made many changes in the plan before the first concrete was poured. A number of unique policies were also instituted. Because Dr. Shouldice started out to be a minister, ministers are treated gratis. And you see that mother and child in the next room? Parents accompanying children here for an operation stay free. You may wonder why we can do it, but we learned that we save more in nursing costs than we spend for the patient's room and board. Children may present difficulties in a hospital environment, but when accompanied by a parent, the parent is happier and so is the child.

While patients and staff were served food prepared in the same kitchen, the staff was required to pick up its food from a cafeteria line placed in the very center of the kitchen. This provided an opportunity for everyone to chat with the kitchen staff several times a day as they picked up a meal or stopped for coffee. Patients were served in the adjoining patient dining room.

According to O'Dell:

We use all fresh ingredients and prepare the food from scratch in the kitchen. Our kitchen staff of three prepares about 100 breakfasts, 200 lunches, and 100 dinners each day at an average raw food cost of $1.10 per meal.

Iona Rees, director of housekeeping, pointed out:

We do all of our own laundry in the building with two full-time employees. And I have only three on my housekeeping staff for the entire facility. One of the reasons for so few housekeepers is that we don't need to change linens during a patient's four-day stay. They are basically well, so there is no soiling of bed linens. Also, the medical staff doesn't want the patients in bed all day. They want the nurses to encourage the patients to be up socializing, comparing notes [for confidence], encouraging each other, and walking around, getting exercise.

Of course, we're in the rooms straightening up throughout the day. This gives the housekeepers a chance to josh with the patients and to encourage them to exercise.

The bottom level of the clinic housed five operating rooms, a laboratory, the patient-recovery room, and a central supply area where surgical instruments were cleaned and sterilized. This was the only area of the entire facility that was not carpeted, to prevent static electricity from forming in areas where potentially explosive anesthetics might be used. In total, the estimated cost to furnish an operating room was no more than $30,000. This was considerably less than for other hospitals requiring a bank of equipment with which to administer anesthetics for each room. At Shouldice, two mobile units were used by the anesthetist when needed. In addition, the complex had one "crash cart" per floor for use if a patient should suffer a heart attack or stroke during his or her hospital stay.

The first floor of the clinic containing admissions and accounting offices, a large waiting room with a capacity for as many as 50 people, and 6 examination rooms. On the second floor of the clinic, situated in much of what was the original house, was found the administrative offices. A third floor contained 14 additional hostel rooms where patients could be held overnight awaiting the assignment of a room and their operations. At such times when the hospital was particularly crowded, doctors were asked to identify those postoperative patients who could be released a day early. Often these were local residents or children.

ADMINISTRATION

Alan O'Dell, while he walked, described his job:

I'm responsible for a little of everything around here. We try to meet people's needs and make this as good a place to work as possible. My door is always open. And members of our staff will come in to seek advice about everything from medical to marital problems.

There is a strong concern for employees here. Nobody is fired. [This was later reinforced by Dr. Shouldice, who described a situation involving two employees who confessed to theft in the hospital. They agreed to seek psychiatric help and were allowed to remain on the job.] As a result, turnover is low.

We don't have a union, but we try to maintain a pay scale higher than the union scale for comparable jobs in the area. For example, our nurses receive from $15,000 to $25,000 per year, depending on the number of years' experience. We have a profit-sharing plan that is separate from the doctors'. Last year the employees divided up $65,000.

If work needs to be done, people pitch in to help each other. A unique aspect of our administration is that I insist that each secretary is trained to do another's work and in an emergency is able to switch to another function immediately and enable the more vital workload to proceed uninterrupted. With the exception of the accounting staff, every secretary, regardless of her or his position in the hospital, is trained to handle the hospital switchboard and work at the reception desk. If necessary, I'll go downstairs and type billings if they're behind. We don't have an organization chart. A chart tends to make people think they're boxed into jobs.[4]

In addition to other activities, I try to stay here one night a week having dinner and listening to the patients to find out how things are really going around here.

Administrative Structure

The hospital was operated on a nonprofit basis and the clinic on a for-profit basis. Dr. Shouldice and Mrs. W. Urquhart, his sister, each owned 50% of each.

O'Dell, as administrator of the hospital, was responsible for all of its five departments: surgery, nursing, administration, maintenance, and housekeeping. Medical matters were the domain of Dr. Obney, the chief surgeon. Both Alan O'Dell and Dr. Obney reported directly to an executive committee composed of Drs. Shouldice and Obney, Alan O'Dell, Ursula Verstraete (director of nursing), and Mrs. Urquhart. The executive committee met as needed, usually twice a month, and in turn reported to an inside board (as shown in *Exhibit 2*). In addition to executive committee members (except Ursula Verstraete), the board included the spouses of Dr. Shouldice and Mrs. Urquhart, two former long-time employees, and Jack MacKay. The board met three times per year, or when necessary.

Operating Costs

It was estimated by the casewriter that the 1983 budgets for the hospital and clinic were close to $2.8 million and $2 million, respectively.[5]

THE MARKET

Hernia operations were among the most common performed on males. In 1979, for example, it was estimated that 600,000 such operations were performed in the United

---

[4] The chart in *Exhibit 2* was prepared by the casewriter, based on conversations with hospital personnel.
[5] The latter figure included the bonus pool for doctors.

States alone. Only in the early 1980s had the hospital begun to organize information about either its client base of 140,000 "alumni" or the market in general.

According to Dr. Shouldice:

> When our backlog of scheduled operations gets too large, we begin to wonder how many people decide instead to have their local doctor perform the operation. Every time we have expanded our capacity, the backlog has declined briefly, only to climb once again. Right now, at 1,200, it is larger than it has ever been at this time of year [January].

The hospital relied entirely on word-of-mouth advertising, the importance of which was suggested by the results of a poll carried out by students of DePaul University as part of a project (*Exhibit 3* shows a portion of these results). Although little systematic data about patients had been collected, Alan O'Dell remarked that "if we had to rely on wealthy patients only, our practice would be much smaller."

Patients were attracted to the hospital, in part, by its reasonable rates. For example, charges for a typical operation were four days of hospital stay at $111 per day, a $450 surgical fee for a primary inguinal (the most common hernia) operation, and a $60 fee for the assistant surgeon.[6] If a general anesthetic was required, an additional fee of $75 was assessed. These were the charges that compared with total costs of $2,000 to $4,000 for operations performed elsewhere.

Round-trip fares for travel to Toronto from various major cities on the North American continent ranged from roughly $200 to $600.

In addition to providing free services to the clergy and to parents of hospitalized children, the hospital also provided annual checkups to its alumni, free of charge. Many of them occurred at the time of the annual reunion. The most recent reunion, featuring dinner and a floor show, was held at a first-class hotel in downtown Toronto and was attended by 1,400 former patients, many of them from outside Canada.

The reunion was scheduled to coincide with the mid-January decline in activity at the hospital, when an average of only 145 operations per week were performed. This was comparable to a similar lull in late summer and contrasted with the peak of activity in September, when as many as 165 operations per week might be performed.

It was thought that patients from outside Canada were discouraged from coming to Toronto in midwinter by often misleading weather reports. Vacations interfered with plans in late summer. For many of the same reasons, the hospital closed for two weeks late in December each year. This allowed time for major maintenance work to be performed. Throughout the year, no operations were scheduled for Saturdays or Sundays, although patients whose operations were scheduled late in the week remained in the hospital over the weekend.

PROBLEMS AND PLANS

When asked about major questions confronting the management of the hospital, Dr. Shouldice cited a desire to seek ways of increasing the hospital's capacity while at the same time maintaining control over the quality of the service delivered, the future role

---

[6]At the time this case was written, a Canadian dollar was worth about 80% of an American dollar.

EXHIBIT 3   SHOULDICE HOSPITAL ANNUAL PATIENT REUNION, JANUARY 15, 1983

Direction: For each question, please place a check mark as it applies to you.

1. Sex   Male   41   95.34%
           Female   2   4.65%

2. Age   20 or less   _____
           21–40   4   9.30%
           41–60   17   39.54%
           61 or more   22   51.16%

3. Nationality
   Directions: Please place a check mark in nation you
   represent and please write in your province, state or
   country where it applies.

   Canada   38   Province   88.37%
   America   5   State   11.63%
   Europe _____   Country _____
   Other   _____   _____

4. Education Level
   Elementary   5   11.63%
   High School   18   41.86%
   College   13.30   30.23%
   Graduate work   7   16.28%

5. Occupation _____

6. Have you been overnight in a hospital other than Shouldice before   Yes   31
   your operation?   No   12

7. What brought Shouldice Hospital to your attention?

   Friend   23   Doctor   9   Relative   7   Article _____   Other   4
           53.49%   20.93%   16.28%   (Please explain) 9.30%

8. Did you have a single   25   or double   18   hernia operation?
                         58.14%   41.86%

9. Is this your first Annual Reunion?   Yes   20   No   23   ⎧ 2–5 reunions – 11 47.83%
                                            46.51%   53.49%   ⎪ 6–10 reunions – 5 21.73%
   If no, how many reunions have you attended? _____   ⎨ 11–20 reunions – 4 17.39%
                                                                   ⎩ 21–36 reunions – 3 13.05%

10. Do you feel that Shouldice Hospital cared for you as a person?

    Most definitely   37   Definitely   6   Very little _____   Not at all _____
                    86.05%   13.95%

11. What impressed you the most about your stay at Shouldice? Please check one answer for
    each of the following.

A. Fees charged for operation and hospital stay
   Very   Somewhat   Not
   Important   10   Important   3   Important   6   Important   24

B. Operation Procedure
   Very   Somewhat   Not
   Important   33   Important   9   Important   1   Important _____
            76.74%   20.93%   2.33%

C. Physician's Care
   Very   Somewhat   Not
   Important   31   Important   12   Important   —   Important   —
            72.10%   27.90%

EXHIBIT 3 **(Continued)**

D. Nursing Care

| Very Important _28_ 65.12% | Important _14_ 32.56% | Somewhat Important _1_ 2.32% | Not Important _____ |

E. Food Service

| Very Important _23_ 53.48% | Important _11_ 25.59% | Somewhat Important _7_ 16.28% | Not Important _2_ 4.65% |

F. Shortness for Hospital Stay

| Very Important _17_ 39.53% | Important _15_ 34.88% | Somewhat Important _8_ 18.60% | Not Important _3_ 6.98% |

G. Exercise; Recreational Activities

| Very Important _17_ 39.53% | Important _14_ 32.56% | Somewhat Important _12_ 27.91% | Not Important _-_ |

H. Friendships with Patients

| Very Important _25_ 58.15% | Important _10_ 23.25% | Somewhat Important _5_ 11.63% | Not Important _3_ 6.987% |

I. "Shouldice Hospital hardly seemed like a hospital at all."

| Very Important _25_ 58.14% | Important _13_ 30.23% | Somewhat Important _5_ 11.63% | Not Important _-_ |

12. In a few words, give the MAIN REASON why you returned for this annual reunion.

_____

_____

_____

of government in the operations of the hospital, the use of the Shouldice name by potential competitors, and the selection of the next chief surgeon.

As Dr. Shouldice put it:

I'm a doctor first and an entrepreneur second. For example, we could refuse permission to other doctors who want to visit the hospital. They may copy our technique and misapply it or misinform their patients about the use of it. This results in failure, and we are concerned that the technique will be blamed for the recurrences. But we're doctors, and it is our obligation to help other surgeons learn. On the other hand, it's quite clear that others are trying to emulate us. Look at this ad. [The advertisement is shown in *Exhibit 4.*]

This makes me believe that we should add to our capacity, either here or elsewhere. Here, for example, we could go to Saturday operations and increase our capacity by 20% or, with an investment of perhaps $2 million and permission from the provincial govern-

EXHIBIT 4   ADVERTISEMENT BY A SHOULDICE COMPETITOR

ment, we could add another floor of rooms to the hospital, expand our number of beds by 50%, and schedule the operating rooms more heavily.

On the other hand, with government regulation being what it is, do we want to invest more money in Toronto? Or should we establish another hospital with similar design outside Canada? I have under consideration a couple of sites in the United States where private hospital operations are more common. Then, too, there is the possibility that we could diversify at other locations into other specialties offering similar opportunities such as eye surgery, varicose veins, or hemorrhoids.

For now, I have my hands full thinking about the selection of someone to succeed Dr. Obney when he retires. He's 65, you know. And for good reason, he's resisted changing certain successful procedures that I think we could improve on. We had quite a time changing the schedule for the administration of Demerol to patients to increase their comfort level during the operation. Dr. Obney has opposed a Saturday operating program on the premise that he won't be here and won't be able to maintain proper control.

Alan O'Dell added his own concerns:

How should we be marketing our services? Right now, we don't. We're even afraid to send out this new brochure we've put together for fear it will generate too much demand.

We know that both patients and doctors believe in what we do. Our records show that just under 1% of our patients are medical doctors, a significantly high percentage. How should we capitalize on that? And should we try to control the misuse of the hospital's name by physicians who say they use our techniques but don't achieve good results? We know it's going on, because we get letters from patients of other doctors claiming that our method didn't work.

On the other hand, I'm concerned about this talk of Saturday operations. We are already getting good utilization of this facility. And if we expand further, it will be very difficult to maintain the same kind of working relationships and attitudes. Already there are rumors floating around among the staff about it. And the staff is not pleased.

We still have some improvements to make in our systems. With more extensive computerization, for example, we could improve our admitting procedures.

The matter of Saturday operations had been a topic of conversation among the doctors as well. Four of the older doctors were opposed to it. While most of the younger doctors were indifferent or supportive, at least two who had been at the hospital for some time were particularly concerned about the possibility that the issue would drive a wedge between the two groups. As one put it, "I'd hate to see the practice split over the issue."

AT&T (A): FOCUSING THE SERVICES SALESFORCE ON CUSTOMERS

Dick Falcone, head of Sales Operations at AT&T, America's largest telecommunications company, had been saying for years that small business would be critical to AT&T's continued preeminence in the marketplace. By mid-1989, after substantial market share drop and a recent spate of ads by competitors such as MCI (Microwave Communications, Inc.), his point began to hit home. Typical ads zeroed in on AT&T's weak spots, e.g.:

How can Goliath ever understand David?

Who can better understand the needs of a small business . . . than a small business?

When was the last time you saw your AT&T rep?

The obvious answer—"never"—underscored a fact that had long worried Falcone: while AT&T had made certain that its large, national customers were served by a face-to-face salesforce, the small business accounts were being handled by its telemarketing department.

Ten or even five years earlier, Falcone agreed, that kind of sales approach may have been adequate. But now, with the irreversible changes happening in the competitive landscape, AT&T had no option but to change with it. As he saw it, these changes were being driven by two related factors: (1) the emergence of small business as the source of growth, productivity and wealth; and (2) fueling this growth, the information and com-

---

This case was written by Professor Sandra Vandermerwe and Dr. Marika Taishoff as a basis for class discussion rather than to illustrate either effective or ineffective handling of a business situation.

munications services offered by AT&T as well as—to an ever growing extent—by competitors entering the newly opened market nearly every week.

Since the United States district court consent decree in 1984 to dismantle AT&T's legal monopoly of most telecommunications services in the U.S., over 300 competitors had entered a market which, for almost 100 years, had been overwhelmingly AT&T's. But, of all these new players, one in particular had become synonomous with "competition": MCI. Many found this fact to be ironic: MCI was a small company which had started out during the '60s in microwave technology applications. Unlike Sprint—another key competitor that was strategically and financially aligned to the telephone manufacturer GTE—MCI had no major partnerships or financial backing. Yet, in less than five years, the company had inched its way into AT&T's market to such an extent that it had achieved double-digit share.[1]

For Falcone, the reasons for MCI's impact in the market were obvious: it had targeted an end of the market where AT&T had traditionally been little involved, and was therefore also unaware of the strength and potential of this small business sector. By the same token, MCI had formed and trained a salesforce specifically for the small end of the market—a sector whose needs from a services' salesforce were, Falcone was convinced, profoundly different from those of the large customers with whom AT&T had historically cultivated relationships.

By the end of 1989, what Dick Falcone had long been advocating finally happened, and he was appointed to create, staff, and lead a brand new unit in AT&T's Business Network Sales division: the Commercial Market Group. By covering the small business market across the United States, he was expected to deliver multi-billion dollar revenue to AT&T annually.

When he began this new journey in January 1990, Falcone was reminded of the old Chinese adverb: "Be careful what you ask for in life: you just might get it."

DE-MONOPOLIZING THE MONOPOLY

Since its inception in 1885, AT&T—the driving force behind the Bell System—functioned as a regulated monopoly providing the bulk of telephone service throughout the U.S. The Bell System had been a vertically integrated monopoly with over one million employees who had assumed they had secure employment. The company's activities included: communications technology research; production and distribution of equipment; installation and maintenance of facilities, as well as provision of the necessary services; and handling accounts and revenues for the entire system. In 1974, antitrust proceedings against AT&T were launched; ten years later, AT&T agreed to divest itself of its Bell Operating Companies that provided local exchange service. And from that agreement, AT&T was dismantled and the Bell System existed no more.

AT&T was allowed to retain $34 billion of the $149.5 billion in assets it had on December 31, 1983. Of its over 1 million employees, only 373,000 remained; even the

---

[1] According to Federal Communications Commission News Report, March 20, 1990.

EXHIBIT 1   ORGANIZATIONAL CHART (SIMPLIFIED)

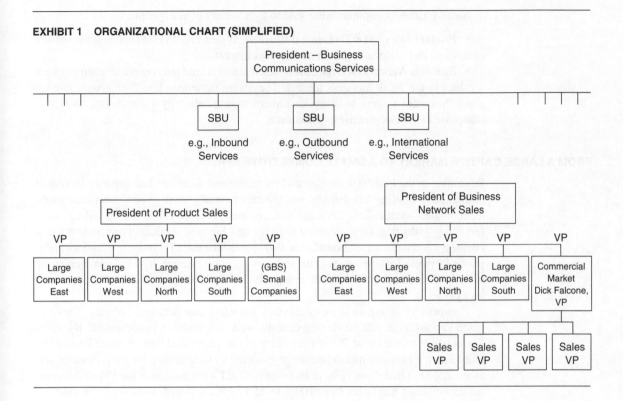

well-known Bell name and logo had to be discontinued. But, in recompense, the company was permitted to pursue more fully the technology being developed at Bell Laboratories.

The newly created AT&T was still the largest telecommunications company in the United States and one of the worldwide leaders in information technology. It had been allowed to retain several activities from the former Bell System, most notably: long-distance services; equipment manufacture and supply; and research and development, including integrated communications and computer solutions. All told, by 1989 the AT&T network handled 135-140 million calls a day.

A constantly changing number of Strategic Business Units (SBUs), each headed by a President and all of them under the direction of AT&T's President of Business Communications Services, could choose either to use AT&T's sales channels or to engage third parties like independent retailers to sell their products and services to the market. The principal SBUs were Inbound Services, Outbound Services, and International Services. (*Refer to **Exhibit 1** for a simplified organization chart.*)

As accelerating leaps in technology allowed ever wider use and different applications of existing lines and cables, services became the key source of innovation at AT&T and at other communication companies.

Small business customers were sold to by a variety of salespeople:

• *Product Sales:* AT&T's General Business Systems (GBS) sold telecommunication equipment and systems to the small business market.

• *Business Network Service Sales:* Telemarketers sold telecommunication network services to the small business market. They were organized into four geographic regions. In contrast, large business customers were handled by a direct, face-to-face—otherwise known as premises—salesforce.

FROM A LARGE CAPTIVE MARKET TO A SMALL COMPETITIVE ONE

Beginning in the mid-'80s, the demand for telecommunications line capacity increased dramatically. Fueling this demand was the exponential growth in new communications technologies—particularly fax machines, computers, video conferencing and tele-conferencing—which, in turn, created a need for new kinds of services. The acceleration in business conducted across boundaries also spurred the need for more international telephone services. Total revenues in the industry grew, on average, by 5% a year beginning in 1984. This was combined with an equally dramatic decrease in communication service prices.

Competitors sprang up in many facets of the telecommunications industry. They targeted various areas and, to varying extents, were successful or unsuccessful. By 1989, Sprint had acquired about 7% of the market in pre-subscribed long-distance lines—i.e., lines which customers had deliberately specified as their choice for long-distance services, and MCI had about 15%. In five years, AT&T's percentage of the 134 million pre-subscribed lines had fallen from 100% to 75%.[2] MCI's inroads were typically ascribed to its almost exclusive focus on small businesses and its ability to undercut AT&T's prices by 1-2 cents. Because MCI was small, as its ads claimed, it did not have to support an infrastructure the size of AT&T's. A number of smaller competitors—about 300 dispersed throughout the country—were primarily regional or niche providers.

Market share in the industry was measured by the number of minutes a line was used. AT&T's share steadily diminished from 98.7% of premium interstate minutes to 65% by the end of 1989.[3]

Throughout the decade of the '80s, the small business market had been growing steadily and, in a stark reversal of previous trends, had overtaken large business as the key source of economic growth. By the end of the '80s, small business was worth $10 billion, with 100% of the growth in employment figures from 1980-1989 due to this sector. Falcone figured that even if AT&T were to recapture 100% of the large business market, the company would not be able to grow, simply because future growth was not taking place in that market.

A survey commissioned by the National Foundation of Women Business Owners had in fact indicated that, if trends continued, by 1992 more people would be employed by female business owners than by all the Fortune 500 companies combined. In Falcone's

---

[2] According to Federal Communications Commission News Report, March 20, 1990.
[3] According to Federal Communications Commission News Report, March 20, 1990.

view, AT&T had lost huge chunks of market share simply because it did not fully appreciate the power and importance of small business. Historically, AT&T had cultivated relationships with a relatively small number of large companies, with whom it had conducted a huge, and therefore, cost-efficient volume of business. Substantial volume was especially important in this market, since large users tended to demand tariff revisions, thus lowering prices. The primary focus of the AT&T salesforce was to sell new products and services to this market as soon as they became technologically feasible and commercially viable.

THE COMMERCIAL MARKET GROUP: TO DEVELOP THE SMALL BUSINESS SECTOR

In late 1989, AT&T determined that the company's future success lay in two areas: expanding business internationally, and regaining and growing the ever-more important small business market share domestically. To achieve this goal, top priority would be given first to winning back those customers who had moved over to the competition.

It was clear to the SBUs that the time had come to meet the just-created demand in marketplace for services designed and delivered specifically for small businesses. The creation of a national sales organization for this market—together with a new set of disciplines to guide it—was, they had decided, the one critical way for the company to remain competitive. The most important step, though, was finding the right person to make it work. It did not take long.

Dick Falcone had been working at AT&T since graduation. He worked for a short period of time at the Massachusetts Institute of Technology's Industrial Guidance Laboratory—and held a bachelors degree in Engineering. He had had a variety of positions at the company across all key disciplines, with considerable time in marketing. Up until 1989, he had been in charge of the national sales support organization at AT&T's GBS division—the organization that sold telephone equipment to small business customers—where he had been responsible for ensuring appropriate training, compensation plans, quotas, and the like for a multi-thousand person salesforce. Just prior to being assigned to the new position, he had designed and established one of the largest information and database systems; it gave all AT&T salespeople anywhere in the U.S. instant access to any and all unrestricted customer files.

When the President of Business Communications Services told him that he had been selected as head of the soon-to-be created Commercial Market Group—responsible for the eight million small business customers nationwide—and, as such, the fifth Vice President in AT&T's Business Network Sales Department, Falcone was ready. Designing and establishing a world-class salesforce, he admitted, interested him far more than implementing technology—even though he was an engineer. The cardinal objective given by the SBUs to the Commercial Market Group was to create and achieve a "winback" strategy: to recapture the market base that had left AT&T.

Falcone, his direct boss (the President of Business Network Sales), and his internal constituents—the SBUs, which he called his "client customers," all concurred that the only way to accomplish this goal was to "get as many feet on the street and into customers' premises as possible." But, where should they start? Falcone recalled that time:

I was given a title, assigned major responsibilities, and presented with an entirely new department to run. There were a few startup problems, though: expectations in the small business market were changing on a daily basis, and we hadn't been keeping up with those new requirements; we had to create a salesforce and train them to sell to those customers and meet their expectations; and to top it all off, we had to do all of this from scratch.

At first, the telemarketing salespeople who had been working in one of the four major regional divisions were realigned into the national Commercial Market Group. Falcone knew that telemarketing was an integral component to meeting the needs of small businesses across the US. The objective was not to dismantle what already existed but to complement it with a direct, face-to-face salesforce.

THE FORMING OF A NEW SALESFORCE: THE FIRST WAVE

Of the 8 million customers who fell into the small business category, about 4 million were very small businesses that were satisfied with telemarketing. The other half typically had more employees and more specialized needs. It was for these customers that a face-to-face salesforce would have to be created. From his own research and from market data from consultants, Falcone knew that he would need at least a multi-thousand-strong force to satisfy these customers.

But, while the Commercial Market Group was a priority for AT&T, the company was also instituting an across-the-board cost-cutting exercise. Hiring an employee base of this magnitude would be difficult. Therefore, rather than look outside, it was decided that the majority of the salesforce should be hired from within.

Falcone put together a marketing program—including brochures, presentations, etc.—throughout AT&T nationwide, offering an option to AT&T employees whose positions were being eliminated and who wanted to recycle their professional competence, as well as to those who basically wanted to do something else with their lives. He asked his sales managers to become personally involved. A salesforce was being created, he announced, that would focus on the growth sector of the American economy and would give each individual the opportunity to grow with it. Surplus headquarters employees, 5,000 in all, from every level of the company—accountants, nurses, middle managers—applied. They were all given a test designed specifically to assess their sales talent and potential. The several thousand who passed then attended a basic, one-month sales training program before being sent to one of the 27 branches across the U.S., from where they would play their role in the "win-back process."

Falcone was fully aware that he was taking a gamble by building the foundations of his salesforce on a group of people who had never sold before. But, he had confidence in AT&T people, their intelligence, their work-ethic and, most importantly, their cultural propensity to serve customers well. "After all, isn't that what quality selling is?" he thought. One of the nurses was an example: she claimed that, despite all of her qualifications and her successful career, she felt that she had been doing the wrong thing all her life; she had always wanted to sell, but never had the chance to do so. She was not going to let this opportunity slip away. Other candidates were less interested in sales *per se* than in changing their careers entirely. One of the accountants bluntly explained that he was tired of dealing with numbers and wanted to work with people instead.

The drive of these people to do something different with their lives encouraged Falcone. Still, he decided not to expect too much too soon. His main objective was to create a physical presence in the marketplace and convince small business customers that AT&T, in creating a salesforce to handle their needs in a uniquely personal way, did indeed care about them. Changing the perception that small businesses had formed of AT&T would, Falcone knew, be sufficient challenge for his people. But, if that goal were successful, it would be the first step toward rebuilding market share.

Setting the Drumbeat . . .

Throughout 1990, Falcone concentrated on creating the framework in which these new salespeople could most effectively work and be evaluated. Four managers who had previously overseen the telemarketers in their respective geographic territories reported to Falcone on a dotted line basis; they reported to his four peers—VPs for each of those regions—on a solid line basis. As he put it:

> I believed in the idea, and I had responsibility for the group, but I didn't have any authority to make decisions: I had to get the agreement from the other four VPs. But that never really stopped me: if I thought it was the right thing to do, I did it. Sometimes that meant counting on the fact that forgiveness is a lot easier to get than permission.

Convinced that only something that is measured gets done, Falcone began thinking about what he should be expecting of his newly created, multi-thousand salesforce. His years at Product Sales' small business division, GBS, had exposed him to this kind of market, yet he did not want to rely on that experience to create a strategy for the Commercial Market Group. He knew that selling services was completely different from selling products and that fighting this year's wars with last year's strategies was a sure route to defeat. So, he decided to start with a clean slate.

Falcone soon began to sense how many customers needed to be contacted and/or visited in a day, as well as how many deals should be signed daily. Still, more needed to be done in order to achieve all of his goals. It was not enough for his people to be "as good" as the competitors—they had to be better. Having a competitive salesforce selling network communication services to small businesses would not satisfy him; he wanted a world-class salesforce as good as that of the best company—regardless of industry—when it came to serving the needs of the small business sector. To meet such a goal, Falcone did several things:

- Using consultants' data, he set best-in-industry performance levels for his people, based on benchmarking against his direct competitors.
- Best-in-class performance standards were also set by identifying, studying, and establishing the benchmark for firms which were not in the industry but serviced the small business sector. He traveled and met with Vice Presidents of Sales from other industries who were selling into the small business market to learn what metrics of performance they used. He was able to do this through the many good relationships AT&T had with other firms. He concluded:

> You have to visit a certain number of potential customers a day and close at least a given amount of deals every day if we are to get the sales we expect. And if we don't, the cash

registers won't be ringing, and we as a group—and as a company—will have to bear the consequences.

• More and better training programs would also be needed. His salesforce was a patchwork quilt of people and experience, and simply setting targets would not suffice for getting consistently high performance. The salespeople would have to be fashioned to meet those targets.

The sales training programs initiated over the past year had undergone a quantum leap, with two or three generational improvements. Now, more than ever, the intent of these courses was not just to demonstrate effective selling techniques but to instill a real sense of team spirit which would differentiate the Commercial Market Group—in mentality, outlook, and results—from the traditional AT&T salesforce. These training courses were entirely paid for by the SBUs.

• A remuneration package was designed to help Falcone achieve his objectives. The salesforce was paid on a 60% salary and 40% commission basis. Falcone decided early on that there would be no limit on how much the high achievers could earn: the more money they brought in, the more they could earn for themselves. Even in that first year of operation, a few salesmen began to stand out as real stars, earning four to five times above average; others were nearer to the 80% mark. Any salesperson who underperformed for a specific period of time was eligible to be reassigned or terminated.

• He also laid out his expectations for branch managers. First and foremost, their responsibility was to motivate and drive the Commercial Market Group salesforce. And although the branch managers were directly responsible for running the branches, Falcone himself also set some key guidelines for them to follow. For instance, to meet the profitability target he expected of them, they had to be able to constantly challenge their employees to do better. As Falcone explained:

> In our lives, the one thing that gives us real satisfaction is stressing our capabilities against some challenge. We are not here to control the salesforce, but to get their commitment by constantly challenging them to do better. Management's *raison d'etre* is to let people be "ever in a state of becoming more," and this can only be done by constantly setting challenging and rewarding hurdles.

Branch managers had been given the mandate to train their people, direct them and offer appropriate career advice. Salesforce satisfaction, Falcone recognized, would be directly related to how well branch managers suceeded in these tasks. Managers would be judged by the overall financial results of their branches.

Integrating the Second Wave

By the end of 1990, market share was still eroding, but at a slower pace than over the past five years. The SBUs insisted that more coverage was needed on the small business front. The sales support requirements in the high end of the market, because of advances in technology, had been lessened. Therefore, they boosted Falcone's salesforce by taking about 15-20% of the sales support away from the four major regional groups and reassigning them to the Commercial Market Group. This second wave that joined the Group was a combination of salespeople—already trained and accustomed to selling at the high end of the market—as well as technical people who were not strictly "sales" people; rather, they were technical support specialists.

The SBUs told the four VPs responsible for large national customers which accounts they thought needed fewer people, based on achieved results and changes in technology. These employees were then sent to the Commercial Market Group to form the "second salesforce wave." More than a thousand people joined Falcone in this way, and now there was a salesforce that Falcone felt was sufficient in number to beat the competitors and satisfy the customer. The training course, by this stage perfected still more, was mandatory for the second wave.

Falcone recalled their reaction to being allocated to the Commercial Market Group, and to being obliged to attend the initial briefings and training sessions:

> It was a real eye opener: here I was, telling them how great this journey was going to be, and they were hating every minute of it. I remember one of my sales managers coming into my office the first day they joined us, and saying he had never seen such an "ugly"— and he didn't mean in physical appearance—group of people in his life. What they were basically saying was that AT&T owed them something: that they were entitled to the job that they wanted, and no one had the right to tell them that they had to work here or there.

Falcone rearranged his entire schedule over the next few months so that he could visit and personally participate in every training group. At each session, he discussed his objectives, requirements and aims for the group, and then gave the salespeople three options.

1 They could decide to stay, consciously seize the opportunity and make the best of it. He emphasized that they would learn something new, perfect their skills and grow, and that he, in turn, would do everything he could to help them succeed. Falcone reiterated that his expectations were high and that nothing would interfere with achieving the results he wanted for the group as a whole. He told them that he was counting on them and would invest in them so that they could invest in themselves. He conveyed his philosophy that what was in it for them was the opportunity to become more than they were, to become even stronger professionals and that, in the final analysis, the value of their improved professionalism would be something that they uniquely owned. They could apply that strength in the future to AT&T or anywhere they chose.

2 They could decide that they just could not work in this kind of market. Perhaps they had done well dealing with large accounts—but the small business market, he emphasized, had its own pace and beat which was rather different. As he put it to them:

> You've got to wake up in the morning, get out there and pound the pavement, and meet as many customers as possible. And you've got to sign a deal—quickly. It's a totally different ball game and I'm not going to hide anything from you. Some may not want to. And if you decide you don't want to do this, we'll help you find something else at AT&T.

3 They could decide not to make a choice: just sit in on the training classes, pass the time away, and then try to get some business. But, Falcone told them, this option would be a mistake. He encouraged them to "either stay, or go, but make a decision. After all, it's your life."

About 50% of the second wave decided not to join the Commercial Market Group. Falcone and his management team successfully placed the majority of them in other functions at AT&T; the remainder left the company.

The Unlearning Process: Moving from Selling Lines to Selling Applications

The typical contacts for the Commercial Market salesforce were the small business firms' presidents who, although they wanted solutions, usually had very little time to give and no in-house technical expertise on hand. As Falcone explained:

> It's not only *what* they need that is different, it's also how and when they need it. And, they don't always even know what they need; their requirements are different, and so is their buying process. The salesperson has to be able to understand, meet, and satisfy the ongoing needs of these customers—in as short a time as possible.

For Falcone, the only way to sell services to this kind of market was by somehow showing the customer the benefits of those services upfront. In his opinion, perfecting this approach would be pivotal for AT&T's overall profitability. As he saw it, AT&T and its competitors all had the same hardware—cables and wires. But, those assets only made a return when customers used them, which—given the nature of the phone business—they inevitably had to do, but only up to a point. Since that limit was money, competitors tended to cut prices to get customers to use the phone more often. Falcone did not want to compete that way, but rather demonstrate results. He wanted to show customers that, even if AT&T was a price leader for some services, it could help them make more money by reaching more people and thus having more customers come to them.

Persuading small business customers successfully, though, meant having a much keener insight into their operations than most salespeople were accustomed to. It also meant not just selling the attributes of a service, but emphasizing the results that customers would get from that service. Falcone called this "application selling," and insisted that even a butcher—who had probably never thought of his phone as a tool to extend his market and improve his results—could be a suitable candidate for such services. AT&T, for instance, could design an advertising campaign whereby existing or potential meat purchasers could call for information, prices and deliveries on a reversed charge, toll-free "800" line. By encouraging customers to use this line free of charge to place orders, the butcher would be getting results he otherwise would never have achieved. Such services, designed on the premise that toll-free "800" numbers could be just as beneficial to small businesses as they had always been to large companies, were a typical example of an application sale.

A completely different example was the "900" service numbers. Here, because of the specific and unique value of the service provided over the line, individual end users paid much more for the call than the use of the line alone. A pharmacy, for instance, installed a 900 number as a service to its customers: at any time of the day or night, if they had any questions about counter-indications from prescribed drugs, or their side effects, they could dial the service.

Some salespeople were apprehensive about being able to determine, in the short time

EXHIBIT 2 ELEVEN POINT EMPLOYEE SATISFACTION SURVEY

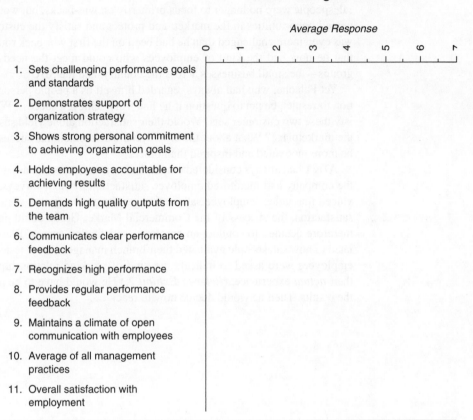

Branch Managers: Nationwide

Average Response

1. Sets challlenging performance goals and standards
2. Demonstrates support of organization strategy
3. Shows strong personal commitment to achieving organization goals
4. Holds employees accountable for achieving results
5. Demands high quality outputs from the team
6. Communicates clear performance feedback
7. Recognizes high performance
8. Provides regular performance feedback
9. Maintains a climate of open communication with employees
10. Average of all management practices
11. Overall satisfaction with employment

period between the expected number of daily customer visits, the specific needs that these customers might have to get the results they were after. Falcone was determined, however, that this skill be learned and applied. Service was more than just efficiency, as had been assumed in the past. It was improving customers' bottom line performance.

TURNING THE CORNER

By the end of the third quarter of 1991, the results of the Commercial Market Group impressed everyone at AT&T. The SBUs, the direct clients of the Group, were especially satisfied with the results, which had exceeded financial expectations. The Group had helped the company turn the corner and had broken the back of market share erosion. The Group had also restored the AT&T name amongst the major contenders in the small business market, which continued to be the key growth sector in the economy. Customer satisfaction surveys continued to place AT&T above competitors.[4]

The SBUs now decided on a new strategy for the Commercial Market Group. Its salespeople were no longer to focus primarily on win-backs, but would also exploit untapped opportunities in the market, and protect and satisfy the customer base. Falcone was even more challenged than he had been on the first win-back round. He was certain that he now had the kind of employees who could meet the needs of both customer groups—the small businesses across the country, and the SBUs.

Yet Falcone, who had always regarded himself as a people person, despite his attention to results, began to question if he had truly achieved success. Was it enough to satisfy these two customer sets? Would their satisfaction alone yield sustainable success in the marketplace? What about the employees who created this success: did they need to be more motivated and inspired than others?

AT&T had always considered employees its most important asset, and so for decades the company had monitored employee satisfaction through surveys. Falcone was convinced that unless employee satisfaction results grew together with those of customer satisfaction, the success of the Commercial Market Group could not be sustained. He therefore decided to conduct an employee satisfaction survey. Eleven key factors, related to how salespeople evaluated their branch managers, were tested on a scale of 0-7: employees were asked to indicate the kind of working relationship they *desired,* and their *actual* experience. (*Refer to* **Exhibit 2.**) He would have to be patient and wait for the results. Then he would decide how to react. . . .

---

[4]Statement about customer satisfaction from Data Communications "Data Comm User Survey," August 1992.

Editor's note: Following this case, Dick Falcone came to the realization (through personal interviews with his salespeople and an employee satisfaction survey) that employee morale wasn't as high as it should be to ensure continued success [AT&T(B)]. He discovered that "people weren't unhappy because the results expected of them were too rigorous, but because those results didn't embrace everything that was important to them." The organization had done very well in satisfying their SBU's (internal customers), but had forgotten that the salespeople were customers too. Results of the survey pointed to the primary source of employee dissatisfaction being their relationships with branch management.

AT&T (C): EMPLOYEES AS CUSTOMERS

Following the employee survey results, Falcone decided to take his top management team to an off-site location to discuss the problem and find a solution. Three days later, they emerged with a newly formulated aim and an overriding sentiment: "Only from the inside out can we achieve our goal of becoming a world-class sales channel." His sales vice presidents aggressively embraced this notion, becoming leaders in advancing and fleshing out the steps needed to move forward. His idea, with their full support, was to convince branch management that meeting employee expectations was as critical to overall success as meeting the expectations of the external and internal customers—i.e., the small businesses and the SBUs. Indeed, the needs of all three had to be understood and met if the Commercial Market Group were to achieve its world-class objectives.

Several weeks later, Falcone assembled his 27 branch managers and met with them over several days, impressing upon them that their roles were coaches and mentors, not overseers and controllers. He emphasized:

> People are the only appreciating assets we really have in the service business, and they're all we can depend on to sell our intangible wares; how these people feel about their jobs and about themselves will inevitably surface at each and every encounter with a customer—and it can't help but affect the outcome of that interface. While you as branch managers can't directly have an influence on the sale itself, you can be, and are responsible for creating the kind of environment where people feel good about themselves and their jobs, are energized and are continuously learning and developing.

To help branch managers think more creatively about the people working for them, Falcone used a crystal—whose special beauty was not created by one individual facet but, rather, by the combination of its facets—to symbolize the variety of aspects that make up any individual and together would create AT&T's small business advantage. He felt that it was only when managers understood their employees in these terms that they could begin to relate to them in an unfettered and relevant way. The professional guidance and career development plans which Falcone considered so essential to the branch managers' responsibilities could then be made less constricting and more meaningful. The aim, he said, should be to discuss what these individuals wanted to do in the next year, or in their lives, not in terms of targets but rather in terms of where they planned to be professionally and personally. Some might opt for following the same course they were currently on; others might suggest something entirely different. Either way, it would fall on the branch manager to discern what was driving the employee so as to individually determine his or her potential to pursue those objectives.

LOCALIZING THE EFFORT: GIVING TOOLS TO THE BRANCHES

Ultimately, Falcone decided, he and his team at headquarters could only do so much to improve results—whether in employee satisfaction, customer satisfaction, or sales effectiveness. The real effort and impetus would have to come from the branches themselves. He could map the direction he wanted the Commercial Market Group to take, but only the local branches could follow through. In order to help them do that, Falcone gave them several tools which had been adapted from those used at the national level. The employee satisfaction and customer satisfaction tools would help the branches get a sense of how well they were doing compared with expectations, so they could work on closing the gaps. The Sales Effectiveness Diagnostic tool would help to measure the sales performance of individuals and so maintain high levels of performance among them.

• *Employee Satisfaction:* In order to make employee satisfaction a part of the infrastructure and values, tool kits were designed and sent to the branch managers to measure employee satisfaction. The object was to make these managers individually responsible for ensuring the best possible results. In Falcone's words, they had to "own" the tools and the results instead of having them thrust upon them. Once the results of these exercises were gathered and analyses made, they were sent on to headquarters.

• *Customer Satisfaction:* Falcone developed a customer satisfaction survey that would be conducted nation-wide on a local level. This survey was sent to each branch, and the managers were responsible for collecting the data, and for tallying and interpreting the results. In addition to measuring customer satisfaction, the survey served as a diagnostic tool for local improvement plans. These were also sent to headquarters.

• *Sales Effectiveness Diagnostic Test:* Known as SEDS, this tool was commissioned from an outside market research and testing agency. It was the first branch-managed diagnostic test designed specifically to assess sales ability in the small business market. Factors were isolated that historically correlated with sales success. These factors, which had led to high performance sales, were then used as a basis for measuring

EXHIBIT 1   SALES EFFECTIVENESS DIAGNOSTICS SYSTEM (SEDS)

PERFORMANCE COMPONENTS

1. **Sales skills**   20%
   Six critical steps demonstrated in the sales process
   - Pre-call Planning
   - Positioning/Building Rapport
   - Data Gathering
   - Proposing/Presenting
   - Closing
   - Finalizing the Call

2. **Performance management**   30%
   What employee has learnt from:
   - Manager's General Coaching
   - Feedback Sessions
   - Problem-solving Discussions

3. **Territory planning and management**   15%
   Skills in defining standards for effective account coverage
   - Territory Planning
   - Teaming
   - Territory Management Reviews
   - Sales Flow/Work Reviews

4. **Activity levels**   10%
   Whether daily contact and sales requirement targets are met

5. **Promotions / programs effectiveness***   15%

6. **Training**   10%
   Product and skill proficiency based on test scores and
   completion percentages
   - Product Proficiency
   - Core Skill Training Course Completions

   * Currently being more specifically defined.

salespeoples' effectiveness and direct ongoing improvement. (Refer to Exhibit 1 for select excerpts from this tool.)

Falcone and his Leadership Team communicated to their branches that the approach
was to inculcate quality and empowerment into their operating style; that they would
provide the tools and infrastructure to enable a branch to "self-diagnose" and, through
empowerment, to "self-improve."

The results of the satisfaction surveys and sales effectiveness diagnostic test were gathered on an annual basis and sent to headquarters. They were used by Falcone to judge the performance of branch managers and decide on their pay. A branch's financial results were no longer therefore the sole determinant of success or failure. Falcone sent public letters of congratulation to branch managers in the top quartile ranking.

CREATING THE VIRTUAL ENVIRONMENT

Falcone continued his visits to the branches, always speaking to as many of the salespeople as possible. Typically he spent 20% of his time with them. He asked them personally what they found pleasant and unpleasant about their work, what they wanted from their jobs, and what was not desirable. One theme that seemed to be echoed by many of the salespeople touched upon the long assumed sacrosanct idea of having to come to work at all. One salesman expressed it this way:

> We don't have to be checked on all the time, having to clock in and clock out like children. We know what we have to do and, as responsible adults and professionals, we can achieve that without having anyone breathe down our necks. Management may think that boxing us in and controlling us is the way to get the kinds of results they want, but they're wrong.

Falcone began to think that "boxing" people in physically also boxed in their individual aspirations and sense of accountability, as well as their competitive drive. It led people to feel that someone down the hall either could fix their problem or would blame them for not having fixed it themselvs. Either way, employees' focus was on the internal structure, and their position in it, rather than where it exclusively had to be—out in the marketplace with individual customers.

Falcone began formulating his ideas on creating a "virtual environment," where people were not physically present in their offices, but "connected" to them electronically—via faxes, PCs with modems, and, of course, telephones. In short, they were not obliged to be physically present every morning from 8 a.m. to 5 p.m. in order to accomplish what had to be done. They would determine the amount of time they spent working and which chunks of time.

Large office blocks to house the salesmen, he explained to his colleagues, were unnecessary for two reasons. Firstly, the fact that AT&T sold on applications and quality didn't obviate its need to keep costs down. For him, virtual offices could improve the quality of work-life primarily while offering a secondary benefit of lower costs. Additionally, he was convinced that office structures were detrimental to the kind of unfettered culture and mindset he had been trying to instill. The message he had been sending to his salespeople all along was that they themselves should act and make decisions as individuals, and be individually accountable for ensuring that those decisions were successful. How they met their target, he emphasized, was ultimately up to them. Operating in a "virtual environment," he maintained, would allow them to truly feel and exercise their individuality.

Several basic variables influenced the speed with which the "virtual environment" could be instituted in all 27 branches. The most important one was the amount of time before the branch's office lease ran out. Ideally, enough lead time and coordination were critical to making a successful transition from a traditional to a "virtual organization." People also had to be supplied with the right equipment, trained, and be comfortable using the technology well in advance of virtualizing operations.

The toughest hurdle would be in making it work on a practical and ongoing basis, and eliminating the very real "separation anxiety" that some employees felt following the virutalization of their workspace. Creating a culture unique to the Commercial Market Group had been one of Falcone's first objectives when he became VP of the Group in 1990. Training sessions had been built around that theme and his extensive visits to the branches had been intended to instill it even further. Maintaining that same kind of cultural cohesiveness in a "virtual environment" required several steps:

- *Informal office rituals* such as impromptu lunches amongst employees and managers were strongly advised. This way, branch managers could liaise with their salesforce and set up individual meetings, lunches, or simple get-togethers on a monthly, at the very least, basis.
- *Keeping the group "together" through technology.* Headquarters sent monthly video cassettes to the branches. Through regular features on new products, services, and evolving corporate objectives, these videos were intended to keep the "virtual" salesforce up-to-date with what was happening in AT&T as a whole. Plans were under way to create an audio cassette which would have the same kind of information but adapted to suit the needs of employees on the road for extended periods.
- *Filmed interviews of employees in situ,* either at the branch or at an employee's virtual office, were made. During these interviews, managers and salesmen were encouraged to speak about those topics which most pleased them, concerned them, or upset them—their recent successes, their frustrations, or specific kinds of problems they had encountered.
- *A "fellowship" program was created* for employees who had been doing well in their jobs and who wanted to take part in project teams to do something entirely different. Falcone took a personal interest in formulating the kinds of projects that would be pursued. They could, for instance, be devoted to determining how to improve the work process amongst clerical workers, or studying the evolving needs of the small business market, or improving communications both within and amongst the branches. These fellowship programs typically lasted six months, at which time the employee would return to his or her original job.

By mid-1992, every branch in the Commercial Market Group operated in a "virtual environment." People productivity figures shot up, and employees were on the whole enthusiastic. Typical comments included:

Before, I wasted three and a half hours a day: the office was an hour's drive from home, and my customers couldn't be reached from 11:30 to 1:00 every day. Now, instead of being in a car at 7 a.m. going to the office, I'm at home doing my targets or talking with customers.

It's the ultimate in flex time. It really lets me work according to my bio-rhythms, and according to when in the day, or night, I happen to perform best—which happens to be from midnight to 4 a.m.—not according to when the office is open.

It lets us do what we've been told we're expected to do: be with customers. So instead of being in an office filling out forms and then trying to squeeze in some time to see real or potential customers, they're getting all our attention now. We come into the office when we feel it's necessary and when we have the time, not when somebody—who doesn't really know anything about what we're doing or what we're trying to sell—tells us it's necessary, or that we've got to spend 40 hours a week inside a cubicle because that's the rule.

MANAGING EMPLOYEE VALUES ON THE ROAD AHEAD . . .

By the fall of 1992, Dick Falcone was less than two years into the journey he had set for himself and for his salesforce. He had achieved and even exceeded many of his objectives, and that was reward in and of itself. Previously, customer satisfaction surveys had shown competitors' ratings improve vis-à-vis AT&T's benchmark. Anecdotal information led Falcone to believe that this trend was beginning to reverse itself. Also, employee satisfaction results for the organization indicated improvement in all categories, with dramatic improvement in several categories. Management leadership improvements were the most significant and dramatic—a clear acknowledgement that the tools and practices which had been put in place were succeeding.

But there was more to do. A conversation with his son had reinforced his conviction that the values of the present generation of employees were sharply different from those of their predecessors. His son had phoned from his part-time job in a computer company to say that he planned to quit. His decision had nothing to do with pay, job conditions, vacation time, employment contracts, or working hours—all of which were excellent. Rather, he was depressed because he was surrounded by "all these people here doing things they really don't want to do and with no opportunity to do anything else." On top of it all, those in "senior" positions at the company simply told them what to do, and never really listened to what people like him wanted to do, or how they wanted to do it. No one seemed happy.

Falcone had heard the same sentiments many a time from his own young salesforce whose still emerging values soon would irrevocably, he was certain, take root and become the norm. As he saw it, the manager of the future would have to be able to find a confluence of individual and professional needs. People would continue to go to work for money, of course, but that would no longer be enough. For them, the *opportunity* to learn and enjoy their work took precedence over all else. After these reflections, Falcone proceeded to jot down some thoughts:

The environment in which AT&T operates has changed dramatically, radically and irreversibly. The stability we used to seek and create just doesn't exist anymore. I don't know if I'll have a job tomorrow, and offering even the illusion of lifetime employment to people is a thing of the past. I tell my people that even if they can't make it, or even if they don't want to, by having worked at AT&T they'll come out a better individual and be able to sell the skills they've acquired here wherever they like. Becoming a successful professional, and a fulfilled human being, is the best offer any company can hope to make to its employees today.

And what we have to bear in mind is that people today are simply not looking for a job in the traditional sense of the word. They are looking for contentment, gratification, growth, the chance to make a contribution. And if we, the people responsible for people in companies, build systems against this, we and our organizations will have absolutely no chance of surviving.

Creating the "virtual office" was, he thought, one step in creating the right kind of system for today's, and especially tomorrow's world. But he wondered whether simply making people feel that they were physically free, and no longer constrained to being in an office building, was enough. Perhaps this sense of freedom had to extend still further and become as much a part of organizational culture as it already was of people's mindsets, attitudes, and values. Falcone summed it up:

The main thing is that people shouldn't feel that they have to stay or feel constrained in any way: if they decide to stay, it's because that's best for them and for AT&T. What we have to do is create an environment where staying with AT&T is clearly the best option, in all respects, for our people to take. But above all else, our employees must feel that they are entirely free to leave: the people who feel that way are the most productive individuals and the ones who stay on the longest.

WOLF FENNER (A): PAN-EUROPEANIZING SERVICE QUALITY

Reciprocity is what service quality is all about in a network model like ours. We try to serve our Italian or German colleagues' clients here in the UK as though they were our own clients. That's the way professional firms like ours work: we do things for each other.

People think we don't have difficulty with consistent pan-European service quality because we have a common philosophy on auditing, set designs for working papers, and standard software. But it takes more than that.

Service quality means different things to different people. In France, what goes into making a good audit may be very different from what it takes in Spain, the UK, or Germany. Each country has its own culture, client sets, standards of operating, and legalities. You just can't talk about service quality in one breath.

We all have the finest intentions when it comes to providing our colleagues' clients with good services. The problem is, we're often too busy to follow through. Our own local clients have still got to come first.

When it comes to multinational clients, it's easier to get local practices to respond to requests for services. But with mid-sized clients, they're likely to be far less enthusiastic: the rewards are less obvious to them, especially if their domestic markets are still thriving.

Most of the middle market have only just begun to think in a pan-European way. It's going to be a slow process. We don't want to be ahead of clients: we've got to move carefully, and weigh everything we do from country to country.

Clients will tolerate some service quality differences, but only up to a point. We must be able to give the same calibre services to all clients everywhere today—irrespective of their size—and quickly, because if we can't, they'll go to someone who can.

EXHIBIT 1   1989 FEES (IN ECU MILLION) AND MARKET SHARE (%) OF THE BIG SIX ACCOUNTING FIRMS

MARKET SHARE OF SIX FIRMS TOTAL 100 IN EACH EC MEMBER STATE

Country	A	B	C	D	E	WF
Belgium	30.5 (23.2)	27.4 (20.8)	27.3 (20.7)	19.4 (14.7)	14.2 (10.8)	12.9 (9.8)
Denmark	49.7 (22.8)	24.9 (11.4)	47.8 (22.0)	13.1 (6.0)	9.8 (4.5)	72.6 (33.3)
France	335.4 (41.3)	119.1 (14.7)	67.06 (8.3)	155.2 (19.1)	74.0 (9.1)	61.5 (7.6)
Germany	208.7 (30.0)	132.9 (19.1)	180.9 (26.0)	79.7 (11.5)	33.3 (4.8)	60.4 (8.7)
Greece	1.2 (17.7)	1.72 (24.5)	1.5 (21.4)	1.7 (24.4)	0.9 (12.1)	NA
Ireland	31.5 (27.4)	19.3 (16.8)	18.0 (15.7)	13.1 (11.4)	24.7 (21.5)	8.2 (7.2)
Italy	52.5 (16.8)	38.7 (12.4)	49.5 (15.8)	114.2 (36.6)	32.0 (10.2)	25.5 (8.2)
Luxembourg	5.2 (19.9)	NA	2.4 (9.2)	3.1 (11.8)	4.3 (16.6)	11.1 (42.5)
Netherlands	227.0 (24.4)	259.4 (27.9)	253.1 (27.2)	27.9 (3.0)	23.7 (2.5)	140.0 (15.0)
Portugal	3.8 (15.1)	6.5 (25.8)	3.3 (13.0)	8.1 (32.0)	3.6 (14.1)	NA
Spain	28.9 (9.7)	26.1 (8.9)	18.4 (6.3)	149.5 (51.0)	51.4 (17.5)	19.2 (6.5)
UK	522.8 (22.1)	405.5 (17.1)	603.7 (25.5)	256.9 (10.9)	381.3 (16.1)	195.2 (8.3)

Source: NERA accounting firm survey, 1989.

BACKGROUND OF THE FIRM: A FEDERATION OF PRACTICES

Wolf Fenner (WF) was created after the merger in the late '80s of two international auditors, Wolf Horning and Fenner & Young. Similar to the experience of numerous firms in the auditing industry, the merger had been driven by the increasingly global audit, tax, and consulting needs of the multinational companies being targeted—those with assets or turnover in the range of ECU 1 billion or more. Because of their rapid growth during the '80s, these multinationals needed accounting firms capable of providing worldwide coverage. For the auditors of such corporations, the most expedient way of ensuring service delivery in those regions where they were not present was through mergers and acquisitions.

By 1991, this wide-scale consolidation in the industry resulted in shrinking what had been known as the Big Eight auditing firms into the Big Six, of which WF was one. (*Refer to* Exhibit 1 *for the 1989 EC market shares of the Big Six firms.*) By 1992, it had over 600 offices in about 100 countries with close to 30,000 audit professionals, 6,000 tax professionals, and 6,000 management consultants. In Europe, it had almost 300 practices in 20 countries, some still maintaining their original names either completely or in part.

WF's international structure was a "federation" of independent national practices—a sort of partnership of partnerships. Each firm (practice), operated autonomously. Practices in some countries were well established, with long traditions and client bases behind them. Others were more recent and were sometimes assumed by foreign colleagues to be less competent and reliable. Within countries, practices had different levels of expertise and competency. Each local practice had responsibility for its own firms within approved strategic plans. Partners drew their compensation from the revenue pool of their country practices, rather than from a global pool.

According to a survey done by WF in London, the purchasing behaviour of the Big Six's multinational clients (in this case, banks) was determined by the perceived competency, professionalism, and involvement of the partners working with them. Equally important was the quality of the work performed by the firm and the partners and the fact that WF was a member of the Big Six. *(The importance of key criteria in client purchasing behaviour, and how clients ranked the Big Six on each of them, is given in Exhibit 2.)* The scope and volume of auditing services needed by the multinationals made these accounts the most enticing ones because they provided the needed critical mass. Therefore, WF had always focused its efforts on them.

All the Big Six firms offered services which were considered essential to the multinational corporation's financial requirements: audit, tax, and management consulting. Typically, *audit services* embraced audit and non-audit accounting; *tax* was split into tax compliance and tax advisory; and *management consulting* generally included information technology, human resources, strategy, operations, and finance & accounting—the so-called advisory services. *(Refer to* Exhibit 3 *for a listing of the typical activities performed by these management advisory firms.)* In most countries, there was a high degree of interdependence between the auditing and tax functions: the financial reports and P&L statements established by the auditing department formed the basis for the tax documentation prepared by the tax professionals. Each WF country practice offered the basic commodities—audit, non-audit accounting, and tax services; the size and needs of the local market determined which of the other value-adding, consulting type services were offered.

The high anticipated growth rate—16% per annum through 1997—for management consulting services as opposed to the persistently low growth forecasts for auditing and accounting is what led the Big Six firms to begin acquiring or adding consulting practices during the late '80s. They believed that adding such activities to their portfolios would improve their cross-selling opportunities and thus enhance their overall hold on the marketplace. In 1989, audit services still accounted for the bulk—anywhere from 50-80%—of individual country practice fees in Europe. *(Refer to* Exhibit 4 *or a comparison of the Big Six auditors in Europe by fee sources.)* The research done by WF in the UK revealed that, in general, many multinational companies would deal with independent firms rather than use their auditors for these consulting services. With growth potential so high in this value-added activity, however, competition was expected to increase steeply over the next decade.

Across the various countries in Europe, the national laws regulating company audit procedures and obligations were different. The Anglo-Saxon countries, for instance, had long made it mandatory for all companies—public and private—to publish and file annual statements that were audited externally. In other countries—such as in the Mediterranean region, the audit requirement by an independent auditor was a relatively recent development and tended to be limited to the large publicly listed companies that made up only a small proportion of all active companies. Different regulatory statutes in European countries also determined which performance data had to be measured, as well

EXHIBIT 2   MULTINATIONAL CLIENT PURCHASING CRITERIA AND COMPETITOR PERFORMANCE

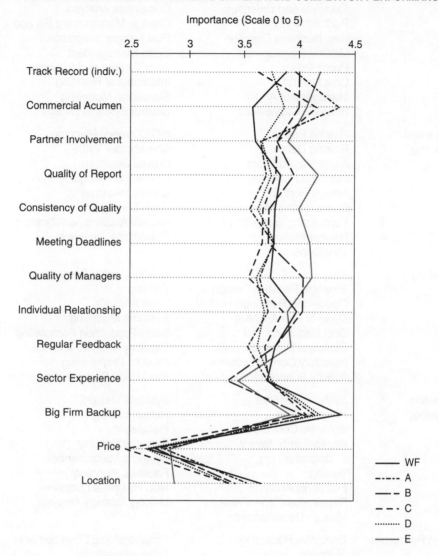

Importance (Scale 0 to 5)

Source: WF, Client Specific Services London, 1993.

EXHIBIT 3   MANAGEMENT CONSULTING SERVICES AND ACTIVITIES IN GENERAL

Service	Typical Activities	
Strategy	M&A Planning	Customer Analysis
	Takeover and Defenses	Competitor Analysis
	Portfolio Analysis	Change Management Service
	New Business Direction	Post Merger Integration
	Mission Development	Crisis Management
	Public Policy	Joint Venture and Alliances
	Cost Control	International Planning
	Management Audits	Simulation Modelling
	Strategic Capabilities	Control Systems Design
Finance and Accounting	Raising Equity	Int'l Currency Planning
	Raising Debt	Shareholder Value
	Asset Management	Capital Structure
	Financial Reporting	Mergers and Acquisitions
	Annual Reports	Capital Investments
	Shareholders Meetings	Cash Management
	Forecasting/Budgeting	Internal Auditing Assistance
	Reorganization	Operational Reviews
	Valuations	
Operations	Plant Layout	Quality Control Programs
	Strategic Facilities Design	Training
	Operations Research Analysis	Work Analysis
	Make or Buy Analysis	Systems Modelling
	Cost Reduction	Sales/Production Forecasting
	Statistical Process Control	Capacity Analysis and Util.
	Inventory Control Systems	Product Engineering
	Activity Subcontracting Anal.	Production Engineering
Information Technology	Systems Analysis	Systems Design
	Programming	Network Design
	Software Conversion	Installation
	Application Software Upgrades	Systems Security
		Systems Maintenance
	Testing	Facilities Planning
	Feasibility Analysis	New Business Direction
	Requirement Specifications	Linking Strategy Analysis
	Mission Development	
Human Resources	Executive Recruiting	Organizational Development
	Temporary Help	Labour Relations
	Employee Leasing	Equal Employment Opportunity
	Outplacement	
	Relocation	Risk Information Services
	Training	Employee Benefits
	Career Guidance/ Development	Job Design
		Remuneration Design

Source: The European Management Consulting Industry, by James Henderson and Professor Ralf Boscheck, 1991 by IMD.

EXHIBIT 4   BREAKDOWN OF FEES, BIG SIX AUDIT CLIENTS

Country	Audit Fee	Non-audit Accounting	Tax Consulting	Corporate Finance	Management Consulting Services	Total Fees from Audit Clients
	%	%	%	%	%	%
Belgium	52	12	23	4	10	100
Denmark	59	14	11	5	11	100
France	82	5	5	5	5	100
Germany	65	5	21	5	5	100
Greece	63	4	13	15	4	100
Ireland	48	13	28	7	5	100
Italy	80	5	5	5	5	100
Luxembourg	69	9	9	0	12	100
Netherlands	57	10	23	5	5	100
Portugal	72	5	9	5	9	100
Spain	60	5	18	5	13	100
UK	51	12	27	5	5	100

Source: NERA accounting firm survey, 1989.

as the professional qualifications necessary to perform auditing and tax services. The unique legal and fiscal environment in each country also determined the kind of expertise auditing firms had to acquire. The fiscal situation in Germany, for instance, made tax services especially important for clients; thus, this area was where the auditing firm was expected to be expert, and offer clear, tangible value.

Longstanding attitudes about the profession affected what clients expected of their auditors. In some countries, the auditing profession had always held a very specific role, and clients expected narrowly defined services from their auditors. In other countries, the opposite was true: because auditing traditionally covered a broader range of activities, clients in these countries assumed that their auditors would do more than prepare financial statements and documents in accordance with legal reporting requirements. They were also expected to explore and identify general business opportunities and financial options for their clients.

The pricing for WF's services was done on a national basis which reflected local and regional cost structures. In Germany, therefore, where the number of professionally accredited, certified accountants was limited, prices tended to be higher than, say, in the UK, where noticeable redundancy existed in the profession. Even without countries, prices could vary: fees were higher in London than in Bristol or Manchester. Prices could also be affected by each local practice's capacity to deliver specific services—especially those related to management consulting, which cost considerably more than the basic services. Amongst those country practices where there was a large local demand, experts were available on site for specialized local auditing and related issues, although duplications from region to region and country to country were becoming increasingly costly. Sometimes expertise may have been brought in from other WF practices.

THE EXPANDING MARKETPLACE: CROSSING BORDERS

WF had always considered its market in three distinct categories. The first market was comprised of small local companies that typically were profitable but not looking for growth outside the country. The middle market companies tended to be growing and even expanding across borders. The multinational market consisted of cross-border operations, and it was this market that WF—like the other Big Six firms—has been targeting.

The middle market in Europe was comprised of approximately 8,750 companies—active in sectors such as construction, chemicals, machinery, fashion, finance, networks, medical equipment, and services. Their sales or assets were in the range of ECU 10 million to ECU 800 million. By the early '90s, the average annual growth rates of these companies across Europe was 6%; among multinational companies, this figure was closer to 4%. Amongst the middle market companies, 700—or 8%—had achieved an average growth rate of 30% per annum over the past three years. These companies were known as the "hidden champions" since, of the multinationals, only 4% had attained a similar level of growth.

The strength and significance of the middle market varied from region to region. In some countries, like Germany, the strength of this sector was steadily becoming more important. In others, such as Italy, Denmark, Sweden, and the Netherlands, these companies had always been the drivers of the economy. Although about 50% of the middle market companies in such countries had European subsidiaries, WF had not really been focusing on their pan-European needs.

By 1992 the middle market's growth became more interesting in other countries. In Britain, for instance, about 35% of middle market companies maintained operations in other European countries. Five years earlier, some UK-based middle market companies may have considered expanding in Europe, but they had not been given that much attention by WF. This had to change, as one WF partner observed:

> In the '80s, the director of a British manufacturer of lifting equipment for lorries would not have seriously thought about setting up an operation in continental Europe. But, once the company started growing and saturating the UK market and began recruiting a new, younger and more professional breed of management, a fresh kind of thinking emerged. Setting up a factory in France, for instance, to improve European presence is now considered a logical next step in their growth strategy by many middle market clients—as opposed to simply trying to capture more and more of the English market. This is the opportunity for us and the accounting industry as a whole.

The increased Europeanization of WF's UK activities led that practice to believe that at least 30% of its mid-sized clients' needs would be for their non-domestic operations by 1998. Pan-European work referred to WF in the UK by its partners in other countries was expected to increase at a similar, if not greater, rate. In countries which had moved more rapidly than England in setting up pan-European operations, the rate of referrals was expected to be even higher.

While middle market clients were still relatively small in terms of their assets and market presence, they had a greater tendency to use auditors other than the Big Six. WF had, however, been doing some work for these clients via requests from such auditors. As the middle market grew and the auditing needs of these companies changed—either because the scope of their audit and fiscal obligations was enlarged, or because they now needed pan-European audit services, some were switching to one of the Big Six firms. Some of these companies, however, were still reluctant to use the larger auditors for two overriding reasons: the Big Six charged higher fees, and they were perceived as mainly positioned for multinational clients, providing services specifically designed for them. The auditor switching rate for mid-sized companies, research had revealed, was considerably higher than it was for multinational companies, which tended to remain loyal to their auditors over longer periods of time. *(Exhibit 5 indicates some of the key reasons why European middle market companies have changed auditors, moving from a smaller firm to one of the Big Six.)*

THE EXPANDING "PRODUCT" BASE: GOING PAN-EUROPEAN

Because middle market companies tended to lack the in-house expertise, managerial and professional support, and resources available to multinationals, it was customary for these mid-sized companies to expect their auditors to provide more than auditing, accounting, and tax services. According to many WF partners, their dealings with such companies tended to be more as general business advisors than as auditors. Because these clients wanted more general assistance, insight, and services related to a wider range of their activities, many WF partners believed that the firm's priorities should be in offering a full range of services, geared specifically to the needs of this market. *(Refer to Exhibit 6 for specific product offerings suggested by five WF European practices.)*

Experience had shown that when mid-sized companies first began going pan-European, their needs from auditing firms were significantly different from those of the multinationals. These firms would generally not have the tax specialists, relocation experts, IT divisions, strategic planning, and legal departments which facilitated the international expansion of the large multinational companies. Regardless of the industry, country of origin, or where in Europe they decided to set up operations, most middle market clients tended to have the same kinds of experiences once they began planning and implementing their European expansion.

As an example, an Italian manufacturer of machine equipment that wanted to set up a small distribution outlet in France might first need to know about French property and labor laws, the tax position of the company and its employees, as well as have some feasibility studies and upfront financing options explored. Once the facility was actually up and running, it would need to have its financial statements audited, tax forms filed regularly and certified. After a few years, it might decide to expand either by growing its operations or by establishing other outlets in another part of that country; later it might have to think about how to prevent takeovers; or, alternatively, it might opt to buy other

EXHIBIT 5   WHY FIRMS HAVE SWITCHED ("CORPORATE TYPE" MIDDLE MARKET COMPANIES WHICH HAVE SWITCHED FROM SMALL TO BIG SIX AUDITOR IN PAST 5 YEARS)

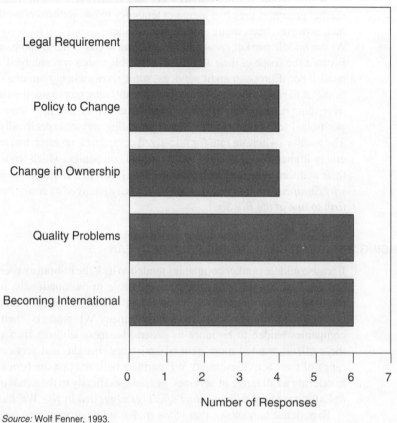

Source: Wolf Fenner, 1993.

companies. And, throughout its operations, the company would occasionally have specialized requirements. For instance, it might need to modernize its facilities, enhance its IT system linkups and processing, or consolidate different financial accounts.

The general auditing and basic financial service needs required by these companies on an ongoing basis were generally performed by the less senior WF partners. When, however, a mid-sized company was beginning to plan the pan-Europeanization of its activities, or later, when it might consider expanding by acquiring local companies or, conversely, avoiding takeover attempts by other companies, partners with specific expertise in these areas were usually required. Once that particular objective had been achieved, these partners could be moved into other projects, while the partners with less exposure to international or specialist activities continued to work with the client. The specific, more senior, expertise could be and was pulled in when required on an ongoing basis.

EXHIBIT 6   PRODUCT OFFERINGS SUGGESTED BY FIVE WF EUROPEAN PRACTICES

Scandinavia:	International Tax Advisory
Italy:	1. Guide to Eastern Europe
	2. Planning for Growth in Europe
	3. Business Check-up
Benelux:	1. Doing Business in European Countries
	2. European Tax Planner
UK:	1. Financing Your Business
	2. Setting Up in Europe
France:	1. International Tax
	2. Planning for Growth in Europe
	3. European Business Guide

Source: Wolf Fenner, Report of Middle Committee on Strategy for the Nineties, 1993.

GIVING SERVICE QUALITY LOCALLY: THE ROLE OF THE CLIENT PARTNER

Within WF, client accounts were handled by designated account managers, or client partners (CPs). The overall responsibility of the CP was to ensure the integrity of the relationship, oversee the profitability of the account, and coordinate the different on-off and ongoing services the client needed. An especially important part of the CP's activities when dealing with middle market clients was to assume the role of "general business advisor," listening to problems, assisting, and giving a broad range of advice.

Typically, the size and nature of the client company would determine the extent and closeness of the CP's involvement in its general operations. Some middle market companies—characteristically owner-managed and in the smaller size range (ECU 10-200 million)—were led by a single "dominant" person. This kind of leader, as the client's founder and managing director, ran the company with a direct interest in all its activities, and the company's growth and profitability were closely linked to his or her management style, capabilities, and knowledge.

Although generally familiar with all the operational aspects of their businesses, these managers were less comfortable when it came to dealing with the financial and fiscal requirements, often depending on the CPs to handle them. Because these aspects were integral to the company's overall performance, the managers expected to be able to call upon and meet with the CP whenever they had a query or problem regarding auditing requirements, account preparation, or the like. It was also common, given the kind of managerial expertise and style in these owner-managed companies, for their directors to call upon a WF CP whenever they had more general managerial or operational issues to explore and resolve. Close relationships between the managing director and WF's CP—characterized by going out together socially, and forging a kind of friendship—were thus the norm when working with such middle market companies. As one partner put it,

When working with these middle market companies, we not only become their auditors and their business advisors—we become their friends. It's understanding the psychology of people which is so important in this market. When it comes to auditing, my client expects someone who can give him the kind of advice he needs on an ongoing basis; if he occasionally requires a very special kind of service, he expects me to send him the experts—from wherever necessary—as long as they can deliver. But for auditing and related services which they need on a regular, almost daily basis, I've simply got to be next door.

These clients generally preferred to have a local WF expert do the work related to running their business, whereas experts from other regions/countries could be called in to do the more specific/unusual work. For instance, as one CP explained: if a distributor near Newcastle wanted work done to improve its warehousing system, it wanted local expertise. But, when it was a specific kind of problem—like designing and using the right kind of IT-based system, or special customs documentation necessary for doing business in other countries—such a client was pleased and indeed often expected that CPs bring in the experts to tell them what to do—regardless of where they came from. The local CP remained these clients' main contact and source of advice, and resource for the cross-border operations as well. A CP described this situation:

These clients want you to know everything about their businesses locally as well as abroad. If something special is needed, they expect you to find someone who has the answer. And if something goes wrong, they want you to supervise—even though, once they're operating somewhere else, technically speaking, there's only so much you can do. It's the locals who then have to perform.

Amongst those mid-sized companies at the larger end of the middle market spectrum—with assets or sales in the range of ECU 200-1000 million, many were less "dominant" in character and more "corporate": they generally had boards of directors, as well as a greater number of professional and managerial level employees with a wider range of specialist and generalist expertise. For these companies, the CP was more of a facilitator and consultant than an expert. These companies considered the CP as someone who performed the basic auditing services and who would pull in the required expertise in specialized areas.

Because most of the management-level employees in these "corporate" type companies had, in all likelihood, worked in other companies and industries, they were already familiar with the Big Six auditors and the advantages of working with them, especially on cross-border activities. They operated under the assumption that WF was an organization that offered absolute competence on all accounting matters, and so expected each WF practice—irrespective of location—to be equally professional and reliable. Some of the executives of such companies could also have worked in other European countries so, when a problem did arise they sometimes would deal directly with WF's partner there to have it investigated and rectified rather than work through their CPs. One CP explained his role in these terms:

On the whole, this particular group of mid-sized clients initially uses you as a link, but after that they usually prefer dealing with the local country practices. They expect that we're kept informed by our foreign colleagues. When handling owner-managed dominant companies, however, it's up to the CP to get colleagues in other countries to perform on a continuous basis. In such clients' eyes, responsibility still remains squarely in the CP's hands. With the corporate type mid-sized companies, the risk is greater: if the local WF people don't perform, we don't necessarily know and, therefore, can't do anything about it. The danger is that the home account may suffer.

Ensuring uncontested service quality throughout WF's European practices was, according to some CPs, difficult to attain. There were even occasions when within the same country there could be a disagreement between how well the client thought a service had been delivered and how well the firm believed it had performed that job. Once activities extended across borders, they claimed, such disagreements would inevitably occur more frequently. A partner expanded on this problem:

> Sometimes getting the locals to perform at what I and my clients think is an adequate service level is easier said than done—and that's through no fault of their own. After all, since different clients have different requirements and expectations in different countries, and partners in different practices have their own cultures, priorities and inherited sets of standards, we'd need a miracle to give 100% service consistency! And, sometimes it's not even our mistake when service quality fails: the client may be late in giving us the necessary documentation and information, but they still complain that we haven't done our job.

Another frequently cited example included differing client requirements, such as expected response times to queries, acceptable degrees of accuracy, or precision in financial reports; an acceptable level in one country could be totally unacceptable for clients from another. As well, some countries simply lacked the capability to deliver the same service quality standards as others. Differing assessments also existed within practices. In Germany, auditors were known to examine reports with an eye to ensuring that everything was right—down to the "last pfennig." In Anglo-Saxon regions, the significance of minor deviations was viewed differently because auditing standards, and the partners' training and mental frame, were based on "true and fair views."

Attitudinal differences also affected how partners in different countries responded to clients and their needs. One partner elaborated:

> The fundamental quality is excellent in most countries, and the people working in these practices are absolutely brilliant from a technical standpoint. It's just that they need to be opened up, to go beyond their narrow view of auditing as just being the rules of accounting or taxes, and to see the potential they have and the opportunities that exist to serve their local clients, and get more involved in the needs and activities of foreign clients.

The intention was always the same: to give the best possible service to all clients. The interpretation of what that meant sometimes put the partners in these practices at potential cross-purposes. And, while most pratices were invariably enthusiastic just after a client from another European country was referred to them, this initial enthusiasm frequently waned. As one partner explained:

> Either there is too much to do for local clients, or the services required by the client are too routine, or the returns simply don't justify the means: when clients are charged for services rendered in other countries, the fee is paid locally. For some country practices, this translates into getting paid at below the local going rates.

Many WF partners argued that the integrity of the relationship between the CP and the client was the only real way of ensuring that the middle market client remained satisfied and the account safe even if cross-country quality problems occurred. When this relationship was strong, a "bank of goodwill" which could withstand some dissatisfaction and disagreement would be created. A CP spoke about this relationship:

> The client must know that he can pick up his phone and complain to someone he relates to and has confidence in. When you have an unhappy client in one country, word gets around to that client in another country, and another. Then, before you know it, that client will say, "WF just can't deliver quality service in today's European environment." It's a creeping disease, a sort of gangrene. That's why, if I know that a certain country practice isn't competent enough to deliver what my client needs, I could end up advising my client to use a competitor. In the long run, it's safer and better: the client ends up trusting me even more, and the relationship is strengthened.

However, notwithstanding this attitude, other partners were beginning to question whether the CP could continue to serve the middle market's increasingly sophisticated pan-European needs. As one executive put it:

> In the future, the role of the CP will be critical to service quality delivery. No matter what the client wants and where the service comes from, someone has to "own" the client relationship and coordinate its needs on an ongoing basis. One of our critical challenges is to decide on this role in both of our middle markets: should the CP be an account manager? an expert? a facilitator? a quality controller? Where should they be located? Should they be used for clients in specific industries or specific countries? How powerful should they be? How can we structure for this? Until we can resolve these issues, we can never make pan-European service quality a reality.
> And probably even more significant is this question: how much can we learn and transfer from our experience with the MNCs? are the principles the same?

THE COUNTRY DESKS: GIVING SERVICES ACROSS EUROPE

The Country Desk concept at WF was launched in the late-'80s as an attempt to have better coordination of the services required by Japanese companies as they rapidly expanded overseas. Many issues surfaced during this expansion: where should the country practice turn when its client needed assistance? Who had the basic language skills and an empathy for the social and cultural traditions that distinguished one country from another, including the way they did business? Who would be responsive—and directly accessible within a WF practice abroad—to the partner's needs as well as those of that partner's clients?

The idea of a "desk"—an actual "place" to turn to when clients needed assistance, advice, or direction—within certain WF practices abroad, dedicated exclusively to serving WF's Japanese clients in those countries, was the solution to these increasingly common occurrences. By the early '90s, the notion of a Desk as a coordinating mechanism to assist European middle market companies in their cross-border expansion began to surface in some WF European practices as well.

Desks were typically established in those practices where non-local, middle market companies were especially active. Of the 400 Danish middle market companies operating in Germany, for instance, 380 were established in northern Germany. For that reason, a "Danish Desk" had been set up in WF Hamburg. It was run by a German-speaking Danish partner, "taking care"—as he put it—of the Danish companies, coordinating their needs, guiding them to the right people in WF Hamburg for their auditing, tax, and special needs. Another function of the Desk was to find opportunities for Danish companies and do some promotional work. The Desk was credited with 75% of the indirect turnover it did, i.e., the time spent by the partner in charge which did not necessarily result in immediate business (giving speeches, writing articles, and meeting with Danish companies in the region). Some practices, like the German Desk in London, followed the Japanese model and dedicated people to that function. In other locations, Desk "members" did not actually sit in a specific spot or have a label—they were a "virtual" team in the sense that they came together, or existed, when needed.

WF in Frankfurt maintained desks for other countries which were active in that area of Germany. For example, the French Desk was run by an audit manager who was French and had experience working with German business people in Frankfurt. A tax expert, he was there to assist both local and French companies with their tax needs, as well as to guide French companies that were setting up in Frankfurt to the right people. Similarly, the English Desk in Frankfurt was coordinated by a UK chartered accountant who would take time from his regular activity to assist English companies in the planning stages of their expansion into Germany.

Most of the Desks at WF in the UK were staffed by a single partner whose chief responsibility lay elsewhere and who managed them as liaison centers between WF in the UK and an overseas country practice. The German Desk in London was probably the most sophisticated one after the Japanese Desk. A small promotional budget was used to publish and distribute informative brochures—in English and German: about the Desk itself *(refer to* Exhibit 7 *for an example of this brochure)*; the services it offered; the peculiarities of UK taxes, property laws, and financial reporting requirements; and the key differences between English and German accounting principles. The names and phone numbers of the members of the Desk in the UK were included on each document. Articles written by the Desk members that were published in German economic and business papers were also compiled for distribution.

The principle which guided this Desk's activities was to gain the confidence of WF's German partners. It was only by establishing a working relationship based on such professional trust and commitment, they believed, that the Desk would become the first choice for German partners whenever their clients in the UK required services, a principle they felt all Desks should ultimately follow. As things stood at WF, there was no unique channel to take whenever a mid-sized company decided to set up business in another country. As an example, if a German chemical manufacturer decided to purchase an English company, it had a variety of options available:

1 The CP of the parent company in Germany could call the international service coordinator in London (every country had one) and ask him to handle it. Depending on the expertise required, the coordinator could either do whatever was necessary himself, or allocate the work to the relevant person in that practice.

EXHIBIT 7   EXAMPLE OF GERMAN DESK IN THE UK BROCHURE

Introducing
our
German Desk

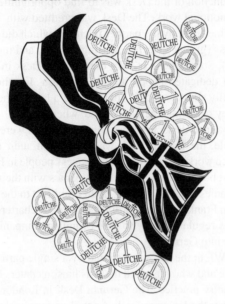

OUR GERMAN FIRM

Our German Desk Team liaise closely with our German firm, Feldpausch & Winkler, which has 1000 staff and offices in 11 German cities (including the new Bundesländer).

- HAMBURG
- BERLIN
- HANOVER
- DUSSELDORF
- FRANKFURT
- NUREMBURG
- HEIDELBURG
- STUTTGART
- MUNICH

FOR FURTHER INFORMATION

Please contact Harry Hornblower at WFI, 100 Charing Cross Road, London, Tel. 44 71 801 48 02.

2 The partner in Germany with a specific expertise in chemical companies could be contacted by the local CP. He could proceed in the same way, finding someone to serve the client in the UK if and when needed.

3 The CP could direct the request to partners who dealt with acquisitions, and they would probably forward it on to the acquisition specialist based in London, and so on.

4 The CP in Germany could hand over the request to the UK Desk in Frankfurt. The Desk could then either contact the person with the relevant expertise in England, or ask the German Desk in London to handle it.

5 The German CP (or the client) could make contact directly with the German Desk in London, who might do the initial work itself or look for a suitable person.

Whether or not the work for the acquisition was handled by the London Desk at the start, the referring or local CP, the client would afterwards be allocated to a local partner.

The partner managing the Desk in the UK was adamant that those working with him and those in the German practices had to get acquainted individually, and not remain just names in a directory. To avoid the conflicts of different traditions and approaches to work, they had to be able to adapt and accommodate them so that the client would receive consistent and beneficial service. In order to promote this kind of relationship, he visited Germany once a year, spending time with each partner so as to foster personal contact.

SETTING PAN-EUROPEAN STANDARDS: IN SEARCH OF SERVICE CONSISTENCY

In the autumn of 1991, WF's Board created a Task Force for mid-sized companies. It consisted of the partners from various countries responsible for coordinating WF's service delivery procedures for such companies throughout Europe. As they saw it, WF had no clear and uniform definition—on an institutional basis—of what the middle market was, what its needs might be, the most effective methods of targeting it, or the services it needed. Nor was WF necessarily recognized by the middle market in all countries as able and committed to serving their needs. The Board was convinced that, unless definitional, operational, and positional gaps were eliminated, WF would be hampered in its pan-European goals.

The first steps were to determine how the individual country practices defined and targeted the middle market, and what kinds of services they offered to meet the needs of that market in their respective locations; how successful or unsuccessful each practice had been in these pursuits; and what the other individual country practices could learn and apply internally. The Task Force then designed a plan, with the intention of trying to harmonize ideas, standards, and procedures which would include:

• Organizing seminars throughout Europe; exchanging information and ideas to try and promote WF as willing and able to serve the middle market at prices the clients were prepared to pay;
• Studying and comparing the methods used by each country practice in targeting its middle market clients, and the success rates of these methods;
• Comparing the standards and criteria used by these practices to determine the levels of consistency among practices;
• Reviewing the quality of work done in every practice to compare standards.

One problem which rapidly surfaced was the lack of real commitment to middle market clients on the part of many practices in Europe. When requested by non-local colleagues to give their clients the services they needed, the reaction of such partners was "what's in it for me?" A member of the Task Force described the problem:

> For a lot of our practices, the prevailing attitude is that the small clients referred by another European practice are simply uneconomical: they just haven't got enough resources to treat a client worth £15,000 in the same way they treat a local one worth £150,000. We've got to overcome that attitude and encourage them to do whatever is needed to serve these clients.

The Task Force believed that, in order to achieve consistent service quality, a certain amount had to be done on a formal basis instead of leaving things only to the informal relationships between partners. But, the question was: how far should WF go and what changes needed to be made so that the firm could hold onto its local business while, at the same time, it captured the new emerging opportunities?

GETTING THE BUGS OUT

In the extermination business, there is
Al Burger and there is everybody else.
What does he know that the others don't?

—Tom Richman

Howard Roth, born and reared in the Bronx, had to work late one evening at the cheap North Miami Beach, Fla., steak house where he was, temporarily and not by choice, the night manager. A new exterminator was coming to attack the resident cockroaches. Roth let the crew in, went for a drink, and came back later to see how things were going. He opened the door and couldn't believe what he saw. "It was the middle of the night," and here were these five guys, filthy dirty, crawling under and into everything, just doing a super job. Jesus Christ, I said to myself. After a while one guy got up off the floor and we started talking. I didn't know it at first, but he was the boss."

Roth switched jobs.

He hired himself, says the boss, Alvin Burger (rhymes with merger). "We're talking and Roth says, 'I'm gonna go to work for you. Anybody who can motivate people to do this kind of work, I want to be associated with him.' "

That was 17 years ago. Today, Miami-based "Bugs" Burger Bug Killers Inc. services nearly 12,000 restaurant and hotel accounts spread over 43 states, and the boss doesn't personally supervise every job anymore. No matter. The work gets done just as it would if he were there.

Al Burger has no MBA and little patience for the financial and administrative details of business. But he has overcome the biggest hurdle facing any small, growth-oriented company whose sole competitive advantage is quality of service. The more than 400 service specialists working for "Bugs" Burger (the company) today are just as motivated, and get just as dirty, as the original crew 17 years ago. Al Burger (the man) couldn't do a better job himself.

Says who?

Reprinted with permission. *INC* Magazine, June 1984, pp 67–72.

The competition, to begin with. " 'Bugs' Burger" says Jim Gillis, owner of All Boston Exterminators, "is number one. There is no number two."

And customers. "Let me put it this way," says Bob Crooks, manager of Gallagher's Restaurant, in Garland, Tex. "You have 'Bugs' Burger, and then you have to go waaay down to get to the second best."

And employees. "I left 'Bugs' Burger and worked for another company," says Alan Rosenberg, a service specialist in Boston who was recently promoted to district manager. "It was a step backward. They had no standards. So I came back. This is the only company I ever saw where the owner and the people on the job all think the same way."

With anticipated 1984 sales of $25 million, "Bugs" Burger is not the largest company in the national pest-control market, estimated at close to $2 billion annually. Orkin Exterminating Co. and Terminix International, both corporate subsidiaries with branch operations or franchises in about 40 states, rack up greater sales: $213 million for Orkin and $160 million for Terminix in 1983. Most of the rest of the industry consists of small, local operators. Indianapolis alone has about 75 pest-control companies. The competition is cutthroat, and the service, according to people with years of experience in the industry, is about the same everywhere: minimal. Most customers assume they will get the same results no matter who they hire, so they hire on price. "Bugs" Burger doesn't operate in that market. "It's like he's a Mercedes," says Gillis, "and you've got a whole lot of Chevettes driving around out there."

"Bugs" Burger's marketing hook is its audacious guarantee—an unconditional promise to eliminate all roach and rodent breeding and nesting areas on the clients' premises, with no payment due until the pests are eliminated. If the company fails, the guarantee says, "Bugs" Burger will refund the customer's last 12 monthly payments and will pay for one year's service by another exterminator of the customer's choice.

The company doesn't promise that a restaurant diner or a hotel guest will never see another roach, but it does promise that if one shows up, it won't be native-born. Should an immigrant bug ride in with the groceries and stroll across a diner's table, "Bugs" Burger pays for the meal and sends the offended gourmet a letter of apology as well as a gift certificate for yet another free meal. "Customers feel like they've hit the state lottery," says the manager of one client restaurant. "They come in the next time and look for the little things." Hotel guests experiencing a similarly close encounter also get their night's lodging free, an apology, and an invitation to return—on the house. To help the company make good on its promises, "Bugs" Burger customers agree in writing to prepare their premises for monthly servicing and are fined if they don't.

Although the company says it has only once had to honor its full guarantee to a customer, it does spend about $2,000 a month reimbursing diners and room guests for reported pest sightings.

The professors and consultants would say that Al Burger has segmented the market and claimed the upscale commercial customers, those who will pay a premium price for superior service, as his niche. His company's monthly fees run four to six times those of its nominal competitors, sometimes more, and an initial "cleanout" charge alone can run four times the regular monthly fee. But Al Burger has not only created a new price structure, he has also taken a business with about as much prestige as, say, garbage collection, and given it respectability among both customers—" . . . 'Bugs' Burger, one of my favorite subjects," responded Boston restaurateur Roger Berkowitz when he was asked about Burger—and employees. "In this company, the serviceman is number one," says Roger Gillen, a "Bugs" Burger employee in the Ft. Lauderdale office.

Al Burger's dad ran a not-very-profitable pest control business in Albany, N.Y. His older brother bought another marginal operation in Miami. In 1954, after high school, two years in the Army, and a spell of selling vacuum cleaners door-to-door, Al Burger moved south to work for his sibling. He lasted five and a half ("miserable") years, quit, went to work for a competitor, and resigned. Immediately, he and Sandee, his wife of two years, formed their own partnership. Al was the marketing and service department; Sandee was the administration. They had, at first, no customers. "Most guys," says Al, "stole them. They planned their moves [to their own companies] so they could take a percentage of their accounts with them. I started from ground zero. I had to live with myself."

Al Burger has always been hobbled by a conscience. Owning his own company had never been a dream, but six years of working for other people had frustrated him. Employers in the pest-control industry, by and large, paid poor wages, provided no training, and were inured to high annual employee turnover rates. Further, in his experience, the service most companies provided their customers was unforgivably poor. The industry, he says, had convinced its customers that the best they could do was keep the critters—roaches and rodents—under control. Burger knew that with a little more time and effort they could be eliminated.

That conviction became the underpinning not just of "Bug" Burger's exterminating techniques, but of the company's marketing and personnel management philosophies as well. Unlike the rest of the industry, which talks about "controlling" pests and holding them to an "acceptable" level, Al Burger sets a standard for his people that is unambiguous and requires no interpretation. While an employee might be uncertain about how many roaches is *some* roaches, *no* roaches is pretty easy to understand.

Moreover, it is an unvarying standard. To guarantee "customer satisfaction," as many companies do, is only to say, "We'll do as little as you let us get by with and only as much as you demand." The customer may be happy, but the serviceman on the route is confronted with working to a standard that varies from one customer to another, which is no standard at all. There is nothing to hold him accountable to, except the whim of client complaints.

Companies frequently answer this dilemma by avoiding the issue of quality standards altogether, instructing employees instead to follow a prescribed routine. In the case of pest extermination, that could mean applying the indicated type and quantity of chemicals to a list of likely breeding areas. Follow the routine, the employee is told, and you can't be criticized—whether the rats and roaches are killed or not. After, the company has promised to do only the best it can, and who is to say what that is?

"Bugs" Burger's quality-control system, an integral part of the company's operations, is extraordinary in itself. But the system exists only to ensure compliance with the unambiguous standard. Take away the standard, or fuzz it up, and the organization, like a basketball team with no hoop to shoot for, loses its purpose.

"I started my business," Al Burger says, "because I thought it was unethical to take money for poor-quality performance. I thought there should be standards and ethics in the industry." When he said so before a meeting of the Florida Pest Control Association in 1960, suggesting to his colleagues and competitors that they could upgrade their service by paying more attention, and more money, to the people they hired, he was hooted off the stage. "I almost cried. I went to the door," Burger says, "and I told 'em I quit."

To this day, Al Burger and the industry he is nominally a part of maintain an unusual relationship. Burger is unforgiving in his criticism. Most owners in the industry, he says, "are former routemen who are thieves and lazy to boot. That's what you've got—a lack of scruples. And why should *their* routemen care? They've probably got their own businesses on the side."

Spokesmen for the industry he reviles don't refute him. "So long as the larger firms demand that their routemen service 18 to 20 accounts a day," says Lee Truman of Indianapolis, a former president of the National Pest Control Association and an industry consultant, "there's no way you can do a professional job. They get by, the customers accept it, and that's pretty much the industry standard. . . . Burger doesn't do anything but use the same techniques all of us could use, and he gets rid of the roaches. . . . We talk professionalism a lot, but we don't practice it."

"In this company," as Roger Gillen, a routeman for 10½ years, says, "the serviceman is number one." Scott Hebenton and Philip Hargrove in Boston, each with less than one year's experience on a route, say much the same. Michelle Kolodny, manager of the company's central office in Miami, says, without prompting, "It's the service specialists that pay my salary." "Nobody is a big shot in this company," says Frank Perez, now the vice-president in charge of service but 17 years ago one of the four employees Howard Roth saw working with Al Burger in that greasy steak house. (Roth himself is now executive vice-president.) "Our service people," Perez adds, "are the privileged class."

And so it goes. No matter who you talk to in the company, before long he or she pays homage to the men and women (about 7% of the service specialists are female) in the field. It could be just lip service, but it isn't.

On paper, the "Bugs" Burger service organization looks unremarkable. It separates the country into four divisions, each division into regions, and regions into districts headed by managers supervising a dozen or so service specialists each. But superimposed on this ordinary structure is a quality-control system of thoroughly frightening proportions.

Service specialists work unsupervised, at night, on schedules they set for themselves. After each routine monthly service call on every account, however, the routeman files a report in which, if he wants to remain a routeman with "Bugs" Burger, he spills everything. Were there any problems with the customer's sanitation practices? Did the routeman have access to all the premises? Did the customer do the necessary preparation? Did the routeman see a roach or a rodent, or evidence of roaches or rodents? Did he kill any roaches or rodents? Does he need any help with the account? As the routeman is told from the time he first interviews for a job with the company, honesty pays. At "Bugs" Burger, mistakes are forgiven, liars are not.

The information filed by the routeman is checked, not once but several times, by managers at various levels. District managers call each customer a day or two after every monthly service. District managers, regional directors, and divisional vice-presidents spend much of their time visiting customers' premises, armed when they arrive with a computer printout of the routeman's reports. The computer printout also includes customer complaints received in Miami. (When customers call "Bugs" Burger from any city in the country except Honolulu, using either the local or toll-free number listed in the phone book, the telephone rings at the Miami corporate headquarters, not at the routeman's home or the local office.) And just to keep all of *those* managers honest, a full-time, two-person quality-control team headed by Al Burger's daughter Susan hopscotches the country calling on customers and filing their own reports. Routemen don't know when, or how frequently, their clients will be called on by someone from management. The only certainty is that they will be called on, and that if there are complaints, Miami will hear about them first.

Naturally, company managers insist that all this checking up is really done for the routeman's benefit. "Our job," says Tom Schafer, vice-president of technical services, which includes quality control, "is to support the service department." Routemen "appreciate" the help these reports and visits give them, assures Perez.

That is exactly the sort of thing you would expect to hear from management. What is surprising, however, is that you get the same story from the field.

"Yeah, it's pressure," says Scott Hebenton in Boston, "but it helps you keep up your standards."

"It gives us that little extra motivation," says Alan Rosenberg. "It would be easy to slack off one night, make it up the next month. But then you think, well, they might call this account *this* month."

Don't they resent it?

"I don't," says Hebenton. "Without it I guess we'd be just like any other company."

An employee-turnover rate of less than 3% last year suggests that most people at "Bugs" Burger feel much the way Hebenton does. Something about this system of management and quality control builds pride instead of resentment among the people whose performance is constantly monitored.

Jack Kaplan, the company's vice-president for human resources, thinks it is a "mentality . . . that says, 'You are critical to the success of this company, and I'm going to make you feel that way from day one.' Most people coming here from different backgrounds aren't used to hearing words like that."

Employees first encounter this attitude during the hiring process, which involves two rounds of interviews, elaborate personality and aptitude testing, a polygraph examination, and thorough explanations of the job and the company—all conducted by officials from Miami headquarters, who eventually turn over the names of qualified applicants (2% or 3% of those who answer the ads) to local service managers for the final decision. The people hired already feel part of an elite group just from having survived what they know is an exhaustive selection process. Further, it is a process that doesn't automatically select the young. "I appreciate it," says Hebenton, hired last year at age 37, "because an older guy has just as good a chance." Kaplan recalls interviewing a 45-year-old woman in Roanoke, Va., who asked, he says, "Would you hire an old broad like me?" They did. "Her district manager says she's fantastic," he adds.

New hires undergo a five-month training program. "It's like boot camp in the Army," says Kaplan, "only it's three times as long and twice as tough." Recently hired service specialists confirm Kaplan's analogy. During the program, they are not assistants, helping someone else. They do real work under the full-time instruction of a field manager. After about three months, new recruits attend a two-week school in Miami, where, one says, "there is no fooling around. You go to class from eight o'clock until six or seven o'clock, then you do your homework and show up again the next morning. It's pretty intense." (Letting no opportunity to exercise a little quality control slip by, company officials test the recruits in Miami, not just to see what they have learned, but also to check the techniques they have been taught by field managers against the company's standards. What public school administrators can't get away with, "Bugs" Burger can.)

Finally, in the sixth month, the new service specialist gets a route. In one sense he is on his own, because the responsibility of keeping customers' premises clear of nesting and breeding pests is ultimately his. Says serviceman Phil Hargrove, "It's like your own little business."

Not quite, but neither are Hargrove and his peers just employees hired to do a high-quality job.

Burger's routemen occupy a unique middle ground. They control the up-side of their working lives—their own schedules, their incomes, and, to a large extent, their career paths within the company. What they don't have, in contrast to most workers and all independent business owners, is any downside risk. They can't lose, and that is why they will accept whatever performance standard the company wants them to meet. Once hired and trained at "Bugs" Burger, the only way you can fail is to lie. Cover up a mistake, slack off and don't report it, or ignore a problem, and you are in trouble. But ask for help, and you have it.

Routemen can talk to their district managers on the telephone or ask them to come to the job site, anytime. Regional directors and divisional vice-presidents always travel with a working uniform in their bags. "They never look at it as a negative," says Scott Hebenton, "if you ask for help." Recently, the company flew eight out-of-state service specialists to Boston to get their Massachusetts licenses so that they would be available to augment the local forces if a job suddenly demanded a larger army. "They spare no expense," says Hargrove, slightly amazed. "Any serviceman knows," says Jack Kaplan, "that if he wants to talk to Mr. Burger, all he has to do is pick up the phone."

Nor does a "Bugs" Burger service specialist worry about losses from conditions beyond his control:

- If a major customer decides to drop the service at the end of his contract, the company subsidizes the routeman's compensation until a replacement is signed on.
- When a salesman badly underestimates the hours required to service a new account, the company subsidizes the routeman for the time he puts in, because it won't allow him to shortcut the service.
- Customers that won't cooperate with a routeman by maintaining sanitary conditions or by preparing the premises for treatment are dropped. The serviceman, again, is subsidized until a new client is found to fill out his route.
- Promotions from service specialist to district manager—and all other promotions within the company—are made on a three-month, or longer, trial basis, with the salary

differential held in escrow during the trial. If a supervisor or, as is more frequently the case, the former routeman decides the promotion isn't working, he gets either his old route back, or a better one. Roger Gillen, an 11-year "Bugs" Burger veteran, tried a management job and left it. "I'm not a management type of person, and you just can't replace a good serviceman." There is no shame at "Bugs" Burger in staying with the job you do well—and for which you are paid well. Servicemen receive $1,200 a month in salary plus 20% of all the monthly gross billings on their routes in excess of $5,100. The average routeman makes $24,000, but $32,000 or more isn't unheard of, according to company sources.

Benefits are impressive, too: full health insurance; disability insurance that pays full salary for three months and 60% thereafter; a pension plan; profit sharing; cost of living adjustments; performance bonuses; and, coming soon, employee equity in an affiliated company selling janitorial supplies.

"An old lady," Al Burger recalls, "told me that if you give without thinking about what you might get back, eventually you'll get back 100 times what you gave. That was Mrs. Lummus. When I was 21, working for my brother, she called. She had a terrible roach problem in Miami Beach, but no money. So I got rid of her roaches, and she made me tea and cookies. I remember what she told me. It's a good thing to carry with you."

High-minded thoughts, of course, do not by themselves ensure business success. While they can inform and influence a management organization, they can't take its place, and Al Burger, he will admit today, is no organizer. In 1978, sales were nearly $6 million, but the business was floundering. Burger realized, with a little help from Howard Roth, that he had reached the limits of his managerial capabilities. "I was panicking, beginning to make mistakes. I was disoriented. I actually had heart palpitations. Too many things were happening that I couldn't cope with. . . . Howard Roth—a guy with a ninth-grade education who really understands people—he sat me down and said, 'Here's a guy that you're going to hire.' "

The guy was Art Graham, who, as president of Pizza Hut Canada Ltd., had just turned the company around. He had worked for "Bugs" Burger briefly in the early '70s, but hadn't appreciated the growth opportunities in the business. In 1978, while Graham was in Miami for the Super Bowl game, Roth persuaded him to come back. Graham built a management structure where none had existed before and pulled the profit margin to 12% of sales within six months, up from 1%. He wrote the company's first business plan and constructed its first annual operating budget.

Al Burger, meanwhile, concentrates on what he does best: marketing and firing up the troops. "Basically," says district director Scott Hebenton, "what Al Burger is, is a service specialist . . . and when he talks to you it's like he's right inside your head. He knows exactly what you're thinking out there on the route. 'Oh, I'm tired. Why not just cut this short and go home.' He's a good motivator."

Both management and motivation remain important. On the marketing front, for example, some of the competition is beginning to catch on to Burger's gimmick—the elimination guarantee—and while they have raised their prices accordingly, "Bugs" Burger is still the premium-price service. The company loses $2 million or more annually in unrenewed contracts as existing customers switch to lower-cost exterminators.

"Bugs" Burger's response to the competition has been to develop some productivity-enhancing equipment for routemen to use, and to map out some innovative, but still confidential, pricing options. The one thing Burger won't allow is cuts in service. "The minute we start doing that," he says, "our standard falls apart. You can't tell a service specialist not to do a good job on one account and then expect him not to do a bad job on the others. People will strive for that elusive level of perfection. All they need is the right attitude, and that all depends on the goals and standards you set for them."

Al Burger, in short, is still a man with a mission. He won't rejoin the national trade association until it changes its name from pest control to pest elimination. "He was a voice in the wilderness," says Lee Truman of Indianapolis, "but now an awful lot of people think he's been right all along."

And despite the competition, he remains cool and self-confident. The owner of one of Honolulu's most expensive restaurants didn't hide his condescending skepticism when Burger first stopped by on a sales call. But Burger had already toured the dining rooms, kitchens, and work areas. He had seen the thumb-size roaches scampering over the glassware, gone unerringly to where the egg cases were hidden, noted that rats had walked across the floured surface of the pie-crust machine leaving paw prints and their distinctive calling cards.

Condescending or not, here was a man, Al Burger knew, who needed and eventually would pay for "Bugs" Burger's kind of service.

INDEX